P9-EGD-609

FOUNDED BY BURNS MANTLE

THE BEST PLAYS OF 2001–2002
JEFFREY ERIC JENKINS
Editor

EDITORIAL BOARD
ROBERT BRUSTEIN
TISH DACE
CHRISTINE DOLEN
MEL GUSSOW
ROBERT HURWITT
JOHN ISTEL
CHRIS JONES
JULIUS NOVICK
MICHAEL PHILLIPS
CHRISTOPHER RAWSON
ALISA SOLOMON
JEFFREY SWEET
LINDA WINER
CHARLES WRIGHT

PAST EDITORS
(1919-2000)
BURNS MANTLE
JOHN CHAPMAN
LOUIS KRONENBERGER
HENRY HEWES
OTIS L. GUERNSEY JR.

CONSULTING EDITOR
HENRY HEWES

PHOTO EDITOR
ROBERT KAMP

LISTINGS EDITORS
RUE E. CANVIN (USA), VIVIAN CARY JENKINS (NEW YORK)

Another time, perhaps: Anne Bancroft in the postponed production of Edward Albee's
Occupant. *Drawing:* © *Al Hirschfeld/The Margo Feiden Galleries Ltd., New York.*
www.alhirschfeld.com

THE BEST PLAYS

OF

2001–2002

EDITED BY JEFFREY ERIC JENKINS

*Illustrated with photographs and
with drawings by* HIRSCHFELD

LIMELIGHT EDITIONS

When other books have been forgot,
our book will still be hot.

—Al Hirschfeld

Spanning four editors and fifty years, his drawings have given
vivid life to the pages of *The Best Plays*. A valued collaborator of
great charm and sparkling wit, he will be sorely missed by us all.

The Best Plays of 2001–2002
is dedicated to the memory of
Al Hirschfeld
1903–2003

INTRODUCTION

IN ANY GIVEN season the theater can still manage to offer us the dramatic highs and lows that continue to lure us back into those large, half-darkened rooms. But in this, our 83rd consecutive year of publication, it is hard to imagine any season that has seen lows such as the year 2001–2002. I'm referring, of course, to the tragedy that struck the United States on September 11, 2001, when terrorists destroyed thousands of lives and billions of dollars worth of property in attacks on New York and Washington.

For a few days, New York and the country hunkered down before the comforting signal of commercial-free television as the shamans of post-postmodern culture tried (somewhat in vain) to help us make sense of our national tragedy. For those of us of a certain age, it was reminiscent of the assassination of President John F. Kennedy: a moment that marked the before-and-after of a new era. And yet, as we send the *Best Plays* to press more than a year after that horrible day, I wonder what has really changed.

This volume is not the place for a tract on the failures and pusillanimity of leadership across the political spectrum in our time of crisis. But this is a work that aims to be a second draft of theater history—presuming journalism always to be the first—and it is our goal to locate the best plays and performances of United States theater within their social and cultural milieu. Our contributors are among the finest writers and thinkers on issues relating to theater and culture, and the diversity of their perspectives gives readers of the *Best Plays* a well-balanced picture of the year in theater in New York and around the country.

II

WITH OUR FORMAT of thoughtful essays and comprehensive reference material in mind, a generous critic puzzled in print over how we might deal with the events of September 11 in our pages. The answer so far: in scattered references. As Mel Gussow points out in his essay on the Off Off Broadway season, it will take some time for our artists to respond to those catastrophic events. But for those of us who attempt to offer cultural context, the world around us becomes a Rorschach test.

Tony Kushner's *Homebody/Kabul*, which deals with the silencing of women by the Taliban in Afghanistan—and by male culture in general— was slated for fall production when the airplanes struck the World Trade Center and the Pentagon. Although the play was sprawling and overambitious in its New York Theatre Workshop debut, its power and its poetry insisted that it have a place among the Best Plays. Jennifer de Poyen, a former National Arts Journalism Fellow, explores the terrain in and around Kushner's still-developing play.

Elsewhere among the Best Plays, contemporary culture was reflected in several plays demonstrating the variety of ways that violence often underpins gender relationships. Charles L. Mee's *Big Love*, which received a 2001 ATCA/Steinberg New Play Citation for an earlier production, came to New York and showed its continued power and humor during the Next Wave Festival at the Brooklyn Academy of Music. Editor and critic John Istel discusses Mee's affinity for combining the classic with the contemporary.

Other plays in our top 10 that focus on the play of gender in our lives and on our stages include *Breath, Boom* by Kia Corthron, *Franny's Way* by Richard Nelson, *The Glory of Living* by Rebecca Gilman, *The Goat, or Who Is Sylvia?* by Edward Albee and *Topdog/Underdog* by Suzan-Lori Parks.

In Corthron's play, we see how poverty, inequity and race combine to influence the way young women survive in "the 'hood." As playwright and critic Michael Feingold shows, the cycle spirals downward from one generation to the next amid a culture of violence and abuse in Corthron's subtle, poetic dramaturgy.

The only violence in *Franny's Way* is the damage done to the spirit when love is found to be untrue. Nelson's coming-of-age story, produced by Playwrights Horizons, was a gentle look back to the late 1950s when a contraceptive diaphragm in the possession of a teenage girl was shocking (and unlikely). Beyond the familiar thematic, though, Nelson counterpoints the elements of adolescent romance with the profound loss (and lingering guilt) experienced by a couple whose child dies in its crib—while the couple are making love. Book and theater critic Charles Wright examines the connections between art, life and literature in this lovely play.

After seeing *The Glory of Living*, one can be forgiven for wanting to take a strong drink (or perhaps a shower). Gilman's 1996 play, which arrived at MCC Theater via a circuitous route, resides far from the rarified atmosphere of Nelson's *Franny*. It charts the dismal life of a young woman—reared in a one-room trailer that doubled as her mother's brothel—who kills other girls at the behest of her sadistic husband. Lurid and depressing as it sounds, it was a powerful theatrical experience based on a true story. Critic and reporter Chris Jones brings Gilman's work into sharper focus.

Edward Albee continues his six-decade journey in the front-rank of US dramatists with his eighth Best Play, *The Goat, or Who Is Sylvia?* In *The Goat*, herein discussed by critic Charles Isherwood, Albee skates along the razor's edge of taste with a tragicomedy about a man who has a sexual affair with the aforementioned beast. By turns funny and horrifying, Albee's play—as many of his works have done across the years—prods the conventions of polite society in an examination of the nature of love and desire. Among the Best Plays, *The Goat* is one of only three to play on Broadway and it alone started there. The other Broadway Best Plays, *Topdog/Underdog* and *Metamorphoses* started Off Broadway—with the latter touring resident theaters before its Off Broadway run.

Our developing theme of sex and violence stretches into Suzan-Lori Parks's *Topdog/Underdog*. Here women are nowhere onstage, although they are hardly absent as distinguished scholar Margaret B. Wilkerson mentions in her essay on the play. In this 2002 Pulitzer Prize-winning play, which was first produced at the Joseph Papp Public Theater, a pair of African-American brothers desperately seek their places in a universe of two as they jostle one another for position. Although women are only mentioned in the play—the brothers' mother, an ex-wife and a girlfriend—they haunt the battles between them. (And it isn't much of a stretch to see the links between the brothers' struggle for primacy and the battles of the young women in Corthron's *Breath, Boom*.)

Brothers also dominate the story of *The Dazzle*, by Richard Greenberg, an imagined tale about Homer and Langley Collyer. The Collyer brothers were famous recluses who died in 1947 amid their clutter-packed mansion on upper Fifth Avenue in Harlem—authorities found 14 grand pianos among the tons of debris carted away after their deaths. Greenberg had the basics of their careers—Homer was an admiralty lawyer, Langley a concert pianist—but he created their dramatic lives in his imagination. Haunting in its elliptical examination of consciousness (and how it is constructed), the play, produced by the Roundabout Theatre Company, was found lacking by most mainstream critics. Critic and scholar Donald Lyons, however, unearths a "difficult, delightful masterpiece" in his essay.

Coming just weeks after the devastation of September 11, Mary Zimmerman's *Metamorphoses*, which takes Ovid (and others) as its inspiration, offered a gentle, reassuring reminder of the cyclic nature of human experience: birth, life, love, death and the hope for something beyond death. It was inevitable that critics would locate it in direct relationship to the terrorist attacks, but that view is ultimately too narrow. Critic and editor Christopher Rawson offers a larger context for understanding the allure of these mythic stories and Zimmerman's magical rendering of them.

Melissa James Gibson's *[sic]* rounds out our selection of 10 plays with a clever work about three 30-somethings trying to get traction in their urban existences. Produced Off Off Broadway by the Soho Rep, *[sic]* presses the envelope of language as Gibson creates a playful verbal score that seems to regard breathing and punctuation as unnecessary evils. Critic Bruce Weber revisits the play and rethinks his perspective on the playwright's gleeful toying with language.

In addition to the 10 Best Plays, we also recognize the remarkable Elaine Stritch and her collaborator, John Lahr, for their work on an extraordinary one-woman show, *Elaine Stritch at Liberty*. Although Stritch's show wasn't strictly a play, it was certainly a well-written and well-structured celebration of a life in the theater. (And what a show!) In a fascinating turn, the production grew in its theatrical power when transferred from the Joseph Papp Public Theater to Broadway. We're pleased to honor Stritch and Lahr for their contribution to the 2001–02 theater season with a Special Citation and an essay by critic Michael Sommers.

When we were considering pieces for selection as Best Plays, it never occurred to us that a trend was developing toward sex (and gender) and violence. It may say more about the consciousness of the editor, who makes the choices, than it does about the nature of theater today and its place in our culture. But in a world of expanding complexities—when technology and economics make greater and greater demands on our time—it becomes ever more important that we pay attention to what it means to be human. As we spend increasing amounts of time isolated before computer and television screens, disconnected from the subtle, active, personal links forged by live performance, the theater becomes a haven for the human spirit— even if it challenges us with ideas or images foreign to our experience.

III

DURING A RECENT classroom discussion, a first-year college student referred to an offhand remark made by another teacher about the "dying theater." The student took for granted that her teacher had stated some sort of truth. What's more likely is that the teacher was making a point about the proliferation of opportunity in film and television, but to some extent the damage was done—as it is done every time this canard is spread.

Credit (or blame) may be due to Moss Hart and George S. Kaufman whose 1938 play gave the theater its moniker of the "fabulous invalid." When Kaufman and Hart wrote their sentimental comedy about a theater's march into decrepitude and resurrection, the number of plays opening each season on Broadway had been in steady decline for a decade—usually pinned to the advent of talking motion pictures. Even though *The Fabulous Invalid* ends with the hope for a new beginning sparked by a rising crop of artists, three generations of theater critics and writers have used the play's title (and the first production's failure) to symbolize whatever might be the current state of the theater.

The Broadway decline that began in 1928—the peak season of record was 1927–28 with 261 productions—has leveled in recent years with the past decade averaging 39 shows per season. But in the 1938–39 season, when *The Fabulous Invalid* was an unlucky 13th production to open, "only" 114 shows opened—exactly half of the 1928–29 season's 228. Taking into consideration the economic depression, fascism on the rise abroad and the diversion of crowds to the World's Fair, Hart and Kaufman can be forgiven their wistfulness for a bygone era and their concern for the health of the theater.

IV

BY NOW, THOUGH, the wise reader of the *Best Plays* series knows that Broadway theater is more about economics than a regenerative experience of the mind and spirit. Indeed, three of the Best Plays for this season played Off Off Broadway, which is increasingly the home for much of our finest writing. Of the other seven, only one—as mentioned above—started on Broadway, the rest came from Off Broadway.

With our colleagues in the American Theatre Critics Association, we also keep close tabs on the developing new plays that arise in theaters across the US. Through the good offices of the Harold and Mimi Steinberg Charitable Trust, we recognize the honorees and finalists of the American Theatre Critics/Steinberg New Play Award and Citations. The Steinberg Charitable Trust also supports the *Best Plays* series through a gift program in which the Trust distributes copies of the book to theater leaders and supporters. We extend our deepest thanks to the Trust and its board (William D. Zabel, Carole A. Krumland, James D. Steinberg, Michael A. Steinberg and Seth M. Weingarten) for making the *Best Plays* a priority for their support.

The collection of data for a volume such as this relies on the labors of many people. Our thanks to Jeffrey Finn Productions (Cast Replacements and Touring Productions), and to Mel Gussow for his expanded essay of the Off Off Broadway theater. Rue E. Canvin, who has worked on the *Best Plays* series since the early 1960s, has expanded her duties with this volume and made the USA section a more comprehensive study of the year in theater around the country. Jonathan Dodd, the longtime publisher of the *Best Plays* series, continues to provide important background information and good advice. My good friend Henry Hewes, himself a former editor of this series and my invaluable consulting editor, never stops thinking of ways to help improve the series.

We are also deeply indebted to all of the press representatives who assisted in the gathering of information for this volume, but I particularly want to acknowledge Adrian Bryan-Brown and Chris Boneau of Boneau/ Bryan-Brown for their unflagging support of the series and its editors.

Thanks also are due to the members of the *Best Plays* editorial board, who give their imprimatur to our work by their presence on the masthead. Thanks as well to those who have offered and provided extra support and assistance to this edition: Robert Brustein, Charles Wright, John Istel, Christopher Rawson, Tish Dace (Hewes Design Awards), Caldwell Titcomb (Elliot Norton Awards), David A. Rosenberg (Connecticut Critics Circle Awards), Alec Harvey (American Theatre Critics/Steinberg New Play Award and Citations), Edwin Wilson (Susan Smith Blackburn Prize), Michael Kuchwara (New York Drama Critics Circle Awards), Henry Hewes (Theater Hall of Fame Awards) and Ralph Newman of the Drama Book Shop (New Plays and Publications).

We congratulate and thank all of the Best Plays honorees who made the 2001–02 season so invigorating to contemplate. Edward Albee, Kia Corthron, Melissa James Gibson, Rebecca Gilman, Richard Greenberg, Tony Kushner, John Lahr, Charles L. Mee, Richard Nelson, Suzan-Lori Parks, Elaine Stritch and Mary Zimmerman all enriched our lives during the season under review. The photographers who capture theatrical images on film and help keep those ephemeral moments alive for historical perspective are also due thanks for their contributions to the greater body of theatrical work. Building on our work from last year, we have included credits with each photograph and indexed the photographers' names for easier reference. Similarly, we continue offering biographical information about each of this volume's essayists and editors in a brief section at the back of the book.

My wife, Vivian Cary Jenkins, continues to serve the theater and the *Best Plays* series as a phenomenal tracker and editor of what's happening in the New York theater. Now a professor in the Health Care Programs at Iona College, she continues to help assemble, collate and check the reference information in this book. It is largely through her efforts, and her love and support, that *Best Plays* continues to appear.

Finally, we dedicate this volume to the memory of Al Hirschfeld, whose work has appeared in 50 volumes of the *Best Plays* series with this edition. We had planned to celebrate Hirschfeld's half-century with the book even before he died in his sleep on January 20, 2003. He was fond of telling *Best Plays* editors that the book was a great way to keep track of the theater drawings he had done in a given year. For thousands of *Best Plays* readers, his drawings not only kept track, but also kept alive theater that was long gone. We extend our deepest sympathies to his family, and our thanks to his representative, Margo Feiden.

Although we live in a time of great uncertainty, with a fearful shadow thrown across the land, we have already begun work on the 2002–03 edition of this book. As we ponder the future of our country and its theater, we fondly think of Hirschfeld and a comment he once made in a bit of doggerel about the *Best Plays*.

> When other books have been forgot,
> our book will still be hot.

Then we smile and it's back to work.

JEFFREY ERIC JENKINS
NEW YORK

Contents

THE SEASON
ON AND OFF
BROADWAY

THE SEASON:
BROADWAY AND OFF BROADWAY

○ ○ ○ ○ ○ *By Jeffrey Eric Jenkins* ○ ○ ○ ○ ○

When the 2001–2002 season got underway, it seemed as if *The Producers*-inspired party might continue indefinitely. After his musical snared a record 12 Tony Awards at the 2001 ceremony, Mel Brooks was asked if he could take the show to London without original stars Nathan Lane and Matthew Broderick. According to *Variety*, Brooks replied, "You may not need them. There's Alan Cumming and Alfred Molina and a whole lot of people who can dance and sing." (And, he might have added, those are just the "A"s.)

To some observers, Brooks's comment carried the pungent aroma of hubris. He seemed to be saying that his show was so brilliant, so dynamic that anyone could pull it off. But it was the 75-year-old Brooks's big night on Broadway, so everyone indulged his hyperbole. What couldn't be foreseen, though, were the stumbles that lay ahead for the producers of *The Producers*—not to mention the challenges we would all meet beginning September 11.

Before the roadblocks faced by the most successful show on Broadway, though, there were the closings that usually come with empty hands after the Tony Awards ceremony. *Jane Eyre*, *A Class Act*, *Bells Are Ringing* and *The Invention of Love* (which actually won a pair of acting Tonys) all closed within the first month of the new season. Not far behind were *King Hedley II*, *Follies*, *George Gershwin Alone* and *One Flew Over the Cuckoo's Nest* (best play-revival Tony).

As the season got underway, the developing tradition of television stars summering on Broadway continued when Tom Selleck opened *A Thousand Clowns* in July. Herb Gardner's play, which was a Best Play in 1961–62, was notable this season mainly for Selleck's desire to play the big stage and his professed love for the now-creaky story.

The play focuses on an incorrigible comedy writer who makes a stab at rearing his precocious nephew. Nicolas King made an interesting acting

BROADWAY SEASON 2002–2003

Productions in a continuing run on May 31, 2003 in bold
Productions honored as Best Plays *selections in italics*

NEW PLAYS (8)
If You Ever Leave Me . . .
   I'm Going With You!
45 Seconds From Broadway
QED
   (Lincoln Center Theater)
Metamorphoses
   (Second Stage Theatre)
The Goat or Who Is Sylvia?
The Smell of the Kill
The Graduate
Topdog/Underdog
   (Joseph Papp Public Theater)

NEW MUSICALS (6)
Urinetown (2000–2001 Best Play)
Mamma Mia!
Thou Shalt Not
By Jeeves
Sweet Smell of Success
Thoroughly Modern Millie

PLAY REVIVALS (12)
A Thousand Clowns
Major Barbara
Hedda Gabler
Dance of Death

PLAY REVIVALS (cont'd)
Noises Off
The Women
The Crucible
Fortune's Fool
The Elephant Man
Morning's at Seven
Private Lives
The Man Who Had All the Luck
   (Roundabout)

MUSICAL REVIVALS (3)
One Mo' Time
Oklahoma!
Into the Woods

SOLO PERFORMANCES (6)
Sexaholix . . . a Love Story
Mostly Sondheim
   (Lincoln Center)
An Almost Holy Picture
   (Roundabout Theatre Company)
Bea Arthur on Broadway:
   Just Between Friends
Elaine Stritch at Liberty
   (Public Theater)
The Mystery of Charles Dickens

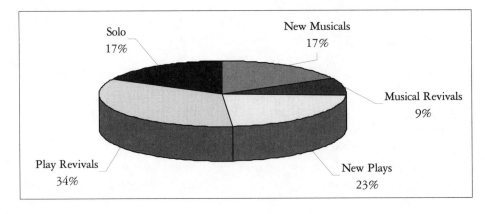

partner for the charming Selleck, even if the youngster seemed to be a pint-sized man of middle age. The company settled in for a scheduled four-month run, unaware of events that were soon to overtake the season.

Roundabout Theatre Company opened its Daniel Sullivan-directed production of George Bernard Shaw's *Major Barbara* the next night with the remarkable Cherry Jones as Barbara Undershaft. Shaw's meditation on the relative nature of morality and notions of the common good, performed well enough to be extended for two weeks beyond its original closing date. Bruce Weber wrote in the *New York Times* that director Sullivan, "seems to work with a baton and a tuning fork, as if a script were a score and the cast a chamber orchestra," and that Jones, "makes Barbara a formidably beatific adversary whose soul-saving agenda may be of the spiritual sort but is backed with steel nonetheless."

The final production to open on Broadway prior to the terrorist attacks of September 11 was Renée Taylor and Joe Bologna's *If You Ever Leave Me . . . I'm Going With You!* A comic tale of the challenges of a show-business marriage, it played a few weeks at the intimate Cort Theatre before succumbing to the post-September 11 bust.

In the Shadows of Terror

ALTHOUGH THE SEASON began with the renewed hope that marks every endeavor, the theater in New York (at all levels, in all venues) was brought to its knees by the terrorist attacks on the World Trade Center and the Pentagon. Coming at a time when tourists—both domestic and international—accounted for nearly 60 percent of all Broadway attendance, fears about air travel and heightened anxiety about traveling to New York (or anywhere) put a big dent in theater attendance. If it weren't for local theatergoers, who took up the slack in the first weeks after the terrorist attacks and helped fill the theaters, things would have been much worse for the Broadway economy. But it probably wasn't simply a sense of civic duty that sent residents of the tri-state area streaming into the city's theaters. In those days following the attacks, many wanted not only to do something to help, but also to be among other people and to connect, to join in some act of human community; to, as E.M. Forster put it in *Howards End*, "Live in fragments no longer." Although politicians and producers painted theater attendance as an act of patriotism, it transcended the symbolic in those days and provided something that may be seen as more valuable: comfort.

Most shows on Broadway missed three performances the week of September 11, with the Roundabout Theatre Company's terrific production of *Major Barbara* closing—as planned—at the end of that week. Although Mayor Rudolph W. Giuliani exhorted New Yorkers to keep on with their lives and invited tourists to come for a visit, drops in attendance and expected attendance began to force closings within a week. On September 23, five shows closed including the marching-band extravaganza *Blast!*; *If You Ever Leave Me . . . I'm Going With You!*; *The Rocky Horror Show*, which would reopen for a holiday run beginning in late October; the two-man Irish acting exercise, *Stones in His Pockets*; and the revival of *A Thousand Clowns*.

Although this shakeout of six shows in two weeks made producers a bit jittery—a natural state for most commercial types—11 new productions opened between September 11 and the end of the year. (For purposes of listing in *Best Plays*, productions such as Patrick Stewart's one-man version of *A Christmas Carol* at the Marquis Theatre are not counted in season totals due to their designation as "benefits." If *Carol* were included, the total would be 12.) A new spate of closings started December 30 when long-running revivals of *Kiss Me, Kate* and *Meredith Willson's The Music Man* folded—as did the lightweight new Andrew Lloyd Webber and Alan Ayckbourn musical, *By Jeeves*. Six more shows followed in the first two weeks of the new year: *Thou Shalt Not*, *Dance of Death*, *45 Seconds From Broadway*, *Hedda Gabler*, *The Women* and (for a second time) *The Rocky Horror Show*. Compared with the same period in 2000–01, roughly from Labor Day until two weeks into the new year, the 2001–02 Broadway season saw a 150 percent increase in the fall season's mortality rate.

One reason that more shows didn't fold is that theatrical labor unions agreed to take pay reductions of 25 to 50 percent in order to help keep them open. Additional help came in the form of $2.5 million given to the League of American Theatres and Producers by the City of New York for the purchase of 50,000 reduced-price tickets. New York State also contributed $1 million in marketing money, but all of the government assistance was directed to Broadway. Meanwhile, Off Broadway and Off Off Broadway theaters struggled on their own to stay open. In March, after the crisis had passed on Broadway, the league returned $1 million to the city, which Mayor Michael Bloomberg funneled to nonprofit arts groups.

Despite the aura of cooperation, however, all was not well in the theater district. The initial union pay-reductions affected only a handful of long-running shows (*Les Misérables*, *Chicago*, *The Full Monty*, *The Phantom of the Opera*, *Rent* and, later, *Kiss Me, Kate*). Productions not involved in the early negotiations found themselves closed out as unions took a wait-and-see attitude about how Broadway would fare. After posting a closing notice,

To the moon: Joe Bologna and Renée Taylor in If You Ever Leave Me . . . I'm Going With You! *Drawing: © Al Hirschfeld/The Margo Feiden Galleries Ltd., New York. www.alhirschfeld.com*

Meredith Willson's The Music Man also received union concessions. As it happened, the reductions lasted only a few weeks before things began to return to normal—whatever that may mean in a post-September 11 world. Some producers, a group often maligned for its miserly impulses, even managed to return some of the pay and royalties that had been waived.

In response to the manner in which the union negotiations were handled, Dodger Theatricals—producer of *Urinetown, Meredith Willson's The Music Man* and *42nd Street*—announced in November that it would withdraw from the league because it had been forced to negotiate its own reductions. Dodger spokesman Adrian Bryan-Brown told *Variety*, "The Dodgers believe that the league doesn't represent their own business interests at this time." Consequently, the league lost approximately $200,000 in annual fees and the Dodgers became the second large Broadway producing organization to decline league membership—Walt Disney Theatrical Productions is the other. The Dodgers aside, though, other producers privately continued to express their frustrations with the way that the negotiations had unfolded.

Given all of this information about bad blood, missing performances, drops in tourism and a flurry of closings, one might be forgiven for assuming that Broadway attendance and profits were headed for record losses. But even with the national economy in a tailspin and with the losses associated with the terrorist attacks, the 2001–02 season still ranks second only to the previous year (2000–01) in box office totals—although season attendance ranked fifth of the past five years. Overall attendance showed a decline of about 8 percent, accounting for nearly a million audience members. With a $2.88 increase in the average ticket price (to $58.63, according to *Variety*), the decreased attendance translated into a mere 3.4 percent reduction in receipts. In an industry that relies on more than half a billion dollars in annual receipts, though, a 3.4 percent drop equals nearly $23 million— which buys a lot of lunches at the Edison Coffee Shop. Considering the bleak outlook in the weeks after September 11, the financial news wasn't as poor as it might have been—and those dark days in September accounted for approximately 9 percent of the total drop in attendance.

Max Bialystock Lives

WHILE WE'RE TRYING to make sense of theatrical dollars, it's as good a time as any to discuss the missteps of *The Producers* team during the 2001–02 season—none of which, by the way, stopped the cash from flowing. At times, though, *The Producers* seemed to have devolved from a slick theatrical machine into the Gang That Couldn't Shoot Straight. First was a new system of exclusive day-of-show tickets to be sold for $480 each in a program initiated in fall 2001. With the creation of a new company, Broadway Inner Circle, Brooks and his partners held 50 tickets per performance to be sold at $400 plus an $80 processing fee—which went to the Brooks-backed company. Producers argued that the high prices and day-of-show availability kept choice tickets out of the hands of scalpers and made sure that the premiums on those exclusive tickets went to the producing team.

Under the best of circumstances, it would have been an appalling turn of events (isn't Broadway already too expensive for most Americans?). But given the terrorist attacks of September 11, the announcement of the new pricing structure seemed a galling grab for loot. (To be fair, the company had planned the new pricing structure before the attacks and reportedly postponed the program's beginning in the wake of them.) As a result, Brooks and company didn't have much in the sympathy bank when a recasting fiasco embarrassed the production (again) in the spring of 2002.

Puppet master: August Strindberg draws Ian McKellen and Helen Mirren in Dance of Death. *Drawing: © Al Hirschfeld/The Margo Feiden Galleries Ltd., New York. www.alhirschfeld.com*

As Nathan Lane's contract was about to expire early in 2002, producers of *The Producers* made the surprising announcement that noted British actor Henry Goodman—a two-time Olivier Award-winner—would be the new Max Bialystock. With all of the talented actors available in this country (Lewis J. Stadlen came immediately to mind), why cross the pond? Tom Viertel told *Variety*, "We don't feel we're particularly vulnerable in any sense. We do believe the show has become the star. And we've seen, from the many performances with understudies, that the show really cooks as long as you've got great actors in these great roles" (there's that hubris thing again). At the time, *The Producers* was operating on an advance of more than $20 million, which would help to cushion the transition from Lane to Goodman. (Lane co-star Matthew Broderick was replaced by television star Steven Weber in the Leo Bloom role.)

New York critics eagerly awaited the date when the new cast would be available for review, but they never got their chance. Two weeks before the critics were due, Goodman was fired on a Sunday afternoon for not getting the laughs—or for not getting the same laughs as Lane. Goodman had given only 30 performances, but the producers had seen enough and turned to understudy Brad Oscar, who had played Max dozens of times when Lane had suffered vocal strain. The new star team faced the critics on cue at the beginning of May and the response was respectful, if unenthusiastic. John Heilpern, who had called the original production the "best time you could ever wish for at the theater," in the *New York Observer*, wrote about the new leads: "My fellow critics have all rolled over wagging their tails to declare *The Producers* as good as ever. If only it were."

Oscar's own story was about as fabulous as they get. He started as an understudy to Ron Orbach, who was the show's original Franz Liebkind before injury forced him out of the pre-Broadway tryout. The understudy then stepped into the role of the wacky Nazi playwright who provides Bialystock and Bloom with the raw material for their planned flop. Oscar received a Tony nomination for his efforts as Liebkind and later found himself channeling Nathan Lane several times a month during the star's health problems. (Some veterans of the Broadway scene claim they still see Lane's spirit hovering over the performance.)

Songs in Their Hearts

THE NUMBER OF Broadway musical productions dropped from 10 last season to 9 this year—the difference was one less revival. But musicals struggled to enthrall critics and hold audiences in the season of September

11. Of the six new musicals to open in the 2001–02 season, two departed after staggering through the holiday season (creating a tidy category of nominees among the other four for the best-musical Tony). Harry Connick Jr.'s *Thou Shalt Not*, a New Orleans retake on Émile Zola's *Thérèse Raquin*, failed to take wing despite a terrific cast and the extraordinary talents of director-choreographer Susan Stroman. The musical—trapped in a Zola-esque netherworld where show music and jazzy riffs battled for primacy—lacked the magic spark necessary to fire the audience's enthusiasm. For something completely different, Andrew Lloyd Webber paired with Alan Ayckbourn to stage a musical entertainment, *By Jeeves*, fit for fanatics of P.G. Wodehouse's Bertie and Jeeves characters. For the rest of us, it was a bit of forced frivolity.

Of the other new musicals, two were remakes of movies (*Sweet Smell of Success* and *Thoroughly Modern Millie*) and a third (*Mamma Mia!*) repackaged ABBA tunes around the thinnest of story lines to create a goofy celebration of 1970s music and baby boomer angst. (You haven't lived until you've experienced the culture schlock of gray-haired suits from Wall Street boogeying to "Waterloo.") The saga of *Sweet Smell* was detailed at length as it worked its way from a pre-Broadway tryout in Chicago toward the Great White Way. The Chicago reviews suggested that the creative team—book writer John Guare, composer Marvin Hamlisch and lyricist Craig Carnelia—had not solved the problem of converting a noirish 1957 film into a snappy, wise-cracking musical. It was one of those projects that makes Broadway heads shake (and tongues wag) in wonder: how did so much talent and potential go so wrong?

After the show opened to a similar critical reception in New York, the producers embarked on a campaign—a battle, really—against New York theater columnists for focusing on the production's many difficulties. In what seemed to some as a bid for sympathy Tony votes, the producers distributed a letter drawing parallels between the evil press in *Sweet Smell* and the evil press at the *New York Times* and the *New York Post*. It made a good story—for the columnists, not the producers—but the storm passed.

In the Broadway run, Guare, a masterly Mr. Fix-It of others' musicals (notably the recent uncredited updating of *Kiss Me, Kate*), seemed handcuffed to a string of tired one-liners; the zany erudition demonstrated in so many of his plays was scarcely in evidence. Critical (and audience) darling John Lithgow—call him Lithgow the Lovable—as the evil gossip columnist J.J. Hunsecker, kept the show's darker elements from sizzling, but it didn't prevent him from landing a Tony Award for best actor in a musical.

The next entry in the remake sweepstakes was the ditzy feel-good musical *Thoroughly Modern Millie*. Based on the 1967 film, *Millie* charts the rise of a girl from Kansas who moves to New York seeking a "modern life," but finds herself battling white slavers and falling in love with Mr. Right. Featuring a cast filled with eager-to-please young performers, *Millie* marked the creation of a bright new musical star in the title role: Sutton Foster. This new light on Broadway has the clearest, most resonant voice heard on a legit stage in many a day—and it's housed, astonishingly, in a slight, almost delicate frame. Foster reminded many people of a young Mary Tyler Moore in performance—although Moore was in the 1967 film version of *Millie*, Julie Andrews played the title role. Foster capped her season of success with the Tony Award for best actress in a musical.

The show received five other Tonys (see our Awards section), including best musical, which was peculiar due to the pastiche nature of the book, score and lyrics. Indeed, in an unusual move by Tony voters, the awards for book and score of a musical went to upstart *Urinetown*'s Greg Kotis and Mark Hollmann. John Rando, who directed *Urinetown*, also snagged the Tony Award for best director of a musical, which showed a remarkable split over the musical categories. The voters seemed to imply that *Millie* was a kind of theme-park show (and voted Tony Awards accordingly) driven by Rob Ashford's choreography, Harriet Harris's outrageous comic performance, Martin Pakledinaz's electric couture, Doug Besterman and Ralph Burns's zippy orchestrations and, of course, Foster's soaring voice. Or did they?

Even though the Tony Awards honor excellence in the Broadway theater, they also have a pocketbook element—and producers, whose pockets are correspondingly filled or emptied, get to vote. In the case of *Millie*, this meant a bonanza of voters due to a $1 million investment in the show by a group known as the Independent Presenters Network—which includes several dozen theater presenters from around the country. Added to the large number of presumed votes for *Millie* based on self-interest, there was also some residual annoyance at one of the producers of *Urinetown*. Dodger Theatricals, which had withdrawn from the League of American Theatres and Producers for reasons detailed above, had reportedly alienated other producers in abandoning the trade group. Some speculated that the bloc voting for *Millie* and Dodger's own action spelled doom at the Tony Awards for *Urinetown* and for the revival of the Stephen Sondheim musical *Into the Woods*, in which Dodger Theatricals also had a leadership role.

Oh, Mama: Louise Pitre and company in Mamma Mia! *Drawing: © Al Hirschfeld/The Margo Feiden Galleries Ltd., New York. www.alhirschfeld.com*

But the Tony voters showed a Solomonic wisdom with which they are rarely credited in splitting the musical awards between *Urinetown* and *Thoroughly Modern Millie*. (Likewise, the superb musical revival of *Into the Woods* beat a shockingly inept revival of *Oklahoma!* in a tiny category of two Tony nominees—so Dodger Theatricals didn't do so poorly after all. The other musical revival, Vernel Bagneris's lively *One Mo' Time*, was dismissed by the mainstream media and departed after only 21 performances.) *Urinetown* was the sole entry to the (really) new musical realm on Broadway after its runs Off and Off Off Broadway. A Best Play from last season, *Urinetown* also faced the daunting task—when it premiered September 20—of being the first show to open on Broadway following the terrorist attacks.

OFF BROADWAY SEASON 2002–2003

Productions in a continuing run on May 31, 2003 in bold
Productions honored as Best Plays *selections in italics*

NEW PLAYS (44)

The Woman in Black
Eat the Runt
The Credeaux Canvas (Playwrights)
Chaucer in Rome (Lincoln Center)
Breath, Boom (Playwrights)
World of Mirth
Blue (Roundabout)
Saint Lucy's Eyes
Topdog/Underdog (Public/NYSF)
First Love (NYTW)
Rude Entertainment (Drama Dept.)
Metamorphoses (Second Stage)
The Shape of Things
Light Years (Playwrights)
Underneath the Lintel
Havana Is Waiting
Everything That Rises Must Converge (NYTW)
Wonder of the World (MTC)
Where's My Money? (MTC)
Everett Beekin (Lincoln Center)
Speaking in Tongues (Roundabout)
True Love
Psych (Playwrights)
Homebody/Kabul (NYTW)
What's on the Hearts of Men
Sorrows and Rejoicings (Second Stage)
Further Than the Furthest Thing (MTC)
The Matchmaker (Irish Rep)
Golden Ladder
Four (MTC)
Necessary Targets
The Dazzle (Roundabout)
Surviving Grace
Mr. Goldwyn
The Carpetbagger's Children
    (Lincoln Center)
Franny's Way (Playwrights)
36 Views (Public/NYSF)
Helen (Public/NYSF)
Blue Surge (Public/NYSF)
The Odyssey (Willow Cabin)
One Shot, One Kill (Primary Stages)

NEW PLAYS (cont'd)

House (MTC)
Garden (MTC)
Boys and Girls (Playwrights)

NEW MUSICALS (9)

Tick, Tick . . . Boom!
Once Around the City (Second Stage)
The Spitfire Grill (Playwrights)
Reefer Madness
Roadside (York)
Summer of '42
The Last Five Years
Prodigal (York)
Menopause: The Musical

PLAY REVIVALS (6)

Measure for Measure (Public/NYSF)
The Ghost Sonata (BAM)
Quartett
The Seagull (Public/NYSF)
Othello (Public/NYSF)
Cymbeline (BAM)

SOLO (7)

Elaine Stritch at Liberty (Public/NYSF)
One Man
The Godfadda Workout
Throw Pitchfork (NYTW)
Ricky Jay on the Stem (Second Stage)
Red Hot Mama (York)
21 Dog Years: Doing Time @ Amazon.com

SPECIALTIES (9)

Slanguage (NYTW)
Puppetry of the Penis
The Complete Works of William Shakespeare
    (Abridged)
Marc Salem's Mind Games, Too
Criss Angel Mindfreak
Carnival (Encores!)
Golden Boy (Encores!)
Pajama Game (Encores!)
Vienna: Lusthaus (revisited) (NYTW)

REVUES (2)

Hello Muddah, Hello Fadduh!
Capitol Steps: When Bush Comes to Shove

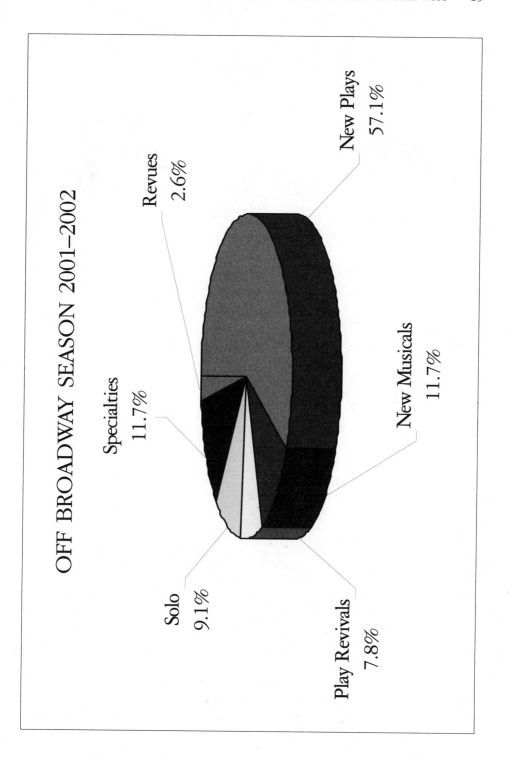

OFF BROADWAY SEASON 2001–2002

New Plays
57.1%

Revues
2.6%

Specialties
11.7%

Solo
9.1%

Play Revivals
7.8%

New Musicals
11.7%

Wonder *women: Sarah Jessica Parker with Amy Sedaris, Marylouise Burke and Kristine Nielsen in* Wonder of the World. *Drawing:* © *Al Hirschfeld/The Margo Feiden Galleries Ltd., New York. www.alhirschfeld.com*

In the hours following the terrorist attacks, members of the pompous punditocracy declared the death of irony saying, in effect, that a new seriousness would now seize our culture as we faced challenges on the scale of our parents and grandparents in the Great Depression and World War II. These pronouncements didn't bode well for *Urinetown*, a musical about a town where no one may go to the bathroom unless they can pay. The show relies on a certain sophistication as it toys with the romantic musical form and ultimately exposes the darker side of "happily ever after"—

pace Stephen Sondheim. But critics and audiences ignored the prognosticators, and the Little Musical That Could continued to survive and prosper. The success of *Urinetown* was due in no small part to the versatility of a talented cast who threw themselves into their roles with gleeful abandon. The resulting performances, especially those of Jeff McCarthy and Spencer Kayden (as Officer Lockstock and Little Sally), kept the audiences aware that "reality" might burst at any moment. It was thrilling theater, even if the murder of one character—he's thrown from a building—was a bit too reminiscent of bodies falling from the sky just a few days earlier in Lower Manhattan. It also brought another Foster to the Broadway stage as a headliner. Hunter Foster, brother to Sutton, starred as Bobby Strong, who takes on the powers that pee—uh, be—and falls in love with heiress Hope Cladwell (Jennifer Laura Thompson).

Broadway Plays: Welcome to the Museum

AS DETAILED IN the summary and chart on page 4, there were 35 new productions on Broadway with 20 productions of nonmusical plays—8 more than last season. A majority of the plays this year, however, were revivals (12). Careful readers will note that the Ivan Turgenev play, *Fortune's Fool*, is listed as a revival in counterpoint to our friends at the Tony Awards, who made it eligible for a new-play award. Although there may never be anything quite as brilliant as the masterly Tony-winning performances by Alan Bates and Frank Langella in the male leads of this production, Mike Poulton's translation does not diverge notably from translations by the estimable Constance Garnett (*A Poor Gentleman*, 1959) and Stephen Mulrine (*One of the Family*, 1998). In the case of Mary Zimmerman's adaptation of Ovid's *Metamorphoses*, authorship clearly lies with Zimmerman, who retains the essence of Ovid and yet locates the play in a context all her own. (Edward Albee, the Tony Award winner for *The Goat, or Who Is Sylvia?*, joked about hoping to meet two of the other nominees whom he had not seen: Turgenev and Ovid.)

Of the 8 new plays on Broadway, 3 are honored as 2001–02 Best Plays (*Metamorphoses, The Goat, or Who Is Sylvia?* and *Topdog/Underdog*). Perhaps 3 out of 8 isn't a bad ratio, but there was a time when all of the Best Plays were routinely Broadway babies. There was also, of course, a time when nearly 200 new plays opened during a season. As the song says, those days are gone. Indeed, two of the honored plays (*Metamorphoses* and *Topdog/Underdog*) first opened Off Broadway. Of the transfers, Mary Zimmerman's magical *Metamorphoses* made the move more seamlessly, losing little of the intimacy it enjoyed at the Second Stage Theatre. But Suzan-Lori Parks's *Topdog*, with its new cast member—rapper-actor Mos Def replaced Don Cheadle when the play moved from the Joseph Papp Public Theater—saw its impact dissipate.

In the Anspacher Theater at the Public, the audience surrounded the action on three sides making Parks's dramaturgy all the more raw and vivid. The proscenium stage of Broadway's Ambassador Theatre removed the spectators from the action and diminished Def's stage presence. Students who sat in the rear mezzanine (i.e., the cheap seats) of the Ambassador often complained that they could barely understand what Def was saying. Those of us in the orchestra could easily see that the superb Jeffrey Wright, as one of the battling brothers, dominated the younger brother played by Def. These Broadway-based drawbacks undermined Parks's story of a struggle for primacy, but the text itself remained a wonder for its poetry and its challenges to ideas about modes of US identity and representation. George C. Wolfe provided his usual deft direction here and in *Elaine Stritch at Liberty*, but he was somehow overlooked in the Tony Award nominations. (In a musical number at the beginning of the Tony Awards ceremony, Def joined a Richard Rodgers medley and added a lyric of his own—sung to the tune of "Brown paper packages/Tied up with string/These are a few/Of my favorite things"):

> G-E-O-R-G-E/Wo-L-F-E/Off or on Broad/You're the Topdog to me.

Edward Albee's *The Goat, or Who Is Sylvia?* started on Broadway and managed to stay there well into the next season. Albee's play, with its faux-shocking subject matter, is really a dark comedy with light tragic undertones in its exploration of the nature of love and societal codes. The important thing for any director or producer of Albee's work to remember is that the playwright creates spoken music requiring actors with superior lingual dexterity. Albee actors must be able to "sing" his arias, but lightly, effortlessly. Unfortunately, the excellent Mercedes Ruehl as the betrayed wife Stevie seemed endlessly entangled in Albee's savory speeches—but no one seemed to mind. Bill Pullman played the goat-loving husband with the studied modulation for which the film actor is well known.

Except for these Best Play productions, seeing a play on Broadway tended to be a trip to the museum. Although plays dominated with 57 percent of the new productions this season, most Broadway plays were revivals and those that weren't (exceptions noted above) broke little new ground. The first new play after September 11 was Neil Simon's whimsical stab at a backstage theater story, *45 Seconds From Broadway*. Set among the denizens of the New York theater scene (patrons, performers, producers) at the Edison Coffee Shop, it relied on Simon's tried-and-true comic formula. Featuring Lewis J. Stadlen as a Jackie Mason clone and the always-fascinating Marian Seldes as a nutty theatrical wannabe, the piece fizzled as a mere collection of theatrical in-jokes that detoured on the way to becoming a compelling play. The collection of actors, though, was a casting agent's dream. In addition to Stadlen and Seldes, audiences were treated to performances by Louis Zorich, Rebecca Schull, Alix Korey, Bill Moor, Lynda Gravátt and David Margulies.

Next up was Peter Parnell's engaging biographical drama, *QED*, starring Alan Alda as physicist Richard Feynman. Performed when the musical *Contact* was dark at Lincoln Center's Vivian Beaumont Theater, *QED* was very nearly a one-man show except for the role of a young female student (played by Kellie Overbey). Alda played the irrepressible Feynman with director Gordon Davidson helping the actor to keep the story interesting and lively as the character spun theories on the relationships between physics, life and death—while facing his own life-threatening illness. With only a couple of shows a week, and a long hiatus during the winter holidays, it must have been hard for *QED* to find its footing. Even so, tickets were often difficult to get.

The least of the new-play offerings on Broadway this season had to be *The Smell of the Kill* by Michele Lowe. This production was notable only for the reunion of Elizabeth Ireland McCann and Nelle Nugent, two trailblazing women producers (of the original Broadway production of *The Elephant Man* in 1979, among others) who had taken a 17-year hiatus from working together in the theater. One headline writer insisted that *Smell* was a play "some women will love and most men will hate." But however much critics might want to make this play about the gender wars, it has two insurmountable problems: 1) we never see the annoying, disgusting husbands whom the wives finally kill (we hear them offstage), and 2) the women aren't very sympathetic (or interesting) characters. It has been far too long since McCann and Nugent joined forces on a production, but it might have been better if they had waited a bit longer.

More than a few members of the theater community, however, thought Terry Johnson's adaptation of the *The Graduate*, was the season's weakest entry. (At some point during the awards season, the producers of *The Graduate* purchased a full-page ad in the *New York Times* trumpeting their lack of honors and the financial success of their show.) But for those of us who saw the play in London, the New York production was a bit of a treat.

Jason Biggs made a fine Benjamin—the London actor seemed to be trying a Dustin Hoffman impression via Woody Allen—and Kathleen Turner was her smoky, sultry, 20-seconds-naked self. The humor of the play carried better on Broadway and, even if there seems to be no good reason to bring a 1960s iconic movie to the stage (except money), it was—surprise!—an entertaining time at the theater. (Now, if someone in New York would only do *Hysteria*, Johnson's twisted comedy about Sigmund Freud and Salvador Dalí.)

Over in the Revival Wing

AS WE MAKE our way through the museum that is Broadway theater in 2001–02, we can take pleasure in the revivals that provided much of the interest this season. After September 11, a desperation enveloped the theater community. As Broadway theater teetered near the edge of the abyss, producers filled the stages with revivals of plays that almost guaranteed success—though most shows were planned far in advance of the terrorist attacks. But in those days of insecurity, everyone wondered what might be the reception for plays such as Henrik Ibsen's *Hedda Gabler* and August Strindberg's *Dance of Death*—neither of them beacons of hope about human relations.

After beating the drum for Kate Burton's portrayal of the prototypical female control freak, Hedda Gabler, when he saw it in Boston early in 2001, *New York Times* critic Ben Brantley moderated his praise a bit when the play opened on Broadway in October. According to others who saw the production several times—it was developed by the Bay Street Theatre, the Williamstown Theatre Festival and the Huntington Theatre Company—Burton's crisp performance evolved from what Brantley called a "stinging portrait of a woman who fears, more than anything else, being ordinary" into a broader, almost comic portrayal. Although there was certainly nothing ordinary about the riveting Burton's characterization, it was unsettling, for example, that Hedda's suicide tended to provoke laughter—and not, it seemed, nervous-tension titters. Jon Robin Baitz's adaptation of the text enlivened the action, Michael Emerson made an almost charming George Tesman and Harris Yulin was a properly unctuous Judge Brack.

Richard Greenberg—celebrated elsewhere in this volume for *The Dazzle*—adapted Strindberg's *Dance of Death* giving it a contemporary ring: at one point, for instance, one character calls another "clueless." But the good fortune of fall theatergoers was in getting to see the larger-than-life stage performances of Ian McKellen and Helen Mirren. Transformation is the key element required in great acting and it was brilliantly on display in McKellen's and Mirren's performances. In what is often referred to as a forerunner to Edward Albee's *Who's Afraid of Virginia Woolf?*, the marvelous pair gave an object lesson in the winding paths traversed by many who attempt long relationships: the petty slights, the mutual loathing—and the unstinting attraction. David Strathairn, as the cousin who comes to call, never quite matched the intensity of the leads, but who could blame him? Most actors would find themselves overmatched by this dynamic (and sexy) duo.

Both of these productions managed to make it through the winter holiday season, but both closed on the same day, January 13. Burton and Mirren were nominated for Tonys, but the revivals to be celebrated at season's end included a fall comedy, and spring-opening comedies and dramas. The revival of Michael Frayn's *Noises Off*, a farce about the backstage antics of a British regional theater troupe, featured a veteran cast including Patti LuPone, Peter Gallagher, Katie Finneran, Faith Prince, Edward Hibbert, Richard Easton and others. The self-conscious good cheer of the comedy,

Tea and matzo balls: Lewis J. Stadlen, Marian Seldes and company in 45 Seconds From Broadway. *Drawing: © Al Hirschfeld/The Margo Feiden Galleries Ltd., New York. www.alhirschfeld.com*

opening at a time when everyone in New York seemed to need a good laugh, was warmly received by critics and audiences. For some, though, including Elysa Gardner of *USA Today*, the "headache started about 10 minutes after the curtain rose. . . . By the end, you're likely to be more dazed than dazzled." Gardner gets no argument from this corner: the fussy staging by Jeremy Sams made *Noises Off* a hard night's work for actors and spectators alike. One who made the work look easy was Finneran as sexy Brooke Ashton, for which the actor won a Tony Award. Finneran's triumph was somewhat vitiated, though, by Robin Pogrebin's report in the *New York Times* that the play had closed before the Tony Awards—it actually ran for three months beyond the ceremony.

The other comic revivals of the season included Clare Boothe Luce's *The Women* (a 1936–37 Best Play), Ivan Turgenev and Mike Poulton's *Fortune's Fool*, Paul Osborn's *Morning's at Seven* (a 1939–40 Best Play) and Noël Coward's *Private Lives*. The Luce play, in a production by the Roundabout Theatre Company, was more interesting to watch than to hear. Derek McLane's clever Art Deco set pieces opened into cushy, satiny rooms with a 1930s New York skyline in the background. Fashion designer Isaac Mizrahi's creations put the "cost" into costumes with arch couture that was largely unflattering to his female clients. Director Scott Elliott seemed dominated by the designer even down to the curtain call, which was in embarrassingly bad taste with the women (and a young girl) taking their bows garbed only in a wide variety of underwear. At times, it also appeared that the director and his team were doing a drag-show parody of Luce's play—except when the luminous Cynthia Nixon was onstage.

Fortune's Fool, as mentioned above, lands in our revival category because it is not a previously unknown or unproduced play. There is something slightly perverse and hegemonistic about reclaiming the work of a 19th-century Russian author and labeling it "original" to the Broadway stage. Ironically, given the competition this season, the producers of *Fortune's Fool*—who petitioned the Tony Awards committee to be considered as a new play—might have done better in the revival category. (We'll let pass without further comment the similarities between Poulton's version and those of Constance Garnett and Stephen Mulrine—neither of which, in any case, played on Broadway.) It was tempting for writers to invoke Anton Chekhov when discussing the play due to the obvious similarities between the playwrights. Both were Russian, familiar with the crumbling feudal class structure and anxious about the changes needed (and coming) to their society.

Twelve steps: John Leguizamo in Sexaholix . . . a Love Story. *Drawing:* © *Al Hirschfeld/ The Margo Feiden Galleries Ltd., New York. www.alhirschfeld.com*

The Russian version of *Fortune's Fool* was banned for nearly 15 years because, according to Mulrine, it was an "indictment of upper class modes and manners." The true joy of *Fortune's Fool* on Broadway—aside from the superb pairing of Bates and Langella—was the clever weaving of issues surrounding class into a psychological narrative of family melodrama. It's a technique that Chekhov himself would later employ in his own plays. In *The Seagull*, Chekhov pays homage to Turgenev when Chekhov's alter ego, Trigorin, says, "And when I die my friends, passing by my tomb, will say, 'Here lies Trigorin. He was a good writer, but inferior to Turgenev.'" In that brief passage, Chekhov acknowledges—with typical indirection—the debt all writers owe to those who came before.

The Lincoln Center Theater production of *Morning's at Seven* provided work for nine mature actors (the youngest character is about 40) and the play is likely to continue to be revived every couple of decades or so for that very reason. Osborn's play is a subtle, old-fashioned piece that gives actors of a certain age roles into which they can sink their teeth. The four sisters of the piece were played with nuanced style by Estelle Parsons, Elizabeth Franz, Frances Sternhagen and Piper Laurie. Three of these actors, Laurie was the exception, competed with one another in the featured actress category for a Tony Award. The ubiquitous Daniel Sullivan showed his steady directorial hand yet again—although Parsons made some discontented noises on a panel discussion during the play's run. Parsons, of course, is also a director, which brings to mind the old joke: How many directors (or actors) does it take to screw in a light bulb? Fifty. One to do it and 49 to say, "I could do it better." The rest of the cast included William Biff McGuire, Christopher Lloyd, Stephen Tobolowsky, Julie Hagerty and Buck Henry in a fine ensemble effort.

It was Coward's *Private Lives* that received the play-revival award at the Tony Awards ceremony. It may also deserve an award for being the most revived modern play in Broadway history: it has been produced a total of seven times including the 1931 premiere. Burns Mantle declined to make it a Best Play all those years ago writing that it is a "deft and amusing farce, but largely dependent upon the personalities and skillful playing of its actors." Producers across the decades have taken Mantle's words to heart casting personalities in the lead roles. No less a personage than the Master himself (Coward, the author) played the lead in the original with Gertrude Lawrence as his Amanda. Laurence Olivier played Victor, the second male lead. Other "personalities" have included Tallulah Bankhead, Tammy Grimes, Maggie Smith, Elizabeth Taylor and Joan Collins. Interestingly, almost all of the Amandas have been bigger celebrities than the Elyots—the exception being Richard Burton (with Taylor) in his final Broadway role (1983).

The 2002 revival of *Private Lives* made a better acting match than in most of those past productions (with apologies to Brian Bedford, Remak Ramsay and Simon Jones). Alan Rickman and Lindsay Duncan had a sizzling chemistry that somehow managed to distract the audience from the forced-perspective of Tim Hatley's luxe settings. Despite occasional reports of uneven performances—up one night, down the next—the production received Tony Awards for best revival, leading actress in a play and scenic design.

As the season drew to a close, three dramas were revived on Broadway that, in a time of insecurity and terror, fittingly considered issues on the minds of many Americans—Arthur Miller's *The Crucible* (a 1952–53 Best Play), Bernard Pomerance's *The Elephant Man* (a 1978–79 Best Play) and Miller's *The Man Who Had All the Luck*. In Richard Eyre's production of *The Crucible*, Liam Neeson and Laura Linney joined forces as John and Elizabeth Proctor, who suffer the tyranny of weak-minded, superstitious society in 17th-century Massachusetts. Eyre's production was perfectly suited to a consideration of the misuse and abuse of power in God's name—particularly at a time when it seemed that religious wars were driving our nation's leadership. The first act of the play seemed slow and ponderous, which is

Diva divine: Barbara Cook in Mostly Sondheim. *Drawing:* © *Al Hirschfeld/The Margo Feiden Galleries Ltd., New York. www.alhirschfeld.com*

Golden gal: Bea Arthur in Bea Arthur on Broadway: Just Between Friends. *Drawing:* © *Al Hirschfeld/The Margo Feiden Galleries Ltd., New York. www.alhirschfeld.com*

a particular stylistic choice that Eyre has made in other productions—but the acting overall was unusually uneven, given the talents of the ensemble at hand. Tim Hatley's dark, foreboding settings reinforced the power and structure of the State. In a cataclysmic moment at the end, though, the setting collapsed in a thunderous effect that allowed light to shine through. It was a metaphorical act indicating that the darkness of *The Crucible*'s culture was soon to dissipate—though too late for Proctor and his family.

Director Sean Mathias returned to Broadway with his second production of the season—the first was *Dance of Death*—in the revival of Bernard Pomerance's *The Elephant Man*. It also marked the return of Billy Crudup, who had been away making films for five years, and of Kate Burton, whose

Hedda Gabler closed three months earlier. Most reviewers commented on the emotional cool of Mathias's production—a trend among the current crop of young directors that we have noted in the past. But in this play about a man's spiritual alienation from society and society's revulsion at his physical form, emotional distancing raised elements of Brechtian theory to powerful human art—extending even to scene titles announced in unison by the cast. The production wasn't of the conventionally uplifting variety often found on television's "family hour." But the clinical, even harsh overtones of Mathias's staging (combined with exceptionally fine and sensitive performances by Crudup and Burton) gave a solid jolt—or should have—to the middle-class sensibilities that fill Broadway theater seats. In days when fear and suspicion seemed abroad in our land, Mathias asked us to consider the nature of strangeness and the other—before we marginalize it, detain it, expel it, kill it, crush it. That jolt, however, is not the sort of thing audiences tend to seek on Broadway. Indeed, the production was far enough outside of the mainstream to make us wonder how it ever made it to Broadway. The likely two-word answer: Billy Crudup.

When Arthur Miller's *The Man Who Had All the Luck* opened November 23, 1944, it was Thanksgiving Day. But gratitude must have come hard to Miller on that weekend, when his producers closed the show after only four performances. Lewis Nichols wrote in the *New York Times* that the author and his director, Joseph Fields, "have not edited out the confusion of the script nor its somewhat jumbled philosophies, nor have they kept it from running over into the ridiculous now and then." For Nichols, the play's complex approach to how success comes—"Luck, or good work, you get your choice," as he put it—made the play difficult to follow and "corny to the extreme." Burns Mantle took a typically more charitable approach when he wrote in *Best Plays* that the play was, "mistakenly withdrawn. . . . It was at least worth a three-week chance to find itself and its public."

Critics in 2002 New York were much kinder to Miller and his play, enjoying the blessing of hindsight that allowed them to place *Luck* in context with his later, more successful work. Miller's main character, David Beeves, is probably more a man of our time than of his own—the play was set in 1938, though the rumble of coming war and the vestiges of economic depression are faint. An auto mechanic, David cannot believe the paths of good fortune that he takes at every juncture: his girlfriend's father (who hates him) dies at an opportune moment, he's helped with a complex, career-making car repair by a mysterious fellow from Austria (Sam Robards

Stritch stretch: Elaine Stritch in Elaine Stritch at Liberty. *Drawing: © Al Hirschfeld/The Margo Feiden Galleries Ltd., New York. www.alhirschfeld.com*

in a Clarence Derwent Award-winning performance), he makes a success of a mink farm when others are failing, etc. Sure, he works hard, but what (or where) is the unseen hand that nudges him this way or that? David constantly asks the question: Why me? Haunted by fear that his luck is going to turn bad at any moment, he also watches as his brother's chances at success evaporate—which hints at the many Miller-written brothers yet to come. Compellingly acted by a large ensemble, with Chris O'Donnell as the doubt-wracked David, *Luck* runs out in the final act when the young playwright ties the drama's loose ends into an attractive (and convenient) bow. Still, it was a pleasure to have an otherwise trying Broadway season end with such a lucid, intelligent production.

Star Turns

THAT THERE WERE as many solo-performer productions as new musicals on Broadway this season shouldn't come as a surprise. Anyone with simple math skills knows that it's much less expensive to do solo shows with their lower production costs. This season's solo pieces included actors in one-man plays (*An Almost Holy Picture* and *The Mystery of Charles Dickens*), one-woman retrospectives by certifiable divas (*Mostly Sondheim, Bea Arthur on Broadway: Just Between Friends* and *Elaine Stritch at Liberty*) and one of the finest comic actors of the younger generation, John Leguizamo, in his second Broadway standup run (*Sexaholix . . . a Love Story*).

Leguizamo got things rolling on the Broadway-solo front with his meditation on love, sex and fatherhood, *Sexaholix*, in December 2001. But Elaine Stritch was already honing her show, *Elaine Stritch at Liberty*, downtown at Off Broadway's Joseph Papp Public Theater. Before the season was over, Stritch would be the reigning champion of the Broadway solo world with a Tony Award, a New York Drama Critics Circle Award and a Special Citation from *Best Plays*. Stritch wasn't the only diva to trod the big stage this season, she was merely the most sensational. *Elaine Stritch at Liberty*, written by the great dame of American theater and her collaborator, John Lahr, covered Stritch's life, loves, alcoholism and career with a musical-comedy style that very nearly made the show into a one-woman musical. Directed with a fine hand by the underappreciated George C. Wolfe, the production managed somehow to be more powerful and more intimate when it transferred to Broadway's 1,297-seat Neil Simon Theatre.

In addition to Stritch, two other divas of the stage, Barbara Cook and Bea Arthur, also reminded theatergoers why we keep going back to sit in those large glow-in-the-dark-rooms. Cook's *Mostly Sondheim* concert demonstrated to the few who were able to see it—similar to Peter Parnell's *QED* mentioned above, she performed in the Vivian Beaumont at Lincoln Center when *Contact* was dark—that she still possesses a rich, powerful soprano and employs it with exquisite theatrical skill. In *Bea Arthur on Broadway: Just Between Friends*, audiences at the intimate 785-seat Booth Theatre were treated to a cozy rendition of Arthur's life in show business. Barefoot and perched on a comfy chair with pianist Billy Goldenberg accompanying her, the woman who helped bring women's issues into the public arena as star of two groundbreaking television shows—*Maude* and *The Golden Girls*—shared a few personal stories, a few jokes, a few songs. It was especially interesting that Arthur and Stritch were appearing simultaneously: the latter told, in her show, how she ruined a job interview for *Golden Girls*. We're left to figure out which role she didn't get.

Kevin Bacon and Simon Callow appeared in the only solo shows that might be termed plays—if they were not so completely something else. Bacon scored points for his nuanced portrayal of a man who has his faith challenged again and again in Heather McDonald's *An Almost Holy Picture* at the American Airlines Theatre. Ultimately, he seems to take comfort in the notion that God's hand is everywhere to be seen—even in his daughter's physical anomaly that provides the play's title. Bacon is an honest, intelligent performer with roots in the theater (*Getting Out*, *Slab Boys*, *Forty Deuce*) and we hope he returns soon with a play. Callow's turn in *The Mystery of Charles Dickens*, by Peter Ackroyd, at the Belasco Theatre was in a lecture format—Dickens himself toured frequently, reading his works to audiences—that allowed the actor to tell Dickens's life story while drawing parallels between it and Dickens's art. It ran a mere 20 performances.

Off the Rialto

OFF BROADWAY STRUGGLED through this troubled season by banging the media drum loudly when Broadway producers got all of the attention in those first days and weeks following September 11. Producer Scott Morfee became an impassioned advocate for the downtown theaters—which is where most of Off Broadway resides—as he tried to keep his production of Glen Berger's thoughtful play, *Underneath the Lintel*, running at the Soho Playhouse. He managed to keep the one-man performance running into the next season. *Lintel* was of particular interest due to its pursuit of a string of human events that eventually lead back to the pursuer and, by implication, to all of humanity. It was a simple, touching production that pointedly reminded post-September 11 audiences of the connections among us all.

Virginia Louloudes, of the theater service organization ART/NY, and many theater leaders outside the mainstream banded together to keep Off and Off Off Broadway alive. Indeed, more than a few downtown theaters found themselves in desperate straits due to their proximity to Ground Zero. Some could not operate during the attempted rescue and the prolonged recovery because of travel restrictions in the disaster zone. Some shows closed for a few days, other shows could not take the pressure and ended their runs altogether.

There were 77 new productions of record Off Broadway during the 2001–02 season, which is five fewer than last year's 82. (See summary and chart on pages 14 and 15.) There was a slight decrease in the number of new musicals, none of which seemed destined for Broadway. But there were more new plays Off Broadway this year. Indeed, Off Broadway has

Gotham gossips: John Lithgow with Brian d'Arcy James at left in Sweet Smell of Success. *Drawing: © Al Hirschfeld/The Margo Feiden Galleries Ltd., New York. www.alhirschfeld.com*

Country rave: Company members in the revival of Oklahoma! *Drawing:* © *Al Hirschfeld/ The Margo Feiden Galleries Ltd., New York. www.alhirschfeld.com*

become the home of the liveliest new playwriting in New York—six of the 10 Best Plays and our Special Citation honoree all started there.

New Plays at Nonprofits

THE FIRST OPENING of the Off Broadway season was a commercial offering that would be hard to call a new play, since *The Woman in Black* had already been running for 12 years in London when it appeared at the Minetta Lane Theatre. A thriller of the play-within-a-play variety, New York critics and audiences weren't excited and it passed in 40 performances. Avery Crozier's *Eat the Runt* transferred from Off Off Broadway in June. Its gimmick of interactive theater—audience members helped choose who played what role, which influenced what happened—kept it running for a respectable 125 performances at the American Place Theatre.

The Off Broadway season really began, though, with the Playwrights Horizons productions of Keith Bunin's *The Credeaux Canvas* and Kia Corthron's *Breath, Boom*. Bunin's play is a character study about art, authenticity and betrayal among three artsy friends. Michael Mayer's solid production couldn't hide the play's flaws, which centered on too many conflicts going in too many directions at once. Annie Parisse and Lee Pace stood out for their sensitive portrayal of lovers whose moment is evanescent. *Breath, Boom*, Corthron's 2001–02 Best Play, is an impressionistic drama about "girl gangstas" who function both as victims and victimizers in a criminal justice system designed apparently to crush the human spirit. Marion McClinton directed the powerful production with Yvette Ganier starring as Prix, an angry teenage girl who grows, with difficulty, into self-awareness.

After *Breath, Boom*, Playwrights Horizons was "homeless" while its new building was under construction. For the rest of the season, Playwrights productions appeared in several venues. The company's next effort—at the Duke on 42nd Street—was a co-production (with the George Street Playhouse) of the Richard Rodgers Award-winning musical *The Spitfire Grill*, by James Valcq and Fred Alley. Based on Lee David Zlotoff's film, *Spitfire* tracks the lives of three rural women who attempt to make new lives for themselves. In the wake of the tragic events of a few weeks earlier (and the sudden death of co-creator Alley several months earlier), the musical's homespun, feel-good tone seem forced and ill-suited to New York—and probably would have even before September 11. The company followed with Billy Aronson's *Light Years* (at Theater Three) a lightweight comedy about four undergraduates making their way to adulthood.

Evan Smith's *Psych* (in Signature Theatre's Peter Norton Space) was a critically undervalued allegory on the price we pay for failing to conform to society's expectations. When a graduate student in psychology learns that nice people not only finish last but get crushed in the bargain, she uses the system to beat the system. Despite director Jim Simpson's best efforts, the play suffered from a subplot about personal betrayal that only obliquely fit with the main story. Heather Goldenhersh was the aptly named Sunny, and Enid Graham played a tightly wound friend who narrates the play and drives the subplot. Playwrights veteran Richard Nelson directed his *Franny's Way* (at Atlantic Theater Company), a coming-of-age tale that echoed the previous season's *Madame Melville*. A 2001–02 Best Play, *Franny's Way* lovingly captured the existential angst of a 1950s teenager and framed it against the writings of famed recluse J.D. Salinger. The delightful Kathleen Widdoes played the adult version of Franny, who narrates the action, as well as Franny's grandmother.

The final Playwrights production of the season also brought Off Broadway's season to a close. Tom Donaghy's *Boys and Girls* (at the Duke on 42nd Street) meandered in Mametian dialogue through the lives of four gay people—two men, two women—who couple and uncouple, contemplate commitment and try to become adults. The result is that none of the characters in the play is particularly attractive—which makes it difficult for audiences to engage the work.

Fool's delight: Frank Langella and Alan Bates in Fortune's Fool. *Drawing: © Al Hirschfeld/The Margo Feiden Galleries Ltd., New York. www.alhirschfeld.com*

Lincoln Center Theater got a bouncy start to the summer with John Guare's *Chaucer in Rome*, a madcap comedy about art, religion, sacrifice and the millennium in modern-day Rome. It's an inverted sequel to his masterpiece, *The House of Blue Leaves*, which featured a visit to New York by the Pope and an AWOL soldier, Ronnie Shaughnessy. In *Chaucer*, Ronnie has become an old, guilt-stricken man named Ron whose son is a painter poisoned by the hazardous materials he uses. Ultimately, Guare gathered enough ideas for (at least) two plays and squeezed them into *Chaucer*. Where this fertile mind will land next is anyone's guess. Richard Greenberg's *Everett Beekin*, an uneven play about American family, identity and assimilation, received an equally unbalanced production at Lincoln Center despite the presence of the exquisite Bebe Neuwirth in a central role.

Horton Foote's *The Carpetbagger's Children*, the final Lincoln Center production of the season, was presented jointly with three resident theater companies: Alley Theatre in Houston, Guthrie Theater in Minneapolis and Hartford Stage in Connecticut. A memory play of monologues spoken by three mid-20th-century Texas sisters—played by Jean Stapleton, Roberta Maxwell and Hallie Foote—the play received the 2002 American Theatre Critics/Steinberg New Play Award. Foote's elegiac play in production had the rhythms of a hot summer day in south Texas, but almost no interaction among the three women who are onstage throughout. For those of us who see new plays as the roadmaps of our culture, helping us to locate where we are and where we may be going, it is of no little concern to see that it took three major companies to produce this one sweet, simple play. How many other new plays—and new playwrights—could have been produced with the resources devoted to *The Carpetbagger's Children*?

The World According to Mee

PLAYWRIGHT CHARLES L. MEE brought his consciousness to the stage with productions of three plays that focused on love from different perspectives. *First Love* started Mee's Season of Loves at the New York Theatre Workshop in a production directed by the playwright's daughter, Erin B. Mee. (The workshop's first production of the season was a performance-art project, modeled on poetry slams, titled *Slanguage*.) In *First Love*, the playwright explored what might happen when two mid-20th-century radicals—who never had time or inclination for it before—fall in love for the first time. Downtown veterans Ruth Maleczech and Frederick Neumann spiced the mix for the cognoscenti, but there was a bleakness to the proceedings that kept audiences at arm's length. Nothing of that sort happened in Mee's two other productions, *Big Love* and *True Love*, which played, respectively, at the Brooklyn Academy of Music's Next Wave Festival and the Zipper Theater (a new performance space in the West 30s). *Big Love* is a 2001 American Theatre Critics/Steinberg New Play Citation honoree and a 2001–02 Best Play for its rollicking take on the gender wars as viewed through the lens of an ancient Greek play (see John Istel's essay in this volume). Mee stayed with the classical influence in *True Love*, a tale of loneliness and desire—inspired by the story of Phaedra and Hippolytus— set in a rural mechanic shop and beauty salon, and punctuated with wild humor and rock music.

New York Theatre Workshop continued its tradition of presenting theater on the cutting edge with an adaptation of Flannery O'Connor's Southern stories, *Everything That Rises Must Converge*, and a one-man tale of African-American brothers growing up with an angry, drunken father, Alexander Thomas's *Throw Pitchfork*. But the post-September 11 theatrical event that captured the attention of the media—both Off and on Broadway was the workshop's production of Tony Kushner's *Homebody/Kabul*. A 2001–02 Best Play choice, *Homebody* gave timely focus to a region and a political ideology that Americans suddenly clamored to understand. Kushner, though, had set his tale in 1998 around the time that the US had bombed suspected terrorist camps in Khost, Afghanistan—and there are no American characters in the play. One line in particular—written many months in advance of the terrorist attacks—about the Taliban coming to New York was said to have given the creative team more than a little anxiety. But they ultimately kept the line—much reported prior to the play's opening—which sent a *frisson* of recognition through the theater when it was recited by the superb Rita Wolf. Kushner continues to polish the play and there have been published reports of another New York run in the future. (See Jennifer de Poyen's essay in this volume.)

Martha Clarke's visionary theater piece, *Vienna: Lusthaus (revisited)*, marked a return to familiar territory for New York theatergoers who saw the 1986 original (*Vienna: Lusthaus*) at St. Clement's and, later, at the Public Theater. For those who missed it last time, the dreamy evocations of turn-of-the-20th-century *Mitteleuropa* in this *Lusthaus* offered a layered perspective on consciousness, fantasy and desire. Set behind a slightly alienating scrim at the front of the stage, the action flowed as in a dream with the movement demonstrating virtuosity both balletic and modern. While one can hardly argue that the piece itself was new work, Clarke's singular perspective—aided by Charles L. Mee's fractured text and Richard Peaslee's haunting music—must make this experience always seem new.

Imperfect Ganesh: Billy Crudup in The Elephant Man. *Drawing: © Al Hirschfeld/The Margo Feiden Galleries Ltd., New York. www.alhirschfeld.com*

Brooklyn Academy of Music again presented its vibrant mixture of cutting-edge world drama in a production of August Strindberg's *The Ghost Sonata* as imagined by the great Swedish director, Ingmar Bergman, and in a Shakespeare's Globe production of *Cymbeline*. *Ghost Sonata* opened in June 2001 and demonstrated once again that the Swedish master is at home on film or on the stage. The stage, of course, offers a density of simultaneous images and immediacy that film cannot approximate. With the Strindberg classic, Bergman strips the drama bare as he did with his phenomenal *Hamlet* at BAM in 1988. It's no coincidence that the two plays are rife with thematics surrounding corruption and the need to cleanse the soul before we shuffle off this mortal coil. The director's work is a seminar in bringing the essential to the stage—and it leaves us longing for more work of its power. The Shakespeare's Globe production of *Cymbeline*, directed by Mike Alfreds, brought to New York the acting company that performs in a re-creation of the original 17th century Globe Theatre. At the BAM Harvey, six actors played all of the many roles in *Cymbeline* simply by making slight adjustments to their physical carriage or vocal delivery. The actors and two musicians—who sat just behind the action playing an array of gongs, cymbals, bells and drums—were all bedecked in white silk pajamas and the aroma of incense wafted throughout the theater, giving a distinctly Asian feel to the production. The audience was kept on its toes by the Globe actors' style of playing to the "groundlings," who stand in a pit at the foot of the stage in London. Since the Harvey Theater is an indoor space with seats, there are no groundlings. But the house lights remained fully illuminated throughout the production engaging the audience more fully with the action onstage. (Other BAM theater productions are covered by Mel Gussow in the Off Off Broadway essay.)

Broadway Aspirations

ROUNDABOUT THEATRE COMPANY, which has a presence both on and Off Broadway, began winding down its multiyear Off Broadway tenancy at the Gramercy Theatre on 23rd Street this season. The final production there was scheduled to be a revival of Edward Albee's *All Over* in the 2002–03 season, and the company will open an Off Broadway space at the American Place Theatre—probably in the 2003–04 season. Charles Randolph-Wright's play with music, *Blue*, opened in June 2001 and ran until September 23, when the rocky theatrical economy forced closings of many productions. Randolph-Wright's play focused on the struggles of an upper-middle-class African-American family and featured fine performances by Phylicia Rashad,

Hill Harper, Howard W. Overshown and others. Australian dramatist Andrew Bovell's *Speaking in Tongues* failed to pique the interest of New York critics despite winning performances by Margaret Colin, Karen Allen, Kevin Anderson and Michel R. Gill. Perhaps its focus on the psychology of betrayal and the dark impulses that lurk beneath the surface of human discourse was too close to home. Similarly, Richard Greenberg's *The Dazzle* (a 2001–02 Best Play) missed with the critics despite the playwright's fascinating exploration of consciousness and its formation in an imagined story about famous New York recluses Homer and Langley Collyer. (See Donald Lyons's essay in this volume.)

Another nonprofit Off Broadway theater with Broadway aspirations, Manhattan Theatre Club, had a less focused season than in the past couple of years. The company, under the leadership of Lynne Meadow and Barry Grove, is embarked upon the reclamation of Broadway's Biltmore Theatre, which will provide MTC with an intimate 650-seat Broadway theater. In its presentations during the 2001–02 season, MTC relied on works developed at other theaters before production at the company's City Center space. David Lindsay-Abaire's *Wonder of the World*, a wacky character comedy about a woman who breaks out of her routine life—though nothing in Lindsay-Abaire's plays is completely routine—romped through a two-month run with Sarah Jessica Parker supported by Marylouise Burke, Amy Sedaris, Kristine Nielsen, Kevin Chamberlin, Alan Tudyk and Bill Raymond. The playwright's signature lunacy is all over the map in *Wonder* and leads us to ponder where the clever, quirky writer goes from here.

John Patrick Shanley's *Where's My Money?* was an angry screech from beginning to end, though not out of character with the playwright's other ruminations on the nature of love and relationships. In Zinnie Harris's *Further Than the Furthest Thing*, directed by Neil Pepe, the idyllic lives of people who inhabit a strategic island are disrupted in the name of progress— which leads to predictable outcomes. Christopher Shinn's *Four*, directed by Jeff Cohen, was unquestionably the most compelling offering of the MTC season in its depiction of two couples—one gay, one straight—who navigate the reefs of sexual preference and racial identity. Most unsettling in *Four*, though, was the older man-younger man seduction (performed with grace and subtlety by Isiah Whitlock Jr. and Keith Nobbs): the elder was in his 40s, the younger still a teen.

Alan Ayckbourn's gimmicky *House* and *Garden*, the final offering of MTC this season, seemed more about the concept than its execution. It was a typical Ayckbourn offering with randy white men of middle age behaving

Beyond Chekhov: Frances Sternhagen, Piper Laurie, Estelle Parsons and Elizabeth Franz in Morning's at Seven. *Drawing: © Al Hirschfeld/The Margo Feiden Galleries Ltd., New York. www.alhirschfeld.com*

like oversexed schoolboys while long-suffering wives continue to suffer. Played simultaneously in two theaters (one a house, the other its garden), between which actors dashed to make certain that they made their cues, the plays demonstrated (above all) that you can get actors to give more than one performance at a time—but pay them just once.

The Joseph Papp Public Theater has long performed the dance of the downtown company with uptown aspirations; sometimes to great success, sometimes less. The 1971 John Guare and Mel Shapiro adaptation of *Two Gentlemen of Verona* and, of course, *A Chorus Line* are a pair of early examples of success. Under the leadership of George C. Wolfe, productions such as *Bring in 'da Noise, Bring in 'da Funk* and *The Tempest* represent notable transfers. Both founder Papp and successor Wolfe also had their share of disappointments. After a 2000–01 season when several Public productions seemed to lack a certain finish, the company came back this year with several strong offerings—including two that moved to Broadway: *Elaine Stritch at Liberty* and *Topdog/Underdog* (see above).

A Tom Stoppard adaptation of *The Seagull*—which played at the New York Shakespeare Festival's Delacorte Theater in the summer of 2001—broke a few hearts when it failed to transfer to Broadway. The Mike Nichols-directed production featured a stellar cast of Meryl Streep, Kevin Kline, Christopher Walken, Natalie Portman, Philip Seymour Hoffman, Stephen Spinella, Marcia Gay Harden, Debra Monk, Larry Pine and John Goodman. Rounding out the summer season for the festival, Billy Crudup and Joe Morton starred in an emotionally cool production of *Measure for Measure* directed by Mary Zimmerman. The Public's other outing with the Bard this season featured Keith David and Liev Schreiber in a taut production of *Othello* directed by Doug Hughes at the Anspacher Theater downtown.

The spring season at the Public brought three very interesting dramas to the attention of New York theatergoers. Naomi Iizuka's *36 Views* was a theatrical ride through the nether regions of the glitzy (and seamy) world of international art dealing. Employing a rich mixture of realism and kabuki-inspired theater technique, director Mark Wing-Davey kept the tension lively as Iizuka's sparkling ideas about art, authenticity and ownership washed over the audience. The play ultimately sprawls at the feet of its ideas, and a dubious conceit about easily duped experts ruined by a fraud keep *36 Views* from reaching greater heights. The scenery design by Douglas Stein combined with costumes by Myung Hee Cho, lighting by David Weiner, sound by Matthew Spiro and projections by Ruppert Bohle to make it one of the most arresting physical productions on any stage this year.

Ellen McLaughlin's *Helen* recounted an alternate story of the woman whose face launched a thousand ships. In McLaughlin's play, Helen has been spirited away to Egypt—a tale that seems to originate from the Greek poet Stesichorus—where she whiles away the time swatting insects and trying to learn the latest news of the Trojan War (which has been over for years). Played by a ravishingly attractive Donna Murphy in flowing blond locks, this Helen is visited by an array of mythic creatures including a black Athena (Phylicia Rashad), Io (Johanna Day) and finally Menelaus (Denis O'Hare). Murphy's Helen was tended by the ever-magnetic Marian Seldes who filled in when the original servant (Mary Louise Wilson) bowed out.

As Suzan-Lori Parks's *Topdog/Underdog* was readied for its Broadway debut, the Public postponed the premiere of her new piece, *Fucking A*, and replaced it with a production of Rebecca Gilman's *Blue Surge*. Directed by Robert Falls, this production originated at Chicago's Goodman Theatre and transferred essentially intact. In *Blue Surge*, Gilman explores the lives of the outsider underclass in a story about police and prostitutes—eventually drawing parallels between the two groups and their placement on the social spectrum.

From its founding in 1979, Second Stage Theatre has focused on giving a second chance to plays that, for whatever reason, did not have an opportunity to shine in their debuts. For nearly 25 years, the company has hewn to that course in addition to providing an artistic home to new voices and established playwrights. In the season under review, Second Stage had a season of odd highs and lows. The highs included the marvelous production of *Metamorphoses* that enjoyed several extensions and later transferred to Broadway and the less-successful production of Athol Fugard's *Sorrows and Rejoicings* (a more accurate title would have dropped the final two words). Fugard's play revolves around the confrontation between a white woman and a black woman who discuss their dead husband and lover—he's the same guy, a white South African man—in a vain attempt to put his spirit to rest. Despite the superb acting of Judith Light, Charlayne Woodard, John Glover and Marcy Harriell, the playwright's mournful tone (an allegory, perhaps, on the death of white rule in South Africa?) left the audience feeling benumbed at the end of two intermissionless hours.

Second Stage's *Once Around the City*, which opened in July 2001, marked the final production of Mark Linn-Baker's tenure as "2001 artistic director." Linn-Baker celebrated by directing *Once*, a musical about an heiress cheated out of her home—where she shelters homeless men—and how she is saved from ruin. When one of the kinder reviews says, "once is definitely enough," we have to think that it probably wasn't the sort of ending that the director had envisioned. The final Second Stage offering of the 2001–02 season was a one-man demonstration of the art of confidence and graft in *Ricky Jay on the Stem*. The stem of the title refers, of course, to Broadway. Ironically, the card-shark and raconteur was decidedly *not* located on Broadway—either geographically or by union designation. But Jay, directed by David Mamet, certainly had plenty of information to impart and mesmerizing tricks to play on his all-too-willing audience.

Endangered Species: Off Broadway Musicals

THE DROP IN production of musicals Off Broadway may be attributable to the effects of September 11. This season saw no revivals of musicals Off Broadway—although there was but one the previous year—and a 25 percent decline of new musicals. In addition to *The Spitfire Grill* and *Once Around the City*, mentioned above, there were song cycles that passed for musicals (*Tick, Tick . . . Boom!* and *The Last Five Years*) as well as several others with more developed books that were still quite thin. In the weeks after September 11, the musical *Reefer Madness* arrived from the West Coast laden with irony that was completely devoid of content. This spoof of an 1936 anti-marijuana film might have made for biting satire in, say, 1970, but the humor is toothless these days—and by October 2001 we knew the devil to be more real, more scary. Like *Bat Boy: The Musical* the season before, *Reefer*'s emptiness produced a few hollow laughs and an overriding sense of ennui. It closed after 25 performances. *Summer of '42,* which followed *Reefer* into the Variety Arts Theatre in December, lasted 47 performances—

Ever after: Molly Ephraim, Vanessa Williams, Stephen DeRosa, Laura Benanti and Gregg Edelman in Into the Woods. *Drawing: © Al Hirschfeld/The Margo Feiden Galleries Ltd., New York. www.alhirschfeld.com*

almost twice as long as its predecessor. *Summer*, however, suffered from a deficiency similar to *Reefer*'s: based on a movie several decades old, it was a dramatic idea well past its moment.

Up at the York Theatre Company, valiant attempts to breathe life into the Off Broadway musical passed essentially for naught. The Tom Jones and Harvey Schmidt musical, *Roadside*, opened in November 2001 and managed 29 performances before disappearing. Based on a play by Lynn Riggs—whose other play, *Green Grow the Lilacs*, became the basis for the musical *Oklahoma!*—the production creaked under the weight of its cornpone story and local-color stereotypes. *Prodigal* was an Australian import about a young man's coming-out and the dangers inherent to depraved life in the big city. The final York entry was a one-woman performance by Sharon McKnight of *Red Hot Mama*, based on the work and life of Sophie Tucker.

Although *Menopause: The Musical* names itself, it might be better characterized as a revue with its use of rewritten lyrics to popular 1960s songs serving a theme about women's passages in middle age. As if to prove the point, the characters have no names but are known by their types: Power Woman, Soap Star, Earth Mother and Iowa Housewife. To its credit, *Menopause* looked poised for a long run as the new season began.

This is probably the place for a midrange baby boomer to decry what's happened to musical composition in the recent past. When we listen to the music of people such as John Kander or Stephen Sondheim—two very different types of musician—we can hear the influences of great composers, operatic composers, modern composers. But when we are subjected to the new these days, the work often sounds like it is created by a Sondheim imitation—not always the sincerest form of flattery, we're persuaded—or, God forbid, an Andrew Lloyd Webber clone (he the musical robber baron of mid-20th-century rock and pop).

When Jonathan Larson—who wrote the one-man shows that became *Tick, Tick . . . Boom!* (with a bit of editing help from playwright David Auburn)—died just before his 1996 musical *Rent* opened, he seemed to be on the verge of forging a new sound for the musical theater. (Is there anyone, except perhaps Larson's grieving family, who thinks the composer wouldn't have wanted and needed to develop *Rent* much more before it went to Broadway?) There are other composers who come to mind when thinking about the possibilities for the musical theater: Jeanine Tesori, Michael John LaChiusa, Andrew Lippa, Adam Guettel, Elliot Goldenthal and Jason Robert Brown. (And why aren't there more women?)

Brown was the author of *The Last Five Years*, a musical *roman à clef* that underwent changes after the composer's ex-wife was chagrined at how she was portrayed. Even with the changes, the female character played by Sherie René Scott came across as weak and simpering, while the presumed doppelgänger of the composer (played by Norbert Leo Butz) appeared as a true artist destined for finer things. Brown and his contemporaries have all begun to develop signature sounds. But what happens if film or television success strikes? Will these committed creators turn their talents to music on demand? Everyone needs to earn a living and to provide for himself. But can the musical theater withstand the continued replication of soundtracks from films transformed for the stage and the Las Vegas-style show music we now often hear?

Off Broadway: The Commerce Department

EVERY THEATER PRODUCER, of course, needs to sell tickets. But for the commercial Off Broadway producer the margin for error is slim indeed. Nonprofit companies can rely on a combination of ticket packages, season ticket sales, donations and earned income to help weather bad weeks at the box office. On the commercial side, there's only the comfort of a fat wallet, a big bank account or understanding backers. All of this probably accounts for the small percentage of new plays premiering outside of nonprofit venues. Of the 44 new plays Off Broadway this season, a little more than a quarter (13) functioned as commercial productions. Of that group, about half started at a nonprofit theater before going commercial.

What makes a commercial Off Broadway run viable? The answer is almost always star power. It's either the star power of the actor(s), the star power of the playwright or some combination of the two. (The exception: vanity productions funded by well-heeled angels.) The days of trying and failing and trying again Off Broadway are well in the past.

Saint Lucy's Eyes, with Ruby Dee, moved to the Cherry Lane Theatre for a brief summer stint in 2001 after a spring run at the Women's Project and Productions. Bridgette A. Wimberly's play about a backroom abortionist showed great promise for the writer's future projects. Neil LaBute's *The Shape of Things* brought the hot film-director back to the stage with another of his trademark wars-of-attrition between the genders. LaBute's cool sensibility often plays more interestingly through the lens of a camera than it does in a room filled with people. He might want to consider allowing someone else to stage his plays because his own direction emphasizes the emotional deadness of his characters. (A suggestion: Joe Mantello.) One of the true losses in the September 11 fallout was the production of Eduardo Machado's *Havana Is Waiting*, a poetic play about a Cuban man who recovers his sense of identity when he returns to Havana decades after he was airlifted to the US. It lasted barely a month partly due to the shift of emphasis in the theater industry to the economic crisis on Broadway. With a bit more time and financial support, *Havana* might have found its audience. But in the weeks after terrorists struck the city, a delicate play about Cuba, the US and American identities had little chance of survival.

Eve Ensler's play about women in war-torn Central Europe, *Necessary Targets*, opened at the Variety Arts in February with a fine cast that included Shirley Knight, Catherine Kellner, Alyssa Bresnahan, Diane Venora and others. Although Ensler takes some dramaturgical shortcuts—particularly in the latter half of the play—that truncate the piece's intellectual (and emotional) core, it still possesses a visceral impact that makes audiences consider who pays the price for wars waged by men. Trish Vradenburg's *Surviving Grace* was a kind of survivor itself. A contrived, sentimental story of a mother's encroaching Alzheimer's Disease, and how it affects her and her daughter, the play opened for a brief moment on Broadway in 1996 as *The Apple Doesn't Fall*. Featuring Illeana Douglas and Doris Belack as the daughter and mother in its Union Square Theatre run this season, the play was generally dismissed by critics (and discerning audience members). A heavy advertising campaign and someone's deep pockets kept the show afloat well into the new season. One of the overlooked gems of the season was Gene Saks's production of *Mr. Goldwyn* at the Promenade Theatre—with Alan King as the malaprop-spouting movie mogul, Samuel Goldwyn. King was essentially alone onstage for the entire two acts—Goldwyn's assistant was capably performed by Lauren Klein in brief snippets—and he offered a refreshingly crisp portrayal of the last of a breed of filmmaker.

Elsewhere Off Broadway there were the usual solo shows, which included Steven Berkoff (*One Man*) returning with a performance of three monologues that paled next to his Shakespearean turn of last season. Seth Isler, a connoisseur of *The Godfather* films, performed a solo version of those films' greatest hits—if you'll pardon the pun—in a run of *The Godfadda Workout* that extended into the new season. Mike Daisey gave us all something to laugh about in an unsettling comic journey through the bowels of the internet economy titled *21 Dog Years: Doing Time @ Amazon.com*.

Specialty performances included the revival of a spoof on the works Shakespeare, a pair of magic acts and three programs of concert versions of classic musicals in the ongoing Encores! series at City Center. There was also a 90-minute performance of two men manipulating their genitalia into various shapes for the "amusement" of the audience—it was sheer torture for those who weren't inebriated (we weren't) or looking for a new career path (we aren't).

Saying Goodbye

EVERY YEAR FOR the past eight decades, the *Best Plays* series has marked the passing of members of the theater and entertainment community in a section called Necrology, which we changed to In Memoriam in last year's edition. Due to the evanescent nature of theatrical art, the manner in which we note the people and performances that have passed our way always seems to fall short. This series, of course, has been an important marker for the past 83 years and it links with George C.D. Odell's monumental *Annals of the New York Stage* to chronicle English-speaking theater back to the early colonial era. Each year *Best Plays* loses a few more of our friends— and by friends we mean anyone who helps to feed the minds, the spirits, the souls of the larger community with works in the theater and the performing arts.

This past year was especially painful to us because we knew many of those who passed from among us. But our loss is even greater when we consider what so many of these people meant to arts and culture in our world today. The simple truth is that we need every soul with us to advocate for the sort of human communion and transformative power we get from the performing arts. Among the lives we celebrate this year we include three important teachers: Martin Esslin, Jan Kott and Paul Hume. Esslin and Kott were original and imaginative thinkers on things theatrical. Esslin defined our perspective for viewing mid-20th-century plays of the avant-garde in his book *The Theatre of the Absurd*, which came to represent a genre of literature. Kott, a Polish-born critic who lived in this country for many years, was an essayist and author whose books—especially *Shakespeare: Our Contemporary*—encouraged artists and theorists alike to consider the many contexts within which drama and theater can be located.

Hume was a music critic for the *Washington Post* who became inadvertently famous when his negative review of a piano recital by Margaret Truman provoked the fiery President Harry S. Truman into giving him hell and threatening to punch him. The unassuming Hume showed the letter to a friend who leaked it to the press—much to the critic's chagrin. Hume was also a teacher of criticism who told his young charges that they must hear everything, read everything, learn everything, if they wished to be a critic in the performing arts. Those of us who took his advice to heart, tell our students the same today.

Others in our special honor roll this year include the amiable sportscaster (and theater reviewer) Dick Schaap. Over the past several years, Schaap was an important particpant in our best-of-bests poll of New York critics and always a pleasure to encounter. John Springer, press agent to film stars (and father of Gary Springer of Springer/Chicoine Public Relations), was one of the all-time great representatives who handled such names as Marilyn Monroe, Judy Garland, Gary Cooper, Henry Fonda and Marlene Dietrich. But beyond his great client list, Springer was known in the business—even by those of us who never worked with him—as a man with unique style and class. The theater community lost an important supporter and friend when John Alun Stevenson died in February. A former film publicist and publishing executive, Stevenson was a significant patron of the theater through his own good works and through those of his wife Isabelle Stevenson, who has served with distinction for many years at the helm of the American Theatre Wing. Irene Worth, whose health problems had curtailed her acting in recent years, worked into her 80s and set a standard for performance that many would do well to emulate.

Finally, though, the loss of Robert Whitehead just a few days after he received a Tony Award for lifetime achievement, was a blow to the entire community. Whenever we discuss the changes in theater across the recent decades, we often lament the loss of the "gentleman producer." Although it generally refers to a time and a style of doing business that antedates the corporate world that is Broadway theater, it is a term that fit the always-dapper Whitehead like a glove. Whitehead forged a life in the theater that included productions dating back to the 1930s as well as several productions of Arthur Miller plays and a tenure leading the Lincoln Center Theater in its early days. Whitehead and his wife, the legendary Zoe Caldwell, were a kind of theatrical royalty. Elegant and sophisticated, the Whiteheads gave any theatrical event—simply by their attendance—a bit more sparkle and a lot more gentility. Although Caldwell illuminates any room with her charismatic presence, that glow is sure to be slightly dimmer without her beloved partner.

Nostalgia and Vision

THE BEAUTY AND heartbreak of the theater is in its essence as a vanishing act, an act of disappearance. As in life itself, theater is forever slipping away, living on only in memory. What we know from research on memory (and, let's face it, our own experience) is that it is unreliable—a prism through which we may shine a light to witness a rainbow of possibilities. As Charles Wright notes in his essay on *Franny's Way*, Tennessee Williams explores the trickiness of consciousness in *The Glass Menagerie*. As Williams's narrator puts it, the play—and memory—is "dimly lighted, it is sentimental, it is not realistic." That isn't a description of a clear-eyed perspective on the world, but it is where we live.

Teachers of acting are forever telling their students to "be in the moment," to "be here now." That, of course, is the true difficulty of the acting art. The problem is as eternal as it is simple: as soon as you have said "now," it is already in the past. The notion of being or thinking or living in the present is itself part of humanity's undying hubris (you see, it's not just the producers of *The Producers*). If we accept what Freud and others have taught us about the nature of consciousness and experience, then every "present moment" is relentlessly redolent of the past. The anxieties of everyday existence—or stage fright, to extend the acting metaphor—aren't based in reality. They are the most discomfiting form of nostalgia.

Still, we seek the loving embrace of nostalgia—the good kind, that is—and what better place to find it than at the theater? Because it is a phenomenon of disappearance, theatrical performance resonates in the mind long after voices have faded from the stage. The critic Eric Bentley recently told of a theatergoing high point that occurred when he was 13 years old. The memory was of John Gielgud playing Shakespeare and its impact echoes with Bentley more than 70 years later—and makes Bentley's audience long to have seen it, too. Of more recent vintage were the Alan Bates and Frank Langella performances in *Fortune's Fool*, which may remain alive with us to the final moments of sentience. But who's to say how much these performances "improve" in the echo chambers of memory?

So it is that we return to the theater, sitting night after night among others. We face forward in the darkness, bathed in the glow of stage lighting, hopeful for the impressions and memories to come. It may be a stretch to suggest that there is something satisfyingly human about leaning from the darkness toward the light, but the alternative should be unacceptable to every one of us.

But what of the theater to come? How will our artists and our audiences respond to a new world of fear and insecurity? Is it really a "new" world? Or are we now, in this country, simply experiencing what many others have faced for many years? The answers, of course, will come in the future. Indeed, at the rate events occur in our world today, some of the answers will have come by the time this book is in readers' hands.

As the future unfolds before us, we may need to take a leap, to stand apart from memory and the lure of nostalgia. In the era ahead, we will need the theater to lead, comment, reflect—and entertain. It can do these things only if we move beyond the museum pieces of the present—however necessary and successful they may be—and listen closely to the new voices that are all around us.

Speaking about new-play development recently, Todd London of New Dramatists invoked a passage written by D.H. Lawrence in *Studies in Classic American Literature*. Part of it captures perfectly our location as audience members, as critics, as lovers of theater:

> It is hard to hear a new voice, as hard as it is to listen to an unknown language. We just don't listen. . . . Out of fear. The world fears a new experience more than it fears anything. Because a new experience displaces so many old experiences.

In order to understand and be understood in our increasingly diverse and challenging world, we know that learning a new language is not only a good idea, it is practically imperative. Leaning forward in the dark, though, we need only breathe—and listen.

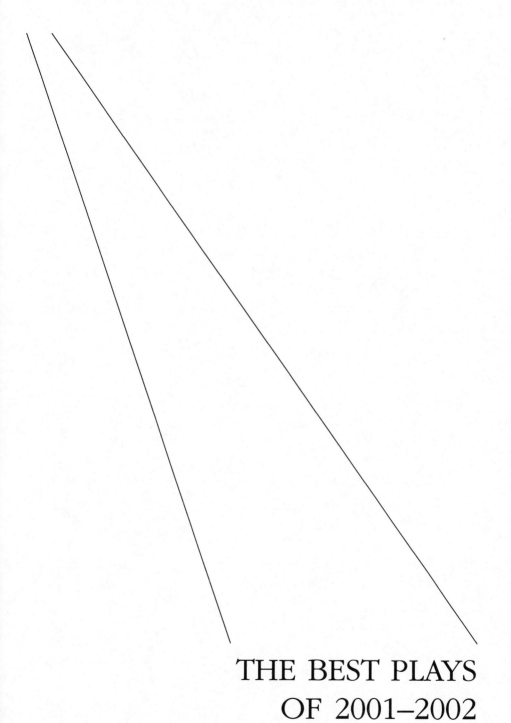

THE BEST PLAYS
OF 2001–2002

2001–2002 Best Play

BIG LOVE

By Charles L. Mee

○ ○ ○ ○ ○

Essay by John Istel

LYDIA: But if we live in a world where it is not possible
to love another person
I don't want to live.

THYONA: All this talk of love.
In the real world,
if there is no justice
there can be no love
because there can be no love
that is not freely offered
and it cannot be free
unless every person has equal standing.

CHARLES L. MEE'S *BIG LOVE* is a stunning, bravura piece of theater. And as the epigraph suggests, it cheekily rewrites New Hampshire's license plate motto to read: "*Love* free or die." That simple and profound sentiment—as kitschy as it may sound—gets a swooping chopper ride through the playwright's fertile imagination in the play inspired by Aeschylus's *The Suppliants*, sometimes translated as *The Suppliant Women*.

Mee is not unlike an experiment-addicted automotive scientist who concocts ever more high-powered vehicles to fill with crash-test dummies. Only in his demolition derbies, the vehicles are works of classical literature—often of Greek origin—that have been souped up, retrofitted and rewired for contemporary audiences. Mee describes his aesthetic predilections this way: "I like plays that are not too neat, too finished, too presentable. My plays are broken, jagged, filled with sharp edges, filled with things that take sudden turns, career into each other, smash up, veer off in sickening turns."

His stage adaptations or "remakings," as he terms them, may include familiar plot lines and characters from Drama 101, like Orestes or Agamemnon or Dido, but they also include bits of advertising copy, political treatises, television scripts, historical writings and extracts from self-help books, as well as other assorted found texts, inspirational jargon and cultural

53

Rockin' 'n' ragin': KJ Sanchez, Carolyn Baeumler and Aimée Guillot in Charles L. Mee's
Big Love. *Photo: Richard Trigg*

detritus. His list of sources for *Big Love* include the works of pop sociologist
Klaus Theweleit, the self-congratulatory platitudes of Leo Buscaglia, the
healing thoughts of Gerald G. Jampolsky, and the vitriol of Valerie Solanus.

Having reviewed the results from many of Mee's experiments, I can
report that *Big Love* may be his purest "smash." There's proof all over the
stage. In the head-spinning production seen at the Brooklyn Academy of
Music's Harvey Theater, glasses, tomatoes, plates, a wedding cake and human
bodies take turns crashing to the ground.

Big Love was the result of a commission from Actors Theatre of Louisville
for its "millennium" Humana Festival of New American Plays in 2000. In
searching for an appropriate topic for such a portentous occasion, Mee
decided to reconfigure one of the oldest dramas in Western civilization.
The Suppliants, like all Greek tragedies, was originally part of a trilogy. In
the extant play, 50 sisters arrive in a distant land, seeking asylum from their
50 cousins who were ready to wed and bed them. The women refused the
men and fled to a foreign country. They are granted asylum in Aeschylus's
play, which ends with the impending arrival of the angry suitors.

Since the last two parts of the trilogy no longer exist, Mee was free to
make up his own ending, though he could draw on ancient Greek accounts
of the missing plays. Updated, *Big Love* becomes an opportunity to address
such contemporary issues as the age-old battle between the sexes, the

plight of refugees around the world, the politics of granting asylum, the ubiquity of rape and violence against women, the role of mercy and forgiveness during a siege, and the question of whether love can survive the most intense brutality. The Louisville production, directed by Les Waters, was redesigned slightly for bigger theaters and in 2001 ran at the Berkeley Repertory Theatre, Chicago's Goodman Theatre, and New Haven's Long Wharf Theatre, before coming to the Brooklyn Academy of Music's Next Wave Festival. Mee also received a $5000 New Play Citation from the American Theatre Critics Association and the Harold and Mimi Steinberg Charitable Trust.

The script of *Big Love* (available, as are all of Mee's plays, on his website www.charlesmee.org) only hints at the incredibly visceral experience of watching it. For example, in the dialogue used as an epigraph, two sisters argue about the circumstances that are necessary for love to exist, and the role love has in any society, a central concern of the play. But how could you guess that the women are standing in blood-spattered wedding dresses amid a stage filled with the carnage from their nuptial night massacre?

Mee's plays often revel in such imagery, filled with juxtapositions, parallels and opposites. Some scenes reflect a cool, formal modernism; others seem overwrought and baroque. Moments of extreme violence and physicality alternate with scenes of intellectual argument or quiet tenderness. Irony and sentiment can, and often do, co-exist in Mee's plays, sometimes uneasily, sometimes barely recognizable to each other, like twins in a Shakespearean comedy. But particularly in *Big Love*, the text, printed in verse-like line breaks, always seems modulated, structured, controlled.

BIG LOVE BEGINS WITH A WOMAN in a wedding gown entering an airy, sun-filled space with a sky-blue, spongy floor occupied solely by a bathtub, as wedding march music plays (Mee suggests something from Mozart's *Marriage of Figaro*). Lydia (Carolyn Baeumler) runs the water, adds bubbles, then strips naked and sinks into the suds. After a moment, a young Italian man enters and is shocked to find a stranger in one of his baths. He introduces himself as Giuliano (Tony Speciale) and wonders if she's a guest of his family. She's confused. She thought this big villa was a hotel. Lydia explains that she and her 49 sisters were in a boat that just landed on the beach below it. Mee writes the scene with a slight comic tone that holds up throughout the play, as if this is just another of those surreal, crazy encounters, in which two people struggle to understand each other.

> LYDIA: We're looking for asylum.
> We want to be taken in here
> so we don't have to marry our cousins.

GIULIANO: You want to be taken in as immigrants?

LYDIA: As refugees.

GIULIANO: Refugees.

LYDIA: Yes.

GIULIANO: From . . .

LYDIA: From Greece.

GIULIANO: I mean, from, you know:
political oppression, or war. . . .

LYDIA: Or kidnapping. Or rape.

GIULIANO: From rape.

LYDIA: By our cousins.

GIULIANO: Well, marriage really.

LYDIA: Not if we can help it.

Moments later, another big entrance occurs: Lydia's two sisters, Olympia (Aimée Guillot) and Thyona (KJ Sanchez), tromp onstage, dragging heavy suitcases and trunks, dressed in tattered wedding attire. They throw the luggage down and break into a full-throttled rendition of the 1960s song,

Men with attitude: J. Matthew Jenkins, Bruce McKenzie and Mark Zeisler in Charles L. Mee's Big Love. *Photo: Richard Trigg*

"You Don't Own Me," singing into their high-heel shoes as if crooning into a mike. Suddenly, one sister throws open a suitcase and begins smashing wedding gifts of china and crystal. It's not only a good example of how Mee mashes together the classic and contemporary, pop music and Mozart, but as he writes in the stage directions, the action is necessary to make clear that the play "is not a text with brief dances and other physical activities added to it, but rather a piece in which the physical activities and the text are equally important to the experience."

As for the text, Mee has admitted in an interview that he's prone to "arias," by which he means long virtuosic speeches whose effect can be like watching circus acts—plate spinners, jugglers, and gymnasts. There are several classic set pieces in *Big Love*. The first occurs when Bella (Lauren Klein), an old woman, enters after the sisters' song. She doesn't look surprised to see the wedding-dressed women, and after asking a few questions begins a long comic monologue about her 13 sons. As she speaks, she shines tomatoes that she pulls from a basket. Each personifies a son. The tomato is either lovingly wiped clean ("he stays home here with his mother") and set carefully or dropped with a splat on the ground ("he moved to America") or almost dropped but then saved ("My eleventh son / he is on television / on a soap opera / with the stories of love affairs / and godknows whatnot," she spits, about to hurl the tomato to the ground before reconsidering his fate: "at least he's not killing people.")

Subsequently, Bella's oldest son Piero (J. Michael Flynn), the man of the house, enters and hears the sisters' plea for protection. He's noncommittal, allowing them to stay at least for dinner. During this scene, as they plead their case, the sisters' personalities become clear, especially as they fit on the feminine to feminist continuum. Olympia may sound like a classic Greek name, but she's the most "contemporary," craving bath lotions and designer footwear.

> OLYMPIA: I know this is not a hotel, so you wouldn't have everything,
> but maybe some Estee Lauder 24 Karat Color Golden Body Creme with Sunbloc,
> or Fetish Go Glitter Body Art in Soiree,
>
> LYDIA: Olympia . . . .
>
> OLYMPIA: or some Prescriptives Uplift Eye Cream, not in the tube: firming,
> Mac lip gloss in Pink Poodle
> just
> some things to make a woman feel
> you know
> fresh

She's like a Greek goddess of capitalist consumption and is the most traditionally feminine. Thyona is the most ardent, uncompromising feminist: "boy babies should be flushed down the toilet at birth," she says at one point. (Here, Mee borrows a line again, this time from himself: essentially the same line can be heard in his play *First Love*.) Lydia moderates between these views, refusing to condemn the entire male species.

> LYDIA: [T]here could be a world where people care for one another
> where men are good to women
> and there is not a men's history
> and a separate women's history
> but a human history
> where we are all together
> and support one another
> nurture one another.

Ironically, her idealistic words are drowned out by the intensifying chop of an unseen helicopter that carries the suitors who are pursuing them: Constantine (Mark Zeisler), betrothed to Thyona; Oed (J. Matthew Jenkins), Olympia's intended partner; and Nikos (Bruce McKenzie), matched with Lydia. They enter wearing military jumpsuits over tuxedos, with US flags on their helmets. They're greeted by a deadpan Lydia: "Oh. You've found us." Although there are no scene or act breaks in this 100-minute piece, the first part of the trilogy would end about here.

Of the newly arrived bridegrooms, Constantine is clearly the leader and the most macho. Mee gives him two long "arias" about a man's role in society and a woman's duty to cleave unto him. The speeches are conservative and reactionary—a viewpoint not heard often in American theater, and Zeisler's performance of them garnered applause (and some hisses). His second speech is harrowing as he argues women should be thankful that they're beaten by men because it can serve as a reminder of the violence men must perpetrate to establish a civilization that will be safe for women. In the first speech, he puts forth the case that he was promised a wife by the sisters' father; and, therefore, the women have no individual choice. They have a fate, which they must embrace.

> CONSTANTINE: Tomorrow will take today by force
> whether you like it or not.
> Time itself is an act of rape.
> Life is rape.
> No one asks to be born.
> No one asks to die.
> We are all taken by force, all the time.
> You make the best of it.
> You do what you have to do.

Bloodied lust: KJ Sanchez (standing), J. Michael Flynn (on tub) and Lauren Klein in Charles L. Mee's Big Love. *Photo: Richard Trigg*

After the arguments, Piero guides the men offstage so they can smoke cigars and negotiate a possible settlement to this conflict. And what ensues next is another "smashing" scene, one that makes audiences audibly gasp, giggle or groan.

> THYONA: This game isn't over till someone lies on the ground
> with the flesh pulled off their bones.
> Men.
> You think you can do whatever you want with me, think again.
> you think that I'm so delicate?
> you think you have to care for me?
> You throw me to the ground
> you think I break?

And with those words, she literally begins throwing herself around the stage floor. She jumps in the air, goes completely limp, and slams to the floor (which we thankfully discover is made from a wrestling mat-like material). Soon all three sisters are hurtling around the stage in a gravity-defying, breathtaking dance of defiance. They shout bits of dialogue about their relationships and feelings toward men as they hurl themselves in the air like rag dolls, falling, rising and starting over again.

This scene is mirrored later in the play by the men, who do their version of the same frenzied dance of frustration. It's occasioned by the women's refusal to compromise. And in perhaps the most memorable bit of staging, as they run, tumble and roll over one another, Oed starts picking up nine-inch circular saw blades (often the means of terrorizing victims in old melodramas or movies) and throws them, one by one, into a back foam wall. Each sticks with a sickening thud.

EVEN THE MINOR CHARACTERS can be fascinating and are invariably given their own great arias. Giuliano, who turns out to be gay, sings "Bewitched, Bothered and Bewildered" and at another moment describes his obsession with Ken and Barbie dolls. Two weekend guests arrive, Eleanor and Leo, both suavely dressed and courteous in manner (Klein and Flynn doubled in these roles). They are bourgeois hedonists who insist on telling the sisters about all the pleasures in life, which in their opinion, are so abundant and available that it's quite useless to be unhappy.

Amid these strange and surreal characters, Lydia and Nikos find in each other the potential for some common ground. Nikos, unlike Constantine, is shy, somewhat sensitive, and prone to stammering. They have one long courtship scene, both funny and touching, during which Lydia shares a crazy dream that includes a Julian Schnabel bridge, Boris Yeltsin, a dog named Chopin, and cell phones. Nikos's response mirrors Mee's bottom-line philosophy when he says, "I think things happen so suddenly sometimes."

In any case, it turns out that Piero can't save the sisters: Constantine, speaking for the suitors, and Thyona, representing the women, refuse to compromise. Piero, therefore, tells the brides to prepare to be married. In response, Thyona convinces the women to unite and murder the men because they are no different than soldiers who break into a house intent on raping the women inside. The tone then veers suddenly again as the oblivious Eleanor enters and helps them prepare their makeup and offers wedding night advice to the girls, including the best sexual position that makes for "very deep penetration / some say the very deepest."

To suggest the 50 couples, a few extra brides and grooms join the wedding party, and within moments a wedding cake is rolled onstage. Eleanor cuts a piece. First Olympia feeds it to Oed and they start dancing; Nikos and Lydia follow. But Thyona takes the cake and smushes it all over Constantine's face, illustrating the inherent hostility in this wedding ritual. He retaliates in kind and soon their responses escalate into full-scale ferocity. She eggs him on sexually; he takes off his clothes. Then, in a carefully choreographed, stylized whirlwind (performed to an ecstatic organ symphony by Widor that's often played at Easter services), the sisters start pulling out kitchen knives and stabbing all the men.

When the chaos clears, the sisters are shocked to discover that not only has Lydia spared her bridegroom, she has consummated her marriage. Thyona is especially infuriated. She sees this as an act of betrayal and insists that in most countries Lydia would be tried for treason. In the play's weakest scene, Bella steps forward to serve as a judge and determine the guilt of the aggrieved parties. Is Lydia wrong to have betrayed her sisters? Or were the sisters wrong for committing such cold-blooded killings? Both Thyona and Lydia argue their cases (it is from this scene that the epigraph was taken).

ONE PROBLEM WITH *BIG LOVE* is that Mee raises serious political issues throughout the play, but always indirectly; and too often the sheer physicality of the play overshadows its intellectual content. For example, at one point Bella tells Piero that he could have done something to prevent the bloodshed. He asks, "What could I have done?" Thus the question of when it's appropriate to intervene in another country's conflicts is raised and abruptly dropped. Piero symbolizes the ineffectuality of so many national leaders, but the audience must faconnect the dots between the stage situation and recent contemporary events.

Individual responsibility for the violence is partially laid at Olympia's manicure-deprived feet. She realizes that she didn't really want to murder her husband: "I was just following orders in a way. / I should kill myself probably / now that I see the kind of person that I am." Here again, there's a quick reference to the way the behavior of the masses, particularly in Germany during World War II, has been dissected and criticized. But instead of broadening these points, Mee has Bella shush everyone and deliver a "verdict." She absolves both Lydia of the charge of betrayal, since she acted out of love. She absolves the sisters from any guilt for their violent act since they had no other choice.

> BELLA: [L]ove trumps all.
> Love is the highest law.
> It can be bound by no other.
> Love of another human being —
> man or woman —
> it cannot be wrong.

Bella tries to make everyone feel better, even Olympia, whom she lauds for sticking with her sisters. Dramatically, it's all a little hard to swallow, although the actual text of Bella's speech has its moving moments.

> BELLA: For we all live together
> and come to embrace
> the splendid variety of life on earth
> good and bad
> sweet and sour
> take it for what it is: the glory of life.
>
> This is why at weddings
> everybody cries
> out of happiness and sorrow
> regret and hope combined.

Bella and Giuliano then offer a long, lyrical list of those things for which humans express the greatest of their qualities—sympathy—including "the hum of insects," "orchestras," and "the earth itself." At the end of this pseudo-benediction, Lydia throws her wedding bouquet and garter before she exits to musical wedding pomp.

It's questionable whether any ending could adequately finish off *Big Love,* considering all its *coups de théâtre.* Seeing it twice only confirms the play's strengths. The BAM audience in particular reacted enthusiastically throughout, whooping and hollering during the most outrageous moments of this amazingly physical production, and even applauding at the end of monologues. It's as close as I've come to experiencing what I imagine Shakespeare's audiences felt while watching say, *The Taming of the Shrew* or *Henry V*; in fact, elements of both these plays—particularly the former's farcical gender arguments and the latter's emboldened militarism—permeate *Big Love.*

In the end, *Big Love* can be seen as Mee's virtuoso theatrical valentine to a world besotted by violence and all manner of atrocities, especially between men and women. In New York, it could be seen as part of a loose, unplanned trilogy by Mee that included *First Love*, produced at the New York Theatre Workshop, and *True Love,* an adaptation of *Hippolytus* and *Phèdre*, at the Zipper Theatre. True to its title, however, *Big Love* ends with the suggestion that the grander the problem or crime, the bigger the love needed to right the ship of state. That may not wash with every clear-eyed pragmatist in the audience—but for most of us, who share a bit of Lydia's romantic idealism, it's a fine way to end a ripping ride.

2001–2002 Best Play

BREATH, BOOM

By Kia Corthron

○ ○ ○ ○ ○

Essay by Michael Feingold

DENISE: When you said you was gonna make a fireworks show. You serious? (*No answer*) I sure as hell couldn't. Set a thing up, then see one a them hot sparks fly off, come fallin down right on top a ya *no!*

(*Pause*)

PRIX: Scariest is the opposite. Black shell. Send it up and somethin' go wrong: it don't explode And in the blacka night, you can't see where it's fallin'. You know that live explosive's on the way back down, right down to ya. You just can't see where it's comin' from.

C HILLING, PROVOCATIVE, UNYIELDING in subject and elliptical in style, Kia Corthron's plays are among the most daring theatrical adventures of our time, and *Breath, Boom*, its explosive power crammed into Playwrights Horizons's tiny Studio Theater, was no exception. Corthron's gifts have meshed with her concerns and her tactics to form an approach not quite like that of any other playwright. Her language, knotty but flexible, merges urban African-American street speech with blips of educated diction, the professional jargon of those her characters encounter, and short, unexpected bursts of poetry. As a woman of color, she writes her passionately contentious works from within an issue-conscious perspective, but she never preaches; the issues, which pour thick and fast out of her taut, urgent scenes, are embedded in the lives of her characters.

Breath, Boom chronicles the story of Prix (pronounced pree), whose name is French for "price" or "prize"—a fact that Corthron, typically, declines to signal or explain for the audience. Life has its price for Prix (played by Yvette Ganier in a stunning, implacable performance) and offers her few prizes. Many would think that she herself is no prize: she is a girl "gangsta," running drugs and engaging in turf wars with rival gangs. When we meet her, in the first of the play's twelve scenes, she is watching while two of her followers, Angel and Malika, beat up a third girl, Comet, who has breached the gang's discipline by announcing her plan to "retire" when she turns 18 (after which, if caught, she can be tried and sentenced as an adult).

Despite this announcement, Comet has left her 18th birthday party at the gang's summons, walking into Prix's trap. Prix, who will go through the play saying little and never smiling, watches the fight with no visible enthusiasm, only "throw[ing] in a few kicks or punches." All she says to her henchwomen is, "Don't kill her." During the beating, her attention is distracted by a fireworks display in the distance; it's Memorial Day weekend. As the action goes on, we will learn that Prix has always been fascinated by fireworks. Malika and Angel join her, gazing raptly at the fireworks while the bleeding Comet lies unconscious nearby.

In the next scene, we see Prix's room, which is covered with her drawings of fireworks and with tiny pipe-cleaner figures that she has made. Angel and Malika gossip while Prix, on the phone, gets information about a gang operation later that night; we discover that Angel is Prix's cousin. A repentant Comet, newly out of the hospital, arrives; she has been let into the building by Prix's mother and her common-law husband, Jerome, whom we hear offstage. Prix, ignoring the other girls, turns to drawing at her desk as Comet tries to get Angel to teach her the gang girl trick of juggling a razor blade on one's tongue. A sharp remark from Prix ("I find a spot a blood on my floor the owner's gonna lose six pints more") ends the game and the rising sound of Prix's mother and Jerome fighting encourages Angel and Malika to leave. But Comet stays, attempting to strike up a conversation.

COMET (*Looking around the room*): You sure like the fireworks.

PRIX: Everybody likes the fireworks.

In one of her rare long speeches, Prix explains Comet's mistake: retiring "ain't a dumb idea. Mouthin' off about it was."

COMET: [. . .] I thought we ain't s'posed to hit on our own[. . . .]

PRIX (*Dry*): Yeah, we ain't s'posed to. See how low you brung us. (*Beat*) Don'tchu know better than to walk into a deserted narrow place, your sisters jus' waitin' for ya?

(*Quiet again.*)

COMET: Whatchu wanna do? Shoot 'em off?

PRIX: Design 'em. (*Works quietly. Then:*) *And* shoot 'em off. Fireworks people ain't a architect, make the blueprint and give to someone else to build. Clothes designer never touch a sewin' machine. A fireworks artist, take your basic chrysanthemum, not to be confused with peonies, the latter comprised a dots but chrysanthemum with

Ms. Firecracker: Yvette Ganier in Kia Corthron's
Breath, Boom. *Photo: Carol Rosegg*

petal tails, the big flower, start with a pistil of orange, then move out
into blue, blue which comes from copper or chlorine, cool blue
burstin' out from orange pistil, blue instantly change to strontium
nitrate red to sodium yellow, cool to warm, warmer and the designer
ain't the joyful bystander, she's right there pushin' the buttons and
while the crowd's oohin' aahin' and this'n she's already on to the
next button.

Here we see the layered social commentary that lies at the heart of Corthron's
best work. Prix lives in a world forever teetering on the edge of violence
where sisterhood—far from feminist notions of collective cooperation—
means dominance and submission. Yet, she manages to carry and nurture
an intricate (and unlikely) dream that offers her creative release. Corthron's
use of the razor-blade trick is a neat metaphor for Prix's balancing act: one
slip and there's blood all over the carpet. The "trick," of course, is the crust
built on the tongue from repeated failures. The playwright alludes, in a

passing phrase, to the blood and scars formed on these women's softest places—and social commentary rises to poetry.

Prix's vision of a colorful, explosive future is interrupted by the shouts and thumps of her mother and Jerome fighting offstage. Before long the battle spills into Prix's room where her mother hides in a closet. Believing the mother has escaped through a window , Jerome sidles up to Prix and wonders aloud "what we do till your mama get back." When he makes a sexual advance on Prix, she slams him against the closet door with surprising force, saying, "I ain't five no more." As the stunned Jerome creeps from the room and we hear him leave the apartment, Prix's mother weeps audibly in the closet.

> PRIX: If you weren't always playin' Helen Keller, bitch, you mighta knowed a long time ago.

Although it has become almost routine for stories about fathers and daughters to include some intimation of sexual abuse, Ganier's matter-of-fact delivery and director Marion McClinton's cool hand prevented the moment from descending to soap opera. The brief exchange gives us insight into what Prix has had to overcome in her young life, but it also sets up the action to follow—which includes Prix visiting her mother in jail, where she lands for killing Jerome.

Prix arrives to visit her mother via her own probation officer, who has insisted on the visit. The mother has presumably killed Jerome for his abuse of Prix, but the young woman wants nothing to do with her mother. We realize that this is a Christmas visit, which Corthron artfully discloses at the end of a conversation between Prix and Angel in the jail's waiting room. It's another example of the skill Corthron demonstrates in placing seemingly ordinary events within an extraordinary context. As Angel and Prix speak in the waiting room—Angel does most of the talking, Prix is characteristically silent—Angel steadily works on a scrapbook. It isn't long before Angel explains that the scrapbook is an ongoing memorial to her siblings and classmates who have died by violence since childhood. For the audience, the dawning recognition—which leads up to a blithe "Merry Christmas"—is powerful.

Much of the play charts Prix's own experience within the criminal justice system. The rest of the first act focuses on her development into an institutional being forced to mouth the psychobabble platitudes of social rehabilitation. Sharing her cell with a former streetwalker, Cat, Prix finds herself haunted by Jerome, whom she "kills" several times in fantasies unnoticed by the cellmate. But even amid the presumed security of a jail for adolescents, there is a constant jostling among the young women, as they seek advantage over one another.

The act ends with Prix and her cellmate in their cell. While Prix reads a black romance novel, Cat talks on, her complaints, including those about Prix ("You the coldest fish I know."), marked by increasing emotional stress. The talk turns to suicides and funerals, inspiring Prix to describe the fireworks display she imagines as her memorial. Lost in her description, Prix does not see that Cat has tied her bedsheets into a knot, fixing one end to a ceiling pipe and the other in a noose around her neck. Noticing Cat for the first time in the silence following her reverie, Prix says tersely, "Jump," as the lights black out.

CORTHRON DIVIDES HER PLAY into two parts: the adolescent world of juvenile hall (Act I) and the even harder-edged reality of adult life (Act II). As Prix grows older—and somewhat less sure that she wants to continue as a gangsta girl—a new generation of young women appear with the assurance of youth. When Prix later encounters younger women in another stint in jail and submits to them, it's easy to recall her on the other side of the dividing line and to see how the cycle continues. In addition, the specter of Jerome continues to haunt her, weakening her, and before long it's clear that she's over-the-hill before she's 30. But in Corthron's world there are plenty of angry, undereducated young women to take her place.

The first scene of the second act finds Prix dealing crack and carrying a gun. Jerome now haunts her as an articulate presence, defending his actions in life. "Shut up!" Prix tells him, "You're mixin' me up." Comet arrives to monitor the phone (on which Prix receives her drug-dealing instructions) while Prix runs an errand.

> COMET: Thought kids I'd give up the life. Welfare sure don't cut it.
> Gotta gangbang supplemental income for the luxuries: food. Diapers.

While Prix is out, the phone rings; Comet panics, thinking she has miscounted the rings, but the expected message does not arrive till after Prix's return. When Prix shoos her off dismissively, Comet explodes: "Don't name me worthless just cuz my personality don't got what yours does: the ice." But we see that the ice is beginning to melt.

In the next scene, Prix has spent the past four years in prison. Her cellmate, Denise, knows of her reputation as an "original gangsta" but is curious about other aspects of Prix's life, notably a recently delivered personal letter, the first she has been known to receive. The letter is from Prix's mother—last seen by her 12 years ago—and says that she has become an addict in prison and now has AIDS.

But that's not the only bad news for Prix. Continuing her drug dealing within the prison, Prix has misheard a signal and passed on the wrong message about the location of a drug pickup. "She's gonna kill me! Fuck!" Prix exclaims, to which Denise sadly replies, "You been in it too long [. . .] Ain't twenty-eight bit old for the gangs?" In an apparent attempt to cheer Prix up—quoted in the epigraph—she changes the subject to Prix's desire to set off fireworks, adding, "I sure as hell couldn't." Prix counters her fear of catching fire with the deeper terror of the unexploded "black shell," which falls unseen and filled fiery danger.

Over the next several scenes, Prix gradually becomes more aware of the costs of her violent, drug-dominated lifestyle. Denise and a crack-fuzzed older convict called Socks sweep floors until Denise is relieved by Prix. After Socks begins babbling, Prix recognizes her—or thinks she does—as one of her original gang members, Malika. Socks, claiming she needs to go to the bathroom, is led off by the guard, leaving Prix alone and unsettled.

In the visitors room, we see Prix's mother, now on the visitors' side, waiting to see her daughter—but Prix does not appear. Mistaking the guard's impassivity for contempt, she lashes out at him: "Some nerve you got, dontchu *dare* label me [. . .] our relationship mother-daughter, nunna your biz—." The guard's call of "*Five*," signaling the end of visiting hours, cuts her off.

In a prison toilet stall, Prix is beaten up and mocked by younger gang girls under the command of Comet's daughter, Jupiter. "I came to your christenin'," Prix tells her. Jupiter forces her to stand on the toilet seat and repeat a jargon-filled, social-worker-influenced "speech"—one we heard her laugh over with Cat in Act I. Jupiter's sidekicks hoot with laughter over a phrase ("we are sisters") until Jupiter cuts them off sharply. When they have left, Jupiter explains to Prix that she did not take a hand in the beating because she is pregnant. Because Prix addresses her by name and mentions her mother, Jupiter explodes in rage, "Like I ever see the bitch between jail and the fosters [. . . .] Dontcha be mentionin' her stupid name to me." Leaving, she slams Prix's head against the side of the toilet.

IN A BRONX PARK at dusk, Prix, now free again and working at a Burger King, has joined Angel and the latter's children (unseen offstage) for a picnic. Each woman says she has a surprise for the other. When Prix opens

Early retirement: Rosalyn Coleman and Yvette Ganier in Kia Corthron's Breath, Boom. *Photo: Carol Rosegg*

her backpack, Angel immediately assumes she has gone back to drug dealing, but Prix is only assembling her surprise—a small-scale fireworks show.

Prix is staring with elation at the last of her handiwork when a girl in a wheelchair, Jo, wheels up to her. "You done it," Jo says, and Prix at first smiles, thinking she means the fireworks, but then realizes that Jo is blaming her for her crippled and disfigured condition. "I don't remember," shouts Prix, as Jo and the friend wheeling her become actively hostile, "Long time ago, lotta stuff blur." As Angel comes to back Prix up, Jo and her friend move off, muttering imprecations. "I don't remember her," Prix tells Angel, "I ain't callin' her a liar, just. . . ." "It's time," says Angel, "Come on." She leads Prix into a narrow corner that, recalling the blind alley of the opening scene, gives Prix a moment of panic when Comet steps out. But Angel and Comet have not come to attack, but to display what they preserved from the household goods thrown out while Prix was in prison: her colored penlights, with which they form a "fireworks" display for her. Though moved, Prix suppresses her sobs.

Outside the Empire State Building shortly before midnight, Prix has come to meet her mother, who has been begging her since adolescence to observe the magical moment when the building's decorative lights are turned off. Prix complains that she has to work the breakfast shift the next day and the subway back to the Bronx comes infrequently. Though guarded, Prix is more communicative with her mother than in earlier scenes; she tells her she has "retired": "Thirty pretty old to still bang in the gangs." The criminal activities that bring her "supplemental income" are now no more than peddling "a few food stamps, bitta herb." Asked if she still thinks about Jerome, Prix replies, "Useta. Not lately." "Different," her mother says about Prix. "Was a time you'da seen that note from me, tossed it in the trash [. . . .] Seems you ain't s'mad no more."

Her mother asks what became of Prix's drawings and pipe-cleaner figures. "Got lost or thrown out while I was in jail," says Prix. Begging her to make some new ones, her mother offers her a huge handful of change.

> PRIX: I toldju not to do that! Panhandlin', Jesus! we ain't fuckin' beggars.
>
> MOTHER: I just thought, maybe you can't afford the pipe cleaners, maybe that why you don't do it no more.
>
> PRIX: Do I look like I got time to fool around, arts and crafts? Grown woman.

"Make one for me," her mother pleads. Prix pointedly looks up at the building and shakes her head no. The chimes of a nearby church are striking midnight. Her mother shouts with redoubled force, "PRIX! YOU MAKE ONE? FOR ME?" Her fervor makes her hand shake, so that the coins fall. Prix's mother kneels to pick them up, but when Prix tries to help, her mother waves her away. As the last chime sounds, the mother, still kneeling, the money again in her hand, looks up intently into Prix's eyes. And just as Prix says "Yes," the Empire State Building's lights begin to go out.

Corthron's impressionistic dramaturgy—which forces the mind of the audience member to blend, shade and otherwise fulfill elements of the story—leaves us with a sense that her characters may yet overcome their circumstances and survive. But her great strength is that she makes us question how these social structures arise, even as she declines to ascend the pulpit of righteous indignation.

2001–2002 Best Play

THE DAZZLE

By Richard Greenberg

○ ○ ○ ○ ○

Essay by Donald Lyons

HOMER: Cuspidors, crushed pince-nez, checkbooks from defunct accounts, pieces of a smashed demi-lunette, plumbing parts, rusted roasted pans, baseballs, spoons, pickling spices—

UP IN HARLEM IN THE EARLY YEARS of the twentieth century there dwelt in a lush Victorian home the two Collyer brothers, who passed their lives in a comfortable obscurity but became proverbial when, after their death, they were discovered to have lived amid a mountain of clutter. This indiscriminate heap is thus, ironically but exuberantly, described by Homer Collyer in Richard Greenberg's amazing *The Dazzle*. This author of such exercises in lugubrious nostalgia as *Three Days of Rain* and *Everett Beekin* seems to have found whole new octaves to his voice in this play. Perhaps working on Strindberg—his adaptation of *Dance of Death* played on Broadway this season—opened his imagination to the kind of macabre but funny madhouse we glimpse in *The Dazzle*.

Greenberg admits that "I know almost nothing" about the real Collyer brothers. In other words, he is a poet of the imagination (like the Collyer brothers themselves); you'd no sooner go to *The Dazzle* for info about Homer and Langley Collyer than you'd consult *Twelfth Night* for mating customs in Illyria or *Volpone* for banking practices in Venice. The play has the lively brilliance of a first-rate imaginative work.

Allen Moyer's droll set, a two-tiered library, perfectly embodied the encroaching lunacy: in the first act, it was still an elegant, if crowded, room with two pianos; later, the clutter took on an entropic chaos on its own. The backstory: Homer, the older, saner (that's saner, not sane) brother was for a time an admiralty lawyer but has, under parental advice, given that up to attend to Langley, his younger brother, a professional pianist and fantasist who has come close to destroying his career by performing too slowly. Lang (as he's known) whines: "I didn't hold the last note long enough."

As the play begins, the two brothers stagger back from a concert, Lang whining the while. With them is Milly, a bright, attractive, talkative

Brother act: Peter Frechette and Reg Rogers in Richard Greenberg's The Dazzle. *Photo: Joan Marcus*

young society woman who has undertaken to investigate, tease and ultimately wed Lang. Milly is a (presumably) invented character who fits the Collyer style with odd perfection. Homer is at first hostile to her: "Can I get you something? A comic book? The Koran?" he asks, half nasty and half genuinely unused to entertaining.

But Molly is cheerful—her cheer with the brothers stems from some terrible experiences in her home we later hear about. She listens as Lang explains how he watches the men returning to fashionable Harlem of an evening:

> LANG: I'll watch the men return from business.
> Especially this is in late fall, and early winter— coats are important— thick collars turned up— and a current of wind— a light current of wind that seems— this is an illusion— that seems to speed them along—
> They are accompanied by leaves. Curled umber and orange and sepia at their feet, sped by the wind— that's *not* an illusion.

This is man of the senses, utterly divorced from human concern. Molly is quite different. Her answering words are: "I come from swine. No, I live among the most remarkably unpleasant people." Homer returns from the kitchen, swearing there is nothing to drink. Milly takes his attitude in good part, saying "I'm not really thirsty." Noticing that his brother and Molly have become rather intimate in his absence, Homer orders Lang to "remove your hand from that lady's coiffure," but Lang objects on the grounds that "I almost have a name for its color." Milly attempts polite conversation.

> MILLY: How exciting it must have been, Admiralty law, I mean.
>
> HOMER: Why?
>
> MILLY: I think the sea is the most exciting thing! The air, all salt, all brackish, and then the weather vanes and . . . Nor'easters and whatnot— isn't it, didn't you find?
>
> HOMER: Admiralty lawyers do not sail.

Various sorts of madness never intersect, and the playing of it here was perfect. Director David Warren evocatively brought out the madness and sadness in each scene. Peter Frechette played Homer as acerbic, eloquent, domineering. Reg Rogers as Lang was giggly but cunning, a man deeply selfish, a man who does not notice such things as the eventual blindness of his brother. Francie Swift was poised and sexy but darkly wounded as Milly; it's an appealing performance in a well-written but under-thought-out role.

THE NEXT SCENE FINDS LANG playing the Minute Waltz in "slightly under three quarters of an hour" and deciding his career is "doomed." Homer, deflecting Milly's questions about his past, quizzes Lang about her. Lang decides he loves her.

> HOMER: Truly?
>
> LANG: Yes. I believe so. There's something . . . miasmic about her.
>
> HOMER: Miasmic?
>
> LANG: Yes. It's her speech! It's when she speaks. You see, she has nothing to say, and she says it incessantly.

Homer now approves of the marriage, for he is worried about the Collyer finances and Milly is "very rich." He invites Milly to the Collyer house for a concert given by musicians whom Lang cannot tolerate. Milly asks "Can we dance?"; Lang's reply is "I doubt it." Milly is additionally perplexed by Homer's attitude to her and to life.

> LANG: Homer is having a tragedy. He's a tragic figure.
>
> [. . .]
>
> MILLY: In what way tragic?
>
> HOMER: Oh, I don't know. I don't understand these things. What is tragedy? I wrote it in a notebook once.

MILLY: Tragedy is— a feeling more than any—

HOMER: Oh yes, I remember! Tragedy is when a few people sink to the level where most people always are.

But Homer is at present playing a part in a comedy. He is spying on the courtship. He hears Milly's invitation to Lang to take advantage of her suddenly topless body ("Do you want to touch? Would you like to touch?") and observes Lang's perversely aesthetic response. Lang drops to his knees and buries his head in her dress. Homer can no longer contain himself.

HOMER: Not the *dress*, idiot, the *girl!*

It is a delirious mix of *The Importance of Being Earnest* and August Strindberg's *Dance of Death*—teasing wit on the edge of madness.

Homer next starts to dance on his own and claims, while dancing, to have been to what he calls Cathay. It is a Cathay of the mind. "Dance with me," he suggests, "Please. I love the whole thing of parlors— and music drifting from nearby rooms— and lighting!" Milly is agreeable. Homer continues fantasizing: "When I was in China I met a girl— [. . .]"

MILLY: Could you slow down—

HOMER: A lovely young girl—

MILLY: What was her name?

Sibling savant: Reg Rogers and Peter Frechette in Richard Greenberg's The Dazzle. *Photo: Joan Marcus*

Homer informs her that the girl was called Cio-Cio-San and that he seduced and abandoned her. "I was handsome, then. And Caucasian. And I could do that sort of thing. It was acceptable," Homer insists. Milly recognizes the story from a play, where the girl was "Nipponese." Homer blithely claims he sold the story for five dollars to a playwright in an oyster bar.

> HOMER: Well, where do you think he got the idea?
>
> [. . .]
>
> MILLY: His— well— his imagination!
>
> HOMER: His imagination! We're talking about a *play*wright! Playwrights don't have imaginations— they're drunken illiterates.

And Homer goes on trying to write the novel of the strange trio.

> HOMER: I would say
> . . .
> You're a silly little rich trollop who likes to tease our cocks.
>
> MILLY: Mr. Collyer!
>
> HOMER: Okay, let me try another one:
> You are the spirit of the avant-garde incarnate . . . a quester after the new; it is by the efforts of you and our likes that the fallen, fractured, machine-wrecked world will once again be made whole.
>
> MILLY: . . . That's better.
>
> HOMER: I don't know. I think before I was closer to the mark.
>
> MILLY: I can leave—
>
> HOMER: But you won't.
> Oh listen:
> You're our *enzyme*. In your presence, reactions take place.

THE TWO ARRANGE an odd, supercilious marriage for Milly and Lang. Homer insists, "I don't care what happens as long as something does. My brother's life is . . . one of . . . piecemeal intensities; I watch him." Milly sees her future as one of patronizing power: "I understand him implicitly. He is an artist, therefore turbulent, strange, possessed by passions unknown to the common run of people. He needs to be cosseted, indulged and surreptitiously held in check." They think they have settled the business; both are relieved and pleased.

On the wedding day Lang, duly attired in morning coat and top hat, is upset (are we surprised?) by the fact that the Wedding March is a march and by Milly's blithe assumption that the couple will live on an estate in Nyack or Dobbs Ferry. Milly promises some sort of compromise and begins to look about her.

MILLY: This *room* really *is* a mess . . .

LANG: I don't think so . . .

MILLY: Look at it— it's a *pig* sty!— What if someone were to wander in from the party? Where's the waste paper basket?

LANG: We don't have a waste paper basket—

MILLY: What do you mean, you don't have a waste paper basket? Everybody has—

LANG: I don't believe in waste paper.

Milly commits the unforgivable atrocity of pulling off and threatening to burn a loose thread, and Lang reacts with "I can't possibly marry you. Not possibly." The last attempt to bring three damaged souls into some rapport with reality has come a cropper.

What was eccentricity has turned into entropy and tragedy as the second act begins. Time has passed. A jungle of junk (newspapers, etc.) has taken possession of the set. Homer sits alone in the darkness, drinking and reflecting on the "diminishment" of his life since the high days of Lang's near marriage.

HOMER: I used to love— on bad days— I used to love— on days when I'd stayed indoors and weltered in my . . . freedoms . . . I used to love to walk around the block. Simply that.

When Lang comes in for dinner, Homer demands that Lang wash first. Lang complains that "you pluck the wrong ingredients from the shelf— once I tasted library paste in the goulash" and decides that "I'm utterly renouncing you and food!" Homer turns the attack:

HOMER: *Look* at this place! Will you— *look* at this place?

LANG: That's all I ever do.
[. . .]
It's *lovely*, Homer. It's sacred.

HOMER: Sacred! You're an atheist!

LANG: God isn't the source of what's sacred.

HOMER: Then what is?

LANG: Things in themselves.

Baffled by this perverse pantheism, Homer asks Lang to read to him (why, we can guess although Lang does not bother to). And Lang reads a sentence each from Ruskin, Gibbon, Locke, Pater, Rousseau, Jonathan Edwards and says "I love our life." Random sentience is his highest bliss.

A changed, white-haired, ill wretch comes by. It is Milly. Homer tells her Lang no longer plays.

HOMER: He's no longer employable. His tempi became too slow.

MILLY: I suppose that's how he heard the music.

HOMER: No.
He couldn't bear to let the notes go.

Milly tells Homer of what happened after the interrupted marriage: of her rape by her father, her confinement, her arranged marriage, her forced abortion, her disowning, her impoverished wandering. The sufferings of her life strike a note of operatic melodrama not entirely reconcilable with the mad sickness of the Collyer brothers. Says Homer to her story: "What a

Collyers aclutter: Reg Rogers and Peter Frechette in Richard Greenberg's The Dazzle. *Photo: Joan Marcus*

corker!" One sees Greenberg's determination to implicate all New York society in the madness and wickedness; one feels he has crossed genres here and mingled, unattractively, the guignol with the tragic.

Homer simply sets three places for the dangerous (dangerous because he is blind and is likely to cook with glue or worse) dinner he's making. Lang announces he's seen a ghost: "I thought I saw that girl"; Homer makes him say whom he means; "the bride," Lang confesses. Homer says, "Oh,

Milly"; Lang reacts to her appearance with a long screech. To Lang's repeated question of why she has come she calmly answers: "This is as good a place as any to die."

> HOMER: Better. Here the difference is so much less marked.
>
> MILLY: An easy passage . . . a slide . . .
>
> HOMER: You won't be dying.
>
> MILLY: Of course I will.

Milly has slipped into a mode of discourse common *chez* Collyer. Her situation is desperate but she speaks with point and precision. She is not, though, for all her mastery of the Collyer-speak, blind to what is before her. Milly realizes that Homer has lost his sight, but remains alive to the humor of the situation:

> MILLY: "Blind Homer"— oh God!
>
> HOMER: I know—incredibly pat, isn't it?
> I find that comforting, somehow. Life goes along—
> happening or . . . not . . . chaotic . . . and then you're all at once
> "Blind Homer!"— Literature in*sists* on itself—

Lang is affronted by all this planning for the future that does not center on him:

> LANG: Homer, an adult woman cannot come and simply live in this
> house— it's an affront to all the decencies!
>
> HOMER: Then I'll marry her.
> If she'll have me.
>
> MILLY (*softly*): Homer—
>
> HOMER (*on bended knee*): Will you marry me, Miss Ashmore?
>
> MILLY: Of course.
>
> LANG: But— *I* was supposed to do that.
>
> HOMER: Too late.
> Oh, this will be fun!
> What did that German say— all history happens twice, first as tragedy,
> then as farce? *We'll* do it *twice* as farce.

And on this note we are back with the importance of being earnest. The mad union is complete just before it begins to disintegrate.

In the last scene, Milly is long dead. More detritus has piled up. The house is being bombarded by cackling urchins. Lang insists, "I've had the most wonderful day!" and recounts his absorption in "the history of sunlight through clear glass."

Homer manages to get a word in edgewise only to insist: "Lang, I'm going to die today." Lang is utterly reluctant to accept this fact—so intensely does he dislike change—and when it happens he refuses to accept it. He insists to the corpse of his brother: "Just don't move. . . Just— please!— don't move. . . ." Oddly enough in their various woundedness and waggishness both Homer and Milly managed to get in some living and even loving before their ends; Lang, impermeable to life and emotion, is left alone.

The play is a difficult, delightful masterpiece.

2001–2002 Best Play

FRANNY'S WAY

By Richard Nelson

○ ○ ○ ○ ○

Essay by Charles Wright

MARJORIE: As we get old, we start to see the [. . .] fragility of—well everything. But when we are young, thank God we are oblivious.

RICHARD NELSON HAS TAKEN a surprising turn. For much of his three decades in the theater, this prolific dramatist, an honorary artistic associate of Britain's Royal Shakespeare Company, wrote plays so argumentative, ironic and arch that audiences mistook him for an Englishman. Lately, though, he is aligning himself with the American tradition of poignancy—the school, if you will, of Tennessee Williams and William Inge.

Over the past five years, notably in *Goodnight Children Everywhere* and *Madame Melville*, Nelson has demonstrated an enhanced capacity to plumb characters' emotions and present even disturbed and morally unhinged figures with tenderness and empathy. This season, in *Franny's Way*, his themes include the irrevocable velocity of life—especially the velocity of youth, so famously wasted on the young—and the fragile nature of human experience. This new comedy-drama is neither as arresting nor profound as the small-scale masterpiece *Goodnight Children Everywhere*, but it nonetheless achieves intense sentiment without sentimentality and shows off the brainy playwright's long undisclosed heart.

Franny's Way was produced in March 2002 for a limited run by the nonprofit Playwrights Horizons, which has staged many of the author's works, from *Jungle Coup* in 1978 to *James Joyce's The Dead* two seasons ago. The play focuses on contrapuntal existential crises in the lives of Franny (Elisabeth Moss), a teenager from upstage New York, and her older first cousin, Sally (Yvonne Woods), an aspiring actress in Manhattan. Franny and Sally are typical of the displaced persons about whom Nelson writes. With customary expectations dislodged by events beyond their control, they're as uprooted as the tourists of *Some Americans Abroad*, as disoriented as the British expatriates in *New England* and as homeless—metaphorically— as the war refugees of *Goodnight Children Everywhere*.

Her way: Elisabeth Moss, Kathleen Widdoes, Jesse Pennington, Domenica Cameron-Scorsese and Yvonne Woods in Richard Nelson's Franny's Way. *Photo: Joan Marcus*

Franny's world has been disrupted by her mother's abandonment and the recent arrival of a less-than-sympathetic stepmother. Rather than facing her disappointments head-on, Franny has distracted herself by writing a steamy novel set in 19th century Yorkshire and embarking on a sexual relationship with a college boy. Franny's cousin Sally, though in her twenties, is coping childishly with grief. Since losing an infant daughter to "crib death" a few weeks before, she has been reclusive, lolling about all day in nightclothes. Sally's husband, Phil (Jesse Pennington), also mourning, has withdrawn from her, unwilling to tolerate physical contact. Sally is unforgiving of Phil's standoffishness, yet unable to explain or justify her own way of dealing with tragedy. Consequently, their marriage is in tatters.

Franny's Way takes place over the two days Franny, her younger sister, Dolly (Domenica Cameron-Scorsese), and their grandmother, Marjorie (Kathleen Widdoes), spend in New York on a condolence visit with Sally and Phil. The play is narrated by Franny at age 60 (also Widdoes), reminiscing about the summer of 1957 when she, age 17, restyled herself as an "homage . . . to the beautiful, frail, lost, fair-skinned, funny, faint-prone heroine of my life and J.D. Salinger's story." It was—or, in the literary present tense, is—a moment at which Franny, like Salinger's Franny and Holden Caulfield in *The Catcher in the Rye*, is poised on the threshold of adulthood, profoundly confused about her own identity and in agony over what is genuine and "phony," both in the world and in her own constitution.

Nelson gives "Older Franny" (as the script calls the narrator) a believable, down-to-earth voice reminiscent of Salinger's first-person storytellers (Holden, for instance, or Buddy Glass, who narrates *Zooey*, "Raise High the Roof Beams, Carpenters," and "Seymour: An Introduction"). Even in the instances where Older Franny's speeches become flowery and overpoetic, she has the sympathetic tone that Salinger strikes so expertly.

> OLDER FRANNY: This death which swept as a tidal wave over the lives of Sally and Phil, was by the time it reached my distant shore— in Millbrook, New York—but a small almost unnoticed ripple. [. . .] I had, after all, other things on my mind that summer. There was a boyfriend, with whom I had had my first sex, and he was now at NYU. And I loved him. Though his letters were beginning to get, if not less frequent, then less—interesting. Was this my fault? Or his? [. . . W]hen Grandma offered to take my sister and me on a trip to New York City, it [. . .] seemed the very understandable fulfillment of a seventeen-year-old's desire, if not need, to get the hell out of Millbrook and be hurtled headlong into that swirl of life called New York.

SALINGER IS A SIGNIFICANT PRESENCE throughout the play. By 1957, when *Franny's Way* takes place, he had been contributing sad, understated, oddly urbane tales to American magazines for more than a decade. His novel, *The Catcher in the Rye*, had been out for six years. Because Salinger's highly original voice jibed ideally with the mid-century *Zeitgeist*, he seemed destined to inherit Ernest Hemingway's dominant place in American fiction.

"Franny," the Salinger story from which Nelson derives his play's title, was published in *The New Yorker* in January 1955. Its companion piece, the novella *Zooey*, appeared in the same publication in May 1957 (a few weeks, it's significant to note, before the action of *Franny's Way*). The two stories portray Franny Glass, youngest of seven gifted siblings, veterans all of a radio quiz program called *It's a Wise Child*, who populate a number of Salinger stories. Franny, like Holden Caulfield, recoils from the corruption she perceives in the adult world and rails against the "phoniness" of those around her.

The sisters in Nelson's play, Franny and Dolly, have arrived in New York with secret agendas—Franny's an assignation and Dolly's a rendezvous with their mother. Nelson's Franny, like Salinger's Franny, suffers an emotional blow while visiting her boyfriend's college: the putative boyfriend doesn't appear and, when Franny telephones him, he reveals that he never intended to keep their date.

> OLDER FRANNY: [H]e'd met this girl, just the weekend before, and he really wished he could tell me in another way—I deserved that— and by the way, there's lots of fun things I could do in New York by myself, did I want a list? And hey, would I like to meet his new girl, she's real real nice, and the two of us would really really get along, and to this day I remember not so much what he said, but the smell in that phone booth, a mixture of stale cigarette smoke, some half-eaten thing that had sat in the sun too long, and urine. Anyway, I hung up on my boyfriend, and threw up in the booth.

Like Salinger's Franny, Nelson's young heroine has a fainting spell and a painful episode in a restaurant ladies' room.

> OLDER FRANNY: [A] tiny, dirty room with a hook to lock the door. I sat on the toilet seat, rubbed a wet towel across my face and tried to

Loss and longing: Jesse Pennington and Yvonne Woods in Richard Nelson's Franny's Way. *Photo: Joan Marcus*

stop crying. [. . .] I think I did faint. But I guess didn't hurt myself when I fell. Someone shouted through the door to see if I was all right. I suppose they'd heard this thud or something or maybe just my sobbing.

Nelson's drama, like *The Catcher in the Rye* and *Franny and Zooey*, presents the clash of values between an adolescent and those with power over her. But Nelson's Franny isn't suffering a profound crisis of the spirit like Franny Glass or Holden Caulfield. This Franny's crisis falls within the normal range of adolescent growing pains. Hurt but enlightened by the boyfriend's betrayal, she is swift to conclude that he's a phony and to apply the same convenient, if simplistic label to others in her ambit, especially her blustering father and meddling stepmother.

> FRANNY: They're idiots. I don't care what they think. They are complete phonies. (*Beat*) And so is Mom.
>
> DOLLY: That's not true.
>
> FRANNY (*to herself, mumbling*): Father and his bitch!

These, however, are offstage phonies. An unexpected telephone call from back home in Millbrook lays the groundwork for the conflict between Franny and her older cousin that establishes Sally as principal onstage phony. This creaky turn of events illustrates how Nelson, so gifted at characterization, is often less adept at plotting.

> SALLY (*Turns to Dolly*): It was your father [on the phone]. [. . .] Do *you* know where [Franny]'s meeting this guy? [. . .] Is he her boyfriend? (*No response*) [. . .] Your stepmother found a letter in Franny's bureau.
>
> DOLLY: What was she doing in Franny's bureau?!
>
> [. . .]
>
> SALLY: He read me part of this letter! How this guy has a friend with an off-campus apartment. How this friend is away this afternoon. How he's got the key, everything but the size of the bed! Your father's so upset. She doesn't know what she's doing. She's a kid.
>
> [. . .]
>
> DOLLY: My stepmother was looking for Franny's diaphragm. (*Sally turns, confused when she hears this.*) Last week she accused Franny of owning one. Franny denied it of course.
>
> SALLY (*suddenly laughs*): Where would Franny get a dia—?
>
> DOLLY: But she brought it with her. So that's why she didn't find it.

Sally, consumed by an older cousin's sense of superiority, pontificates to her visitors. "I see right through you," she tells Franny, "I see who you are—*and* who you think you are. And there's a real big discrepancy, my dear." In his *New York Times* review, Ben Brantley focused on that line as an instance of Freudian projection in which Sally's voice, "devastatingly phony," sounds "like a girl playing matron."

NELSON'S LITERARY STYLE isn't as schematic as Salinger's; he doesn't make particular characters—at least not onstage characters—bear the whole burden of human phoniness. Nelson's onstage characters are unfailingly complex, with at least a degree of inauthenticity in each. Sally's posturing, for instance, is a ploy to obscure her grieving, little-girl heart and her feeling that she's inadequate to the demands of adulthood.

The playwright understands Franny's ache to be adult; and his sympathetic portrait of her includes moments in which she strikes pseudo-sophisticated poses because she's profoundly uncertain what it means to be grown-up. Franny's mix of the genuine and the phony is clearest in her exchanges with Phil, whom she judges to be her fellow member of the anti-phonies brigade.

> PHIL: "Franny." I think that's really neat, by the way. [. . .] Changing your name. Because of the Salinger story. I think it's an incredible story.
>
> FRANNY: Me too.
>
> PHIL: Obviously or you wouldn't have—.
>
> FRANNY: Do you think she's pregnant or having a nervous breakdown? In the story.
>
> [. . .]
>
> PHIL: I know. I—maybe it's both.
>
> FRANNY: That's good. I hadn't thought of that.
>
> PHIL: That's—what a lot of people think now. Anyway, it's a neat thing to do. If only my name were Zachery, then I could—
>
> BOTH: —be called Zooey!

Franny flirts with Phil and then, in an attempt to storm the barricades of adulthood, applies a sexual full-court press, only to discover that, though aroused and sorely tempted, he won't capitulate to her advances. "No, I can't [. . .] this isn't right. This is wrong," he says. The flirtation is significant on both sides. When Phil breaks away from Franny's embrace and rushes into the bedroom he shares with Sally, he discovers that communion with a soulmate (Franny) has mitigated his grief, jump-started his libido, and freed him to reconcile—that is, resume conjugal relations—with Sally. It's another example of facile plotting by Nelson (comparable, in fact, to Salinger's facile conclusion of *Zooey*); and, in this easy resolution, Nelson

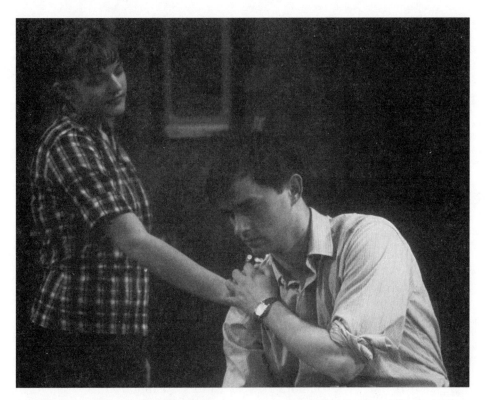

A look, a touch: Elisabeth Moss and Jesse Pennington in Richard Nelson's Franny's Way. *Photo: Joan Marcus*

casts Franny in the salvific role that Zooey plays in Salinger's novella. In the final scene of *Franny's Way*, set the next morning, Phil acknowledges his obligation to Franny (and their kinship in the anti-phonies league) by giving her his copy of the hard-to-find back-issue of *The New Yorker* containing *Zooey*. Clutching this totem, Franny leaves New York wiser than when she arrived and destined, one suspects, to return to New York to stay.

AS WITH NELSON'S PREVIOUS DRAMA, *Madame Melville*, *Franny's Way* is cast in the mold of Tennessee Williams's *The Glass Menagerie*. At once whimsical and gritty, *Franny's Way* attempts to rejigger the "memory play" for a new millennium by coupling this classic dramatic form with contemporary sensibility. In memory plays—recent examples including Brian Friel's *Dancing at Lughnasa* and Warren Leight's *Side Man*—an adult narrator reflects upon a watershed in his past. "The scene is memory and is therefore nonrealistic," writes Williams in stage directions for *The Glass Menagerie*. "Memory takes a lot of poetic license," he adds. "It omits some details;

others are exaggerated, according to the emotional value of the articles it touches, for memory is seated predominantly in the heart."

While the bulk of *Franny's Way* adheres to the conventions of *The Glass Menagerie*, the play opens with a scene structurally separate from what follows and so stylistically divergent that it seems like a curtain-raiser. Nelson doesn't even introduce his narrator until after this brutally naturalistic prologue, which is played in semidarkness. The reason for this dramaturgical choice is obscure. As exposition, the prologue is superfluous, since the background of the sisters' visit and the married couple's problems are addressed efficiently in the narrator's monologue that follows. Reminiscent of the unnerving onstage depiction of incest in Nelson's *Goodnight Children Everywhere*, the scene feels as if it's grafted onto the larger, more elegiac drama. Though executed with the playwright's usual skill, it seems like an attempt to balance the old-fashioned form of the other seven scenes with something that's up-to-the-minute.

Franny's Way may represent Nelson in a new, less intellectual mode, but the dramatist's erudition remains evident. He scatters blue-chip literary associations throughout the text, creating pungent intertextual ironies for those inclined to analyze them. Besides his allusions to *The Glass Menagerie* and *Franny and Zooey*, Nelson also includes elements of homage to Mary McCarthy, Philip Roth, and the vast tradition of mid-century American magazine fiction. The diaphragm that causes so much consternation in *Franny's Way* has antecedents in Mary McCarthy's 1954 *Partisan Review* short story, "Dottie Makes an Honest Woman of Herself," and Philip Roth's 1959 novella, *Goodbye, Columbus*, published initially in *The Paris Review*. Franny's offstage stepmother in *Franny's Way* is a near relation of Mrs. Patimkin, the bureau-ransacking mother in *Goodbye, Columbus*. These allusions evoke an era in which serious fiction writers and public intellectuals, such as Salinger and Edmund Wilson—both discussed prominently in the dialogue of Nelson's play—enjoyed a cachet now accorded to movie stars and mobsters. It was a time when both mass circulation magazines and egghead journals challenged the conformity and anti-intellectualism brought on by the political climate of the Cold War.

The most significant literary association in *Franny's Way* is Salinger himself, whom Franny and Phil discuss in the penultimate scene.

> FRANNY: What do you think he's going to write next? [. . .] Could be a million things. There's so much we don't know about—the twins. Waker? In the conscientious objectors camp? What's that about? I think what Salinger's got to do is start putting things together. Show how the Glass family fits together. Right now it's just—bits, fragments—.

PHIL: Fantastic bits—.

FRANNY: True. But I think he's only begun something. . . . Something that is going to define our time.

What Phil and Franny can't foresee—and what the spectator can't avoid—is that eight years later, in 1965, the 46-year-old Salinger would cease publishing new work and disappear from public view. Though living in New Hampshire and, reportedly, still writing fiction, he has now been absent almost forty years from the literary scene. As a result, he is not Papa Hemingway's successor; and, though widely read by generations of adolescents, he occupies a marginal position in American letters. Salinger's midlife departure and spooky silence mean that, for the present at least, his achievement consists of nothing more than those unintegrated fragments of which Franny speaks. The specter of Salinger's unfulfilled promise looms large in *Franny's Way*, a bitter contrast to the exuberance, the aspirations, and the utterly convincing naïveté of Nelson's heroine.

Unlike most of Nelson's recent output, *Franny's Way* premiered in the United States rather than England. The production's first-class staging, directed by the author, went a long way toward masking the shortcomings in what is, apart from the anomalous prologue, a generally well-constructed script. Thomas Lynch, the seemingly ubiquitous stage designer, created a Sullivan Street walk-up that was squalid in a distinctively New York City way. Lighting guru Jennifer Tipton supported Lynch in masterly fashion, displaying special atmospheric delicacy in three scenes played somewhere between darkness and half-light. Sound man Scott Lehrer evoked the ambience of the Village with soulful melodies and round-the-clock offstage racket. Widdoes, seldom seen on stage in recent years but well-remembered for her 1972 Beatrice opposite Sam Waterston's Benedick in Central Park and on Broadway, was surrounded by a talented ensemble, strikingly youthful and technically strong.

In a different theater season, *Franny's Way* might have transferred to a commercial engagement, as *Goodnight Children Everywhere* and *James Joyce's The Dead* recently did. Ben Brantley's all-important *Times* review lauded the play as a "sensitively drawn portrait of love in the age of J.D. Salinger" and called Nelson a "keen-eyed observer of the pretensions, sexual competitiveness and the self-centered cruelty in being young that haunts the memory years later." Mixed notices from other quarters, coupled with the deepening economic recession, discouraged commercial producers. *Franny's Way* received a Drama Desk Award nomination as "outstanding play," but vanished after seven weeks.

2001–2002 Best Play

THE GLORY OF LIVING

By Rebecca Gilman

○ ○ ○ ○ ○

Essay by Chris Jones

LISA: You tell 'em what you want but they ain't gonna believe it.
They'll know just by looking at me. They'll know that it didn't even
occur to me that I didn't hafta to do it.

B Y THE TIME DIRECTOR Philip Seymour Hoffman's well-received MCC
Theater production opened in November 2001—the play's New York
debut—Rebecca Gilman's *The Glory of Living* already had enjoyed a long
life both across the Atlantic and in the Midwestern hinterlands.

One of her earliest plays, the creation of this lean but disturbing drama
predated several other Gilman plays that made their ways to New York
much more quickly—including such dramas as *Spinning Into Butter*, *Boy
Gets Girl* (a 2000–01 Best Play) and, most recently, *Blue Surge*.

In many ways, this unusual production chronology has given New
York audiences a convoluted sense of the prolific playwright's career
trajectory. For *The Glory of Living*, which is set in rural Alabama, is perhaps
the simplest of Gilman's works—her later plays tend to have more characters
and more ambitious dramatic canvases. And even though Gilman's later
plays have attempted to make forays into the tricky sociopolitical worlds of
gender politics and the latent racism of liberals, the themes of *The Glory of
Living* can be distilled into something much simpler.

This may be a graphic, emotionally disturbing and unflinching
exploration of child abuse, sexual deviance and serial murder. But, even
though it may appear to be dealing only with a specific socioeconomic
milieu, *The Glory of Living* is a play about the utter inability of American
society to permit its children to grow up as children. In the final analysis,
the play betrays a palpable sweetness amid its shocking language and plot.

Gilman's detractors have tended to argue that her desire to engage
her audience in topical discussion and deliberation often gives rise to plot
contrivances, polemicized characters and overly smooth narratives. And,
indeed, both *Boy Gets Girl* (which deals with a blind date who turns out to

Lost girl: Anna Paquin in Rebecca Gilman's The Glory of Living. *Photo Joan Marcus*

be a stalker) and *Spinning Into Butter* (which considers the closeted quality of liberal racism on a college campus) are plays based around a specific issue.

Some critics have argued that the exploration of a single social problem tends to drive the plays' *raison d'etre* at the expense of their naturalistic credibility. Characters in these Gilman works frequently take particular ideological positions and often maintain their views throughout the dramas— as if they were mouthpieces for one aspect of the playwright.

But one could not say the same about *The Glory of Living*, the rawest of Gilman's works to date. In some ways, the play makes a case against the death penalty—especially for persons who commit crimes as juveniles. And one could reasonably see the work as a plea for sympathy for those who commit crimes, as well as for the victims. But whereas the troubled dean in *Spinning Into Butter* directly indicates her angst (and thus the theme of the play), the leaner and sparser *Glory of Living* avoids such direct polemics. And, as many critics acknowledged, *Glory*'s message is thus more powerful.

THE GLORY OF LIVING was given its American premiere in 1996 in a memorable production at the tiny Circle Theatre in Forest Park, Illinois (a suburb 10 miles west of downtown Chicago). Few people saw the work in its initial production, directed with low-budget lucidity and uncompromising power by Robin Stanton, a director now based on the West Coast.

At the time, Gilman was just another struggling Chicago writer feeding her love of playwriting by working temp jobs. But *The Glory of Living* was enough to convince anyone who wandered into the prosaic Illinois storefront that its author was a significant new presence in American playwriting.

In 1999, London audiences discovered much the same thing—Kathryn Hunter's United Kingdom premiere of the play at the Royal Court Theatre constituted Gilman's first significant exposure to British audiences and critics. The play was exceptionally well received on both sides of the Atlantic, winning the M. Elizabeth Osborn Award from the American Theatre Critics Association for the best new play of the year by a new writer.

To some degree, the play falls into the category of American gothic—a stereotype beloved in particular by British critics. For the London audience, at least, it offered further evidence of the dysfunction of rural Americans. And it did so in a violent fashion that was entirely at home in a theater that had provided a warm welcome for the tortured dramatic work of Sarah Kane.

Yet unlike other plays of this type, which often sensationalize their villains or ensnare their lower-class characters in Southern stereotypes (and thus play well to the smugness of theatrical sophisticates in northern cities like New York or Chicago), Gilman tells her story with an almost clinical realism. If some of her later plays follow a more predictable path, *The Glory of Living* constantly confounds the audience's expectations.

The authorial message, though, is abundantly clear: we all bear responsibility for the young people whose childhoods have been stolen by a society that no longer nurtures its young. *The Glory of Living* is all the more disturbing because of its basis in historical fact—it's a fictional tale that's based nonetheless on the youngest person ever to be sentenced to death in the state of Texas.

THE CENTRAL CHARACTER of the play is a teenage girl named Lisa (played in New York by Anna Paquin, in a significant deviation from the actor's early career choices). When we first meet her, the lanky 15-year-old Alabaman is chatting with an older man named Clint (Jeffrey Donovan) who is passing the time while his friend, Carl (David Aaron Baker) has sex with Lisa's prostitute mother, Jeanette (Erika Rolfsrud) behind the blanket that divides their trailer. The blanket is only a dismal parody of a boundary line—Jeanette uses her daughter to make small talk with her johns and to usher these sexual customers in and out. Despite her young age, Lisa has clearly cultivated a timeworn cynicism as a manner of survival:

> CLINT: Your Mama always do that sorta stuff with you right in the room.
>
> LISA: It ain't the same room.
>
> CLINT: It's the same room, darlin'.
>
> LISA: She does it but I don't care.
>
> JIM (off): Oh that's nice.
>
> (Pause. CLINT and LISA stare at the television.)
>
> That is, that's nice. Come on an' take your panties off too honey.
>
> LISA: I really don't mind on account of it happens all the time.
>
> (Pause.)
>
> So I guess I'm kinda used to it.

By the second scene of the play, years have passed. And a married Lisa and Clint are seen shacked up together in a cheap and dirty motel. Lisa has given birth to twins—which are apparently being kept with Clint's mother. At first it appears that Lisa and Clint are merely embroiled in a dysfunctional relationship involving abuse. But then a 15-year-old girl emerges from behind the bed and it quickly becomes clear that, during the time that has passed since the first scene, Lisa has somehow been coerced into picking up a succession of vagrant teenage girls for Clint's sexual pleasure.

Like Lisa, the nameless new girl has been abused as a child—this time by a friend of her mother who forced her to lie on the couch while he touched her. Once Clint is done raping his newest victim, Lisa appears to treat the girl with gentleness. But, as the girl is replaced by other girls in subsequent fast-paced scenes, it becomes clear to the audience that Lisa not only finds girls for Clint, but she also kills them after her husband is through having his way. After having so done, she feels remorse on a regular basis and tends to call the police:

> LISA: Hello? This is the police station . . . Um, no, I don't guess it's an emergency. I just got some information. It's about a girl. Up at Kentwood. State Park. Up there. There's a, there's a um . . . missin' girl up there. She was at the Harpstead Home. She ran away from there. No ma'am. I don't know her name. But I seen her body up there. (Pause. Then quickly.) No ma'am, I can't give you my name. You just, you just got to go up there, if you go up there through the main park part, up ta the parkin' lot, and then there's a lookout spot?

Go up there and look down in the canyon and you'll see where they
dumped her body. Down there. You'll see her if you go up there and
look.
(*She hangs up quickly.*)

In fairly short order, the police track down who has been making
these calls—and they arrive at a motel room where Clint and Lisa are staying.
Interrogated alone at the police station (since he didn't do any of the actual
killing himself, Clint is able to plead to much lesser charges), Lisa puts up
no credible defense. About to request the death penalty for this youthful
murderer, the incredulous police try to understand her motivation, which
she blithely and naively explains as follows:

BURROWS: Why did you kill her?

LISA: Clint tole me to.

BURROWS: You do everything he tells you to do.

LISA: Yeah.

BURROWS: Why?

LISA: 'Cause.

BURROWS: Because you love him?

LISA: No, sir.

BURROWS: Why then?

LISA: You don't want to know.

BURROWS: Oh yes I do.

LISA: He'd a killed me. If I hadn't done it.

BURROWS: But you said he was "off" somewhere.

LISA: Yeah.

BURROWS: Then why didn't you just let the girl go?

LISA (*this idea is new to her*): I dunno. It's just that . . . he would of
known.

BURROWS: How?

LISA: I'm a bad liar.

BURROWS: Christ.

Somehow, Clint turned his child-bride into a murderer whose taciturn
answers feel strangely logical even as they make no sense whatsoever. But
uncomfortable with the thought of leaving bodies unburied, Lisa proves
insufficiently duplicitous to get away with the crimes—or to ensure that
Clint, the instigator of the murders, gets any share of the blame.

Lisa's court-appointed lawyer, a sympathetic man named Carl, tries to
get Lisa to explain to a jury that the killings were a result of Clint's horrendous

abuse. But she lacks the ability to help him construct an argument. Instead, she laughs inappropriately and insists that all the lawyer's efforts will be futile, as quoted in the epigraph.

Convicted and on death row, Lisa's only solace is a tiny red toy piano that was given to her as her small child, she says, by her long-absent father, although he never taught her how to play. Carl tries to get Lisa to focus on her appeal, but she thinks only of the piano, her most precious possession. And it's only when Carl tries to teach Lisa to play that he finally gets the attention of a doomed young client, destroyed by those who killed her childhood.

It's this climactic scene that carries by far the most emotional weight in the play. Since she has never been taught to value her life or sense its possibilities, there's little use to Carl filing a successful appeal for Lisa. But as the child-criminal says in her own words, she appreciates that he makes the attempt. No one else has cared in the past. And after suggesting in the preceding scenes that her central character is little more than a surly cipher for abuse uninterested in her own fate, Gilman deftly delays the revelation of Lisa's stunted emotional inner-life.

The audience does not expect a warm scene with the attorney (who turns out to be the only responsible adult in the entire play), and the relationship feels all the more emotionally powerful because previous relationships in the play have been so cold. Carl and Lisa speak only in short sentences and cover no matters of obvious profundity. But since the two characters take on parent and child roles, the scene functions as an ironic counterpart for all that has gone before. The world has clearly failed this girl.

It's not unusual in dramatic writing for killers to have vulnerabilities or a certain sweetness. But even with her lean dialogues, Gilman offers a glimpse of the Lisa that might have been. And, therefore, the audience has to rethink its expectations. Accompanied at times by a flickering television set and ever-changing mountains of material debris (all of its productions to date have kept one foot in naturalism but also allowed the psychological subtext to have an influence on design and direction), *The Glory of Living* tells its terrible story with a relentless intensity. It is a tough-nosed and uncompromising play filled with graphic and disturbing imagery and, it sometimes seems, more horrible images around every twist and turn. The picture of Lisa, the young killer, is avowedly unsentimental. Indeed, one gets the sense that the writer was trying desperately to avoid any such notions—even at the expense of her play's commercial appeal.

Yet for all of its brutality, *The Glory of Living* lives on in memory because of its palpable compassion for Lisa's plight—her desperation for childish pleasure at the end of the play, even as she is about to die, is intensely moving.

Written at a time when victim's rights were very much in vogue—and when unforgiving policies toward crime were all the rage, *The Glory of Living* managed to make its audience understand that not all criminals are fully culpable. Indeed, by presenting a bevy of characters who misunderstand or abuse Lisa, the play suggests that society always ignores its own responsibility to criminals who also qualify as victims.

This notion of abdicated responsibility has informed many of Gilman's other plays. In *Blue Surge*, also seen in New York during the season under review, Gilman concocted a story of policemen arresting and becoming emotionally entangled with prostitutes in a faceless Midwestern town. Gilman's main point in the play—seen at the Joseph Papp Public Theater in a production directed by Robert Falls of Chicago's Goodman Theatre—is that cops and hookers are not the moral opposites one finds in melodramatic Hollywood movies. Rather, Gilman suggests that they are cut from the same social cloth—even to the point of having high-school friends in common and sharing the usual dysfunctional families. All are struggling in a world that has little time for people without the requisite smarts or diplomas.

Those same ideas are very much present in *The Glory of Living*, a play about the dispossessed inevitably preying on their own kind. In some ways, writers who take on the white lower classes face an uphill battle against the American theater establishment, which tends to shy away from such figures unless they are infused with the romanticism of the American West or indulge in comedic Irish theatrics that can make an audience feel superior. To its credit, *The Glory of Living* eschews such cheap tricks—which may partly account for its choice as a Pulitzer Prize finalist in 2002.

Despite the lean canvas, the simple structure and the brief scenes, and without every resorting to crude sociopolitical polemics, this early but strikingly mature Gilman play brilliantly observes that it is the flaws of society—and, most specifically, the ineptitude of parents—that bring about the hell caused by those who kill mainly because they were denied the right ever to be children.

2001–2002 Best Play

THE GOAT, OR WHO IS SYLVIA?

By Edward Albee

○ ○ ○ ○ ○

Essay by Charles Isherwood

STEVIE: We prepare for . . . things, for lessenings, even; inevitable . . . lessenings, and we think we can handle everything, whatever comes along, but we don't know, do we! Do we!

MARTIN: No; no, we don't.

FOR QUITE SOME TIME, the only element disturbing the sunny mood of marital accord in Edward Albee's *The Goat, or Who Is Sylvia?* is the peculiar look on the face of Martin Gray, the esteemed architect who is the play's protagonist. Is it caused by mild nausea, midlife malaise (he's just reached 50) or merely forgetfulness, as he claims? Set aside for a moment Martin's visible unease, and we see a disarmingly cheery portrait of spousal complacency. Martin and Stevie are no George and Martha; indeed they are the polar opposite of that combative couple from *Who's Afraid of Virginia Woolf?*, the 1962 play that won Albee his first Tony, four decades before he would win him his second with *The Goat*.

As the couple banters idly on this average morning in their graciously appointed home, all of the surface signals of marital contentment—something almost uniformly absent from the Albee *oeuvre*—shine forth. Martin and Stevie share the same sane attitude toward Martin's success. They share the same sane attitude toward the homosexuality of their 17-year-old only son. They have similarly sharp minds and sharp wits, and when they happen upon the subject of marital infidelity, they embark instantly on a parody of a scene from Noël Coward.

MARTIN: I've fallen in love!

STEVIE: I knew it!

MARTIN: Hopelessly!

STEVIE: I knew it!

MARTIN: I fought against it!

STEVIE: Oh, you poor darling!

MARTIN: Her name is Sylvia!

She's a what? *Bill Pullman and Mercedes Ruehl in Edward Albee's* The Goat, or Who Is Sylvia? *Photo: Carol Rosegg*

STEVIE: Sylvia? Who is Sylvia?
MARTIN: She's a goat.

Stevie exits in a gale of laughter, but Martin, as the audience for this much-talked-about play already knows, is in deadly earnest. He is in fact in love with a goat—conducting a sexual liaison with a goat, too, preposterous as the fact is—and the repercussions of this appalling admission will drive this savagely funny play to its devastating conclusion.

The outrageousness of the conceit was an audacious choice, even a dangerous one for a playwright who has been criticized for dabbling in arcane symbolism and willful obscurity, from the abstruse gothic milieu of *Tiny Alice* (which is jokingly alluded to here in a reference to a "large Alice") to the surrealistic dreamscape of his most recent work, *The Play About the Baby.* Academic analysts and average audience members alike could take refuge in assuming the goat was merely a symbol, a metaphor; the play merely a literary exploration of an idea, not intended to depict actual experience.

But Albee's language tells us otherwise: it is unusually crisp and accessible, vernacular and precise, largely devoid of the dense textures that typify much of his work. Albee points to the specificity of language time and again throughout *The Goat* as all of its characters trade commentary—even in the midst of dire emotional combat—on syntax and word usage. A couple of references to the danger of mixing metaphors can be seen as Albee's sly admonition to the audience: sometimes a goat is in fact a goat.

INDEED, IN ITS STRAIGHTFORWARD approach to the ideas it confronts, *The Goat* is in many ways an atypical work in the Albee *oeuvre*. Perhaps most notably—and most distressingly for some critics—Albee's humor here is uncharacteristically blunt and quip-laden. The play, which is divided into three scenes and played without an intermission, has as its centerpiece a scorching confrontation between Martin and Stevie.

Martin had confessed his secret to his best friend Ross at the conclusion of the play's first scene. Ross immediately sends a letter to Stevie alerting her to the improbable, distasteful truth. With occasional interruptions from their bewildered and anguished son, Stevie proceeds to verbally lacerate her husband, demanding an explanation for this unfathomable phenomenon. But she repeatedly cuts off Martin's desperate attempts to communicate his experience. Stevie pounds him with volleys of sarcasm that keep the belly laughs coming and turn the scene—in David Esbjornson's world premiere production on Broadway—into a rollicking comic crowd-pleaser.

Quoting Ross's letter, in which he writes that he's sure she'd rather hear it from a dear friend, Stevie quips, "As opposed to what? The ASPCA?" To Martin's ardent protestations that he does indeed still love her, she witheringly replies, "But I'm a human being; I have only two breasts; I walk upright; I give milk only on special occasions." Mercedes Ruehl's ferocious and committed performance met the play's joking humor head-on, her timing worthy of a great Borscht Belt comic.

The question arises: Is Albee pandering to his audience? Is he sweetening the bitter pill of his grotesque subject matter by allowing theatergoers to vent their discomfort through mindless laughter? To assume so is to underestimate a playwright who has spent decades of his career exiled from the acceptance of mainstream audiences and mainstream critics. If Albee were a playwright driven by the need for a wide popular audience, he would have begun cracking jokes long ago.

But Albee did note, in interviews prior to the play's opening, that he was interested in "testing the tolerance" of the audience. He might almost have said testing its humanity, for as the play evolves into a complex and layered inquiry into the nature of love, and its mysterious alliance to sexuality, the empathy of the audience—of the human race—becomes a central subject.

In order to fully engage the audience, to get us to sign up for the test, if you will, Albee first must seduce us into entering into the strange reality of the story. His canny tactic is to invite us to delight in Stevie's very funny, natural and utterly human reaction to her husband's outrageous confession.

Do we remain comfortable in our disgust with Martin's aberrant sexuality, content to bask happily in Stevie's merciless ridicule? (The audience, unlike Stevie, also has the option of exiling Martin's experience to the land of symbolism, and reactions to the play included quite a few commentators—with some textual support—who pointed to the name "Billy" and decided the play was actually about a man's incestuous love for his son.) Or does the laughter begin to stick in the throat, as we witness a man's anguished plea for the least celebrated but perhaps most noble and necessary form of love—understanding—go unheeded by the very people he loves most? Martin's betrayal of Stevie is the action that sets the play on its ultimately tragic course, but it may be Stevie's betrayal of Martin that is the more harrowing comment on the human capacity for cruelty, our inability to offer true compassion—when it is most desperately needed—even to those whom we hold most dear.

The first testing point for the audience—whose sympathies are naturally drawn to Stevie both by the nature of Martin's offense and the searingly

Goat song: Mercedes Ruehl and Bill Pullman in Edward Albee's The Goat, or Who Is Sylvia? *Photo: Carol Rosegg*

funny outrage with which she greets it—comes as Martin tries to honestly respond to Stevie's demands for an explanation by talking about his visit to a therapy group for people with similar fixations. He speaks with sad sympathy of a woman who was violently abused by the men in her family, and formed a relationship with a dog; of a man so grossly ugly that human intercourse was out of the question; of a pair of farm-raised brothers for whom sex with animals had become a habit that they couldn't shake despite their shame.

But Stevie, whose heart and mind are clouded by hurt, reacts with violence. Verbal at first—"Goat-fuckers anonymous!" she sneers—her rancor eventually becomes physical, as Stevie rises repeatedly to vent her anger and disgust by smashing crockery. Her outrage only grows when Martin points out how his experience diverges from that of the other members of the support group.

> MARTIN: I didn't understand why they were there—why they were all so . . . unhappy; what was wrong with . . . being in love . . . like that.

Stevie's rage—and her despair—reach the breaking point when Martin begins finally to describe his meeting with his four-legged lover, Sylvia, and the convolutions in his soul that it set in motion.

> MARTIN: I knelt there, eye level, and there was a . . . a what?! . . . an understanding so intense, so natural [. . .] an understanding so natural, so intense that I will never forget it, as intense as the night you and I finally came at the same time.

Note the emphasis on the word "understanding." When Martin concludes by saying, "I love you. And I love her. And there it is," the razor-tongued Stevie finally must abandon language. She is reduced to a series of howls born of "a combination of rage and hurt," as the playwright describes them in the text.

Here is where Albee's play brings forth one of its most provocative ideas, that love, in whatever form it takes, is an imperative that cannot be denied, an event so overpowering in its truth that social strictures, cultural context and even personal will are powerless to deny it. Pleading with Stevie for understanding in one breath, apologizing to her in the next, Martin cannot justify his experience, but he steadfastly refuses to deny its significance, its authenticity. Calling the encounter an "epiphany," he continues: "When it happens there's no retreating, no holding back." The suggestion that his love for Sylvia is fundamentally equivalent to his love for Stevie is repellent to her, impossible for her to understand.

STEVIE: I'm your type and so is she; so is the goat. So long as it's female, eh? So long as it's got a cunt it's all right with you!

MARTIN: A soul! Don't you know the difference?! Not a cunt, a soul!

STEVIE: You can't fuck a soul.

MARTIN: No; and it isn't about fucking.

Of course, if love is an abstraction without any inherent moral or immoral value, its manifestations in human experience—sex included—are terribly concrete, and inevitably freighted with a moral charge. And while the play questions the idea that Martin's experience of love, as with many others condemned by various cultures at various times, is inherently wrong, it also acknowledges that in the context of his life it has tragic consequences for which he is ultimately responsible. Martin remarked of his encounter with Sylvia that "it relates to nothing," but he discovers soon enough that it relates to everything.

IN DISCUSSING THE PLAY before and during its Broadway run Albee said he toyed with subtitling it *Notes Toward a Definition of Tragedy*. The phrasing is a bit grandiose—Albee's tongue was somewhat in cheek, one suspects—but the playwright ornaments the play with enough classical allusions to indicate his intention, however playfully, to trace the dramatic lineage of his story back to the Greeks. The word tragedy, as many critics pointed out, derives from the Greek for "goat song"; John Arnone's set for the Broadway production gently alluded to classical Greek architecture in its use of columns; and when Ross wonders, early in the first scene, at a strange rushing sound, Martin jokes grimly that it's probably "the Eumenides."

In his book *The Life of the Drama*, Eric Bentley wrote, "In tragedy man is an angel, but also a beast; and the two wrestle." The idea finds an echo in *The Goat*. Martin speaks of the soul; Stevie insists on sex. When she describes their predicament as being "about you being an animal," Martin calmly replies, "I thought I was [. . .] I thought we all were animals." He goes on to describe himself as "greatly troubled" and "deeply divided." It sometimes seems there are as many definitions of tragedy as there are examples of it, but certainly it can be agreed that tragedy concerns itself with humanity in the grip of extraordinary circumstances. By this broad definition, *The Goat* qualifies as tragic.

In fact, the extremity of Albee's proposition suggests that the playwright is seeking in *The Goat* to affirm that tragedy—let's define it for our purposes as the depiction of a person of moral stature being brought low by an encounter with the profound mystery of human experience—has a place in contemporary culture and can still move us with its primal power. With daily newspapers filled with stories that turn the most shocking circumstances into banalities, we can still be shaken, be awed, be filled with "pity and terror" by the dilemma of a human being confronting the extraordinary in life. Albee is trying to shock us into an awareness that yes, the deeper mysteries of life are still abroad in the world; more importantly, they still cry out for compassion—the nobler form of pity.

But compassion—and the forgiveness that might follow from it—is in noticeably short supply in *The Goat*. Instead it is revenge, a dominant theme in tragedy from the Greeks onward, that plays a powerful part in the action of the play. It turns out that the Eumenides are hardly necessary here; Stevie, a woman of notable resourcefulness and efficiency, dispenses with their help in exacting revenge on the man who has undone her. "You have brought me down to nothing!" she cries at the conclusion of the play's second scene, "and I will bring you down with me!" These are terrible words, and they are followed up by terrible action.

Before Albee ushers Martin's tragedy through to its agonizing conclusion, though, the play pauses—during the third and last scene—to expand on some of the troubling issues it has raised regarding the nature of love and sexuality. Dramatically, there may be something unsatisfactorily digressive about this scene, which involves Martin, Billy and Ross in a combative discussion about the infinite possibilities of sexuality, and the unthinking cruelty with which society condemns all behavior that the majority regards as aberrant. There is a blunt, consciousness-raising aspect to some of the dialogue. But it plays an important part in the emotional and intellectual development of the play.

With Stevie and her outraged hurt finally offstage, Martin at last gets a chance to unburden his heart, and the audience is allowed to take the full measure of the man without having to view him through the scornful eyes of his wife. It is here that the excellence of Bill Pullman's performance in the Broadway production shone forth most commandingly (unfortunate as it was that Pullman's performance wasn't granted even a Tony nomination, it was also somehow appropriate: in its subtlety and sensitivity, its moral integrity even, the performance was truly in a class by itself). What we see is a man who, through his painful and unusual experience, has come to an infinitely compassionate understanding of the complicated nature of love and sex.

His hard-won wisdom is called upon when Billy, distraught at the sudden destruction of his previously comfortable and comforting world, falls into his father's arms and, seeking the succor of paternal affection, begins kissing his father with an ardency that suddenly, for just the flash of an instant, seems to turn sexual. Martin gently disengages from him; Billy stammers an apology; Martin holds out his arms again, in perfect understanding.

But Ross, who has silently witnessed this tortured encounter between a loving father and son, reacts with accusatory disgust. Martin tries to explain:

> MARTIN: This boy is hurt! I've hurt him and he still loves me! He loves his father and if it . . . clicks over and becomes—what?—sexual for just a moment, so what? So fucking what?

Ross responds with knee-jerk repellence, sneering, "You're sicker than I thought." Martin goes on to speak about a man who realized, with horror, that he was inadvertently becoming aroused by the movement of a baby—his own—being dandled on his lap. Ross comes back with another sneer: "Is there anything you people don't get off on?"

The answer, of course, is no. Finally losing his grasp of grammatical niceties, Martin explodes:

> MARTIN: Is there anything anyone doesn't get off on, whether we admit it or not—whether we know it or not? Remember Saint Sebastian with all the arrows shot into him? He probably came! God knows the faithful did!

It is only by facing up to the endlessly complicated varieties of sexuality that the dangerous and destructive possibilities in sex—as in all kinds of human behavior—can be averted. The impulse to deny, to dismiss with laughter, to hush up the unpleasant truth, is what allows the destructive aspects of sexuality to run rampant. (Interestingly, *The Goat* opened just a few months before the Catholic Church would be rocked by the scandals involving its policy of covering up for abusive priests.)

MARTIN FINALLY COMES TO ADMIT that his behavior was "sick" and "compulsive," but nevertheless believes that with the sympathetic understanding of the "best friend" to whom he turned in his befuddlement and shame, he could have conquered his impulses, recognized that his "epiphany" was ultimately a destructive one. But Ross met his appeal with unthinking judgment, ridicule, disgust (as, ultimately, did Stevie) and the cynical advice to cut it out lest he be caught. Thus was destroyed any chance Martin might have had to redeem his life. "I could have worked it out," Martin says. "And now nothing can ever be put back together! Ever!"

The irrevocable truth of those words is made clear when Stevie re-enters, covered in blood and dragging behind her Sylvia's corpse. Hate, revenge and incomprehension have had their way; love, compassion and understanding are vanquished. Martin keens in anguish over the death of his beloved, but it is his own fate that is most heartrending. Just before Stevie's arrival, he turned away from Ross and asked, "Does nobody understand what happened? [. . .] Why can't anyone understand this, that I am alone . . . all . . . alone!" The tragic note is struck; in recognition of his fate, Martin Gray raises the specter of Oedipus, self-blinded and suffering, disappearing into the wilderness, exiled forever from the warmth of human companionship and the possibility of compassion.

2001–2002 Best Play

HOMEBODY/KABUL

By Tony Kushner

○ ○ ○ ○ ○

Essay by Jennifer de Poyen

KHWAJA (*Translating*): We must suffer under the Taliban so that the U.S. might settle a twenty-year-old score with Iran.

MAHALA (*Not waiting for Khwaja to finish*): You love the Taliban so much, bring them to New York! Well, don't worry, they're coming to New York! Americans!

PRISCILLA: I'm English.

MAHALA: English, America, no difference, one big and one small, same country, America say, Britain do, women die, dark-skin babies die, land mine, Stinger *projectile*, British American so what? So what you say?!

BEFORE SEPTEMBER 11, 2001, Afghanistan was a country whose politics and history were of little interest to most Americans, the ancient city of Kabul a hard-to-place locale on the far shores of exoticism. When word got out in 1999 that Tony Kushner had written a new play called *Homebody/Kabul*, theaters across the country lined up to produce it not expressly to bring stories of Talibs, mullahs and mujahideen to American stages, but because audiences had been waiting almost a decade for a worthy successor to the playwright's epoch-defining *Angels in America*.

Then history intervened. Two planes struck the twin towers of the World Trade Center; another pierced the Pentagon; still another, apparently headed for Washington, crashed into a field in Pennsylvania. Everybody—suddenly, painfully—recognized Afghanistan as home to the ur-terrorist Osama bin Laden, his Al Qaeda network and the brutally repressive Taliban regime. And everyone wanted to hear from Kushner who, having known what we did not, might help us interpret what we now only feared.

So we all brought September 11 to the New York Theatre Workshop when *Homebody/Kabul* made its debut at the end of 2001. Even before the official opening, a little more than two months after the terrorist attacks, observers were calling the play "eerily" and "chillingly" prescient. (So often was the phrase repeated that the playwright has suggested he might adopt

Day tripper: Linda Emond in Tony Kushner's Homebody/Kabul. *Photo: Joan Marcus*

the drag name Eara Lee Prescient.) But in an afterword to the published edition of the play (Theatre Communications Group), Kushner rejects the assertion that he knew the unknowable, and insists that he did not tweak his work, which is set in 1998–99, to accommodate and comment on the terrorist attacks. "[T]he information required to foresee, long before 9/11, at least the broad outline of serious trouble ahead," he writes, "was so abundant and easy of access that even a playwright could avail himself of it."

If *Homebody/Kabul* was not a dramatic work that foretold the horror of the terrorist attacks on New York and Washington, then what did we find at the East Village theater? A play fired by moral indignation about living conditions under the Taliban and the West's complicity in the rise of fundamentalism in that politically, economically and culturally devastated country. Or two plays, really, as the criticism went. Act I, set in a London drawing room, is a delirious, wide-ranging, poetic monologue spoken by an unassuming, slightly frumpy woman known only as the Homebody, who ultimately decamps for Afghanistan. Acts II and III are set in rubble-strewn, Taliban-oppressed Kabul at the time of the 1998 US bombing of terrorist camps in Khost, Afghanistan. (The bombing raids, history may recall, started a few days after President Bill Clinton, faced with impeachment, was forced to acknowledge his affair with a White House intern.)

The second and third acts are of a piece: a sprawling, ambitious account of the Homebody's family on a subsequent quest to find her—dead or alive. Many viewers complained that the play fizzles after Act I, and that the rest is intermittently brilliant, but also long-winded, unfulfilled and schematic. (The published version and subsequent productions of the play bring the first scene from Act II into Act I, among other changes, but for now, I will direct my remarks at the structure of and response to the play's premiere in New York.) Even to this sympathetic viewer, it seemed as if Kushner, like Coleridge, had begun work on his play in a surge of dream- and drug-saturated inspiration and then completed it slowly, laboriously and unsatisfyingly in the cold light of day.

The monologue, inspired in style and substance by Nancy Hatch Dupree's eloquent and piquant guidebook, *An Historical Guide to Kabul*, was written first—though likely not, given Kushner's avowed aversion to drugs, in an altered state. Kushner composed the monologue for a friend, the British actress Kika Markham, who performed it as a one-act play in London; only later did it serve as a springboard for the larger work. The monologue is an outpouring—rhythmic, astute, funny and sad—of the playwright's copious research and reflections on Afghanistan. It is also a closely observed, moving portrait of a woman's search for identity. The rest of the play, according to Kushner, was harder to discover and harder to write. It is, on the page and the stage, less accomplished than the monologue.

As the title suggests (both in form and content), the play's structure is dialectical, positing two different worldviews. And each segment is written in a distinct style. The Homebody's monologue, which incorporates historical information, is largely a product of the character's imagination. Composed in heightened, intellectualized prose, it is both breathtaking and absurd. The rest of the play, which recites the too-close-for-comfort facts of Afghanistan circa 1998, is written in sober, no-nonsense language. Act I provides the backdrop for the later acts, which then give context to the Homebody's emotional drama. Each segment depends upon the other. Although Kushner's brief epilogue is a tantalizing synthesis of the preceding action, the play's ultimate interpretation is left to the viewer.

AT THE NEW YORK PREMIERE, the first act, performed by the astonishing Linda Emond, was unadulterated pleasure, a virtuosic dance between playwright and actor. It was a duet in another sense as well, pairing the Homebody's readings from an outdated guidebook of Kabul (liberally borrowing from Dupree's lucid, sardonic text) with the character's multivalent reflections on her life and the world at large.

During the first night critics' performance, the audience offered rapt attention as Emond, perched on a hard-back chair in an English sitting room, animated Kushner's imaginative portrait of a self-effacing woman of middle age. Cradling an old book in her hands like a precious gift, she detailed her unhappy marriage and troubled daughter; her readings on Kabul and her theories about the march of history; her visit to a London shop to purchase hats for a party and an imagined voyage to Afghanistan with the toasted-almond-scented shopkeeper.

Audiences who recall the lonely mind-traveler Harper from *Angels in America* will recognize the Homebody as an archetype of Kushner's imagination. Yet, such is the range and specificity of his writing that we quickly come to feel we know the Homebody personally. As she removes from her shopping bag a series of beautiful Afghan hats, we mourn her rotten marriage, bemoan her bad self-esteem, sympathize with her "inexcusable and vague" love for the world, and revel in the linguistic and intellectual flights that so annoy her husband—whom she calls "the near-mute purveyor of reproachful lids-lowered glances."

Knowledgeable as she is, the Homebody is not *knowing*; the story she thinks she's telling—about the hats, Afghan history, her fantasized journey to Kabul—is the least of her tale. In recounting her pursuit of the hats, she

Revoicing woman: Dylan Baker and Rita Wolf in Tony Kushner's Homebody/Kabul. *Photo: Joan Marcus*

ruminates on our craving for objects "made by people who believe, as I do not, as *we* do not, in magic." The Homebody, who expounds (and digresses) on everything, goes on to discuss the uses of magic, the nature of being and the modernist corruption of traditional culture—all without drawing breath.

She reads passages from the outdated guidebook, whose vestigial, irrelevant information she finds "irresistible, ghostly, dreamy, the knowing what *was* known before the more that has since become known overwhelms." She tells of the bloody and bitterly divisive history of Afghanistan, complete with tales of "obstreperous worshippers of Zoroaster" and "the Greco-Bractian Confusion"—intriguing phrases that Kushner took directly from Dupree's guidebook. And she ruminates on our tendency to "romp about, grieving, wondering," but mostly remaining "suspended in the Rhetorical Colloidal Forever that agglutinates between Might and Do."

> HOMEBODY: What has this century taught the civilized if not contempt for those who merely contemplate; the lockup and the lethal injection for those who Do.

The monologue ends with a loving description of Kabul by the 17th century Persian poet Sa'ib-I-Tabrizi, and it brought many in the audience to tears. We had all seen the images of a desperately poor, war-ravaged and environmentally decimated Afghanistan. Here, though, was a poet's testament to Kabuli gardens so lush that "[e]ven Paradise is jealous of their greenery." How could we not, in a sense, become the Homebody, able to "love love love love the world," and at the same time despair at its horrors?

This is Kushner at his best, rhapsodically weaving together an outrageous surfeit of ideas in perceptive, and often dead funny, language. Almost every line suggests a fresh theme, a new direction. There's an evolving dialectic in play—between skepticism and faith, male and female, private lives and official histories, psychological dynamics and political fiats, stasis and action, might and do. But the most insistent themes are our need (and inability) to communicate with each other; the voicelessness of (and violence against) women; the search for home and the insistent pull of Otherness; and the persistence of grief, of sorrow—and also of hope.

These themes, which arise again in Acts II and III in a different guise, are expressed with astonishing empathy and insight through the Homebody, who is portrayed as both compellingly individual and an archetype of Western consciousness. Married to a man of ultra-rational impulses, she is the embodiment of a cultural belief in the primacy of individuals—whose actions and experiences can be explained in psychodynamic terms, rather than through an analysis of socioeconomic and political forces. Shaped by the myth of radical individualism, the Homebody is unable to see the social conditions that also shape her—and so she blames herself for everything.

The Homebody's appetite for self-effacement seems to impel an ill-advised trip to Afghanistan, which ends in her mysterious disappearance and—if the gruesome official report is to be believed—death by beating and dismemberment. In the New York version, Act II opened with the lengthy post-mortem description of her injuries and death, creating a jarring transition from her cozy home to danger-filled Kabul. In the published edition, the same speech—delivered by the Kabuli Dr. Qari Shah (Joseph Kamal) to the Homebody's family and others—forms the end of Act I.

ONCE IN KABUL, we are again in a cloistered chamber, this time a barren hotel room from which the grieving husband, Milton (Dylan Baker), and daughter, Priscilla (Kelly Hutchinson), intend to conduct a search for the Homebody's remains. At first we don't see Priscilla; she is veiled behind a bed sheet while the men discuss her mother's fate. But once the mullah and doctor leave, their horrific descriptions of the Homebody's mutilated body hanging in the air, she tears down the sheet and begins to question whether her mother is really dead. Not satisfied with the official report, she runs out into the streets armed only with the guidebook and a burqa. Her father, Milton, overcome by hopeless grief, lounges in the hotel room with Quango (Bill Camp), a louche, lonely decadent who is more grateful for the company than helpful in determining what has happened to the missing woman.

Most of the rest of the action centers on Priscilla's determined search and Milton's equally determined cloistering in his barracks-style hotel room. Here the play bogs down, as these two underwritten, stupid-Westerner characters—not strongly embodied by Hutchinson and Baker—are asked to carry the plot. Camp's Quango, who has the most ridiculous name and pathetic fate, provides exquisite and much-needed comic relief. Most interesting are the Afghan characters—principally, Priscilla's Tajik guide, Khwaja (the excellent Yusef Bulos), who persuades her to convey his Esperanto poems (or are they anti-Taliban intelligence documents?) and the desperate librarian Mahala (Rita Wolf, in a ferocious performance) out of the country.

In New York, it fell to director Declan Donnellan to tease out the connections between Kushner's uneven scenes, and to guide the actors in giving voice to sometimes underwritten roles. He wasn't always successful; the segments' shared themes were less than clear. Moreover, Hutchinson couldn't carry the weight of her central role, and Baker struggled to put flesh on the barebones Milton.

And yet nearly a year later, I still recall Hutchinson's fierce, sneakered Priscilla wandering amid black-clad fundamentalist aggressors and Baker's Milton, slugging booze from a bottle while Camp's Quango—who seems straight out of a Graham Greene novel—cooks drugs on the floor beside him. Once again we have a dialectical opposition, as Priscilla, a modern-day Antigone, thrusts herself into a hostile world of men to demand the return of her mother's body for proper burial. Milton, meanwhile, tacitly takes on the veiled passivity of Afghan women as envisioned by the Taliban.

IN *HOMEBODY/KABUL*, language is abundant, dazzlingly descriptive—and a tower of Babel. The Homebody, who loves antiquated words from her guidebook, speaks with such irritatingly "rhapsodic effulgence" (her words) that her husband, who is most at ease talking with and about computers, hardly speaks to her. In Kabul, one man speaks in Dari, another in Pashtun, still another in Arabic. Mahala, desperate to escape the murderously antifemale climate in her formerly civilized native land, mingles Pashtun, German, French and English as she pleads with Priscilla to help her emigrate. That these passages are sometimes translated for the questing Brits and the audience, and sometimes not, dramatizes Kushner's theme of the difficulty people have understanding each other.

Khwaja, who may be a spy, writes poetry—or whatever—in Esperanto. He loves that the universal language is "homeless, stateless, a global refugee patois." He tells Priscilla, who has hired him to help find her mother:

> KHWAJA: When I write in Esperanto I am transported to a time when such a thing as a dream of universal peace did not seem immediately crazy. And not even the news that yet another child has trod upon a land mine or has been caught in crossfire can disperse the dovelike murmuring sounds of it. I am moved to compose another lament, in Esperanto, another hymn to peace.

Why was Kushner so drawn to Afghanistan? In an interview with the *New York Times Magazine*, the playwright describes Afghanistan as a place that has held fascination for many people in many times. His imagination was also kindled by Dupree's guidebook. And for Kushner, as for many left-leaning intellectuals, Afghanistan is a leading example of the dangers of cynical US intervention: a country decimated by Cold War power struggles and rapacious, post-Cold War opportunism that has sapped the region's resources and lent power to fundamentalists.

> MAHALA: America buys this, bombs, from Communist Chinese to sell in secret to Taliban through Pakistan. Afghanistan kill the Soviet Union for you, we win the "Cold War" for you, for us is not so cold, huh?

I suspect, too, that the stark horror of the Taliban's treatment of women allowed Kushner to draw into sharp relief his more universal concern for women's lives and the corrosive power of misogyny. Despite her dazzling prolixity, the Homebody cannot make herself heard. Priscilla seems to emulate her mother by imitating her mind-bending double-speak, but she remains invisible to her father, who anesthetizes himself with drink and drugs in their hotel room while she runs around Kabul in a burqa. Mahala, begging Priscilla to help her escape, may speak a handful of languages, but like all of the women of Afghanistan she has been silenced by the Taliban.

FOR ALL OF HIS POLITICAL PASSION, Kushner doesn't present these themes in straightforward, unambiguous terms. His female characters, while more interesting and complex than their male counterparts, are not entirely sympathetic. Once we see the Homebody through the eyes of her husband and daughter, she becomes more complete, more human and therefore flawed like the rest of us. Although we empathize with Priscilla, she is often unlikable—emotionally volatile, culturally insensitive and disagreeably self-involved. And Mahala may have lied and allowed a man to die in her desperate attempt to get out of Afghanistan. Ultimately, though, the women are the protagonists; the men are ineffectual bit players (Milton, Quango) and pernicious forces (Dr. Qari Shah, the mullah Aftar Ali Durranni).

These women, Kushner suggests, are all in desperate search of a home—not some sentimentalized Arcadia, but an existence grounded in recognition of, and respect for, their right to be who they are. The Homebody seldom leaves her house, yet feels so rudderless, so comfortless, so alien in her body, that she abruptly takes flight for Kabul. Mahala, who understands perfectly the conditions of her existence, seeks salvation as a refugee in England. And Priscilla's search for her mother—dead or alive—is ultimately a search for herself, her own place in the world. Even Quango expresses this quest for a sense of belonging, albeit in a perverse manner. As he tells Milton Ceiling, he came to Afghanistan "to do good,'" and was hooked like a fish to a lure on heroin. "[W]hy else," he says as he offers Milton a bowl of opium, "would I be here?"

Longing and loss are the twin pillars of the play's emotional landscape; anger, grief, confusion and shame color almost every scene as the various characters struggle to come to terms with what they've lost, and what they hope to find. A drunken Milton, bereft at the loss of his wife and the gulf between him and his daughter, dismisses both of them as revenge-seeking bloodsuckers. Zai Garshi, an actor forbidden by the Taliban to practice his trade, collapses into tears as he listens to a contraband compact disc of Frank Sinatra singing "Come Fly With Me."

> ZAI GARSHI: AAAAH, MY KABUL, MY BEAUTIFUL BEAUTIFUL KABUL, WHERE HAVE THEY TAKEN YOU, AAAAAH, AAAAH, MY LONGING FOR YOU IS KILLING ME!

Ultimately, for Kushner, there is suffering, but there is also hope. This is not to be confused with mere sentimentality, which is the choice, as Quango suggests in Act III, of wayward believers like the Talibs. In his 2002 commencement address at Vassar College, the playwright argues that "hope isn't a choice, it's a moral obligation, a human obligation, an obligation to the cells in your body. [. . .] Real, vivid, powerful, thunderclap hope, like the soul, is at home in darkness, is divided; but lose your hope and you lose your soul." Hope is being alive to the moral choices available to, and required of, human beings.

At the end of *Homebody/Kabul*, back in the Ceilings' sitting room, Mahala has taken the place of the Homebody. Dressed like a Londoner, legs crossed with ankles showing, she is sitting in the Homebody's chair, living in her home. By definition a nonbeing in the misogynistic, Taliban-controlled Afghanistan, Mahala has nonetheless begun to read the Koran again; she is, of her own volition, "becoming Muslim again."

This is a fascinating, and ambiguous development. Is she Kushner's vision of a recreated Western consciousness, a person who is politically engaged, historically informed, liberated but aware of the precious gift of freedom? And what of Priscilla, who returns to her childhood home to confront Mahala about her political activity in Afghanistan, and inform her father, from whom she is estranged, that she has found a job, is getting by? She has roused herself from her self-hating stupor, but she remains tormented by her mother's uncertain fate, her own uncertain future; she has resolved only to resume living, and nothing more. When Priscilla suggests that the appeal of the Taliban, for Afghans, is certainty, and that "uncertainty kills," Mahala has a hard-won, but also hopeful, reply.

> MAHALA: As does certainty.
> They're like the communists, the Taliban. One idea for the whole world. The Dewey Decimal System is the only such system.
>
> PRISCILLA: It provides no remedy.
>
> MAHALA: Only it provides knowing, and nothing more.
> (*Little pause*)

I am gardening now! To a Kabuli woman, how shall I express what
these English gardens mean?
Your mother is a strange lady; to neglect a garden. A garden shows
us what may await us in Paradise.

PRISCILLA: She read instead.

MAHALA: I have examined her library. Such strange books.
I spend many hours. The rains are so abundant.
In the garden outside, I have planted all my dead.

2001–2002 Best Play

METAMORPHOSES

By Mary Zimmerman

○ ○ ○ ○ ○

Essay by Christopher Rawson

PHAETON'S THERAPIST: It has been said that the myth is a public dream, dreams are private myths. Unfortunately we give our mythic side scant attention these days. [. . .] So it remains important and salutary to speak not only of the rational and easily understood, but also of enigmatic things: the irrational and ambiguous. To speak both privately and publicly.

PRIMAL YET SOPHISTICATED, Mary Zimmerman's *Metamorphoses* is accessible and a lot of fun, but its blend of private dream and public myth touches the heart. Although Phaeton's Therapist is rather a fool (you can hear it in her pedantic tone), in the ironic, story-drenched world of Ovid—as selected and re-imagined by Zimmerman—even fools can speak wisdom.

But before language it speaks with shimmering images: a large rectangular pool, blond wooden decking, a painterly swath of sky, a small crystal chandelier and a tall dark door. The first four are water, earth, air and fire—the basic elements of ancient physics and also the scenic essence of this engagingly theatrical, teasingly thoughtful and warmly entertaining play.

After a short invocation of inspiration, both Ovid's big 12,000-line poem and Zimmerman's small 90-minute play begin, like Genesis and other creation stories, with the four elements in chaos, hopelessly confused. After God (or "the natural order," as Ovid wisely waffles) separates land from sea and turns on the celestial lights, scene designer Daniel Ostling's enigmatic door opens to admit a new chaos—humankind. More specifically, Zimmerman's Zeus, pausing in postgenerative satisfaction over the traditional cigarette, looks out on the freshly arranged world, with "each order of creature settling into itself," and says, "A paradise it would seem, except one thing was lacking: words."

Words? That's not what Ovid says, but how could he object? For him, as for Zimmerman, words are essential, the medium of story, which is their

Gods' blessings: Members of the company in Mary Zimmerman's Metamorphoses. *Photo: Joan Marcus*

shared element. Humankind isn't needed until there's a story to tell. So the creators—God, Nature, Ovid, Zimmerman—invoke man, and the stories commence. The considerable charm and visual dream of Zimmerman's suggestive staging would be nothing without its storytelling base.

Of course, she draws from a deep well. There is no richer compendium in the western literary heritage than the *Metamorphoses*, written by Ovid (43 BCE–17 CE) at the height of his career and ranking with such great anthologies as the Old Testament, Homer, *Mahabarata*, *Decameron* and *Arabian Nights*. Zimmerman previously dramatized the *Arabian Nights* and Homer's *Odyssey*. "Their longevity is the proof of their immediacy," she has said, recognizing that Ovid's stories were already ancient when he wove the voluptuous quilt of his *Metamorphoses*. "I'm not intimidated by these big old stories," she says. "I'm just one of the participants in a thousand-year chain."

Indeed, take away *Metamorphoses* and half of the subjects of old master paintings would disappear; Chaucer, Spenser and Milton would shrink; Shakespeare would be impoverished. Shakespeare's generation proved its narrative and descriptive skills—along with indulging its taste for genteel erotica—in a craze for imitative Ovidian narratives of sexual pursuit, of which Shakespeare's *Venus and Adonis* and Marlowe's *Hero and Leander* are only the best known.

THERE ARE HUNDREDS OF TALES intertwined in Ovid, though it's hard to count precisely, because they are embedded within each other—sometimes in sequence, sometimes in overlapping bunches—their profusion mimicking the world's abundance. Ovid's epic poem tumbles along with energy, wit, curiosity and invention from the mists of early myth to legends of historic times. Most stories tell of transformation, almost all generated by love or lust or whatever the sexual principle of ongoing creation may be. Sex fascinates Ovid as much as any recent novelist, and whenever we turn to the insights of Freud and Jung for explanation, we discover our modern wisdom anticipated in his text.

Of all of Ovid's riches, Zimmerman—a Chicago-based theater artist who teaches performance studies at Northwestern University and who won a 1998 MacArthur "genius grant"—picks eight major tales and related snippets. Most of the names are familiar (Midas, Orpheus and Eurydice, Cupid and Psyche, Phaeton) but the characters and situations are beyond familiar, they're archetypal.

As her base text, Zimmerman avoids the famous classic or modern translations in favor of David R. Slavitt's 1994 American version, which is rendered in light, flexible hexameter verse. It's beyond this essay to detail how she cut and transformed Slavitt's fine, brisk language as she developed the script for performance at Northwestern, in 1996, and later for Chicago's Lookingglass Theatre. But even a cursory check reveals that her changes are determined mainly by compression and colloquial clarity, and that she feels free to supply passages of her own to fill in gaps.

You cannot separate her text from its staging, because they grew together under the hand of the director-playwright. Designer Ostling's pool is as important as Slavitt's words. T.J. Gerckens's lights have transformative power, setting mood, varying that swath of sky. Mara Blumenfeld's flowing costumes can be funny as well as lovely, and Willy Schwarz's connective music (pan pipes, of course) and the atmospheric sound by Andre Pluess and Ben Sussman are inextricable. "God," Zimmerman has said about the play's design, "is in the details."

Zimmerman directs with lively variety, drawing on tragedy, romance, sex, wit, elegy and farce. She interrogates everything—you feel this in the language, which can be slangy, weighty, poignant or melodious. Its occasional self-mockery is especially Ovidian. But her chief interrogation (call it deconstruction if you must) comes in subjecting some stories to alternate takes, as with Phaeton—a whiny rich kid floating in a pool, caught between his psychoanalyst and sun-god father.

Nothing is more faithful to Ovid than this apparent modernizing, because that's what he does, too, delicately layering reverence, storytelling agility, tongue-in-cheek wit and sophisticated skepticism. He is the original Roman postmodernist, loving the old stories but always cocking a wry eye at their fabulous excess. Zimmerman's mode—as realized by her supple ensemble of 10 actors, all capable of sweetness and modest demeanor—is more ingenuous than Ovid. More even than he, Zimmerman believes in these stories as stories. Her crew of shifting narrators and hearers express various degrees of skepticism or belief, but the balance always comes down on the side of wide-eyed wonder.

Still, the wit of Zimmerman's anachronisms helps counter sentimentality. As in Ovid, her layering insures against seeming to take the tales at face value; but that deprecatory gesture frees us to enjoy and even believe. After all, we recognize these types: Vertumnus the besotted lover, Alcyon the grieving spouse, Midas the driven acquisitive. We know fathers and sons give each other a hard time, whether or not we believe Phaeton actually drove the chariot of the sun. In other words, we slip easily into metaphorical mode. It's a habit of centuries.

LONG BEFORE CRITICS ALLEGORIZED Christian scripture, they honed their interpretive tools on Ovid. *Metamorphoses* is such fun, it had to be saved from condemnation as pagan fiction by promoting its hidden seriousness. Hence the elaborate medieval tradition that culminated in the encyclopedic *Ovide Moralisé*, which turned Ovid from entertainer into philosopher, just as Juvenal was turned from lurid scold into principled prophet.

But any interpretation must be lightly worn, because, for all its art, *Metamorphoses* is most artful in the seeming artlessness of its narrative. The seamlessness of the staging carries all before it, starting with the elemental inevitability of that pool. Zimmerman confirms that the pool came first and she chose her stories to exploit its possibilities. It can turn idyllic or tempest-tossed, dramatic or contemplative, as the agile ensemble members wade and soak, pause and drift, cavort and splash.

The poolside decking is where the world of the play meets the audience, usually through the mediation of various narrators, regaling other ensemble members with their ancient tales. These hearers represent us, modeling our own eagerness and resistance. Meanwhile the other observers, the gods, appear farther off, on a platform above the sky (a modern approximation of the god walk of Greek theater). But the major human characters stumble about right in the water, fully engaged with their own obsessions.

Off Broadway, *Metamorphoses* debuted in the proscenium space at Second Stage Theatre, with its stadium-style seating. It might have seemed too delicate and intimate to survive the transfer to Broadway, but

Daddy's girl: Chris Kipiniak as Cinyras and Anjali Bhimani as Myrrha in Mary Zimmerman's Metamorphoses. *Photo: Joan Marcus*

transformation, after all, is its major theme. The thrust-stage mounting at Circle in the Square remained charming, except that those sitting on the sides missed how the sky looms behind the pool.

For all of Ovid's modernity and casual accessibility, he is still partly exotic. So Zimmerman mediates by making her narrative figures women—girlish, motherly or priestess-like—who threaten less and promise more than men. She specifies an ensemble of five men and five women, but it is the women, early on in the guise of villagers doing laundry by the pool, who both spin the stories and attend with eager ears. "Let me glimpse the secret and speak better than I know how," the first teller says—and that "speak" is a conscious softening of the usual grand epic formula, "I sing." No one is grand, here, not even the authorial tale-tellers.

Zimmerman's second speaker, the scientist who describes creation, is also a woman. Then the first narrator returns to invoke the story of Midas (Raymond Fox). (Actors names, given with only one of the many roles each plays, are from the original Broadway cast.) In Ovid, we don't meet Midas until the 11th book, but Zimmerman's Ovid is distilled, an epic journey shrunk into telling snapshots. And the contemporary note is struck right away.

> MIDAS: It wasn't always this way with me—the boats, the houses by the sea, the summer cottages and the winter palaces, the exotic furnishings, the soft clothes, the food and—
> (*To his daughter, bouncing a red ball.*)
> Honey, can you stop that now? Be still now. Daddy's talking.
> (*Back to audience.*)
> Excuse me. The outrageous food and two-hundred-year-old wine. No, it wasn't always like this. I came up from poor and worked hard all my life.

IT'S ALL VERY FAMILIAR, very contemporary. Then the magic happens: Silenus enters, a being from another dimension, a familiar happy drunk but with panache that takes us from Midas's prosaic world back toward myth. Bacchus enters next and the dialogue turns contemporary again.

> MIDAS: [G]rant me that everything I touch, everything I put my hand to, will turn to solid gold.
>
> (*Long pause.*)
>
> BACCHUS: That's a really, really bad idea.

But because Midas has aided Bacchus's follower, Silenus, the god grants his wish. For all of its supernatural trappings, *Metamorphoses* is about humans. The gods can only watch, as do we, in bemusement that quickly converts to alarm when Midas's comic obsession turns tragic, his daughter transformed to rigid gold in his arms. Zimmerman frequently turns on a dime like this, whipping us from comic to tragic or past to present. Nonetheless, she keeps it light. These gods (and this storyteller) are more benign than in, say, Greek tragedy. Midas has a moment of despair, then sets off to find redemption. Disaster comes quickly, but there's always another story to savor. Music soothes the transitions. We are flattered into god-like detachment as the fables unfurl.

THE SECOND STORY is of Alcyon (Louise Lamson) and Ceyx, the perfect couple brought to despair by separation and death. They live "in a monotony of happiness"—one of Zimmerman's typically pungent phrases—but in spite of her pleas, Alcyon must wave goodbye as Ceyx sails off on a journey, "while the ribbon of black water widened between the ship and shore." In

Daddy dearest: Erik Lochtefeld as Apollo (standing) and Doug Hara as Phaeton in Mary Zimmerman's Metamorphoses. *Photo: Joan Marcus*

Ovid, we learn a great deal about Ceyx, but here, he is just a questing husband whose journey occasions lively stagecraft: Poseidon and henchmen whip the pool into a froth, wetting a few in the front row, as Ceyx's ship meets its fate.

Back home, Alcyon waits. Aphrodite (Felicity Jones) cues a comic interlude, sending Iris off to ask the grotesque Sleep (who lives at "the heart of an almost painted stillness") for some magic to show Alcyon her husband's death. A ghost Ceyx is conjured, and the comic bathos of Sleep gives way to the cool pathos of husband and wife meeting in a dream, preparing us for their ultimate transformation into wave-skimming seabirds.

A similar meld of comic and bitter distinguishes the third story, Erysichthon and Ceres. In revenge for his cutting down her sacred tree, the goddess turns him over to gaunt Hunger. Made insatiable, Erysichthon (Chris Kipiniak) sells his mother into slavery, but in another comic interlude, Poseidon saves her. ("This is the kind of sweet, unbidden praise the gods adore," moralizes a narrator.) It's very funny until the final horrid image when Erysichthon prepares to eat himself, a chilling emblem of ecological depradation.

The tale of Orpheus (Erik Lochtefeld) and Eurydice (Mariann Mayberry) is more elaborate. "Ovid, AD 8" says the narrator, introducing Ovid's version of the sweet singer's fruitless journey into the underworld to reclaim his dead wife. "Is this a story of love and how it always goes away?" the narrator asks. "Is this a story of how time can move only in one direction?" And finally, "Is this a story of an artist, and the loss that comes from sudden self-consciousness or impatience?" Actually, these possibilities barely touch on the meanings of this famous story of human mutability; the power of Orpheus's music isn't even mentioned. But Zimmerman does insert another view, Rainer Maria Rilke's 1908 meditation on the same story, which focuses instead on Eurydice:

> EURYDICE: She was deep within herself. [. . .] Being dead filled her
> beyond fulfillment. [. . .] She was already loosened like long hair,
> poured out like fallen rain, shared like a limitless supply.

The play's rhythms shift as this elegiac voice cuts across the lightly jokey Ovidian tone. By departing from Ovid, Zimmerman reaffirms her allegiance to what is most Ovidian—constant change. So it is natural that the next story, the sixth, compensates for Orpheus's tragedy by being jollier, though including its own dark antithesis. This is the tale of Pomona and Vertumnus, introduced by an interlude in which silent Narcissus enters, sees his reflection in the pool and freezes in self-admiration, requiring that he be carried out while a potted narcissus comes in to take his place. Call it a passing joke for the cognoscenti.

Vertumnus (Kyle Hall), god of springtime, is an inventive suitor for frolicsome Pomona, wood nymph of his dreams. He tries many disguises to catch her attention, finally falling back on that essential Ovidian technique—storytelling—regaling her with the darkly cautionary tale of

Myrrha (Anjali Bhimani) and her incestuous desire for her father, Cinyras. The inevitable nursemaid (Lisa Tejero) helps Myrrha feed her lust, then the aghast father tries to drown her (more splashing). We return to Pomona, who, we discover, isn't much impressed by Vertumnus's tale. But freed of his disguise, he appeals to her after all. In this case, storytelling isn't as effective as sexual attraction.

Next comes the story of Phaeton (Doug Hara), the comic heart of Zimmerman's play. The preppy lad floats idly, his therapist in poolside attendance. "Go on," she says. And Phaeton does, at self-pitying length. His telling is so banal ("I never knew him [Apollo, his sun-god father], and he wasn't really around. I mean, not *around* around") that the therapist's interjected musings almost seem plausible before gradually curdling into self-important jargon.

> THERAPIST: Where better might we find a more precise illustration of the dangers of premature initiation than in this ancient tale of alternating parental indulgence and neglect? [. . .]
> When he matures beyond the customary Eden of the mother breast, the child seeks to individuate beyond its unfolding gate. [. . .]
> The conventional exordium of the initiate from latent to realized potential is inevitably accompanied by a radical realignment of his emotional relationship with the imago of parental authority.

This turgid theorizing contrasts deliciously with Phaeton, who gabbles on like a teenager, and with Apollo, standing aside in effulgent glory, singing snatches of Mozart intermingled with descriptions of Phaeton's fatal adventure.

But this is the same therapist who also waxes wise on myth and dream. Her defense of "the irrational and ambiguous" provides a perfect segue to Zimmerman's penultimate tale, Eros and Psyche. The mimed story is accompanied by hushed, terse questions and answers between two poolside watchers. The naked Eros sleeps on a raft; Psyche brings in a small candelabra, disobeying his injunction not to look at him; Aphrodite condemns her to suffer; but eventually Zeus makes all well. The narrator allegorizes: "The soul wanders in the dark, until it finds love. And so, wherever our love goes, there we find our soul." That's too pat, of course; for once, Zimmerman's sweetness proves resistible.

PSYCHE HERSELF INTRODUCES THE FINAL STORY, "a coda, if you will," the sweet tale of Baucis and Philemon, the classical equivalent of the Good Samaritan. As the pool gradually fills with small floating candles, the unwitting elderly couple serve their guests a modest supper.

NARRATOR THREE: Philemon set out a plate of olives, green ones and black, and a saucer of cherry plums.

NARRATOR FOUR: Then there was cabbage and some roasted eggs. [. . .]

NARRATOR FIVE: For dessert there were nuts, figs, dates, and plums.

NARRATOR ONE: And a basket of ripe apples.

NARRATOR TWO: Remember how apples smell?

At that moment in performance, you hear the audience take a collective breath, remembering that smell. Under the Zimmerman/Ovidian spell, it has become a community. *Metamorphoses* stirs emotions but then calms them, sensitizing us but also lowering our emotional temperature. When the entire ensemble speaks for the transformed Baucis and Philemon, apotheosized into whispering leaves, it speaks also for us: "Let me not outlive my own capacity for love."

The true coda then follows: Midas reappears. Our pool has become the pool at the end of the earth where Bacchus told him he might be cured. He is. His daughter revives in a ceremony of love reaffirmed. In an interview, Zimmerman quoted her mentor, Frank Galati, "You need to lose the trail of bread crumbs in order for enchantment to occur—to be a little lost." As was Midas, so are we all lost from time to time. Like us, *Metamorphoses* meanders, seeming to lose its way, but it never does. Following it, neither do we.

2001–2002 Best Play

[SIC]

By Melissa James Gibson

○ ○ ○ ○ ○

Essay by Bruce Weber

> THEO: I didn't like either one of them at first but then one of them
> sublet their way into my building and then the other got the other an
> apartment and somehow we were all neighbors and when you share
> a landlord with people you have of course a Built-In Common Enemy
> and there's just about nothing more bond-inducing than Sharply
> Focussed Ill Will.

WHEN I FIRST WROTE about Melissa James Gibson's tangy talkfest, *[sic]*, I evidently misapprehended the playwright's intentions. Speeches like the one above—smirky, shrewd, a little pouty and a little defiant—are typical of all three of the play's principal characters, Theo and his two apartment house neighbors, Babette and Frank. And I interpreted this as the rhetoric of the young and ironic, contemporary 20-somethings, a generation that grew up skeptical of just about everything and particularly averse to sincerity.

That the three characters were all struggling with love, professional ambition and money also made me think they were new to adulthood, in the midst of experiencing the postcollege shock that afflicts many people when they move to the big city, discover no one was waiting for them and realize the world owes them nothing. The talented and funny trio of actors in Daniel Aukin's production at Soho Rep in the fall of 2001—Dominic Fumusa (Theo), Christina Kirk (Babette) and James Urbaniak (Frank)—all affected the kind of vivacity in their despair that only the young can muster. (The production felt defiantly celebratory from the beginning; Soho Rep is a mere few blocks from Ground Zero and *[sic]* was one of the first plays to open in TriBeCa after September 11.) In any case, the play, I thought, achieved something rare—a mature perspective on the experience of immaturity.

I still think that, actually, though it turns out—I learned this from the author's introduction to the script—that Theo, Babette and Frank are not, in the playwright's imagination, quite the fledgling adults they seemed to

Mighty neighborly: Dominic Fumusa, Christina Kirk and James Urbaniak in Melissa James Gibson's [sic]. *Photo: Paula Court*

me to be. They're in their mid-*thirties,* which makes one view their predicaments quite differently.

Specifically, their lack of personal achievements is not meant to be so ordinary or understandable; rather these are lives bordering on genuine failure. And this spins the characters away from the universal and sympathetic. They're not so easy to identify with; nor are they so precocious. Instead they come across as desperate and rather immature. And they are all self-aware enough to recognize this, to worry that they are pathetic. This alters the play's subject. In the author's mind, it is evidently about confronting a life of disappointment; in mine, at least when I first saw it, it was about impatience. In Gibson's purview *[sic]* is a dark comedy; in mine it's a rather light one.

Curiously, I'm not sure it matters. That is, the play works marvelously either way, if the characters are around 25 or a decade older. And that's because Gibson's primary gift is not for plot; there is none, really, in *[sic]*. Nor is it for character. There isn't much to differentiate, actually, among Theo, Babette and Frank aside from a few biographical details: Frank is gay. Babette owes everyone money. Theo married early but his wife left the house one day and never came back.

Rather, Gibson's main talent is for language. She has a great ear for the vocabulary and cadences of the educated wiseass class and the tone of voice that communicates hopefulness beneath a façade of disinterest. The dialogue is written mostly in the meandering breathlessness of quick-minded talkers excited by their stream-of-consciousness cleverness.

Gibson relishes the flexible grammar of talk, the nuances of emphasis and innuendo. Her script—the literal script—mostly disdains punctuation, capitalizes words in mid-sentence for whatever subtle properties that implies, organizes her lines frequently into free verse. She delights in subverting the traditional sentence with interruptions ("Could I borrow hi Babette your Cassette Tape Player?" Frank asks) or a general disdain of punctuation: "It's true we did Socialize without you last night"—this is Babette and Frank confessing to a lonely, paranoia-prone Theo (who has the hots for Babette)— "but only because we were meeting to plan an impromptu surprise party for you having nothing to do with your birthday and having everything to do with your being You Theo You"

On the page this sends the message that words are important, that they have all sorts of properties that can aid in or obscure communication and meaning. But this idea is manifest on the stage as well. When I saw the play performed, perhaps my foremost reaction was that Gibson was a rare playwright in showing such a high degree of respect for air time onstage; that is, she makes every line count.

In spite of overlapping dialogue and characters who are perpetually interrupting each other and finishing one another's sentences, there aren't any speeches that feel like place holders. Even the most expository passages are delivered with ancillary functions. The jokes are good because the lines are polished, and you get the clear idea that every one of them is the result of tinkering, experimenting with things like the number of syllables or the repetition of consonant sounds.

This becomes grand license for the performers to experiment, to interpret. The dialogue, with its interruptions, sentence shards and idea fragments, means, I think, to reproduce a kind of thinking out loud, and it suggests that there is a community of people who understand it and who understand they have a language of their own.

Indeed, more than their ages, the real distinguishing mark of Theo, Babette and Frank is that they are naturally verbal. It isn't that they have great vocabularies, exactly. It's more that they have a taste for talk, an instinct for verbal wit in a contemporary mode. They're all quick thinkers, but they aren't big thinkers, or even particularly good thinkers. They don't really think about much. Mostly, their ideas consist of the linguistic tropes with which they make their observations.

When Theo, an aspiring composer whose pinnacle of success has been a commission to write a theme for a thrill park ride (which he can't seem to finish), feels put upon by his friends, he defends his dignity with a self-aware grandiosity: "Are you saying the average pimply prepubescent doesn't deserve a real musical score for his amusement park ride experience?"

Frank, who aspires to be an auctioneer, seems to get an almost erotic thrill from the tongue-twisting assignments he gets from mail-order instruction tapes: "Sally sought some seeds to sow but sadly soon it snowed" or "Course your cousin couldn't kiss you cause you can't kiss kin"

And Babette, perhaps the most verbally deft of the three, and the character who seems most resigned to the reality that a gift for language and $1.50 will get her on the subway, shows her fundamental wisdom in a wonderfully shrewd social observation.

"If you can spell bourgeois, then you're bourgeois," she says. Like the playwright, Babette is a clever young woman, smitten with the nuances of language, right down to the individual letters and punctuation marks. Her joke about the word "bourgeois" is carried even further by Gibson; no one who sees the play in a theater will know this, but in the script, the word is spelled incorrectly. If you need another clue that [sic] is a play on words (get it?), there it is.

INDEED, BABETTE SEEMS a likely stand-in for Gibson in [sic]; she's the lone woman, the lone professional wordsmith. A frustrated scholar, Babette is ostensibly putting the finishing touches on an academic tome that considers the history of the world as a series of temper tantrums—as though life on earth proceeded from human big bangs.

You can see how an aspiring playwright, someone like Gibson, a New Yorker who was 36 when [sic] opened and was working as a teacher to support her playwriting, would, half with pride, half with self-mockery, turn herself into a fictional character this way. In any case, that would explain the keenness of her sense of how smart, poor, aspirants to conventional success live in New York City; she's a member of the tribe. And in its way, *[sic]* is as informative as an insider's sociological report.

City dwellers will recognize in the play the signature socialization pattern of single urban adults, the creation of communities almost at random, based on such unpredictable variables as where you can afford to live, how neighborly your neighbors turn out to be, who the friends of the friends of your friends are. As a result, most people who live in the city do so with a network of personally important acquaintances—a veterinarian, the woman at the dry cleaner, the nut case who lives next door—buzzing around like a haze of mosquitoes inside their heads.

These are the people who make up the lion's share of urban personal experience. And so the universe for each of us gets small, and sooner or later we begin to measure ourselves against our companions in the little world we know. This is why the city feels—to a lot of us who live here— like a gigantic and insoluble jigsaw puzzle, and the pieces are all of the interlocking universes that accompany these individual lives. It's impossible to untangle; people get lost in the city's thick vines all the time. (Yes, yes, it's a jungle out there.)

[Sic] illustrates this beautifully. Just outside the small circle of the three protagonists are the shared figures in their lives, influential shadows all.

One is the upstairs neighbor, an elderly woman named Mrs. Jorgenson who is something of an inspiration to them all with her open-mindedness, friendliness and curiosity. After her death halfway through the play, she becomes a kind of angelic presence overseeing the goings-on in the apartment house. (In Aukin's production at the Soho Rep, her spirit seemed to take up residence in a light bulb.) And all of this happens without her ever speaking or appearing onstage.

Two other key figures are the couple who are breaking up in a neighboring apartment. In Gibson's script, they are known as the "airshaft couple," because they are never seen; their cryptic dialogue simply wafts with the mysterious currents of the ventilation system into the apartments of Babette, Theo and Frank.

Aukin, however, had the idea to create a two-tiered stage, and to place the couple in three rooms beneath the tiny broom closets of the three protagonists. The juxtapositions—the sullen, monosyllabic conversation of the couple as they divide up their belongings versus the nonstop prolixity of the three single people; the misery of a bad marriage versus the misery of being alone—are pungent in any case, but Aukin's staging added layers of meaning.

For one thing, the faces of the downstairs couple are scarcely visible. The sightlines cut them off from the audience at the neck—an emotionally distancing effect. And second, placing them below the main characters sets them off against the angelic Mrs. Jorgenson. It may sound heavy-handed that the three main characters are poised between heaven and hell, but the suggestion is made deftly, and it works to deepen the play's subject, which is nothing less than the overly circumscribed way that many people lead their lives.

THE FINAL OUTSIDER IN THE PLAY is also never seen, but he's keenly important as the catalyst that brought the three principals together. He is only a presence on the telephone—we never hear him, either—but he is constantly on the mind of everyone else. This is Larry, a shop owner who was recently Frank's boyfriend, who has loaned Babette a lot of money and who is Theo's confidant. Among the secrets that Larry doesn't keep about Theo is that his wife has walked out on him. Another is that Theo is saving up his money to be frozen, a la Ted Williams. These crossed circumstances result in a hilarious sequence of explanatory speeches to the audience:

> BABETTE: Before I knew Frank Larry told me he was saving up / money to be frozen

> THEO: I'd heard from Larry that this girl / Babette this woman was an editor who specialized in incredibly / obscure subject matter which I understood to / mean that she was mostly out of work

> BABETTE: It took a month or two before I understood that it was some guy / Theo who was saving up to be Frozen not / some guy Frank

> FRANK: Larry said something about some guy / having lost his wife / literally

> THEO: Larry told me that he'd been seeing some guy named Frank for a while but that things were going Disastrously

> FRANK: I asked Larry what do you mean he lost his wife Did she die Did / he leave her somewhere Were they at a / Mall

> THEO: Larry's pretty unlucky in love but / This Guy Frank sounded particularly awful

> FRANK: Larry and I were doing Really Well at that point except / I wondered about his friends who to a one sounded like a bunch of Losers

Cheek by jowl: James Urbaniak and Dominic Fumusa and Christina Kirk in Melissa James Gibson's [SIC]. *Photo: Paula Court*

BABETTE: I was worried about Larry seeing a guy who sounded like such a / Loser I mean a Profound Loser Profoundly depressed / and in Profound Denial / Larry also told me that the guy who was saving up to be Frozen / also lost his wife / What do you mean Lost His Wife / At the Mall or something

THEO: I started to get this paranoid / feeling that Larry was telling everybody my / personal business

This passage, which occurs early on in the play, is a lovely capsule of Gibson's accomplishment in *[SIC]*. Before they knew each other, these three characters belonged together, and in this passage we see why. Each is lost but self-aware. So they use what they have—their blunt verbal dexterity—to stave off loneliness and desperation. They talk in order to cling to their self-esteem, to prove their worth to themselves, to compete in the tiny world they live in within the big world they aspire to.

And whether they are in their 20s and life's novices, or in their 30s and life's losers, anyone who enjoys theater, no matter what age, will feel acutely in their company. For the thing drawing them together—and us to watch them—is a shared relish of what, sadly, the world outside no longer values much: words.

2001–2002 Best Play

TOPDOG/UNDERDOG

By Suzan-Lori Parks

○ ○ ○ ○ ○

Essay by Margaret B. Wilkerson

LINCOLN: First thing you learn is what is. Next thing you learn is what aint. You don't know what is you don't know what aint, you don't know shit.

FROM THE FIRST ENCOUNTER, *Topdog/Underdog*—its title arranged as mirror images—warns that we are entering a world turned on end whose reflected images will challenge our perceptions. Playwright Suzan-Lori Parks is a wordsmith who knows how the language of a dominant culture can entrap and betray. So she plays with words and with history, recognizing that some of us live both inside and outside of those constructed realities. This 2002 Pulitzer Prize-winning Best Play probes the idea of America and challenges its audience to question what is real and what isn't about those constructions.

Parks, who has written more than 15 plays, won two Obies and a MacArthur "genius" award, displays her talents in thought-provoking ways that continue to unfold long after the play itself has ended. Tony Award-winning director George C. Wolfe, who first came to prominence as playwright of *The Colored Museum*, understands the edgy comedy of this play and mines its deeper resonances.

Topdog/Underdog made compelling theater in the 2001–02 season whether in its Off Broadway premiere at the Joseph Papp Public Theater's intimate Anspacher space or on the large proscenium stage of Broadway's Ambassador Theatre. Engaging and entertaining, it hurtled through a tale of desire, aspiration, disappointment and death carried by rapid-fire dialogue shrouded in illusion. Lincoln, the older brother, was ably performed in both productions by Jeffrey Wright—an incredibly versatile actor. Don Cheadle, the talented film and stage actor, played Booth, the younger brother, at the Public Theater. When *Topdog/Underdog* transferred to Broadway, Mos Def, a film and television actor best known as a hip-hop artist, took over the latter role, attracting a younger audience to the theater.

137

Cash stash: Don Cheadle and Jeffrey Wright in the Off Broadway production of Suzan-Lori Parks's Topdog/Underdog. *Photo: Michal Daniel*

Ostensibly, the play is about the relationship and competition between two brothers, Lincoln and Booth, who survive on the legitimate income of one and the clever thievery of the other. Both could make a handsome living playing three-card monte, the shell game of cards in which the spectator bets that his or her eyes are as fast as the hands of the dealer and that a quick glance will identify the winning card. Lincoln is a master of the scam who, in his heyday, won $1000 a day with the able assistance of his team of homies. He quit the cards, however, after the shooting death of his partner and vowed never to return to them.

From the beginning, the brothers' names suggest an inevitability reinforced by the fact that "Link"—as Booth refers to him—plays the historical figure of President Lincoln in an arcade where customers pay to play the role of Booth and assassinate him. Brother plays are well established in modern US drama, beginning with Eugene O'Neill's *Beyond the Horizon* (which won the second Pulitzer Prize) and including Sam Shepard's *True West*. Far from O'Neill's treatment of brothers competing for the love of a woman, Parks's play uses the absence of women as a comment on the brothers' social, emotional and sexual condition. *Topdog/Underdog* is closer to the Shepard drama, which suggests a critique of the West with its suburban setting literally and figuratively on the edge of civilization (complete with coyotes howling in the background).

Topdog/Underdog invites us to think beyond the personal drama onstage and to contemplate familial and national ties bound together through blood and beyond. Parks has written about Lincoln and Booth before in *The America Play*—produced in 1994 at Yale Repertory Theatre—introducing them as characters in a theme park. In *Topdog/Underdog*, she follows Lincoln home to discover the life behind the pretense, a performance that, in fact, works for this young man.

SET IN THE "HERE AND NOW," the play takes place in Booth's shabby one-room apartment with no bath or running water. There is a single bed— more like a cot—which is Booth's; Lincoln sleeps on a reclining chair. Except for a small wooden chair, there is no other furniture in the room. The show opens with a blast of loud "urban" music and Booth awkwardly playing three-card monte, desperately trying to coordinate hand, eye and banter. He speaks the dealer role better than he handles the cards and, of course, in his imaginary scenario beats the sucker soundly, winning the loot.

Lincoln has quietly entered dressed in his frayed Abraham Lincoln costume, his face covered with chalk-white make-up, watching his brother from behind. Sensing something behind him, Booth, in one fluid move, whirls, pulls a gun from his pants and, displaying a quickness and grace that he can't seem to muster for the shell game, points it at Lincoln. In the show's first minutes, the audience has shifted from innocent laughter to the edge of horrifying violence. The pace is set and we are on an emotional roller coaster right up to the end of the play.

The five scenes that follow deepen and complicate the relationship of the two brothers by juxtaposing moments of true comedy with instances of startling clarity. For example, the second scene opens with Booth bringing in the bounty from his most recent "shopping spree": two suits complete with accessories, that he has worn out of the store (under his regular clothes). As spectators, we laugh at his antics and are amazed at his audacity and ability. But when the men eagerly try on their new clothes, Lincoln reverses an American truism.

> LINCOLN: They say the clothes make the man. All day long I wear that getup. But that don't make me who I am. [. . .] Worn suit, not even worn by the fool that Im supposed to be playing, but making fools out of all those folks who come crowding in for they chance to

> play at something great. Fake beard. Top hat. Don't make me into no
> Lincoln. I was Lincoln on my own before any of that.

As much as the audience wants to believe Link, when he puts on the new suit that Booth has stolen for him, we the audience do "see" him differently—in our eyes the clothes do make the man. He looks like a new person—and one with real potential. It is a startling, self-reflective moment that simultaneously challenges our view of the men and questions the sincerity of our values.

Sex and death pervade the atmosphere and the dialogue of this play. In the third scene both subjects are explicitly connected. Booth, a dreamer

Fantasy hustler: Mos Def in the Broadway production of Suzan-Lori Parks's Topdog/Underdog. *Photo: Michal Daniel*

who invents elaborate stories about his sexual prowess and his relationship with Grace, his former girlfriend, brags about his "evening to remember" and their sexual intimacies. Link constantly goads and taunts him, knowing that his brother is fantasizing. The brothers quickly turn to trading barbs with Link ridiculing Booth's weapon as a pop gun and Booth equating the blanks used by shooters in the arcade with the sexual impotence that cost Link his marriage.

The gun becomes the symbol of sexual potency as well as a weapon of death. Then, in a macabre moment of humor, Booth gets Lincoln to practice some new and interesting "dying" moves so that he can save his job. (His boss is threatening to replace him with a wax dummy.) He "shoots" Lincoln several times—with his finger—and Lincoln tries various ways of dying, all of which are comical. As audience, we laugh a bit uneasily at his antics even as Booth tries to get him to take the exercise more seriously. Finally, Booth shouts at him.

> BOOTH: Hold yr head or something, where I shotcha. Good. And look at me! I am the assassin! *I am Booth!!* Come on man this is life and death! Go all out!

But Lincoln's performance is too realistic for Booth (and for the audience), and they stop the enactment. Too much realism scares the customers, says Lincoln. While his antics under Booth's tutelage are comical, they clearly foreshadow what is to come. We laugh, but with anxiety and fearful anticipation.

By intermission, we know that Link is likely to be replaced by a wax dummy and that he fears losing his "sit-down job with benefits," even though he hates his boss's demeaning treatment and his insistence that Link pay for any damage to his costume. Link prefers legitimate employment with its relative certainties, but he is drawn to the cards like an alcoholic to drink. The last image as the audience takes a break is Link playing three-card monte alone, hustling himself.

FOLLOWING INTERMISSION, THE PLAY QUICKLY moves from the brothers' high expectations and dreams to disappointment and bitter reality. The lights go up on a transformed room with Booth waiting for Grace to arrive for a dinner complete with china, crystal and silver that he has stolen. Lincoln, who has in fact lost his job to a wax dummy from a mail order catalogue, enters.

> BOOTH: Hey, Graces on her way. You gotta go.
>
> LINCOLN: I'll stay until she gets here. I'll act nice. I wont embarrass you.
>
> BOOTH: You gotta go.
>
> LINCOLN: What time she coming?
>
> BOOTH: Shes late. She could be here any second.
>
> LINCOLN: I'll meet her. I met her years ago. I'll meet her again.
>
> (*Rest*)
>
> How late is she?
>
> BOOTH: She was supposed to be here at 8.
>
> LINCOLN: Its after 2 a.m. Shes — shes late.

It's a moment of laughter for the audience, but a pause of recognition passes over the brothers as their disappointments sink in, and they begin to recall the gritty and pathetic years of their childhood. Link remembers their parents who struggled against "something out there that they liked more than they liked us [. . .] against moving towards that more liked something."

> LINCOLN: We moved out of that nasty apartment into a house. A whole house. It wernt perfect but it was a house and theyd bought it and they brought us there and everything we owned figuring we could be a family in that house and them things, them two separate things each of them was struggling against would just leave them be. Them things would see thuh house and be impressed and just leave them be.

But it got to be too much, "the whole family mortgage bills going to work thing," says Booth, and the parents abandoned their teenage sons, leaving each an inheritance of $500 in cash. The boys, then, have been on their own since they were 16 and 11. They pause as they remember that all they have had for the past 15 or more years is each other. At this vulnerable moment, teaming up to exploit three-card monte sounds good and Link starts teaching Booth the game from the bottom up, explaining the full setup and follow through.

But Booth's ineptitude becomes apparent once more, and Link laughs at his lack of skill, reminding him of an $800 mistake he made years ago when they worked together briefly. Booth's frustration with the game and his anger at Grace spill over, and he leaves abruptly to go and find her, claiming that he is his own man—and not like Lincoln. Link, left in the room alone, throws the cards faster and faster as the play moves swiftly and determinedly to its conclusion.

The final scene is full of sudden revelations and reversals. Lincoln enters drunk and high on success; he's returned to three-card monte and brandishes a roll of bills that he's won. Booth, who has overheard his bragging, announces that Grace has begged him to marry her and that Lincoln will have to move out of the apartment. Lincoln doesn't resist at all, but quickly begins to pack his clothes. Like a raging stream-of-consciousness, the conversation rushes from one experience to another with the logic of the subconscious in a jumble of thoughts and memories. Ever present is an undercurrent of recognition and sadness that they are about to break their lifelong bond. The torrent of words climaxes as the brothers challenge each other to a last game of three-card monte.

> BOOTH: I got yr shit and Ima go out there and be thuh man and you aint gonna be nothing.

Brotherly rap: Mos Def and Jeffrey Wright in Suzan-Lori Parks's Topdog/Underdog. *Photo: Michal Daniel*

LINCOLN: Set it up!

In a classic showdown, the brothers face each other in the ultimate test of their skill. Link is clearly the topdog at the game, but unexpectedly Booth picks the winning card, surprising his brother. Booth, buoyed by his success and anxious to make sure it is real, challenges Link to bet the wad of bills he's just won. Link agrees, but to his surprise, Booth decides to bet his $500 inheritance still wrapped in his mother's stocking. But before he puts the inheritance on the box, he reveals the story behind it: that it was money from his mother's "Thursday man" to clean up a mistake. Booth never mentions abortion, but the language clearly implies it. Whatever happened, she told Booth she was giving him a $500 inheritance. So when he bets that inheritance against Link's skill as a dealer, he bets any illusions he has about his mother and, by extension, about Grace.

Link throws the cards and Booth, thrown off by Link suddenly questioning whether they are actually brothers, picks the wrong card. Link scoops up the stocking and starts laughing at Booth—boasting that he still has the moves. Then, when he realizes that Booth has never untied the stocking to see the actual money, Link ridicules his naivete and proceeds to open it even though Booth begs him not to. But Link pursues, "teaching" his brother about life.

LINCOLN: She coulda been jiving you, bro. Jiving you that there really *was* money in this thing. [. . .] Its like thuh cards. [. . .] Cause its thuh first move that separates thuh Player from thuh Played. And thuh first move is to know that there aint no winning [. . .] the only time you pick right is when thuh man lets you. And when its thuh real deal, when its thuh real fucking deal, bro, and thuh moneys on the line, that's when thuh man wont want you picking right. He will want you picking wrong so he will make you pick wrong. Wrong wrong wrong.

Lincoln holds the knife high ready to cut the stocking—and the audience holds its breath. Booth is chuckling with him, but then in a sudden reversal, suddenly blurts out, almost non-chalantly, that he shot and killed Grace.

BOOTH: I popped her. [. . .] Who thuh fuck she think she is doing me like she done? Telling me I don't got nothing going on. I showed her what I got going on. Popped her good. Twice. Three times.

Lincoln, sensing the volatility of this moment, tries to give the stocking back. But Booth has gone over the edge. Bolstered by the gun's potency, he stops Link's laughter in his throat and shouts that he's the man, commanding Lincoln to open the stocking. But just as Lincoln brings the knife down, Booth grabs him from behind, Lincoln utters a quiet "Dont," and Booth shoots him. Booth continues to talk to the dead Lincoln telling him that he's going out on the street to make a name for himself as "3-card" and that he'll be famous like Link was. But when he bends down to take back the money he lost, he crumples, recognizing the enormity of his act. The lights go down on Booth holding Lincoln's body and sobbing over him.

TOPDOG/UNDERDOG HAS MANY LAYERS working simultaneously: historical, psychoanalytical, mythical. It constantly challenges us to question what we know and how we know it. As in three-card monte, we're never quite sure where the winning card—the truth—is, but we know it's there somewhere and that the dealer knows where it's located. Do you trust the con man or do you try to beat him at his game?

Lincoln and Booth are so named as a joke by their father. But it is a profound and prophetic joke that places this dysfunctional black family within a larger dysfunctional American family. Lincoln and Booth are not strangers but rather caught up in a history that they inherited. The historical Booth's assassination of Lincoln is tied up in a history of slavery that becomes a major cause of the Civil War. It is a family war that turned neighbor against neighbor, state against state, brother against brother.

The phony Honest Abe that Link portrays in the arcade resonates with the question of President Lincoln's intentions in freeing the slaves: Was it an act of morality, of compassion or a military tactic to break the back of the South? The historical Booth is now known to be an average actor who gained fame through his assassination of Lincoln. Linked forever in history, which is the topdog, which the underdog? And what of the shooters in the arcade? What sick fantasies and historical denial are implied by their actions? Our perceptions of family, both onstage and in the national sense, and their contentious interdependence are rocked in this play between what we think we know about history and what we want to believe about our place in it.

> LINCOLN: People are funny about they Lincoln shit. Its historical. People like they historical shit in a certain way. They like it to unfold the way they folded it up. Neatly like a book. Not raggedy and bloody and screaming.

This troubled black family becomes a metaphor for a nation and world struggling to find a unity that both acknowledges and crosses historical divides.

On a superficial level, *Topdog/Underdog* is simply a play about a maladjusted black family, complete with irresponsible parents and antisocial children. But there is a deeper, subtler resonance. As the play hurtles toward its foregone conclusion, Lincoln and Booth become almost mythic in dimension, which is partly suggested by angular, shadowy production lighting that casts an other-worldly glow. Lincoln's amazingly quick hands are magical and ritualistic. At one point, he stands in shadows observing Booth's efforts to locate the winning card, his words suggesting that he is trying to lead Booth to a fuller understanding of his life, of his choices.

The ever-present themes of sex and death, and Link's emotional distance from Booth raise the specter of a powerful deity, Gede—a loa (or powerful spirit) of Afro-Caribbean religions—who occasionally possesses those with a deep psychic connection to his archetypal energy. Fittingly, Gede is the god of sex and death who deals with the continuation of life in this world and rules the world of the dead. Known by his dress—shabby tails, top hat and clownish behavior—he is the court of last appeal when there is a life-threatening illness that needs healing or when there are difficult questions that need sound, reliable and honest answers. He can also help to enhance sexual potency or heal sexual repression. Like Link, Gede protects children. Known for facing the truth, he uses humor to expose it.

Gede is never mentioned in this play by name, but another deity is. In the first scene, Lincoln suggests that Booth name himself after Shango, the thunder god. Shango represents the courage to work through fear and to face personal transformation. Followers call on him for personal power and for justice. Drummers and dancers call on him for inspiration. Passionate procreation is also his specialty. Lincoln's choice of this name for his brother connotes a profound understanding of Booth's deepest desires and needs. Invoking the name of Shango might have helped Booth to become the graceful, fast-moving card dealer and lover that he hoped to be. Shango might also have helped him to accept the truth about his illusions—without killing the messenger.

The play's tragic ending is hard to take because we have come to care about these vibrant, intelligent, troubled young men. Although they are certainly responsible for their own choices, they have had to make them within a confusing, frustrating context in which even the "real" is topsy-turvy. Lincoln, for instance, describes seeing his shooters reflected upside down in a shiny box on the wall in front of him.

Topdog/Underdog draws heavily on vaudevillian and minstrel traditions of the 19th and 20th centuries with its one-liners, comic routines and costume changes. From the first scene, Lincoln's appearance in partial white face signals both minstrelsy and its decline. Booth's characterization as a booster-hustler fits this genre as well. Minstrelsy masked or hid natural skin color and true identities—but not talent—so its evocation in the play reinforces Parks's playfulness as she toys with illusion and the audience's perceptions of history.

Although Parks says that this play is about family and healing, it is difficult to see the latter quality within the narrative itself. That healing comes from the power of transformation that begins with self-knowledge, both as individuals and as a nation. We must question our assumptions, behaviors, ideals and ideas—in other words, the challenges that a Gede presents to us. We must seriously ask ourselves what we know.

As in the shell game, we must ask who's on top, who's on the bottom? Who's in control? What's "real?" Who's winning? Who's losing? And, as important, why? Do we want to play this game? The Lincoln/Gede figure challenges us to see beyond the illusion. The healing, Parks suggests, lies in asking all those difficult and painful questions, stripping away illusions and challenging our most sacrosanct assumptions.

2001–2002 Special Citation

ELAINE STRITCH AT LIBERTY

By Elaine Stritch and John Lahr

○ ○ ○ ○ ○

Essay by Michael Sommers

ELAINE: You know what helped? You know what really helped me? Booze. It's scary up here. OK? OK, so you're scared. You drink. You're not scared. What is the problem? So-o-o . . . I never set foot on a stage without a drink! Or any place else, come to think of it.

WATCHING ELAINE STRITCH PERFORM—so fierce, so fearless—you'd never think that anything has ever frightened this peerless artist. But for decades, anxiety shadowed her hike across the peaks and occasional swamps of a remarkable 55-year Broadway career.

To paraphrase one of the 20 or so songs that the lady delivered in her stunning solo show *Elaine Stritch at Liberty*: good times and bum times, she's seen them all, and my dear, she's still here.

Mixing funny, bittersweet autobiography with music, Stritch first wowed the crowds at the Joseph Papp Public Theater in the fall. Then she moved her act uptown to the Neil Simon Theatre in February, where she triumphantly filled the 1,300-seat house with her sardonic personality.

Out she strides, this self-described "existential problem in tights" now in her late 70s; a slim, edgy, long-legged, lemon-blonde dame in a white silk shirt. Drawling a dry "Yeah, well . . . ," Stritch introduces her world with a sharp rendition of "There's No Business Like Show Business" spiked with barbs upon its realities.

Stritch knows the Broadway bottom-line better than most. A convent-reared gal bitten by the acting bug in a sunken living room in suburban Detroit, Stritch made her way to Manhattan where she briefly and disastrously dated Marlon Brando in drama school.

"No, nobody has ever been as young as I was that night," she recalls. "Not ever."

Shortly after graduation, Stritch made her Broadway debut in a 1947 musical revue. She scored a hit warbling "Civilization," a comic ditty about a native who dismisses inventions like padded bras and the nuclear bomb,

147

Winning ways: Elaine Stritch in Elaine Stritch at Liberty. *Photo: Michal Daniel*

chanting "Bongo, bongo, bongo, I don't wanna leave the Congo." Recreating the number with its minstrelsic original choreography, Stritch shows how she made such an impact at the starting gate of her career.

And the great backstage stories roll out. Like the one about Stritch understudying Ethel Merman in *Call Me Madam* while singing "Zip" in *Pal Joey* and madly commuting between performances of the former show in New York and the latter during its New Haven tryout—in a blizzard. "And you wonder why I drank?" she asks.

Belying her reputation, Stritch maintains that she wasn't all that sophisticated.

> ELAINE: 1970. *Company!* "The Ladies Who Lunch"—"A matinee, a Pinter play, perhaps a piece of Mahler's." I thought Mahler's was . . . Mahler's Pastry Shop, 47th Street and Broadway. The ladies had lunch, went to a matinee, saw a Pinter play, and went around the corner for a cup of tea and a piece of Mahler's. When I brought this up to Mr. Sondheim, he said, "Elaine, I have to go to the bathroom."

During her semi-chronological saga, Stritch evokes the greats who have crossed her path. A suave, mandarin-faced Noël Coward, complete with clipped accents and admonishing finger-wag, is Stritch's most masterly impression. Her steely George Abbott, bleary Judy Garland, wincing Stephen Sondheim and hard-as-nails Merman are other sharp cameos.

Maintaining a wry, no-nonsense persona, Stritch does not neglect to recreate herself at various stages. Softness colors Stritch's voice as she recalls her early years and huskiness creeps in whenever she speaks of romance.

Of course, Stritch's career hasn't been all showstoppers tailored just for her talents by Sondheim and Coward, although she brilliantly performs signature numbers such as "The Ladies Who Lunch" and "Why Do the Wrong People Travel?"

There's the time that Stritch willfully blew her audition for the *Golden Girls* television pilot. And the debacle of a ghastly summer stock staging of *The Women* in Ohio where the other stars forced her out.

Stritch serves up the inside dish on rueful love affairs, including the mistake of dumping her 1950s fiancé Ben Gazzara in favor of Rock Hudson, with whom she was filming *A Farewell to Arms* in Italy.

> ELAINE: He liked me. He did. He took me out—a lot. I was in heaven. I mean, seeing Rock Hudson come down a winding staircase at the Grand Hotel in Rome in a tux to take me to dinner. I mean, come on. It was just too much. *Arrivederci*, Ben Gazzara! And we all know what a bum decision that turned out to be.
>
> Oh, God! Maybe, if I'd had a Diet Coke or two somewhere along the way, I might have made some grown up decisions about a lot of things. But I didn't.

She freely admits that booze fueled most of her life.

> But I had rules. I was very disciplined about all of this. Especially up here. Anyplace else, who cares, who's counting? But up here two drinks: one before the curtain, the other at intermission, a little back up. That was it. Well, three maybe if I had the eleven o'clock number.

Ultimately, a near-fatal diabetic seizure a few years ago scared Stritch off the firewater for good. She found true love, too, in a 10-year marriage to British actor John Bay that ended with his early death. And finally, she made some kind of peace with herself.

For those who work around Times Square, Stritch's reputation as a tempestuous soul is legend. It was said, for instance, that she rejected two sets of dressing room furniture before getting what she liked at the Neil Simon Theatre. To insiders, her show proved to be an extremely artful portrait of a difficult artist who, despite her supreme gifts, has driven many of her associates nuts.

But so what? In a two hours-plus soliloquy, Stritch tells her version, illuminating crucial moments with musical numbers rendered in her distinctive scotch-sour tones.

Stritch does not waste time explaining her artistry. She just does it. To applause that stops the show cold several times, Stritch demonstrates the supernatural power possessed by stars of her pre-amplification vintage. In performance, Stritch summons energy from the very basement beneath her feet and sends that personal voltage crackling to the farthest row.

An unforgettable visit with one helluva lady—and the best-reviewed event of the New York theater season—*Elaine Stritch at Liberty* was not devised by her lonesome. The distinguished theater critic for the *New Yorker*, John Lahr, helped to craft the piece. Actually, the program billing reads "Constructed by John Lahr" followed immediately underneath with the line "Reconstructed by Elaine Stritch."

Still there: Elaine Stritch in Elaine Stritch at Liberty.
Photo: Michal Daniel

No less than George C. Wolfe—one of the best directors around—channeled and paced the star's energies with great savvy. Subtly brushing the event with theatricality, Wolfe staged Stritch within a bare environment of backstage bricks and pipes designed by Riccardo Hernández and shaded her with glowing lighting by Jules Fisher and Peggy Eisenhauer. Jonathan Tunick's witty arrangements for nine fine musicians enhanced the songs. And what a great batch of songs: "All in Fun," "But Not for Me," "If Love Were All" and "There Never Was a Baby Like My Baby" to name a few.

Lovingly showcased by such collaborators, an honest-to-God legend proved (as if she needed to) that there's never been anyone quite like

Elaine Stritch on Broadway—and quite possibly on Earth. For her indefatigable efforts, Stritch received a long-overdue Tony Award, a New York Drama Critics Circle Award and many other deserved accolades.

Most important, night after night at the end of every performance, thrilled viewers complied with the command from that *Company* song in Stritch's repertoire: "Everybody rise."

Everybody did, cheering.

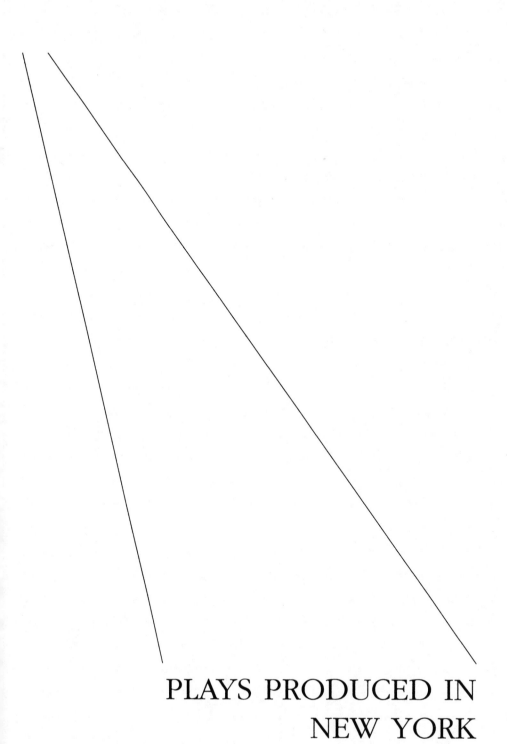

PLAYS PRODUCED IN
NEW YORK

PLAYS PRODUCED ON BROADWAY

○ ○ ○ ○ ○

FIGURES IN PARENTHESES following a play's title give the number of performances. These figures do not include previews or extra nonprofit performances. In the case of a transfer, the Off Broadway run is noted but not added to the figure in parentheses.

Plays marked with an asterisk (*) were still in a projected run June 1, 2002. Their number of performances is figured through May 31, 2002.

In a listing of a show's numbers—dances, sketches, musical scenes, etc.—the titles of songs are identified wherever possible by their appearance in quotation marks (").

HOLDOVERS FROM PREVIOUS SEASONS

BROADWAY SHOWS THAT WERE RUNNING on June 1, 2001 are listed below. More detailed information about them appears in previous *Best Plays* volumes of the years in which they opened. Important cast changes since opening night are recorded in the Cast Replacements section of this volume.

*Les Misérables** (6,281). Musical based on the novel by Victor Hugo; book by Alain Boublil and Claude-Michel Schönberg; lyrics by Herbert Kretzmer; original French text by Alain Boublil and Jean-Marc Natel; additional material by James Fenton. Opened March 12, 1987.

*The Phantom of the Opera** (5,984). Musical adapted from the novel by Gaston Leroux; book by Richard Stilgoe and Andrew Lloyd Webber; music by Andrew Lloyd Webber; lyrics by Charles Hart; additional lyrics by Richard Stilgoe. Opened January 26, 1988.

*Beauty and the Beast** (3,306). Musical with book by Linda Woolverton; music by Alan Menken; lyrics by Howard Ashman and Tim Rice. Opened April 18, 1994.

*Rent** (2,540). Transfer from Off Broadway of the musical with book, music and lyrics by Jonathan Larson. Opened Off Off Broadway January 26, 1996 and Off Broadway February 13, 1996 where it played 56 performances through March 31, 1996; transferred to Broadway April 29, 1996.

*Chicago** (2,311). Revival of the musical based on the play by Maurine Dallas Watkins; book by Fred Ebb and Bob Fosse; music by John Kander; lyrics by Fred Ebb; original production directed and choreographed by Bob Fosse. Opened November 14, 1996.

*The Lion King** (1,932). Musical adapted from the screenplay by Irene Mecchi, Jonathan Roberts and Linda Woolverton; book by Roger Allers and Irene Mecchi; music by Elton John; lyrics by Tim Rice; additional music and lyrics by Lebo M, Mark Mancina, Jay Rifkin, Julie Taymor and Hans Zimmer. Opened November 13, 1997.

*Cabaret** (1,707). Revival of the musical based on the play by John van Druten and stories by Christopher Isherwood; book by Joe Masteroff; music by John Kander; lyrics by Fred Ebb. Opened March 19, 1998.

Fosse (1,092). Dance revue with choreography by Bob Fosse; conceived by Richard Maltby Jr., Chet Walker and Ann Reinking; artistic advisor, Gwen Verdon. Opened January 14, 1999. (Closed August 25, 2001)

Annie Get Your Gun (1,046). Revival of the musical with book by Herbert and Dorothy Fields as revised by Peter Stone; music and lyrics by Irving Berlin. Opened March 4, 1999. (Closed September 1, 2001)

Kiss Me, Kate (881). Revival of the musical with book by Sam and Bella Spewack, music and lyrics by Cole Porter. Opened November 18, 1999. (Closed December 30, 2001)

Riverdance on Broadway (605). Return engagement of the dance and music revue with music and lyrics by Bill Whelan. Opened March 16, 2000. (Closed August 26, 2001)

*Aida** (910). Musical suggested by the Giuseppe Verdi opera; book by Linda Woolverton, Robert Falls and David Henry Hwang; music by Elton John; lyrics by Tim Rice. Opened March 23, 2000.

*Lincoln Center Theater** production of *Contact** (903). Dance play by Susan Stroman and John Weidman; written by John Weidman. Opened March 30, 2000.

Meredith Willson's The Music Man (698). Revival of the musical with book, music and lyrics by Meredith Willson; story by Meredith Willson and Franklin Lacey. Opened April 27, 2000. (Closed December 30, 2001)

The Dinner Party (366). By Neil Simon. Opened October 19, 2000. (Closed September 1, 2001)

*Proof** (252). Transfer from Off Broadway of a play by David Auburn. Opened October 24, 2000.

*The Full Monty** (664). Musical with book by Terrence McNally; music and lyrics by David Yazbek. Opened October 26, 2000.

*The Tale of the Allergist's Wife** (654). Transfer from Off Broadway of a play by Charles Busch. Opened November 2, 2000.

The Rocky Horror Show (356). Book, music and lyrics by Richard O'Brien. Opened November 15, 2000. (Closed September 23, 2001) Re-opened October 30, 2001. (Closed January 6, 2002)

Jane Eyre (209). Musical with book by John Caird; music and lyrics by Paul Gordon; additional lyrics by John Caird. Based on the novel by Charlotte Brontë. Opened December 10, 2000. (Closed June 10, 2001)

A Class Act (105). Musical with book by Linda Kline and Lonny Price; music and lyrics by Edward Kleban. Opened March 11, 2001. (Closed June 10, 2001)

Lincoln Center Theater production of **The Invention of Love** (108). By Tom Stoppard. Opened March 29, 2001. (Closed June 30, 2001)

Stones in His Pockets (201). By Marie Jones. Opened April 1, 2001. (Closed September 23, 2001)

Roundabout Theatre Company production of **Follies** (116) Revival of the musical with book by James Goodman; music and lyrics by Stephen Sondheim. Opened April 5, 2001. (Closed July 14, 2001)

One Flew Over the Cuckoo's Nest (120). Revival of the play by Dale Wasserman; based on the novel by Ken Kesey. Opened April 8, 2001. (Closed July 29, 2001)

Bells Are Ringing (69). Revival of the musical with book and lyrics by Betty Comden and Adolph Green; music by Jule Styne. Opened April 12, 2001. (Closed June 10, 2001)

Blast! (176). Marching band musical entertainment with music by various authors. Opened April 17, 2001. (Closed September 23, 2001)

*The Producers (461). Musical with book by Mel Brooks and Thomas Meehan; music and lyrics by Mel Brooks. Opened April 19, 2001.

George Gershwin Alone (96). One-man performance piece on the life of George Gershwin. Book by Hershey Felder; music and lyrics by George Gershwin and Ira Gershwin. Opened April 30, 2001. (Closed July 22, 2001)

King Hedley II (72). By August Wilson. Opened May 1, 2001. (Closed July 1, 2001)

*42nd Street (447). Revival of the musical based on the novel by Bradford Ropes and the 1933 movie; book by Michael Stewart and Mark Bramble; music by Harry Warren; lyrics by Al Dubin. Opened May 2, 2001.

PLAYS PRODUCED JUNE 1, 2001–MAY 31, 2002

A Thousand Clowns (84). Revival of the play by Herb Gardner. Produced by Jeffrey Richards, Raymond J. Greenwald, Norma Langworthy, James Fuld Jr., Irving Welzer, Kardana/Swinsky Productions, in association with Theater Previews at Duke, at the Longacre Theatre. Opened July 11, 2001. (Closed September 23, 2001)

Murray Burns	Tom Selleck	Sandra Markowitz	Barbara Garrick
Nick Burns	Nicolas King	Arnold Burns	Robert LuPone
Albert Amundson	Bradford Cover	Leo Herman	Mark Blum

Understudies: Ms. Garrick—Lauren Bone; Messrs. Cover, LuPone, Blum—Eric Siegel; Mr. Selleck—Russ Anderson; Mr. King—Harley Adams.

Directed by John Rando; scenery, Allen Moyer; costumes, Martin Pakledinaz; lighting, Brian MacDevitt; sound, Peter Fitzgerald; casting, Liz Woodman; production stage manager, Jane Grey; press, Jeffrey Richards Associates.

Time: April 1962. Place: Murray's apartment and Arnold's office in Manhattan. Presented in three parts.

A writer for a children's television program struggles to maintain his free-spirited lifestyle while rearing his precocious nephew. A 1961–62 *Best Plays* choice, the original Broadway production opened at the Eugene O'Neill Theatre (4/5/1962; 428 performances).

Roundabout Theatre Company production of **Major Barbara** (74). Revival of the play by George Bernard Shaw. Todd Haimes artistic director, Ellen Richard managing director, Julia C. Levy executive director of external affairs, at American Airlines Theatre. Opened July 12, 2001. (Closed September 16, 2001)

Lady Britomart Undershaft .... Dana Ivey	Snobby Price .... James Gale
Stephen Undershaft .... Zak Orth	Jenny Hill .... Kelly Hutchinson
Morrison .... Denis Holmes	Peter Shirley .... Richard Russell Ramos
Barbara Undershaft .... Cherry Jones	Bill Walker .... David Lansbury
Sarah Undershaft .... Henny Russell	Mrs. Baines .... Beth Dixon
Charles Lomax .... Rick Holmes	Bilton .... Brennan Brown
Adolphus Cusins .... Denis O'Hare	Factory Workers .... Eli Gonda,
Andrew Undershaft .... David Warner	Jeremy Furhman, Jeremy Lewit,
Rummy Mitchens .... Jenny Sterlin	Brian Shoaf

Directed by Daniel Sullivan; scenery, John Lee Beatty; costumes, Jane Greenwood; lighting, Brian MacDevitt; original music, Dan Moses Schreier; associate artistic director, Scott Ellis; production stage manager, Roy Harris; press, Boneau/Bryan-Brown, Adrian Bryan-Brown.

Time: 1906. Place: England. Presented in two parts.

Revival of George Bernard Shaw's play about the relative nature of morality and notions of the common good. First produced in New York at the Playhouse (12/9/1915).

If You Ever Leave Me . . . I'm Going With You! (53). By Renée Taylor and Joe Bologna. Produced by Martin Melzer, Stephen Melzer, Leonard Soloway and Steven Levy at the Cort Theatre. Opened August 6, 2001. (Closed September 23, 2001)

Performed by Renée Taylor and Joe Bologna.

Directed by Ms. Taylor and Mr. Bologna; scenery, Kenneth Foy; costumes, Alvin Colt; lighting, Ken Billington; sound, Jon Gottlieb; associate producers, Larry Scott, Bob Bender, Donald R. DeCiccio, Sandra L. DeCiccio; production stage manager, Fredric H. Orner; press, Pete Sanders Group, Pete Sanders, Erin Dunn.

Presented without intermission.

Ninety-minute comedy covering the pleasures and pitfalls of a show-business marriage.

*Urinetown (290). Transfer from Off Broadway of the musical with book and lyrics by Greg Kotis; music and lyrics by Mark Hollmann. Produced by the Araca Group and Dodger Theatricals, in association with TheaterDreams, Inc., and Lauren Mitchell, at the Henry Miller. Opened September 20, 2001.

Officer Lockstock .... Jeff McCarthy	Little Becky Two Shoes;
Little Sally .... Spencer Kayden	Mrs. Millennium .... Jennifer Cody
Penelope Pennywise .... Nancy Opel	Robbie the Stockfish;
Bobby Strong .... Hunter Foster	Business Man #1 .... Victor W. Hawks
Hope Cladwell .... Jennifer Laura Thompson	Billy Boy Bill;
Mr. McQueen .... David Beach	Business Man #2 .... Lawrence Street
Senator Fipp .... John Deyle	Old Woman;
Old Man Strong;	Josephine Strong .... Kay Walbye
Hot Blades Harry .... Ken Jennings	Officer Barrel .... Daniel Marcus
Tiny Tom;	Caldwell B. Cladwell .... John Cullum
Dr. Billeaux .... Rick Crom	
Soupy Sue;	
Cladwell's Secretary .... Rachel Coloff	

Orchestra: Ed Goldschneider conductor, piano; Paul Garment clarinet, bass clarinet, alto sax, soprano sax; Ben Herrington tenor trombone, euphonium; Tim McLafferty drums, percussion; Dick Sarpola bass.

Understudies: Mr. McCarthy—Don Richard, Peter Reardon; Ms. Kayden—Jennifer Cody, Erin Hill; Mr. Foster—Peter Reardon, Victor W. Hawks; Ms. Thompson—Erin Hill, Rachel Coloff; Mr. Cullum—Don Richard, Daniel Marcus; Ms. Opel—Kay Walbye, Rachel Coloff; Mr. Beach—Rick Crom, Lawrence Street; Mr. Marcus—Victor W. Hawks, Don Richard; Mr. Deyle—Rick Crom, Don Richard; Ms. Walbye—Rachel Coloff, Erin Hill; Mr. Crom—Peter Reardon, Lawrence Street; Ms. Cody—Erin Hill; Mr. Hawks—Lawrence Street, Peter Reardon; Ms. Coloff—Erin Hill; Mr. Street— Peter Reardon.

Directed by John Rando; choreography, John Carrafa; scenery, Scott Pask; costumes, Jonathan Bixby, Gregory Gale; lighting, Brian MacDevitt; sound, Jeff Curtis, Lew Meade; fight direction, Rick Sordelet; orchestrations, Bruce Coughlin; musical direction, Edward Strauss; music coordination, John Miller; casting, Jay Binder, Cindi Rush, Laura Stanczyk; production stage manager, Julia P. Jones; stage manager, Matthew Lacey; press, Boneau/Bryan-Brown, Adrian Bryan-Brown, Jim Byk, Jackie Green, Martine Sainvil.

Presented in two parts.

A town with a water shortage finds itself paying dearly for one of the most basic human needs in this eco-satire and spoof of Broadway musicals. A 2000–01 *Best Plays* choice and winner of three 2002 Tony Awards (for book, score and director). Originally presented as part of the 1999 New York International Fringe Festival before a 2001 Off Broadway engagement (see Plays Produced Off Broadway section).

ACT I

Scene 1: Amenity #9, the poorest, filthiest urinal in town
"Urinetown" .... Lockstock and Company
"It's a Privilege to Pee" .... Penny and the Poor
"It's a Privilege to Pee" (Reprise) .... Lockstock and the Poor
Scene 2: The good offices of Urine Good Company
"Mr. Cladwell" .... Cladwell, McQueen, Hope and UGC Staff
Scene 3: .... A street corner
"Cop Song" .... Lockstock, Barrel and the Cops
"Follow Your Heart" .... Hope and Bobby
Scene 4: Amenity #9, the poorest, filthiest urinal in town
"Look at the Sky" .... Bobby and the Poor
Scene 5: The good offices of Urine Good Company
"Don't Be the Bunny" .... Cladwell and UGC Staff
Scene 6: Amenity #9, the poorest, filthiest urinal in town
Act I Finale .... Ensemble

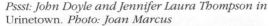

Pssst: John Doyle and Jennifer Laura Thompson in Urinetown. *Photo: Joan Marcus*

ACT II

Scene 1: A secret hideout
"What Is Urinetown?" .... Ensemble
Scene 2: A secret hideout
"Snuff That Girl" .... Hot Blades Harry, Little Becky Two Shoes
and the Rebel Poor
"Run Freedom Run" .... Bobby and the Poor
"Follow Your Heart" (Reprise) .... Hope
Scene 3: The good offices of Urine Good Company
"Why Did I Listen to That Man?" .... Penny, Fipp, Lockstock, Barrel, Hope
Scene 4: A secret hideout
"Tell Her I Love Her" .... Little Sally and Bobby
Scene 5: Various
"We're Not Sorry" .... The Rich and the Poor
"We're Not Sorry" (Reprise) .... Cladwell and Penny
"I See a River" .... Hope and the Ensemble

Hedda Gabler (117). Adapted by Jon Robin Baitz from the play by Henrik Ibsen; based on a literal translation by Anne-Charlotte Hanes Harvey. Produced by Randall L. Wreghitt, Harriet Newman Leve, Gallin Productions, USA Ostar Theatricals and Bob Boyett, in association with Bay Street Theatre, Huntington Theatre Company and the Williamstown Theatre Festival, at the Ambassador Theatre. Opened October 4, 2001. (Closed January 13, 2002)

Berta .... Maria Cellario	Mrs. Elvsted .... Jennifer Van Dyck
Miss Julia Tesman .... Angela Thornton	Judge Brack .... Harris Yulin
George Tesman .... Michael Emerson	Servant .... Claire Lautier
Hedda Tesman .... Kate Burton	Eilert Lovborg .... David Lansbury

Understudies: Ms. Burton—Tina Benko; Messrs. Emerson, Lansbury and Ms. Lautier—Patrick Boll; Ms. Thornton—Maria Cellario; Mr. Yulin—Martin LaPlatney; Mses. Van Dyck, Cellario—Claire Lautier.

Directed by Nicholas Martin; scenery, Alexander Dodge; costumes, Michael Krass; lighting, Kevin Adams; sound, Jerry M. Yager; original music, Peter Golub; casting, Amy Christopher; production stage manager, Kelley Kirkpatrick; press, Boneau/Bryan-Brown, Adrian Bryan-Brown, Jim Byk, Jackie Green, Ellen Levene, Aaron Meier.

Time: Late 1800s. Place: The Tesman home, Christiania, Norway. Presented in two parts.

Ibsen's tale of an unhappy housewife who seeks vicarious thrills as she attempts to influence the destiny of others. First New York English-language production at the Fifth Avenue Theatre, March 30, 1898. Elizabeth Robins played the title role.

Dance of Death (108). Adapted by Richard Greenberg from the play by August Strindberg. Produced by the Shubert Organization, Roger Berlind, USA Ostar Theatricals and Chase Miskin at the Broadhurst Theatre. Opened October 11, 2001. (Closed January 13, 2002)

Edgar, an army captain .... Ian McKellen	Maja .... Anne Pitoniak
Alice, his wife .... Helen Mirren	Jenny .... Keira Naughton
Kurt, her cousin .... David Strathairn	Sentry .... Eric Martin Brown

Standbys: Mr. McKellen—Edmond Genest; Ms. Mirren—Suzanna Hay; Mses. Naughton, Pitoniak—Alicia Roper; Messrs. Strathairn, Brown—James Riordan.

Directed by Sean Mathias; scenery and costumes, Santo Loquasto; lighting, Natasha Katz; sound and original music, Dan Moses Schreier; casting, Ilene Starger; production stage manager, Arthur Gaffin; press, Barlow-Hartman Public Relations, John Barlow, Michael Hartman, Bill Coyle.

Time: Autumn 1900. Place: The Captain and Alice's home—a fortress on an island off the coast of Sweden. Presented in two parts.

Gilded cage: Kate Burton and Harris Yulin in Hedda Gabler. *Photo: T. Charles Erickson*

A married couple experience love as an emotional torment that leads—after a twisted journey—back to one another. The first English-language production of record in New York played at Off Broadway's Key Theatre (9/13/1960; 112 performances). Abe Vigoda and Jennie Davis played the battling couple. An earlier adaptation, *The Last Dance* by Peter Goldbaum and Robin Short, played at the Belasco Theatre (1/27/1948; 7 performances).

*Mamma Mia! (256). Musical with book by Catherine Johnson; music and lyrics by Benny Andersson and Björn Ulvaeus, some songs with Stig Anderson. Produced by Judy Craymer, Richard East and Björn Ulvaeus for LittleStar, in association with Universal, at the Winter Garden Theatre. Opened October 18, 2001.

Sophie Sheridan	Tina Maddigan	Pepper	Mark Price
Ali	Sara Inbar	Eddie	Michael Benjamin Washington
Lisa	Tonya Doran	Harry Bright	Dean Nolen
Tanya	Karen Mason	Bill Austin	Ken Marks
Rosie	Judy Kaye	Sam Carmichael	David W. Keeley
Donna Sheridan	Louise Pitre	Father Alexandrios	Bill Carmichael
Sky	Joe Machota		

The Ensemble: Meredith Akins, Stephan Alexander, Kim-e J. Balmilero, Robin Baxter, Brent Black, Tony Carlin, Bill Carmichael, Meghann Dreyfuss, Somer Lee Graham, Hollie Howard, Kristin McDonald, Adam Monley, Chris Prinzo, Peter Matthew Smith, Yuka Takara, Marsha Waterbury.

Orchestra: David Holcenberg conductor, keyboard; Rob Preuss associate music director, keyboard 3; Steve Marzullo keyboard 2; Myles Chase keyboard 4; Doug Quinn guitar 1; Jeff Campbell guitar 2; Paul Adamy bass; Gary Tillman drums; David Nyberg percussion.

Understudies: Ms. Maddigan—Meghann Dreyfuss, Somer Lee Graham; Ms. Inbar—Kim-e J. Balmilero, Kristin McDonald; Ms. Doran—Meredith Akins, Yuka Takara; Ms. Pitre—Marsha Waterbury; Ms. Mason—Leslie Alexander, Marsha Waterbury; Ms. Kaye—Robin Baxter, Marsha Waterbury; Mr. Machota—Adam Monley, Peter Matthew Smith; Mr. Price—Stephan Alexander, Jon-Erik Goldberg; Mr. Washington—Chris Prinzo, Peter Matthew Smith; Mr. Nolen—Tony Carlin, Bill Carmichael; Mr. Marks—Brent Black, Tony Carlin; Mr. Keeley—Brent Black, Tony Carlin.

Swings: Barrett Foa, Jon-Erik Goldberg, Janet Rothermel.

Gleesome threesome: Karen Mason, Louise Pitre and Judy Kaye in Mamma Mia! *Photo: Joan Marcus*

Directed by Phyllida Lloyd; choreography, Anthony Van Laast; scenery and costumes, Mark Thompson; lighting, Howard Harrison; sound; Andrew Bruce and Bobby Aitken; musical supervision, Martin Koch; music direction, David Holcenberg; music coordination, Michael Keller; associate director, Robert McQueen; associate choreographer, Nichola Treherne; casting, Tara Rubin Casting; press, Boneau/Bryan-Brown, Adrian Bryan-Brown, Steven Padla, Jackie Green, Karalee Dawn.

Time: A wedding weekend. Place: A tiny Greek Island. Presented in two parts.

Songs of the 1970s pop group ABBA strung together in a story of baby boomer wisfulness and a girl's search for her unknown father.

MUSICAL NUMBERS
(in alphabetical order)

"Chiquitita"
"Dancing Queen"
"Does Your Mother Know"
"Gimme! Gimme! Gimme!"
"Honey, Honey"
"I Do, I Do, I Do, I Do, I Do"
"I Have a Dream"
"Knowing Me, Knowing You"
"Lay All Your Love on Me"
"Mamma Mia"
"Money, Money, Money"

"One of Us"
"Our Last Summer"
"Slipping Through My Fingers"
"S.O.S."
"Super Trouper"
"Take a Chance on Me"
"Thank You for the Music"
"The Name of the Game"
"The Winner Takes it All"
"Under Attack"
"Voulez-Vous"

Lincoln Center Theater production of **Thou Shalt Not** (85). Musical by Susan Stroman, David Thompson and Harry Connick Jr.; based on *Thérèse Raquin* by Émile Zola; book by David Thompson; music and lyrics by Harry Connick Jr. André Bishop artistic director, Bernard Gersten executive producer, at the Plymouth Theatre. Opened October 25, 2001. (Closed January 6, 2002)

Flim Flam .... J.C. Montgomery	Camille Raquin .... Norbert Leo Butz
Papa Jack .... Ted L. Levy	Officer Michaud .... Leo Burmester
Monsignor .... Patrick Wetzel	Oliver... Brad Bradley
Sass .... Rachelle Rak	Suzanne .... JoAnn M. Hunter
Sugar Hips .... Davis Kirby	Antoine .... Patrick Wetzel
Laurent LeClaire .... Craig Bierko	Busker .... Ted L. Levy
Therese Raquin .... Kate Levering	Sanctify Sam .... Ted L. Levy
Madame Raquin .... Debra Monk	

Ensemble: Timothy J. Alex, Brad Bradley, Dylis Croman, Michael Goddard, Amy Hall, Ellen Harvey, Amy Heggins, JoAnn M. Hunter, Cornelius Jones Jr., Davis Kirby, Ted L. Levy, J.C. Montgomery, Rachelle Rak, Kelli Severson, Patrick Wetzel.

Orchestra: Phil Reno conductor; Gregory J. Dlugos associate conductor; Jonathan Levine, Jerry Weldon, Dave Schumacher, Sal Spicola reeds; Joe Magnarelli, Derrick Gardner, John Reid trumpet; John Allred, Joe Barati trombone; Philip Fortenberry, Gregory J. Dlugos keyboards; Benjamin Franklin Brown bass; Brian Grice drums; Walter "Wally" Usiatynski percussion; Martin Agee concertmaster; Cenovia Cummins violin; Maxine Roach viola; Roger Shell cello.

Swings: Pam Bradley, James Hadley, Emily Hsu, Kent Zimmerman.

Standby: Messrs. Bierko, Butz—David New.

Understudies: Ms. Levering—Dylis Croman, Kelli Severson; Mr. Bierko—Timothy J. Alex; Mr. Butz—Timothy J. Alex, Brad Bradley; Ms. Monk—Pam Bradley, Ellen Harvey; Mr. Burmester—J.C. Montgomery, David New; Mr. Bradley—James Hadley, Patrick Wetzel; Mr. Levy (Papa Jack)—Timothy J. Alex, Kent Zimmerman; Ms. Hunter—Dylis Croman, Emily Hsu; Mr. Levy (Sanctify Sam)—J.C. Montgomery.

Directed and choreographed by Ms. Stroman; scenery, Thomas Lynch; costumes, William Ivey Long; lighting, Peter Kaczorowski; sound, Scott Lehrer; orchestrations and arrangements, Harry Connick Jr.; music direction, Phil Reno; music coordination, John Miller; associate director and choreographer, Tara Young; casting, Tara Rubin Casting; production stage manager, Peter Wolf; assistant stage managers, Lisa Buxbaum, Mark Dobrow; press, Philip Rinaldi, Barbara Carroll.

Time: 1946–47 Place: New Orleans, in and around the Ninth Ward. Presented in two parts.

Steamy, jazz-inflected retelling of Zola's tale of lust, betrayal, murder and madness.

ACT I

Scene 1: French Quarter Jazz Club
"It's Good to Be Home" .... Flim Flam, Papa Jack and Ensemble
Scene 2: The backyard of the Broken Tea Cup
"I Need to Be In Love" Ballet .... Therese
Scene 3: The Broken Tea Cup
"My Little World" .... Madame Raquin
"While You're Young" .... Laurent
"I Need to Be in Love" .... Therese
Scene 4: The Broken Tea Cup
"The Other Hours" .... Laurent
Scene 5: The bedroom
"The Other Hours" Ballet .... Laurent and Therese
Scene 6: The bedroom
"All Things" .... Camille
Scene 7: French Quarter
"Sovereign Lover" .... Therese, Laurent, Busker and Ensemble
Scene 8: The parlor
"I've Got My Eye on You" .... Madame Raquin and Camille
Scene 9: The alley
Scene 10: The backyard of the Broken Tea Cup
Scene 11: Mardi Gras
"Light the Way" .... Ensemble
"Take Her To the Mardi Gras" .... Laurent, Camille, Therese and Ensemble
Scene 12: Lake Pontchartrain
"Tug Boat" .... Camile and Therese

ACT II

Scene 1: French Quarter Jazz Club
Scene 2: The morque
"Tug Boat" (Reprise) .... Laurent
Scene 3: Madame's sitting room
"My Little World" (Reprise) .... Madame Raquin
Scene 4: The funeral
"Won't You Sanctify" .... Sanctify Sam and Ensemble
"Time Passing" .... Therese, Laurent, Madame Raquin and Ensemble
Scene 5: The Broken Tea Cup
"Take Advantage" .... Officer Michaud
Scene 6: The bedroom
Scene 7: The Ninth Ward
"Oh! Ain't That Sweet" .... Camille
Scene Eight: The bedroom
Scene 9: The wharf
"Thou Shalt Not" Ballet .... Therese, Laurent and Ensemble
Scene 10: The parlor, 4 a.m.
Scene 11: The parlor, 8 p.m.
Scene 12: French Quarter Jazz Club
"It's Good to Be Home" (Reprise) .... Camille

By Jeeves (73). Musical with book and lyrics by Alan Ayckbourn; music by Andrew Lloyd Webber; based on the Jeeves stories by P.G. Wodehouse. Produced by Goodspeed Musicals, Michael P. Price producer, at the Helen Hayes Theatre. Opened October 28, 2001. (Closed December 30, 2001)

Bertie Wooster .... John Scherer
Jeeves .... Martin Jarvis
Honoria Glossop .... Donna Lynne Champlin
Bingo Little .... Don Stephenson
Gussie Fink-Nottle .... James Kall
Sir Watkyn Bassett .... Sam Tsoutsouvas

Madeline Bassett .... Becky Watson
Stiffy Byng .... Emily Loesser
Harold "Stinker" Pinker .... Ian Knauer
Cyrus Budge III (Junior) .... Steve Wilson
Other Personages .... Tom Ford,
        Molly Renfroe, Court Whisman

Orchestra: Michael O'Flaherty conductor, piano; F. Wade Russo associate conductor, keyboard; Eddie Salkin reeds; Jack Cavari guitar; Brian Cassier bass; Brad Flickinger drums, percussion.

Understudies: Messrs. Scherer, Stephenson, Kall—Tom Ford, Jamison Stern; Mses. Loesser, Watson, Champlin—Cristin Mortenson, Molly Renfroe; Messrs. Jarvis, Wilson, Tsoutsouvas, Knauer—David Edwards, Court Whisman.

Swings: Cristin Mortenson, Jamison Stern.

Directed by Mr. Ayckbourn; choreography, Sheila Carter; scenery, Roger Glossop; costumes, Louise Belson; lighting, Mick Hughes; sound, Richard Ryan; music supervision and direction, Michael O'Flaherty; music coordination, John Miller; music arrangements, David Cullen and Andrew Lloyd Webber; casting, Sarah Hughes and Warren Pincus; production stage manager, Daniel S. Rosokoff; press, Barlow-Hartman Public Relations, John Barlow, Michael Hartman, Jeremy Shaffer.

Time: This very evening. Place: A church hall, later to represent a London flat. Presented in two parts.

Musical version of Jeeves stories by Mr. Wodehouse that show the English upper class to be helpless, harmless ninnies who must be rescued by their loyal, sensible servants. First performance at the Stephen Joseph Theatre in Scarborough, May 1996.

ACT I

"A False Start" .... Bertie
"Never Fear" .... Bertie, Jeeves
"Travel Hopefully" .... Bertie, Bingo
"That Was Nearly Us" .... Honoria
"Love's Maze" .... Stiffy, Bertie and Company
"The Hallo Song" .... Bertie, Budge, Gussie

ACT II

"By Jeeves" .... Bertie, Bingo, Gussie
"When Love Arrives" .... Bertie, Madeline
"What Have You Got to Say, Jeeves?" .... Bertie, Jeeves
"Half a Moment" .... Harold, Stiffy
"It's a Pig!" .... Honoria, Madeline, Bassett, Gussie, Bertie
"Banjo Boy" .... Company
"The Wizard Rainbow Finale" .... Company

Farce faces: Peter Gallagher and Patti LuPone in
Noises Off. *Photo: Joan Marcus*

*Noises Off (242). Revival of the play by Michael Frayn. Produced by Ambassador
Theatre Group and Act Productions, Waxman Williams Entertainment, Dede Harris/
Morton Swinsky, USA Ostar Theatricals and Nederlander Presentations, Inc., at the
Brooks Atkinson Theatre. Opened November 1, 2001.

Dotty Otley .... Patti LuPone
Lloyd Dallas .... Peter Gallagher
Garry Lejeune .... Thomas McCarthy
Brooke Ashton .... Katie Finneran
Poppy Norton-Taylor .... Robin Weigert

Belinda Blair .... Faith Prince
Frederick Fellowes .... Edward Hibbert
Tim Allgood .... T.R. Knight
Selsdon Mowbray .... Richard Easton

Standbys: Ms. Lupone—Barbara Sims; Mr. Gallagher—Doug Stender; Messrs. McCarthy, Knight—
Michael Bakkensen; Mses. Finneran, Weigert—Virginia Louise Smith; Ms. Prince—Barbara Sims;
Mr. Hibbert—Ross Bickell, Doug Stender; Mr. Easton—Ross Bickell.

Directed by Jeremy Sams; scenery and costumes, Robert Jones; lighting, Tim Mitchell; sound,
Fergus O'Hare; associate producers, Pre-Eminence, Incidental Colman Tod, Jane Curtis/Ann Johnson;

casting, Jim Carnahan; production stage manager, David O'Brien; press, Barlow-Hartman Public Relations, Michael Hartman, John Barlow, Wayne Wolfe.

Time: Three months of a theatrical tour. Place: Three regional theaters in England. Presented in two parts.

Farcical take on the challenges—love, lust, inept actors, ego clashes—facing a touring theater company in England. A *Best Plays* choice for 1983–84, the original Broadway production opened at the Brooks Atkinson Theatre (12/11/83; 553 performances).

Roundabout Theatre Company production of **The Women** (77). Revival of the play by Clare Boothe Luce. Todd Haimes artistic director, Ellen Richard managing director, Julia C. Levy executive director of external affairs, at the American Airlines Theatre. Opened November 8, 2001. (Closed January 13, 2002)

Jane .... Heather Matarazzo	Mrs. Morehead .... Mary Louise Wilson
Sylvia	1st Salesgirl .... Ann Talman
(Mrs. Howard Fowler) .... Kristen Johnston	2nd Salesgirl .... Barbara Marineau
Nancy Blake .... Lisa Emery	Miss Shapiro .... Cheryl Stern
Peggy (Mrs. John Day) .... Amy Ryan	1st Saleswoman .... Julie Halston
Edith	2nd Saleswoman .... Susan Bruce
(Mrs. Phelps Potter) .... Jennifer Coolidge	Miss Myrtle (a model) .... Adina Porter
Mary	Crystal Allen .... Jennifer Tilly
(Mrs. Stephen Haines) .... Cynthia Nixon	1st Model (negligee) .... Jen Davis
Mrs. Wagstaff .... Barbara Marineau	2nd Model (corset) .... Kelly Mares
Olga .... Jennifer Butt	A Fitter .... Jennifer Butt
1st Hairdresser .... Gayton Scott	Princess Tamara .... Roxanna Hope
2nd Hairdresser .... Roxanna Hope	Exercise Instructress .... Gayton Scott
Pedicurist .... Cheryl Stern	Maggie .... Mary Bond Davis
Mud Mask .... Julie Halston	Miss Watts .... Susan Bruce
Euphie .... Adina Porter	Miss Trimmerback .... Ann Talman
Miss Fordyce .... Jane Cronin	A Nurse .... Adina Porter
Little Mary .... Hallie Kate Eisenberg	Lucy .... Julie Halston

Girls will be: Lisa Emery, Lynn Collins, Kristen Johnston, Cynthia Nixon, Jennifer Tilly, Rue McClanahan in The Women. *Photo: Joan Marcus*

Countess De Lage .... Rue McClanahan	2nd Woman .... Susan Bruce
Miriam Aarons .... Lynn Collins	Sadie .... Cheryl Stern
Helene .... Rosanna Hope	Cigarette Girl .... Adina Porter
1st Girl ....Jennifer Butt	Dowager............................... Barbara Marineau
2nd Girl .... Gayton Scott	Debutante .... Roxanna Hope
1st Woman .... Julie Halston	Girl in Distress.............................. Ann Talman

Understudies: Mses. Matarazzo, Stern, Scott—Jen Davis; Ms. Johnston—Julie Halston; Mses. Emery, Coolidge—Jennifer Butt; Mses. Ryan, Hope—Kelly Mares; Ms. Nixon—Ann Talman; Mses. Marineau, Davis, Talman—Jane Cronin; Mses. Bruce, Butt, Porter—Cheryl Stern; Ms. Cronin—Brandy Mitchell; Ms. Eisenberg—Madeline Rogan; Mses. Wilson, McClanahan—Barbara Marineau; Ms. Tilly—Roxanna Hope; Mses. Collins, Halston—Gayton Scott.

Directed by Scott Elliott; scenery, Derek McLane; costumes, Isaac Mizrahi; lighting, Brian MacDevitt; sound and musical arrangements, Douglas J. Cuomo; casting, Jim Carnahan; production stage manager, Peter Hanson; stage manager, Valerie A. Peterson; press, Boneau/Bryan-Brown, Adrian Bryan-Brown, Matt Polk, Jackie Green, Karalee Dawn, Cindy Valk.

Time: 1930s. Place: New York City and Nevada. Presented in two parts.

Acid-tinged (and tongued) chronicle of life amid a group of women who take pleasure in the betrayals and humiliations of their "sisters." A 1936–37 *Best Plays* choice, the original Broadway production opened at the Ethel Barrymore Theatre (12/26/1936; 657 performances).

45 Seconds From Broadway (73). By Neil Simon. Produced by Emanuel Azenberg, Ira Pittelman, James Nederlander, Scott Nederlander and Kevin McCollum at the Richard Rodgers Theatre. Opened November 11, 2001. (Closed January 13, 2002)

Mickey Fox .... Lewis J. Stadlen	Cindy ....Judith Blazer
Andrew Duncan .... Dennis Creaghan	Rayleen .... Marian Seldes
Bernie ....Louis Zorich	Charles W. Browning III .... Bill Moor
Solomon Mantutu .... Kevin Carroll	Zelda ....Rebecca Schull
Megan Woods ....Julie Lund	Bessie James .... Lynda Gravátt
Arleen .... Alix Korey	Harry Fox .... David Margulies

Understudies: Mr. Stadlen—Adam Grupper; Mses. Seldes, Schull—Maggie Burke; Messrs. Zorich, Margulies—Herbert Rubens; Ms. Gravátt—Tonye Patano; Mses. Blazer, Korey—Marisa Redanty; Mr. Carroll—Teagle F. Bougere; Messrs. Moor, Creaghan—James A. Stephens; Ms. Lund—Rhea Seehorn.

Entre nous: *Marian Seldes and Lewis J. Stadlen in* 45 Seconds From Broadway.*Carol Rosegg*

Directed by Jerry Zaks; scenery, John Lee Beatty; costumes, William Ivey Long; lighting, Paul Gallo; sound, Peter J. Fitzgerald; associate producer, Ginger Montel; casting, Jay Binder Casting; stage manager, J. Philip Bassett; press, Bill Evans and Associates, Jim Randolph, Terry M. Lilly.

Time: The four seasons. Place: A coffee shop in New York. Presented in two parts.

Comic celebration of the famous Broadway theater district coffee shop, located in the Edison Hotel, known as the "Polish Tea Room."

*Lincoln Center Theater production of **QED** (35). By Peter Parnell; inspired by the writings of Richard Feynman and Ralph Leighton's *Tuva or Bust!* André Bishop artistic director, Bernard Gersten executive producer, at the Vivian Beaumont Theater. Opened November 18, 2001.

Richard Feynman .... Alan Alda   Miriam Field .... Kellie Overbey

Understudy: Ms. Overbey—Piper Brooks.

Directed by Gordon Davidson; scenery, Ralph Funicello; costumes, Marianna Elliott; lighting, D. Martyn Bookwalter; sound, Jon Gottlieb; creative consultant, Ralph Leighton; casting, Daniel Swee; stage manager, Robin Veith; press, Philip Rinaldi, Barbara Carroll.

Time: June 1986. Place: California Institute of Technology, Pasadena. Presented in two parts.

Physicist Richard Feynman's musings on the nature of life, death and science in a play that is nearly a one-man performance. Using an intermittent schedule, *QED* was performed in the Vivian Beaumont Theater when *Contact* was dark. The production also took a hiatus during winter holidays. *QED* was commissioned by and had its world premiere at the Mark Taper Forum.

Sex mad: John Leguizamo in Sexaholix . . . a Love Story. *Photo: Joan Marcus*

Sexaholix . . . a Love Story (67). By John Leguizamo. Produced by Tate Entertainment Group, Inc., at the Royale Theatre. Opened December 2, 2001. (February 10, 2002)

Performed by Mr. Leguizamo.

Directed by Peter Askin; costume consultant, Santiago; lighting, Kevin Adams; production stage manager, Pat Sosnow; press, Bill Evans and Associates, Bill Evans, Jim Randolph, Terry M. Lilly.

Presented in two parts.

Comedic observations on race, culture, intermarriage, family and sex.

Lincoln Center Theater production of **Mostly Sondheim** (9). André Bishop artistic director, Bernard Gersten executive producer, at the Vivian Beaumont Theater. Opened January 14, 2001. (Closed February 11, 2002)

Performed by Barbara Cook.

Musicians: Wally Harper music director, piano; Jon Burr bass.

Presented without intermission.

Concert performance of songs by Stephen Sondheim and others. Scheduled for return engagement in 2002–03 season.

Prayer power: Kevin Bacon in An Almost Holy Picture. *Photo: Joan Marcus*

Roundabout Theatre Company production of **An Almost Holy Picture** (68). By Heather McDonald. Todd Haimes artistic director, Ellen Richard managing director, Julia C. Levy executive director of external affairs, at the American Airlines Theatre. Opened February 7, 2002. (Closed April 7, 2002)

Samuel Gentle .... Kevin Bacon   Samuel Gentle (alt.) .... John Dossett

Directed by Michael Mayer; scenery, Mark Wendland; costumes, Michael Krass; lighting, Kevin Adams; sound, Scott Myers and Robert Kaplowitz; original music, Mitch Greenhill; associate director, Todd Lundquist; production stage manager, Roy Harris; stage manager, Kimberly Russell; press, Boneau/Bryan-Brown, Adrian Bryan-Brown, Matt Polk, Amy Dinnerman.

Time: The present. Place: The grounds of a cathedral and other places. Presented in two parts.

One-man performance of a story of trial and faith.

Bea Arthur on Broadway: Just Between Friends (65). By Bea Arthur and Billy Goldenberg, in collaboration with Charles Randolph Wright. Produced by Daryl Roth, M. Beverly Bartner and USA Ostar Theatricals at the Booth Theatre. Opened February 17, 2002. (Closed April 14, 2002)

Performed by Bea Arthur with Billy Goldenberg on piano.

Production consultants, Mark Waldrop and Richard Maltby Jr.; scenery, Ray Klausen; lighting and sound, Matt Berman; press, Barlow-Hartman Public Relations, John Barlow, Michael Hartman, Jeremy Shaffer.

Presented without intermission.

Autobiographical perspective on the life and career of Bea Arthur.

I'm over here! Elaine Stritch and Bea Arthur in their respective solo shows. Elaine Stritch photo: Michal Daniel; Bea Arthur photo: Joan Marcus

Elaine Stritch at Liberty (69). Transfer from Off Broadway of the solo performance piece by Elaine Stritch and John Lahr. Produced by John Schreiber, Creative Battery, Margo Lion, Robert Cole, in association with Dede Harris/Morton Swinsky, Cheryl Wiesenfeld, and the Joseph Papp Public Theater/New York Shakespeare Festival, at the Neil Simon Theatre. Opened February 21, 2002. (Closed May 26, 2002)

Performed by Elaine Stritch.

Orchestra: Rob Bowman conductor, piano; Les Scott, Richard Heckman, John Campo woodwinds; Stu Satalof, Kamau Adilifu trumpet; John Gale trombone; Louis Bruno bass; Willard Miller drums, percussion.

Directed by George C. Wolfe; scenery, Riccardo Hernández; costumes, Paul Tazewell; lighting, Jules Fisher and Peggy Eisenhauer; sound, Acme Sound Partners; orchestrations, Jonathan Tunick; music direction, Rob Bowman; music coordination, Seymour Red Press; associate producers, Roy Furman, Jay Furman, Mark Krantz, Charles Flateman; production stage manager, James D. Latus; press, Carol R. Fineman.

Presented in two parts.

Autobiographical perspective on the life and passions of Elaine Stritch. Originally presented Off Broadway by the Joseph Papp Public Theater/New York Shakespeare Festival in its Newman Theater (11/6/2001; 50 performances; see Plays Produced Off Broadway section). A *Best Plays* special citation honoree for 2001–02 (see essay by Michael Sommers in this volume). Received a special citation from the New York Drama Critics Circle and a Tony Award for special theatrical event.

MUSICAL NUMBERS
(in alphabetical order)

"All in Fun" ....Jerome Kern and Oscar Hammerstein II
"Broadway Baby" .... Stephen Sondheim
"But Not For Me" .... George Gershwin and Ira Gershwin
"If Love Were All" .... Noël Coward
"Can You Use Any Money Today?" .... Irving Berlin
"Civilization" .... Carl Sigman and Bob Hilliard
"Horray for Hollywood" .... Richard A. Whiting and Johnny Mercer
"I'm Still Here" .... Stephen Sondheim
"I've Been to a Marvelous Party" .... Noël Coward
"I Want a Long Time Daddy" .... Porter Grainger
"The Little Things You Do Together" .... Stephen Sondheim
"Something Good" .... Richard Rodgers
"The Ladies Who Lunch" .... Stephen Sondheim
"The Party's Over" ....Jule Styne, Betty Comden and Adolph Green
"There Never Was a Baby Like My Baby" .... Jule Styne, Betty Comden and Adolph Green
"There's No Business Like Show Business" .... Irving Berlin
"This Is All Very New to Me" .... Albert Hague and Arnold B. Horwitt
"Why Do the Wrong People Travel" .... Noël Coward
"Zip" .... Richard Rodgers and Lorenz Hart

*Metamorphoses (101). Transfer from Off Broadway of the play by Mary Zimmerman; based on a translation by David R. Slavitt of Ovid's *Metamorphoses*. Produced by Roy Gabay, Robyn Goodman, Allan S. Gordon, Élan V. McAllister, Dede Harris/Morton Swinsky, Ruth Hendel, Sharon Karmazin, Randall L. Wreghitt/Jane Bergère, in association with Second Stage Theatre, Carole Rothman artistic director; Carol Fishman managing director, at Circle in the Square. Opened March 4, 2002.

Myrrha and others .... Anjali Bhimani	Erysichthon and others .... Chris Kipiniak
Midas and others .... Raymond Fox	Alcyon and others .... Louise Lamson
Hermes and others .... Kyle Hall	Orpheus and others .... Erik Lochtefeld
Phaeton and others .... Doug Hara	Eurydice and others .... Mariann Mayberry
Aphrodite and others .... Felicity Jones	Therapist and others .... Lisa Tejero

Heavenly shower: Members of the company in Metamorphoses. *Photo: Joan Marcus*

Understudies: Mses. Lamson, Jones, Tejero—Tara Falk; Messrs. Hall, Hara—Mario Campanaro; Messrs. Kipiniak, Fox, Lochtefeld—Gregory Derelian; Mses. Bhimani, Mayberry—Julienne Hanzelka Kim.

Directed by Ms. Zimmerman; scenery, Daniel Ostling; costumes, Mara Blumenfeld; lighting, T.J. Gerckens; sound, Andre Pluess and Ben Sussman; composer, Willy Schwarz; production stage manager, Debra A. Acquavella; stage manager, Anjali Bidani; press, Richard Kornberg and Associates, Richard Kornberg, Tom D'Ambrosio, Don Summa.

Presented without intermission.

Contemporary adaptation of Ovid's *Metamorphoses* with inspiration from Rainer Maria Rilke's "Orpheus, Eurydice, Hermes" (translated by Stephen Mitchell), Joseph Campbell, Carl Jung, Sigmund Freud and James Hillman. *Metamorphoses* was originally produced by Lookingglass Theatre Company, Chicago. Current production transferred after a run at Off Broadway's Second Stage Theatre (10/9/2001; 96 performances; see Plays Produced Off Broadway section). A 2001–02 *Best Plays* choice (see essay by Christopher Rawson in this volume).

Smooth singin': Rosalind Brown and Vernel Bagneris in One Mo' Time. *Photo: Carol Rosegg*

One Mo' Time (21). Revival of the musical with book by Vernel Bagneris; music and lyrics by various artists. Produced by the Williamstown Theatre Festival, Michael Ritchie producer, in association with Bob Boyett, at the Longacre Theatre. Opened March 6, 2002. (Closed March 24, 2002)

Papa Du	Vernel Bagneris	Theatre Owner	Wally Dunn
Ma Reed	B.J. Crosby	Bertha	Roz Ryan
Thelma	Rosalind Brown		

Orchestra: Mark Braud trumpet; Conal Fowkes piano; Orange Kellin clarinet; Walter Payton tuba; Kenneth Sara drums, percussion.

Standbys: Mr. Bagneris—Eugene Fleming; Mses. Crosby, Ryan—Aisha de Haas; Ms. Brown—Enga Davis; Mr. Dunn—John Ahlin.

Choreography, Eddie D. Robinson; scenery, Campbell Baird, costumes, Toni-Leslie James; lighting, John McKernon; sound, Kurt B. Kellenberger; musical supervision, Mr. Kellin; musical arrangements, Lars Edegran and Mr. Kellin; vocal arrangements, Mr. Edegran and Topsy Chapman; casting, Amy Christopher; production stage manager, Grayson Meritt; press, the Pete Sanders Group, Pete Sanders, Glenna Freedman, Rick Miramontez.

Time: 1926. Place: The Lyric Theatre, New Orleans. Presented in two parts.

Musical that juxtaposes backstage life and onstage performances by African-American performers in the Theatre Owners Booking Association circuit.

ACT I

Overture: "Darktown Strutters Ball" .... Band
(Sheldon Brooks)

"Honky Tonk Town" .... Papa Du, Ma Reed, Thelma
(Charles McCarron and Chris Smith)

"Kiss Me Sweet" .... Papa Du, Thelma
(Armand J. Piron and Steve J. Lewis)

"Don't Turn Your Back on Me" .... Bertha
(Andy Razaf and Clarence Williams)

"Jenny's Ball" .... Ma Reed
(Quenton Reed)

"Cake-Walking Babies" .... Papa Du, Ma Reed, Thelma
(Chris Smith, Henry Troy and Clarence Williams)

"I've Got What It Takes" .... Thelma
(Hezekiah Jenkins and Clarence Williams)

"See See Rider" .... Ma Reed
(Ma Rainey)

"He's in the Jailhouse Now" .... Papa Du
(Toots Davis and Ed Stafford)

"He's Funny That Way" .... Thelma
(Neil Moret, Richard A. Whiting)

"Tiger Rag" .... Band
(Edwin B. Edwards, James D. LaRocca, W.H. Ragas, Anthony Sbarbaro and Larry Shields)

"Kitchen Man" .... Bertha
(Andy Razaf and Alex Bellenda)

"Wait Till You See My Baby Do the Charleston" .... Ma Reed, Bertha, Thelma
(Rousseau Semmois, Clarence Todd and Clarence Williams)

ACT II

Entr'acte: "Muskrat Ramble" .... Band
(Edward "Kid" Ory)

"Black Bottom" .... Papa Du, Ma Reed, Bertha
(Ray Henderson, Lew Brown, B.G. DeSylva)

"Louise Louise" .... Band (vocal, Mr. Braud)

"Get On Out of Here (The Party)" .... Papa Du, Ma Reed, Bertha, Thelma
(Wesley Williams)

"Weary Blues (Shake It and Break It)" .... Band (vocal, Mr. Braud)
(Artie Matthews)

"New Orleans Hop Scop Blues" .... Papa Du
(George W. Thomas)

"Hindustan" .... Band (dance, Ma Reed)
(Oliver G. Wallace and H. Weeks)

"What It Takes to Bring You Back" .... Papa Du, Bertha
(Spencer Williams)

"Everybody Loves My Baby" .... Thelma
(Jack Palmer and Spencer Williams)

"Right Key But the Wrong Keyhole" .... Bertha
(Eddie Green and Clarence Williams)

"After You've Gone" .... Ma Reed
(Henry Creamer and J. Turner Layton)
"My Man Blues" .... Bertha, Thelma
(Bessie Smith)
"Papa De Da Da" .... Papa Du, Ma Reed, Bertha, Thelma
(Spencer Williams, Clarence Williams and Clarence Todd)
"Muddy Water" .... Ma Reed, Bertha
(Harry Richman, Peter de Rose, Jo Trent)
"A Hot Time in the Old Town Tonight" .... Papa Du, Ma Reed, Bertha, Thelma
(Theo A. Metz)

*The Crucible (92). Revival of the play by Arthur Miller. Produced by David Richenthal,
Jennifer Manocherian/Harriet Newman Leve/Bob Boyett, Max Cooper, Allan S. Gordon,
Roy Furman, Us Productions, Élan V. McAllister, Adam Epstein, Margo Lion, in association
with Dede Harris/Morton Swinsky, Clear Channel Entertainment, Old Ivy Productions,
Jujamcyn Theaters, Jeffrey Ash, Dori Berinstein/Roni Selig, Margaret McFeeley Golden/
Michael Skipper, Gene Korf, Robert Cole, and by special arrangement with the
Roundabout Theatre Company, at the Virginia Theatre. Opened March 7, 2002.

Reverend Parris .... Christopher Evan Welch	Reverend John Hale ..... John Benjamin Hickey
Betty Parris .... Betsy Hogg	Elizabeth Proctor .... Laura Linney
Tituba .... Patrice Johnson	Francis Nurse .... Frank Raiter
Abigail Williams .... Angela Bettis	Ezekiel Cheever .... Henry Stram
Susanna Walcott .... Kristen Bell	Marshal Herrick .... Jack Willis
Mrs. Ann Putnam .... Jeanne Paulsen	Hopkins .... Stephen Lee Anderson
Thomas Putnam .... Paul O'Brien	Judge Hathorne .... J.R. Horne
Mercy Lewis .... Sevrin Anne Mason	Voice of Martha Corey .... Lise Bruneau
Mary Warren .... Jennifer Carpenter	Deputy Governor Danforth .... Brian Murray
John Proctor .... Liam Neeson	Girl in Courtroom .... Laura Breckenridge
Rebecca Nurse .... Helen Stenborg	Sarah Good .... Dale Soules
Giles Corey .... Tom Aldredge	

Understudies; Mr. Neeson—Paul O'Brien; Mses. Linney, Paulsen, Soules—Lise Bruneau; Mr.
Murray—J.R. Horne; Mesrs. Hickey, Welch, Stram, Anderson—Michael Winther; Messrs. O'Brien,
Welch, Willis—Stephen Lee Anderson; Ms. Bettis—Jennifer Carpenter; Messrs. Horne, Aldredge,
Raiter, Stram—MacIntyre Dixon; Mses. Mason, Bell, Hogg—Laura Breckenridge; Ms. Carpenter—
Kristen Bell; Mses. Johnson, Bruneau—Marsha Stephanie Blake; Ms. Stenborg—Dale Soules.

Directed by Richard Eyre; scenery and costumes, Tim Hatley; lighting, Paul Gallo; sound, Scott
Myers; original music, David Van Tieghem; associate producers, Toby Simkin, Erick Falkenstein;
casting, Daniel Swee; production stage manager, Susie Cordon; press, Richard Kornberg and
Associates, Richard Kornberg, Don Summa.

Time: 1692. Place: Locations around Salem, Massachusetts. Presented in two parts.

Revival of Arthur Miller's 1953 meditation on the nature of community norms and their
enforcement. A 1952–53 *Best Plays* choice, the original Broadway production opened at the Martin
Beck Theatre (1/22/1953; 197 performances).

*The Goat, or Who Is Sylvia? (94). By Edward Albee. Produced by Elizabeth Ireland
McCann, Daryl Roth, Carole Shorenstein Hays, Terry Allen Kramer, Scott Rudin, Bob
Boyett, Scott Nederlander, Jeffrey Sine/ZPI at the Golden Theatre. Opened March 10,
2002.

Stevie .... Mercedes Ruehl	Ross .... Stephen Rowe
Martin .... Bill Pullman	Billy .... Jeffrey Carlson

Standbys: Mr. Pullman—Richard Thompson; Ms. Ruehl—Felicity LaFortune; Mr. Rowe—Stephen
Schnetzer; Mr. Carlson—Todd Swenson.

Directed by David Esbjornson; scenery, John Arnone; costumes, Elizabeth Hope Clancy; lighting,
Kenneth Posner; sound, Mark Bennett; casting, Bernard Telsey Casting; production stage manager,
Erica Schwartz; press, Shirley Herz Associates, Sam Rudy.

Presented without intermission.

A man's life and family are turned to chaos when his longing for a four-legged creature comes to light. Honored as a best play by the New York Drama Critics Circle and the Tony Awards. A 2001–02 *Best Plays* choice (see essay by Charles Isherwood in this volume).

*Sweet Smell of Success (90). Musical with book by John Guare; music by Marvin Hamlisch; lyrics by Craig Carnelia; based on the novella by Ernest Lehman, and the MGM/UA motion picture with screenplay by Clifford Odets and Ernest Lehman. Produced by Clear Channel Entertainment, David Brown, Ernest Lehman, Marty Bell, Martin Richards, Roy Furman, Joan Cullman, Bob Boyett, East of Doheny, Bob and Harvey Weinstein at the Martin Beck Theatre. Opened March 14, 2002.

J.J. Hunsecker .... John Lithgow	Charlotte Von Habsburg .... Michelle Kittrell
Sidney Falco .... Brian d'Arcy James	Otis Elwell .... Eric Michael Gillett
Susan .... Kelli O'Hara	Lester .... Steven Ochoa
Dallas .... Jack Noseworthy	Kello .... David Brummel
Rita .... Stacey Logan	Club Zanzibar Singer .... Bernard Dotson
Madge .... Joanna Glushak	Cathedral Soloist .... Kate Coffman-Lloyd
Abigail Barcley .... Elena L. Shaddow	Senator .... Allen Fitzpatrick
Billy Van Cleve .... Michael Paternostro	Senator's Girlfriend .... Jill Nicklaus
Pregnant Woman .... Jamie Chandler-Torns	J.J.'s Vaudeville Partner .... Jennie Ford
Pepper White's Escort .... Eric Sciotto	Press Agent .... Timothy J. Alex

Medium hot: Brian d'Arcy James and members of the ensemble in Sweet Smell of Success. *Photo: Paul Kolnik*

Orchestra: Jeffrey Huard conductor; Ron Melrose piano, associate conductor; Joel Fram keyboard 2, assistant conductor; Steve Bartosik drums; Ted Nash, Dennis Anderson, Charles Pillow, Ken Dybisz, Ron Janelli reeds; Bob Millikan, Larry Lunetta trumpet; Michael Davis, Randy Andos trombone; Douglas Purviance bass trombone; Roger Wendt, French horn; Clay Ruede cello; John Beal bass; Bill Hayes percussion.

Swings: Mark Arvin, Lisa Gajda, Laura Griffith, Drew Taylor.

Understudies: Mr. Lithgow—Allen Fitzpatrick; Mr. James—Frank Vlastnik; Ms. O'Hara—Elena L. Shaddow; Mr. Noseworthy—Eric Sciotto; Ms. Logan—Jill Nicklaus.

Directed by Nicholas Hytner; choreography, Christopher Wheeldon; scenery and costumes, Bob Crowley; lighting, Natasha Katz; sound, Tony Meola; orchestrations, William David Brohn; musical direction, Jeffrey Huard; music coordination, Michael Keller; associate choreographer, Jodi Moccia; executive producers, Beth Williams and East Egg Entertainment; associate producers, Producers Circle, Allen Spivak and Larry Magid; casting, Mark Simon; press, Barlow-Hartman Public Relations, Michael Hartman, John Barlow, Wayne Wolfe.

Time: 1952. Place: New York City. Presented in two parts.

Musical adaptation of the noirish 1957 Burt Lancaster-Tony Curtis film about the corruptions of the media and its power.

ACT I

"The Column"	J.J., Sidney and Ensemble
"I Could Get You in J.J."	Sidney
"I Cannot Hear the City"	Dallas
"Welcome to the Night"	J.J., Sidney and Ensemble
"Laughin' All the Way to the Bank"	Club Zanzibar Singer
"At the Fountain"	Sidney
"Psalm 151"	J.J. and Sidney
"Don't Know Where You Leave Off"	Dallas and Susan
"What If"	Susan and Ensemble
"For Susan"	J.J.
"One Track Mind"	Dallas
"I Cannot Hear the City" (Reprise)	Sidney
"End of Act I"	Ensemble

ACT II

"Break It Up"	J.J., Sidney and Ensemble
"Rita's Tune"	Rita
"Dirt"	Ensemble
"I Could Get You in J.J." (Reprise)	Sidney
"I Cannot Hear the City" (Reprise)	Susan and Dallas
"Don't Look Now"	J.J. and Ensemble
"At the Fountain" (Reprise)	Sidney and Ensemble
"End of Act II"	J.J., Susan, Sidney and Ensemble

*Oklahoma! (82). Revival of the musical with book and lyrics by Oscar Hammerstein II; music by Richard Rodgers; based on the Lynn Riggs play *Green Grow the Lilacs*. Produced by Cameron Mackintosh at the Gershwin Theatre. Opened March 21, 2002.

Aunt Eller	Andrea Martin	Susie	Bradley Benjamin
Curly	Patrick Wilson	Slim	Kevin Bernard
Laurey	Josefina Gabrielle	Aggie	Amy Bodnar
Ike Skidmore	Ronn Carroll	Joe	Stephen R. Buntrock
Will Parker	Justin Bohon	Sam	Nicolas Dromard
Jud Fry	Shuler Hensley	Chalmers	Merwin Foard
Ado Annie Carnes	Jessica Boevers	Ellen	Rosena M. Hill
Ali Hakim	Aasif Mandvi	Jake	Chris Holly
Gertie Cummings	Mia Price	Mike	Michael Thomas Holmes
Andrew Carnes	Michael McCarty	Kate	Elizabeth Loyacano
Cord Elam	Michael X. Martin	Armina	Audrie Neenan
Corky	Matt Allen	Rosie	Rachelle Rak
Jess	Clyde Alves	Tom	Jermaine R. Rembert

Vivian	Laura Shoop	Lil' Titch	Julianna Rose Mauriello
Emily	Sarah Spradlin-Bonomo	Travis	Stephen Scott Scarpulla
Fred	Greg Stone	Desiree	Lauren Ullrich
Sylvie	Kathy Voytko	Maverick	William Ullrich
Lucy	Catherine Wreford		

Orchestra: Kevin Stites conductor; Paul Raiman associate conductor, keyboard; Charles duChateau assistant conductor, cello; Martin Agee concertmaster; Cenovia Cummins, Xin M. Zhao, James Tsao violin; Ken Burward-Hoy viola; Sarah Carter cello; Peter Donovan bass; Ed Joffe, Matt Dine, John J. Moses, Steve Kenyon, Thomas Sefcovic reeds; Don Downs, Tino Gagliardi trumpet; Keith O'Quinn trombone; Lawrence DiBello, Peter Schoettler, French horn; Perry Cavari drums; James Baker percussion; Greg Utzig guitar, banjo; Grace Paradise harp.

Understudies: Mr. Wilson—Stephen R. Buntrock, Greg Stone; Ms. Gabrielle—Amy Bodnar, Laura Shoop; Ms. Martin—Audrie Neenan; Mr. Hensley—Merwin Foard, Michael X. Martin; Ms. Boevers—Kathy Voytko, Catherine Wreford; Mr. Bohon—Matt Allen, Nicolas Dromard; Mr. Mandvi—Michael Thomas Holmes, Tony Yazbeck; Messrs. McCarty, Carroll—Harvey Evans.

Swings: Dylis Croman, Rommy Sandhu, Jennifer West, Tony Yazbeck.

It's OK! Members of the company in Oklahoma! *Photo: Michael LePoer Trench*

Directed by Trevor Nunn; choreography, Susan Stroman; scenery and costumes, Anthony Ward; lighting, David Hersey; sound, Paul Groothuis; fight direction, Malcolm Ranson; original orchestrations, Robert Russell Bennett; musical supervision, David Caddick; music direction, Kevin Stites; dance music arrangements, David Krane; music coordination, John Miller; associate choreographer, Warren Carlyle; executive producers, David Caddick, Nicholas Allott, Matthew Dalco; casting, Tara Rubin Casting, Johnson-Liff Associates; production stage manager, Mahlon Kruse; press, the Publicity Office, Marc Thibodeau, Bob Fennell, Michael S. Borowski, Candi Adams.

Time: Near the turn of the 20th century. Place: The Oklahoma Territory. Presented in two parts.

Revival of the classic 1943 Rodgers and Hammerstein musical about Americans carving a life on the frontier. The current production premiered at London's Royal National Theatre in 1998. A 1942–43 *Best Plays* choice, the original Broadway production opened at the St. James Theatre (3/31/1943; 2,212 performances).

ACT I

Overture .... Orchestra
"Oh, What a Beautiful Mornin'" .... Curly
"The Surrey with the Fringe on Top" .... Curley, Laurey and Aunt Eller
"Kansas City" .... Will, Aunt Eller and the Boys
"I Cain't Say No" .... Ado Annie
"Many a New Day" .... Laurey and the Girls
"It's a Scandal! It's a Outrage!" .... Ali Hakim and Farmers
"People Will Say We're in Love" .... Curly and Laurey
"Poor Jud Is Daid" .... Curly and Jud
"Lonely Room" .... Jud
"Out of My Dreams" Ballet .... Laurey, the Girls and Dream Figures

ACT II

"The Farmer and the Cowman" .... Aunt Eller, Andrew Carnes, Curly,
Will, Ado Annie, Ike Skidmore and Company
"All er Nothin'" .... Will and Ado Annie
"People Will Say We're in Love" (Reprise) .... Curly and Laurey
"Oklahoma" .... Curly, Laurey, Aunt Eller and Company
Finale Ultimo .... Entire Company

Husband hunters: Lisa Emery and Jessica Stone in The Smell of the Kill. *Photo: Joan Marcus*

The Smell of the Kill (40). By Michele Lowe. Produced by Elizabeth Ireland McCann, Nelle Nugent, Milton and Tamar Maltz, and USA Ostar Theatricals, at the Helen Hayes Theatre. Opened March 26, 2002. (Closed April 28, 2002)

Debra	Claudia Shear	Danny; Marty	Patrick Garner
Milly	Jessica Stone	Jay	Mark Lotito
Nicky	Lisa Emery		

Understudies: Mses. Shear, Stone, Emery—Julie Boyd, Liz Larsen; Messrs. Garner, Lotito—James Mountcastle.

Directed by Christopher Ashley; scenery, David Gallo; costumes, David C. Woolard; lighting, Kenneth Posner; sound, Dan Moses Schreier; fight direction, Rick Sordelet; casting, Johnson-Liff

Associates; production stage manager, David Hyslop; press, Boneau/Bryan-Brown, Adrian Bryan-Brown, Jackie Green, Martine Sainvil.

Presented without intermission.

Comedy about three upper-middle-class women who take revenge on their clueless, retro husbands. Originally produced at the Cleveland Play House.

*Fortune's Fool (69). Adapted by Mike Poulton from the play by Ivan Turgenev. Produced by Julian Schlossberg, Roy Furman, Ben Sprecher, Ted Tulchin, Aaron Levy, Peter May, Bob Boyett, James Fantaci at the Music Box Theatre. Opened April 2, 2002.

Above Stairs
Vassily Semyonitch Kuzovkin .... Alan Bates
Ivan Kuzmitch Ivanov .... George Morfogen
Olga Petrovna .... Enid Graham
Pavel Nikolaitch
  Yeletsky ("Paul") .... Benedick Bates
Flegont Alexandrovitch
  Tropatchov .... Frank Langella

Karpatchov ("Little Fish") .... Timothy Doyle
Below Stairs
Praskovya Ivanova .... Lola Pashalinski
Nartzis Konstantinitch
  Trembinsky .... Edwin C. Owens
Pyotr .... Jeremy Hollingworth
Servants .... Beth Bartley, Ann Ducati,
      Patrick Hallahan, John Newton

Standbys: Mr. A. Bates—Edwin C. Owens, Jeff Talbott; Mr. Langella—Edwin C. Owens.

Understudies: Mr. Langella—Timothy Doyle; Mr. B. Bates—Jeremy Hollingworth, Patrick Hallahan; Messrs. Doyle, Hollingworth—Patrick Hallahan; Ms. Graham—Beth Bartley; Messrs. Morfogen, Owens—John Newton; Ms. Pashalinski—Ann Ducati; Servants—Jeff Talbott.

Directed by Arthur Penn; scenery, John Arnone; costumes, Jane Greenwood; lighting, Brian Nason; sound, Brian Ronan; original music, Kramer; associate producers, Rita Gam and Jill Furman; casting, Howard/Schecter/Meltzer; production stage manager, Jane Grey; press, the Publicity Office, Bob Fennell, Marc Thibodeau, Candi Adams, Michael S. Borowski.

Time: Mid-19th century Russia. Place: A country house. Presented in two parts. Adaptation of an Ivan Turgenev play—alternately translated as *A Poor Gentleman* (Constance Garnett, 1959) and *One of the Family* (Stephen Mulrine, 1998)—about a member of the aristocracy who suffers the slights of the contemptuous (and contemptible) bourgeosie. Originally presented at Rich Forum in Stamford, Connecticut, in association with Stamford Center for the Arts.

Soon parted: Timothy Doyle, Frank Langella and Alan Bates in Fortune's Fool. *Photo: Carol Rosegg*

Here's to you: Kathleen Turner in The Graduate.
Photo: Joan Marcus

*The Graduate (66). Adapted by Terry Johnson from the novel by Charles Webb, and the screenplay by Calder Willingham and Buck Henry. Produced by John Reid and Sacha Brooks, by special arrangement with StudioCanal, at the Plymouth Theatre. Opened April 4, 2002.

Benjamin Braddock	Jason Biggs	The Bartender;	
Mr. Braddock	Murphy Guyer	The Priest;	
Mr. Robinson	Victor Slezak	The Motel Manager	John Hillner
Mrs. Braddock	Kate Skinner	The Assistant Desk Clerk	Kelly Overton
Mrs. Robinson	Kathleen Turner	The Bellhop;	
Elaine Robinson	Alicia Silverstone	The Man in Bar	Judson Pearce Morgan
The Hotel Clerk;		The Stripper	Susan Cella
The Bar Patron;			
The Psychiatrist	Robert Emmet Lunney		

Understudies: Mses. Turner, Skinner—Susan Cella, Jurian Hughes; Mr. Biggs—Judson Pearce Morgan; Ms. Silverstone—Kelly Overton; Mr. Guyer—John Hillner, Larry Cahn; Ms. Cella—Jurian Hughes, Kelly Overton; Men—Larry Cahn; Women—Jurian Hughes.

Directed by Terry Johnson; scenery and costumes, Rob Howell; lighting, Hugh Vanstone; sound, Christopher Cronin; songs, Paul Simon, performed by Simon and Garfunkel; other music and songs, Barrington Pheloung and original artists; associate producers, Clear Channel Entertainment, StudioCanal; casting, Howard/Schecter/Meltzer; stage manager, Karen Moore; press, Barlow-Hartman Public Relations, John Barlow, Michael Hartman, Bill Coyle.

Time: 1960s. Place: California. Presented in two parts.

Coming of age story set in the angst-ridden, youth-worshipping era of the 1960s. First produced in 2000 at the Gielgud in London's West End.

*Topdog/Underdog (62). Transfer from Off Broadway of the play by Suzan-Lori Parks. Produced by Carole Shorenstein Hays, Waxman Williams Entertainment, Bob Boyett, Freddy De Mann, Susan Dietz/Ina Meibach, Scott Nederlander, Ira Pittelman, in association with Hits Magazine, Kelpie Arts, Rick Steiner/Frederic H. Mayerson, at the Ambassador Theatre. Opened April 7, 2002.

Lincoln .... Jeffrey Wright   Booth .... Mos Def

Standbys: Mr. Wright—Kevin Jackson; Mr. Def—Jeremiah W. Birkett.

Directed by George C. Wolfe; scenery, Riccardo Hernández; costumes, Emilio Sosa; lighting, Scott Zielinski; sound, Dan Moses Schreier; executive producers, Alexander Fraser, Greg Holland; casting, Jordan Thaler/Heidi Griffiths; production stage manager, Rick Steiger; press, Boneau/Bryan-Brown, Chris Boneau, Amy Jacobs, Jim Mannino, Juliana Hannett.

Time: Here. Place: Now. Presented in two parts.

A pair of African-American brothers struggle for survival and primacy in their marginal existence. Originally produced Off Broadway by the Joseph Papp Public Theater/New York Shakespeare Festival in its Anspacher Theater (7/26/2001; 45 performances). 2002 Pulitzer Prize Award in drama. A 2001–02 *Best Plays* choice (see essay by Margaret B. Wilkerson in this volume).

Sibling revelry: Mos Def and Jeffrey Wright in Topdog/Underdog. *Photo: Michal Daniel*

*The Elephant Man (54). Revival of the play by Bernard Pomerance. Produced by David Aukin for Act Productions, Waxman Williams Entertainment, Manhattan Theatre Club, Bob Boyett, Steve Martin and Joan Stein, in association with Boston Court Theatre/Eileen T'Kaye, Daniel H. Cohen, June Curtis, Hot Springs Ventures, Inc., at the Royale Theatre. Opened April 14, 2002.

Frederick Treves .... Rupert Graves   London Policeman .... Nick Toren
Carr Gomm;   Pinhead Manager;
  Belgian Policeman .... Edmond Genest   London Policeman;
Ross; Bishop Walsham How .... Jack Gilpin   Will; Lord John .... James Riordan
John Merrick .... Billy Crudup   Pinhead; Mrs. Kendal .... Kate Burton

Pinhead; Miss Sandwich;
  Duchess; Princess Alexandra ......Jenna Stern
Pinhead .... Lynn Wright

Belgian Policeman;
Conductor; Snork;
Countess .... Christopher Duva

All other parts played by the ensemble.

Understudies: Messrs. Crudup, Duva, Riordan—Nick Toren; Mr. Graves—Stevie Ray Dallimore; Ms. Burton—Jenna Stern; Messrs. Genest, Gilpin, Riordan, Toren—Joe Vincent; Ms. Stern—Lynn Wright.

Directed by Sean Mathias; scenery and costumes, Santo Loquasto; lighting, James F. Ingalls; sound, David Shapiro for ADI Group; original music, Philip Glass; projections, Michael Clark; associate producers, Ken Denison, Alexander Fraser; casting, Ilene Starger; production stage manager, Arthur Gaffin; press, Boneau/Bryan-Brown, Adrian Bryan-Brown, Susanne Tighe, Adriana Douzos.

Time: 1884–90. Place: London and Belgium. Presented without intermission. The emotional journey of a man who suffers from a congenital disfigurement that gradually snuffs out his life. Originally produced in London in 1977 by the Foco Novo and the Hampstead Theatre. A 1978–79 *Best Plays* choice, the first Broadway production opened at the Booth Theatre (4/19/1979; 916 performances), where it transferred after an Off Broadway run at the Theatre at St. Peter's Church (1/14/1979; 73 performances).

Dissed figure: Rupert Graves and Billy Crudup in The Elephant Man. *Photo: Joan Marcus*

*Thoroughly Modern Millie (50). Musical with book by Richard Morris and Dick Scanlan; new music by Jeanine Tesori; new lyrics by Dick Scanlan; based on the story and screenplay by Richard Morris for the Universal Pictures film. Produced by Michael Leavitt, Fox Theatricals, Hal Luftig, Stewart F. Lane, James L. Nederlander, Independent Presenters Network, Libby Adler Mages/Mari Glick, Dori Berinstein/Jennifer Manocherian/Dramatic Forces, John York Noble and Whoopi Goldberg at the Marquis Theatre. Opened April 18, 2002.

Millie Dillmount .... Sutton Foster   Jimmy Smith .... Gavin Creel

Ruth .... Megan Sikora
Gloria .... JoAnn M. Hunter
Rita .... Jessica Grové
Alice .... Alisa Klein
Ethel Peas .... Joyce Chittick
Cora .... Catherine Brunell
Lucille .... Kate Baldwin
Mrs. Meers .... Harriet Harris
Miss Dorothy Brown .... Angela Christian
Ching Ho .... Ken Leung
Bun Foo .... Francis Jue
Miss Flannery .... Anne L. Nathan
Mr. Trevor Graydon .... Marc Kudisch
Speed Tappists .... Casey Nicholaw,
                                                    Noah Racey
The Pearl Lady .... Roxane Barlow

The Letch .... Noah Racey
Officer .... Casey Nicholaw
Muzzy Van Hossmere .... Sheryl Lee Ralph
Kenneth .... Brandon Wardell
Mathilde .... Catherine Brunell
George Gershwin .... Noah Racey
Dorothy Parker .... Julie Connors
Rodney .... Aaron Ramey
Dishwashers .... Aldrin Gonzalez,
                                Aaron Ramey, Brandon Wardell
Muzzy's Boys .... Gregg Goodbrod,
                                Darren Lee, Dan LoBuono,
    John MacInnis, Noah Racey, T. Oliver Reid
Daphne .... Kate Baldwin
Dexter .... Casey Nicholaw
New Modern .... Jessica Grové

Ensemble: Kate Baldwin, Roxane Barlow, Catherine Brunell, Joyce Chittick, Julie Connors, David Eggers, Gregg Goodbrod, Aldrin Gonzalez, Jessica Grové, Amy Heggins, JoAnn M. Hunter, Alisa Klein, Darren Lee, Dan LoBuono, John MacInnis, Casey Nicholaw, Noah Racey, Aaron Ramey, T. Oliver Reid, Megan Sikora, Brandon Wardell.

Orchestra: Michael Rafter conductor, music director; Lawrence Goldberg associate conductor, piano; Charles Descarfino assistant conductor, percussion; Lawrence Feldman, Walt Weiskopf, Dan Willis, Allen Won woodwinds; Craig Johnson, Brian O'Flaherty, Glenn Drewes trumpet; Larry Farrell, Jeff Nelson trombone; Brad Gemeinhardt, French horn; Belinda Whitney, Eric DeGioia, Laura Oatts, Karl Kawahara, Mary Whitaker violin; Stephanie Cummins, Anik Oulianine cello; Emily Mitchell harp; Ray Kilday bass; Jack Cavari guitar; Warren Odze drums.

Standby for Mses. Ralph, Harris—Sharon Scruggs.

Understudies: Ms. Foster—Catherine Brunell, Susan Haefner; Mr. Creel—Aaron Ramey, Brandon Wardell; Ms. Christian—Kate Baldwin, Jessica Grové; Mr. Kudisch—Gregg Goodbrod, Aaron Ramey; Mr. Leung—Francis Jue, Darren Lee; Mr. Jue—JoAnn M. Hunter, Darren Lee; Ms. Nathan—Julie Connors, Susan Haefner.

Happy feet: Sutton Foster and the company of Thoroughly Modern Millie. *Photo: Joan Marcus*

Swings: Melissa Bell Chait, J.P. Christensen, Susan Haefner, Matt Lashey.

Directed by Michael Mayer; choreography, Rob Ashford; scenery, David Gallo; costumes, Martin Pakledinaz; lighting, Donald Holder; sound, Jon Weston; orchestrations, Doug Besterman and Ralph Burns; music coordination, John Miller; associate producers, Mike Isaacson, Kristin Caskey, Clear Channel Entertainment; casting, Jim Carnahan; press, Barlow-Hartman Public Relations, John Barlow, Michael Hartman, Jeremy Shaffer.

Time: 1920s. Place: New York City. Presented in two parts.

Musical based on a 1967 film about a kid from Kansas who struggles to survive amid adversity in the Big Apple. This production premiered in October 2000 at the La Jolla Playhouse in La Jolla, California. Winner of six 2002 Tony Awards including best musical, choreography, orchestrations, costumes, featured actress and leading actress. (See Awards section for details.)

ACT I

Overture .... Orchestra
Scene 1: A New York City street
   "Not for the Life of Me" .... Millie
   "Thoroughly Modern Millie" .... Millie and Ensemble
        (music by James Van Heusen, lyrics by Sammy Cahn)
Scene 2: The Hotel Priscilla lobby
   "Not for the Life of Me" (Reprise) .... Ruth, Gloria, Rita, Alice, Cora and Lucille
   "How the Other Half Lives" .... Miss Dorothy and Millie
Scene 3: The laundry room of the Priscilla
   "Not for the Life of Me (Reprise) .... Ching Ho and Bun Foo
Scene 4: The Sincere Trust Insurance Co.
   "The Speed Test" .... Mr. Graydon, Millie, Miss Flannery and Office Workers
        (music by Arthur Sullivan, lyrics by Dick Scanlan)
Scene 5: The 12th floor of the Priscilla
   "They Don't Know" .... Mrs. Meers
Scene 6: A New York City street
Scene 7: The Tie-One-On-Club
   "The Nuttycracker Suite" .... Millie, Miss Dorothy, Jimmy,
                           Gloria, Alice, Ruth and Speakeasy Patrons
        (by Jeanine Tesori, based on the music by Peter Ilych Tchaikovsky)
Scene 8: A jail
   "What Do I Need with Love?" .... Jimmy
Scene 10: Muzzy's Penthouse
"Only in New York" .... Muzzy
Scene 11: The penthouse terrace
   "Jimmy" .... Millie
      (music and lyrics by Jay Thompson, additional music by Jeanine Tesori,
                additional lyrics by Dick Scanlan)
Scene 12: The 12th floor of the Priscilla

ACT II

Entr'acte .... Orchestra
Scene 1: The Sincere Trust Insurance Co.
   "Forget About the Boy" .... Millie, Miss Flannery and Typists
   "I'm Falling in Love with Someone" .... Mr. Graydon and Miss Dorothy
        (music by Victor Herbert, lyrics by Rita Johnson Young)
Scene 2: The window ledge
   "I Turned the Corner" .... Jimmy and Millie
   "I'm Falling in Love with Someone" (Quartet) .... Millie, Jimmy,
                            Mr. Graydon and Miss Dorothy
Scene 3: The 12th floor of the Priscilla
   "Muqin" .... Mrs. Meers, Ching Ho and Bun Foo
     (music and lyrics by Sam Lewis, Joe Young and Walter Donaldson;
               additional lyrics by Dick Scanlan)

Scene 4: The floor show and kitchen at Café Society
"Long as I'm Here with You" .... Muzzy, Millie and Ensemble
Scene 5: Muzzy's dressing room at Café Society
"Gimme Gimme" .... Millie
Scene 6: The dining room at Café Society,
Scene 7: The Hotel Priscilla lobby
Scene 8: The laundry room of the Priscilla
"The Speed Test" (Reprise) .... Millie, Mr. Graydon, Jimmy and Muzzy
Finale: "Thoroughly Modern Millie" .... Jimmy, Miss Dorothy and Moderns

Sisters' 'hood: Estelle Parsons, Elizabeth Franz, Frances Sternhagen and Piper Laurie in Morning's at Seven. *Photo: Joan Marcus*

*Lincoln Center Theater production of ***Morning's at Seven** (46). Revival of the play by Paul Osborn. André Bishop artistic director, Bernard Gersten executive producer, at the Lyceum Theatre. Opened April 21, 2002.

In the house at the left:
Theodore Swanson .... William Biff McGuire
Cora Swanson .... Estelle Parsons
Aaronetta Gibbs .... Elizabeth Franz

In the house at the right:
Ida Bolton .... Frances Sternhagen

Carl Bolton .... Christopher Lloyd
Homer Bolton .... Stephen Tobolowsky
Others:
Myrtle Brown .... Julie Hagerty
Esther Crampton .... Piper Laurie
David Crampton .... Buck Henry

Cora, Aaronetta, Ida and Esther are sisters.

Understudies: Mses. Sternhagen, Franz—Barbara Caruso; Messrs. Henry, McGuire, Lloyd—Jack Davidson; Mses. Laurie, Parsons—Rita Gardner; Ms. Hagerty—Linda Marie Larson; Messrs. Tobolowsky, Lloyd—David Manis.

Directed by Daniel Sullivan; scenery John Lee Beatty; costumes, Jane Greenwood; lighting, Brian MacDevitt; sound, Scott Myers; casting, Daniel Swee; press, Philip Rinaldi, Barbara Carroll.

Time: 1938. Place: Two backyards in a small Midwestern town. Presented in two parts.

Revival of a gentle comedy of midwestern manners and mores, with parts for nine mature actors. A 1939–40 *Best Plays* choice, the original Broadway production opened at the Longacre Theatre (11/30/1939; 44 performances). A 1980 revival at the same theater as the current production, earned Tony Awards for best revival and best director (Vivian Matalon).

The Mystery of Charles Dickens (20). By Peter Ackroyd. Produced by Ambassador Theatre Group, Act Productions and Pre-Eminence Ltd. at the Belasco Theater. Opened April 25, 2002. (Closed May 12, 2002)

Performed by Simon Callow.

Directed by Patrick Garland; scenery and costumes, Christopher Woods; lighting, Nick Richings; production stage manager, Frank Hartenstein; press, Boneau/Bryan-Brown, Adrian Bryan-Brown, Susanne Tighe, Karalee Dawn.

Presented in two parts.

A discourse on the life and times of Charles Dickens in his own words and the words of his characters.

The Dickens: Simon Callow in The Mystery of Charles Dickens. *Photo: Joan Marcus*

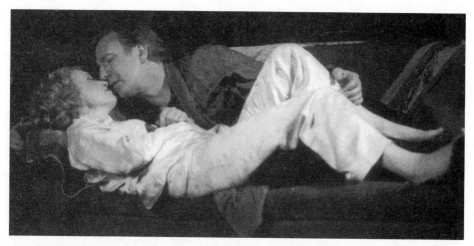

Privacy, please: Lindsay Duncan and Alan Rickman in Private Lives. *Photo: Joan Marcus*

*Private Lives (34). Revival of the play by Noël Coward. Produced by Emanuel Azenberg, Ira Pittelman, Scott Nederlander, Frederick Zollo, Nicholas Paleologos, Dana Broccoli/ Jeffrey Sine, James Nederlander, Kevin McCollum, Jeffrey Seller, and Duncan C. Weldon and Paul Elliott for Triumph Entertainment Partners, Ltd., at the Richard Rodgers Theatre. Opened April 28, 2002.

Sibyl	Emma Fielding	Amanda	Lindsay Duncan
Elyot	Alan Rickman	Louise	Alex Belcourt
Victor	Adam Godley		

Directed by Howard Davies; scenery, Tim Hatley; costumes, Jenny Beavan; lighting, Peter Mumford; sound, John A. Leonard; music, Paddy Cunneen; fight coordinator, Terry King; associate producer, Ginger Montel; production stage manager, Bonnie Panson; press, Bill Evans and Associates, Bill Evans, Jim Randolph.

Time: 1930s. Place: A hotel terrace in France and Amanda's flat in Paris. Presented in two parts.

When an acerbic divorced couple discover the flames of love for one another still burn hotly— even as they honeymoon with new mates—verbal and sexual fireworks ensue. The current production received three Tony Awards including best revival of a play, leading actress, and scenic design. First produced in New York at the Times Square Theatre (1/27/1931; 256 performances). Noël Coward, Gertrude Lawrence, Laurence Olivier and Jill Esmond starred.

*Into the Woods (37). Revival of the musical with book by James Lapine; music and lyrics by Stephen Sondheim. Produced by Dodger Theatricals, Stage Holding/Joop van den Ende and TheaterDreams, Inc. at the Broadhurst Theatre. Opened April 30, 2002.

Narrator	John McMartin	Cinderella's Father	Dennis Kelly
Cinderella	Laura Benanti	Mysterious Man	John McMartin
Jack	Adam Wylie	Wolves	Gregg Edelman,
Milky-White	Chad Kimball		Christopher Sieber
Baker	Stephen DeRosa	Rapunzel	Melissa Dye
Baker's Wife	Kerry O'Malley	Rapunzel's Prince	Christopher Sieber
Cinderella's Stepmother	Pamela Myers	Granny	Pamela Myers
Florinda	Tracy Nicole Chapman	Cinderella's Prince	Gregg Edelman
Jack's Mother	Marylouise Burke	Steward	Trent Armand Kendall
Little Red Ridinghood	Molly Ephraim	Horse	Jennifer Malenke
Witch	Vanessa Williams		

Cow eyes: Chad Kimball (in cow costume) and Adam Wylie in Into the Woods. *Photo: Joan Marcus*

Orchestra: Paul Gemignani conductor; Annbritt duChateau associate conductor, keyboard 1; Mark Mitchell assistant conductor, keyboard 2; Marilyn Reynolds concertmaster, violin 1; Mineko Yajima violin 2; Richard Brice viola 1; Shelley Holland-Moritz viola 2; Deborah Assael cello; John Beal bass; Les Scott flute; Amy Zoloto clarinet; John Campo bassoon; Ron Sell, French horn 1; Nancy Billman, French horn 2; Dominic Derasse trumpet; Paul Pizutti percussion.

Understudies: Mr. McMartin—Stephen Berger, Dennis Kelly; Ms. Benanti—Melissa Dye, Kate Reinders; Mr. Wylie—Adam Brazier, Chad Kimball; Mr. Kimball—Jennifer Malenke, Kate Reinders; Mr. DeRosa—Stephen Berger, Trent Armand Kendall; Ms. O'Malley—Linda Mugleston, Amanda Naughton; Ms. Myers—Linda Mugleston; Ms. Chapman—Jennifer Malenke; Ms. Burke—Linda Mugleston, Pamela Myers; Ms. Ephraim—Melissa Dye, Kate Reinders; Ms. Williams—Tracy Nicole Chapman, Linda Mugleston; Mr. Kelly—Stephen Berger, Trent Armand Kendall; Ms. Dye—Jennifer Malenke, Kate Reinders; Mr.Edelman—Adam Brazier, Christopher Sieber; Mr. Sieber—Adam Brazier, Chad Kimball; Mr. Kendall—Stephen Berger, Adam Brazier; Ms. Malenke—Adam Brazier.

Directed by Mr. Lapine; choreography, John Carrafa; scenery, Douglas W. Schmidt; costumes, Susan Hilferty; lighting, Brian MacDevitt; sound, Dan Moses Schreier; projections, Elaine J. McCarthy; special effects, Gregory Meeh; illusion, Jim Steinmeyer; fight direction, Rick Sordelet; orchestrations, Jonathan Tunick; music direction, Mr. Gemignani; executive producer, Dodger Management Group, associate producer, Lauren Mitchell; casting, Jim Carnahan, press, Boneau/Bryan-Brown, Adrian Bryan-Brown, Amy Jacobs, Susanne Tighe, Juliana Hannett.

Time: Once upon a time. Place: A far-off kingdom. Presented in two parts.

Classic fairy tales brought to musical life before crossing into the dark side of happily ever after. 2002 Tony Award for best musical revival. This production originally presented at the Ahmanson Theatre, Los Angeles, California. A 1987–88 *Best Plays* choice, the original Broadway production opened at the Martin Beck Theatre (11/5/1987; 765 performances).

ACT I

Prologue: "Into the Woods"	Company
"Hello, Little Girl"	Wolves, Little Red Ridinghood
"I Guess This Is Goodbye"	Jack
"Maybe They're Magic"	Baker's Wife
"Our Little World"	Witch, Rapunzel

"I Know Things Now"	Little Red Ridinghood
"A Very Nice Prince"	Cinderella, Baker's Wife
"Giants in the Sky"	Jack
"Agony"	Cinderella's Prince, Rapunzel's Prince
"It Takes Two"	Baker, Baker's Wife
"Stay With Me"	Witch
"On the Steps of the Palace"	Cinderella
"Ever After"	Narrator, Company

ACT II

Prologue: "So Happy"	Company
"Agony"	Cinderella's Prince, Rapunzel's Prince
"Lament"	Witch
"Any Moment"	Cinderella's Prince, Baker's Wife
"Moments in the Woods"	Baker's Wife
"Your Fault"	Jack, Baker, Witch, Cinderella, Little Red Ridinghood
"Last Midnight"	Witch
"No More"	Baker, Mysterious Man
"No One Is Alone"	Cinderella, Little Red Ridinghood, Baker, Jack
Finale: "Children Will Listen"	Witch, Company

Oh, lucky man: James Rebhorn, Mason Adams, Chris O'Donnell, Samantha Mathis and Richard Riehle in The Man Who Had All the Luck. *Photo: Joan Marcus*

*Roundabout Theatre Company production of **The Man Who Had All the Luck** (35). Revival of the play by Arthur Miller. Todd Haimes artistic director, Ellen Richard managing director, Julia C. Levy executive director of external affairs, at the American Airlines Theatre. Opened May 1, 2002.

David Beeves	Chris O'Donnell	Aunt Belle	Mary Catherine Wright
J.B. Feller	Richard Riehle	Pat Beeves	James Rebhorn
Shory	Dan Moran	Amos Beeves	Ryan Shively

Hester Falk	Samantha Mathis	Gustav Eberson	Sam Robards
Dan Dibble	Mason Adams	Augie Belfast	David Wohl
Andrew Falk	Edward James Hyland		

Understudies: Mr. O'Donnell—Ryan Shively; Mr. Rebhorn—Edward James Hyland; Messrs. Shively, O'Donnell—Will Bozarth; Messrs. Adams, Hyland, Riehle—Philip LeStrange; Messrs. Wohl, Moran, Robards—Blake Robbins; Mses. Mathis, Wright—Catherine Wadkins.

Directed by Scott Ellis; scenery, Allen Moyer; costumes, Michael Krass; lighting, Kenneth Posner; sound, Eileen Tague; fight direction, Rick Sordelet; original music, Tom Kochan; casting, Amy Christopher; production stage manager, Andrea J. Testani; stage manager, Brendan Smith; press, Boneau/Bryan-Brown, Adrian Bryan-Brown, Matt Polk, Amy Dinnerman.

Time: Several years in the late 1930s. Place: Midwest. Presented in three parts.

A man who feels that he has had more than his share of blessings struggles to understand why. The current production was first presented at the Williamstown Theatre Festival in July 2001. First produced in New York at the Forrest Theatre (11/23/1944; 4 perfomances).

PLAYS PRODUCED OFF BROADWAY

○ ○ ○ ○ ○

For the purposes of *Best Plays* listing, the term "Off Broadway" signifies a show that opened for general audiences in a mid-Manhattan theater seating 499 or fewer and 1) employed an Equity cast, 2) planned a regular schedule of 8 performances a week in an open-ended run (7 a week for solo shows and some other exceptions) and 3) offered itself to public comment by critics after a designated opening performance.

Figures in parentheses following a play's title give number of performances. These numbers do not include previews or extra non-profit performances. For the current edition, these numbers also take into account closings and reopenings of shows affected by the terrorist attacks of September 11, 2001. Most performance interruptions occurred the week of the attacks—usually affecting two or three performances—although a few productions took longer breaks.

Plays marked with an asterisk (*) were still in a projected run on June 1, 2002. The number of performances is figured from press opening through May 31, 2002.

In a listing of a show's numbers—dances, sketches, musical scenes, etc.— the titles of songs are identified wherever possible by their appearance in quotation marks (").

HOLDOVERS FROM PREVIOUS SEASONS

OFF BROADWAY SHOWS that were running on June 1, 2001 are listed below. More detailed information about them appears in previous *Best Plays* volumes of appropriate date. Important cast changes since opening night are recorded in the Cast Replacements section of this volume.

The Fantasticks (17,162; longest continuous run of record in the American theater). Musical suggested by the play *Les Romanesques* by Edmond Rostand; book and lyrics by Tom Jones; music by Harvey Schmidt. Opened May 3, 1960. (Closed January 13, 2002)

*Perfect Crime** (6,254). By Warren Manzi. Opened October 16, 1987.

*Tony 'n' Tina's Wedding** (4,654). By Artificial Intelligence. Opened February 6, 1988.

*Blue Man Group (Tubes)** (5,212). Performance piece by and with Blue Man Group. Opened November 17, 1991.

*Stomp** (3,464). Percussion performance piece created by Luke Cresswell and Steve McNicholas. Opened February 27, 1994.

191

*I Love You, You're Perfect, Now Change (2,448). Musical revue with book and lyrics by Joe DiPietro; music by Jimmy Roberts. Opened August 1, 1996.

*Late Nite Catechism (1,115). By Vicki Quade and Maripat Donovan. Opened October 3, 1996.

*De La Guarda (1,549). Spectacle devised by De La Guarda (Pichon Baldinu, Diqui James, Gabriel Kerpel, Fabio D'Aquila, Tomas James, Alejandro Garcia, Gabriella Baldini). Opened June 16, 1998.

*Naked Boys Singing! (1,206). Musical revue conceived by Robert Schrock; written by various authors. Opened July 22, 1999.

*The Donkey Show (862). Musical conceived and created by Randy Weiner and Diane Paulus; adapted from William Shakespeare's *A Midsummer Night's Dream*. Opened August 12, 1999.

*The Vagina Monologues (1,105). By Eve Ensler. Opened October 3, 1999.

*Our Sinatra (1,037). Musical revue conceived by Eric Comstock, Christopher Gines and Hilary Kole; music and lyrics by various authors. Opened December 19, 1999.

*The Syringa Tree (583). By Pamela Gien. Opened September 14, 2000.

Maybe Baby, It's You (163). By Charlie Shanian and Shari Simpson. Opened November 9, 2000. (Closed June 30, 2001)

Forbidden Broadway 2001: A Spoof Odyssey (552). Musical revue created and written by Gerard Alessandrini. Opened November 18, 2000. (Closed February 6, 2002)

The Play About the Baby (245). By Edward Albee. Opened February 2, 2001. (Closed September 1, 2001)

Bat Boy: The Musical (260). Musical with story and book by Keythe Farley and Brian Flemming; music and lyrics by Laurence O'Keefe; licensed under agreement with *Weekly World News*. Opened March 21, 2001. (Closed December 2, 2001)

*Love, Janis (457). Musical based on the book by Laura Joplin; adapted and directed by Randal Myler. Opened April 22, 2001.

Uncle Bob (80). Revival of the play by Austin Pendleton. Opened April 23, 2001. (Closed July 1, 2001)

Madame Melville (61). By Richard Nelson. Opened May 3, 2001. (Closed June 24, 2001)

Urinetown (58). Musical with book and lyrics by Greg Kotis; music and lyrics by Mark Hollmann. Opened May 6, 2001. (Closed June 25, 2001)

Lobby Hero (136). Transfer of the play by Kenneth Lonergan. Opened May 8, 2001. (Closed September 2, 2001)

Six Goumbas and a Wannabe (241). By Vincent M. Gogliormella. Opened May 10, 2001. (Closed December 9, 2001)

New York Theatre Workshop production of **Nocturne** (38). By Adam Rapp. Opened May 16, 2001. (Closed June 17, 2001)

Manhattan Theatre Club production of **Blur** (46). By Melanie Marnich. Opened May 17, 2001. (Closed June 24, 2001)

Manhattan Theatre Club production of **Glimmer, Glimmer and Shine** (54). By Warren Leight. Opened May 24, 2001. (Closed July 8, 2001)

Brooklyn Academy of Music presentation of a **Royal National Theatre** production of **Hamlet** (5). Revival of the play by William Shakespeare. Opened May 30, 2000. (Closed June 2, 2001)

PLAYS PRODUCED JUNE 1, 2001–MAY 31, 2002

The Woman in Black (40). By Stephen Mallatratt; adapted from the novel by Susan Hill. Produced by Don Gregory at the Minetta Lane Theatre. Opened June 4, 2001. (Closed July 8, 2001)

Arthur Kipps .... Keith Baxter   The Actor .... Jared Reed

Directed by Patrick Garland; scenery, James Noone; costumes, Noel Taylor; lighting, Ken Billington and Brian P. Monahan; sound, Christopher Walker; production stage manager, J.P. Elins; press, Bill Evans.

Presented in two parts.

An actor tries to help a lawyer exorcise a ghostly female presence in a play within the play. A London production had been running for more than 12 years when the New York production opened.

Eat the Runt (125). By Avery Crozier. Produced by Matthew von Waaden, Weil Richmond and Matthew Richmond at the American Place Theatre. Opened June 5, 2001. (Closed October 7, 2001)

CAST: Kelli K. Barnett, Linda Cameron, LaKeith Hoskin, Weil Richmond, Thom Rivera, Keesha Sharp, Curtis Mark Williams, Jama Williamson.

Understudies—Andrew Robbins, Joy Styles.

Directed by Matthew von Waaden; scenery, Jerome Martin; costumes, Courtney McClain; lighting, Michele Disco; music and sound design, Timothy Cramer; associate producer, Margaret Perry; production stage manager, Adam Crosswirth; press, Patt Dale.

Time: The present. Place: In an art museum. Presented in two parts.

Office politics, sexual desires and other complications come into play when someone interviews for a job at a museum. The audience chose which actor played which role.

Con artist: Lee Pace and Annie Parisse in The Credeaux Canvas. *Photo: Joan Marcus*

Playwrights Horizons production of **The Credeaux Canvas** (16). By Keith Bunin. Tim Sanford artistic director, Leslie Marcus managing director, William Russo general manager. Opened June 5, 2001. (Closed June 17, 2001)

Amelia	Annie Parisse	Jamie	Glenn Howerton
Winston	Lee Pace	Tess	E. Katherine Kerr

Directed by Michael Mayer; scenery, Derek McLane; costumes, Michael Krass; lighting, Kenneth Posner; sound, Scott Myers; fight direction, J. Steven White; casting, James Calleri; production stage manager, J. Philip Bassett; press, Publicity Office, Bob Fennell, Marc Thibodeau, Michael S. Borowski, Candi Adams.

Time: The present. Place: An attic apartment on East 10th Street in New York City. Presented in two parts.

A tale of emotional betrayal and artistic corruption among the disaffected twentysomething set.

Lincoln Center Theater production of **Chaucer in Rome** (61). By John Guare. André Bishop artistic director, Bernard Gersten executive producer, at the Mitzi E. Newhouse. Opened June 7, 2001. (Closed July 29, 2001)

Matt	Jon Tenney	Renzo	Ümit Çelebi
Sarah	Carrie Preston	Dolo	Polly Holliday
Pete	Bruce Norris	Ron	Dick Latessa
Il Dottore; Father Shapiro;		Pilgrims; Fellows	Ümit Çelebi, Susan Finch,
Joe; Charlie	Lee Wilkof		Mark Fish, Nancy McDoniel,
Il Tassinaro	Antonio Edwards Suarez		Tim McGeever, Antonio Edwards Suarez

Understudies: Mr. Tenney—Baylen Thomas; Ms. Preston—Claire Lautier; Messrs. Norris, Wilkof (Joe), Suarez—Tim McGeever; Messrs. Latessa, Wilkof (Father Shapiro, Charlie)—Bill Cwikowski; Ms. Holiday—Nancy McDoniel; Mr. Wilkof (Il Dottore)—Ümit Çelebi; Mr. Çelebi—Antonio Edwards Suarez; (Pilgrim, Fellow)—Claire Lautier, Baylen Thomas, Bill Cwikowski.

Directed by Nicholas Martin; scenery, Alexander Dodge; costumes, Michael Krass; lighting, Donald Holder; original music and sound, Mark Bennett; casting, Daniel Swee and Amy Christopher; stage manager, Michael Brunner; press, Philip Rinaldi, Brian Rubin.

Time: 2000. Place: Rome. Presented without intermission.

Comedy about expatriate American artists and frenzied religious pilgrims who seek authentic communion in millennial Rome. First presented 7/28/1999 by Williamstown Theatre Festival in Massachusetts.

Playwrights Horizons production of **Breath, Boom** (25). By Kia Corthron. Tim Sanford artistic director, Leslie Marcus managing director, in the Studio Theater. Opened June 10, 2001. (Closed July 1, 2001)

Jerome	Russell Andrews	Cat; Girl with Pepper;	
Jupiter	Pascale Armand	Jo's Friend	Donna Duplantier
Shondra; Pepper; Jo	Dena Atlantic	Prix	Yvette Ganier
Malika; Socks	Kalimi A. Baxter	Fuego; Denise	Abigail López
Mother	Caroline S. Clay	Comet	Heather Alicia Simms
Angel	Rosalyn Coleman		

Directed by Marion McClinton; scenery and lighting, Michael Philippi; costumes, Katherine Roth; sound, Ken Travis; fight direction, David Leong; casting, James Calleri; production stage manager, Jane Pole; press, Publicity Office, Bob Fennell, Marc Thibodeau, Michael S. Borowski, Candi Adams.

Presented in two parts.

Drama about girl gangsters and how they survive on the margins of society and within the criminal justice system. A 2001–02 *Best Plays* choice (see essay by Michael Feingold in this volume).

Ticking away: Jerry Dixon, Raúl Esparza and Amy Spanger in Tick, Tick . . . Boom! *Photo: Joan Marcus*

Tick, Tick . . . Boom! (215). Book, music and lyrics by Jonathan Larson. Produced by Victoria Leacock, Robyn Goodman, Dede Harris, Lorie Cowen Levy and Beth Smith, at the Jane Street Theatre. Opened June 13, 2001. (Closed January 6, 2002)

Jonathan	Raúl Esparza	Michael	Jerry Dixon
Susan; Karessa	Amy Spanger		

Orchestra: Stephen Oremus conductor, keyboard; Matt Beck guitar; Konrad Adderly bass; Craddock Clayton drums.

Understudies: Messrs. Esparza, Dixon—Charlie Pollock; Ms. Spanger—Nicole Bradin.

Directed by Scott Schwartz; choreography, Christopher Gattelli; scenery, Anna Louizos; costumes, David Zinn; lighting, Kenneth Posner; sound, Jon Weston; musical director, orchestrator and arranger, Stephen Oremus; script consultant, David Auburn; associate producers, Ruth and Stephen Hendel, Stephen Semlitz and Cathy Glaser; casting, David Caparelliotis; production stage manager, Ed Fitzgerald; press, Richard Kornberg and Associates, Richard Kornberg, Don Summa.

Time: 1990. Place: The edge of Soho. Presented without intermission.

Musical revue stitched together by Mr. Auburn from solo shows performed by Mr. Larson himself.

MUSICAL NUMBERS

"30/90"	Jonathan
"Green Green Dress"	Jonathan, Susan
"Johnny Can't Decide"	Jonathan, Susan, Michael
"Sunday"	Jonathan, Diner Patrons
"No More"	Michael, Jonathan
"Therapy"	Jonathan, Susan
"Play Game"	Jonathan
"Real Life"	Michael
"Sugar"	Jonathan, Karessa, Counter Guy
"See Her Smile"	Jonathan, Susan, Michael
"Come To Your Senses"	Karessa
"Why"	Jonathan
"30/90" (Reprise)	Jonathan
"Louder Than Words"	Jonathan, Michael, Susan

Power players: Billy Crudup and Joe Morton in Measure for Measure. *Photo: Michal Daniel*

The Joseph Papp Public Theater/New York Shakespeare Festival production of **Measure for Measure** (10). Revival of the play by William Shakespeare. George C. Wolfe producer, Fran Reiter executive director, Rosemarie Tichler artistic producer, at the Delacorte Theater. Opened June 17, 2001. (Closed June 28, 2001)

Vincentio .... Joe Morton	Friar Peter .... Robert Colston
Escalus .... Herb Foster	Isabella .... Sanaa Lathan
Angelo .... Billy Crudup	Elbow .... Tom Aulino
Lucio .... John Pankow	Froth .... Daniel Pearce
Gentlemen .... Darren Pettie,	Justice; Barnardine .... Traber Burns
Victor Quinaz, Eric Alperin	Boy .... Dennis Michael Hall
Mistress Overdone;	Mariana .... Felicity Jones
Francisca .... Julia Gibson	Abhorson .... Glenn Fleshler
Pompey .... Christopher Evan Welch	Ensemble .... Eric Alperin, Gregory Bratman,
Claudio .... Daniel Pino	Bryan Cogman, Sanjit De Silva,
Juliet .... Cote de Pablo	Dale Ho, Nicole Lowrance,
Provost .... Christopher Donahue	Jenn Perkins, John Livingston Rolle

Directed by Mary Zimmerman; scenery, Daniel Ostling; costumes, Mara Blumenfeld; lighting, T.J. Gerckens; sound, Acme Sound Partners; original music, Michael Bodeen; production stage manager, Charles Means; press, Carol R. Fineman, Tom Naro.

Presented in two parts.

Dark drama about the corrupting effects of lust and power. First New York presentation of record was given 3/27/1818 at the Park Theatre.

Brooklyn Academy of Music presentation of **The Ghost Sonata** (5). Revival of the play by August Strindberg. Bruce C. Ratner chairman of the board, Karen Brooks Hopkins president, Joseph V. Melillo executive producer, at the BAM Harvey Theater. Opened June 20, 2001. (Closed June 24, 2001)

The Old Man	Jan Malmsjö	Johansson	Örjan Ramberg
The Student	Jonas Malmsjö	Bengtsson	Ingvar Kjellson
The Milkmaid	Virpi Pahkinen	Posh Man	Anders Beckman
The Doorman's Wife	Gertrud Mariano	The Cook	Margareta Hallin
The Dead Man	Nils Eklund	The Fiancee	Margreth Weivers-Norström
The Dark Lady	Gerthi Kulle	Ensemble	Maria Alm-Norell,
The Young Lady	Elin Klinga		Sven-Erik Eriksson, Carl-Lennart Fröbergh,
The Colonel	Per Myrberg		Per Hedefalk, Henrik Sjögren, Ulf Strandberg
Mummy	Gunnel Lindblom		

Directed by Ingmar Bergman; choreography, Virpi Pahkinen; scenery, Göran Wassberg; costumes, Anna Bergman; lighting, Pierre Leveau; stage manager, Tomas Wennerberg; press, Elena Park, Melissa Cusick, Fateema Jones, Tamara McCaw, Kila Packett.

Mummy's curse: Gunnel Lindblom and Jan Malmsjö in The Ghost Sonata. *Photo: Bengt Wanselius*

Presented with no intermission.

Drama about the debilitating corruptions that lie beneath the surface lives of the bourgeoisie. Performed in Swedish with simultaneous English translation. First New York production of record was given 1/5/1924 at the Provincetown Playhouse as *The Spook Sonata* and was presented by Kenneth Macgowan, Robert Edmond Jones and Eugene O'Neill.

World of Mirth (45). By Murphy Guyer. Produced by Amy Danis and Mars Theatricals, Inc. at Theatre Four. Opened June 21, 2001. (Closed July 29, 2001)

Sweeney	Mark Johannes	Patch	Jack Willis
Buffy Starr	Deirdre O'Connell	Ken Harley	John Elsen
Emmett	George Bartenieff	Kaspar Kelly	Victor Slezak
Augie	Kieran Campion	Marcey	Angela Gots

Directed by Dona D. Vaughn; scenery, Michael Brown; costumes, Tracy Christensen; lighting, James Vermeulen; sound, Bruce Ellman; fight director, B.H. Barry; production stage manager, Matthew Lacey; press, Cromarty and Company, Peter Cromarty, Alice Cromarty.

Drama about the dark undercurrents of life as viewed through the eyes of a clown in a carnival.

Quartett (5). By Heiner Muller; translated by Marc von Henning. Produced by RPN Globe at the BAM Harvey Theater. Opened June 28, 2001. (Closed July 1, 2001)

CAST: Daniel McDonald, Chandler Vinton, Omar Metwally and Suzanne Packer.

Directed by Gabriella Maione; scenery, Jean Paul Chambas; costumes, Catherine Zuber; lighting, Robert Wierzel; sound, Peter Cerone and Michael Galasso; music, Mr. Galasso; dramaturg, Arthur Holmberg; production stage manager, James Mountcastle; press, Barlow-Hartman Public Relations, Joe Perrotta.

Presented without intermission.

Bemused and bewitched: Phylicia Rashad, Messeret Stroman and Michael McElroy in Blue. *Photo: Joan Marcus*

Mr. Muller's 1980 free adaptation of *Les Liaisons Dangereuses* presented amid a flood of visual images.

Roundabout Theatre Company production of **Blue** (98). By Charles Randolph-Wright. Todd Haimes artistic director, Ellen Richard managing director, Julia C. Levy executive director of external affairs, at the Gramercy Theatre. Opened June 28, 2001. (Closed September 23, 2001)

Reuben Clark (adult) .... Hill Harper	Sam Clark III .... Howard W. Overshown
Reuben Clark (young);	LaTonya Dinkins .... Messeret Stroman
Blue Williams Jr. .... Chad Tucker	Samuel Clark Jr. .... Randall Shepperd
Peggy Clark .... Phylicia Rashad	Tillie Clark .... Jewell Robinson
Blue Williams .... Michael McElroy	

Standbys: Mses. Rashad, Robinson—Elizabeth Van Dyke; Messrs. Harper, Overshown, Shepperd—Robert Tyree; Ms. Stroman—Jennifer Hunter.

Directed by Sheldon Epps; scenery, James Leonard Joy; costumes, Debra Bauer; lighting, Michael Gilliam; sound, Kurt Eric Fischer; music, Nona Hendryx; lyrics, Ms. Hendryx, Mr. Randolph-Wright; casting, Jeremy Rich and Pat McCorkle; production stage manager, Jay Adler; press, Boneau/Bryan-Brown, Adrian Bryan-Brown, Matt Polk, Jackie Green, Karalee Dawn, Cindy Valk.

Time: The late 1970s; 15 years later; a few years later. Place: Kent, South Carolina. Presented in two parts.

Family drama with music about the struggles within an upper-middle-class African-American family.

Second Stage Theatre production of **Once Around the City** (16). Musical with book and lyrics by Willie Reale; music by Robert Reale. Carole Rothman artistic director, Mark Linn-Baker 2001 artistic director, Carol Fishman managing director, Alexander Fraser executive director, in association with Ron Kastner and Robert Boyett. Opened July 10, 2001. (Closed July 22, 2001)

Charlie; Brandebaine .... William Parry	Rudy .... Michael Potts
Phyllis; Eve .... Anna Stone	Hank .... Geoffrey Nauffts
Luis .... Peter Jay Fernandez	Margaret; Dolores.................... Anne Torsiglieri
John .... Patrick Garner	Bill .... Michael Mandell
Mario .... Joe Grifasi	David .... Michael Magee
Elizabeth .... Brandy Zarle	Gwen .... Jane Bodle
Nicky .... Harry Althaus	Mrs. Merkin .... Sandra Shipley
Ernie .... John Bowman	

Directed by Mark Linn-Baker; choreography, Jennifer Muller; scenery, Adrianne Lobel; costumes, Paul Tazewell; lighting, Donald Holder; sound, Jon Weston; music direction and orchestrations, Rick Fox; music coordinator, Seymour Red Press; production stage manager, Alexander Lyu Volckhausen; stage manager, Megan Schneid; press, Richard Kornberg and Associates, Richard Kornberg, Tom D'Ambrosio.

Presented in two parts.

Musical about a good-hearted heiress cheated out of her home, where she shelters homeless men, and how her problem is resolved.

Saint Lucy's Eyes (45). By Bridgette A. Wimberly. Produced by Angelina Fiordellisi and Cherry Lane Theatre Company, in association with Women's Project and Productions, at the Cherry Lane. Opened July 26, 2001. (Closed September 2, 2001)

Grandma .... Ruby Dee	Bay .... Willis Burks II
Young Woman .... Toks Olagundoye	Woman .... Sally A. Stewart

Directed by Billie Allen; scenery, Beowulf Boritt; costumes, Alvin B. Perry; lighting, Jane Reisman; music and sound, Michael Wimberly; stage manager, John Handy; Springer/Chicoine Public Relations, Susan Chicoine, Joe Trentacosta.

Presented in two parts.

A woman who performs illegal abortions struggles to survive as times change around her. Originally produced Off Off Broadway 4/5/2001 by Women's Project and Productions.

New York Theatre Workshop production of **Slanguage** (16). By Universes (Gamal Abdel Chasten, Lemon, Flaco Navaja, Mildred Ruiz and Steven Sapp). James C. Nicola artistic director, Lynn Moffat managing director. Opened July 23, 2001. (Closed August 5, 2001)

Featuring Universes (Gamal Abdel Chasten, Lemon, Flaco Navaja, Mildred Ruiz and Steven Sapp).

Directed by Jo Bonney; scenery, Scott Pask; lighting, James Vermeulen; sound, Darron L. West; projections, Batwin and Robin Productions; production stage manager, Katherine Lee Boyer.

Presented without intermission.

Poetry slam meets performance art when language of the streets is celebrated in a stream of brief scenes.

Grace's comin': Jeffrey Wright and Don Cheadle in the Off Broadway production of Topdog/Underdog. *Photo: Michal Daniel*

The Joseph Papp Public Theater/New York Shakespeare Festival production of **Topdog/Underdog** (45). By Suzan-Lori Parks. George C. Wolfe producer; Fran Reiter executive director, in the Anspacher Theater. Opened July 26, 2001. (Closed September 2, 2001)

Booth .... Don Cheadle   Lincoln .... Jeffrey Wright

Directed by George C. Wolfe; scenery, Riccardo Hernández; costumes, Emilio Sosa; lighting, Scott Zielinski; sound, Dan Moses Schreier; associate producers, Bonnie Metzgar, John Dias; casting, Jordan Thaler, Heidi Griffiths; production stage manager, Rick Steiger; press, Carol R. Fineman, Tom Naro, Kris Diaz.

Time: Now. Place: Here. Presented in two parts.

A pair of African-American brothers struggle for survival and primacy in their marginal existence. Transferred to Broadway's Ambassador Theatre 4/7/2002 (see Plays Produced on Broadway section). Winner of the 2002 Pulitzer Prize in Drama. A 2001–02 *Best Plays* choice (see essay by Margaret B. Wilkerson in this volume).

Hello Muddah, Hello Fadduh! (124). Revival of the musical revue by Doug Bernstein and Rob Krausz; music and lyrics by Allan Sherman. Produced by Jennifer Dumas and Jack Cullen at the Triad Theater. Opened August 2, 2001. (Closed November 18, 2001)

Harvey	Larry Cahn	Sheila	Kristie Dale Sanders
Sarah	Leslie Lorusso	Phil	Jimmy Spadola
Barry	Kevin Pariseau		

Directed by Mr. Krausz; scenery, William Barclay; costumes, Michael Louis; lighting, Phil Monat; production stage manager, Jason Cohen; press, Keith Sherman and Associates, Miller Wright.

Presented in two parts.

Revival of the musical revue that uses Mr. Sherman's novelty songs to tell the life stories of a couple in Florida retirement. Originally opened Off Broadway 12/5/1992 at Circle in the Square Downtown for 235 performances.

The Joseph Papp Public Theater/New York Shakespeare Festival production of **The Seagull** (13). Revival of the play by Anton Chekhov; adapted by Tom Stoppard. George C. Wolfe producer, Fran Reiter executive director, Rosemarie Tichler artistic producer, at the Delacorte Theater. Opened August 12, 2001. (Closed August 26, 2001)

Arkadina	Meryl Streep	Polina	Debra Monk
Trigorin	Kevin Kline	Dorn	Larry Pine
Sorin	Christopher Walken	Shamrayev	John Goodman
Nina	Natalie Portman	Yakov	Henry Gummer
Konstantin	Philip Seymour Hoffman	Servants	Morena Baccarin,
Medvedenko	Stephen Spinella		Vitali Baganov, Craig Bockhorn,
Masha	Marcia Gay Harden		Mark H. Dold, Sharon Scruggs

Directed by Mike Nichols; scenery and costumes, Bob Crowley; lighting, Jennifer Tipton; sound, Acme Sound Partners; music, Mark Bennett; production stage manager, Peter Lawrence; press, Carol R. Fineman, Tom Naro.

Time: 19th century. Place: Russia. Presented in two parts.

A new version of the 1896 play by Mr. Chekhov featuring a starry cast of actors. The first New York presentation of record was given 5/20/1916 by the Washington Square Players at the Bandbox Theatre.

Passion rookies: Jennifer Hall, Frederick Neumann and Ruth Maleczech in First Love. *Photo: Joan Marcus*

New York Theatre Workshop production of **First Love** (26). By Charles L. Mee. James C. Nicola artistic director, Lynn Moffat managing director. Opened September 9, 2001. (Closed September 30, 2001)

Harold .... Frederick Neumann   Melody ....Jennifer Hall
Edith .... Ruth Maleczech

Directed by Erin B. Mee; scenery, Klara Zieglerova; costumes, Christine Jones; lighting, Christopher Akerlind; sound, Bo Bell; production stage manager, Judith Schoenfeld; press, Richard Kornberg and Associates, Don Summa.

Presented without intermission.

Two senior citizens discuss politics and cultural change as they fall in love for the first time.

Spitfire riches: Garrett Long, Steven Pasquale, Phyllis Somerville and Liz Callaway in The Spitfire Grill. *Photo: Joan Marcus*

Playwrights Horizons production of **The Spitfire Grill** (15). Musical with book by James Valcq and Fred Alley; music by Mr. Valcq; lyrics by Mr. Alley; based on the film by Lee David Zlotoff. Tim Sanford artistic director, Leslie Marcus managing director, William Russo general manager, by special arrangement with the George Street Playhouse, at the Duke on 42nd Street. Opened October 2, 2001. (Closed October 14, 2001)

Percy Talbott.................................. Garrett Long   Effy Krayneck .... Mary Gordon Murray
Sheriff Joe Sutter ....Steven Pasquale   Shelby Thorpe ....Liz Callaway
Hannah Ferguson .... Phyllis Somerville   The Visitor ....Stephen Sinclair
Caleb Thorpe .... Armand Schultz

Orchestra: Andrew Wilder conductor, keyboard; Antoine Silverman violin; Deborah Sepe cello; Greg Utzig guitar, mandolin; Charles Giordano accordion.

Directed by David Saint; choreography, Luis Perez; scenery, Michael Anania; costumes, Theoni V. Aldredge; lighting, Howell Binkley; sound, Scott Stauffer; musical director, Mr. Wilder; orchestrations, Mr. Valcq; music coordinator, John Miller; associate producer, Ira Weitzman; casting,

James Calleri; production stage manager, Thomas Clewell; press, Publicity Office, Bob Fennell, Marc Thibodeau, Michael S. Borowski, Candi Adams.

Time: The recent past. Place: Rural Wisconsin. Presented in two parts.

Young woman faces challenges as she adjusts to post-prison life in a small town. First produced by the George Street Playhouse, 11/5/2000. Recipient of the 2001 Richard Rodgers Award for production.

ACT I

"A Ring Around the Moon" .... Percy
"Something's Cooking at the Spitfire Grill" .... Company
"Out of the Frying Pan" .... Percy
"When Hope Goes" .... Shelby
"Ice and Snow" .... Caleb, Joe and Effy
"The Colors of Paradise" .... Percy and Shelby
"Digging Stone" .... Caleb
"This Wide Woods" .... Joe and Percy
"Forgotten Lullaby" .... Hannah
"Shoot the Moon" .... Hannah and Company

ACT II

"Come Alive Again" .... Hannah and Company
"Forest for the Trees" .... Joe
"Wild Bird" .... Shelby
"Shine" .... Percy
"Way Back Home" .... Hannah
Finale .... Company

Drama Dept. production of **Rude Entertainment** (31). By Paul Rudnick. Douglas Carter Beane artistic director, Michael S. Rosenberg managing director, at Greenwich House Theater. Opened October 3, 2001. (Closed October 28, 2001)

Mr. Charles, Currently of Palm Beach
Mr. Charles .... Peter Bartlett
Shane .... Neal Huff

Very Special Needs
Timmy .... Neal Huff
Trent .... Peter Bartlett

Katinka .... Harriet Harris

On the Fence
Matthew .... Neal Huff
Eleanor .... Harriet Harris
Paul .... Peter Bartlett

Directed by Christopher Ashley; scenery, Allen Moyer; costumes, Gregory A. Gale, lighting, Kirk Bookman; sound, Laura Grace Brown; stage manager, Sarah Bittenbender; press, Boneau/Bryan-Brown, Chris Boneau, Steven Padla, Aaron Meier.

Presented without intermission.

Comic sketches lampooning contemporary gay life. *Mr. Charles, Currently of Palm Beach* was first produced in 1998 by Ensemble Studio Theatre, New York City.

*Puppetry of the Penis (273). By David Friend and Simon Morley. Produced by David J. Foster and Ross Mollison, in association with Johnson Temple Productions, at the John Houseman Theater. Opened October 5, 2001.

CAST: Wendy Vousden, Simon Morley, David "Friendy" Friend, Justin Morley.

Production design, Andrew Dunn and Thomas Milazzo; associate producer, Mr. Milazzo; production stage manager, Janey Rainey; press, Boneau/Bryan-Brown, Adrian Bryan-Brown, Jackie Green, Martine Sainvil.

Presented in two parts.

Sometimes the title says it all.

Wild about the weed: John Kassir and Kristen Bell in Reefer Madness. *Photo: Joan Marcus*

Reefer Madness (25). Musical with book Kevin Murphy and Dan Studney; music by Mr. Studney; lyrics by Mr. Murphy. Produced by James L. Nederlander and Verna Harrah, in association with Nathaniel Kramer and Terry Allen Kramer and Dead Old Man Productions, at Variety Arts Theatre. Opened October 7, 2001. (Closed October 28, 2001)

Lecturer	Gregg Edelman	Placard Girl	Roxane Barlow
Jimmy	Christian Campbell	Ralph	John Kassir
Mary	Kristen Bell	Ensemble	Andrea Chamberlain,
Jack; Jesus	Robert Torti		Jennifer Gambatese,
Mae	Michele Pawk		Paul Leighton,
Sally	Erin Matthews		Michael Seelbach

Swings: Robert Gallagher, Molly Zimpfer.

Understudies: Mr. Edelman—Robert Gallagher; Mr. Campbell—Paul Leighton, Michael Seelbach; Ms. Bell—Jennifer Gambatese, Molly Zimpfer; Mr. Torti—Robert Gallagher, Paul Leighton; Ms. Pawk—Andrea Chamberlain, Erin Matthews; Ms. Matthews—Andrea Chamberlain, Molly Zimpfer; Mr. Kassir—Robert Gallagher, Paul Leighton; Ms. Barlow—Andrea Chamberlain, Molly Zimpfer.

Directed by Andy Fickman; choreography, Paula Abdul; scenery, Walt Spangler; costumes, Dick Magnanti; lighting, Robert Perry; sound, Lew Mead; fight direction, Rick Sordelet; music direction, David Manning; orchestrations, Nathan Wang and Mr. Manning; casting, Jim Carnahan; stage manager, Ritchard Druther; press, Richard Kornberg and Associates, Richard Kornberg, Tom D'Ambrosio, Don Summa.

Time: 1936. Place: The good ol' USA. Presented in two parts.

Stage-musical parody of the 1936 anti-marijuana propaganda film.

ACT I

Scene 1: A High School Auditorium
"Reefer Madness!" .... Lecturer and Company
Scene 2: A Back Yard
"Romeo and Juliet" .... Jimmy and Mary
Scene 3: A Reefer Den
"The Stuff" .... Mae
Scene 4: A Five-and-Dime Store
"Down at the Ol' Five-and-Dime" .... Lecturer, Jimmy, Jack and Company
Scene 5: A Reefer Den
"Jimmy Takes a Hit" .... Sally, Jimmy, Jack, Mae, Ralph and Lecturer
"The Orgy" .... Company
Scene 6: A Schoolyard, A Park, A Suburban Home
Scene 7: A Church
"Lonely Pew" .... Mary
"Listen to Jesus, Jimmy" .... Jesus and Company

SCENE 8: .... A REEFER DEN
"Lullabye" .... Sally's Baby
Scene 9: A Street
"Dead Old Man" .... Jimmy and Company
Scene 10: A Driveway
Act I Finale .... Company

ACT II

Scene 1: A City Street, A Train Station
"Jimmy on the Lam" .... Mary, Jimmy, Ralph, Sally, Mae and Company
"The Brownie Song" .... Jimmy and Company
Scene 2: A Five-and-Dime Store
"Down at the Ol' Five-and-Dime" (Reprise) .... Lecturer
Scene 3: .... A Reefer Den
"Little Mary Sunshine" .... Ralph and Mary
"Romeo and Juliet" (Reprise) .... Jimmy and Mary
Scene 4: A Reefer Den
"Murder" .... Company
"The Stuff" (Reprise) .... Mae and Jack
Scene 5: An Execution Chamber
"Listen to Jesus, Jimmy" (Reprise) .... Jesus, Jimmy and Company
"Tell 'em the Truth" .... Company
Scene 6: An Auditorium
"Reefer Madness!" (Reprise) .... Lecturer and Company

Second Stage Theatre production of **Metamorphoses** (96). By Mary Zimmerman, based on Ovid. Carole Rothman artistic director, Carol Fishman managing director. Opened October 9, 2001. (Closed December 30, 2001)

Myrrha and others	Anjali Bhimani	Erysichthon and others	Chris Kipiniak
Midas and others	Raymond Fox	Alcyon and others	Louise Lamson
Hermes and others	Kyle Hall	Orpheus and others	Erik Lochtefeld
Phaeton and others	Doug Hara	Eurydice and others	Heidi Stillman
Aphrodite and others	Felicity Jones	Therapist and others	Lisa Tejero

Directed by Ms. Zimmerman; scenery, Daniel Ostling; costumes, Mara Blumenfeld; lighting, T.J. Gerckens; sound, Andre Pluess and Ben Sussman; composer, Willy Schwarz; production stage manager, Anjali Bidani; stage manager, Brian Klevan Schneider; press, Richard Kornberg and Associates, Richard Kornberg, Tom D'Ambrosio, Don Summa.

Presented without intermission.

Contemporary adaptation of Ovid's *Metamorphoses* with inspiration from Rainer Maria Rilke's "Orpheus, Eurydice, Hermes" (translated by Stephen Mitchell), Joseph Campbell, Carl Jung, Sigmund Freud and James Hillman. *Metamorphoses* was originally produced by Lookingglass Theatre Company, Chicago. Transferred to Broadway's Circle in the Square Theatre 3/4/2002 (see Plays Produced on Broadway section). A 2001–02 *Best Plays* choice (see essay by Christopher Rawson in this volume).

Shape shifter: Rachel Weisz and Paul Rudd in The Shape of Things. *Photo: Joan Marcus*

The Shape of Things (118). By Neil LaBute. Produced by Susan Quint Gallin, Sandy Gallin, Stuart Thompson, Ben Sprecher and USA Ostar Theatricals, at the Promenade Theatre. Opened October 10, 2001. (Closed January 20, 2002)

Evelyn	Rachel Weisz	Jenny	Gretchen Mol
Adam	Paul Rudd	Philip	Frederick Weller

Directed by Mr. LaBute; scenery, Giles Cadle; costumes, Lynette Meyer; lighting, James Vermeulen; sound, Fergus O'Hare; production stage manager, Jane Grey; press, Richard Kornberg and Associates, Richard Kornberg, Don Summa.

Presented without an intermission.

Another skirmish in Mr. LaBute's ongoing gender war in which issues of power, control and artistic responsibility collide. Originally staged 5/24/2001 at the Almeida Theatre Company, London.

Zany Will: Jeremy Shamos (kneeling), David Turner and Peter Ackerman in The Complete Works of William Shakespeare (Abridged). Photo: Carol Rosegg

The Complete Works of William Shakespeare (Abridged) (256). Revival of Shakespearean parody by Adam Long, Daniel Singer and Jess Winfield. Produced by Jeffrey Richards, Christopher Gould, Raymond J. Greenwald, Norma Langworthy and Jamie deRoy at Century Center for the Performing Arts. Opened October 15, 2001. (Closed May 26, 2002)

CAST: Peter Ackerman, Jeremy Shamos, David Turner. At certain performances: Mark Fish, Jamie Iglehart, Brian Shoaf.

Directed by Jeremy Dobrish; scenery, Steven Capone; costumes, Markas Henry; lighting, Michael Gottlieb; original music and sound, Lewis Flinn; slide projections, Richard Fahey; movement and fight choreography, Tony Stevens; associate producer, Howard R. Berlin; casting, Bernard Telsey Casting; production stage manager, Katherine Lee Boyer; press, Jeffrey Richards Associates.

Presented in two parts.

Free-wheeling ride through Shakespearean characters and situations aimed at crowd-pleasing belly laughs. First produced in New York 6/13/1991 at Marymount Manhattan Theatre as part of the New York International Festival of the Arts.

Life lessons: Anne Marie Nest, Ian Reed Kesler, Paul Bartholomew, Sarah Rose in Light Years. *Photo: Joan Marcus*

Playwrights Horizons production of **Light Years** (17). By Billy Aronson. Tim Sanford artistic director, Leslie Marcus managing director, William Russo general manager, at Theater Three. Opened October 21, 2001. (Closed November 4, 2001)

Courtney	Anne Marie Nest	Doug	Paul Bartholomew
Daphne	Sarah Rose	Michael	Ian Reed Kesler

Directed by Jamie Richards; scenery, Narelle Sissons; costumes, Amela Baksic; lighting, Michael Lincoln; sound, Laura Grace Brown; fight direction, dance consultant, Luis Perez; production stage manager, Michael Schleifer; press, Publicity Office, Bob Fennell, Marc Thibodeau, Michael S. Borowski, Candi Adams.

Time: Freshman, sophomore and senior years. Place: A college. Presented without intermission.

Four young people struggle to define themselves in a three-scene comedy about college days. *Light Year: Part One* was originally presented by Ensemble Studio Theatre.

*Underneath the Lintel (252). By Glen Berger. Produced by the Soho Playhouse, Scott Morfee, Tom Wirtshafter and Dana Matthow. Opened October 23, 2001.

Librarian .... T. Ryder Smith

Understudy–Glen Berger

Directed by Randy White; scenery, Lauren Helpern; costumes, Miranda Hoffman; lighting, Tyler Micoleau; sound, Paul Adams; projection design, Elaine J. McCarthy; production stage manager, Richard A. Hodge; press, Shirley Herz Associates.

Presented without intermission.

A librarian goes in search of the borrower of a book that is overdue by 123 years and discovers the world and his connections to it.

Havana Is Waiting (38). By Eduardo Machado. Produced by Barbara Ligeti and Angelina Fiordellisi at the Cherry Lane Theatre. Opened October 24, 2001. (Closed November 25, 2002)

Federico	Bruce MacVittie	Ernesto	Felix Solis
Fred	Ed Vassallo	Percussion	Richard Marquez

Directed by Michael John Garcés; scenery, Troy Hourie; costumes, Elizabeth Hope Clancy; lighting, Kirk Bookman; sound, David M. Lawson; associate producer, Annette Tapert; production stage manager, Charles M. Turner III; press, Springer/Chicoine Public Relations, Susan Chicoine, Joe Trentacosta.

Time: December 1999. Place: New York City and Havana.

A middle-age Cuban native searches for his roots when he returns to his homeland 40 years after he was airlifted to the United States. First presented as *When the Sea Drowns in Sand* at the 2001 Humana Festival of New American Plays.

New York Theatre Workshop production of **Everything That Rises Must Converge** (24). By Flannery O'Connor; based on three of her short stories: "A View of the Woods," "Greenleaf" and "Everything That Rises Must Converge." James C. Nicola artistic director, Lynn Moffat managing director. Opened October 30, 2001. (November 18, 2001)

Actor One	Isiah Whitlock Jr.	Actor Five	Laura Hicks
Actor Two	Michael Moran	Actor Six	Michael Rogers
Actor Three	Kelli Rae Powell	Actor Seven	John McAdams
Actor Four	Ayeje Lavonne Feamster	Actor Eight	Ledlie Borgerhoff

Directed by Karin Coonrod; scenery, Marina Draghici; costumes, P.K. Wish; lighting, Christopher Akerlind; sound, Tony Geballe; production stage manager; Jennifer Rae Moore; press, Richard Kornberg and Associates, Don Summa.

Presented in three parts.

Presentation of three stories, with no adaptation, that show the gradual encroachment of the mid-20th century on the mores of the Old South.

Front of the bus: Laura Hicks, Ledlie Borgerhoff and John McAdams in Everything That Rises Must Converge.*Photo: Joan Marcus*

Wonder woman: Sarah Jessica Parker and Kevin Chamberlin in Wonder of the World.
Photo: Joan Marcus

Manhattan Theatre Club production of **Wonder of the World** (76). By David Lindsay-Abaire. Lynne Meadow artistic director, Barry Grove executive producer, at City Center Stage I. Opened November 1, 2001. (Closed January 5, 2002)

Cass Harris	Sarah Jessica Parker	Glen	Bill Raymond
Kip Harris	Alan Tudyk	Captain Mike	Kevin Chamberlin
Lois Coleman	Kristine Nielsen	Barbara; Helicopter Pilot;	
Karla	Marylouise Burke	Three Waitresses; Janie	Amy Sedaris

Directed by Christopher Ashley; scenery, David Gallo; costumes, David C. Woolard; lighting, Ken Billington; music and sound, Mark Bennett; fight director, Rick Sordelet; casting, Nancy Piccione/David Caparelliotis; production stage manager, Kate Broderick; press, Boneau/Bryan-Brown, Chris Boneau, Steven Padla, Jackie Green, Aaron Meier.

Presented in two parts.

Wacky young woman escapes her unfulfilling life, exchanging her husband's sexual peculiarities for the macabre kookiness she encounters along the way.

The Joseph Papp Public Theater/New York Shakespeare Festival production of **Elaine Stritch at Liberty** (50). Musical revue by Elaine Stritch and John Lahr; songs by various authors (see below). George C. Wolfe producer, Fran Reiter executive director, in the Newman Theater. Opened November 6, 2001. (Closed January 13, 2002)

Featuring Elaine Stritch.

Directed by George C. Wolfe; scenery, Riccardo Hernández; costumes, Paul Tazewell; lighting, Jules Fisher and Peggy Eisenhauer; sound, Acme Sound Partners; orchestrations, Jonathan Tunick; music direction, Rob Bowman; music coordinator, Seymour Red Press; production stage manager, Rick Steiger; press, Carol R. Fineman, Tom Naro, Ian Rand.

Autobiographical perspective on the life and passions of Elaine Stritch. Transferred to Broadway's Neil Simon Theatre 2/21/2002 (see Plays Produced on Broadway section). A *Best Plays* special citation honoree for 2001–02 (see essay by Michael Sommers in this volume). Received a special citation from the New York Drama Critics Circle and a Tony Award for special theatrical event.

MUSICAL NUMBERS

"All in Fun"	Jerome Kern and Oscar Hammerstein II
"Broadway Baby"	Stephen Sondheim
"But Not For Me"	George Gershwin and Ira Gershwin
"If Love Were All"	Noël Coward
"Can You Use Any Money Today?"	Irving Berlin
"Civilization"	Carl Sigman and Bob Hilliard
"Hurray for Hollywood"	Richard A. Whiting and Johnny Mercer
"I'm Still Here"	Stephen Sondheim
"I've Been to a Marvelous Party"	Noël Coward
"I Want a Long Time Daddy"	Porter Grainger
"The Little Things You Do Together"	Stephen Sondheim
"Something Good"	Richard Rodgers
"The Ladies Who Lunch"	Stephen Sondheim
"The Party's Over"	Jule Styne, Betty Comden and Adolph Green
"There Never Was a Baby Like My Baby"	Jule Styne, Betty Comden and Adolph Green
"There's No Business Like Show Business"	Irving Berlin
"This Is All Very New to Me"	Albert Hague and Arnold B. Horwitt
"Why Do the Wrong People Travel"	Noël Coward
"Zip"	Richard Rodgers and Lorenz Hart

Manhattan Theatre Club production of **Where's My Money?** (79). By John Patrick Shanley. Lynne Meadow artistic director, Barry Grove executive producer, in association with Labyrinth Theater Company, City Center Stage II. Opened November 7, 2001. (Closed January 13, 2002)

Sidney	David Deblinger	Marcia Marie	Florencia Lozano
Celeste	Yetta Gottesman	Tommy	Chris McGarry
Henry	Erik Laray Harvey	Natalie	Paula Pizzi

Understudies: Mr. Deblinger—Chris McGarry; Messrs. Harvey, McGarry—Jason Manuel Olazabál; Mses. Gottesman, Lozano, Pizzi—Sara Surrey.

Directed by Mr. Shanley; scenery, Michelle Malavet; costumes, Mimi O'Donnell; lighting, Sarah Sidman; sound Eric DeArmon; fight direction, Blaise Corrigan; casting, Nancy Piccione/David Caparelliotis; production stage manager, Dawn M. Wagner; press, Boneau/Bryan-Brown, Chris Boneau, Steven Padla, Jackie Green, Aaron Meier.

Presented in two parts.

Angry comic take on the torments of marital (and other) relationships. Originally produced 7/9/2001 by New York's Labyrinth Theater Company.

Lincoln Center Theater production of **Everett Beekin** (62). By Richard Greenberg. André Bishop artistic director, Bernard Gersten executive producer at the Mitzi E. Newhouse Theater. Opened November 14, 2001. (Closed January 6, 2002)

Ma; Waitress	Marcia Jean Kurtz	Jack; Bee	Jeff Allin
Sophie; Celia,		Miri; Laurel	Jennifer Carpenter
Anna's older daughter	Robin Bartlett	Jimmy; Ev	Kevin Isola
Anna; Nell,			
Anna's younger daughter	Bebe Neuwirth		

Understudies: Ms. Kurtz—Nancy Franklin; Mses. Bartlett, Neuwirth—Deborah Offner; Mr. Allin—Jack Koenig; Ms. Carpenter—Kate Arrington; Mr. Isola—Kieran Campion.

Directed by Evan Yionoulis; scenery, Christopher Barreca; costumes, Teresa Snider-Stein; lighting, Donald Holder; music and sound, Mike Yionoulis; casting, Daniel Swee; stage manager, Denise Yaney; press, Philip Rinaldi.

Time: Late 1940s; 1990s. Place: Lower East Side of Manhattan; the Pacific. Presented in two parts.

Comedy about two generations of a Jewish family on the path to assimilation and the obscure connections that lie beneath the surface of their relationships. First presented 9/8/2000 at South Coast Repertory, Costa Mesa, Calif.

Cheating hearts: Kevin Anderson and Margaret Colin in Speaking in Tongues. *Photo: Joan Marcus*

Roundabout Theatre Company production of **Speaking in Tongues** (77). By Andrew Bovell. Todd Haimes artistic director, Ellen Richard managing director, Julia C. Levy executive director of external affairs, at the Gramercy Theatre. Opened November 15, 2001. (January 20, 2002)

Jane; Valerie .... Karen Allen	Sonja; Sarah .... Margaret Colin
Leon; Nick .... Kevin Anderson	Pete; Neil; John .... Michel R. Gill

Standbys: Men—Paul Schoeffler; Women—Dee Pelletier.

Directed by Mark Clements; scenery, Richard Hoover; costumes, Jess Goldstein; lighting, Brian MacDevitt; music and sound, Scott Myers; casting, Amy Christopher; production stage manager, Jay Adler; stage manager, Leslie C. Lyter; press, Boneau/Bryan-Brown, Adrian Bryan-Brown, Matt Polk, Jackie Green, Karalee Dawn, Cindy Valk.

Time: The present. Place: A coastal city in the United States. Presented in two parts.

A relationship drama focusing on the psychology of betrayal and what may lurk in the character of ourselves and those around us. First produced in 1996 by the Griffin Theatre Company in Sydney, Australia.

True Love (61). By Charles L. Mee. Produced by Jeanne Donovan at the Zipper Theatre. Opened November 27, 2001. (Closed January 20, 2002)

Polly	Laurie Williams	Bonnie	Jayne Houdyshell
Edward	Jeremiah Miller	Phil	Dallas Roberts
Shirley	Laura Esterman	Alicia	Halley Wegryn Gross
Red Dicks	Paul Mullins	Richard	Roy Thinnes
Jim	Christopher McCann		

Understudies: Messrs. Roberts, McCann—James Sobol.

Musicians: Crispin Cioe keyboard, saxophone, vocals; George Gilmore guitar, vocals; Charles Giordano keyboard, accordion; Robin Gould III drums.

Directed by Daniel Fish; choreography, Peter Pucci; scenery, Christine Jones; costumes, Kaye Voyce; lighting, Jane Cox; sound, Robert Kaplowitz; musical direction, Mr. Cioe; co-producer, Tessa Blake; casting, Janet Foster; production stage manager, Babette Roberts; press, Richard Kornberg and Associates, Don Summa, Tom D'Ambrosio, Erin Dunn.

Presented without intermission.

Wild reinterpretation of the story of Phaedra and Hippolytus punctuated by angry, energetic rock-and-roll songs and set in a garage filled with characters of the working class.

Roadside (29). Musical with book and lyrics by Tom Jones; music by Harvey Schmidt. Based on the play *Roadside* by Lynn Riggs. Produced by the York Theatre Company, James Morgan artistic director, Peter Poliakine managing director, in association with Lyric Stage, at the Theatre at St. Peter's. Opened November 29, 2001. (Closed December 23, 2001)

Miz Foster	Jennifer Allen	Amos K. Buzzey Hale	James Hindman
Red Ike	Ryan Appleby	Hannie Raider	Julie Johnson
Pap Raider	G.W. Bailey	Texas	Jonathan Beck Reed
Black Ike	Steve Barcus	The Verdigree Marshal	William Ryall
Neb, the Jailer	Tom Flagg		

Musicians: John Mulcahy conductor, piano; Joe Brent fiddle, guitar, banjo, mandolin; Mike Kennan bass; Barry Mitterhoff guitar, banjo, mandolin, harmonica.

Directed and choreographed by Drew Scott Harris; scenery, James Morgan; costumes, Suzy Benzinger; lighting, Mary Jo Dondlinger; orchestrations, Joseph Brent and Peter Larson; musical direction, Mr. Mulcahy; casting, Norman Meranus; production stage manager, Scott F. Dela Cruz; press, Keith Sherman and Associates, Dan Fortune.

Time: Early 1900s. Place: Oklahoma Territory. Presented in two parts.

Musical version of a play about Oklahoma country folk by Mr. Riggs , whose *Green Grow the Lilacs* became *Oklahoma!*

ACT I

"Uncle Billy's Travellin' Family Show"	Pap and Company
"Roadside"	Pap, Buzzey, Hannie, Ikes
"Here Am I"	Hannie, Buzzy
"I Don't Want to Bother Nobody"	Texas, Pap and Ikes
"Smellamagoody Perfume"	Hannie, Texas and Buzzey
"Smellamagoody Perfume" (Reprise)	Hannie
"Lookin' at the Moon"	The Ikes
"I'm Through With You"	Hannie and Texas
"Peaceful Little Town"	Neb and Miz Foster
"I Toe the Line"	Marshal, Texas, Neb and Miz Foster
"I'm Through With You" (Reprise)	Hannie, Texas, Neb and Miz Foster

ACT II

Entr'acte	The Band
"Back to Our Story"	Pap and the Ikes
"Personality Plus"	Buzzey

"Another Drunken Cowboy" .... Texas
"The Way It Should Be" .... Pap and Texas
"My Little Prairie Flower" .... The Ikes
"All Men Is Crazy" .... Hannie
"Ain't No Womern But You" .... Texas and Hannie
"Borned" .... Texas
"Wild and Reckless" .... Texas and All
"Peaceful Little Town" (Reprise) .... Neb, Miz Foster, Buzzey, Marshal
"The Way It Should Be" (Reprise) .... Texas, Hannie and All
"Roadside" (Reprise) .... All

Marc Salem's Mind Games, Too (48). Solo performance of mentalist act by Marc Salem. Produced by Mr. Salem, Anita Waxman and Elizabeth Williams at the Duke on 42nd Street. Opened December 3, 2001. (Closed January 13, 2002)

Featuring Mr. Salem with scenery by Ray Recht. Presented without intermission.
Return of Mr. Salem and his bag of psychological tricks.

Say your prayers: Kate Forbes and Keith David in Othello. *Photo: Michal Daniel*

The Joseph Papp Public Theater/New York Shakespeare Festival production of **Othello** (24). Revival of the play by William Shakespeare. George C. Wolfe producer. Opened December 9, 2001. (Closed December 30, 2001)

Roderigo	Christopher Evan Welch	Lodovico	Dan Snook
Iago	Liev Schreiber	Gratiano	Thomas Schall
Barbantio	Jack Ryland	Desdemona	Kate Forbes
Othello	Keith David	Montano	Thom Sesma
Cassio	Jay Goede	Emilia	Becky Ann Baker
Duke of Venice	George Morfogen	Bianca	Natacha Roi

Ensemble: Corey Behnke, Paul Vincent Black, Mark H. Dold, Robert Steffen, Remy Auberjonois, Lea Coco, Gregory Derelian

Directed by Doug Hughes; scenery, Neil Patel; costumes, Catherine Zuber; lighting, Robert Wierzel; music and sound, David Van Tieghem; fight direction, Rick Sordelet; production stage manager, Buzz Cohen; press, Carol R. Fineman, Tom Naro, Ian Rand.

Presented in two parts.

Revival of the popular Shakespeare play about manipulation, jealousy and murder. First performed 11/1/1604 at the court of King James I. The first New York presentation of record was 12/30/1751 by Robert Upton at the Theatre in Nassau Street.

*Criss Angel Mindfreak (243). By Criss Angel. Produced by Tableau Entertainment at the World Underground Theatre of the World Wrestling Federation. Opened December 13, 2001.

CAST: Mr. Angel and Kirk L. McGee, Svetlana Alexandra, Tatyana Senchihina, Ken Romo, Costa Sarantakos.

Directed by Mr. Angel; choreography, Deanne Lay, scenery, John Farrell; costumes, Barak Stribling; lighting, Jules Fisher and Peggy Eisenhauer; music, Mr. Angel and Klayton; creature design, Steve Johnson; special effects, Thaine Morris, Pete Cappadocia, Elia Popov; production stage manager, Larry Baker.

Mentalist and special effects performance.

Playwrights Horizons production of **Psych** (17). By Evan Smith. Tim Sanford artistic director, Leslie Marcus managing director, William Russo general manager, in the Peter Norton Space. Opened December 16, 2001. (Closed December 30, 2001)

Bill; Michael;	Sunny Goldfarb .... Heather Goldenhersh
Gar; Advocate .... Danny Burstein	Molly Salter .... Enid Graham
Dominque; Jana;	Desiree; Karen; Jennifer .... Katie Kreisler
Barbara Stafford;	Todd Cox;
Therapist .... Marissa Copeland	Profound Psychotic .... Damian Young

Directed by Jim Simpson; scenery, Kyle Chepulis; costumes, Claudia Brown; lighting, Frances Aronson; music and sound, Scott Myers; production stage manager, James FitzSimmons; press, Publicity Office, Bob Fennell, Michael S. Borowski.

Presented without intermission.

A nice (if quirky) young woman suffers the taunts and humiliations of jaded, embittered people she encounters—until she stops her tormentors cold.

Summer of '42 (47). Musical with book by Hunter Foster; music and lyrics by David Kirshenbaum; based on novel and screenplay by Herman Raucher. Produced by Mitchell Maxwell and Victoria Maxwell, Robert Eckert, Michael A. Jenkins, Kumiko Yoshii, James L. Simon, Mark Goldberg, Andrea Pines, in association with Robert Bernstein and Sibling Entertainment, Inc., at the Variety Arts Theatre. Opened December 18, 2001. (Closed January 27, 2002)

Hermie .... Ryan Driscoll	Gloria .... Erin Webley
Dorothy .... Kate Jennings Grant	Oscy .... Brett Tabisel
Pete .... Greg Stone	Benjie .... Jason Marcus
Aggie .... Celia Keenan-Bolger	Mr. Sanders; Walter Winchell .... Bill Kux
Miriam .... Megan Valerie Walker	

Orchestra: Lynne Shankel conductor, keyboard; John DiPinto associate conductor, keyboard; Chris MacDonnell reed; Peter Prosser cello; MaryAnn McSweeney bass; Joe Mowatt percussion.

Understudies: Messrs. Driscoll, Tabisel, Marcus—Joe Gallagher; Mses. Grant, Walker, Keenan-Bolger, Webley—Kelli Sawyer; Messrs. Kux, Stone—Buddy Crutchfield.

Directed and choreographed by Gabriel Barre; scenery, James Youmans; costumes, Pamela Scofield; lighting, Tim Hunter; sound, Jim Van Bergen; orchestrations, vocal arangements and music direction, Ms. Shankel; associate choreographer, Jennnifer Cody; associate producer, Fred H. Krones; casting, Jim Carnahan, Warren Pincus; production stage manager, Gail Eve Malatesta; press, Springer/Chicoine Public Relations, Gary Springer, Susan Chicoine, Joe Trentacosta, Ann Guzzi, Michelle Moretta.

Time: Summer 1942. Place: An island off the coast of New England. Presented in two parts.

Musical based on the novel and 1971 movie about a boy's passage into manhood one heart-throbbing summer during World War II. Originally presented by Goodspeed Musicals 8/10/2000 in Chester, Connecticut.

ACT I

Scene 1: The Beach
Opening .... Company
"Here and Now" .... Hermie, Oscy and Benjie
"Will That Ever Happen to Me?" .... Hermie
Scene 2: The Pier
"You're Gonna Miss Me" .... The Girls
"Little Did I Dream" .... Pete and Dorothy
Scene 3: The Island
"The Walk" .... Hermie and Dorothy
"Like They Used To" .... Hermie and Dorothy
"I Think I Like Her" .... Hermie
Scene 4: The Movies
"The Heat" .... The Girls
"The Movies" .... Hermie, Aggie, Oscy and Miriam
Scene 5: Dorothy's House
"Man Around the House" .... The Girls
"Someone to Dance with Me" .... Dorothy and Hermie

ACT II

Scene I: Oscy's Bedroom
"Unfinished Business" .... Oscy, Hermie and Benjie
Scene 2: Mr. Sanders's Drugstore
"Make You Mine" .... The Girls
"The Drugstore" .... Hermie and Mr. Sanders
Scene 3: The Beach
"The Campfire" .... Hermie
Scene 4: .... Dorothy's Porch
"Promise of the Morning" .... Dorothy
Scene 5: .... Dorothy's House and The Beach
"Oh Gee, I Love My GI" .... The Girls
"The Dance" .... Instrumental
Finale .... Company

New York Theatre Workshop production of **Homebody/Kabul** (86). By Tony Kushner. James C. Nicola artistic director, Lynn Moffat managing director. Opened December 19, 2001. (Closed March 3, 2002)

The Homebody .... Linda Emond
Dr. Qari Shah .... Joseph Kamal
Mullah Ali Aftar Durranni .... Firdous Bamji
Milton Ceiling .... Dylan Baker
Quango Twistleton .... Bill Camp
Priscilla Ceiling .... Kelly Hutchinson
A Munkrat .... Dariush Kashani
Khwaja Aziz Mondanabosh .... Yusef Bulos
Zai Garshi; The Marabout .... Sean T. Krishnan
Mahala .... Rita Wolf
A Border Guard .... Jay Charan

Understudies: Messrs. Baker, Camp—Edmund C. Davys; Mr. Bamji—Joseph Kamal; Messrs. Bulos, Krishnan, Kamal, Charan—Dariush Kashani; Mr. Kashani—Jay Charan; Ms. Hutchinson—Autumn Dornfeld.

Directed by Declan Donnellan; scenery, Nick Ormerod; lighting, Brian MacDevitt; sound, Dan Moses Schreier; production stage manager, Martha Donaldson. Richard Kornberg and Associates, Richard Kornberg, Don Summa.

Time: August 1998. Place: London and Kabul just before and just after the American bombardment of the suspected terrorist training camps in Khost, Afghanistan.

Drama about an Englishwoman who "disappears" into her fantasies, which leads her family to Afghanistan and into confrontation with that culture's dangerous realities. A 2001–02 *Best Plays* choice (see essay by Jennifer de Poyen in this volume).

What's on the Hearts of Men (8). By Malik Yoba and A. Rahman Yoba. Produced by Performing Arts Productions, Dia Theatricals and Malik Yoba, at the Beacon Theatre. Opened January 29, 2002. (Closed February 3, 2002)

Jerome Jones	Malik Yoba	Carmen	Stephanie Mills
Al Washington	BeBe Winans	Trina	Julie Dickens
Charles Ramsey,		Vanessa	Patricia Cuffie
known as Boo	Michael LeMelle		

Directed by Mr. Yoba and George Faison; scenery, Felix Cochren; costumes by Rahimah Yoba; lighting, Marshall Williams; sound, Sound of Authority.

Family drama about African-American men dealing with issues of sex, fatherhood and responsibility.

One Man (29). Solo performance by Steven Berkoff. Produced by the Culture Project at 45 Bleecker. Opened January 31, 2002. (Closed March 10, 2002)

Directed by Mr. Berkoff; lighting, Giselda Beaudin; production stage manager, Paul J. Nye Pouthier; press, the Jacksina Company, Judy Jacksina.

Presented in two parts.

"The Tell-Tale Heart," "The Actor" and "The Dog" enacted by Mr. Berkoff.

Second Stage Theatre production of **Sorrows and Rejoicings** (32). By Athol Fugard. Carole Rothman artistic director, Carol Fishman managing director. Opened February 4, 2002. (Closed March 3, 2002)

Allison	Judith Light	Rebecca	Marcy Harriell
Marta	Charlayne Woodard	Dawid	John Glover

Directed by Mr. Fugard; scenery and costumes, Susan Hilferty; lighting, Dennis Parichy; production stage manager, Alison Cote; stage manager, Amy Patricia Stern; press, Richard Kornberg and Associates, Richard Kornberg, Tom D'Ambrosio, Don Summa.

Time: The present. Place: The living room of a large and comfortable house in a Karoo village in the heartland of South Africa.

Presented without intermission.

The white wife and black mistress (and housekeeper) of a white South African man conduct an emotional séance after his death. Originally produced 5/1/2001 at the McCarter Theatre, Princeton, New Jersey.

Manhattan Theatre Club presentation of **Further Than the Furthest Thing** (64). By Zinnie Harris. Lynne Meadow artistic director, Barry Grove executive director, at City Center Stage I. Opened February 5, 2002. (Closed March 31, 2002)

Rebecca Rogers	Jennifer Dundas	Bill Laverello	Robert Hogan
Francis Swain	Dan Futterman	Mill Lavarello	Jenny Sterlin
Mr. Hansen	Peter Gerety		

Understudies: Mr. Futterman—Marcus Chait, Gareth Saxe; Ms. Sterlin—Mikel Sarah Lambert; Ms. Dundas—Aidan Sullivan; Messrs. Hogan, Gerety—Kenneth Ryan.

Tourists at home: Robert Hogan and Jenny Sterlin in Further Than the Furthest Thing. *Photo: Joan Marcus*

Directed by Neil Pepe; scenery, Loy Arcenas; costumes, Laura Bauer and Bobby Tilley II; lighting, James F. Ingalls; music and sound, Scott Myers; dramaturg, Paige Evans; production stage manager, Harold Goldfaden; press, Boneau/Bryan-Brown, Chris Boneau, Jim Byk, Jackie Green, Aaron Meier.

Time: 1960s. Place: A remote island in the Atlantic; England. Presented in two parts.

A rustic island community is spoiled and its people corrupted by their encounter with 20th century modernity. First production of record opened 7/28/2000 at the Tron Theatre, Glasgow, before runs at the Edinburgh Festival Fringe 2000 and at the Royal National Theatre.

City Center Encores! presentation of **Carnival** (5). Concert version of musical with book by Michael Stewart; music and lyrics by Bob Merrill; based on material by Helen Deutsch. Judith E. Daykin president and executive director; Jack Viertel artistic director, at City Center. Opened February 7, 2002. (Closed February 10, 2002)

CAST: Brian Stokes Mitchell, Anne Hathaway, Debbie Gravitte, David Margulies, David Costabile, Douglas Sills, Peter Jacobson, Philip LeStrange, Lloyd Culbreath, Angelo Fraboni, Peter Gregus, Julio Monge, Timothy Robert Blevins, Sara Gettelfinger, Liz McCartney, William Ryall, Enrique Brown, Blake Hammond, Carol Lee Meadows, Cynthia Sophiea, Jessica Leigh Brown, Emily Hsu, Tina Ou, Rebecca Spencer, Stephanie D'Abruzzo, Kevin Ligon, Andrew Pacho, John Tartaglia.

Coffee Club Orchestra: Rob Fisher musical director.

Directed and choreographed by Kathleen Marshall; scenery, John Lee Beatty; costumes, Martin Pakledinaz; lighting, Peter Kaczorowski; sound, Scott Lehrer; concert adaptation, Wendy Wasserstein; puppets, Jim Henson Company; orchestrations, Philip J. Lang; music coordinator, Seymour Red Press; production stage manager, Peter Hanson.

Concert version of the musical about an orphan girl who finds love and a sense of family in a carnival. It first opened on Broadway 4/13/1961 for 719 performances at the Imperial Theatre.

Irish Repertory Theatre presentation of the **Machine Theatre Company** production of **The Matchmaker** (57). By Phyllis Ryan; adapted from the novella *Letters of a Matchmaker* by John B. Keane. Charlotte Moore artistic director, Ciarán O'Reilly producing director. Opened February 10, 2002. (Closed March 31, 2002)

Featuring Anna Manahan and Des Keogh.

Directed by Michael Scott; scenery, Michael McCaffery; costumes, Synan O'Mahoney; original music, Mr. Scott; associate producer, Matthew Gale; production stage manager, John Brophy; press, Barlow-Hartman Public Relations, Jeremy Shaffer, Richard Callison.

Presented in two parts.

Adaptation of an epistolary novella about a wise, compassionate matchmaker and his clients. First production of record 5/28/2001 at the Gaiety Theatre, Dublin, before a run at the Edinburgh Festival Fringe 2001.

Golden Ladder (32). By Donna Spector. Produced by Donald H. Goldman at the Players Theatre. Opened February 12, 2002. (Closed March 10, 2002)

Cathy Bronson	Amy Redford	Bernard Bronson	Neal Lerner
Aaron Feldman	Michael Anderson	Laura Bronson	Annie McGovern
Carol Havens; Hotel Clerk	Christi Kelsey	Mary Scaccia	Marjan Neshat

Directed by Thomas G. Waites; scenery and lighting, Barry Arnold; costumes, Laura Frecon; sound, David A. Gilman; stage manager, Terri Mintz; press, Media Blitz, Beck Lee.

Coming-of-age comedy about a girl, raised Christian, who discovers Jewish branches in her family tree.

Manhattan Theatre Club production of **Four** (48). By Christopher Shinn. Lynne Meadow artistic director; Barry Grove executive producer, in association with the Worth Street Theater Company, at City Center Stage II. Opened February 19, 2002. (Closed March 31, 2002)

Opposites attract: Armando Riesco and Pascale Armand in Four. *Photo: Joan Marcus*

Abigayle	Pascale Armand	Dexter	Armando Riesco
June	Keith Nobbs	Joe	Isiah Whitlock Jr.

Directed by Jeff Cohen; scenery, Lauren Helpern; costumes, Veronica Worts; lighting, Traci Klainer; sound, Paul Adams; music, David Van Tieghem; casting, Nancy Piccione/David Caparelliotis; production stage manager, Jason Scott Eagan; press, Boneau/Bryan-Brown, Chris Boneau, Jim Byk, Jackie Green, Aaron Meier.

Presented without intermission.

Four people, two couples, reach beyond societal boundaries of race and sexual preference as they attempt to find human connection. *Four* was first presented at London's Royal Court Theatre 11/26/1998. The original New York production was presented by the Worth Street Theater Company 7/1/2001, in association with Hugh Hayes.

Women in war: Maria Thayer, Alyssa Bresnahan (standing), Catherine Kellner, Sally Parrish in Necessary Targets. *Photo: Joan Marcus*

Necessary Targets (61). By Eve Ensler. Produced by Harriet Newman Leve, Willa Shalit, Bob Boyett, in association with Suze Orman, Melissa Howden, Beth E. Dozoretz/ Jane Fonda/Pat Mitchell, Dori Berinstein/Douglas P. Teitelbaum, at the Variety Arts Theatre. Opened February 28, 2002. (Closed April 21, 2002)

J.S.	Shirley Knight	Seada	Mirjana Jokovic
Melissa	Catherine Kellner	Azra	Sally Parrish
Jelena	Alyssa Bresnahan	Nuna	Maria Thayer
Zlata	Diane Venora		

Directed by Michael Wilson; scenery, Jeff Cowie; costumes, Susan Hilferty; lighting, Howell Binkley; music and sound, John Gromada; casting, Cindy Tolan; associate producers, Andrew Shalit, Carol Kaplan, Margaret McFeeley Golden/Michael Skipper; production stage manager, Pamela Edington; press, Publicity Office, Bob Fennell, Marc Thibodeau, Michael S. Borowski, Candi Adams.

Presented without intermission.

Seven women thrown together in war-torn Central Europe find conflict and common ground. First presented 11/28/2001 at Hartford Stage in Connecticut.

The Last Five Years (73). Musical with music and lyrics by Jason Robert Brown. Produced by Arielle Tepper, Marty Bell, in association with Libby Adler Mages/Mari Glick, Rose/Land Productions at the Minetta Lane Theatre. Opened March 3, 2002. (Closed May 5, 2002)

Kathleen .... Sherie René Scott   Jamie .... Norbert Leo Butz

Orchestra: Jason Robert Brown conductor, piano; Dorothy Lawson associate conductor, cello I, percussion, celeste; Gary Sieger acoustic guitar; Mairi Dorman cello II, percussion; Randy Landau electric bass; Christian Hebel violin, percussion.

Understudies: Ms. Scott—Nicole Van Giesen; Mr. Butz—D.B. Bonds.

Directed by Daisy Prince; scenery and costumes, Beowulf Boritt; lighting, Christine Binder; sound, Duncan Edwards; orchestrations, Mr. Brown; musical director, Thomas Murray; casting, Mark Simon; production stage manager, Patty Lyons; press, Barlow-Hartman Public Relations, John Barlow, Michael Hartman, Jeremy Shaffer.

Presented without intermission.

An artistic couple meet, fall in love and separate in a song cycle encompassing 14 scenes. Originally presented 5/23/2001 at Northlight Theatre Company, Skokie, Illinois.

Take five: Norbert Leo Butz in The Last Five Years.
Photo: Joan Marcus

MUSICAL NUMBERS

Scene 1	"Still Hurting"
Scene 2	"Jamie's Song'
Scene 3	"See I'm Smiling"
Scene 4	"Moving Too Fast"
Scene 5	"A Part of That"
Scene 6	"The Schmuel Song"
Scene 7	"A Summer in Ohio"
Scene 8	"The Next Ten Minutes"

Roundabout Theatre Company production of **The Dazzle** (80). By Richard Greenberg. Todd Haimes artistic director, Ellen Richard managing director, Julia C. Levy executive director of external affairs, at the Gramercy Theatre. Opened March 5, 2002. (Closed May 12, 2002)

Homer Collyer .... Peter Frechette   Milly Ashmore .... Francie Swift
Langley Collyer .... Reg Rogers

Understudies: Mr. Rogers—John Feltch, Adrian LaTourelle; Mr. Frechette—Adrian LaTourelle, John Feltch; Ms. Swift—Christi Craig.

Directed by David Warren; choreography, Karen Azenberg; scenery, Allen Moyer; costumes, Gregory A. Gale; lighting, Jeff Croiter; sound, Robert Murphy; music, Lawrence Yurman; casting, Amy Christopher and Bernard Telsey Casting; production stage manager, Jay Adler; press, Boneau/ Bryan-Brown, Adrian Bryan-Brown, Matt Polk, Amy Dinnerman.

Time: Early 20th century. Place: A home in Harlem. Presented in two parts.

An eccentric pair of brothers withdraw from life into a domestic cocoon filled with the detritus of modern life—which finally includes themselves. Originally presented 7/26/2000 by New York Stage and Film Company and the Powerhouse Theater at Vassar.

Stormy weather: Mark Rylance and company in Cymbeline. *Photo: John Tramper*

Brooklyn Academy of Music presentation of the **Shakespeare's Globe** production of **Cymbeline** (14). Revival of the play by William Shakespeare. Alan H. Fishman chairman of the board, Karen Brooks Hopkins president, Joseph V. Melillo executive producer at the BAM Harvey Theater. Opened March 5, 2002. (Closed March 17, 2002)

CAST: Jane Arnfield, Terry McGinity, Fergus O'Donnell, John Ramm, Mark Rylance, Abigail Thaw.

Musicians: Irita Kutchmy and Claire van Kampen.

Directed by Mike Alfreds; choreography, Glynn MacDonald; costumes and properties, Jenny Tiramani; lighting, Donald Holder; music, Ms. van Kampen; stage manager, Kim Beringer; press, Sandy Sawotka, Melissa Cusick, Fateema Jones, Tamara McCaw, Kila Packett.

Revival of the Shakespeare play that demonstrates humanity's reliance on happenstance (and a bit of help from the great beyond). Earliest known performance was at the Globe Theatre in 1611. The first New York presentation of record was 12/28/1767 by the American Company (David Douglass played Iachimo, Lewis Hallam II played Posthumus) at the John Street Theatre.

Prodigal (24). Musical with book and lyrics by Dean Bryant, music by Mathew Frank. Produced by the York Theatre Company, James Morgan artistic director, at the Theatre at the St. Peter's. Opened March 12, 2002. (Closed March 31, 2002)

Ken Flannery;	Harry Flannery	David Hess
Zach Marshall	Christian Borle	Luke Flannery	Joshua Park
Maddy Sinclair	Kerry Butler	Piano	Mathew Frank
Celia Flannery	Alison Fraser		

Directed and scenery by Mr. Morgan; costumes, Daniel Lawson; lighting, Edward Pierce; casting, Norman Meranus; production stage manager, Scott F. Dela Cruz; press, Keith Sherman and Associates, Scott Klein.

Presented without intermission.

Coming-out musical about a young Australian who finds the wicked city's temptations to be overwhelming. Originally presented in Australia by Ztudio and Stacey Testro International.

Overture	Pianist
"Picture Postcard Place"	Luke, Celia, Harry, Kane
"Happy Families"	Luke, Celia, Kane, Harry
"Picture Postcard Place" (Reprise)	Celia, Luke, Kane, Harry
"Run With the Tide"	Luke
"Brand New Eyes"	Maddy
"Brand New Eyes" (Reprise)	Luke, Maddy
"When I Was a Kid"	Maddy, Zach, Luke
"My Boy"	Harry, Celia, Kane, Luke
"Out of Myself"	Zach, Luke
"Set Me Free"	Zach, Luke
"Epiphany"	Luke, Celia, Harry, Maddy
"Happy Families" (Reprise)	Celia
"Love Them and Leave Them Alone"	Celia
"Where Does It Get You?"	Luke, Celia
"Maddy's Piece"	Maddy
"Lullaby"	Harry
Finale	Luke, Maddy, Celia, Harry

New York Theatre Workshop production of **Throw Pitchfork** (16). Solo performance by Alexander Thomas. James C. Nicola artistic director, Lynn Moffat managing director. Opened March 12, 2002. (Closed March 24, 2002)

Featuring Alexander Thomas.

Directed by Lenora Pace; scenery, Troy Hourie; lighting, Ben Stanton; sound, Jerry M. Yager; production stage manager, Jonathan Donahue; press, Richard Kornberg and Associates, Don Summa.

Presented without intermission.

A young African-American man recounts the men in his life who helped and hindered his development.

*Surviving Grace (92). By Trish Vradenburg. Produced by Nina Benton at the Union Square Theatre. Opened March 12, 2002.

Kate Griswald	Illeana Douglas	Jack Griswald	Jerry Grayson
Grace Griswald	Doris Belack	Sam Gelman	Armand Schultz

My mother, myself: Doris Belack and Illeana Douglas in Surviving Grace. *Photo: Joan Marcus*

Lorna .... Cynthia Darlow   Madge Wellington;
Lenny; Marty; Various Doctors;   Nurse Pam .... Linda Hart
  Morton Seligman .... James Hindman

    Understudies: Mses. Belack, Hart—Lois Markle; Mses. Douglas, Hart, Darlow—Jennifer Regan; Mr. Grayson—Richard M. Davidson; Mr. Schultz and others—Peter Bradbury.

    Directed by Jack Hofsiss; scenery, David Gallo; costumes, Ann Hould-Ward; lighting, Russell H. Champa; music and sound Guy Sherman/Aural Fixation; executive producer, Richard Frankel; casting, Jay Binder; production stage manager, Joshua Halperin; press, Barlow-Hartman Public Relations, John Barlow, Michael Hartman, Joe Perrotta.

    Time: The present and memory. Place: New York, New Jersey, Miami, Chicago and Washington, DC. Presented in two parts.

    Relationship comedy about a family struggling with the mother's approaching Alzheimer's Disease. Opened and closed on Broadway 4/14/1996 as *The Apple Doesn't Fall.*

*Mr. Goldwyn (93). By Marsha Lebby and John Lollos. Produced by David Brown for the Manhattan Project, Ltd., and Ben Sprecher for Emma Luke Productions, LLC, in association with Michael Gardner, at the Promenade Theatre. Opened March 12, 2002.

Samuel Goldwyn .... Alan King   Helen .... Lauren Klein

    Understudy: Ms. Klein—Jan Leslie Harding.

    Directed by Gene Saks; scenery, David Gallo; costumes, Joseph G. Aulisi; lighting, Michael Lincoln; sound, T. Richard Fitzgerald; associate producers, David Jaroslawicz, Carol Fleisig, Aaron Levy; casting, Deborah Brown; production stage manager, Daniel S. Rosokoff; press, Publicity Office, Bob Fennell, Marc Thibodeau, Candi Adams, Michael S. Borowski.

    Time: 1952. Place: Goldwyn Studios, Hollywood. Presented in two parts.

Include him out: Alan King in Mr. Goldwyn. *Photo: Carol Rosegg*

Samuel Goldwyn waxes malapropistic in this near-solo celebration of Hollywood's golden age. Originally presented 7/27/2001 by New York Stage and Film Company and the Powerhouse Theater at Vassar.

City Center Encores! presentation of **Golden Boy** (5). Concert version of musical with book by Clifford Odets and William Gibson; music by Charles Strouse; lyrics by Lee Adams; based on the play by Mr. Odets. Judith E. Daykin president and executive director; Jack Viertel artistic director, at City Center. Opened March 21, 2002. (Closed March 24, 2002)

CAST: Alfonso Ribeiro, Anastasia Barzee, Norm Lewis, William McNulty, Paul Butler, Wayne Pretlow, Thursday Farrar, Michael Potts, Rob Bartlett, Joseph R. Sicari, Morgan Burke, Kamar de los Reyes, Karine Plantadit-Bageot, Julio Monge, Eric Anthony, Kristine Bendul, Chaundra Cameron, Kyra DaCosta, Manuel Herrera, Erik Houg, Terace Jones, Gelan Lambert Jr., Vicky Lambert, Sharon Moore, April Nixon, Devin Richards, Angela Robinson, Janelle Anne Robinson, J.D. Webster, Patrick Wetzel.

Coffee Club Orchestra: Rob Fisher musical director.

Directed by Walter Bobbie; choreography, Wayne Cilento; scenery, John Lee Beatty; costumes, William Ivey Long; lighting, Peter Kaczorowski; sound, Acme Sound Partners; concert adaptation, Suzan-Lori Parks; fight direction, Michael Olajide; music coordinator, Seymour Red Press; orchestrations, Ralph Burns and Don Sebesky; production stage manager, Peter Hanson.

Concert version of the musical adaptation of Mr. Odets's play about a boxer torn between work and musical passion. It first opened on Broadway 10/20/1964 at the Majestic Theatre for 568 performances—Sammy Davis Jr. starred.

Three sisters: Jean Stapleton, Roberta Maxwell and Hallie Foote in Horton Foote's The Carpetbagger's Children. *Photo: Jim Caldwell*

*Lincoln Center Theater presents the Alley Theatre, Guthrie Theater and Hartford Stage production of ***The Carpetbagger's Children** (77). By Horton Foote. André Bishop artistic director, Bernard Gersten executive producer, at the Mitzi E. Newhouse Theater. Opened March 25, 2002.

Cornelia	Roberta Maxwell	Sissie	Hallie Foote
Grace Anne	Jean Stapleton		

Understudies: Mses. Maxwell, Foote—Jennifer Harmon; Ms. Stapleton—Sandra Shipley.

Directed by Michael Wilson; scenery, Jeff Cowie; costumes, David C. Woolard; lighting, Rui Rita; sound John Gromada; casting, Cindy Tolan and Daniel Swee; stage manager, Michael Brunner; press, Philip Rinaldi.

Time: Mid-20th century. Place: Harrison, Texas. Presented without intermission.

Trio of interspersed monologues in which three sisters wax nostalgic about the passing of time with the petty hurts and tiny victories that accumulate in a full life. Mr. Foote's play was the 2002 ATCA/Steinberg New Play Award honoree. First presented 6/6/2001 at the Alley Theatre, Houston, Texas.

*The Godfadda Workout (76). Solo performance by Seth Isler. Produced by East of Doheny, in association with Woody Fraser, at the American Place Theatre. Opened March 25, 2002.

Featuring Seth Isler.

Directed by Susan Jane Sullivan; costumes and lighting, Mr. Isler and Ms. Sullivan; sound, Jerry Houser; press, Springer/Chicoine Public Relations, Susan Chicoine, Joe Trentacosta.

Billed as a parody in 12 rounds, one performer plays scenes from Francis Ford Coppola's *The Godfather.*

Playwrights Horizons production of **Franny's Way** (32). By Richard Nelson. Tim Sanford artistic director, Leslie Marcus managing director, William Russo general manager, at the Atlantic Theater. Opened March 26, 2002. (Closed April 21, 2002)

Older Franny	Kathleen Widdoes	Young Franny, age 17	Elisabeth Moss

Granny's girls:Domenica Cameron-Scorsese, Kathleen Widdoes and Elisabeth Moss in Franny's Way. *Photo: Joan Marcus*

Dolly (her sister),	Phil (Sally's husband) .... Jesse Pennington
age 15 .... Domenica Cameron-Scorsese	Marjorie (Franny, Dolly and
Sally (her cousin) .... Yvonne Woods	Sally's grandmother) .... Kathleen Widdoes

Directed by Mr. Nelson; scenery, Thomas Lynch; costumes, Susan Hilferty and Linda Ross; lighting, Jennifer Tipton; sound, Scott Lehrer; casting, James Calleri; production stage manager, Jane Pole; press, Publicity Office, Bob Fennell, Michael S. Borowski.

Time: Summer, 1957. Place: An apartment on Sullivan Street, Greenwich Village. Presented without intermission.

Memory play about a young woman's awakening passion for life and literature set against an emotional backdrop of family loss. A 2001–02 *Best Plays* choice (see essay by Charles Wright in this volume).

The Joseph Papp Public Theater/New York Shakespeare Festival production of **36 Views** (22). By Naomi Iizuka. George C. Wolfe producer, in association with Berkeley Repertory Theatre, in the Newman Theater. Opened March 28, 2002. (Closed April 14, 2002)

Darius Wheeler .... Stephen Lang	Claire Tsong .... Elaine Tse
Setsuko Hearn .... Liana Pai	Elizabeth Newman-Orr .... Rebecca Wisocky
John Bell .... Ebon Moss-Bachrach	Owen Matthiassen .... Richard Clarke

Directed by Mark Wing-Davey; scenery, Douglas Stein; costumes, Myung Hee Cho; lighting, David Weiner; sound, Matthew Spiro; projections, Ruppert Bohle; associate producers, Bonnie Metzgar, John Dias; casting, Jordan Thaler/Heidi Griffiths, Amy Potozkin; production stage manager, John C. McNamara; press, Carol R. Fineman, Tom Naro, Elizabeth Wehrle.

Notions of cultural possession and authenticity are interrogated in this play about an adventurer who deals in Asian national treasure. First presented 9/12/2001 by Berkeley Repertory Theatre in California.

Sleight of hand: Stephen Lang and Liana Pai in 36 Views. Photo: Michal Daniel

*Menopause: The Musical (66). Musical revue with book and lyrics by Jeanie Linders; music by various popular artists. Produced by Mark Schwartz and TOC Productions, in association with Brent Peek, at Theatre Four. Opened April 4, 2002.

Power Woman ....Joy Lynn Matthews	Earth Mother ....Joyce A. Presutti
Soap Star .... Mary Jo McConnell	Iowa Housewife .... Carolann Page

Orchestra: Jana Zielonka piano, keyboard; Diana Herald drums; Audry Perry bass guitar.

Understudies: Nancy Slusser, Wanda L. Houston.

Directed by Kathleen Lindsey; choreography, Patty Bender; scenery, Jesse Poleshuck; costumes, Martha Bromelmeier; lighting, Michael Gilliam; sound, Johnna Doty; musical direction, Corinne Aquilina; production stage manager, Christine Catti; press, Shirley Herz Associates, Shirley Herz, Nancy Khuu, Kevin McAnarney.

Place: Bloomingdale's, New York City. Presented without intermission.

Celebration of women of a certain age in 1960s (and a few later) pop tunes that have been given a lyrical facelift. The original 2001 production opened in Orlando, Florida.

The Joseph Papp Public Theater/New York Shakespeare Festival production of **Helen** (16). By Ellen McLaughlin. George C. Wolfe producer, in Martinson Hall. Opened April 8, 2002. (Closed April 21, 2002)

Helen .... Donna Murphy	Athena .... Phylicia Rashad
Servant... Marian Seldes	Meneleus .... Denis O'Hare
Io...Johanna Day	

Directed by Tony Kushner; scenery, Michael Yeargan; costumes, Susan Hilferty; lighting, Scott Zielinski; sound, Gina Leishman; associate producers, Bonnie Metzgar, John Dias; casting, Jordan Thaler/Heidi Griffiths; production stage manager, C.A. Clark; press, Carol R. Fineman, Tom Naro, Elizabeth Wehrle.

Time: 17 years after the inception of the Trojan War. Place: Egypt. Presented in two parts.

An alternative, comic tale of Helen languishing in an Egyptian hotel long after the Trojan War has been decided.

Brooding beauty: Donna Murphy and Marian Seldes in Helen. *Photo: Michal Daniel*

The Joseph Papp Public Theater/New York Shakespeare Festival production of **Blue Surge** (25). By Rebecca Gilman. George C. Wolfe producer, in the Anspacher Theater. Opened April 22, 2002. (Closed May 12, 2002)

Sandy	Rachel Miner	Doug	Steve Key
Curt	Joe Murphy	Beth	Amy Landecker
Heather	Colleen Werthmann		

Directed by Robert Falls; scenery, Walt Spangler; costumes, Birgit Rattenborg Wise; lighting, Michael Philippi; sound, Richard Woodbury; associate producers, Bonnie Metzgar, John Dias; casting, Jordan Thaler/Heidi Griffiths; production stage manager, Katherine Lee Boyer; press, Carol R. Fineman, Tom Naro, Elizabeth Wehrle.

Time: Present. Place: A mid-sized city in the midwest. Presented in two parts.

Star-crossed relationship drama between prostitutes and policemen living on the margins of society. First presented 7/9/2001 by the Goodman Theatre, Chicago, Illinois.

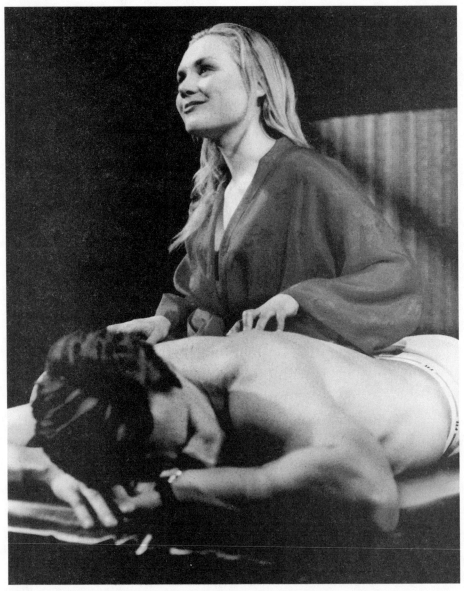

Officer down: Joe Murphy and Rachel Miner in Blue Surge. *Photo: Michal Daniel*

City Center Encores! presentation of **Pajama Game** (5). Concert version of musical with book by George Abbott and Richard Bissell; music and lyrics by Richard Adler and Jerry Ross; based on the novel *7½ Cents* by Richard Bissell. Judith E. Daykin president and executive director; Jack Viertel artistic director, at City Center. Opened May 2, 2002. (Closed May 5, 2002)

CAST: Brent Barrett, Karen Ziemba, Daniel Jenkins, Ken Page, Deidre Goodwin, Mark Linn-Baker, Gina Ferrall, Fred Burnell, Jennifer Cody, Katie Harvey, Edgar Godineaux, Herman Payne, Rebecca Baxter, Timothy Breese, Tony Capone, Caitlin Carter, Susan Derry, Joe Farrell, Anne Hawthorne, Joy Hermalyn, Ann Kittredge, Kirk McDonald, April Nixon, Marc Oka, Tina Ou, Jessica Perrizo, Josh Prince, Devin Richards, Rebecca Robins, Angela Robinson, J.D. Webster, Patrick Wetzel.

Coffee Club Orchestra: Rob Fisher musical director.

Directed by John Rando; choreography, John Carrafa; scenery, John Lee Beatty; costumes, David C. Woolard; lighting, Ken Billington; sound, Scott Lehrer; concert adaptation, David Ives; orchestrations, Don Walker; music coordinator, Seymour Red Press; production stage manager, Peter Hanson.

Concert version of the musical about love, labor and corporate abuse of workers. It first opened on Broadway 5/13/1954 at the St. James Theatre for 1,063 performances.

*Second Stage Theatre production of ***Ricky Jay on the Stem** (30). Solo performance by Ricky Jay. Carole Rothman artistic director; Carol Fishman managing director. Opened May 2, 2002.

Featuring Ricky Jay.

Directed by David Mamet; scenery, Peter S. Larkin; lighting, Jules Fisher and Peggy Eisenhauer; effects, Jim Steinmeyer; production stage manager, Matthew Silver; press, Richard Kornberg and Associates.

Presented in two parts.

Presentation of Mr. Jay's prodigious knowledge of games of skill and confidence along with a history lesson about the seamier side of Broadway.

*The Odyssey (30). By Derek Walcott; adapted from Homer. Produced by Willow Cabin Theatre Company at Theatre at St. Clement's. Opened May 5, 2002.

CAST: John Bolger, Jim Butz, Michael Hunsaker, Caralyn Kozlowski, Liza Lapira, Novella Nelson, Chuck Patterson, Michael Pemberton, Andrew Polk, Linda Powell, Joanna Rhinehart, Adriana Sevan, Jed Sexton, Lou Sumrall, Sullivan Walker, Cornell Womack.

Directed by Edward Berkeley; scenery, Beowulf Boritt; costumes, Hilary Rosenfeld; lighting, Matthew McCarthy; music, Cesar Manzano; press, Keith Sherman and Associates, Brett Oberman.

Mr. Walcott's distinctive take on the wanderings of Ulysses following the Trojan War. First presented by the Royal Shakespeare Company at the Other Place, Stratford-upon-Avon, 7/2/1992.

*New York Theatre Workshop production of ***Vienna: Lusthaus (revisited)** (27). By Martha Clarke; music by Richard Peaslee; text by Charles L. Mee. James C. Nicola artistic director, Lynn Moffat managing director. Opened May 8, 2002.

CAST: Vivienne Benesch, Erica Berg, Elzbieta Czyzewska, Mark DeChiazza, George de la Peña, Philip Gardner, Richmond Hoxie, James Lorenzo, Denis O'Hare, Jimena Paz, Andrew Robinson, Paola Styron, Julia Wilkins.

Musicians: Jill Jaffe violin; Daniel Barrett cello; Steven Silverstein woodwinds; Stewart Schuele, French horn; Nina Kellman harp.

Standbys: Mr. Robinson—Mark DeChiazza, James Lorenzo.

Directed by Ms. Clarke; scenery and costumes, Robert Israel; lighting, Paul Gallo; music direction, Jill Jaffe, production stage manager, Jennifer Rae Moore; press, Richard Kornberg and Associates, Don Summa.

Hypnotic theatrical evocation of Vienna at the turn of the 20th century. First presented as *Vienna: Lusthaus* 4/8/1986 by Music-Theatre Group at St. Clement's, it later transferred to the New York Shakespeare Festival's Newman Theater 6/15/1986.

*Red Hot Mama (27). Solo performance by Sharon McNight; based on the work of Sophie Tucker. Produced by the York Theatre Company, James Morgan artistic director, at the Theatre at St. Peter's. Opened May 8, 2002.

Artist's musing: Jimena Paz and Paola Styron in Vienna: Lusthaus (revisited). *Photo: Joan Marcus*

Featuring Sharon McNight.

Directed by Jay Berkow; scenery, Mary Houston; costumes, Patti Whitelock; lighting, Mary Jo Dondlinger; music director, Louis Goldberg; arrangements, Stan Freeman; production stage manager, Scott F. Dela Cruz; press, Keith Sherman and Associates.

Performance of the songs of Sophie Tucker, the "Last of the Red Hot Mamas."

*21 Dog Years: Doing Time @ Amazon.com (27). Solo performance by Mike Daisey. Produced by David J. Foster, Martian Entertainment and Peter Cane at the Cherry Lane Theatre. Opened May 9, 2002.

Featuring Mike Daisey.

Directed by Jean-Michele Gregory; scenery, Louisa Thompson; lighting, Russell H. Champa; associate producers, Steve Farbman, Tom Lightburn, Adam Weinstock; press, Boneau/Bryan-Brown, Chris Boneau, Jackie Green, Jim Byk, Martine Sainvil.

Presented without intermission.

A former dot-com employee comically ruminates on the oddities of the "new economic model."

*Capitol Steps: When Bush Comes to Shove (18). By Bill Strauss, Elaina Newport and Mark Eaton. Produced by Eric Krebs, in association with Capitol Steps, at the John Houseman Theatre. Opened May 16, 2002.

Mayor Michael R. Bloomberg;
George Bush Sr.;
Alan Greenspan; others .... Mike Carruthers
Hillary Clinton;
Gail Norton; others .... Ann Johnson
Laura Bush;
Elizabeth Dole; others .... Tracey Stephens

Bill Clinton; Sen. Strom Thurmond;
others .... Mike Tilford
President Bush;
Jerry Falwell; others .... Jamie Zemarel

Woof: Mike Daisey in 21 Dog Years: Doing Time @ Amazon.com. *Photo: Melanie Grizzel*

Directed by Mr. Strauss, Ms. Newport and Mr. Eaton; scenery, R.J. Matson; lighting, Krista Martocci; costumes, LindaRose Payne; sound by Jill B.C. DuBoff; press, Jeffrey Richards Associates.

Satirical sketches on the state of politics and politicians. First version presented at a Senate Christmas party in 1981.

*Primary Stages production of ***One Shot, One Kill** (12). By Richard Vetere. Casey Childs artistic director, in association with Morton Wolkowitz. Opened May 20, 2002.

Major Mark Royce .... Michael Cullen Nicole Harris .... Andrea Maulella
Sergeant Nick Harris .... Robert Montano

Directed by Joe Brancato; scenery, Tony Straiges; costumes, Curtis Hay; lighting, Jeff Nellis; music and sound, Johnna Doty; casting, Stephanie Klapper; production stage manager, Tanya Gillette; press, Barlow-Hartman Public Relations, John Barlow, Michael Hartman, Joe Perrotta.

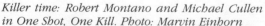

Killer time: Robert Montano and Michael Cullen in One Shot, One Kill. *Photo: Marvin Einhorn*

Perfect for politics: Nicholas Woodeson behaves badly with Olga Sosnovska (top) and Veanne Cox (bottom) in House *(top) and* Garden *(bottom). Photos: Joan Marcus*

Time: Now. Place: The US Marine Corps Scout/Sniper School, Quantico, Virginia. Presented without intermission.

Drama about a sniper, who loses control of his emotions, and his relationships with his wife and his commanding officer.

*Manhattan Theatre Club productions of ***House** and ***Garden** (12). By Alan Ayckbourn. Lynne Meadow artistic director, Barry Grove executive producer, at City Center Stage I (*House*) and City Center Stage II (*Garden*). Opened May 21, 2002.

Izzie Truce	Patricia Conolly	Sally Platt	Bryce Dallas Howard
Giles Mace	Michael Countryman	Trish Platt	Jan Maxwell
Joanna Mace	Veanne Cox	Lindy Love	Ellen Parker
Barry Love	John Curless	Lucille Cadeau	Olga Sosnovska
Pearl Truce	Laura Marie Duncan	Warn Coucher	James A. Stephens
Jake Mace	Carson Elrod	Fran Briggs	Sharon Washington
Gavin Ryng-Mayne	Daniel Gerroll	Teddy Platt	Nicholas Woodeson

Children: Alla Carponter-Walker, Edie Feinstein, Ronan Greenwood, Aliza Goldberg, Madeleine Hamingson, Matthew Hollis, Gillian Jakab, Sofia Kelley Johnson, Hillary Jost, Josh Marmer, Chandler Rosenthal, Emma Sadler, Daniel Stern.

Understudies: Mses. Howard, Duncan—Sarah Avery; Mr. Elrod—Kieran Campion; Mses. Maxwell, Cox, Sosnovska—Marie Danvers; Mses. Parker, Conolly, Washington—Deborah Mayo; Messrs. Countryman, Gerroll—Don Sparks.

Directed by John Tillinger; scenery, John Lee Beatty; costumes, Jane Greenwood; lighting, Duane Schuler; sound, Bruce Ellman; music, John Pattison; fight direction, Rick Sordelet; casting, Nancy Piccione/David Caparelliotis; production stage manager (*House*) James FitzSimmons; production stage manager (*Garden*), Barclay Stiff; press Boneau/Bryan-Brown, Chris Boneau, Jim Byk, Jackie Green, Aaron Meier.

Time: Saturday, August 14. Place: An English house and garden. Each of the two plays was presented in two parts.

Boy and boy: Malcolm Gets and Robert Sella in Boys and Girls. *Photo: Joan Marcus*

A pair of comedies, performed simultaneously on adjacent stages, in which the hapless members, friends and hangers-on of an English household are put through their farcical paces—at a gallop. *House* and *Garden* were first presented in June 1999 at the Stephen Joseph Theatre, Scarborough.

*Playwrights Horizons production of ***Boys and Girls** (4). By Tom Donaghy. Tim Sanford artistic director, Leslie Marcus managing director, William Russo general manager, at the Duke on 42nd Street. Opened May 28, 2002.

Reed .... Robert Sella   Shelly .... Carrie Preston
Jason .... Malcolm Gets   Bev .... Nadia Dajani

Directed by Gerald Gutierrez; scenery, Douglas Stein; costumes, Catherine Zuber; lighting, David Weiner; sound, Aural Fixation; fight director, Rick Sordelet; casting, James Calleri; production stage manager, Marjorie Horne; press, Publicity Office, Bob Fennell, Marc Thibodeau, Michael S. Borowski, Candi Adams.

Tale of four gay people—two men, two women—who couple and uncouple in various ways as they edge unwillingly toward maturity.

CAST REPLACEMENTS
AND TOURING COMPANIES
○ ○ ○ ○ ○
Compiled by Jeffrey Finn Productions

T HE FOLLOWING IS A LIST of the major cast replacements of record in productions that opened in previous years, but were still playing in New York during a substantial part of the 2001–02 season; and other New York shows that were on a first-class tour in 2001–02.

The name of each major role is listed in *italics* beneath the title of the play in the first column. In the second column directly opposite appears the name of the actor who created the role in the original New York production (whose opening date appears in *italics* at the top of the column). Indented immediately beneath the original actor's name are the names of subsequent New York replacements—with the date of replacement when available.

The third column gives information about first-class touring companies. When there is more than one roadshow company, #1, #2, etc., appear before the name of the performer who created the role in each company (and the city and date of each company's first performance appears in *italics* at the top of the column). Their subsequent replacements are also listed beneath their names in the same manner as the New York companies, with dates when available.

AIDA

	New York 3/23/00	*Minneapolis, MN 4/6/01*
Aida	Heather Headley	Simone
	Maya Days 9/13/01	Paulette Ivory
	Simone 1/29/02	
Radames	Adam Pascal	Patrick Cassidy
		Jeremy Kushnier
Amneris	Sherie René Scott	Kelli Fournier
	Taylor Dayne	
	Idina Menzel 9/13/01	
	Felicia Finley 1/29/02	
Mereb	Damian Perkins	Jacen R. Wilkerson
	Delisco	
Zoser	John Hickok	Neal Benari

ANNIE GET YOUR GUN

	New York 3/4/99	*Dallas, TX 07/25/00*
Buffalo Bill	Ron Holgate	George McDaniel
	Christopher Councill 9/99	
	Dennis Kelly 1/00	
	Conrad John Schuck	
Frank Butler	Tom Wopat	Rex Smith
	Brent Barrett	Tom Wopat 10/31/00
	Tom Wopat 6/23/01	
Dolly Tate	Valerie Wright	Susann Fletcher
	Michelle Blakely	Julia Fowler 5/8/01
	Valerie Wright	
	Kerry O'Malley	
Tommy Keeler	Andrew Palermo	Eric Sciotto
	Randy Donaldson	Randy Donaldson 1/9/01
	Eric Sciotto	Sean Michael McKnight 4/3/00
Winnie Tate	Nicole Ruth Snelson	Claci Miller
	Claci Miller	Carolyn Ockert 12/27/00
Charlie Davenport	Peter Marx	Joe Hart
Annie Oakley	Bernadette Peters	Marilu Henner
	Susan Lucci	Karyn Quackenbush 4/3/01
	Bernadette Peters 1/18/00	
	Cheryl Ladd	
	Reba McEntire	
	Crystal Bernard 6/23/01	

BEAUTY AND THE BEAST

	New York 4/18/94	*Minneapolis 11/7/95*
		Closed 3/7/99
		#3 Tulsa 9/7/99
Beast	Terrence Mann	Fred Inkley
	Jeff McCarthy	Roger Befeler
	Chuck Wagner	#3 Grant Norman
	James Barbour	
	Steve Blanchard	
Belle	Susan Egan	Kim Huber
	Sarah Uriarte	Erin Dilly 2/11/98
	Christianne Tisdale	#3 Susan Owen
	Kerry Butler	Danyelle Bossardet
	Deborah Gibson	
	Kim Huber	
	Toni Braxton	
	Andrea McArdle	
	Sara Litzsinger	
Lefou	Kenny Raskin	Dan Sklar
	Harrison Beal	Jeffrey Howard Schecter
	Jamie Torcellini	Aldrin Gonzalez
	Jeffrey Howard Schecter	#3 Michael Raine
	Jay Brian Winnick 11/12/99	Brad Aspel
	Gerard McIsaac	
	Brad Aspel	

Gaston	Burke Moses	Tony Lawson
	Marc Kudisch	#3 Chris Hoch
	Steve Blanchard	Edward Staudenmayer
	Patrick Ryan Sullivan	
	Christopher Seiber	
	Chris Hoch 12/10/02	
Maurice	Tom Bosley	Grant Cowan
	MacIntyre Dixon	#3 Ron Lee Savin
	Tom Bosley	
	Kurt Knudson	
	Tim Jerome	
	J.B. Adams 11/12/99	
Cogsworth	Heath Lamberts	Jeff Brooks
	Peter Bartlett	#3 John Alban Coughlan
	Gibby Brand	Ron Bagden
	John Christopher Jones	
	Jeff Brooks 11/12/99	
Lumiere	Gary Beach	Patrick Page
	Lee Roy Reams	David DeVries
	Patrick Quinn	Gary Beach
	Gary Beach	David DeVries
	Meshach Taylor	#3 Ron Wisniski
	Patrick Page	Jay Russell
	Paul Schoeffler	
	Patrick Page	
	Bryan Batt	
	Rob Lorey 5/7/02	
Babette	Stacey Logan	Leslie Castay
	Pamela Winslow	Mindy Paige Davis 2/15/97
	Leslie Castay	Heather Lee
	Pam Klinger	#3 Jennifer Shrader
	Louisa Kendrick	
	Pam Klinger	
Mrs. Potts	Beth Fowler	Betsy Joslyn
	Cass Morgan	Barbara Marineau 7/2/97
	Beth Fowler	#3 Janet MacEwen
	Barbara Marineau 11/12/99	
	Beth Fowler	

CABARET

	New York 3/19/98	Los Angeles 2/99
Emcee	Alan Cumming	Norbert Leo Butz
	Robert Sella 9/17/98	Jon Peterson 1/2/00
	Alan Cumming 12/1/98	
	Michael Hall 6/8/99	
	Matt McGrath 10/17/01	
	Raúl Esparza 10/26/01	
	John Stamos 4/29/02	
Sally Bowles	Natasha Richardson	Teri Hatcher
	Jennifer Jason Leigh 8/20/98	Joely Fisher 9/4/99
	Mary McCormack 3/2/99	Lea Thompson 3/19/00
	Susan Egan 6/17/99	Kate Shindle 7/11/00
	Joely Fisher 6/2/00	Andrea McArdle 1/23/01

	Lea Thompson 8/2/00	
	Katie Finneran 11/21/00	
	Gina Gershon 1/19–6/17/01	
	Kate Shindle 6/19/01	
	Brooke Shields 7/3/01	
	Molly Ringwald 12/18/01	
	Jane Leeves 4/29/01	
Clifford Bradshaw	John Benjamin Hickey	Rick Holmes
	Boyd Gaines 3/2/99	Jay Goede 10/16/99
	Michael Hayden 8/3/99	Hank Stratton 1/23/01
	Matthew Greer 1/19/01	
Ernst Ludwig	Denis O'Hare	Andy Taylor
	Michael Stuhlbarg 5/4/99	Drew McVety 10/16/99
	Martin Moran 11/9/99	
	Peter Benson 1/19/01	
Fraulein Schneider	Mary Louise Wilson	Barbara Andres
	Blair Brown 8/20/98	Alma Cuervo 9/4/99
	Carole Shelley 5/4/99	Barbara Andres 6/08/01
	Polly Bergen	
Fraulein Kost	Michele Pawk	Jeanine Morick
	Victoria Clark 5/4/99	Lenora Nemetz 2/20/00
	Candy Buckley	
Herr Schultz	Ron Rifkin	Dick Latessa
	Laurence Luckinbill 5/4/99	Hal Robinson 9/4/99
	Dick Latessa 11/9/99	
	Larry Keith	
	Hal Linden	

CHICAGO

	New York 11/14/96	*#1 Cincinnati 3/25/97* *#2 Ft. Myers, FL 12/12/97*
Roxie Hart	Ann Reinking	#1 Charlotte d'Amboise
	Marilu Henner	Belle Calaway
	Karen Ziemba	Ann Reinking 4/22/99
	Belle Calaway	Belle Calaway 5/18/99
	Charlotte d'Amboise	Sandy Duncan 4/22/99
	Sandy Duncan 8/12/99	Ann Reinking 5/1/99
	Belle Calaway 1/18/00	Belle Calaway 6/1/99
	Charlotte d'Amboise 3/24/00	Sandy Duncan 7/13/99
	Belle Calaway	Belle Calaway 8/3/99
	Nana Visitor	Nana Visitor 11/16/99
	Petra Nielsen 10/8/01	Tracy Shane 1/4/00
	Nana Visitor 11/19/01	#2 Karen Ziemba
	Belle Calaway 1/13/02	Nancy Hess
	Denise Van Outen 3/18/02	Charlotte d'Amboise
	Belle Calaway 4/22/02	Amy Spanger 11/10/98
		Charlotte d'Amboise 11/24/98
		Amy Spanger 12/1/98
		Chita Rivera 2/2/99
		Marilu Henner 7/6/99
		Charlotte d'Amboise 8/24/99
		Marilu Henner 12/22/99
		Nana Visitor 1/3/00

Velma Kelly

Bebe Neuwirth
  Nancy Hess
  Ute Lemper
  Bebe Neuwirth
  Ruthie Henshall 5/25/99
  Mamie Duncan-Gibbs 10/26/99
  Bebe Neuwirth 1/18/00
  Donna Marie Asbury 3/23/00
  Sharon Lawrence 4/11/00
  Vicki Lewis
  Jasmine Guy
  Bebe Neuwirth
  Donna Marie Asbury
  Deidre Goodwin
  Vicki Lewis
  Deidre Goodwin 6/29/01
  Anna Montanaro 7/9/01
  Deidre Goodwin 9/14/01
  Donna Marie Asbury
  Roxane Carrasco 1/13/02
  Deidre Goodwin 3/18/02

#1 Jasmine Guy
  Janine LaManna
  Jasmine Guy
  Donna Marie Asbury
  Stephanie Pope
  Jasmine Guy 7/7/98
  Stephanie Pope 7/14/98
  Mamie Duncan-Gibbs 1/12/99
  Deidre Goodwin 2/16/99
  Ruthie Henshall 4/22/99
  Deidre Goodwin 5/18/99
  Ruthie Henshall 4/22/99
  Deidre Goodwin 6/1/99
  Donna Marie Asbury 10/12/99
  Vicki Lewis 11/16/99
  Roxane Carrasco 1/4/00
  Vicki Lewis 3/14/00
  Roxane Carrasco 3/21/00
#2 Stephanie Pope
  Jasmine Guy
  Stephanie Pope
  Khandi Alexander 8/4/98
  Donna Marie Asbury 9/29/98
  Stephanie Pope 2/2/98
  Ute Lemper 2/19/99
  Stephanie Pope 4/5/99
  Mamie Duncan-Gibbs 8/3/99
  Jasmine Guy 8/24/99
  Marianne McCord 12/22/99
  Vicki Lewis 1/3/00

Billy Flynn

James Naughton
  Gregory Jbara
  Hinton Battle
  Alan Thicke
  Michael Berresse
  Brent Barrett
  Robert Urich 1/11/00
  Clarke Peters 2/1/00
  Brent Barrett 2/15/00
  Chuck Cooper
  Brent Barrett 7/2/01
  Chuck Cooper 8/27/01
  George Hamilton 11/12/01
  Eric Jordan Young 1/18/02
  Ron Raines 3/26/02
  George Hamilton 5/21/02

#1 Obba Babatunde
  Alan Thicke
  Michael Berresse 8/18/98
  Alan Thicke 8/25/98
  Destin Owens 10/13/98
  Alan Thicke 10/27/98
  Destin Owens 1/26/99
  Adrian Zmed 2/16/99
  Hal Linden 8/6/99
  Gregory Jbara 8/17/99
  Robert Urich 10/19/99
  Lloyd Culbreath 1/4/00
  Alan Thicke 1/18/00
  Lloyd Culbreath 2/29/00
  Alan Thicke 3/14/00
  Clarke Peters 3/21/00
#2 Brent Barrett
  Michael Berresse 11/3/98
  Brent Barrett 11/24/98
  Michael Berresse 12/1/98
  Ben Vereen 2/19/99
  Hal Linden 8/31/99
  Gregory Jbara 1/3/00
  Clarke Peters

Amos Hart

Joel Grey
  Ernie Sabella
  Tom McGowan

#1 Ron Orbach
  Michael Tucci
  Bruce Winant 12/22/98

	P.J. Benjamin	Ray Bokhour 10/19/99
	Ernie Sabella 11/23/99	P.J. Benjamin 4/4/00
	P.J. Benjamin	#2 Ernie Sabella
	Tom McGowan	Ron Orbach
	P.J. Benjamin	Tom McGowan
	Ray Bokhour 7/30/01	Ron Orbach
	P.J. Benjamin 8/13/01	P.J. Benjamin 11/10/98
		Joel Grey 12/1/98
		P.J. Benjamin 12/29/98
		Ernie Sabella 2/2/99
		Michael Tucci 8/24/99
		P.J. Benjamin 1/3/00

Matron "Mama" Morton — Marcia Lewis

	Roz Ryan	#1 Carol Woods
	Marcia Lewis	Lea DeLaria
	Roz Ryan	Carol Woods 8/4/98
	Marcia Lewis	#2 Avery Sommers
	Roz Ryan	Marcia Lewis 2/2/99
	Marcia Lewis	
	Jennifer Holliday 6/18/01	
	Marcia Lewis 8/27/01	
	Roz Ryan 11/16/01	
	Michele Pawk 1/14/02	
	Alix Korey 3/4/02	

Mary Sunshine — D. Sabella

	J. Loeffelholz	#1 M.E. Spencer
	R. Bean	D.C. Levine
	A. Saunders	M.E. Spencer 7/7/98
	J. Maldonado	R. Bean 7/28/98
	R. Bean	A. Saunders 10/13/98
	A. Saunders 1/2/02	R. Bean 10/20/98
	R. Bean 1/14/02	J. Maldonado 10/27/98
		J. Roberson 2/9/99
		M. Von Essen 5/12/99
		J. Maldonado 10/12/99
		M. Agnes 1/4/00
		#2 D.C. Levine
		M.E. Spencer 2/2/99
		D. Sabella 9/7/99

CONTACT

	New York 3/30/00	*San Francisco 5/15/01*
Girl in Swing	Stephanie Michaels	Mindy Franzese Wild
	Joanne Manning 1/29/02	
Servant	Seán Martin Hingston	Keith Kuhl
Aristocrat	Scott Taylor	Andrew Asnes
		Dan Sutcliffe
Wife	Karen Ziemba	Meg Howrey
	Charlotte d'Amboise	
Husband	Jason Antoon	Adam Dannheiser
	Danny Mastrogiorgio	
Head Waiter	David MacGillivray	Gary Franco
Michael Wiley	Boyd Gaines	Alan Campbell
	D.W. Moffett 9/13/01	Daniel McDonald 3/19/02
	Alan Campbell 3/19/02	

| *Girl in Yellow Dress* | Deborah Yates | Holly Cruikshank |
| | Colleen Dunn 9/4/01 | Deborah Yates 5/14/02 |

42ND STREET

	New York 5/2/01
Peggy Sawyer	Kate Levering
	Meredith Patterson
Julian Marsh	Michael Cumpsty
Billy Lawler	David Elder
Dorothy Brock	Christine Ebersole
	Beth Leavel 1/2/02
	Christine Ebersole 3/12/02

THE FULL MONTY

	New York 10/26/00	*Toronto 5/21/01*
Jerry Lukowski	Patrick Wilson	Rod Weber
	Will Chase	
Dave Bukatinsky	John Ellison Conlee	Daniel Stewart Sherman
	Daniel Stewart Sherman	Michael J. Todaro
Malcolm MacGregor	Jason Danieley	Danny Gurwin
	Danny Gurwin	Geoffrey Nauffts
Ethan Girard	Romain Frugé	Chris Diamantopoulos
	Chris Diamantopoulos	Christopher Hanke
Harold Nichols	Marcus Neville	Steven Skybell
	Steven Skybell	Robert Westenberg
Noah T. Simmons	André De Shields	Larry Marshall
	Larry Marshall	Cleavant Derricks
Jeanette Burmeister	Kathleen Freeman	Kaye Ballard
	Jane Connell	Carol Woods

KISS ME, KATE

	New York 11/18/99	*New Haven 6/21/01*
Fred; Petruchio	Brian Stokes Mitchell	Rex Smith
	Burke Moses 1/30/01	
Lilli; Katherine	Marin Mazzie	Rachel York
	Carolee Carmello 3/29/01	
Lois Lane; Bianca	Amy Spanger	Nancy Anderson
	JoAnn M. Hunter 4/24/01	Jenny Hill
Bill Calhoun; Lucentio	Michael Berresse	Jim Newman
	David Elder 9/19/00	Kevin Neil McCready
	Michael Berresse 12/19/00	
Hattie	Adriane Lenox	Susan Beaubian
	Mamie Duncan-Gibbs	

LES MISÉRABLES

New York 3/12/87	*Tampa 11/28/88*
Jean Valjean	Colm Wilkinson	Gary Barker
	Robert Marien 3/12/97	Gregory Calvin Stone 3/3/97
	Ivan Rutherford 9/9/97	Colm Wilkinson 7/15/98
	Robert Marien 12/12/97	Ivan Rutherford 1/19/99
	Craig Schulman 3/3/98	Randal Keith
	Fred Inkley 9/8/98	
	Tim Shaw 9/7/99	
	J. Mark McVey 3/7/00	
	Ivan Rutherford 4/23/01	
	J. Mark McVey 1/29/02	
Javert	Terrence Mann	Peter Samuel
	Christopher Innvar 10/15/96	Todd Alan Johnson 3/31/97
	Robert Gallagher 12/6/97	Stephen Bishop 8/3/99
	Philip Hernandez 10/27/98	Philip Hernandez
	Gregg Edelman 9/7/99	Joseph Mahowald
	Shuler Hensley 11/14/00	
	Philip Hernandez 11/19/01	
Fantine	Randy Graff	Hollis Resnik
	Juliet Lambert 3/12/97	Lisa Capps 3/24/97
	Lisa Capps 4/15/98	Holly Jo Crane
	Alice Ripley 9/8/98	Susan Gilmour 6/2/98
	Susan Gilmour 3/9/99	Joan Almedilla 3/2/99
	Alice Ripley 3/23/99	Thursday Farrar
	Jane Bodle 9/7/99	Joan Almedilla
	Jacquelyn Piro 4/23/01	Jayne Paterson
Enjolras	Michael Maguire	Greg Zerkle
	Stephen R. Buntrock 3/12/97	Brian Herriott
	Gary Mauer 12/8/98	Kurt Kovalenko
	Stephen R. Buntrock 4/6/99	Michael Todd Cressman
	Christopher Mark Peterson 6/21/99	Matthew Shepard 12/8/98
	Ben Davis 9/10/01	Kevin Earley 1/19/99
	Christopher Mark Peterson 1/7/02	Stephen Tewksbury 2/15/00
Marius	David Bryant	Matthew Porretta
	Peter Lockyer 3/12/97	Rich Affannato 8/12/96
		Steve Scott Springer
		Tim Howar
		Stephen Brian Patterson
Cosette	Judy Kuhn	Jacquelyn Piro
	Cristeena Michelle Riggs 3/12/97	Kate Fisher 9/9/96
	Tobi Foster 11/6/98	Regan Thiel
	Sandra Turley 2/5/01	Stephanie Waters
Eponine	Frances Ruffelle	Michele Maika
	Sarah Uriarte Berry 3/12/97	Rona Figueroa 3/31/97
	Megan Lawrence 6/19/98	Jessica-Snow Wilson 5/19/99
	Kerry Butler 12/11/98	Sutton Foster 1/19/99
	Megan Lawrence 2/25/99	Diana Kaarina 3/21/00
	Rona Figueroa 6/3/99	Dina Morishita
	Megan Lawrence 6/24/99	Ma-Anne Dionisio
	Jessica-Snow Wilson 8/31/99	
	Rona Figueroa 9/14/99	
	Jessica Boevers 12/7/00	
	Catherine Brunell 8/10/00	

Dana Meller 12/13/01
Diana Kaarina 1/13/02

THE LION KING

	New York 11/13/97	#1 Los Angeles, CA 10/19/00 #2 Gazelle Company 4/27/02
Rafiki	Tsidii Le Loka Thuli Dumakude 11/11/98 Sheila Gibbs	#1 Fuschia #2 Fredi Walker-Browne
Mufasa	Samuel E. Wright	#1 Rufus Bonds Jr. #2 Alton Fitzgerald White
Sarabi	Gina Breedlove Meena T. Jahi 8/4/98 Denise Marie Williams Meena T. Jahi	#1 Marvette Williams #2 Jean Michelle Grier
Zazu	Geoff Hoyle Bill Bowers 10/21/98 Robert Dorfman Tony Freeman	#1 William Akey #2 Jeffrey Binder
Scar	John Vickery Tom Hewitt 10/21/98 Derek Smith	#1 John Vickery #2 Patrick Page
Banzai	Stanley Wayne Mathis Keith Bennett 9/30/98 Leonard Joseph Curtiss I' Cook	#1 Jeffrey Polk #2 James Brown-Orleans
Shenzi	Tracy Nicole Chapman Vanessa S. Jones Lana Gordon	#1 Carla Renata Williams #2 Jacquelyn Renae Hodges
Ed	Kevin Cahoon Jeff Skowron 10/21/98 Jeff Gurner Timothy Gulan	#1 Price Waldman Jim Raposa 12/2/01 #2 Wayne Pyle
Timon	Max Casella Danny Rutigliano 6/16/98 John E. Brady	#1 Danny Rutigliano #2 John Plumpis
Pumba	Tom Alan Robbins	#1 Bob Bouchard #2 Blake Hammond
Simba	Jason Raize Christopher Jackson	#1 Clifton Oliver #2 Josh Tower
Nala	Heather Headley Mary Randle 7/7/98 Heather Headley 12/8/98 Bashirrah Creswell Sharon L. Young	#1 Moe Daniels Jewl Anguay 10/3/01 #2 Kissy Simmons

MEREDITH WILLSON'S THE MUSIC MAN

	New York 4/27/00
Harold Hill	Craig Bierko Eric McCormick 5/8/01 Robert Sean Leonard 6/7/01

Marian Paroo	Rebecca Luker
Marcellus	Max Casella
	Joel Blum 1/5/01
Mayor Shinn	Paul Benedict
	Kenneth Kimmins 4/10/01
Eulalie Shinn	Ruth Williamson
	Ruth Gottschall 8/17/00
Tommy Djilas	Clyde Alves
	Manuel Herrera 4/10/01
Zaneeta Shinn	Kate Levering
	Cameron Adams 2/20/01

THE PHANTOM OF THE OPERA

New York 1/26/88

#1 *Los Angeles 5/31/90*
#2 *Chicago 5/24/90*
#3 *Seattle 12/13/92*

The Phantom   Michael Crawford
  Thomas James O'Leary 10/11/96
  Hugh Panaro 2/1/99
  Howard McGillin 8/23/99

#1 Michael Crawford
    Franc D'Ambrosio 3/28/94
#2 Mark Jacoby
    Rick Hilsabeck
    Craig Schulman 1/30/97
    Ron Bohmer 9/97
    Davis Gaines 8/98
#3 Franc D'Ambrosio
    Brad Little
    Ted Keegan
    Brad Little
    Ted Keegan
    Brad Little

Christine Daae   Sarah Brightman
  Sandra Joseph 1/29/98
  Adrienne McEwan (alt.) 4/21/97
  Adrienne McEwan 8/2/99
  Sarah Pfisterer (alt.)
  Sarah Pfisterer 1/17/00
  Adrienne McEwan (alt.)
  Sandra Joseph 10/30/00
  Lisa Vroman (alt.) 10/30/00
  Adrienne McEwan (alt.) 7/9/01
  Sarah Pfisterer 8/6/01
  Beth Southard 3/25/02
  Lisa Vroman 4/22/02

#1 Dale Kristien
    Lisa Vroman 12/2/93
    Cristin Mortenson (alt.)
    Karen Culliver (alt.) 6/3/97
#2 Karen Culliver
    Sandra Joseph 3/26/96
    Marie Danvers 1/13/98
    Teri Bibb 4/98
    Susan Owen (alt.) 9/24/96
    Rita Harvey (alt.) 3/98
    Marie Danvers 6/98
    Susan Facer (alt.) 6/98
#3 Tracy Shane
    Kimilee Bryant
    Amy Jo Arrington
    Tamra Hayden (alt.)
    Marie Danvers (alt.)
    Megan Starr-Levitt (alt.)
    Rebecca Pitcher
    Kathy Voytko
    Julie Hanson

Raoul   Steve Barton
  Gary Mauer 4/19/99
  Jim Weitzer 4/23/01
  Michael Shawn Lewis 11/2/01

#1 Reece Holland
    Christopher Carl 7/2/96
#2 Keith Buterbaugh
    Lawrence Anderson

> Jason Pebworth 1/13/98
> Lawrence Anderson 7/98
> #3 Ciaran Sheehan
> Jason Pebworth 1/29/97
> Jim Weitzer
> Jason Pebworth 7/22/98
> Richard Todd Adams 3/31/99
> Jim Weitzer 1/12/00
> John Cudia
> Tim Martin Gleason

THE PRODUCERS

New York 4/19/01

Max	Nathan Lane Henry Goodman 3/19/02 Brad Oscar 4/16/02
Leo	Matthew Broderick Steven Weber 3/19/02
Ulla	Cady Huffman
Roger	Gary Beach
Carmen Ghia	Roger Bart
Franz	Brad Oscar John Treacy Egan

Replacement players: Brad Oscar and Steven Weber in The Producers. *Photo: Paul Kolnik*

PROOF

	New York 10/24/00	*Seattle 10/15/01*
Robert	Larry Bryggman Patrick Tovatt 6/12/01	Robert Foxworth
Catherine	Mary-Louise Parker Jennifer Jason Leigh	Chelsea Altman
Hal	Ben Shenkman Josh Hamilton	Stephen Kunken
Claire	Johanna Day Seana Kofoed	Tasha Lawrence

RENT

	New York 4/29/96	*#1 Boston 11/18/96 closed 9/5/99 #2 La Jolla 7/1/97*

Roger Davis	Adam Pascal
	Norbert Leo Butz
	Richard H. Blake (alt)
	Manley Pope 12/1/98
		#1 Sean Keller
		    Manley Pope 3/14/97
		    Christian Anderson
		    Dean Balkwill
		#2 Christian Mena
		    Cary Shields
		    Christian Mena
		    Cary Shields
		    Jeremy Kushnier 3/8/01

Mark Cohen	Anthony Rapp
	Jim Poulos
	Trey Ellett 5/15/00
	Matt Caplan 5/19/02
		#1 Luther Creek
		    Christian Anderson
		    Trey Ellett
		#2 Neil Patrick Harris
		    Kirk McDonald
		    Scott Hunt
		    Matt Caplan 2/1/00

Tom Collins	Jesse L. Martin
	Michael McElroy
	Rufus Bonds Jr. 9/7/99
	Alan Mingo Jr. 4/10/00
	Mark Leroy Jackson 1/15/01
	Mark Richard Ford 2/3/02
		#1 C.C. Brown
		    Mark Leroy Jackson
		#2 Mark Leroy Jackson
		    Dwayne Clark
		    Horace V. Rogers
		    Mark Richard Ford 6/13/99

Benjamin Coffin III	Taye Diggs
	Jacques C. Smith
	Stu James 3/13/00
		#1 James Rich
		    Dwayne Clark
		    Brian Love
		#2 D'Monroe
		    Brian Love
		    Carl Thornton
		    Stu James
		    Brian Love 2/29/00

Joanne Jefferson	Fredi Walker
	Gwen Stewart
	Alia León
	Kenna J. Ramsey
	Danielle Lee Greaves 10/4/99
	Natalie Venetia Belcon 10/2/00
	Myiia Watson-Davis 10/28/01
		#1 Sylvia MacCalla
		    Kamilah Martin
		#2 Kenna J. Ramsey
		    Monique Daniels
		    Danielle Lee Greaves
		    Jacqueline B. Arnold

Angel Schunard	Wilson Jermaine Heredia	#1 Stephan Alexander
	Wilson Cruz	Shaun Earl
	Shaun Earl	Evan D'Angeles
	Jose Llana	Shaun Earl
	Jai Rodriguez	#2 Wilson Cruz
	Andy Senor 1/31/00	Andy Senor
	Jai Rodriguez 3/10/02	Pierre Bayuga
		Shaun Earl 11/23/99
Mimi Marquez	Daphne Rubin-Vega	#1 Simone
	Marcy Harriell 4/5/97	Laura Dias
	Krysten Cummings	Daphne Rubin-Vega
	Maya Days	Sharon Leal
	Loraine Velez 2/28/00	#2 Julia Santana
	Karmine Alers 12/31/01	Saycon Sengbloh 11/30/99
		Dominique Roy 12/5/00
Maureen Johnson	Idina Menzel	#1 Carrie Hamilton
	Sherie René Scott	Amy Spanger 6/5/97
	Kristen Lee Kelly	Erin Keaney
	Tamara Podemski	#2 Leigh Hetherington
	Cristina Fadale 10/4/99	Carla Bianco
	Maggie Benjamin 10/28/01	Leigh Hetherington
		Cristina Fadale
		Michelle Joan Smith 9/28/99
		Erin Keaney 4/7/00
		Maggie Benjamin 9/12/00

THE ROCKY HORROR SHOW

New York 11/15/00

Frank 'N' Furter	Tom Hewitt
	Terrence Mann
Janet Weiss	Alice Ripley
	Kristen Lee Kelly
Brad Majors	Jarrod Emick
	Luke Perry 6/26/01
	Jarrod Emick 7/3/01
Riff Raff	Raúl Esparza
	Mark Price
	Sebastian Bach
Magenta	Daphne Rubin-Vega
Columbia	Joan Jett
	Kristen Lee Kelly
	Ana Gasteyer 6/12/01
	Liz Larsen
Rocky	Sebastian LaCause
	Jonathan Sharp
Dr. Scott; Eddie	Lea DeLaria
	Jason Wooten

THE TALE OF THE ALLERGIST'S WIFE

New York 11/2/00

| Mohammed | Anil Kumar |
| | Charles Daniel Sandoval 5/28/02 |

Marjorie	Linda Lavin
	Valerie Harper 7/31/01
	Rhea Perlman 5/28/02
Ira	Tony Roberts
	Richard Kind 5/28/02
Frieda	Shirl Bernheim
	Chevi Colton 5/28/02
	Rose Arrick (alt.)
Lee	Michele Lee
	Marilu Henner 5/28/02

FIRST-CLASS NATIONAL TOURS

THE BEST LITTLE WHOREHOUSE IN TEXAS

Wallingford, CT 2/13/01

Mona Stangley	Ann-Margret
Sheriff Dodd	Gary Sandy
Jewel	Avery Sommers
Governor	Ed Dixon
Angel	Terri Dixon
Doatsey Mae	Roxie Lucas
Shy	Jan Celene Little
Mayor Poindexter; Senator Wingwoah	Matt Landers

CINDERELLA

Tampa Bay, FL 11/28/00

Cinderella	Deborah Gibson
	Jamie-Lynn Sigler 3/6/01
	Jessica Rush
Prince	Paolo Montalban
Fairy Godmother	Eartha Kitt
King	Ken Prymus
Queen	Leslie Becker
Stepmother	Everett Quinton
Grace	NaTasha Yvette Williams
Joy	Alexandra Kolb
	Sandra Bargman
Lionel	Victor Trent Cook
	Brooks Ashmanskas 5/8/01

COPENHAGEN

Los Angeles 11/27/01

| *Margrethe Bohr* | Mariette Hartley |
| *Niels Bohr* | Len Cariou |

Werner Heisenberg   Hank Stratton

DIRTY BLONDE

Washington, DC 12/9/01

Jo; Mae	Claudia Shear
	Sally Mayes
Charlie; Others	Tom Riis Farrell
Frank; Ed; Others	Bob Stillman

FIDDLER ON THE ROOF

Detroit, MI 10/24/00

Tevye	Theodore Bikel
Golde	Susan Cella
	Maureen Silliman 12/9/01
Lazar Wolf	John Preece
Yente	Miriam Babin
	Mimi Bensinger 1/15/02
Chava	Dana Lynn Caruso
	Sara Schmidt 4/17/01
Perchik	Daniel Cooney
	Jonathan Hadley 11/16/01
Fyedka	Brad Drummer
	Justin Patterson 5/28/01
	Brad Drummer 11/16/01
Hodel	Tamra Hayden
	Rachel Jones 11/16/01
Motel	Michael Iannucci
Tzeitel	Eileen Tepper

GUYS AND DOLLS

Vienna, VA 8/28/01

Nathan Detroit	Maurice Hines
Adelaide	Alexandra Foucard
Sky Masterson	Brian Sutherland
Sarah Brown	Diane Sutherland

MAMMA MIA!

#1 San Francisco, CA 11/14/00
#2 Providence, RI 2/26/02

Donna Sheridan	#1 Louise Pitre
	Dee Hoty
	#2 Monique Lund
Sam Carmichael	#1 Gary P. Lynch
	#2 Don Noble

Sophie Sheridan	#1 Tina Maddigan Michelle Arvena #2 Kristie Marsden
Sky	#1 Adam Brazier Ryan Silverman #2 Chris Bolan
Rosie	#1 Gabrielle Jones #2 Robin Baxter
Tanya	#1 Mary Ellen Mahoney #2 Ellen Harvey
Harry Bright	#1 Lee MacDougal Mark Zimmerman #2 James Kall
Bill Austin	#1 David Mucci Craig Bennett #2 Pearce Bunting

THE ODD COUPLE

Little Rock, AR 11/07/01

Florence Unger	Barbara Eden
Olive Madison	Rita McKenzie

SATURDAY NIGHT FEVER

Chicago 03/06/01

Tony Manero	Richard H. Blake
Stephanie Mangano	Jeanine Meyers
Annette	Aileen Quinn
Bobby C	Jim Ambler

SOUTH PACIFIC

St Paul, MN 7/23/01

Nellie Forbush	Erin Dilly Amanda Watkins
Emile de Becque	Michael Nouri Robert Goulet
Bloody Mary	Amelia McQueen Gretha Boston
Joe Cable	Lewis Cleale

TOMMY

Los Angeles 12/18/01

Tommy	Michael Seelbach
Mrs. Walker	Lisa Capps
Captain Walker	Michael Berry

Acid Queen	Monique L. Midgette
Cousin Kevin	Daniel Levine
Sally Simpson	Cara Cooper

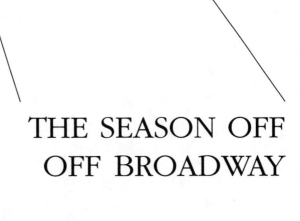

THE SEASON OFF
OFF BROADWAY

THE SEASON OFF OFF BROADWAY

○ ○ ○ ○ ○ *By Mel Gussow* ○ ○ ○ ○ ○

ALONG WITH ALL OF THE PERSONAL TRAGEDIES of September 11, there was great economic fallout. Businesses suffered, not least of all those involved in the performing arts. While attendance dipped on Broadway—and then was buoyed somewhat by the end of the season— Off Off Broadway theaters never fully recovered, and some, especially those in the downtown area, ended or at least temporarily suspended their operations. Part of the problem, of course, was that theatergoers were reluctant to spend their evenings anywhere near the frozen zone, but there was also a general economic failure for those companies already operating on a marginal budget.

It was generally agreed that artists would need to take their time to respond to the acts of terrorism. In December, however, *The Guys*, a tribute to the firemen who lost their lives in the rescue operation, opened as a workshop at the Flea Theater, where it was directed by Jim Simpson, the company's artistic director. The author was Anne Nelson, a journalist and a teacher of journalism at Columbia University. Her first play, it was simply a dialogue between a fireman and an editor who is helping him to write a eulogy to fallen comrades. Because of its timely subject matter and its changing cast of stars, the play soon became a theatrical event, drawing uptown audiences to this fringe theater.

Although *The Guys* was earnest and heartfelt, it did not fulfill its dramatic potential. It would have benefited from more originality in the writing or, on the other hand, it could have been a straightforward documentary, as later was so effective in various television films dealing with September 11. Instead, it occupied a middle ground, falling short both as theater and journalism. What made it of continuing interest were the actors who participated. It opened with Sigourney Weaver and Bill Murray—sitting on stage, scripts in hand—and the two of them added an emotional line that was well hidden in the play. Best known as a comic actor, Murray was especially touching in his role as a survivor grasping for something to hold on to. Other actors followed them in the roles, including Susan Sarandon,

Tim Robbins, Bill Irwin, Anthony LaPaglia, Swoosie Kurtz, Tom Wopat and Amy Irving. The play proved to be so popular that its run was extended again and again.

Parenthetically, before September 11, Simpson had gone about one of his early traditions at the Flea, rediscovering obscure plays from the past, in this case, Lillian Mortimer's *No Mother to Guide Her*, a melodrama from the early 20th century. Expecting a kind of American *Wild Oats* (that delightful Royal Shakespeare Company rediscovery), I found . . . not much of anything. The play was a thicket of twists, momentarily made passable by a few of the actors, namely Leila Howland as a manipulative con artist named Bunco and Cori Clark Nelson in the romantic lead.

But to return to theater responding to the moment: far more effective in an indirect way was the musical *Islands*, which gave only one performance at the New Victory Theater. Created by John Wulp (an experienced New York producer, director and designer) and Cindy Bullens (a songwriter and singer), the show began as a community enterprise for the residents of the island of North Haven in Maine. It featured a cast of local residents: teachers and parents, the mailman as narrator and many school children. Through Wulp's book and agile direction, Bullens's melodic score and a talented cast of nonprofessionals, the musical far exceeded expectations. It offered an intimate and captivating look at people who choose to live on islands, and at least tangentially think of them as sanctuaries. Because of September 11, the Maine troupe's scheduled visit to New York was almost cancelled. Then, it was decided to bring it to New York as a kind of tribute from one island (North Haven) to another (Manhattan). Either touring or in a return to New York, *Islands* deserves to have a future life.

Elizabeth Swados, who was one of the initial encouragers of the island musical (but did not participate in it), returned late in the season with her new work in progress, *The Violence Project*. As she has in previous years, beginning with *Runaways*, she created this musical in collaboration with nonprofessionals, in this case New York City school children. *The Violence Project* toured schools and made a brief stop at La MaMa, where Swados has done much of her previous work. Diligent and well-intentioned, the show dealt with varieties of violence among children and began with a scene of a girl beating her doll, while she was being beaten by her mother. In performance, the work seemed sprawling and unfocused—this was not *Runaways*—but the spirit was tonic and several of the songs and scenes lingered in one's mind. In one striking moment, a jigsaw version of the World Trade Center towers crumbled; "Secrets, Lies and Muffled Cries" was a final song of hope.

THE SEASON, BEFORE SEPTEMBER 11, began on a salutary note with the Lincoln Center Festival. Its high point was a festival within the festival featuring plays by Harold Pinter. As a successor to the Samuel Beckett festival of several seasons ago at Lincoln Center, the Pinter series offered nine plays—with Pinter represented as a playwright, actor and director—and 10 films written by him. The plays ranged from his first, *The Room*, to his latest, *Celebration*, and included a masterly revival of *The Homecoming*. Ian Holm, who created the role of Lenny, an especially unsavory member of the *Homecoming* family, moved up to the role of the domineering father.

Celebration, cited as an outstanding OOB production, was a return of Pinter to a comic mode after such somber works as *Moonlight* and *Ashes to Ashes*. In this spirited comedy, couples (two brothers married to two sisters) celebrate and clash in an upscale restaurant. Filled with Pinterly strokes—things said and things unsaid—*Celebration* had a twist of the absurd. It was deftly directed by the author. His surrogate onstage is a waiter, who repeatedly interrupts the diners with hilarious reflections on his grandfather, who seemingly (but not really) knew everyone from T.S. Eliot to Elisha Cook Jr. That part of the play was direct from life. Many years ago, as an unemployed actor, Pinter worked as a waiter until the day that he interrupted a conversation among diners to interject his knowledge of Franz Kafka. He was fired for his efforts—not so the waiter in the play. Lindsay Duncan, later to score a huge success (and a Tony Award) in the Broadway revival of *Private Lives* did a virtuosic turn in the Pinter plays, as a dowdy housewife in *The Room* and a glamorous partygoer in *Celebration*.

Another highlight of the Lincoln Center Festival was a performance of *Edda*, Icelandic tales adapted by Benjamin Bagby and Ping Chong, and enacted by Bagby. Though admittedly specialized, it was a magical retelling of eerie stories, in which threats are omnipresent. Equally offbeat was *POEtry*, a salute to Edgar Allan Poe by Robert Wilson and Lou Reed, at the Brooklyn Academy of Music. Visually striking—as always—Wilson went all out on sets, costumes, lights and strange effects, including the motif of a headless man. The stories included "The Tell-Tale Heart" and "The Cask of Amontillado," filtered through Wilson's imagination and elevated by Reed's song cycle. Also part of BAM's Next Wave Festival was the United States debut of *Cloudstreet*, an Australian epic, adapted by Nick Enright and Justin Monjo from the novel by Tim Winton. This five-hour marathon told the story of two families in the 1940s and 1950s, and by inference was a metaphor for Australia itself during this time. Using some of the techniques of *Nicholas Nickleby*, *Cloudstreet*—despite the acclaim it had received in London—turned out to be uninspired and impossibly elongated.

Far more interesting—and innovative—was Tadashi Suzuki's freely interpretative version of *Electra* at the Japan Society (in repertory with *Oedipus*). The scene was a madhouse and patients came clacking onstage in wheelchairs—almost like a production number from *The Producers*. The audience laughed, and then gradually the laughter curdled, as Suzuki revealed a highly emotional and relevant view of a Greek classic, one that at moments paid homage to Peter Brook's celebrated Beckettian production of *King Lear*.

The New York International Fringe Festival, in August, was the most ambitious Off Off Broadway project of the season, featuring some 180 shows at 20 theaters and performance spaces, including such oddities as *Debbie Does Dallas*, a stage version of the porno film; *Elephant Man: The Musical* and *21 Dog Years: Doing Time @ Amazon.com*, which later had an Off Broadway run.

Next in ambition was the Ionesco Festival created by Edward Einhorn, artistic director of the Untitled Theater Company. During a three-month period, more than a dozen theaters throughout New York City—including the Pearl, the Jean Cocteau, the Connelly, Here and the Untitled—presented nearly 40 plays by Eugène Ionesco: the famous works (*Rhinoceros*, *Exit the King*, *The Chairs*, *The Bald Soprano*) and the lesser known (*To Prepare a Hard Boiled Egg*, *The Picture*). At the same time, Ionesco films were shown and there were several seminars. I moderated one at the Players with Tina Howe, Israel Horovitz, David Ives and Richard Foreman, a thought-provoking discussion in which Foreman played devil's advocate against a background of fervid Ionesco admirers.

BEING CLOSE TO GROUND ZERO, the Soho area was directly affected by the fallout from the attack. In November, the Soho Rep on Walker Street presented Melissa James Gibson's *[sic]*, which dealt with three young people in close quarters in a New York apartment house, brought together by circumstance into friendship. There was talent here and eccentric dialogue, some of it overlapping, but the story was thin and repetitive. Gibson evidently aspired to a kind of Alan Ayckbourn cleverness but settled for quirkiness. Nevertheless, *[sic]* is honored in this volume as a 2001–02 Best Play.

In contrast, Jessica Goldberg's *Good Thing*, presented by the New Group, opened our eyes to an unfamiliar world, and did so in imaginative ways. This slice of sad (not really sordid) life among the dysfunctional and drug addicted was keenly observed and acted with a sense of reality and immediacy. An early marriage, unwanted pregnancy, dropouts almost accidently becoming a family—this is characteristic Goldberg country. The youthful characters, confused and unsure about their future, were contrasted to an older married couple, who, despite their experience, had no answers, no solutions—only middleage platitudes. As directed by Jo Bonney, and featuring Chris Messina, Alicia Goranson, Cara Buono and Hamish Linklater, *Good Thing* merited a citation as an outstanding OOB production.

At the end of the season, the New Group returned with another provocative play, *Smelling a Rat* by Mike Leigh. Written in 1988, it finally arrived in New York, after the New Group had presented Leigh's later *Ecstasy* and *Goose-Pimples*, and after the author had been firmly established as a film auteur. Scott Elliott seems to have a special affinity for Leigh's idiosyncratic approach to theater. The playwright described *Smelling a Rat* an antifarce, which means that the play does not work for laughs (but they come anyway). In it, a wealthy exterminator (Terence Rigby) returns home early from a holiday and finds his apartment invaded by various intruders. People jump into closets and otherwise spook each other, but nothing much happens. The exterminator's reclusive son hardly ever speaks, his son's girlfriend giggles, the boss's hired hand spouts mouthfuls of large words. But taken all together, the play and performance establish a mood on the outer edges of absurdism, and there were vivid performances by Rigby and by Michelle Williams (a star on television's *Dawson's Creek*) as the girlfriend in question.

True Love, one of Charles L. Mee's trilogy of "love plays," also deals with dysfunctionalism, but in a desultory fashion. This was an uninvolving series of monologues and dialogues mostly about sex (and mostly about incest) that took place, for some reason, in a garage. At the core is a variation on *Phèdre*, not directly evoked until the final scene between husband, wife and stepson. As it turned out, the garage was the most interesting aspect of the production, filled with gewgaws and gimcracks that might have been envied by a collector like Richard Foreman.

FOR THE 50TH PRODUCTION of his Ontological-Hysteric Theater, Foreman created *Maria del Bosco: A Sound Opera (Sex & Racing Cars)*, a fascinating exploration into the world of fashion and ballet—and yes there is a racing car (and he did not forget the sex). As elliptical as ever, Foreman retains his title as the champion of the avant garde, someone who has stubbornly and insightfully gone his own way for more than 30 years. There is no linear movement here, but there is movement, in a piece that is more choreographic than usual. As Foreman explained in an essay, his characters are trying to "escape through impulsive behavior," and are told repeatedly to resist the present, and, presumably to look to the future.

I caught up to the show at the end of its long run, and, as always, the theater was filled with Foreman enthusiasts. A young man seated behind me seemed to be trying to seduce his date through his knowledge of Foreman. She had never seen one of his plays before and her companion explained that Foreman was "a philosopher poet from another time" (he must have read that somewhere), who dealt in both images and intellectual ideas. "Cool," she said. "Cool." And indeed it was. Then Foreman came out and asked the audience to turn off their beepers and cell phones, partly, one suspects, so as not to interfere with his own beeps, blurts and musical soundtrack. An OOB citation for outstanding production goes to Foreman and his latest postexistential experience.

On other stages, New York's experimental theater was represented by the Wooster Group's *To You, the Birdie!* the company's deconstruction of Racine's *Phèdre* (which went to London after its stand in Brooklyn) and by *Ecco Porco*, the latest in Lee Breuer's "animations," with animals at the center (beavers, dogs and now pigs). (*Phèdre* and *Cymbeline* were among the classics most frequently revived this season.) The Irish Repertory Theatre brought back Hugh Leonard's *A Life* and the Mint Theater Company offered rare revivals of *Rutherford and Son* and *No Time for Comedy*.

Drawers-room comedy: Cheryl Lynn Bowers and Kristine Nielsen in Steve Martin's The Underpants. *Photo: Dixie Sheridan*

Continuing its policy of investigating and reinventing classics, Classic Stage Company presented Neal Bell's *Monster*, a new version of Mary Shelley's *Frankenstein*, directed by Michael Greif. The high point of the season at this enterprising theater was the world premiere of *The Underpants*, Steve Martin's adaptation of Carl Sternheim's *Bloomers*, a pre-absurdist German play from 1910. The play was commissioned and directed by Barry Edelstein, CSC artistic director. Sternheim had wanted to be the German Molière—that's how Martin approached his adaptation and how the actors played it—though from the evidence here Sternheim still posed no competition for the French master. Byron Jennings was the pompous, self-deluding husband (like Molière's Orgon in *Tartuffe*), fussily and amusingly browbeating his neglected wife (Cheryl Lynn Bowers). While watching the king on parade, she accidentally dropped her underpants. That becomes something of a public scandal—and also provokes a high degree of male admiration, even from the king himself. This was a frenetic, frequently funny farce, with many of the choice comic moments coming from Kristine Nielsen as a nosy neighbor. As adapter, Martin juggled and jettisoned aspects of the original and wrote several new scenes. As an actor, he could have played all of the male roles, or at least most of them: men turned on by the thought of dropped drawers.

CSC followed *The Underpants* with *Room*, one of Anne Bogart's series of biodramas about artists (others have dealt with Robert Wilson, Robert Rauschenberg and Leonard Bernstein). *Room* was about Virginia Woolf, and her *A Room of One's Own* was a primary source of Jocelyn Clarke's adaptation. As played by Ellen Lauren, this is Bogart's impressionistic view of the closeted and depressive world of Woolf. The set—an almost bare room—had, as intended, an aura of loneliness, and a sad, mournful mood was firmly established. But Lauren is no Eileen Atkins, whose *A Room of One's Own* (1991) was a transforming event, and a paradigm of the art of acting. In the case of *Room*, the actress lacked variety in her voice, speaking on a schoolmarm-ish level, and she was directed into awkward poses as well as balletic movement. Some of this was effective, other moments were self-conscious, and the play seemed far longer than its 90 minutes. The strongest moment was a passage delivered as a Beckettian stream of consciousness (as in *Not I*), which underscored the character's incipient madness.

For several seasons, The Actors Company Theatre (or TACT) has been reinvestigating the theatrical past, presenting staged readings of plays by Shaw, Anouilh and others. With *Long Island Sound*, a forgotten work by Noël Coward, TACT emerged into full public view—and it was a mistake.

This purported comedy inspired by a weekend Coward once spent on Long Island, is unworthy of its author, and it was shabbily directed by Scott Alan Evans. In a large, hyperactive cast, only Simon Jones (in the lead) and Delphi Harrington emerged with their dignity intact.

Stephen Belber, one of many promising playwrights to emerge from the writing program at Juilliard (led by Marsha Norman and other playwrights), was represented by *Tape*. In a curious reversal, the movie version had previously been released. (The play premiered at the 2000 Humana Festival of New American Plays in Louisville, Kentucky.) In the Naked Angels production directed by Geoffrey Nauffts, the play proved to be a stageworthy effort. A study of date rape and its effect on three people, including the rapist and the raped, it was taut both in the writing and the acting (by Dominic Fumusa, Josh Stamberg and Alison West).

The Vineyard Theatre—which in past seasons presented the New York premieres of Edward Albee's *Three Tall Women* and Paula Vogel's *How I Learned to Drive*—both Pulitzer Prize-winners, continued to devote its attention to new work. Cornelius Eady and Diedre Murray, who created the musical *Running Man*, were represented by *Brutal Imagination*, based on Eady's poem of that title, about racism. *Swimming With Watermelons*, written and directed by Diane Paulus (who also directed *Brutal Imagination*) and Randy Weiner, was a musicalized variation on the story of Paulus's parents, who fell in love in Japan after World War II. Doug Wright, author of *Quills*, returned with *Unwrap Your Candy*, four one-acts that seemed mild fare compared to his past, often outrageous efforts. The most evocative of the short plays was a long one-act about a rental agent and a killer (Leslie Lyles and Reg Rogers). Wright also offered a fairly funny sketch about a fetus that speaks.

LATELY THERE HAVE BEEN MANY PLAYS about the world of art, most auspiciously Naomi Iizuka's *36 Views* at the Public Theater. One problem with such a subject is, of course, how to deal with the art itself, how to demonstrate the creative act onstage. With *Lapis Blue Blood Red*, Cathy Caplan tried and failed, although she had a minimal success with the scenic background. The play was about Artemisia Gentileschi, one of the earliest and most famous female artists. In 17th century Italy, she lived and worked with her father Orazio, a better known painter of their time, and she brought a charge of rape against one of his protégés. The writing in the piece was mock poetic and the rape trial lost momentum as it unfolded. The performances were overwrought, except for Meg Glenn and Erica Bey,

Reel west? Ethan Hawke and Arliss Howard in The Late Henry Moss. *Photo: Susan Johann*

who played the two ages of Artemisia. Wisely, designer David Barber filled the stage with copies of the artist's work. But this was not the play the subject deserved. Simultaneously, Artemisia's world was in breathtaking evidence at an exhibition of work by both father and daughter at the Metropolitan Museum of Art.

The Signature Theatre Company—which devotes each season to a single playwright—took two years off from its central mission, to offer new plays by its house playwrights. The 2001–2002 season, the second of these departures from Signature's norm, began with Sam Shepard's *The Late Henry Moss*. It's a familiar Shepard story (as in *True West*) about two brothers in conflict and, in this case, united against an unsympathetic father. The play begins as a mystery, exploring how the father died, and for two acts it holds our interest, but the third sputters to a conclusion as the father appears in a flashback—alive and mean as ever. Ethan Hawke shone as the younger brother, but the best moments were with two minor characters, a cab driver (Clark Middleton) and an Hispanic neighbor (José Perez).

At the Signature, *The Late Henry Moss* was followed by Edward Albee's *Occupant*, a biographical play starring Anne Bancroft as Louise Nevelson. When Bancroft became ill, performances were suspended, then reinstituted, but the play was never opened to reviewers. Undoubtedly it will return.

The Signature season closed with John Guare's *A Few Stout Individuals*, cited as an outstanding OOB production. An epic fantasy about Ulysses S. Grant, the play is, at times, satirical and farcical, farfetched and down to earth and filled with humor and passion. In other words, it is definitively a work by Guare. The story, apparently based on fact, concerns Mark Twain, acting as publisher, trying to get Grant to write his memoirs. The problem is that Grant is at the point of being delusionary and only has brief moments of lucidity. In Grant's mind, the Emperor and Empress of Japan are present in New York (rather than in the past, in Japan), and they take part in the confrontation that surrounds the central character. Around him circle his dutiful wife (Polly Holliday) and his warring family. Donald Moffat, stepping in and out of reality, was a persuasive Grant and William Sadler was an ideal Twain, complete with twang and bluster. Some aspects of the writing were ineffective, like a sculptor (Ümit Çelebi) who is anxious about finishing his bust of Grant and continually tries to enter the room and Grant's life. But the play is tantalizing, a hearty Guarian exploration of memory, history and war.

For 25 years, the Ensemble Studio Theatre has presented its annual marathon of one-act plays, introducing new writers and also giving established playwrights a chance to flex their talents in the short form. In this year's festival, as always, there were good plays as well as those that should never have moved onto a stage in such unfinished fashion. This season, the marathon was distinguished by works from two versatile veterans and longtime EST contributors, Romulus Linney and Horton Foote.

Linney's *Lark*, drawn from a novel by Willa Cather, was a sensitive story of artistic yearning, about a young pianist who turns out to be a singer. In the play, Winslow Corbett made her auspicious New York debut. Although Foote's *The Prisoner's Song* was only 40 minutes long, it had the sweep and lyricism of one of the author's full-length plays, and is cited as an outstanding OOB production. A young couple in Harrison, Texas (the locus of so many of Foote's fine plays) is borderline hopeless. The husband (Tim Guinee) is unable to find a job, the wife (Mary Catherine Garrison) is scraping by and slowly losing her equilibrium. Where can they turn for surcease? A possible benefactor enters their life—the town's rich man (Michael P. Moran), whose daughter was a schoolmate of the young wife. He promises employment but is really only seeking a substitute daughter. In a sense, these three characters (and a landlady) are all prisoners of their own lives and illusions. The future is bleak, but the play—beautifully staged (by Harris Yulin) and acted—is subtle and poignant.

Grant's tomb: Polly Holliday and Donald Moffat in John Guare's A Few Stout Individuals. *Photo: Susan Johann*

DRAMA MOVED OUT OF THEATERS and into an art gallery, with an exhibition at Exit Art gallery on lower Broadway. The exhibition focused on the work of six experimental directors, all of whom have had their work presented Off Off Broadway: Richard Foreman, Robert Wilson, Anne Bogart, Meredith Monk, Peter Schumann (of the Bread and Puppet Theatre) and Reza Abdoh. As curated by Norman Frisch, the displays—some animated— were designed as self-portraits of the artists. Each was represented by a large, walk-in environment that conjured the spirit and also the specificity of the work. In a sense, it was the equivalent of those moments in movies by Buster Keaton or Woody Allen, in which people watching a movie suddenly walk into the screen and become part of the action. Entering the gallery, we are onstage with the various directors.

With Foreman, the space was like a setting for one of his plays, a curio cabinet of intricate motifs. One walked under the director's signature string that traverses his stage and faced walls filled with jottings from his journals and memories of *Rhoda in Potatoland*, an early seminal work. Lining the space were Foreman's authorial precepts, "10 Things I Hate About the Theater," which offers clues to the nature of his art. Number 6 is "Narrative form being the rule, as opposed to the more potent strategies of theme and variation." In other words, stop looking for a storyline in his work.

In Bogart's display, the walls were lined with an open photo album of memories of past shows, including an early version of *The Lower Depths* that she called *At the Bottom*. In it, she wondered "what would happen if a bunch of East Village skinhead punks found the play and decided to perform it once a week in a deserted basketball court." In this environment one had flashes of memory of various Bogart experiments: *No Plays No Poetry*, her tribute to Brecht, as well as such regional theater excursions as her vivid reinterpretation of Elmer Rice's *The Adding Machine*. Then there were the Bogarts I missed, such as her event in Bern, Switzerland, where, we are told, "audiences met at the top of a hill above Bern's train station and encountered scenes as they walked down towards the building where most of the play would take place."

Wilson's contribution was a kind of sculpture garden of chairs from various productions (*The Life and Times of Joseph Stalin, Death, Destruction and Detroit*), some of them hanging from the ceiling, set against a storyboard scroll from *The Civil Wars*. In the background, one could hear the intoning of dialogue from that dramatic opera. Peter Schumann's exhibit was like walking into the Bread and Puppet workshop—a large room packed with white totemic figures shadowed by messages of political dissent. In Abdoh's room, excerpts from his violent works were screened, and Monk featured an intriguing line-up of shoes worn by her in various productions: sandals, sneakers, sabots, boots and flippers. Next to this display were three "singing suitcases": open the lids and hear the humming. In each instance, a visitor was presented with a complete and evocative picture of the director at work. In a sense, the environments were transformed into performances.

THE DEATHS OF TWO WIDELY DISPARATE ARTISTS who were basic to Off Off Broadway marked the season with a certain finality. The first, in September, was of Stuart Sherman, an avatar of the avant-garde, a theatrical miniaturist who created landscapes in cameo. In his tabletop exercises, he acted as a kind of sidewalk pitchman, showing postcards of his world and in environmental pieces he offered impressionistic soundings of Chekhov and other writers. All this gave him a special spot as a kind of serendipitous suitcase artist.

The second death, which occurred in October, was not discovered until February, and that was the strange disappearance of Leonard Melfi, who had been a pillar of the early Off Off movement (along with Sam Shepard and Lanford Wilson), and had at least briefly been on Broadway.

After being taken to Mt. Sinai Hospital for emergency treatment, Melfi died suddenly. Despite having cards of identity, he was buried at Potters Field, without any relatives or friends being notified. Word finally reached Melfi's brother, John, many months later in the playwright's hometown of Binghamton, New York. Finally, Melfi's body was found, exhumed and then buried on the family plot. Throughout his life, Melfi had written about outcasts and wanderers on the city streets, many of whom resembled the playwright himself. The real life story of the mysterious death and lost body was the kind of tragic farce that would have appealed to him as a writer. In many ways he was an archetypal playwright of his time and in May, there was a celebration of Melfi at Ellen Stewart's La MaMa, where he began his career in the 1960s.

At the memorial, Ellen Stewart, Crystal Field, Paul Foster, and actors who had appeared in Melfi's plays, paid homage to their friend and colleague. The theater was filled with faces from the past: H.M. Koutoukas, Jeff Weiss, Nicky Paraiso, as well as Melfi's relatives. Barbara Eda-Young, the original waif in Melfi's most enduring work, *Birdbath*, reprised a scene from that play. Robert Heide, another playwright of the period, read a message from Edward Albee: "Years ago there were many serious and daring individuals under 30. When they were not seeing plays by Beckett, Ionesco and Genet, they were seeing plays by each other." It was, he said, "a wild and vital time" and "no one was more wild and vital than Leonard."

The scene at the Melfi celebration was like a homecoming for survivors of the Off Off Broadway movement, many of whom continue to be active. Melfi himself may have the last word. At his death, he left *The Violinist*, an unproduced full-length work, about an aged blind violinist, a lonely young woman and an alcoholic playwright who in common with many of his characters is a variation on the playwright himself. Coincidentally, La MaMa, a cornerstone of Off Off Broadway, was in the middle of its 40th anniversary season. La MaMa and Ellen Stewart herself are living proof of the continuing vitality of this arena for experimentation.

PLAYS PRODUCED OFF OFF BROADWAY
AND ADDITIONAL NYC PRESENTATIONS
○○○○○
Compiled by Vivian Cary Jenkins

BELOW IS A COMPREHENSIVE SAMPLING of 2001–02 Off Off Broadway productions in New York. There is no definitive "Off Off Broadway" area or qualification. To try to define or regiment it would be untrue to its fluid, exploratory purpose. The listing below of hundreds of works produced by more than 130 OOB groups and others is as inclusive as reliable sources will allow, however, and takes into account all leading Manhattan-based, new-play producing, English-language organizations.

The more active and established producing groups are identified in **bold face type**, in alphabetical order, with artistic policies and the names of its leaders given whenever these are a matter of record. Each group's 2001–02 schedule, with emphasis on new plays and with revivals of classics usually omitted, is listed with play titles in CAPITAL LETTERS. Often these are works-in-progress with changing scripts, casts and directors, sometimes without an engagement of record (but an opening or early performance date is included when available).

Many of these Off Off Broadway groups have long since outgrown a merely experimental status and offer programs that are the equal in professionalism and quality (and in some cases the superior) of anything in the New York theater. These listings include special contractual arrangements such as the showcase code, letters of agreement (allowing for longer runs and higher admission prices than usual) and, closer to the edge of the commercial theater, so-called "mini-contracts." In the list below, available data has been provided by press representatives and company managers.

A large selection of lesser-known groups and other shows that made appearances Off Off Broadway during the season appears under the "Miscellaneous" heading at the end of this listing.

Amas Musical Theatre. Dedicated to bringing people of all races, creeds, colors, religious and national origins together through the performing arts. Rosetta LeNoire founder, Donna Trinkoff producing artistic director.

> LITTLE HAM. Based on Langston Hughes's play of the same name. November 28, 2001. Book by Dan Owens based on a concept by Eric Krebs; music by Judd Woldin; lyrics by Richard Engquist and Judd Woldin. Directed by Eric Riley; choreography, Leslie Dockery; scenery, Edward T. Gianfrancesco; costumes, Bernard Grenier; lighting, Richard Latta; music direction, David Alan Bunn; orchestrations and arrangements, Luther Henderson. With Ben

271

A man's life: Buddy and Larry Clarke in The Dog Problem. *Photo: Carol Rosegg*

Blake, D'Ambrose Boyd, Venida Evans, Carmen Ruby Floyd, Jerry Gallagher, André Garner, Danielle Lee Greaves, Julia Lema, Kevyn Morrow, Stacey Sargeant, Joy Styles, Lee Summers, Richard Vida, Joe Wilson Jr.

Atlantic Theater Company. Produces new plays or reinterpretations of classics that speak to audiences in a contemporary voice on issues relfecting today's society. Neil Pepe artistic director, Hilary Hinckle managing director.

THE DOG PROBLEM. By David Rabe. June 6, 2001. Directed by Scott Ellis; scenery, Allen Moyer; costumes, Michael Krass; lighting, Brian Nason; sound, Eileen Tague; fight director, Rick Sordelet; production stage manager, Darcy Stephens. With Joe Pacheco, Larry Clarke, David Wike, Victor Argo, Tony Cucci, Andrea Gabriel, Robert Bella.

AN ADULT EVENING OF SHEL SILVERSTEIN. By Shel Silverstein. October 17, 2001. Directed by Karen Kohlhaas; scenery, Walt Spangler; costumes, Miguel Angel Huidor; lighting, Robert Perry. With Jordan Lage, Alicia Goranson, Jody Lambert, Josh Stamberg, Maryann Urbano and Kelly Maurer.

HOBSON'S CHOICE. By Harold Brighouse. January 13, 2002. Directed by David Warren. With Brian Murray, Martha Plimpton, David Aaron Baker, Peter Maloney, Amy Wilson, Katie Carr, Darren Pettie, Jim Fragione, Christopher Wynkoop, Aedin Moloney, Austin Lysy.

THIS THING OF DARKNESS. By Craig Lucas and David Schulner. May 30, 2002. Directed by Mr. Lucas; scenery, John McDermott; costumes, Candice Donnelly; lighting, Christopher Akerlind; sound, Scott Myers. With Daniel Eric Gold, Larry Keith, Mary McCann, Chris Messina, Thomas Jay Ryan, Ralph Waite.

Brooklyn Academy of Music Next Wave Festival. Since 1981, this annual three-month festival has presented more than 200 events, including more than 50 world premieres. Featuring leading international artists, it is one of the world's largest festivals of contemporary performing arts. Bruce C. Ratner chairman, Karen Brooks Hopkins president, Joseph V. Melillo executive producer.

CLOUDSTREET. By Tim Winton. October 2, 2001. Adapted by Nick Enright and Justin Monjo. Directed by Neil Armfield; scenery, Robert Cousins; costumes, Tess Schofield; lighting, Mark Howett; sound, Gavin Tempany; choreography, Kate Champion. With Wayne Blair, Roy Billing, John Gaden, Claire Jones, Gillian Jones, Kris McQuade, Christopher Pitman and Daniel Wyllie.

THE THEFT OF SITA. By Nigel Jamieson. October 17, 2001. Music composed by Paul Grabowsky in association with I Wayan Gde Yudane from an original idea from Nigel Jamieson and Paul Gravowsky. Directed by Mr. Jamieson; scenery, Julian Crouch; lighting Damien Cooper. With I Made Sidia, Peter Wilson, Paul Moore, Steve Howarth and Udo Foerster (puppeteers) and Shelly Scown and I Gusti Putu Sudarta (vocalists).

CORROBOREE. Directed and choreographed by Stephen Page. October 24, 2002. Composed by David Page and Steve Francis; scenery, Peter England, John Markovic and Mr. Page; lighting, Karen Norris and Joseph Mercurio; costumes, Jennifer Irwin.

NEEDCOMPANY'S KING LEAR. By William Shakespeare. October 31, 2001. Directed by Jan Lauwers; choreography, Carlotta Sagna; scenery, Mr. Lauwers; costumes, Lot Lemm; lighting, Dries Vercruysse; sound, Dré Schneider. With Tom Jansen, Josse De Pauw, Simon Versnel, Grace Ellen Barkey, Anneke Bonnema, Carlotta Sagna, Hans Petter Dahl, Misha Downey, Dick Crane, Tijen Lawton, Timothy Couchman.

ONCE UPON A TIME IN CHINESE AMERICA. Written by Fred Ho and Ruth Margraff. November 7, 2001. Directed by Mira Kinsley; music and concept, Mr. Ho; scenery, Michael Forrest Kurtz and Kun-Feng (Tony) Chen; martial arts choreography, Jose Figueroa; lighting, Allen Hahn; costumes, Kenneth Chu. With Chen Jack, Gee Shin, Miao Hin, Li Wen Mao and Ng Mui.

MASURCA FOGO. A piece by Pina Bausch. November 8, 2001. Directed and choreographed by Ms. Bausch; scenery, Peter Pabst; costumes, Marion Cito.

POEtry. Book, music and lyrics by Lou Reed. November 27, 2001. Directed and designed by Robert Wilson; music direction, Mr. Reed; lighting by Mr. Wilson and Heinrich Brunke; costume and mask design, Jacques Reynaud.

Bit of cobbler? David Aaron Baker and Martha Plimpton in Hobson's Choice. *Photo: Carol Rosegg*

Kafka opera: John Duykers (center, with papers) In the Penal Colony. *Photo: Chris Bennion*

BIG LOVE. By Charles L. Mee. An adaptation of Aeschylus' *The Suppliant Women*. November 30, 2001. Directed by Les Waters; scenery, Ann Smart; costumes; James Schuette; lighting, Robert Wierzel; sound, Robert Milburn and Michael Bodeen. With Carolyn Baeumler, Tony Speciale, Aimée Guillot, KJ Sanchez, Lauren Klein, J. Michael Flynn, Bruce McKenzie, Mark Zeisler, J. Matthew Jenkins, Amy Landecker, Lusia Strus, Adrian Danzig, Chuck Stubbings.

Classic Stage Company. Reinventing and revitalizing the classics for contemporary audiences. Barry Edelstein artistic director. Beth Emelson producing director.

IN THE PENAL COLONY. By Philip Glass; based on the original story by Franz Kafka; libretto by Rudolph Wurlitzer. June 14, 2001. Directed by Joanne Akalaitis; scenery, John Conklin; costumes, Susan Hilferty; lighting, Jennifer Tipton; sound, Dominic CodyKramers. With Tony Boutté, Sterling K. Brown, John Duykers, Jesse J. Perez, Eugene Perry, Herbert Perry and Steven Rishard.

MONSTER. By Neal Bell. Based on Mary Shelley's *Frankenstein*. January 27, 2002. Directed by Michael Greif; scenery, Robert Brill; costumes, Jess Goldstein; lighting, Kenneth Posner; sound, Erika H. Sellin. With Jake Weber, Michael Cullen, Christopher Donahue, Annie Parisse, Michael Pitt, Jonno Roberts and Christen Clifford.

THE UNDERPANTS. By Carl Sternheim, adapted by Steve Martin. April 4, 2002. Directed by Barry Edelstein; scenery, Scott Pask; costumes, Angela Wendt; lighting, Russell H. Champa; sound, Elizabeth Rhodes. With Patrick Boll, Cheryl Lynn Bowers, Christian Camargo, William Duell, Bryon Jennings, Kristine Nielsen and Lee Wilkof.

ROOM. Based on the writings of Virginia Woolf. Adapted by Jocelyn Clarke. May 23, 2002. Directed by Anne Bogart; scenery, Neil Patel; costumes, James Schuette; lighting, Christopher Akerlind; sound, Darron L. West. With Ellen Lauren.

Drama Dept. A collective of actors, directors, designers, stage managers, writers and producers who collaborate to create new works and revive neglected classics. Douglas Carter Beane artistic director, Michael S. Rosenberg managing director.

MUSIC FROM A SPARKLING PLANET. July 19, 2001. Directed by Mark Brokaw; scenery, Allen Moyer; costumes, Michael Krass; lighting, Kenneth Posner; sound, Janet Kalas; original music, Lewis Flinn. With J. Smith-Cameron, T. Scott Cunningham, Ross Gibby, Josh Hamilton and Michael Gaston.

Ensemble Studio Theatre. Membership organization of playwrights, actors, directors and designers dedicated to supporting individual theater artists and developing new works for the stage. More than 200 projects each season, ranging from readings to fully-mounted productions. Curt Dempster artistic director.

MARATHON 2001 (SERIES C). Scenery, Warren Karp; costumes, Christopher Peterson; lighting, Greg MacPherson; sound, Robert Gould. June 9, 2001.

GRIEF. By Craig Lucas. Directed by Tom Rowan. With Delphi Harrington, Neal Huff and Christopher Orr.

LARRY'S CHARM. By Edward Allan Baker. Directed by Ron Statson. With Lynn Cohen, Tessa Gyhlin and Maria Gabriele.

LATE NIGHT IN THE WOMEN'S RESTROOM OF THE JUNGLE BAR. By David Riedy. Directed by Eileen Myers. With Melinda Page Hamilton, Jen Drohan, Diana LaMar and Kevin Shinick.

INVITATION TO A FUNERAL. By Julie McKee. Directed by Deborah Hedwall. With Kathleen Doyle and Susan Pellegrino.

THE SECRET ORDER. By Bob Clyman. April 4, 2002. Directed by Jamie Richards; costumes, Amela Baksic; scenery, Bruce Goodrich; sound, Robert Gould; lighting, Michael Lincoln. With Liam Craig, James Murtaugh, Amy Love, Joe Rooks.

MARATHON 2002 (SERIES A). Scenery, Jennifer Varbalow; costumes, Amela Baksic; lighting, Greg MacPherson; sound, Robert Gould. May 8, 2002.

LARK by Romulus Linney.

WHY I FOLLOWED YOU by Lisa-Maria Radano.

Sound baubles: J. Smith-Cameron in Music From a Sparkling Planet. *Photo: Joan Marcus*

Manhattan mixer: Charles Nelson Reilly in Save It for the Stage: The Life of Reilly. *Photo: Gar Campbell*

REUNIONS by Billy Aronson.

SALVAGE BASS by Brian Silberman.

MARATHON 2002 (SERIES B). May 22, 2001.

AM LIT OR HIBERNOPHILIA by Dan O'Brien. Directed by Kevin Confoy. With Tom Bloom.

THE PRISONER'S SONG by Horton Foote. Directed by Harris Yulin. With Mary Catherine Garrison, Tim Guinee, Marceline Hugot, Michael P. Moran.

ADAPTATION by Roger Hedden. Directed by Billy Hopkins. With Ian Reed Kesler, Fiona Gallagher, Dennis Boutsikaris, Brooke Smith, Spencer Garrett.

SALVATION by Bill Bozzone. Directed by Keith Reddin. With Katie Walder, Rishi Mehta, Alex Feldman.

INTAR. Identifies, develops and presents the talents of gifted Hispanic-American theater artists and multicultural visual artists. Max Ferra artistic director.

THE ALAMO PIECE. by Sigfrido Aguilar and Jim Calder. January 4, 2002. With Mr. Aguilar and Mr. Calder.

TIES THAT BIND (three plays in rep). May 26, 2002. YOUNG VALIANT by Oliver Mayer. Directed by Michael John Garcés. With Romi Dias, Alain Rivas, Donald Silva. CUCHIFRITO by Eduardo Andino. Directed by Angel David. With Carlo Alban, Ana Maria Correa, Joel Friedman, Henry Leyva, Marilyn Sanabria. A TO B by Ricardo A. Bracho. Directed by Ela Troyano. With Leith Burk, Carlos Valencia.

Irish Repertory Theatre. Aims to bring works by Irish and Irish American masters and contemporary playwrights to a wider audience and to develop new works focusing on a whide range of cultural experiences. Charlotte Moore artistic director, Ciarán O'Reilly producing director.

A LIFE. By Hugh Leonard. June 28, 2001. Directed by Charlotte Moore; scenery, Dan Kuchar; lighting, Gregory Cohen; costumes, Linda Fisher; sound, Murmod, Inc. With Jarlath Conroy, David Costelloe, Paddy Croft, Pauline Flanagan, John Keating, Heather O'Neill, Derdriu Ring and Fritz Weaver.

THE IRISH . . . AND HOW THEY GOT THAT WAY. By Frank McCourt. August 28, 2001. Directed by Charlotte Moore. With Peter Cormican, Terry Donnelly, Bob Green, Mark Hartman, Donna Kane and Ciarán O'Reilly.

SAVE IT FOR THE STAGE: THE LIFE OF REILLY. By Charles Nelson Reilly and Paul Linke. October 3, 2001. Directed by Mr. Linke; scenery, Patrick Hughes; lighting, Gregory Cohen; costumes, Noel Taylor, sound, Murmod, Inc. With Mr. Reilly.

THE STREETS OF NEW YORK . By Dion Boucicault. November 18, 2001. Adapted for the stage and directed by Charlotte Moore. Scenery, Hugh Landwehr; costumes, Linda Fisher; lighting, Clifton Taylor; sound, Murmod, Inc. With Peter Cormican, Ray DeMattis, Terry Donnelly, Danielle Ferland, Margaret Hall, Michael Halling, Donna Kane, John Keating, Christopher Lynn, Kristin Maloney, Ciarán O'Reilly and Joshua Park.

THAT . . . AND THE CUP O' TEA: AN EVENING WITH CARMEL QUINN. Conceived and performed by Ms. Quinn. November 14, 2001.

PIGTOWN. By Mike Finn. April 28, 2002. Directed by Charlotte Moore; scenery, James Morgan; costumes, Robin L. McGee; lighting, Kirk Bookman. With Jarlath Conroy, Dara Coleman, David Costelloe, Terry Donnelly, Rosemary Fine, Laura James Flynn, Christopher Joseph Jones, John Keating, Aedin Moloney, Declan Mooney, Anto Nolan.

The Joseph Papp Public Theater/New York Shakespeare Festival. Schedule of special projects, in addition to its regular Off Broadway productions. George C. Wolfe producer, Fran Reiter executive director, Rosemarie Tichler artistic producer.

New Work Now! Festival of New Play Readings.

GIRL SCOUTS OF AMERICA. By Andrea Berloff and Mona Mansour. April 28, 2002.

TALE OF 2 CITIES: AN AMERICAN JOYRIDE ON MULTIPLE TRACKS. By Heather Woodbury. April 29, 2002.

THE RATS ARE GETTING BIGGER. By Julia Edwards. May 1, 2002.

THE MUCKLE MAN. By Roberto Aguirre-Sacasa. May 2, 2002.

Orange Lemon Egg Canary. By Rinne Groff.

80 Teeth, 4 Feet and 500 Pounds. By Gustavo Ott, translated by Heather McKay. May 4, 2002.

A HUMAN INTEREST STORY, OR THE GORY DETAILS AND ALL. By Carlos Murillo. May 5, 2002.

WELL. By Lisa Kron. May 7, 2002.

PYRETOWN. By John Belluso. May 8, 2002.

HAZELLE ON EDGE. By Hazelle Goodman. May 9, 2002.

LATE. By Sarah Ruhl. May 10, 2002.

SEBASTIAN. By Alejandro Morales. May 11, 2002.

THE BEAUTY OF THE FATHER. By Nilo Cruz. May 12, 2002.

New Composers Now!: Thirty-Minute Excerpts from Works-in-Progress.

FLORIDA. By Randall Eng and Donna Di Novelli. May 6, 2002.

THE TUTOR. By Andrew Gerle and Maryrose Wood. May 6, 2002.

SUNDAY, A MUSICAL FABLE. By Bruce Monroe and Alva Rogers. May 6, 2002.

Joe's Pub. Schedule included:

CALLALOO. Edited by Charles H. Rowell. October 7, 2001. With John Edgar Wideman, Rita Dove. INSHALLAH. Solo performance by Sandra Bernhard. January 16, 2002. DAPHNE RUBIN-VEGA. February 9, 2002. TONI BLACKMAN. February 15, 2002. ECHO. February 15, 2002. With Joy Askew, Takiya Nakamura. POETRY SOCIETY OF AMERICA'S WRITERS ON POETS: KENNETH KOCH AND JONATHAN LETHEM. February 20, 2002. CHRIS WHITLEY. February 20, 2002. PABLO ZIEGLER. February 21, 2002. With Pablo Aslan, Satoshi Takeishi. GIANT SAND. February 22, 2002. With Howie Gelb. BURNT SUGAR. February 23, 2002. With Lisala Beatty, Vijay Iyer, Vernon Reid, Greg Tate. URBAN COMEDY CURE. February 23, 2002. With Peter Berman, Todd Lynn, Ben Bailey, Bill Burr. GLEN PHILIPS. February 24, 2002. EVERTON SYLVESTER AND SEARCHING FOR BANJO. February February 24, 2002. With Booker King, Danny Sadownick, Paul Shapiro. February 24, 2002. GALT MACDERMOT. February 25, 2002. With New Pulse Jazz Band. LEA DELARIA. February 25, 2002. BETTY RULES. February 26, 2002. NORA YORK. February 28, 2002. With Steve Tarshis, Charles Giordano, Dave Hofstra, Peter Grant, Claire Daily. JUSTIN BOND AND THE FREUDIAN SLIPPERS. February 28, 2002. VOX POPULI. March 1, 2002. With Dean Bowman, David "Fuze" Fiuczynski. JANITA. March 1, 2002. ANTONY AND THE JOHNSONS. March 2, 2002. WILLIAM TOPLEY. March 2, 2002. BILL FRISELL. March 4, 2002. With Viktor Krauss, Kenny Wollesen. NORAH JONES. March 6, 2002. CHOCOLATE GENIUS. March 6, 2002. With Marc Anthony Thompson. LOUIE AUSTIN. March 6, 2002. With Mario Neugebauer and Patrick Puslinger. ANGÉLIQUE KIDJO. March 7, 2002. CY COLEMAN. March 8, 2002. CI JIAN. March 10, 2002. GAVIN DE GRAW. March 13, 2002. Polygraph Lounge. March 14, 2002. With Rob Schwimmer and Mark Stewart. SOUL EROTICA. Curated by Monique Martin. March 16, 2002. LOS HOMBRES CALIENTES. March 17, 2002.With Bill Summers and Irvin Mayfield. DAVE DOUGLAS NEW QUINTET. March 18, 2002. With Chris Potter, Uri Caine, James Genus, Clarence Penn. NATALIE BLALOCK. March 18, 2002. OSCAR BROWN JR. AND MAGGIE BROWN. March 20, 2002. DAPHNE RUBIN-VEGA. March 22, 2002. BIG TIT. March 23, 2002. With Sue Costello, Deidre Sullivan, Kate Rigg. NEW TRENDS IN MODERN JEWISH SONG. March 24, 2002. With Frank London and Lorin Sklamberg, Rob Schwimmer, Marilyn Lerner, Dave Wall. LOS MUÑEQUITOS DE MATANZAS. March 26, 2002. NYCSMOKE. March 26 2002. ED HARCOURT. March 28, 2002. MATTHEW SHIPP. With March 28, 2002. William Parker, Daniel Carter, Chris Flam. TAMMY FAYE STARLITE. March 29, 2002. MARTHA REDBONE. March 30, 2002. MORLEY. March 31, 2002. SMOKEY 7 MIHO. March 31, 2002. ANTI-POP CONSORTIUM. April 2, 2002. GREG WALLOCH AND ALLISON CASTILLO. April 3, 2002. STEPHEN BRUTON. April 3, 2002. JULIAN FLEISHER AND HIS RATHER BIG BAND. April 4, 2002. DIAMANDA GALAS. April 5, 2002. JOEY MCINTYRE. April 5, 2002. JOHN HOLLENBECK – THE CLAUDIA QUINTET. April 7, 2002.

Jewish Repertory Theater. Presents plays in English relating to the Jewish expereience. Ran Avni artistic director.

A NAUGHTY KNIGHT. Musical with book by William Martin; music and lyrics by Chuck Strand, based on a fable by Mark Twain. May 17, 2001. Directed by Mr. Martin; scenery and costumes, Frank J. Boros; lighting, Jason Kankel; sound, Randy Hansen. With Rebecca Kupka, Mark Manley, Christopher J. Hanke, Gordon Joseph Weiss, Rebecca Rich, Kurt Domoney, Paul Romero and John Michael Coppola.

La MaMa Experimental Theater Club (ETC). A busy workshop for experimental theater of all kinds. Ellen Stewart founder and director.

Schedule Included:

BITTERROOT. Musical by Paul Zimet; composed by Peter Gordon; based on the life of Meriwether Lewis. Directed by Mr. Zimet. June 9, 2001. Scenery, Christine Jones; lighting, Leonore Doxsee; costumes, Kiki Smith. With William Badgett, Ellen Maddow, Isaac Maddow-Zimet, Tina Shepard, Jeffrey Reynolds, Ryan Dietz, Randy Reyes, Michelle Rios and Hunyup Lee.

RENO. One-woman show written and performed by Reno. October 15, 2001. Restaged at the Zipper Theater (April 22, 2002).

FERDYDURKE. By Witold Gombrowicz, adapted by Allen J. Kuharski. November 10, 2001. Directed by Witold Mazurkiewicz and Janusz Oprynski; scenery, Jerzy Rudzki; lighting and sound, Mr. Oprynski and Jan Szamryk; music, Borys Somerschaf. With Jacek Brzezinski, Mr. Mazurkiewicz, Jaroslaw Tomica and Michal Zgiet.

STAR MESSENGERS. Musical by Paul Zimet; composed by Ellen Maddow. December 2, 2001. Directed by Mr. Zimet; choreography, Karinne Keithley; scenery, Nic Ularu; costumes, Kiki Smith; lighting, Carol Mullins.With William Badgett, Court Dorsey, David Greenspan, Christine Ciccone. Ryan Dietz, Marcy Jellison, Karinne Keithley, Ms. Maddow, Randy Reyes, Michelle Rios.

THE SOUND OF THE SUN. By Arthur Maximillian Adair. January 31, 2002. With Mr. Maximillian, Einy Aam. Lara Benusir, Alta L. Bode, Marissa Buffone, Antonio Cerezo. Aundré Chin, Richard Cohen, Evaleena Dann, S-Dog, Brian Duggan, Foster, Sara Galassini, Zimena Garnica, Denise Greber, Tim Herlihy, Jake Incao, Jiyang Kim, Tom Lee, Julia Martin, Juan Merchan, La Nena, Scott Gannon Patton, Rolando Politti, Eugene the Poogene, Federico Restrepo, James Rowland, Paul Savas, Meave Shelton, Sara Wilson Sherwin, Yukio Tsiji, Nella Vinci, Angela Wendt, Saria Young, Stefano Zazzera, Hadaaz Zucker.

EROTIC ADVENTURES IN VENICE. By Mario Fratti. February 7, 2002. Directed by Dan Friedman; scenery, Floyd Gumble. With Dave DeChristopher, Mika Duncan, Jennifer Herzog, Zenobia Shroff, Ross Stoner, Caroline Strong.

DOUBLE AGENCY. Created by Peggy Shaw and Lois Weaver in collaboration with Suzy Willson and Paul Clark. February 27, 2002 MISS RISQUÉ directed by Ms. Willson with additional direction by Stormy Brandenberger; scenery, Annabel Lee; lighting, Aideen Malone; costumes, Susan Young. IT'S A SMALL HOUSE AND WE'VE LIVED IN IT ALWAYS directed by Ms. Willson; lyrics; Ms. Shaw and Ms. Weaver; costumes, Sarah Blenkinsop; lighting, Ms. Malone. With Ms. Shaw, Ms. Weaver.

THE HAMLET PROJECT. By William Electric Black (aka Ian James). February 28, 2002. Music, Valerie Ghent; arrangements by Mr. Black, Tony Mann, Giselle Hamburg; choreograpy, Triebien Pollard; costumes, Beth Leward; fight choreography, James Manley. With Oberon K.A. Adjepong, Chris Brady, Eamonn Farrell, Michael Noon, Walter Pagan, Stephen Reyes, Sean Seibert, George Sosa, Brian Walker, Vanessa Burke, Liz Davito, Susanna Harris, Lauren Jacobs, Melissa Leiter, Erin Logemann, Mikey McCue, William Pagan, Lauren Porter, Eily Tuckman, Joni Weisfeld, Katharyn Yew.

TUMOR BRAINIOWICZ. By Stanislaw Ignacy Witkiewicz; translated by Daniel Gerould. February 28, 2002. Directed by Brooke O'Harra; music, Brendan Connelly. With Brian Bickerstaff, Mary Bonner Baker, Rob Marcato, Matt Shapiro, Mary Regan, Nicky Paraiso, Zakia Babb-Bornstein, and the voices of Isaac Zimet-Maddow and Misako Takashima.

THE RISE AND FALL OF TIMUR THE LAME. By Theodora Skipitares. March 14, 2002. Composed by David First; lighting, Pat Dignan. With Sanjeeva Poojary, Lisa Kerrer; narrators, Michael Moran, George Drance.

PI = 3.14. Conceived by Yoshiko Chuma. March 16, 2002. Text by Ms. Chuma, Bonnie Sue Stein and the company. Directed by Ms. Chuma; scenery, Tom Lee; costumes, Gabriel Berry; lighting, Pat Dignan; sound, Jacob Burckhardt. With Tea Alagic, Jim DiBiasio, Ms. Chuma, Wazhmah Osman, Ivan Talijancic, Maggie McBrien, Jenny Smith.

HOWLING. Created by Virlana Tkacz, Sayan Zhambalov, Erzhena Zhambalov, Watoku Ueno. March 16, 2002. Directed by Ms. Tkacz; movement, Katja Kolcio; music, Erzhena Zhambalov; scenery and lighting, Mr. Ueno. With Eunice Wong, Meredith Wright, Angela Lewis, Stephanie Summerville, Anais Alexandra Tekerian.

KISS SHOT. Musical by Jim Neu and Neal Kirkwood. April 4, 2002. Directed by Keith McDermott; scenery, Donald Eastman; lighting, Carol Mullins. With Monte Blane, Belle Russe, Mr. Neu, Charles Allcroft.

BOW DOWN. By Joe Brady. April 4, 2002. Directed by Raine Bode; scenery, Arthur Adair, lighting, Federico Restrepo; costumes, Denise Greber. With Mark Gallop, Paul Savas, Anne Moore, Uma Incrocci, Tommy Lonardo, Brian Glover, Neely Hepner, Tate Henderson, Mo Pula, Andy Rothkin, Antonio Cerezo, Melissa Glassman, Charlie Berfield.

CRACKS. Direction, choreography and scenery by Issey (Itzik) Nini. April 18, 2002 Costumes Mr. Nini and Susan Lazar; music by Mr. Nini, Stefano Zazzera, Greg Christo. With Mr. Nini, Amanda LePore, Jonathan Nosan.

Seguiriya, the Heart Beats. Conceived by Shigeko Suga. April 25, 2002. Directed by Ms. Suga; scenery, Jun Maeda; costumes, Denise Greber. With Mieko Seto, Naomi Shibata, Minouche Waring, Kumi Kuwahata, Aundré Chin, Bret Boyle, Lisa Ann Williamson, Antonio Cerezo, Mitsunari Sakamoto.

ONE NIGHT STANDS: THE BOOK OF JOB. Book, music and lyrics by Danny Ashkenasi. April 8, 2002. With Julie Alexander, Mr. Ashkenasi, Ian August, Joel Briel, Ryan Connolly, Allison Easte, Darra Herman, Anita Hollander, Jennie Im, Jamie Mathews. MISS MOBILE. By Emil Hrvatin. April 15, 2002. UNCLE MOON and AUNTIE ANGUS. April 29, 2002. With Trey Kay, Fritz Van Orden, Scott Selig, Carl Riehl, Jane Young, Henry Tenney, Bryan Costello, Doug Safranek, Christopher Caines.

Lincoln Center Festival 2001. An annual international summer arts festival offering classic and contemporary work. Nigel Redden director.

Harold Pinter Festival

A KIND OF ALASKA. By Mr. Pinter. July 16, 2001. Directed by Karel Reisz; scenery and costumes, Liz Ascroft; lighting, Mick Hughes. With Brid Brennan, Stephen Brennan, Penelope Wilton.

ONE FOR THE ROAD. By Mr. Pinter. July 16, 2001. Directed by Robin Lefevre; scenery and costumes, Liz Ascroft; lighting, Mick Hughes. With Mr. Pinter, Lloyd Hutchinson, Indira Varma, Rory Copus.

THE HOMECOMING. By Mr. Pinter. July 18, 2001. Directed by Robin Lefevre; scenery, Eileen Diss; costumes, Dany Everett; lighting, Mick Hughes. With Ian Holm, Ian Hart, John Kavanagh, Jason O'Mara, Lia Williams, Nick Dunning.

MONOLOGUE. By Mr. Pinter. July 19, 2001. Directed by Gari Jones; scenery, Eileen Diss; costumes, Dany Everett; lighting, Mick Hughes. With Henry Woolf.

The Room. By Mr. Pinter. July 24, 2001. Directed by Mr. Pinter; scenery, Eileen Diss; costumes, Dany Everett; lighting, Mick Hughes; sound, John A. Leonard. With Keith Allen, Lindsay Duncan, George Harris, Steven Pacey, Lia Williams, Henry Woolf.

CELEBRATION. By Mr. Pinter. July 24, 2001. Directed by Mr. Pinter; scenery, Eileen Diss; costumes, Dany Everett; lighting, Mick Hughes; sound, John A. Leonard. With Keith Allen, Lindsay Duncan, Dany Dyer, Steven Pacey, Nina Raine, Emily Strawson, Andy de la Tour, Indira Varma, Thomas Wheatley, Lia Williams, Susan Woodridge.

LANDSCAPE. By Mr. Pinter. July 25, 2001. Directed by Karel Reisz; scenery, Eileen Diss; costumes, Dany Everett; lighting, Mick Hughes. With Stephen Brennan, Penelope Wilton.

Mountain Language. By Mr. Pinter. July 26, 2001. Directed by Katie Mitchell; scenery, Vicki Mortimer; lighting, Paule Constable; sound, Gareth Fry. With Daniel Cerqueira, Neil Dudgeon, Gabrielle Hamilton, Anastasia Hille, Paul Hilton, Geoffrey Streatfield, Tim Treloar.

Ashes to Ashes. By Mr. Pinter. July 26, 2001. Directed by Katie Mitchell; scenery, Vicki Mortimer; lighting, Paule Constable; sound, Gareth Fry. With Neil Dudgeon, Anastasia Hille.

Mabou Mines. Mabou Mines is a theater company creating new works based on original and existing texts. The company was established in 1970. The current artistic directorate includes Lee Breuer, Sharon Fogarty, Ruth Maleczech, Frederick Neumann and Terry O'Reilly.

PETER AND WENDY. By J.M. Barrie, adapted by Liza Lorwin. February 7, 2002. Directed by Lee Breuer; scenery, Julie Archer; costumes, Sally Thomas; sound, Edward Cosla; music, Johnny Cunningham. With Karen Kandel; puppeteers, Basil Twist, Jane Catherine Shaw, Sam Hack. Lute Ramblin', Sarah Provost, Jessica Chandlee Smith, Jenny Subjack.

MCC Theater. Dedicated to the promotion of emerging writers, actors, directors and theatrical designers. Robert LuPone and Bernard Telsey artistic directors, William Cantler associate artistic director.

> The Glory of Living. By Rebecca Gilman. November 15, 2001. Directed by Philip Seymour Hoffman; scenery, Michelle Malavet; costumes, Mimi O'Donnell; lighting, James Vermeulen; original music and sound, David Van Tieghem. With Anna Paquin, Jeffrey Donovan, David Aaron Baker, Erika Rolfsrud, Brittany Slattery, Alicia Van Couvering, Jenna Lamia, Larry Clarke, Andrew McGinn, Myk Watford. A 2001–2002 *Best Plays* choice and finalist for the Pulitzer Prize in Drama, see essay by Chris Jones in this volume.

> A LETTER FROM ETHEL KENNEDY. By Christopher Gorman. May 16, 2002. Directed by Joanna Gleason; scenery, Jeff Cowie; costumes, Martin Pakledinaz; lighting, Michael Chybowski; original music, David Van Tieghem; sound, Jill B.C. DuBoff. With Jay Goede, Anita Gillette, Randy Harrison, Stephen Baker Turner, Bernie McInerney.

> RUNT OF THE LITTER. By Bo Eason. January 31, 2002. Directed by Larry Moss; scenery, Neil Patel; lighting, David Gipson; sound, Bruce Ellman. With Mr. Eason.

Melting Pot Theater Company. Presents multicultural theater in an effort to reflect the ethnic diversity of the city. Larry Hirschhorn artistic director.

> TINTYPES. Musical conceived by Mary Kyte with Mel Marvin and Gary Pearle. November 28, 2001. Directed by Nick Corley; choreography, Jennifer Paulson Lee; scenery, Michael Brown; costumes, Daryl Stone; lighting, Jeff Croiter. With Johmaalya Adelekan, Josh Alexander, Mark Lotito, Michele Ragusa, Christine Rea.

> MISS EVERS' BOYS. By David Feldshuh. March 13, 2002. Directed by Kent Gash; scenery, Emily Beck; costumes, Earl Jerome Battle; lighting, William R. Grant III, sound, Abe Jacob. With Adriane Lenox, Daryl Edwards, Byron Easley, Chad L. Coleman, Helmar Augustus Cooper, J. Paul Boehmer and Terry Alexander.

Mint Theater Company. Committed to bringing new vitality to worthy but neglected plays. Jonathan Bank artistic director.

> MACBETH. By William Shakespeare. July 31, 2001. Directed by Rebecca Patterson; scenery, Louisa Thompson; lighting, Mark Barton; fight direction, Deborah S. Keller and DeeAnn Weir. With Virginia Baeta, Sheila Lynn Buckley, Aysan Çelik, Heather Grayson, Jacqueline Gregg, Stacie Hirsch, Lisette Merenciana, Jina Oh, Karen Pruis, Ami Shukla, Katlan Walker, DeeAnn Weir, Tessa Zugmeyer.

> THE VOICE OF THE TURTLE. By John van Druten. November 23, 2001 Directed by Carl Forsman; scenery, Nathan Heverin; costumes, Theresa Squire; lighting, Josh Bradford; sound, Stefan Jacobs. With Elizabeth Bunch, Megan Byrne and Nick Toren.

> MURDER IN BAKER STREET. By Judd Woldin. February 27, 2002. Directed by Ike Schambelan; scenery, Merope Vachlioti; lighting, Marc Janowitz; costumes, Bryen Shannon; sound, Gary Bergman. With Melanie Boland, Jerry Lee, George Ashiotis, Richard Simon, Michael Dee, Nicholas Viselli.

> NO TIME FOR COMEDY. By S.N. Behrman. March 19, 2002. Directed by Kent Paul; scenery, Tony Andrea; costumes, Jayde Chabot; lighting; Peter West; sound, Jane Shaw. With Simon Booking, Hope Chernov, Diane Ciesla, Leslie Denniston, Ted Pejovich, Shawn Sturnick, Jason Summers.

New Dramatists. An organization devoted to playwrights. Members may use the facilities for projects ranging from private cold readings of their material to public script-in-hand readings. Listed below are readings open to the public. Todd London artistic director, Joel Ruark director of administration and finance, Paul A. Slee executive director.

> GOODBYE MY ISLAND. By Deborah Brevoort. June 1, 2001 Composed by David Friedman. With Chuck Cooper, Merwin Foard, James Fall, Peter Cormican, Allison Fischer, Eleanor Glockner, Virginia Ann Woodruff, Luisa Tedoff, Joan Barber, Lilli Cooper, Shelby Wong, Chris Valiando.

UMKOVU. By Eisa Davis. June 6, 2001 Directed by Michael John Garcés. With Rob Campbell, Laura Flanagan, Bertrand Wang, J. Kyle Manzay, Nilaja Sun, Michole White, Joe Latimore, Reyes Escamilla.

ROAR. By Betty Shamieh. June 7, 2001. Directed by Emily Morse. With Yusef Bulos, Dariush Kashani, Liza Lapira, Sabrina Le Beauf, Shaheen Vaaz, Lindsay Soson.

KEEPERS. By J. Holtham. June 8, 2001. Directed by Tom Rowan. With Mandy Siegfried, Chris Messina, Anthony Mackie, Nancy Wu.

WHEATLEY. By Lonnie Carter. June 11, 2001. Directed by Sharon Scruggs. With Mr. Carter, Matthew Korahais, Jill Kotler, Oni Faida Lampley, April Matthis, Forrest McClendon, Michael Rodgers.

BIRTHMARKS. By Sarah Treem. June 12, 2001. Directed by Kirsten Kelly. With Lynn Cohen, John Daggett, Addie Johnson, Maria Thayer.

IN THE PIGEON HOUSE. By Honour Kane. June 14, 2001. With Ms. Kane, Elizabeth Whyte, Paul Vincent Black, Caroline Winterson.

SPOTLIGHT ON A GIRL. By Candice Baugh. June 15, 2001. Directed by Linsay Firman.

IF HE CHANGED MY NAME. By Edgar Nkosi White. June 20, 2001. Directed by Walter Jones. With Waliek Crandall, Glenda Dixon, Fryday, Amy Leonard, Bobbi Owens, Andrew Platner, Lisa White, Paul G. Winston.

SLOW FAST WALKING ON THE RED EYE. By Caridad Svich. June 21, 2001. Directed by Rebecca Brown. With Carla Harting, Bryant Richards, Todd Cerveris, Gretchen Lee Krich, Carolina McNeely.

TRANSMISSION 0500 / TO THE BLUE PENINSULA. By Caridad Svich. September 19, 2001. Directed by Anne Kauffman. With Michael Bakkensen, Carla Harting, Jonathan Tindle, Nina Hellman, Michael McCartney, Jennifer Morris.

DOG ACT. By Liz Duffy Adams. October 1, 2001. Directed by Rebecca Patterson. With Keith Davis, Isabel Keating, Sarah Lord, Erica Sheffer (stage directions), Myra Lucretia Taylor, Jonathan Tindle, Rufus Tureen.

(900). By Zakiyyah Alexander. October 4, 2001. Directed by Seret Scott. With Eric Martin Brown, Caroline S. Clay, Donna Duplantier, Gretchen Lee Krich, Curtis McClarin, Angela Pietropinto, Randy Reyes, Shaheen Vaaz.

I'D GO TO HEAVEN IF I WERE GOOD. By Carole Thompson. October 10, 2001. Directed by Ben Harney. With Nathan Dyer, Yvonne Facey, Amaris Harney, Robin Johnson, Devry Robinson, Pawnee Sills.

BIOGRAPHY. By Don Wollner. October 11, 2001. Directed by Mr. Wollner. With Reed Birney, Joel Colodner, Cidele Curo.

SALT. By Peta Murray. October 15, 2001. Directed by Debbie Saivetz. With Paul Vincent Black, Judith Roberts, Kate Skinner.

THE WOMEN OF LOCKERBIE. By Deborah Brevoort. October 22, 2001. Directed by Ms. Brevoort. With Traber Burns, Kathleen Chalfant, Lynn Cohen, Jurian Hughes, Patrick Husted, Angela Pietropinto, Judith Roberts, Erica Sheffer.

DON'T PROMISE. By Silvia Gonzales S. Directed by Kim Rubinstein. With Laura Flanagan, Gary Brownlee, Jillian Crane, Patrick Brinker, Ron Riley, Jay Edwards, Autumn Dornfeld, Welker White.

EAST OF THE SUN WEST OF THE MOON: THE LOVE SONG FOR LANGSTON HUGHES. By Edgar Nkosi White. October 24, 2001. Directed by Dana Manno. With Eric McLendon, Brenda Thomas, Arthur French, Abba Elethea, Gabriel Walsh, Lazaro Perez, Mike Smith, Chénana Manno, Von Jacobs, David Salvesdrive, Sean Schulich, Herman Chavez, Jezebel Montero, Aleta LaFarge, Jim Moody, Marcia McBroom.

LORCA IN A GREEN DRESS. By Nilo Cruz. October 25, 2001. Directed by Mr. Cruz. With George de la Peña, Isabel Keating, David Zayas, Carlos Orizondo, Mercedes Herrero, Simeon Moore, Gary Perez, La Conja.

THE POETS HOUR. By Dmitry Lipkin. October 29, 2001. Directed by Mark Brokaw. With Helen Stenborg, Leslie Ayvazian, Tom Mardirosian, Thomas Schall, Meg Gibson, Irma St. Paule, Larry Bryggman, Kelly Hutchinson.

SMITH AND BROWN. By Carlyle Brown. October 30, 2001. Directed by Mr. Brown. With Louise Smith, Keith Davis, Melinda Wade.

EL GRITO DEL BRONX. By Migdalia Cruz. November 2, 2001. Directed by Michael John Garcés. With David Anzuelo, Carlos Molina, Amarelys Perez, Priscilla Lopez, Zabryna Guevara, Michael Ray Escamilla, Akili Prince.

THE SUNGATHERERS. By Tim Acito. November 15 2001. Directed by David Levine. With Laila Robins, George de la Peña, Jim True Frost, Jodie Markell, David Turner, Nicole Alifante, Jeremy Shamos.

JUSTICE. By Herman Daniel Farrell III. November 15, 2001. Directed by Seret Scott. With Marissa Matrone, Jillian Crane, Eunice Wong, Myra Lucretia Taylor, Charles Randall, Ian August, Armando Riesco, Ari Edelson, Irma St. Paule.

2B4U. By Mark Druck. November 27, 2001. Directed by Mr. Druck. With Jay Stuart, Betty Miller, Polly Lee, Canan Erguder, Susan McCallum, Shade Vaughn, Howard Ross.

ARRIVALS AND DEPARTURES. By Rogelio Martinez. December 4, 2001. Directed by David Levine. With Florencia Lozano, Tony Gillan, John Ortiz.

THE WOUNDED BODY. By Bruce Walsh. December 4, 2001. Directed by Christopher Bamonte. With Billie Roe, Jerry Zellers, Sarah Rome, Todd Allen Durkin, Josh Liveright, Gregg Weiner.

THE SILENT CONCERTO. By Alejandro Morales. December 6, 2001. Directed by Lisa Portes. With Christopher Rivera, Sarah Dandridge, Scott Ebersold, Chris Henry Coffey, Nate Mooney.

INBETWEEN. By J. Holtham. December 7, 2001. Directed by Sarah Elkasef. With Kim Donovan, Chris Wight, Amy Staats, Eric Scott, Ian Reed Kesler.

BOLLYWOOD. By Lonnie Carter. December 10, 2001. Directed by Loy Arcenas. With Oni Faida Lampley, Tanya Selvaratnam.

HENRY FLAMETHROWA. By John Belluso. December 12, 2001. Directed by Mark Brokaw. With Jessica Hecht, Daniel Jenkins, Keith Nobbs.

Goodbye My Island. By Deborah Brevoort. January 8, 2002. With Chuck Cooper, James Fall, Allison Fischer, Bill McKinley, Scott Johnson, Joan Barber, Eleanor Glockner, Peter Cormican, Katie Gessinger, Stephanie Weems, Christian Valiando, Lilli Cooper, Aaron Schweitzer.

BROOKLYN BRIDGE. By Melissa James Gibson. January 9, 2002. Music by Barbara Brousal. Directed by Melissa Kievman. With Elizabeth Bunch, William Badgett, Joanna P. Adler, Patrick Husted, Michelle Rios, Barbara Brousal, Livia Scott, Skip Ward, Adam Sorensen.

TENNESSEE DESCENDING. By Leslie Kramer. Directed by Ethan McSweeney. With Sam Tsoutsouvas, Jenna Lamia, Nance Williamson, Kurt Rhoads, Jack Ferver, Patrick McMenamin (stage directions).

MARSUPIAL GIRL. By Lisa D'Amour. January 11, 2002. Music by Sxip Shirey. Directed by Katie Pearl. With April Matthis, Babo Harrison, Ben Schnieder, Sarah K. Chalmers, Maria Elena Ramirez.

TRICK OF FATE. By Stuart Vaughan. January 15, 2002. With Robert Lavelle, Jennifer Chudy, John FitzGibbon, Lauren Lovett, Joseph Culliton, Michael Milligan, Anne Vaughan (stage directions).

HIGH CEILINGS. By Jillian Crane. January 30, 2002. Directed by Marya Cohn. With Robert O'Gorman, Steve Cell, Jennifer Morris, Kevin Thomas, Lou Liberatore, Judith Hawking, Gareth Saxe, Celia Howard, Gerry Goodstein, Larry Bull, Alex Kranz (stage manager).

4 YOR LOVE. By Mary Gallagher. February 7, 2002. Directed by David Levine. With Gretchen Lee Krich, John McAdams, Tertia Lynch, Ron Riley, Donna Duplantier, Chris McKinney, Laura Kindred.

COYOTE GOES SALMON FISHING. By Deborah Brevoort. February 12, 2002. Directed by Ms. Brevoort. With Natalie Venetia Belcon, Culver Casson, Will Erat, J.D. Webster, James Sasson.

LAUGHING PICTURES. By Matthew Maguire. February 15, 2002. With Florencia Lozano, Victoire Charles, Paula Pizzi, Donan Whelan, Steven Rattazzi, Fattah Dihann, T. Ryder Smith, Ben Masur, Edward O'Blenis.

COURSE MAJEURE. By Gordon Dahlquist. February 20, 2002. With Annie McAdams, Molly Powell, Gary Brownlee, Alana Jerins, John McAdams.

Brown University MFA Readings. February 26, 2002. Artistic Director Ruth Margraff. GETTING AWAY. By Kamili Feelings. Directed by Dominic Taylor. With Erica N. Tazel, Akili Prince, Saidah Arrika Ekulona, Danyon Davis, Ron Brice. WEIGHTLESS. By Christine Evans. Directed by Tim Farrell. With Duane Boutté, Keith Nobbs, Lynne McCollough, Brian Delate, Katie Kreisler. THE ACCIDENT. By Kelly Doyle. Directed by David Levine. With Laura Kindred, Edmund C. Davys, Kit Flanagan, Josh Stark, Marin Ireland, Armando Riesco, Jack Ferver, Kelly Doyle. STOP. MOTION. By Robert Quillen Camp. Directed by Steve Cosson. With Christina Kirk, Cam Kornman, James Urbaniak, Brian Sgambati, Ron Riley, Damian Baldet, Travis York, Mia Barron.

SOMETHING SIMPLE, PLAIN-SPOKEN. By Caridad Svich. March 13, 2002. Directed by Hayley Finn. With Carolyn Baeumler, Michael J.X. Gladis, Gretchen Lee Krich, Chris Messina.

PENETRATE THE KING. By Gordon Dahlquist. March 22, 2002. Directed by David Levine. With Laura Kindred, John McAdams, Molly Ward, Michael Stuhlbarg, Ron Riley, Joseph Goodrich, Laurie Williams.

COMPOSER/LIBRETTIST STUDIO. By Eisa Davis, Melissa James Gibson, Keith Glover, Joseph Goodrich, Karen Hartman; composed by Peter Knell, Elodie Lauten, Jeffrey Lependorf, Graham Reynolds, Jeffrey Stock. March 23, 2002. Music director, Roger Ames. With Ron Bagden, Angel Desai, Naomi Gurt Lind, Tracey Moore, James Stovall.

MEDEA. By Joseph Goodrich. April 12, 2002. Directed by Nick Faust. With Vanessa Skantze, Matthew Francisco Morgan, Ron Gural, David Johnson, Molly Powell, Dale Soules.

Van Lier Readings. April 16, 2002
INBETWEEN. By J. Holtham. Directed by Seret Scott. With Joanna Liao, Patrick Darragh, Vanessa Aspillaga, Danyon Davis, Armando Riesco. THE BLACK EYED. By Betty Shamieh. Directed by Seret Scott. With Roxanne Raja, Jenny Bacon, Vanessa Aspillaga, Sabrina Le Beauf. UMKOVU. By Eisa Davis. Directed by Michael John Garcés. With Rob Campbell, Kevin Carroll, Donna Duplantier, Jennifer Gibbs, Tim Kang, Joe Latimore, Alfredo Narciso, Michole White.

AUTODELETE:// BEGINNING DUMP OF PHYSICAL MEMORY//. By Honour Kane. April 22, 2002. Directed by David Levine. With Gretchen Lee Krich, Matthew Stadelmann, John Daggett, Fergus Loughnane.

FLIGHT. By Patrick White. April 26, 2002. Directed by David Levine. With David Johann, Ron Simons, John Andrew Morrison, Donna Duplantier, Jim Iorio, Jay Alvarez, Matthew Francisco Morgan, Erin McLaughlin, Danny Boyd Beaty, Amarelys Perez.

ILLUMINATING VERONICA. By Rogelio Martinez. April 29, 2002. Directed by Ted Sod. With Eduardo Machado, Octavio Solis, Antonia Rey, KJ Sanchez, Vivia Font, Victor Argo.

THE LUCIFER PLAY. By JoSelle Vanderhooft. April 29, 2002. Directed by Clare Lundberg. With Yael Teplow, Celia Peters, Louis Cancelmi, Michael Bell, Andrew Grusetskie.

RESTORING THE SUN. By Joe Sutton. May 3, 2002. Directed by Ethan McSweeney. With Ken Marks, Helen Coxe, Ned Eisenberg, Tim Jerome.

SPIN. By Karl Gajdusek. May 6, 2002. Directed by Pam McKinnon. With Peggy Scott, Charles Hyman, Michael Stuhlbarg, Jenna Stern, Anne Dudek.

The Half-Life of Memory. By Jason Lindner. May 6, 2002. Directed by Karin Coonrod. With Tom Pearl, Ned Eisenberg, David Patrick Kelly, Mia Barron, Tom Nelis, Vivienne Benesch, Gary Brownlee, Ed Vassallo.

EARTHQUAKE CHICA. By Anne Garcia-Romero. May 9, 2002. Directed by Leah C. Gardiner. With Judy Reyes, Al Espinosa.

New Federal Theater. Dedicated to integrating minorities into the mainstream of American theater through training artists and presenting plays by minorities and women to integrated, multicultural audiences. Woodie King Jr. producing director.

EVERY DAY A VISITOR. By Richard Abrons. June 7, 2001. Directed by Arthur Strimling; scenery, Robert Joel Schwartz; lighting, Shirley Prendergast; costumes, Dawn Robyn Petrlik. With Lisa Bostnar, Tom Brennan, John Freimann, Sylvia Gassell, Kenneth Gray, Helen Hanft, Joe Jamrog, Jerry Matz, Anthony Spina, Fiona Walsh.

URBAN TRANSITION: LOOSE BLOSSOMS. By Ron Milner. April 7, 2002. Directed by Woodie King Jr.; scenery, Robert Joel Schwartz; lighting, Shirley Prendergast; costumes, Evelyn Nelson. With Jerome Preston Bates, Chadwick Aharon Boseman, Joseph Edward, Dianne Kirksey, Sade Lythcott, George Newton, Monica Soyemi.

New Group. Launches fresh acting, writing and design talent and provides an artistic home for artists. Committed to cultivating a young and diverse theatergoing audience by providing accessible ticket prices. Scott Elliott artistic director, Andy Goldberg associate artistic director, Elizabeth Timperman producing director.

GOOD THING. By Jessica Goldberg. December 16, 2001. Directed by Jo Bonney; scenery, Neil Patel; costumes, Mimi O'Donnell; lighting, James Vermeulen; sound, Ken Travis. With Betsy Aidem, John Rothman, Alicia Goranson, Chris Messina, Cara Buono, Hamish Linklater.

SMELLING A RAT. By Mike Leigh. May 19, 2002. Directed by Scott Elliott; scenery, Kevin Price; costumes, Eric Becker; lighting, Jason Lyons; composer, Tom Kochan. With Terence Rigby, Brian F. O'Byrne, Gillian Foss, Eddie Kaye Thomas, Michelle Williams.

Pan Asian Repertory Theatre. Celebrates and provides opportunities for Asian-American artists to perform under the highest professional standards and to create and promote plays by and about Asians and Asian Americans. Tisa Chang artistic producing director.

FORBIDDEN CITY BLUES. Musical by Alexander Woo; lyrics by Mr. Woo; music by Ken Weiler. March 20, 2002. Directed by Ron Nakahara; scenery, Eric Renschler; costumes, Ingrid Maurer; lighting, Victor En Yu Tan; sound, Peter Griggs. With José Ramon Rosario, Rick Ebihara, Kate Chaston, Perry Yung, Fay Ann Lee, Julia McLaughlin, Peter Von Berg, Les J.N. Mau, Scott C. Reeves.

Performance Space 122. Exists to give artists of a wide range of experience a chance to develop work and find an audience. Mark Russell artistic director.

IN ON IT. By Daniel MacIvor. October 2, 2001. Directed by Mr. MacIvor; lighting, Kimberly Purtell; sound and music; Richard Feren. With, Mr. MacIvor, Darren O'Donnell.

DRUMMER WANTED. By Richard Maxwell. November 15, 2001. Directed by Mr. Maxwell; songs by Mr. Maxwell; scenery, Angela Moore; costumes, Tory Vazquez; lighting, Michael Schmelling. With Ellen LeCompte and Peter Simpson.

ECCO PORCO. By Lee Breuer. January 16, 2002. Directed by Mr. Breuer. Composed by Bob Telson, Eve Beglarian and Casey Neel; scenery, Manuel Lutgenhorst; costumes, Elizabeth Bourgeois; lighting, Kevin Taylor; sound, Eric Shim. With Black-Eyed Susan, Honora Fergusson, Clove Galilee, Karen Kandel, Ruth Maleczech, Maude Mitchell, Frederick Neumann, Terry O'Reilly, Barbara Pollitt.

Primary Stages. Dedicated to new American plays by new American playwrights. Casey Childs artistic director.

BYRD'S BOY. By Bruce J. Robinson. June 11, 2001. Directed by Arthur Masella; scenery, Narelle Sissons; costumes, Judith Dolan; lighting, Peter West; original music and sound, Donald DiNicola. With David McCallum and Myra Lucretia Taylor.

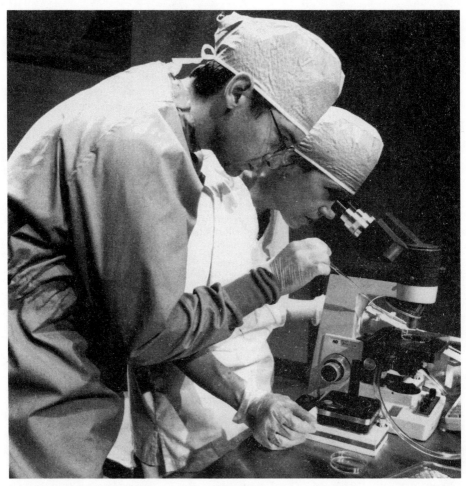

Hands of God: David Adkins and Ann Dowd in An Immaculate Misconception. *Photo: Marvin Einhorn*

AN IMMACULATE MISCONCEPTION. By Carl Djerassi. October 1, 2001. Directed by Margaret Booker; scenery, G.W. Mercier; costumes, Laura Crow; lighting, Deborah Constantine; sound and music, Lewis Flinn. With David Adkins, Ann Dowd, Adam Rose, Thomas Schall.

Puerto Rican Traveling Theater. Professional company presenting bilingual productions of Puerto Rican and Hispanic playwrights, emphasizing subjects of relevance today. Miriam Colon Valle founder and producer.

Schedule included:

LA LUPE: MY LIFE, MY DESTINY. By Carmen Rivera. June 27, 2001. Directed by Luis Caballero, translated by Raúl Davila; scenery, Salvatory Tagliarino; costumes, A. Christina Giannini and Natasha Guruleva; lighting, Maria Cristina Fusté; sound, Frank Rodriquez. With Sally Díaz, Gilberto Arribas, Eddie Marrero, Monica Pérez-Brandes and Marly Rivera, Hector Máximo Rodriguez, Jimmy Delgado, Johnny Rivero.

Signature Theatre Company. Dedicated to the exploration of a playwright's body of work. James Houghton artistic director.

THE LATE HENRY MOSS. By Sam Shepard. September 24, 2001. Directed by Joseph Chaikin; choreography, Peter Pucci; scenery, Christine Jones; costumes, Teresa Snider-Stein; lighting, Michael Chybowski; music and sound, David Van Tieghem and Jill B.C. DuBoff. With Guy Boyd, Sheila Tousey, Arliss Howard, Ethan Hawke, José Perez, Clark Middleton, Michael Aronov, Tim Michael, Luke Notary.

*A FEW STOUT INDIVIDUALS. By John Guare. May 12, 2002. Directed by Michael Greif; scenery, Allen Moyer; costumes, Gabriel Berry; lighting, James Vermeulen; sound and music, David Van Tieghem. With James Yaegashi, Donald Moffat, William Sadler, Polly Holliday, Tom McGowan, Michi Barall, Ümit Çelebi, Charles Brown, Amy Hohn, T.J. Kenneally, Mark Fish, Clark Middleton, Cheryl Evans.

Soho Rep. Dedicated to new and cutting edge US playwrights. Daniel Aukin artistic director, Alexandra Conley executive director.

[SIC]. By Melissa James Gibson. November 20, 2001. Directed by Daniel Aukin; scenery, Louisa Thompson; costumes, Kim Gill; lighting, Matt Frey, sound, Robert Murphy. With James Urbaniak, Dominic Fumusa, Christina Kirk, Jennifer Morris, Trevor A. Williams. A 2001–2002 *Best Plays* choice, see essay by Bruce Weber in this volume.

ATTEMPTS ON HER LIFE. By Martin Crimp. April 22, 2002. Directed by Steve Cosson; scenery, Robert Pyzocha; costumes, Kaye Voyce; lighting, Thomas Dunn; sound, Ken Travis. With Christopher McCann, Sara Barnett, T. Ryder Smith, Tracey A. Leight, Damian Baldet, Aysan Çelik, Jayne Houdyshell.

Theatre for the New City. Developmental theater and new experimental works. Crystal Field executive director.

CANDIDA AND HER FRIENDS. By Mario Fratti. June 7, 2001. Directed by Michael Hillyer; scenery, Mark Symczak; lighting, Jason A. Cina; costumes, Roi "Bubi" Escudero. With Brian Runbeck, Caroline Strong, Neil Levine, Alex McCord and Toks Olagundoye.

THE PATIENTS ARE RUNNING THE ASYLUM. By Crystal Field. August 4, 2001. Directed by Ms. Field; music composed and arranged by Joseph Vernon Banks; design, Mary Blanchard and Walter Gurbo; sound, Joy Linscheid and David Nolan; costumes, Alessandra Nichols and Ruth Muzio. August 4, 2001.

BABES IN AMERICA. By Carole Clement. September 13, 2001.Directed by Max Daniels. With Kate Lunsford, Paula Nance, Alexandra Leeper, Lisa Rock, Samuel Ward, Ryan Paulson and Joseph Jude Zito.

PETER PAN. By J.M. Barrie. November 22, 2001. Directed by Jim Niesen; choreography, Sarah Adams; scenery, Ken Rothchild; costumes, Christianne Myers; lighting, Randy Glickman. With Danny Bacher, Josh Bacher, Rezelle Caravaca, Michael-David Gordon, Missy Jayme, Jack Lush, Sven Miller, Patrena Murray and Damen Scranton.

THE INSURRECTION MASS WITH FUNERAL MARCH FOR A ROTTEN IDEA (A SPECIAL MASS FOR THE AFTERMATH OF THE EVENTS OF SEPT. 11). December 18, 2001. Directed by Peter Schumann. With Strawberry Cantubo, Adam Cook, Susie Dennison, Vasilos Gletsos, Susan Hirschmugl, Jason Norris, Michael Romanyshyn, Maria Schumann, Lydia Stein.

DREAM STAR CAFÉ. By Jack Agueros. January 31, 2002. Directed by Crystal Field. With Elizabeth Ruf, Dalia Ruiz, Michael Vazquez, Primy Rivera.

THE SHORT VIOLENT LIFE OF MARGIE GOOD. By Jimmy Camicia. April 6, 2002 Directed by Harvey Tavel; scenery, Mark Marcante; lighting, Alexander Bartenieff. With Crystal Field, Craig Meade, Irma St. Paule, Mary Tierney, Althea Vythuys, Dorothy Cantwell, Darby Dizard, Marian Sarach.

THE MURALS OF ROCKEFELLER CENTER. By Jim Niesen and members of the Irondale Ensemble Project. April 24, 2002. Directed by Mr. Niesen; scenery, Ken Rothchild; costumes, T. Michael Hall; lighting, Randy Glickman; music, Walter Thompson. With Danny Bacher,

Prodigal baby: Henry Stram, Reg Rogers and Michi Barall in Unwrap Your Candy. *Photo: Carol Rosegg*

Josh Bacher, Michael-David Gordon, Missy Jayme, Jack Lush, Sven Miller, Patrena Murray, Damen Scranton.

CHOCOLATE IN HEAT: GROWING UP ARAB IN AMERICA. By Betty Shamieh. August 26, 2001. Directed by Damen Scranton. With Ms. Shamieh and Piter Fattouche.

The Vineyard Theatre. Multi-art chamber theater dedicated to the development of new plays and musicals, music-theater collaborations and innovative revivals. Douglas Aibel artistic director, Barbara Zinn Krieger executive director, Jeffrey Solis managing director.

UNWRAP YOUR CANDY. Four one-acts written and directed by Doug Wright. October 8, 2001. Scenery, Michael Brown; costumes, Ilona Somogyi; lighting, Phil Monat; sound, David Van Tieghem and Jill B.C. DuBoff; music, Mr. Van Tieghem. With Reg Rogers, Leslie Lyles, Michi Barall, Henry Stram and Darren Pettie. Also includes LOT 13: THE BONE VIOLIN, WILDWOOD PARK and BABY TALK.

BRUTAL IMAGINATION. Musical adapted by Cornelius Eady and Diane Paulus; music by Diedre Murray; from Mr. Eady's poem. January 9, 2002. Directed by Ms. Paulus; scenery, Mark Wendland; costumes, Ilona Somogyi; lighting, Kevin Adams; sound, Brett Jarvis and David A. Gilman. With Joe Morton, Sally Murphy.

SWIMMING WITH WATERMELONS. By Randy Weiner, Diane Paulus and members of Project 400. April 11, 2002. Directed by Mr. Weiner. Scenery, Myung Hee Cho; costumes, Ilona Somogyi; lighting, Michael Chybowski; sound, Brett Jarvis. With Emily Hellstrom, Rachel Benbow Murdy, Anna Wilson, Jordin Ruderman.

Women's Project and Productions. Nurtures, develops and produces plays written and directed by women. Julia Miles artistic director, Georgia Buchanan managing director.

THE STRANGE CASE OF MARY LINCOLN. Musical by June Bingham; music and lyrics by Carmel Owen. October 19, 2001. Directed by Victoria Pero. With Chris Clavelli, David Hess, Mark Ledbetter, Karen Murphy, Peter Samuel, Gayle Turner.

CARSON MCCULLERS (HISTORICALLY INACCURATE). By Sarah Schulman. January 20, 2002. Directed by Marion McClinton; scenery, Neil Patel; costumes, Toni-Leslie James; lighting, Donald Holder; sound, Janet Kalas. With Michi Barall, Rosalyn Coleman, Barbara Eda-Young, Leland Gantt, Tim Hopper, Rick Stear and Anne Torsiglieri.

MISCELLANEOUS

ABINGDON THEATRE COMPANY. *The Mooncalf* by Elisabeth Karlin. October 24, 2001. Directed by Sturgis Warner; with Michael Chernus, Kit Flanagan, Liz Morton, Barbara Rosenblat, Guy Strobel and Debrah Waller. *The Parker Family Circus* by Jan Buttram. February 13, 2002. Directed by Taylor Brooks; with Lori Gardner, Rita Gardner, Debbie Jaffe, Carole Monferdini, Michael Pemberton and Bryan Schany.

THE ACTING COMPANY. *The Taming of the Shrew* by William Shakespeare. May 9, 2002. Directed by Eve Shapiro. *Pudd'nhead Wilson,* adapted by Charles Smith; based on the novel by Mark Twain. May 15, 2002. Directed by Walter Dallas; with Coleman Zeigen, Roslyn Ruff, Michael Lluberes, Michael Abbott Jr., Jordan Simmons, Christen Simon, Jimmon Cole.

THE ACTING SHAKESPEARE COMPANY. *Measure for Measure* by William Shakespeare. April 21, 2002. Directed by Nona Shepphard; with Joanna Bonaro, Tali Friedman, Anna Kepe, Demetrius Martin, Ian Bok, Alice Brickwood, Garth Hewitt, Kerri Ann Murphy, Joe Paulik, Kristin Proctor, Michael Anthony Rizzo, Benjamin Rosen, Benjamin Woodlock, Samantha Wright, Andy English, Trey Ziegler.

THE ACTORS COMPANY THEATRE (TACT). *The Waltz of the Toreadors* by Jean Anouilh. October 5, 2001. Directed by Scott Alan Evans; with Cynthia Darlow, Francesca DiMauro, Cynthia Harris, Simon Jones, Greg McFadden, Eve Michelson, James Murtaugh, Margaret Nichols, Gregory Salata, Lyn Wright. *Time and the Conways* by J.B. Priestley. January 18, 2002. Directed by Will Pomerantz;

Too much fun: Simon Jones and company in Long
Island Sound. *Photo: Joan Marcus*

with Delphi Harrington, Simon Jones, Eve Michelson, Margaret Nichols, John Plumpis, Scott Schafer, Lyn Wright, Mary Bacon, Allison Cimmet, Andrew Dolan. *Look Homeward, Angel* by Ketti Frings; based on the novel by Thomas Wolfe. March 8, 2002. Directed by Scott Alan Evans; with Mary Bacon, Simon Billig, Nora Chester, Cynthia Darlow, Jack Koenig, Darrie Lawrence, James Murtaugh, Margaret Nichols, Joseph Siravo, Lyn Wright, Jamie Bennett, Ken Bolden, Paul DeBoy, Kathryn Phillip, James Prendergast, William Wise. *Widowers' Houses* by George Bernard Shaw. March 8, 2002. Directed by Simon Jones; with Greg McFadden, Gregory Salata, Scott Schafer, Genevieve Elam, Michael Frederic, Gretchen Michelfeld, James Prendergast. *Long Island Sound* by Noël Coward. May 13, 2002. Directed by Scott Alan Evans; with Cynthia Darlow, Kyle Fabel, Delphi Harrington, Cynthia Harris, Simon Jones, Jack Koenig, Darrie Lawrence, Greg McFadden, James Murtaugh, Margaret Nichols, Scott Schafer, Rob Breckenridge, Suzanne Geraghty, Julie Halston, Brent Harris, Darren Kelly, Barbara Marineau, Patricia O'Connell, Patricia Randell, Charles Tuthill, Rebecca Wisocky.

THE ACTORS PLAYGROUND. *Grace's Curse* by Jolie Jalbert. November 4, 2001. Directed by Jose Element; with Heather Aldridge, Ms. Jalbert, Brooke Marie Procida, Mary Holmstrom, Rob Maitner, Michael Goldfried, Cynthia Pierce. *Brilliant Traces* by Cindy Lou Johnson. February 14, 2002. Directed by Guido Venitucci; with Heather Aldridge, Robert Harriell.

ALTERED STAGES. *Single Bullet Theory* by Mike Bencivenga. April 9, 2002. Directed by John McDermott.

AMERICAN PLAYWRIGHTS THEATRE. *Champagne and Caviar* by Frances Galton. August 18, 2001. With Alice Gold, Kerry Prep, Jacqueline Sydney. DISSONANT DOUBLES: AN EVENING OF SHORT PLAYS CELEBRATING WOMEN'S HISTORY MONTH. March 14, 2002. *Sincerity,* written and directed by Mario Fratti. *Places We've Lived* by Milan Stitt. Directed by Richard Harden. *Champagne and Caviar* written and directed by Frances Galton. *Mimi & Me* by Kitty Dubin. Directed by Andrea Andresakis. *Star Collector* by Sally Carpenter. Directed by Jeff Davolt. With Emelise Aleandri, Barney Fitzpatrick, Alice Gold, Carissa Guild, Melissa Hurst, Effie Johnson, Chuck Muckle, Jeff O'Malley, Jacqueline Sydney, Louis Vuolo.

AQUILA THEATRE COMPANY. *Much Ado About Nothing* by William Shakespeare. June 28, 2001. Adapted and directed by Robert Richmond; with Alex Webb, Shirleyann Kaladjian, Lisa Carter, Richard Willis, Anthony Cochrane, Louis Butelli, Nathan Flower, Cameron Blair.

ARCLIGHT THEATER. *Homecoming* by Lauren Weedman. January 21, 2002. Directed by Maryann Lombardi; with Ms. Weedman.

BANK STREET THEATER. *Edward III* by William Shakespeare. July 10, 2001. Directed by Heather Anne McAllister and Kelly McAllister; with Jessica Colley, Jamison Lee Driskill, John Marigliano, Heather Anne McAllister, Ms. McAllister, John Patrick Moore, Stacey Plaskett, Matthew Rankin, W. Emory Rose and Sara Thigpen. UNITY FEST 2001. December 6–December 30, 2001. (Program A.) *The Contents of Your Suitcase* by Daphne R. Hull. Directed by Donna Jean Fogel. *The History of Us* by Andres J. Wrath. Directed by Donna Jean Fogel. *Lettuce Spray* by Jim Doyle and directed by Tony Hamilton. *The Faces of Ants* by Chay Yew. Directed by James McLaughlin. *Wasting Time* by Peter Mercurio. Directed by John Jay Buol. *Auntie Mayhem* by David Pumo. Directed by Donna Jean Fogel. (Program B.) *St. Anthony and the Appendix* by Robin Rice Lichtig. Directed by James McLaughlin; with Frank Anthony Polito, Leila Mansury, Ann Chandler, Tony Hamilton. *F2F* by Linda Eisenstein. Directed by Donna Jean Fogel; with Gisele Richardson. *Refreshments* by Peter Mercurio. Directed by Brenda D. Cook; with John Jay Buol, Tony Hamilton. *Not Exactly Strangers* by Andres J. Wrath. Directed by Brenda D. Cook; with Ivan Davila, Christopher Lawrence Kann. *Stacked: A Deviant Doctoral Dissertation* by Lisa Haas. Directed by James McLaughlin; with Bekka Lindström. *Blow* by Chay Yew. Directed by Dennis Smith; with Steven Eng, Virginia Wing, Keith Lorrel Manning. (Program C.) *Rug Store Cowboy* by Gary Garrison. Directed by Courtenay A. Wendell; with Tony Hamilton, James McLaughlin. *Evergreen* by Amy A. Kirk. Directed by Bekka Lindström; with Donna Jean Fogel, Courtenay A. Wendell. *Pick-Up Times* by Anton Dudley. Directed by Courtenay A. Wendell; with Nicholas Warren-Gray, Michael Rivera. *Class Dismissed* by Rich Orloff. Directed by Donna Jean Fogel; with Keith Lorrel Manning, Frank Anthony Polito. *Never Said* by Kim Yaged. Directed by Anton Dudley; with John Jay Buol, Ivan Davila, Hope Lambert, Bekka Lindström. *White* by Chay Yew. Directed by Anton Dudley; with Patrick Wang. *Falling to Pieces: The Patsy Cline Musical* book and lyrics by Ellis Nassour; original score by George Leonard. Directed by Dan Wackerman. NEW YORK STORIES IN BLACK AND WHITE (AN EVENING OF ONE ACT PLAYS). May 29, 2002–June 23, 2002. *Breakdown* by Bill Bozzone. Directed by Keno Rider; with John Fedele, Raymond Jordan. *In the Garden at St. Luke's* by Stan Lachow. Directed by Leann Walker; with Ms. Walker, Quillan. *The Spelling Bee* by Philip Vassallo. Directed by Leann Walker; with John Fedele, Raymond Jordan.

BLUE HERON THEATER. *Kings* by Christopher Logue. June 7, 2001. Adapted and directed by James Milton; with James Doherty and Michael T. Ringer. *A Prophet Among Them* by Wesley Brown. June 25, 2001. Directed by Marie Thomas; with Reggie Montgomery, Harvy Blanks, Perri Gaffney, Tom Titone, Dina Comoli and Marlon Cherry. *Two Rooms* by Lee Blessing. November 4, 2001. Directed by Roger Danforth; with Thomas James O'Leary, Monica Koskey and Beth Dixon and Steve Cell. *The Cure at Troy* by Seamus Heaney. February 4, 2002. Directed by Kevin Osborne; with Jolie Garrett, Rainard Rachele, Ian Oldaker, Sue Berch, Karla Hendrick, Margot White. *Broken Boughs* by Clay McLeod Chapman. March 3, 2002. Directed by Charles Loffredo; with Patricia Randell, Heather Grayson, Matt Tomasino, Hanna Cheek, Joe Sangillo. *The Mooncalf* by Elisabeth Karlin. November 6, 2001. Directed by Sturgis Warner; with Guy Strobel, Kathy Lichter, Debrah Waller, Liz Morton, Steven Boyer, Barbara Rosenblat. BOROUGH TALES: BROOKLYN (CONCEIVED BY WHITE BIRD PRODUCTIONS). March 14, 2002. *Twelve Brothers* by Jeffrey M. Jones and Camila Jones. Directed by Page Burkholder. *Rapunzel* by Melissa James Gibson. Directed by David Levine. *The Little Matchgirl* by Lynn Nottage. Directed by Daniela Varon. *Snow White* by Onome Ekeh. Directed by Dave Simonds. *Lucky Hans* by Margie Duffield. Directed by Jean Wagner. *Hannah and Gretel* by Creative Theatrics' Performance Team and John Istel. Directed by Welker White. With Amie Bermowitz, Rayme Cornell, Robert Hatcher, Tony Reilly, Christian Rummel, Jackie Sutton, Kathryn Velvel.

BROKEN WATCH PRODUCTIONS. *Boys' Life* by Howard Korder. September 10, 2001. Directed by Drew DeCorleto; with Leo Lauer, Andrew J. Hoff, Jeremy Koch, Jeslyn Kelly, Danielle Savin, Alli Steinberg, Teresa Goding.

THE BUILDERS ASSOCIATION. *Xtravaganza* compiled and directed by Marianne Weems. April 20, 2002. With Moe Angelos, Aimee Guillot, Peter A. Jacobs, Heaven Phillips, Jeff Webster, Brahms "Bravo" LaFortune.

CAP 21 THEATER. *I Love My Wife* book and lyrics by Michael Stewart; music composed and arranged by Cy Coleman. May 28, 2002. Directed and choreographed by John Znidarsic; with Julie Beckham, Matt Kuehl, J. Brandon Savage, Elizabeth Shaw, Jared Stein, Spiff Wiegand.

CENTER STAGE. *3 Sisters Lounge*, based on Anton Chekhov's *The Three Sisters*. September 6, 2001. Directed by John Issendorf; with Browne Smith, Becca Greene, Paula Ehrenberg, Barbara Sauermann, Steve Snerling, Roger Nasser, Jason St. Sauver, Tom Bartos, Jenny Bold.

CENTURY CENTER FOR THE PERFORMING ARTS. OH, SHAW, DON'T BE A COWARD, GO WILDE! IBSEN'S WATCHING (staged readings). *Heartbreak House* by George Bernard Shaw. June 5, 2001. Directed by Alfred Christie; with Keir Dullea, Mia Dillon. *Major Barbara* by George Bernard Shaw. June 6, 2001. Directed by Marco Capalbo. *Mrs. Warren's Profession* by George Bernard Shaw. June 12, 2001. Directed by Sue Lawless; with Tammy Grimes. *Blithe Spirit* by Noël Coward. June 13, 2001. Directed by Alfred Christie; with Tammy Grimes. *Peer Gynt (Part 1)* by Henrik Ibsen. June 14, 2001. Directed by Alex Lippard. *Look After Lulu* by Noël Coward. June 19, 2001. Directed by Steve Ramshur. *Present Laughter* by Noël Coward. June 20, 2001. Directed by Emily Hill. *Peer Gynt (Part 2)* by Henrik Ibsen. *Lady Windermere's Fan* by Oscar Wilde. June 26, 2001. Directed by Alex Lippard. *Salome* by Oscar Wilde. June 27, 2001. Directed by Joel Friedman. *Hedda Gabler* by Henrik Ibsen. October 9, 2001. Directed by Alex Lippard; with Blake Lindsley, Max Vogler, Barbara Haas, Nick Stannard, Maxine Prescott, Jessica Damrow, Christopher Mullen. *Little Eyolf* by Henrik Ibsen. February 10, 2002. Directed by Steve Ramshur; with Kurt Rhoads, Linda Marie Larson, Naomi Peters, Gabriel Maxson, Jonathan Press, Joyce Feurring. *The Master Builder* by Henrik Ibsen. March 10, 2002. Directed by J.C. Compton; with George Cavey, Harmony Schuttler, Paden Fallis, Dennis Parlato, Wendy Barrie-Wilson, David Jones, Tami Dixon. *John Gabriel Borkman* by Henrik Ibsen. April 14, 2002. Directed by Max Montel; with Eric Frandsen, Amber Gross, Charlotte Hampden, Richard Leighton, Cecelia Riddett, Kate Suber, Robert Thompson.

CHASHAMA THEATER. *The Witch of Edmonton* by William Rowley, Thomas Dekker and John Ford. November 1, 2001. Directed by Rosey Hay; with Susan Moses, Christiania Cobean, R. Paul Hamilton, James Hay, Daniel Huston, Patrick Lacey, Brad Lemons, Nicole Marsh, Tracey Paleo, Sonda Staley, Adam Swiderski, Anthony Vitrano, Peter Zazzali. *Mrs. Feuerstein* by Murray Mednick. January 8, 2002. Directed by Roxanne Rogers; with Maria O'Brien, Lynnda Ferguson, Dan Ahearn, David Little, Samantha Quan, Kevin Shinick.

CHELSEA PLAYHOUSE. *Christmas With the Crawfords*. Created by Richard Winchester, written by Wayne Buidens and Mark Sargent. November 20, 2001. Directed by Donna Drake; with Joey Arias, Connie Champagne, Trauma Flintstone, Max Grenyo, Chris March, Matthew Martin, Mark Sargent and Jason Scott. *Embers* by Catherine Gropper. January 30, 2002. Directed by Helena Webb; with Nada Rowand, Michael Graves, Kenneth Wilson-Harrington, Melissa Wolff.

CHERRY LANE ALTERNATIVE. 2001 MENTOR PROJECT. *Strange Attractors* by David Adjmi (Craig Lucas, mentor). June 6, 2001. Directed by Richard Caliban; with Joanna P. Adler, Andrew Heckler, Michael Marisi, and Adrienne Shelly. *The Allegory of Painting* by Cybele Pascal (Marsha Norman, mentor). June 20, 2001. Directed by Leigh Silverman; with Janine Barris-Gerstl, Angel Desai, Caitlin Gibbon, Tony Hoty, Jerusha Klemperer, John Leone, Annie McAdams, Cody Nickel, Michael T. Ringer, and Garret Savage. SPECIAL PROJECT. *Sixty Minutes in Negroland* written and performed by Margo Jefferson. October 1, 2001. Directed by Eduardo Machado and Tatyana Yassukovich. YOUNG PLAYWRIGHTS FESTIVAL 2001. November 23, 2001. *Johnny Likaboot Kills His Father!!* by Yelena Elkind. Directed by Richard Caliban; with Michael Mosley, Steven Hauck, Cynthia Hood. *Conference Time* by Jeb G. Havens. Directed by Padraic Lillis; with Michael Mosley, Brad Malow, Ann Hu, Geoffrey Molloy, Sarah Bragin. *Gorgeous Raptors* by Lucy Alibar-Harrison. Directed by Beth F. Miles; with Geoffrey Molloy, Shannon Emerick, Sarah Bragin, Cynthia Hood, Ann Hu, Steven Hauck, Robin L. Taylor. *Nursery* by Julia Jarcho. Directed by Brett W. Reynolds; with Cynthia Hood, Shannon Emerick, Geoffrey Molloy, Brad Malow, Robin L. Taylor. BLACK HISTORY MONTH. February 20, 2002. *Pickling* by Suzan-Lori Parks. Directed by Allison Eve Zell; with Jaye Austin-Williams. *Harriet's Return* by Karen Jones-Meadows. Directed by Saundra McClain; with Denise Burse-Fernandez. WOMEN'S HISTORY MONTH. March 13, 2002. *Fuente* by Cusi Cram. Directed by Shilarna Stokes; with Vanessa Aspillaga, Sanjiv Jhaveri, Selenis Leyna, James Martin, Nathan Perez. *Ethel Rosenberg* by Lu Hauser. Directed by Joan Micklin Silver. 2002 MENTOR PROJECT. *Out of Sterno* by Deborah Zoe Laufer (Marsha Norman, mentor). April 2, 2002. Directed by Eleanor Reissa; with Charles Borland, Dale Carman, Debbie Gravitte and Emily Loesser. *99 Histories* by Julia Cho (David Henry Hwang, mentor). April 23, 2002. Directed by Maria Mileaf, with Elaina Erika Davis, Joel de la Fuente, Ann Hu, Mia Katigbak, Darren Pettie and Mia Tagano. *Sixteen Wounded* by Eliam Kraiem (Michael Weller, mentor). May 14, 2002. Directed by Matt

August; with Mia Barron, Jane Burd, Edward A. Hajj, Dylan Dawson, Jonathan Hova, Jim Moie, Martin Rayner, Chime Serra and John Phillips.

CLASSICAL THEATER OF HARLEM. *Hamlet* by William Shakespeare. July 27, 2001. Directed by Alfred Preisser; with J. Kyle Manzay, Quonta Shanell Beasley, Arthur French, Brian Homer, Damon Kinard, Rome Neal, Dan Snow, Adam Wade and Lanette Ware. *Native Son* by Richard Wright. February 1, 2002. Adapted and directed by Christopher McElroen; with Johnnie Mae, Ben Rivers, Jim Ganser, Arlene Nadel, Sulai Lopez, Dana Watkins, Robert Heller, Damien Smith, George C. Hosmer. *Medea* by Euripides. April 5, 2002. Adapted by Alfred Preisser. Directed by Mr. Preisser; with Arthur French and April Thompson.

CLEMENTE SOTO VELEZ CULTURAL CENTER. *The Four Little Girls* by Pablo Picasso. October 17, 2001. Directed by R. Michael Blanco and Carol Blanco; with Joan Lunoe, Mary Murphy, Carol Blanco and Kathryn Gayner. *Anna Bella Eema* by Lisa D'Amour. September 30, 2001. Directed by Katie Pearl. *Midnight Brainwash Revival* by Kirk Wood Bromley. December 28, 2001. Directed by Joshua Spafford. *The Bomb* by Josh Fox. February 28, 2002. Directed by Mr. Fox; with Sophie Amieva, Gina Hirsch, Peter Lettre, Patrick McCaffrey, Aya Ogawa, Robert Saietta, and Aaron Mostkoff. *Soon My Work* by Josh Fox. Directed by Mr. Fox; with Jason Fisher, Patrick McCaffrey, Alex Fox, Joe Sanchez. *Icarus & Aria* by Kirk Wood Bromley. March 20. 2002. Directed by Joshua Spafford.

CONNELLY THEATRE. CHEKHOV NOW FESTIVAL. *Uncle Vanya*. November 10, 2001. Directed by Cynthia Croot; with C. Andrew Bauer, Margot Ebeling, Ed Jewett, Harriet Koppel, John Lenartz, Gail Neil, April Sweeney, Gary Wilmes. *AuNT Vanya*. November 11, 2001. Directed by David Karl Lee; with Zoe Jenkin, C.S. Lee, Debra Ann Byrd, T.L. Lee, Alan Nebelthau, Amanda Allan, Craig Schoenbaum, Veronika Duka, Sondra Gorney, Eric Michael Kockmer. *Bloody Poetry* by Howard Brenton. October 8, 2001. Directed by David Travis. *Our Town* by Thornton Wilder. February 16, 2002. Directed by Jack Cummings III; with Barbara Andres, Tom Ligon, Emma Orelove, Jeff Edgerton, Robyn Hussa, Mark Ledbetter, Joanna Lee, Richard Martin, Matt Nowosielski, Carl Palmer, Monica Russell, Julie Siefkes, Jonathan Uffelman, James Weber, John Wellmann, Chuck Wilson, Matt Yeager, Van Zeiler.

CULTURE CLUB. *Birdy's Bachelorette Party* by Mark Nasser with Suzanna Melendez and Denise Fennel. May 17, 2002. Directed by Ms. Melendez; with Maria Barrata, Wass M. Stevens, Melissa Short, Jamie Sorrentini, Alice Moore, Michael Gargani, Frank Rempe, Ms. Fennel, Christopher Campbell, Scott Bilecky, Reed Hutchins.

CURRICAN THEATRE. *Sex and Other Collisons* by Trista Baldwin. June 7, 2001. Directed by Nela Wagman; with Sarah Buff, Whitney Buss, Anna Cody, Joe Fuer, Peter Humer, Matt Neely, Mike Szeles.

THE DIRECTORS COMPANY. *Kilt* by Jonathan Wilson. April 10, 2002. Directed by Jack Hofsiss; with Chris Payne Gilbert, Tovah Feldshuh, Herb Foster, Jamie Harris and Kathleen Doyle.

DIXON PLACE. *The Moon in Vain*; inspired by Anton Chekhov's *The Seagull*. August 7, 2001. Directed by Lee Gundersheimer; with Rae C. Wright and Ethan Cohn. *Uppa Creek* by Keli Garrett. September 15, 2001. Directed by Dominic Taylor; with Ms. Garrett, Amy Fellers, Yvonne Jung, Bradford Olson, Kaipo Schwab, Ron Riley, Rodney Owens, Gwen Mulamba. *Five 'Til* by Edwin Lee Gibson. November 3, 2001. Directed by Daphne Richards; with Mr. Gibson, Robert Blumenthal, Lynnard Williams, Terrence Williams, Amatusami Kari, Keisha Spraggin. *Rosa* by George Emilio Sanchez. February 8, 2001. Directed and performed by Mr. Sanchez. *Soppin' Juice* by Mark Holt. March 16, 2002. Directed by James Busby; with Coby Koehl, Ken Kincaid.

DOUGLAS FAIRBANKS THEATER. *Mr. President*. Musical with book by Howard Lindsay and Russel Crouse; music and lyrics by Irving Berlin; adapted by Gerard Alessandrini. August 2, 2001. Directed and musical staging by John Znidarsic and Mr. Alessandrini; with Jono Mainelli, Clif Thorn, Michael West, Amanda Naughton, Whitney Allen, Eric Jordan Young, Stuart Zagnit.

EDGE THEATER COMPANY. *Life is a Dream* by Pedro Calderón de la Barca; translated by John Clifford. January 31, 2002. Directed by Carolyn Cantor; with Sturgis Adams, Andrew Grusetskie, Guisseppe Jones, Andres Munar, Dustin Tucker, Kathryn Zamora-Benson, Arthur Aulisi, Jenn Harris, Omar Metwally, Ben Schenkkan, Aliza Waksal.

FLATIRON PLAYHOUSE. *Not in Front of the Baby* by Stephen Gaydos. April 8, 2002. Directed by Paul Zablocki; with Joe Fuer, Jeremy Peter Johnson, Rana Kazkaz, Jenna Kalinowski, Kelly McAndrew, Matt Neely, Jeannie Noth, Christopher Swift.

THE FLEA THEATER. *No Mother to Guide Her* by Lillian Mortimer. August 23, 2001. Directed by Jim Simpson; with Joe Holt, Leila Howland, Jennifer McKenna, Cori Clark Nelson, Beth Tapper, Sam Marks, Dean Strange. *Ajax (por nobody)* by Alice Tuan. October 12, 2001. Directed by Jim Simpson; with Joanie Ellen, Sam Marka, Alfredo Narciso, Kristin Stewart, Siobhan Towey. *The Guys* by Anne Nelson. January 17, 2002. Directed by Jim Simpson; with Bill Murray and Sigourney Weaver. *Nighttown* by Susan Mosakowski. May 11, 2002. Directed by Ms. Mosakowski; with Matthew Maguire, Michael Ryan.

45TH STREET THEATRE. *A Magic Place in a New Time* by Robert Lesser. January 26, 2002. Directed by Robert Armin; with Susan Gordon, Kaitlin O'Neal, Dean Fiore, Michael Karp, Celia Howard, John O'Creagh, Chuck Ardezzone, Eloise Iliff, George Santana. *The Ninth Circle* by Edward Musto. March 26, 2002. Directed by Tom Herman; with Beth Beyer, Gene Forman, Jay Greenberg, Stephen Innocenzi, Heidi James, Darren Kelly, Whalen J. Laurence, Rick Lawrence, Rodrigo Lopresti, Andrea Maybaum, John D. McNally, Anne Rutter.

45 BLEECKER. *Three Dark Tales* by Theatre O. April 9, 2002. Directed by Joseph Alford; with Mr. Alford, Sarah Coxon, Lucien MacDougall, Carolina Valdés. *Measure for Measure* by William Shakespeare. April 21, 2002. Directed by Nona Shepphard; with Joanna Bonaro, Tali Friedman, Anna Kepe, Demetrius Martin, Ian Bok, Alice Brickwood, Garth Hewitt, Kerri Ann Murphy, Joe Paulik, Kristin Proctor, Michael Anthony Rizzo.

FOUNDRY THEATRE. *Talk*. By Carl Hancock Rux. April 9, 2002. Directed by Marion McClinton; with Karen Kandel, Maria Tucci, Reg E. Cathey, James Himelsbach, Anthony Mackie and John Seitz.

GENE FRANKEL THEATRE. *Santa Claus is Coming Out* by Jeffrey Solomon. November 26, 2001. Directed by Emily Weiner; with Mr. Solomon. *Unequilibrium* by Alexander Lyrus and Robert McCaskill. January 28, 2002. Directed by Mr. McCaskill; with Mr. Lyrus.

GORILLA REPERTORY THEATRE. *Othello* by William Shakespeare. July 9, 2001. Directed by Christopher Carter Sanderson; with John Roque, Joel de la Fuente, Mel Duane Gionson, Andrew Pang, Joshua Spafford, James Saito, Ariel Estrada, Tina Horii, Joel Carino, Tess Lina, Jennifer Kato. *Cymbeline* by William Shakespeare. July 18, 2001. Directed by Christopher Carter Sanderson; with Michael Colby Jones, Katherine Gooch, Tim Moore, Rohana Kenin, Tom Staggs, Brian O'Sullivan, Sean Elias-Reyes, Greg Petroff. *Ubu is King!* by Alfred Jarry; adapted by Christopher Carter Sanderson. July 21, 2001. Directed by Mr. Sanderson. *A Midsummer Night's Dream* by William Shakespeare. August 13, 2001. *The Death of King Arthur* by Matthew Freeman. September 20, 2001. Directed by Christopher Carter Sanderson; with Sean Elias-Reyes, Sarah Dandridge, Michael Colby Jones, Tom Staggs, Aubrey Chamberlin, Tim Moore and Rohana Kenin.

GREENWICH STREET THEATER. *Some Voices* by Joe Penhall. November 12, 2001. Directed by Kevin Kittle; with Victor Villar-Hauser, Patrick Tull, Mike Finesilver, David Costelloe and Laoisa Sexton. *Scab* by Sheila Callaghan. March 11, 2002. Directed by Hayley Finn; with Shannon Burkett, Sasha Eden, David Wheir, Anne Carney and Flora Diaz. TWO PLAYS IN REP. *The Doctor of Rome* by Nat Colley. May 2, 2002. Directed by Ralph Carhart. *The Merchant of Venice* by William Shakespeare. Directed by Ralph Carhart; with Susan Hyon, Derek Johnsen, Juliet King, Rob Langeder, Brian Linden, Lanie MacEwan, Michael Mendelson, Lawrence Merritt, Matthew Pendergast, John Peterson, Miles Phillips, Dara Seitzman, Lou Tally, Franklin John Westbrooks. *Syndrome* by Kirk Wood Bromley; based on a concept by Joshua Lewis Berg. January 23, 2002. Directed by Rob Urbinati; with Joshua Lewis Berg.

GROVE STREET PLAYHOUSE. *Hello Herman* by John Buffalo Mailer. November 3, 2001. Directed by Thomas Kail; with Jim Isler, John Newman, Nafeesa Monroe, Christina Pabst, Jonathan Mosley, Kady Duffy, Peter Cambor, Alexis Raben, Bob LaVelle, Neil Stewart, Anthony Veneziale, Sidney Williams.

HENRY STREET SETTLEMENT. *Dead End* by Sidney Kingsley. October 18, 2001. Directed by David Gaard. MASKUNMASK: THREE ONE-ACT PLAYS. November 15, 2001. *The Happy Journey* by Thornton Wilder, directed by Seth Sharp; *And Where Was Pancho Villa When You Really Needed Him?* by Silviana Wood, directed by Alexandra Lopez; *The Flying Doctor* by Molière, directed by Saundra McClain. *Urban Transition: Loose Blossoms* by Ron Milner. April 7, 2002. Directed by Woodie King Jr.; with Jerome Preston Bates, Chadwick Boseman, Joseph Edward, Dianne Kirksey, Sade Lythcott, George Newton, Monica Soyemi.

HERE ARTS CENTER. *U.S. Drag* by Gina Gionfriddo. June 17, 2001. Directed by Pam MacKinnon; with Ian Helfer, Effie Johnson, Vin Knight, Meg MacCary, Annie McNamara, Maria Striar, Erich Strom, Mather Zickel. *Woman Killer* by Chiori Miyagawa. September 9, 2001. Directed by Sonoko Kawahara; with Crispin Freeman. *The Bakkhai* by Euripides. September 18, 2001. Directed by René Migliaccio; with Dana Marie Abbatiello, Noelle Adamoschek, Maya Alexander, Suzanne Aptman, Cecilia Biagini, Vanessa Eichler, Bertie Ferdman, Cheryl Fidelman, Jay Gaussoin, Rob Grace. *TimeSlips* by Anne Basting. November 4, 2001. Directed by Christopher Bayes; with Hope Clarke, John Freimann, Jodie Lynne McClintock, Michael Shelle, Sheriden Thomas and Judith Van Buren. *The Star Play* by Michael Arthur. November 2, 2001. Directed by Sonnet Blanton; with Lisa Hargus, Rebekkah Ross, Janelle Schremmer, Troy Schremmer. *Novel* by Nick Bellitto. December 2, 2001. Directed by Lorca Peress; with Gena Bardwell, Michael Citriniti and Peter Reznikoff. CULTUREMART 2002. *Confessions of a Reluctant Buddhist* by Daniel Levy. January 3, 2002. *Desk* by Aaron Landsman. January 5, 2002. Performed by Mr. Landsman. *Just Like a Man* by Fernando Maneca. January 5, 2002. Directed and performed by Mr. Maneca. *Margaret* by Damon Kiely/Real Time Theater. January 5, 2002. *The Don Quixote Project* by Peculiar Works Project. January 7, 2002. *Stars of the Sweet Decline* by the Paul Warner Performance Group. January 9, 2002. *Comedian from a Crumbling Empire* by Kristin Page Stuart. January 10, 2002. Performed by Ms. Stuart. *Radio Wonderland* by Joshua Fried. January 11, 2002. *Suite Devo* created and performed by Troika Ranch. January 11, 2002. *The Unbidden and Unhinged* by Aviva Geisman/Drastic Action. January 12, 2002. *Psychotherapy Live!* by Lisa Levy. January 28, 2002. Performed by Ms. Levy. *Lapis Blue Blood Red* by Cathy Caplan. February 11, 2002. Directed by Paul Smithyman; with Natalie Arkus, Erica Berg, Peter Blomquist, Michael Dempsey, Meg Gibson, Dustin Smith, Scott Sowers, C.J. Wilson, Chandler Vinton. *Fanatics* created and performed by Ellen Beckerman & Company. March 10, 2002. Directed by Ellen Beckerman; with James Saidy, Margot Ebling, Josh Conklin, C. Andrew Bauer, Shawn Fagan. *Calabi-Yau* by Susanna Speier. March 27, 2002. Directed by Tony Torn; with Michael Kraskin, Hai Ting Chinn, John S. Hall, Rob Grace, Ms. Speier, James Urbaniak. *Dead Tech*; based on Henrik Ibsen's *The Master Builder* by Kristin Marting and Celise Kalke. February 4, 2002. Directed by Ms. Marting; with Dmetrius Conley-Williams, Daphne Gaines, Trey Lyford, Holly Twining, Richard Toth, Zishan Uguria. *Hatched*; based on Angela Carter's *Nights at the Circus*. April 12, 2002. Directed by Richard Crawford. *And Then You Go On* by Bob Jaffe. April 29, 2002. Directed by Peter Wallace; with Mr. Jaffe. *Life During Wartime* by Dominic Orlando. May 16, 2002. Directed by Karin Bowersock; with Mark Leydorf, Carla Tassara, Kimberly Jay Thomas, Gerald Marsini, Darius Stone. *The Right Way to Sue* by Ellen Melaver. May 19, 2002. Directed by Anne Kauffman; with Kelly AuCoin, Stephanie Brooke, Robert English, T.R. Knight, Caitlin Miller, Jennifer Morris. *Self Defense* by Carson Kreitzer. May 29, 2002. Directed by Randy White; with Lynne McCollough, Carolyn Baeumler, Stephen Bradbury, Carolyn DeMerice, Dan Illian, Dee Pelletier, Melle Powers, Mark Zeisler.

HUDSON GUILD THEATRE. *A Comedy of Eros* by Paul Firestone. January 27, 2002. Directed by Harland Meltzer; with Jordan Charney, Joan Copeland, Andrea Leigh, Paul Romero, Jennifer Dorr White, Travis Wood. *Illyria*, musical by Peter Mills; based on William Shakespeare's *Twelfth Night*. April 12, 2002. Directed by Cara Reichel; with Ames Adamson, Rich Affannato, Kate MacKenzie, Kate Bradner, Matthew Alexander, Sarah Corey, Arik Luck, Jason Mills, Leon Land Gersing, Courter Simmons.

IMMIGRANTS' THEATRE PROJECT. *Cracking Mud is Pinching Me* by Haya Husseini. Directed by Marcy Arlin. *The Bermuda Triangle* by Nora Amin. January 10, 2002. Directed by Lucinda Kidder. *The Black Eyed* by Betty Shamieh. January 14, 2002. Directed by Hayley Finn. *The Boat People* by Nahed Nayla Naguib. January 15, 2002. Directed by Kiebpoli Calnek. *Abaga* by Torange Yeghiazarian. *Portrait of a Marriage* by Fatma Durmush. January 21, 2002. Directed by Shilarna Stokes. *Edewede* by Juliana Okah. January 22, 2002. Directed by Bridgit Evans. *LuLu LoLo Takes Her Hat Off to the Fair Sex-Unfair Victims* by LuLu LoLo. March 21, 2002. Performed by Ms. LoLo.

THE INDEPENDENT THEATER. *Sex, Drugs, Rock & Roll* by Eric Bogosian. April 9, 2002. Directed by Jason Summers; with Luis-Daniel Morales.

INNOCENT THEATER. *The Vortex* by Noël Coward. June 20, 2001. Directed by Trip Cullman; with Nick Merritt, Dean Nolen, Alexandra Oliver, Tessa Auberjonois, Kathryn Gracey, Louis Cancelmi, James Kaliardos, Andrew Shulman and Elisabeth Waterston.

INSIDE ARTS. *Drinks Before Dinner* by E.L. Doctorow. February 28, 2002. Directed by Darcelle Marta; with Todd Bazzini, Karin Bowersock, David Palmer Brown, Bethany Caputo, Nancy Collins, Dee Dee Friedman, Sean Geoghan, Gerald Marsini, Gabriella Tapcov, Veronica Venture.

INTAR 53. *Two* by Ron Elisha. October 11, 2001. Directed by Bernice Rohret. With Mark Hammer, Tibor Feldman, and Irene Glezos.

IRISH ARTS CENTER. *The Revenge Tour* with Niall Tobín. September 12, 2001. *The Nualas*. October 8, 2001. With Josephine O'Reilly, Susan Collins and Anne Gildea. *The Kings of the Kilburn High Road* by Jimmy Murphy. March 17, 2002. Directed by Jim Nolan; with Sean Lawlor, Eamonn Hunt, Brendan Conroy, Noel O'Donovan, Frank O'Sullivan.

JEAN COCTEAU REPERTORY. *Arms and the Man* by George Bernard Shaw. December 16, 2001. Directed by Ernest Johns; with Amanda Jones, Marlene May, Carey Van Driest, Jason Crowl, Edward Griffin, Michael Surabian, Mark Rimer, Harris Berlinsky. *Oedipus the King* by Sophocles. Opened February 17, 2002. *Dance of Death* by August Strindberg; translated by Edwin Bjorkman. February 17, 2002 . Directed by Karen Lordi; with Craig Smith, Elise Stone, Jason Crowl and Kathryn Foster. *The Marriage of Figaro* by Beaumarchais; translated by Rod McLucas. April 12, 2002. Directed by David Fuller; with Christopher Black, Amanda Jones, Mark Rimer, Kathryn Foster, Michael Surabian.

JOHN HOUSEMAN THEATER. *Good Time Blues*. Concept and direction by Eric Krebs. February 13, 2002. With Genovis Albright, Madame Pat Tandy.

JOHN MONTGOMERY THEATRE COMPANY. *Sex Ed* by Suzanne Bachner. July 12, 2001. Directed by Trish Minskoff; with John Houfe, Alex McCord, Danny Wiseman. *Circle* by Suzanne Bachner. February 18, 2002. Directed by Trish Minskoff; with Bob Celli, Judy Charles, Thaddeus Daniels, Felicia Scarangello, Judy Charles, Danny Wiseman.

JOSE QUINTERO THEATRE. *A Gilbert and Sullivan Christmas Carol*; based on the Charles Dickens's *A Christmas Carol*. Book and lyrics by Gayden Wren; music by Arthur Sullivan. December 2, 2001. Directed by Mr. Wren; with Jonathan Baldwin, Hayley Chapple, Jonathan Demar, Kenneth Finegan, Kenneth W. Gartman, Hannah Hammel, Barry Kaplan, Cecily Kate, Jim Luddy, Kaia Monroe, Jermel Nakia, Matthew Nelson, Robert Charles Rhodes, Jill Skivington, Heather Thompson. *The Suicide Bomber* by Tuvia Tenenbom. November 16, 2001. Directed by Mr. Tenenbom, with Lameece Issaq, James Sears, Run Shayo, David Sitler. *Tape* by Stephen Belber. January 8, 2002. Directed by Geoffrey Nauffts; with Dominic Fumusa, Josh Stamberg and Alison West. *Damien* by Aldyth Morris. February 7, 2002. Directed by Peter John Cameron; with Casey Groves. *Cloud Nine* by Caryl Churchill. March 22, 2002. Directed by Mina Hartong; with Sam Hurlbut, Frances Anderson, Jason Woodruff, Elissa Lash, Jamie Watkins. SHAKESPEARE UNPLUGGED: THE HISTORY CYCLE. *Richard II, Henry IV Parts 1 and 2* by William Shakespeare. April 9, 2002. Directed by Joanne Zipay and Ivanna Cullinan; with Leese Walker, Jane Titus, Laurie Bannister-Colón, Sheriden Thomas, Lea C. Franklin, Vicki Hirsch, Vince Gatton, Bill Galarno, David Huber, Peter Zazzali, Rachel O'Neill, Claudia Peyton, Vanessa Elder, Kevin Till, Richard Kass, Christopher Bell, David Godbey, Jennifer Jonassen.

KIVA COMPANY. *Marisol* by José Rivera. February 15, 2002. Directed by Melissa Boswell and Jane Steinberg; with Ariel Brooke, Tracey Renee Mathis, Emily Parker, Jessica Ramirez-Turner, Brian Sacca, Hilary Ward.

KRAINE THEATRE. *Managers* by Kevin Mandel. September 8, 2001. Directed by Lily Warren; with Jennifer Carta, Steve Cell, Norma Fire, Benim Foster, Kelly Overton, Mandy Steckelberg, Dustin Tucker.

LABYRINTH THEATER COMPANY. *Where's My Money?* by John Patrick Shanley. July 11, 2001. Directed by Mr. Shanley, with David Deblinger, Yetta Gottesman, Florencia Lozano, Chris McGarry, John Ortiz, Paula Pizzi. Production restaged Off Broadway at Manhattan Theatre Club (November 7, 2001). *A Winter Party* by John Patrick Shanley. December 12, 2001. Directed by John Gould Rubin; with the company. THE BARN SERIES FESTIVAL. March 13–24, 2002. *August is a Thin Girl* by Julie Marie Myatt; directed by Joe Salvatore. *Memoire* by Tomokoh Miyagi, directed by John Gould Rubin. *Like It Was Yesterday* by Daniel Harnett, directed by David Anzuelo. *How to Catch a Monkey* by Michael Puzzo, directed by Chris McGarry. *Harlem Ain't Nuttin but a Word* by Russell Jones, directed by Beresford Bennett. *F**king Love* by Justin Reinsilber. *Culture Bandit*, written and performed by Vanessa Hidary. May 28, 2002. Directed by Mariana Hellmund. *Darwaza*, written and performed by Ajay Naidu. May 28, 2002. Directed by David Anzuelo.

MANHATTAN ENSEMBLE THEATER. *The Castle* by Franz Kafka. Translated by Aaron Leichter and Petra Lammers from Max Brod's script; adapted by David Fishelson and Mr. Leichter. January 17, 2002. Directed by Scott Schwartz; with William Atherton, E.J. Carroll, Catherine Curtin, Mireille Enos, Gina Farrell, Sean McCourt, Jim Parsons, Steven Rosen, Raynor Scheine, Grant James Varjas, Dan Ziskie. *The Golem* by H. Leivick; translated by Joseph C. Landis; adapted by David Fishelson. April 1, 2002. Directed by Lawrence Sacharow; with Michael Milligan, Joseph McKenna, Robert Prosky, David Little, Jeff Ware, Ian Pfister, Steven Rosen, David Heuvelman, Ben Hammer, Brandon Demery, Lynn Cohen, Norma Fire, Stuart Rudin, Rosemary Garrison.

MAVERICK THEATER. *I Sing!*, a musical by Eli Bolin, Sam Forman and Benjamin Salka. June 14, 2001. Directed by Mr. Salka; with Billy Eichner, Jeff Juday, Jodie Langel, Michael Raine, Meredith Zeitlin. *Colored Contradictions* by Danny Boyd Beaty. April 16 2002. Directed by Lenora Pace; with Mr. Beaty.

MA-YI THEATER COMPANY. *Watcher* by Han Ong. June 4, 2001. Directed by Loy Arcenas; with Mia Katigbak, Marty Zentz, Orlando Pabotoy, Gilbert Cruz, Virginia Wing, Jojo Gonzalez, Anthony Ruivivar, Ching Valdes-Aran and Harvey Perr. *The Square* by Bridget Carpenter, Ping Chong, Constance Congdon, Kia Corthron, Maria Irene Fornes, Philip Kan Gotanda, Jessica Hagedorn, David Henry Hwang, Craig Lucas, Robert O'Hara, Han Ong, José Rivera, Diana Son, Alice Tuan, Mac Wellman and Chay Yew. October 27, 2001. Directed by Lisa Peterson; with David Wilson Barnes, Joel de la Fuente, Saidah Arrika Ekulona, Michael Ray Escamilla, Fiona Gallagher, Wai Ching Ho, Jennifer Ikeda, Ken Leung, Hamish Linklater, Ching Valdes-Aran, Henry Yuk and Janet Zarish.

MCGINN/CAZALE THEATRE. *Key West* by Dan O'Brien. September 18, 2001. Directed by Daniel Gerroll. *Monsieur Ibrahim and the Flowers of the Koran* by Eric Emmanuel Schmitt; translated by Stephane Laporte. October 2, 2001. Directed by Maria Mileaf. *Bintou* by Koffi Kwahulé; translated by John Clifford. October 9, 2001. Directed by Leah C. Gardiner. *The Bread of Winter* by Victor Lodato. October 16, 2001. Directed by Loy Arcenas. *Smashing* by Brooke Berman. October 30, 2001. Directed by Michael John Garcés. *No.11 (Blue & White)* by Alexandra Cunningham. January 17, 2002. Directed by David Aukin; with Hilary Edson, Liza Lapira, Arthur McDonald, Shauna Miles, Nell Mooney, Armando Riesco, Joey Shea, Robin L. Taylor, Katie Walder. *Miss Evers' Boys* by David Feldshuh. March 16, 2002. Directed by Kent Gash; with Adriane Lenox, Daryl Edwards, Byron Easley, Chad L. Coleman, Helmar Augustus Cooper, J. Paul Boehmer, Terry Alexander. *In the Absence of Spring* by Joe Calarco. May 19, 2002. Directed by Mr. Calarco; with Sophie Hayden, Jason Trevor Oswalt, Gene Farber, Lizzy Cooper Davis, Minda Harden, Michelle Federer, Chris Stack.

METROPOLITAN PLAYHOUSE. *The Woman* by William C. deMille; adapted by David Zarko. June14, 2001. Directed by Mr. Zarko; with Kristin Stewart, Russell Hamilton, David Heckel, Leo Bertelsen, Annette Previti, Tod Mason, Tom Staggs, Sam Kitchin, Ken Bolden, Mike Nowak. *Oedipus Rex* by Sophocles; adapted by Alex Roe. October 14, 2001. Directed by Ian Marshall; with Andy Stewart-Jones, Matt Daniels and Casey Grove. *Salem*, written and directed by Alex Roe. October 31, 2001. With David Carson and DeBanne Brown. *The Faith Healer* by William Vaughn Moody. March 23, 2002. Directed by Keith Oncale; with Henry Afro-Bradley, Roy Bacon, Scott Barrow, Katherine Brecka, Darra Herman, Michael Karp, Tod Mason, Colleen Russell, Jenni Tooley and Susan Willerman. *Dom Juan* by Molière. April 14, 2002. Directed by Alex Roe; with Tom Staggs, George Sheffey, Stephanie Dorian, Sean Dill and Stephanie Cervellino.

MOONWORK THEATER. *Julius Caesar* by William Shakespeare. March 20, 2001. Directed by Gregory Wolfe. *Voices from the Hill*; adapted from Edgar Lee Masters's *Spoon River Anthology*. Directed by Gregory Wolfe; music by Andrew Sherman and Rusty Magee; with Mason Pettit, Aloysius Gigl, Lynn Eldredge, Elizabeth Zins, Noel Velez, Jeannie Goodman, Victoria Adams, Christopher Yates.

NEIGHBORHOOD PLAYHOUSE. *The Madwoman of Chaillot* by Jean Giraudoux; adapted by Maurice Valency. October 8, 2001. Directed by Roy Steinberg; with Anne Jackson, Kim Hunter, Alvin Epstein, Roger Serbagi, Ben Hammer, Catherine Wolf and Sloane Shelton.

NUYORICAN POETS CAFÉ. *Showing Out* by Timothy Reed. April 11, 2002. Adapted by Rome Neal. Directed by Mr. Neal; with Christiana Blain, Cassandra Hume, Michael A. Jones, Nikki Bell, Letha Rose, Jaymie Garner, Maxx.

NEW DIRECTIONS THEATER. *Random Harvest* by Richard Willett. June 25, 2001. Directed by Elizabeth Beckwith; with Patricia Randell, Ann Talman, Patrick Welsh, Kate Downing, Jay Alvarez, Jonathan Kandel.

NEW GEORGES. *The Holy Mother of Hadley New York* by Barbara Wiechmann. September 10, 2001. Directed by Rachel Dickstein; with Mary Shultz, Gretchen Lee Krich, Nicole Halmos, Maria Striar, Gary Brownlee, Andrea Maulella, Alan Benditt, Malachy Cleary, Christopher Mattox, Julia Prud'homme, Richard Toth.

NEW YORK INTERNATIONAL FRINGE FESTIVAL. August 10–August 25, 2001. Schedule included: *The Ballad of Larry the Flyer*, written and performed by the Lexington Group; directed by David Riedy; with Chris Belden, Kathryn Gayner, Holli Harms, Tom Paitson Kelly, Sonya Rokes and Cole Wheeler. *21 Dog Years*, written and performed by Mike Daisey. Directed by Jean-Michele Gregory. Later staged Off Broadway at the Cherry Lane Theatre (May 9, 2002). *The Adding Machine* by Elmer Rice; adapted and directed by Jonathan Silver; with Cynthia Carrol, Paul Marcarelli, Jessamyn Blakeslee, Joshua Dickens and Dan da Silva. *Debbie Does Dallas*, musical adapted by Susan L. Schwartz from the screenplay by Maria Minestra. Directed by Brock Enright; with Ms. Schwartz, Allison Du Val, Ariel Sheldon, Renata Hinrichs, Theresa Young, Tonya Canada, Jill Madeo, Marian Heller, Gary Widlund, Tim Beemer, Matthew Armstrong, Ross Steeves, Bryant MacMillan, Jonathan Hyland, Adam Chandler and Theodore Bouloukos II. *Einstein's Dreams*, adapted by Ralf Remshardt, David Gardiner and Paul Stancato from the novel by Alan Lightman. Directed and choreographed by Mr. Stancato; with Charlie Coniglio, Drew D'Andrea, Leigh Elliot, Jennifer Sorika Horng, Joe LaRue, Rebecca Olympia, Brian Rhinehart, Tamar Schoenberg, Elizabeth Wolf. *Loader #26* by Roberto Marinas. Directed by Vijay Mathew; with Brett Christensen, Keith Stevens, Derek Straat. *Equal Protection*, written and directed by Ann Warren; with Darcy Bledsoe, Lisa Catherine Clark, Joe Rejeski, Lynn Clayton, Helene Galek. *Preview of Murder*, based on the story by Robert Leslie Bellem; adapted by Dawne Seifert; with Matt Wagner, Jon Hemingway, Robert Watts, Mike Gold, Ms. Seifert, John Dowgin and Terry Burch. *The Elephant Man: The Musical*, book by Jeff Hylton and Tim Werenko, lyrics by Mr. Hylton, music by Paul Jones, Mr. Hylton. Directed and designed by James Riggs; with Kenneth Dine, D.P. Duffy III, Mr. Hylton, Jenna Morris. *Sic*, written and performed by Nick Boraine. Directed by Charmaine Weir-Smith. *Fifty Minutes* by Lucas Rockwood. Directed by Sherri Kronfeld; with Tigran Eldred, Jessica Faller, Raymond Hamlin, Guy Larkin, Mick Preston, Dawn Vicknair. *A Piece of My Heart* by Shirley Lauro. Directed by Nancy S. Chu; with Marc Diraison, Amy McKenna, Marco Jo Clate, Robin Dawn Arocha, Sarah Sims, Christine Rodgers, Gisela Adisa. *Jim Carroll's The Basketball Diaries* by Jim Carroll; adapted, directed and performed by Pascal Ulli. *Doing Justice,* written and performed by Adina Taubman. Directed by Beth Manspeizer. *Snapshot* by Samantha Swan. Directed by Christopher Comrie; with Sergio Gallinaro, Joanne Latimer, Steven Puchalski, Ms. Swan. *Woosh!* written and performed by Ryan Egan. *Zoo* by Margarita Manwelyan and Jessica Rotondi. Directed by Ms. Rotondi; with Tiffany May, Alva French, Jay Curtis, Ms. Manwelyan, Haskell King, M. Donelson Renda, Jeromy Barber, Crystal Williamson, Michael Andrews, Jimmy Bopp, Myorah Middleton, Andy Brown, Alyson Riffey, Emily Gustafson, Mia Lottringer. *Fuck You or Dead Pee Holes*, written and directed by John Bowman, Adam Hardman, Ranya Ritchie. Co-directed by Raymond Sanchez; with Mr. Hardman, Mr. Bowman, Jeff Dickinson, Marc Landers, Ms. Ritchie, Nicole Marshall, Vanessa Meryn-Cohn, Jodie Fletcher, Raymond Sanchez, Kellie Starowski, Joel Freidrich, Rob McDonald, Rigo Irizarry, Jae Henson, Nick Nace, Diane Langan, Johanna Buccola, Brion Vytlacil, Brian Corr, McCready Baker, Ann Enzminger.

NEW YORK THEATRE WORKSHOP. *Finally Flannery* by Barbara Suter. November 11, 2001. Directed by Michael Sexton; wfith Ms. Suter, Nancy Robinette.

OHIO THEATER. *The Train Play* by Liz Duffy Adams. January 13, 2002. Directed by Jonathan Silverstein; with Quincy Tyler Berstine, Keith Davis, Gibson Frazier, Nicole Halmos, Austin Jones, Mark Leydorf, Ryan Shogren, Ami Shukla. *Dance, My Darling, Dance* by Stephanie Gilman and K Tanzer. March 13, 2002. Directed by Ms. Gilman and Ms. Tanzer. *Glamour* by John O'Keefe. April 9, 2002. Directed by Katherine Owens; with Bruce DuBose, Tracy Arnold, Suzanne Thomas, Vincent Daly. *Red Death* by Lisa D'Amour. May 5, 2002. Directed by Anne Kauffman; with Mel Jurdem, Meghan Love, John McAdams, Robert Alexander Owens, Mary Shultz, Maria Striar.

ONTOLOGICAL-HYSTERIC THEATER. *Maria del Bosco* by Richard Foreman. January 10, 2002. Directed by Mr. Foreman; with Juliana Francis, Okwul Okpokwasili, Funda Duyal, Frank Boudreaux, Ryan Holsopple, Youssef Kerkour, Zachary Oberzan, Thom Sibbit.

PARADISE THEATER COMPANY. *What the Hell's Your Problem?: An Evening with Dr. Bob Nathelson* by Tom Noonan. March 28, 2002. Directed by Mr. Noonan; with Grant James Varjas, Jay DiPietro, John Good, Cellis Mills, Rhonda Keyser, Eileen O'Connell, Kendall Pigg, Hollis Welsh, Mr. Noonan.

THE PEARL THEATRE COMPANY. *Exit the King* by Eugène Ionesco; translated by Donald Watson. September 13, 2001. Directed by Joseph Hardy; with Celeste Ciulla, Robert Hock, Michael Nichols, Carol Schultz, Sue Jin Song, Ray Virta. *Iphigeneia at Aulis* by Euripides; translated by W.S. Merwin and George E. Dimock Jr. November 19, 2001. Directed by Shepard Sobel; with Dan Daily, Carol Schultz, Sue Jin Song, Robert Hock, Albert Jones, Melissa Maxwell, Celeste Ciulla, Michael Nichols, Scott Whitehurst. *The Phantom Lady* by Pedro Calderón de la Barca; translated by Edwin Honig. January 21, 2002. Directed by René Buch; with Ray Virta, Dominic Cuskern, Celeste Ciulla, Robin Leslie Brown, Jason Manuel Olazábal, Aaron Ganz, Dan Daily, Rachel Botchan, Emily Gray. *Romeo and Juliet* by William Shakespeare. April 4, 2002. Directed by Shepard Sobel; with Edward Seamon, Dominic Cuskern, Celeste Ciulla, Robin Leslie Brown, Rachel Brown, Joanna Camp, Andy Prosky, Matt Mundy, Scott Whitehurst, Eric Sheffer Stevens, Evan Robertson, Ray Virta, Christopher Moore, Christopher Rivera, Andrew Firda, Robert Hock, John Wylie, James Doherty. *Much Ado About Nothing* by William Shakespeare. April 23, 2002. Directed by J.R. Sullivan; with Edward Seamon, Dominic Cuskern, Celeste Ciulla, Robin Leslie Brown, Rachel Brown, Joanna Camp, Andy Prosky, Matt Mundy, Scott Whitehurst, Eric Sheffer Stevens, Evan Robertson, Ray Virta, Christopher Moore, Christopher M. Rivera, Andrew Firda, Robert Hock, John Wylie, James Doherty.

PHIL BOSAKOWSKI THEATRE. *The Norman Conquests: Round and Round the Garden.* April 4, 2002. *Table Manners.* April 6, 2002. *Living Together.* April 6, 2002. By Alan Ayckbourn. Directed by Lise McDermott; with Dan Patrick Brady, Christina Cass, Ledger Free, Kathryn Gayner, Nick Mouyiaris, Christine Verleny.

PRESENT COMPANY THEATORIUM. *Leo Oscar's Backyard* by Leslie Bramm. October 21, 2001. Directed by Pamela S. Butler; with Christopher Yeatts, Hadas Gil-Bar, George G. Colucci, Bart Mallard, Reggie Barton, Kymberly Harris Riggs.

PROSPECT THEATER COMPANY. *The Three Sisters* by Anton Chekhov; adapted by Shawn René Graham and John-Martin Green. March 8, 2002. Directed by Mr. Green; with Joyce Lee, Robin Miles, Carolyn Roberts, Kalimi A. Baxter, Daniel Carlton, Rafael Clements, Benard Cummings, Michael Early, Arthur French, Jesse Kearney, Rudy Marsalis, Rhonda Akanke McLean-Nur, Gregory Mikell, Dennis Reid.

PROVINCETOWN PLAYHOUSE. *Johan Padan and the Discovery of the Americas* by Dario Fo; translated by Ron Jenkins. September 6, 2001. Directed by Mr. Jenkins; with Thomas Derrah.

PULSE ENSEMBLE THEATRE. Outdoor Shakespeare Series. *Macbeth* by William Shakespeare. August 11, 2001. Directed by Alexa Kelly; with Brian Richardson, Natalie Wilder, Bryan Brendle, Jayne Corey, Amanda Dubois, Aaron J. Fill, Nicole Godino, Molly Harrington, Tom Jasorka, Mark Vaughn, Nathan M. White, Pamela Anne Wild, Jim Wiznieweski. *A Midsummer Night's Dream* by William Shakespeare. August 18, 2001. Directed by Alexa Kelly; with Kolawole Ogundiran, Becky Leonard, Danielle Stille, Jim Wiznieweski, Steve Abbruscato, Joseph Capone, Jay Colligan, Oscar de la Colon, David Grosso, Christian Desmond, Gretchen Greaser, Linda Past. *The Tempest* by William Shakespeare. April 19, 2002. Directed by Alexa Kelly; with Nalina Mann, Brian Richardson, Joy Jones, Andrew Stuart-Jones, Oberon K.A. Adjepong, Jeremy Beck, Joshua Billig, Evermore Black, Mark Cirnigliaro, Ellen Hayes, Leslie Jones, Andrew Narston, Nicholas Paczar, Linda Past, Noëlle Teagno, Adam Wyler.

RATTLESTICK PRODUCTIONS. *Down South* by Doug Field. June 28, 2001. Directed by Rick Sparks; with Alice Vaughn, Anthony De Santis, Erin McLaughlin, Dean Fortunato, Audrey Rapoport and David Bicha. *Neil's Garden* by Geoffrey Hassman. November 20, 2001. Directed by Rod Kaats; with William Bogert and Michael Warren Powell. *Finder's Fee* by Wesley Moore. February 3, 2002. Directed by Leigh Silverman; with Christopher Duva, Linda Powell, Tom Reynolds, Rob Sedgwick.

SANFORD MEISNER THEATRE. *Habeas Corpus* by Alan Bennett. November 1, 2001. Directed by Steven Keim; with Neal Arluck, Mary Aufman, Carrie Brewer, Denise DeMirjiam, David Godbey,

Anne F. Kavanagh, Brian Linden, Brad Makarowski, Robert Meksin, Kelly Miller, Kimberly Reiss. *Belly Up* by Tom Bondi and Mark Holt. February 2, 2002. Directed by James Busby; with Messrs Bondi and Holt.

STARFISH THEATREWORKS. *Building* by Gail Noppe-Brandon. February 27, 2002. Directed by Ms. Noppe-Brandon; with Robert Jason Jackson, Keith Crowningshield, Kathleen Murphy Jackson, James Doberman, Rosemary Loar, James Rich, Jennifer Mudge Tucker, Blanca Camacho, Nikki Walker, Joe O'Brien.

78TH STREET THEATRE LAB. *Snatches* by Laura Strausfeld. August 16, 2001. Directed by Ms. Strausfeld; with Jean Taylor, Patricia A. Chilsen. PERMANENT VISITOR (FESTIVAL OF PLAYS BY AND ABOUT DAWN POWELL). January 18, 2002. *Jig Saw* by Dawn Powell. Directed by Donna Linderman. *An Artist's Life and Other Cautionary Tales About the Theatre* by Kira Obolensky. Directed by Will Pomerantz. *As We Were Saying (Or Were We?)* by Laura Strausfeld. Directed by Eileen Phelan. *Women at Four O'Clock* by Dawn Powell. Directed by Eric Nightengale. *Straight Up . . . and With a Twist* by Dawn Powell. THE SERVICE PROJECT (AN EVENING OF SHORT PLAYS). April 16, 2002. *Down Here* by Melody Cooper. *Kuwait* by Vincent Delaney. *McIntyre's* by Suzanne Bradbeer. *The Regular* by Joanna Cherensky. *A Perfect World* by Carol Scudder. *Mutant Sex Party* by Edward Manning. *Service Order* by Brian Dykstra. *Satisfaction Guaranteed* by Kerry Logan. *La Mouche* by Stephen Bittrich. *Bumbershoot* by P. Seth Bauer. Directors: Hamilton Clancy, Carol Halstead, Rob Wilson and Crystal Gandrud. With Julie Alexander, Scott Baker, Magaly Colimon, Colleen Cosgrove, James Davies, Tom Demenkoff, Phil Douglas, Bill Green, Melora Griffis, Carol Halstead, Karen Kitz, John Lewis, Bradford Olson, Oz Phillips, Dan Teachout, Erik Van Wyck, Stacy Wallace, Rob Wilson. *LibidOff* by Dawson Moore. April 28, 2002. Directed by Don K. Williams; with Paul Kropfl, Sarah Lewis, Michael E. Lopez, Kira Onodera, Matthew Porter. *Thin Walls* by Alice Eve Cohen. May 25, 2002. Directed by Elizabeth Margid; with Ms. Cohen.

SHOW WORLD THEATER CENTER. WORLDLY ACTS (FIVE ONE-ACT PLAYS). June 20, 2001. *The Mystery at the Middle of Ordinary Life* by Don DeLillo. Directed by Anastasia Traina; with Ali Marsh, Joe LoTruglio. *Who's on Top* by Elizabeth Dewberry. Directed by Shira-Lee Shalit; with Daniella Rich, Matthew Rauch. *Boise, Idaho* by Sean Michael Welch. Directed by Lizzie Gottlieb; with Jennifer Dundas, Peter Jacobson, Glenn Kessler, Daniel Baker. *Daniel on a Thursday* by Garth Wingfield. Directed by AnnaCatherine Rutledge; with Jack Merrill, Matthew Del Negro. *The Stolen Child* by Amanda Beesley. Directed by Laramie Dennis; with Mike Weaver, Linda Powell. *In the Boom Boom Room* by David Rabe. February 11, 2002. Directed by Renee Phillippi; with Eileen O'Connell, John D'Arcangelo, Vera Beren, Meghan Love, Alison Saltz, Masha Sapron, JB Becton, Peter Lewis, Conn Horgan, Carlo Adinolfi, Joanne Gibson and Willie Caldwell. *Portia Coughlan* by Marina Carr. March 7, 2002. Directed by Aaron Beall; with Mercedes McAndrew, Paul Obedzinski, Marina McCreery, Joseph Small, Fergus Loughnane, Caraid O'Brien, Dorothy Stasney, Ruth Kullerman, Kevin Hagan, Benn Stovall.

STORM THEATRE COMPANY. *Henry IV* by Luigi Pirandello. October 5, 2001. Directed by John Regis; with Dan Berkey, Evangelia Costantakos, Laurence Drozd, Carl Pasbjerg, Paul Burns, Stephen Logan Day, Adriane Urdos, Brett Hemmerling, Hugh Brandon Kelly, Bill Roulet, Cary Seward, Eric Thorne, Brian Whisenant. *Gillette* by William Hauptman. January 18, 2002. Directed by Peter Dobbins; with John Riggins, Eric Alperin, Kevin Villers, Shaula Chambliss, Genia Michaela, Eric Thorne.

SYNAPSE THEATRE COMPANY. *Bloody Poetry* by Howard Brenton. October 10, 2001. Directed by David Travis; with Adrian LaTourelle, Erik Steele, Adrienne Dreiss, Lael Logan, Omar Metwally, Michelle Federer.

TARGET MARGIN THEATER. *Crazy Day Or the Marriage of Figaro* by Beaumarchais, translated by Target Margin Theater. November 17, 2001. Directed by David Herskovits; with Rinne Groff, Robert Alexander Owens, Paul Vincent Black, Yuri Skujins, Kwana Martinez, Alvaro Heinig and Joyce Lee. THE RING: THE OPERATIC ERA LABORATORY by Richard Wagner. January 23, 2002. *Ring Cycle* conceived and directed by Rattazzi Brothers. *Siegfried's Nerve* adapted by Lucas Hnath; directed by Jyana S. Gregory. *Über* music and lyrics by Ethan Hein; directed by Franklin Y. Hundley II. *Boca* directed by Yuri Skujins. *Valkyrie Or What Happens When a Good-Natured Goddess Goes Bad* adapted by Aaron Tugendhaft, Susanna Gellert and Chloe Johnston; directed by

Mind poison: Michael Stuhlbarg and Boris McGiver in Cymbeline. *Photo: Gerry Goodstein*

Ms. Gellert. *The Sandman* by E.T.A. Hoffmann. May 8, 2002. Composed by Thomas Cabannis; libretto by Douglas Langworthy and David Herskovits. Directed by Mr. Herskovits; with Rachel Mondanaro, Jay Johnson, Byron Singleton, Gregory Rahming, Violetta Zambetti, Christian Sebek.

THEATER AT ST. CLEMENT'S CHURCH. *Something Cloudy, Something Clear* by Tennessee Williams. October 5, 2001. Directed by Anatole Fourmantchouk; with Stass Klassen, Elissa Piszel, Joe Mihalchick, Chandler Vinton, Richard Guerreiro. *Good Thing* by Jessica Goldberg. December 18, 2001. Directed by Jo Bonney; with Betsy Aidem, John Rothman, Alicia Goranson, Chris Messina, Cara Buono, Hamish Linklater.

THEATRE FOR A NEW AUDIENCE. *Cymbeline* by William Shakespeare. January 20, 2002. Directed by Bartlett Sher; with Robert Stattel, Andrew Weems, Michael Stuhlbarg, Earl Hindman, Boris McGiver, Pete Starrett, Roderick Hill, Randy Danson, Erica N. Tazel, Peter Francis James, Philip Goodwin, Thomas M. Hammond. *Andorra* by Max Frisch; translated by Michael Feingold. April 7, 2002. Directed by Liviu Ciulei; with David Barlow, Bill Buell, Justin Campbell, Jeffrey Fierson, Rafael Kalichstein, Laurie Kennedy, Nicholas Kepros, Peter Kybart, Maggie Lacey, Andrew McGinn, Boris McGiver, David Don Miller, Simeon Moore, Pamela Nyberg, Chip Persons, Jesse Steccato, Henry Strozier, Chandler Williams.

THEATRE OF THE RIVERSIDE CHURCH. *The Creation of the World and Other Business* by Arthur Miller. October 5, 2001. Directed by Oleg Kheyfets; with Paul Sparks, Tony Torn, Tom Pearl, Kent Alexander, Valerie Stanford, Preston Dane.

TRIBECA PLAYHOUSE. *The Feign'd Courtesans* by Aphra Behn. March 29, 2002, 2002. Directed by Rebecca Patterson; with Lauren Jill Ahrold, Virginia Baeta, Fatima Bazzy, Valentina McKenzie, Maureen Porter, Beverley Prentice, Jill Repplinger, Gisele Richardson, Ami Shukla, Carey Urban, DeeAnn Weir, Tessa Zugmeyer. MRS. SHAKESPEARE AND MRS. BEHN. *Love Arm'd, Aphra Behn & Her Pen* by Karen Eterovich. Performed by Ms. Eterovich. *Mrs. Shakespeare (Will's First & Last Love)* by Yvonne Hudson. Directed by Robert Edward Burns, with Ms. Hudson. April 2, 2002. *Tartuffe* by Molière; adapted and directed by Jeff Cohen; with Gerald Anthony, Keith Reddin, Jen Ryan, Crista Moore.

TRILOGY THEATRE. *Tallboy Walkin'* by Joshua James. September 8, 2001. Directed by Nick Corley; with Lou Carbonneau, Sharif Rashed, Ato Essandoh, James McCauley, Garrison Phillips. *Japa-Rica* by Masayasu Nakanishi and Robert Baumgardner. February 7, 2002. Directed by Mr. Baumgardner; with Mr. Nakanishi.

28TH STREET THEATER. *Blue Window* by Craig Lucas. July 11, 2001. Directed by Julia Gibson; with Hope Chernov, Marcia DeBonis, Katy Hansz, Marin Hinkle, Neal Huff, Jason Kolotouros, Josh Stamberg.

29TH STREET REP. *The Last Barbecue* by Brett Neveu. September 22, 2001. Directed by Tim Corcoran; with Peyton Thomas, Elizabeth Elkins, Leo Farley, Barbara Meyers, Moira MacDonald. *Fool for Love* by Sam Shepard. May 2, 2002. Directed by Tim Corcoran; with David Mogentale, Elizabeth Elkins, Stephen Payne, Tony DeVito.

UPSTAIRS AT 54. *Dragapella Starring the Kinsey Sicks* by Ben Schatz, Irwin Keller, Maurice Kelly and Chris Dilley. October 17, 2001. Directed by Glenn Casale; with Messrs Schatz, Dilley, Kelly and Keller.

URBAN STAGES. *Circumference of a Squirrel* by John Walch. February 19, 2002. Directed by T.L. Reilly; with Paul Sparks. *The Sweepers* by John C. Picardi. April 2, 2002. Directed by Frances Hill; with Dana Smith, Brigitte Viellieu-Davis, Donna Davis, Ivy Vahanian, Matt Walton.

VERSE THEATER MANHATTAN. *War Music* by Christopher Logue, based on Homer's *Iliad*. September 8, 2001. Adapted and directed by James Milton; with Jo Barrick, Angela Moore, Marybeth Bentwood.

WALKERSPACE. *Bluebeard and Other Less Grisly Tales of Love* by Liz Steinberg. September 9, 2001. Directed by Ms. Steinberg; with Kate Baldwin, Erin Cardillo, Deanna Pacelli, Kate Arrington, Melissa Creighton, Lucia Rich, Aaron Clayton, Daniel Goldstein, Peter Russo, Ailsa Muir.

WESTBETH THEATRE CENTER. *Are You Dave Gorman?* by Dave Gorman. October 4, 2001. With Mr. Gorman. *Kiki and Herb: There's a Stranger in the Manger!* November 29, 2001. With Justin Bond and Kenny Mellman. *Homecoming* by Lauren Weedman. January 21, 2002. Directed by Maryann Lombardi; with Ms. Weedman. *Bewilderness* by Bill Bailey. March 7, 2002. With Mr. Bailey.

WINGS THEATRE COMPANY. *Tango Masculino* by Clint Jefferies. April 11, 2002. Music by Mr. Jefferies; original compositions by Paul L. Johnson. Directed by Jeffrey Corrick; with Miguel Belmonte, Stephen Cabral, Roberto Cambeiro, Samantha Clarke, Angel Comas, Ivan Davila, Mickey Goldhaber, Maureen Griffin, JoHary Ramos, Gustavo Santamarina, Karen Stanion, Paul Taylor.

THE WOMEN'S SHAKESPEARE COMPANY. *'Tis Pity She's a Whore* by John Ford; adapted by R.J. Tolan. March 18, 2002. Directed by Mr. Tolan.

WOOSTER GROUP. *To You, the Birdie!*, based on Paul Schmidt's translation of Racine's *Phèdre*. February 19, 2002. Directed by Elizabeth LeCompte; with Francis McDormand, Kate Valk, Willem Dafoe, Ari Fliakos, Scott Shepherd, Suzzy Roche, Koosil-ja Hwang, Dominique Bousquet.

WORKING THEATER. FREE MARKET (EIGHT SHORT WORKS). June 4, 2001. Directed by Joseph Megel. *Fire Drill* by William Wise; with Godfrey L. Simmons Jr. *20/20 Sex Care* by Karen Sunde; with Eunice Wong, Lourdes Martin, Mr. Simmons. *Day of Our Dead* by Elaine Romero; with Ms. Martin, Constance Boardman. *Kickin Summit* by OyamO; with Mr. Simmons, Ms. Boardman, Arthur French, Ms. Wong, Felix Solis, Ms. Martin. *Free Market* by Jim Grimsley; with Mr. Simmons, Mr. Solis, Ms. Wong. *Give Us This Day* by Julie Jensen; with Mr. French, Ms. Wong. *Poodles* by Sachi Oyama; with Mr. Solis, Ms. Boardman, Mr. Simmons. *The Border Crossers Lounge* by Guillermo Reyes; with Mr. Solis, Mr. Simmons, Ms. Martin, Ms. Boardman, Ms. Wong, Mr. French.

WORTH STREET THEATER COMPANY. *Four* by Christopher Shinn. July 1, 2001. Directed by Jeff Cohen; with Keith Nobbs, Vinessa Antoine, Isiah Whitlock Jr., Armando Riesco. *Tartuffe* by Molière; adapted by Mr. Cohen. January 16, 2002. Directed by Mr. Cohen; with Jennifer Bassey, Crista Moore, Adam Hirsch, Liam Christopher O'Brien, Sarah K. Lippmann, Jim Hazard, Jen Ryan, Keith Reddin, James Rana, Gerald Anthony, Jeff Taylor.

ZIPPER THEATER. *True Love* by Charles L. Mee. November 28, 2001. Directed by Daniel Fish; with Laurie Williams, Jeremiah Miller, Laura Esterman, Paul Mullins, Christopher McCann, Jayne Haudeyshell, Dallas Roberts, Halley Wegryn Gross, Roy Thinnes. *Reno: Rebel Without a Pause* by

Reno. April 22, 2002. With Reno. *Downtown Dysfunctionals Episode 2: Baby Buddha*, musical by Richard Sheinmel; music and lyrics by Randy Lake, C. Colby Sachs, Davia Sacks, Mr. Sheinmel, Clay Zambo. April 25, 2002. Directed by Mark Steven Robinson; with Todd Butera, Jennifer Houston, James Lawson, Gregory Marcel, Mardie Millit, Jim Taylor McNickle, Allison Mulrain, Erika Beth Phillips, Sunrize Highway.

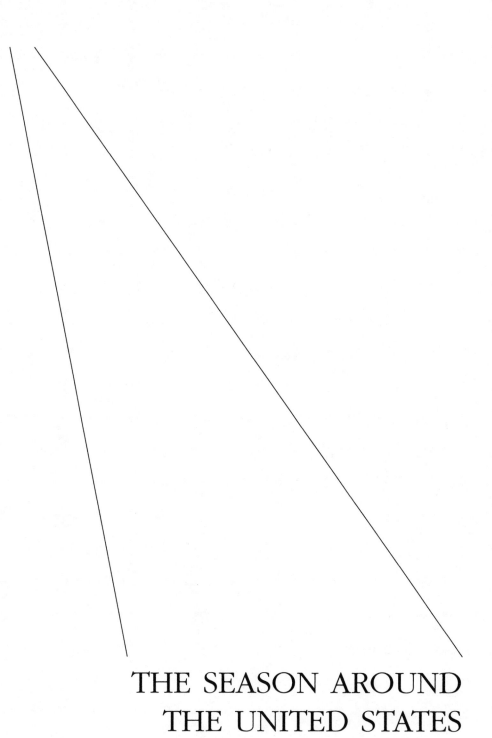

THE SEASON AROUND
THE UNITED STATES

AMERICAN THEATRE CRITICS/STEINBERG NEW PLAY AWARD AND CITATIONS

○ ○ ○ ○ ○

A DIRECTORY OF NEW-PLAY PRODUCTIONS IN THE UNITED STATES

THE AMERICAN THEATRE CRITICS ASSOCIATION (ATCA) is the organization of drama critics in all media throughout the United States. One of the group's stated purposes is "To increase public awareness of the theater as a national resource." To this end, ATCA has annually cited outstanding new plays produced around the US, which were excerpted in our series beginning with the 1976–77 volume. As we continue our policy of celebrating playwrights and playwriting in *Best Plays* essays, we offer essays on the recipients of the 2002 American Theatre Critics/Steinberg New Play Award and Citations. The ATCA/Steinberg New Play Award of $15,000 was awarded to Horton Foote for his play *The Carpetbagger's Children*. ATCA/Steinberg New Play Citations were given to Jeffrey Sweet for *The Action Against Sol Schumann* and to Murray Mednick for *Joe and Betty*. Citation honorees receive prizes of $5,000 each.

The ATCA awards are funded by the Harold and Mimi Steinberg Charitable Trust, which supports theater throughout the United States with its charitable giving. The ATCA/Steinberg New Play Award and Citations are given in a ceremony at Actors Theatre of Louisville. Essays in the next section—by Michael Grossberg (Columbus *Dispatch*), Richard Christiansen (*Chicago Tribune*) and Michael Phillips (*Chicago Tribune*)—celebrate the ATCA/Steinberg honorees.

ATCA's ninth annual M. Elizabeth Osborn Award for a new playwright was voted to Mia McCullough for *Chagrin Falls*, produced by the Stage Left Theatre in Chicago. Ms. McCullough received her award during a February luncheon at Sardi's in New York.

Of the new scripts nominated by ATCA members for the ATCA/ Steinberg prizes, six were selected as finalists by the 2001 ATCA New Plays Committee before making their final citations. Other finalists included: *The*

Dew Point by Neena Beber, produced by Gloucester Stage Company in Massachusetts; *Jerusalem* by Seth Greenland, produced by the Cleveland Play House; and *Chagrin Falls* by Mia McCullough, produced by Stage Left Theatre in Chicago.

The process of selecting these outstanding plays is as follows: any American Theatre Critics Association member may nominate the first full professional production of a finished play (not a reading or an airing as a play-in-progress) during the calendar year under consideration. Nominated 2001 scripts were studied and discussed by the New Plays Committee chaired by Alec Harvey (*Birmingham News*), Jackie Demaline (*Cincinnati Enquirer*), Marianne Evett (Cleveland *Plain Dealer*, retired), Barbara Gross (freelance, *Washington Post*), Claudia W. Harris (freelance, *Back Stage*), Robert Hurwitt (*San Francisco Chronicle*), Elizabeth Maupin (*Orlando Sentinel*), Michael Phillips (*Chicago Tribune*) and Herb Simpson (Rochester, N.Y., *City Newspaper*). These committee members made their choices on the basis of script rather than production. If the timing of nominations and openings prevents some works from being considered in any given year, they may be eligible for consideration the following year if they haven't since moved to New York.

2002 ATCA/Steinberg New Play Award

THE CARPETBAGGER'S CHILDREN
By Horton Foote

○ ○ ○ ○ ○

Essay by Michael Grossberg

CORNELIA: Did you see the plaque the Historical Society is putting up on our house? We're the oldest house in town now. There used to be ten or fifteen older some right on this street but they were all sold off long ago, and replaced by filling stations and God knows what all. Oh, well.

IN MORE THAN A HALF-CENTURY of evocative playwriting, Horton Foote has eschewed the epic to concentrate on small observations brimming with compassion and bittersweet insight about everyday life.

From *The Trip to Bountiful* and his autobiographical nine-play cycle *The Orphans' Home* to the Pulitzer Prize-winning *The Young Man From Atlanta*, Foote's 66 plays mine lonely characters and complex family ties while reflecting a universal longing for a sense of place.

Born and raised in Wharton, Texas, Foote found his primary theatrical territory surrounding him in the social attitudes, status anxieties, romances and relationships that define and constrain small-town America—especially in the Southern-influenced East Texas that Foote knows so well.

In *The Carpetbagger's Children*, one of his simplest and subtlest plays, Foote returns to his favorite setting of Harrison, Texas (a fictionalized Wharton). Three surviving sisters tell overlapping stories of how their Union-soldier father left them with a mixed blessing: ample property and position as the town's wealthiest family, but at the price of a problematic outsider status in post-Confederacy Texas.

The sisters' father developed a sincere friendship with a Confederate colonel, but his Northern background and use of his position as tax collector to buy out desperate Confederate families prompted gossip and community grievances that would reverberate through the decades to the detriment of his descendants.

At once a monologue play and a memory piece about the ravages of time, *Children* is disarmingly simple and charmingly modest. In

309

Problem child: Jean Stapleton in Horton Foote's The Carpetbagger's Children. *Photo: Jim Caldwell*

approximately 90 minutes without intermission, Foote builds a well-knit ensemble piece with a relentless emotional arc that invites audiences to listen closely. Those who choose to do so—not everyone will respond positively to the narrative's seeming passivity—will identify with the sisters' decency and dignity while forgiving their foolishness and shortsightedness.

Three seasoned actresses appeared in the 2001 world premiere at Houston's Alley Theatre, which commissioned the play. They continued under Michael Wilson's fluid direction in subsequent productions at Minneapolis's Guthrie Theater, Connecticut's Hartford Stage and a 2002 Off Broadway run at Lincoln Center Theater.

Jean Stapleton (a Foote veteran from Off Broadway's *Night Seasons* and *The Roads to Home* and film versions of *Lily Dale* and *The Habitation of Dragons*) played rebellious sister Grace Anne, whose poorly chosen marriage distances her from the family and its fortune. Although reduced to poverty, she doesn't lose her playful spirit.

Roberta Maxwell played Cornelia, the controlling middle sister who is asked by her father to take charge of the family's finances. While her responsibilities give her power over the family, they also imprison her.

Daughter Hallie Foote—who starred in her father's *The Death of Papa* and *The Last of the Thorntons*—played Sissie, the sweetly ineffectual youngest sister.

> SISSIE: I'm the baby. I always liked being the baby. I liked being told what to do, and what not to do, what to think and what not to think. My daughter got angry at me once and said Sissie, she always called me Sissie, never Mama, Sissie I don't think you have ever had a thought or an opinion of your own. Ever. I expect that's right. When Grace Anne eloped with Jackson Le Grand I thought to myself I could never do anything like that. Never upset Papa or Mama or my sister like that. I had such a happy childhood.

Foote is known for his strong portraits of women, especially older women, and *Children* offers especially rich portraits, full of elegiac feeling. These sisters are fascinatingly alive however greatly their opportunities have been limited and their lives shaped by events beyond their control.

Each sister alternates as narrator, offering complementary but also contradictory perspectives about what really shifted their family from its position of privilege in the last half of the 1800s to its financial and emotional deterioration during the first decades of the 1900s.

STRUCTURED AS THREE MONOLOGUES that move back and forth in time, *Children* tantalizingly offers only a few moments in which the sisters directly interact, leaving audiences hungry for more. The minimalism is reinforced by the spare set—an isolating triangle of three chairs, with each actress sitting in one corner, and a centerpiece of a table with family pictures.

Inevitably, any play about three sisters begs comparison to Chekhov's *The Three Sisters*—and *Children* is very much a conscious homage. With a similarly evocative blend of tragedy and quiet comedy, Foote dramatizes his sisters' stories with more compassion and hopefulness.

From the start, in the monologue that opens the play and introduces the core characters, Foote establishes the mood of idealized but mournful nostalgia, hints at the unavoidable subjectivity of his overlapping stories and introduces recurring notes of musicality and mortality:

> CORNELIA: [. . .] Whenever I hear dance music I think of Beth. She loved to dance. I never learned to dance. Grace Anne danced and Sissie but Beth was the loveliest dancer I ever saw. Beth was Papa's favorite when she was alive, no question about that. Mama's too. Mine. Brother's. [. . .] She went away one winter to visit some cousins in St. Louis and stayed seven months. We missed her so—let her stay as long as she wants, Papa said, she's having a good time. She deserves it. We were such a happy family then it seemed to me.

In Foote as in Chekhov, appearances are deceiving and happiness is evanescent.

Each of the Thompson sisters is decent and goodhearted, but they are all reluctant to face certain truths about their family's history—which leads to sad consequences. The sisters' most conflicted stories indirectly illustrate how the perceived sins of the father are paid for by succeeding generations.

Even seemingly savvy Cornelia receives her comeuppance, at once financial and romantic, at the hands of Leon Davis, a suitor and promoter who disappears with her heart and an unintended "dowry" on the eve of a sister's marriage.

Occasionally, during or between their monologues, Grace Anne sews, Sissie sings and Cornelia studies and writes in her ledger at a desk. These are really the only tokens of action onstage. By design, the most eventful family upheavals—the death of a beloved fourth daughter, marriages, business failures, an elopement, a bloody fight, a lawsuit, a swindle—take place offstage and in memory.

Foote's elegant entry into the recently popular monologue-play genre may be little more than "talk and talk and talk"—to take part of Cornelia's opening monologue out of context—but what talk! Many revelatory insights and rich nuggets of character and wit can be gleaned from the sisters' torrents of run-on sentences and chatty loops of biased remembrance.

UNLIKE MOST FOOTE PLAYS, this one's shifting perspectives reflect a delicate nonlinear structure. As film director Akira Kurosawa did in *Rashomon*, Foote generates some mystery by questioning the reliability of alternate memories and stories about the same events. As each sister subtly retells her story, she reshapes the past in ways less painful and more flattering to her faltering pride. Toward the end, the sisters' invalid mother has retreated into fantasy, subconsciously preferring an idealized version of family history to the sting of reality.

Such a retreat, added to other defeats and losses, casts a pall over the survivors.

> GRACE ANNE: Sissie died. She went to sleep one night and never woke up. Sissie's daughter went to live with her father in Houston and Cornelia was alone in that big old house with just Mama. Once in a while Cornelia would bring Mama over to see me and Mama was talking all the time now about Beth and Papa and Sissie like they were still alive. She had Papa now a general in the Union Army and that he had been invited by the town of Harrison to come in after the Civil War to bring order to the town and to the county. [. . .] She goes on like this sometimes day and night she said.

Like Foote's other plays and his Academy Award-winning screenplays (*To Kill a Mockingbird, Tender Mercies*), *The Carpetbagger's Children* is suffused with empathy and understanding about the ways that ordinary people cope with life's setbacks and disappointments. Foote has always preferred to explore the consequences of poor behavior and bad decisions without casting blame. There are no villains here, only flawed human beings struggling to catch up with rapidly changing times but sadly falling behind.

With his emblematic tale of sibling rivalries and shifting family loyalties, Foote offers cautious hope about the ability of even flawed characters to carry on and find some sense of place and solace.

TIME OFTEN BRINGS a wiser perspective. For decades, Foote's writing has been concise, assured, reflective and observant. Now at 86, Foote conveys deepening wisdom in his mournful conclusion, which evokes elements of Shakespeare's final tragedies.

Tough one: Roberta Maxwell in Horton Foote's The Carpetbagger's Children. *Photo: Jim Caldwell*

The baby: Hallie Foote in Horton Foote's The Carpetbagger's Children. *Photo: Jim Caldwell*

Children can be appreciated as a *King Lear* retold from the point of view of the three daughters, with Cornelia resembling a modern-day humanized variant of Cordelia. In what might be described as a senior playwright's ruefully ironic Foote-note to *Lear*, Foote dramatizes the perverse consequences when Cornelia struggles to honor her father's wishes by refusing to divide his estate. Despite her success in preserving her father's land, the family's health, wealth and happiness are destroyed. No matter what we do, it seems, life ends with loss.

Perhaps only a seasoned playwright approaching the final stages of life could be so deeply attracted to such a dark theme or infuse it with such tender insight, cautious hope and abiding love for humanity.

"O, the Clanging Bells of Time" is the song most often sung in the play, repeatedly by Sissie and finally by Cornelia at her mother's deluded request. The lyrics underline the play's wintry themes of endurance and resilience:

> Oh, the clanging bells of time,
> Night and day they never cease
> We are wearied with their chime,
> For they do not bring us peace
> And we hush our breath to hear,
> And we strain our eyes to see.

Ultimately, how relevant is a post-Civil War drama to the early 21st century? In this restless new epoch of unexpected change and catastrophic loss, when the pace of life has quickened to a blur and many displaced people are fearful of forgetting their roots, the Chekhov of small-town America offers us a welcome lesson and example.

By drawing today's audiences into an era of our history with a slower pace and a stronger sense of place, *Children* reminds us that every generation must face the dislocations of change with as much decency and dignity as it can summon.

2002 ATCA/Steinberg New Play Citation

THE ACTION AGAINST SOL SCHUMANN
By Jeffrey Sweet

○ ○ ○ ○ ○

Essay by Richard Christiansen

AARON: Jesus, how are people supposed to know who they are if
they don't know what's happened before? Whether we like it or not,
we live in times that came out of other times, we're part of something.
Isn't it better to have some inkling of what?

JEFFREY SWEET'S DRAMA deals with the Holocaust; but it takes place
mostly in Brooklyn, 40 years after the end of World War II, and its principal
characters are not only survivors of the Nazi death camps, but the children
of one particular survivor, who discover that they have inherited a complex,
haunting, bitter legacy from their father.

Sweet based his play about an aged immigrant Jew accused of being
a Nazi collaborator on a real-life case, and his drama, in 25 scenes, moves
with documentary urgency.

A longtime member of the playwrights' ensemble of Victory Gardens
Theater in Chicago, Sweet also has an abiding fascination with the economic
narrative techniques of improvisational comedy and story theater, and he
has harnessed their methods here to give his work a staccato immediacy.
In its premiere at the 195-seat Victory Gardens on March 26, 2001, the
ensemble of nine actors physically and verbally powered the action ahead
by introducing characters, noting the time and place of the action and
bringing on the few essential bits of furniture for each scene. This swift
group action, which brings the audience straight into the action, helps give
the drama a pressing sense of being there.

But *The Action Against Sol Schumann* is not a living newsreel. It is a
play—firmly anchored in the US tradition of dramas about families in crisis—
that seeks to explore with a clear head the major issues of revenge,
retribution, guilt and forgiveness that are the aftermath of the Holocaust.

In Sweet's story, Sol Schumann is indeed guilty of crimes against
humanity, but he is more a figure of pathos than a villain. One of the play's
prime virtues is its belief that crime and punishment are not so easily fixed
in this tangled history. There is a deeply felt understanding of and sympathy

317

Father and sons: Eli Goodman, Bernie Landis and Robert K. Johansen in Jeffrey Sweet's The Action Against Sol Schumann. *Photo: Liz Lauren*

for everyone, especially Sol's two American-born sons, whose lives are shaken and whose views are upended by actions that took place under terrible circumstances many miles away and many years in the past.

THE PLAY BEGINS with a wild-card scene. Mrs. Shapiro, an older woman we do not see again after this opening shot, confronts a government official on the street and, in high agitation, insists that a man living in her building is a Nazi. We later learn that Paul, the man she accuses of ignoring the case, works for the Office of Special Investigations and is charged with identifying and prosecuting illegal immigrants—such as Nazi war criminals—who lied in order to enter the United States after World War II. Paul delicately tries to explain to the woman that there is no hard evidence against the target of her fury, but she will have none of it and leaves him in great anger, scornfully shouting, "You, the Nazis. One government and another. No difference."

With this hint of dark things to come, the play zeroes in on its central arena, the Brooklyn family of Sol Schumann (Bernie Landis), a devout Jew, a loving father of two grown sons and a survivor of the Holocaust.

Aaron (Robert K. Johansen) is a bachelor, an intelligent, street-smart substitute teacher in some if the toughest sections of the New York City public school system. He's also an intense liberal activist, so appalled in this year of 1985 by President Reagan's planned visit to the military cemetery in Bitburg, Germany—where some members of the Nazis' vicious SS troops are buried—that he is flying to Germany on his own to join a group of Americans protesting Reagan's visit.

His brother, Michael (Eli Goodman), is a successful accountant and much less devout, much less involved in Jewish affairs. He has a gentile wife and a more relaxed attitude. This causes tension between the brothers, so much so that Michael at one point sarcastically says to Aaron, "OK, fine; you're the righteous Jew and I'm the assimilated sell-out." Michael tells his wife, Kate, "I am not my brother." And later:

> MICHAEL: You can't just put [people] in easy categories—good, bad. Besides, some people are good because it's been easy for them to be good. They've never faced a hard choice. And maybe, if they did face one, maybe they wouldn't have measured up.

Both men, however different they are from each other, are devastated when they learn that their father, a prisoner in the Ordenhaupt concentration camp during the war, has been accused by some fellow survivors of having been a kapo, a Jew who acted as an often brutal accomplice of the Germans' death-dealing police in the camps.

Worse, when confronted with the accusation, Sol Schumann admits that he was indeed a kapo. He is one of those people who had faced a hard choice. "Do you think it was a job I asked for? Something I wanted?," he asks his sons. "They said, 'Schumann, you. You will do this.' You didn't refuse them. Not if you wanted to live. I had to live. My sister, mother, my father, their mother and fathers—all gone. Only me. The whole family. All gone. Only me. I had to live."

At this point, midway in the drama, after a detailed interrogation by Paul at the OSI office, the action against Sol Schumann is formally presented. Sol is accused of illegally entering the United States and his citizenship is to be stripped from him. He is charged with serving as a supervisory kapo at Ordenhaupt, in which post he "participated in persecution by brutalizing and physically abusing prisoners."

THE LAST HALF OF THE PLAY is concerned with the unraveling of the Schumann family as the two sons try to cope with the truth about the sins of their father. Standing outside the family circle, but very much involved in the case and acting as sounding boards for the sons' agony, are two women: Diane, a reporter from a liberal monthly; and Leah, an attorney, who has had a brief relationship with Aaron. Against the wishes of her mother, a concentration camp survivor, Leah decides to serve as Sol's lawyer.

Also linked to the case are Frieder, a camp survivor hellbent on bringing Sol to judgment and making him suffer for his past acts, and the somewhat shadowy figure of Reiner. (Both of these contrasting characters were portrayed in the original production with equal veracity by Richard Henzel.) Reiner's a suave character who, in an informal meeting, mentions to Paul that he and "some of the people I'm associated with" question the wisdom of prosecuting Sol Schumann.

> REINER: There are some who feel that this can only encourage anti-Semites. "Look. You see, those Jews, give them the opportunity, they even turn on each other. Some of them—no better than Nazis."

Paul responds that Reiner is promoting a dangerous notion.

> PAUL: [. . . T]he idea that if you're Jewish—if you're born Jewish, you couldn't be capable of such things. That to be born a Jew carries with it a presumption of moral superiority. To be separate from, better than others by virtue of ethnicity or nationality.
>
> REINER: And you see a danger in this?

Without sin? Anthony Fleming III, Robert K. Johansen, Eli Goodman, Bernie Landis, Kati Brazda, Amy Ludwig, Roslyn Alexander, Richard Henzel and Melissa Carlson Joseph in Jeffrey Sweet's The Action Against Sol Schumann. *Photo: Liz Lauren*

PAUL: Seem to me that's not too far from what the Germans believed.

And their meeting, the only scene in which Reiner appears, is over.

At first enraged by his father's confession, Aaron is now desperately trying to find witnesses, camp survivors, who might testify in Sol's defense. He cannot believe that Sol would engage is such cruel acts, and he is appalled when Leah suggests that Sol fly to another country before the proceedings begin, in order to be out of the government's jurisdiction.

He gets a bit of hope when Diane, who has formed an attachment to the case (and to Aaron), gives him the name of a survivor who might be of help. She is Rivka Gauer (Roslyn Alexander, in another moving character role), an aged woman living in Toronto. When Aaron and Diane fly there to interview her, she tells them in a tape-recorded conversation that Sol Schumann, who came from her village, saved her life in the camp. But she will not testify, she says. "You don't want me to tell what I saw, what I know."

> RIVKA: You're going to hear terrible things at the trial. But what I feel you must know is that it wasn't your father who did these things. Not the same person who brought you up. Not the same boy I knew. [. . .] The things he was forced to see. A mother, murdered in front of his eyes. A father shot. Something broke. That's what I believe. That's what you must believe. Or how could he have done such things?
>
> AARON: But they made him—the Germans.
>
> RIVKA: No, he did these things even when the Germans were not there. When there was no reason. But that's what I mean; there was no reason. When there's no reason, all that's left is madness.

Returning home after this crushing encounter, Aaron tells his brother the bad news. Michael responds, "So how can it be right to go after someone, punish someone for something he doesn't even know he did?"

But Aaron is inconsolable. For him, the case is over. All he can say, with rue and irony, is:

> AARON: You know, flying back down, all I could think—he did these things and he survived. He survived because—crazy or not— he did these things. And here we are. You and I—the two of us—we are alive because he did these things.

THERE IS ONE FINAL MEETING with Sol, who has heard his sons talking and who has come down to see Aaron. There are a few pleasantries, a quick hug and then Aaron is gone. This silent scene, played with tremendous force by Landis and Johansen, is the emotional peak of the play, a final, mournful reunion of father and son before the deluge of events that follow.

Diane, immediately in the following scene, tells the audience what happened next. Aaron, a savvy teacher who knew better than to take on a tough kid with a weapon, challenged a knife-wielding teenager in a high school cafeteria and was stabbed to death.

Quickly, we learn that Sol suffered a stroke at Aaron's funeral and can now barely speak. The case against him has been dropped. He has relinquished his citizenship, but he will not be deported. In the hospital, Sol is visited by Michael and Kate, who promise him cheerily that they will come to see him regularly. Sol is left alone.

In a rush of melodrama, however, the vengeful Frieder, furious in his belief that Sol has not been sufficiently punished, enters the room, wheels the stricken man out of the hospital and to the edge of a curb (actually the edge of the stage), intending to push Sol (who does not recognize him) into the oncoming traffic.

But Michael, having returned to the hospital room and having learned that "a friend" had taken Sol out for a walk, breaks through at the last moment to rescue Sol and to shove Frieder to the ground. Assured that his father is all right, Michael next offers Frieder his hand, which Frieder angrily rejects.

But then, as the playwright describes the sorrow and the pity of the closing scene:

> Frieder begins to get up, but loses his balance. Michael catches him in his arms, holds him. Frieder holds on to Michael and begins to weep. The sound comes pouring out of him. Sol sits mute in his chair. The lights intensify on the three of them. The rest of the ensemble stands, witnesses in silhouette. The lights fade.

2002 ATCA/Steinberg New Play Citation

JOE AND BETTY

By Murray Mednick

○ ○ ○ ○ ○

Essay by Michael Phillips

> BETTY: Listen to me, Emile. Listen to your mother. Your father's family is against me, who has suffered and put up with a lot. As you know. I don't have a husband who does right, I don't have a father, my sisters have disowned me, you're all I have. You're all I have, Emile. I never wanted to move here from Brooklyn, where I had a life, but your father insisted, he made me do it, and here we are, in the freezing cold, with nothing. I've lost touch, I've lost contact. With my life. Which was in Brooklyn.

THE CATSKILLS ARE THE HILLS forever alive with the sound of rimshots, canoe paddles hitting the water, and Steve and Eydie harmonizing. Across much of the 20th century one Jewish comic after another honed his shtick at resorts such as Grossinger's, surrounded by bucolic mountain greenery. For generations of New Yorkers in particular, the Catskills symbolized stress relief of both the indoor and outdoor variety. It was a Jewish Forest of Arden, with one-liners.

Relief, however, is hard to come by in Murray Mednick's *Joe and Betty*, surely the most unrelenting play ever set in this part of the world. Mednick peels back the familiar Catskills image, revealing something else: A family, based on the writer's own, comprised of Brooklyn Jews lost in the woods.

In spirit Mednick's play—strange, unsettling, distinctive—is more akin to the lean, working-class anguish found in a Franz Xaver Kroetz work such as *Through the Leaves* or *Mensch Meier*, than anything typically American. Yet *Joe and Betty* at its core is as American as apple pie, albeit a pie spiked with vinegar. It is a Jewish family story, set in 1951, pulled straight from Mednick's own fraught childhood, relayed in the disarming, punchy rhythms of a nightclub routine.

Here are the opening lines, spoken by Joe, a sometime movie-house projectionist, and Betty, his beleaguered wife and unstable guardian of their six kids. They are in their cramped apartment, next door to a nightclub where the "colored" gather.

Show me the money: Annabelle Gurwitch and John Diehl in Murray Mednick's Joe and Betty. *Photo: David Weininger*

BETTY: Did you get paid?

JOE: I got paid.

BETTY: Thank God.

JOE: Sure!

BETTY: How much?

JOE: Fifty bucks.

BETTY: Where is it?

JOE: It's in my pocket.

BETTY: Take it out of your pocket.

JOE: Where it belongs.

BETTY: And put it into my pocket.

The Brasmans are behind in their rent. The landlady, Mollie Kaplan, apparently has turned off the heat. Betty and Joe argue, painfully, though casually, as if discussing food shopping or the weather. "You should be committed," Joe says to Betty. "Someone will come out of the future and strangle you."

Scene two finds Betty and Joe playing poker with their neighbors, Stan and Dot. Five of the Brasman kids are sleeping nearby, offstage. "Emile is out," Betty says of the unseen character modeled on Mednick himself, a rebellious and bookish preteen. "Where I don't know."

The talk turns to the subject of the plumber Eddie Popolowksi, revealed later to be having an affair with Stan and Dot's underage daughter. The men in this Catskills town—Mednick grew up in Woodridge—desperately lack grounding; as Betty says, by rote, whenever the subject turns to men, "They take advantage." Joe and Betty tell their old story about why they got married. In Brooklyn, Joe went to Betty's mother, who told him: "You wanna fool around with Betty, then marry her." Everybody laughs.

MEDNICK, ONE OF THE FOUNDERS of the Padua Playwrights project of Los Angeles, keeps the screws tight in every scene of *Joe and Betty*. The goal, Mednick once said of writing, is "realism-plus," and in this work the plus comes from the sense that we're eavesdropping on a corrosive relationship spiraling downward. Yet the jabbing rhythm of the talk sounds as if it is supposed to be funny. Much of the play is a doubletalk routine, only the routine is deadly.

"You abuse me," says Betty, a memorably lost soul in sleepy-eyed Annabelle Gurwitch's portrayal. (Gurwitch played Betty in Los Angeles and, in June 2002, Off Broadway.)

"I abuse you?" replies Joe, a disarmingly genial creep in actor John Diehl's hands. (Diehl co-starred with Gurwitch in Los Angeles and New York.) "There's nothing to abuse."

A later scene between Betty and Dot hints at the world outside the Brasman's claustrophic walls. "It's not like America here," Dot says of their town. "In the winter there's no jobs. In the summer we get tourists." In an aside, Dot mutters to the audience: "One kind of tourist. From New York." Earlier in the same exchange Dot, the gentile, lets slip a reference to being surrounded by "kikes." Betty can only retort with a mirthless "ha, ha, ha."

Betty, disowned by her family, is losing her grip on her life. Emile, her oldest child, likes spending time with Joe's mother, but Betty disapproves: Her mother-in-law "hates and blames me," she says. In Act II Joe's mother dies, and Joe is crazed with grief. He threatens suicide, wielding a knife to his chest. The landlady comforts Joe, though the squalor of Joe and Betty's apartment reminds landlady Mollie of her Warsaw childhood. The apartment is freezing, as always. Mollie walks over to the radiator and turns the knob. Out comes the heat. The Brasmans had heat all along; they just didn't know it. It's a horribly funny moment.

The next scene finds Joe, Stan and Joe's car-salesman brother, Irv, all wearing yarmulkes, back from the brothers' mother's funeral. Irv's own marriage has gone sour, and he is leaving his place in Florida for a new life in California. Stan, janitor at the movie theater where Joe works part-time, dreamily imagines California: "Warm, with oranges." It is a long way from the Catskills.

Joe screws around on Betty, and Betty knows it. Joe may also be sexually abusing his daughter, Marie. (Mednick treats this intimation carefully.) Emile, meantime, withdrawn since his grandmother's death, has begun acting out at school, getting in one fistfight after another. He also has head-lice, unthwarted by Betty's kerosene hair-washings. A visit from a

Brooding Betty: Annabelle Gurwitch in Murray Mednick's Joe and Betty. *Photo: David Weininger*

school social worker brings to Betty a firm reminder to take better care of her children: "We are Jews, after all. We try to take care. (*Pause.*) There are things we believe in." But locked inside her life, Betty cannot see her way clear to a better one.

At once direct and verbally stylized, *Joe and Betty* relates to the coming-of-age familial rites of David Mamet's *The Cryptogram*, where a young boy struggles to comprehend the breakup of his parents' marriage. Here, though, the boy in question isn't part of the action. Mednick's Emile listens, from his room, and his parents talk to him (to us; the room is somewhere in the audience) privately, trying to make amends for a virtually unamendable circumstance.

Mednick never lets the audience off easy in *Joe and Betty*. The director of the New York edition, Guy Zimmerman, wrote in his program notes that "not much happens" in the play. The play, he wrote, "isn't about the characters getting anywhere." (This drove some of the reviewers nuts.) Mednick ends *Joe and Betty* where it began, with the couple locked in verbal battle—only now, the abusive Joe's threat of institutionalizing the abusive Betty has become a reality. The banter takes on a mournful, elegiac quality. Mednick allows Betty a memory of better days, when she was closer to her own, vastly imperfect family, on DeKalb Avenue in Brooklyn. "We lived there," she says. "Me and Joey, we had our own apartment. [. . .] Downstairs they had pushcarts. Downstairs was a fruit and vegetable stand." You could hear the el train, she says.

In the mid-1960s, as an Off Off Broadway maverick working with Sam Shepard and others, Mednick once disdained the notion of the stage serving as a mirror to real life. "What is happening onstage is not a mirror, it's what's happening," he said. *Joe and Betty* is the sort of quasirealistic, quasistraightforward memory play Mednick would never have written in the 1960s or 1970s. Yet its consciously performative texture—the frequent asides to the audience, the nervous, blackly comic rhythms, described by one Los Angeles critic as "Pinter in the Catskills"—transcends realism. It is realism-plus, scored to harsh but precise verbal music made by a writer who, like Mamet busing tables at Second City a decade or two later, once worked as a Catskills busboy.

First seen in a workshop at Atlanta's Seven Stages in 1996, *Joe and Betty* was successfully produced in 2001 by Mednick's own Padua Playwrights at 2100 Square Feet, a nondescript 65-seat space in Los Angeles's Fairfax district, the postwar Jewish heart of the city. In June 2002, with many of the LA cast members, *Joe and Betty* received its New York premiere at the Jose Quintero Theatre on West 42nd Street.

"The dialogue just poured out of me at breakneck speed," Mednick said to the *Jewish Journal of Greater Los Angeles*. "The play came out whole." The writing, he said, was fed by his memories of the adults he observed growing up in the Catskills, adults governed by "a desperate, destructive anxiety and hysteria that had been handed down, the cumulative result of generations of impoverishment and persecution." This, Mednick said, "took its extreme form in my parents."

FROM SUCH STUFF, nightmares are made—and then shaken off, if the boy becomes a writer. Mednick lived to tell the tale his own way, with a rhythmic snap reminiscent of Clifford Odets and a firsthand sense of what it was like to grow up among the walking wounded, in the shadow of the Depression, World War II and the Holocaust. Mednick hasn't so much come out of the future to strangle his parents, as he has struggled, bracingly, with an audacious brand of gallows humor, to remember how it all looked and sounded.

A DIRECTORY OF NEW-PLAY
PRODUCTIONS
○ ○ ○ ○ ○
Compiled by Rue E. Canvin

PROFESSIONAL PRODUCTIONS JUNE 1, 2001–MAY 31, 2002 of new plays by a variety of resident companies around the United States. The companies supplied information on casts and credits, which are listed here in alphabetical order, by state, of 76 producing organizations. Date given is opening date. Most League of Resident Theatres (LORT) and other regularly producing Actors Equity groups were queried for this comprehensive directory. Active United States theater companies not included in this list either did not present new (or newly revised) scripts during the year under review or had not responded to our query by July 1, 2002. Productions listed below are world premieres, United States premieres, regional premieres or substantial revisions. Theaters in the United States are encouraged to submit proposed listings of new works and new adaptations, in addition to the premieres indicated above, to the editor of the *Best Plays* series.

ALABAMA

Alabama Shakespeare Festival, Montgomery
Kent Thompson artistic director, Alan Harrison managing director

Southern Writers Project, June 28, 2001.

THE VENUS DE MILO IS ARMED. By Kia Corthron.

New Voices, October 11–14, 2001.

THE BELL BEFORE SUMMER. By Alan Newton. Read by the playwright.

IN OCEAN SPRINGS. By Elyzabeth Wilder. Read by the playwright.

THIS OAK TREE. By Kelley Pounders. Director, Gwen Orel.

LITTLE CLIFF. By Eric Schmiedl. Adapted from stories by Clifton Taulbert. Director, Chuck Patterson.

AARONVILLE DAWNING. By Linda Byrd Kilian. Director, Kent Thompson.

EIGHTY-SIX. By Javon Johnson. Director, Carlyle Brown.

HOMEMADE LOVE. By Syd Rushing. Director, Gregg T. Daniel.

Southern Writers Project Workshop, March 22–24, 2002.

THE FULA FROM AMERICA. By Carlyle Brown. Read by the author.

AN OLE SOUL, A YOUNG SPIRIT. By John Henry Redwood. Director, Tiffany Trent.

IAGO. By James McLure. Director, Kent Thompson.

LITTLE CLIFF. By Eric Schmiedl. Adapted from stories of Clifton Taulbert. Director, Margaret Ford-Taylor.

THE DREAMS OF SARAH BREEDLOVE. By Regina Taylor. Director, Shirley Joe Finney.

SHILOH RULES. By Doris Baizley. May 17, 2002 (world premiere). Director, John D. Dennis; scenery, Emily Beck; costumes, Kristine Kearney; lighting, Liz Lee; composer, Thom Jenkins; sound, Scott Robertson; dramaturg, Gwen Orel; stage managers, Mark D. Leslie, Cheryl Lynn Bauman.

LucyGale Scruggs .... Kaitlin O'Neal	Cecilia Pettison .... Greta Lambert
Clara May Abbott .... Dawn Didawick	Officer Wilson .... Caroline S. Clay
Meg Barton .... Jen Faith Brown	Widow Beckwith .... Sonja Lanzener

Time: 1862. Place: Shiloh, Tennessee.

ARIZONA

Arizona Theatre Company, Tucson
David Ira Goldstein artistic director, Jessica L. Andrews managing director

GHOSTS. By Henrik Ibsen; translated by Lanford Wilson. October 13, 2001 (world premiere). Director, Marshall Mason; scenery, David Potts; costumes, Laura Crow; lighting, Dennis Parichy; sound, Brian Peterson.

Helen .... Ruth Reid	Regina .... Kelly McAndrew
Oswald Alving .... Jason Kuykendall	Engstrand .... Bob Sorenson
Manders .... Daren Kelly	

Time: A rainy day in early autumn. Place: The Alving estate at Rosenvold on a fjord in rural Norway. Two intermisssions.

Genesis: New Play Reading Series. (Produced with the Scottsdale Center for the Arts.)
TRUCKER RHAPSODY. By Toni Press-Coffman. April 16, 2002. Director, Samantha K. Wyer.

Reginald Denny .... Bob Sorenson	Terry Barnett;
Damian Williams .... Kwane Vedrene	Georgiana Williams .... Lillie Richardson
Riot 208 .... Shaikh Brown	Reader .... Michael Tennant
Titus Murphy .... Ken Love	

THE RECIPE MAN. By Kate Dahlgren. April 30, 2002. Director, Philip J. Taylor.

Arthur .... Ken Love	Actor 4 .... Ben Tyler
Actor 1 .... Roberto Guajardo	Actor 5 .... Jeff Goodman
Actor 2 .... Christopher Haines	Reader .... Philip J. Taylor
Actor 3 .... Mark Broadley	

FRUIT SALAD. By Ashley Davidson. May 13, 2002. Director, Philip J. Taylor.

Daryl .... Kyle Sorrell	Kate; Rita .... Lillie Richardson
Cheryl; Mary .... Erin Curry	Ed; Bill............................... Christopher Haines
Lilly; Charlie .... Patti Hanon	Barry .... Ken Love

CALIFORNIA

American Conservatory Theater, San Francisco
Carey Perloff artistic director

NO FOR AN ANSWER. Musical with book, music and lyrics by Marc Blitzstein. October 25, 2001 (world premiere). Director, Carey Perloff; choreography, Francine Landes; scenery, Elizabeth Mead; costumes, Cassandra Carpenter; lighting, Peter Maradudin; sound, Cliff Caruthers; musical director, Peter Maleitzke; dramaturg, Paul Walsh; stage manager, Katherine Riemann.

CAST: Heidi Armbruster, Jennifer Charles, Michael Chmiel, Michael Goncalves Davis, Ryan Farley, Julie Fitzpatrick, Coley Grundman, Sara Hauter, Sara Homayoon, Neil Edward Hopkins, Adam Ludwig, Jed Orlemann, Renee Penegor, Nathan Peterman, Bradford J. Shreve, Sky Soleil, Finnerty Steeves, Jessica Diane Turner, Melissa Von Siegel, T. Edward Webster.

Place: Diogenes Social Club, Crest Lake, New York. One intermission.

FOR THE PLEASURE OF SEEING HER AGAIN. By Michel Tremblay; translated by Linda Gaboriau. May 12, 2002. Director, Carey Perloff; scenery, Ralph Funicello; costumes, Judith Dolan; lighting, James F. Ingalls; sound, Garth Hemphill.

CAST: Olympia Dukakis, Marco Barricelli.

Berkeley Repertory Theatre, Berkeley
Tony Taccone artistic director, Susan Medak managing director

36 VIEWS. By Naomi Iizuka. September 12, 2001 (world premiere). Director, Mark Wing-Davey; scenery, Douglas Stein; costumes, Myung Hee Cho; lighting, David Weiner; sound, Matthew Spiro; projections, Ruppert Bohle; dramaturg, Luan Schooler; stage manager, Michael Suenkel. Presented in association with the Joseph Papp Public Theater/New York Shakespeare Festival.

Darius Wheeler	Bill Camp	Claire Tsong	Elaine Tse
Setsuko Hearn	Liana Pai	Owen Matthiassen	Peter Donat
John Bell	Ebon Moss-Bachrach	Elizabeth Newman-Orr	Rebecca Wisocky

One intermission.

NOCTURNE. By Adam Rapp. October 17, 2001 (West Coast premiere). Director, Mark Brokaw; scenery, Neil Patel; costumes, Donna Marie; lighting, Mark McCullough; music and sound, David Van Tieghem; stage manager, Cynthia Cahill.

The Son .... Anthony Rapp

No intermission.

L'UNIVERSE. April 17, 2002. Conceived and written by Paul Magid and Howard Jay Patterson. Director, Carys Kresny; scenery, Christopher Barreca; costumes, Susan Hilferty; lighting, Peter Maradudin; sound, Dominic CodyKramers; music, Douglas Wieselman, Mark Ettinger, production stage manager, Kristina Wicke.

Featuring The Flying Karamazov Brothers.

HOMEBODY/KABUL. By Tony Kushner. April 24, 2002 (West Coast premiere). Director, Tony Taccone; scenery, Kate Edmunds; costumes, Lydia Tanji; lighting, Peter Maradudin; sound, Matthew Spiro; score, Paul Godwin; production dramaturg, Luan Schooler; script dramaturgy, Oskar Eustis and Mande Michelle Hackett; stage managers, Michael Suenkel and Shona Mitchell.

The Homebody .... Michelle Morain
Dr. Qari Shah;
  Marabout .... Julian Lopez-Morillas
Mullah Ali Afta Durranni .... Hector Correa
Milton Ceiling .... Charles Shaw Robinson
Quango
  Twistleton .... Bruce McKenzie (4/10–6/9)
                     Rod Gnapp (6/11–7/14)

Priscilla Ceiling .... Heidi Dippold
A Munkrat; A Border Guard .... Rahul Gupta
Khwaja Aziz Mondanabosh .... Harsh Nayyar
Zai Garshi .... Waleed Zuaiter
Mahala .... Jacqueline Antaramian

  Two intermissions.

East West Players, Los Angeles

Tim Dang producing artistic director, Al Choy managing director

RED. By Chay Yew. October 3, 2001 (Los Angeles premiere). Director, Mr. Yew; special choreography, Chua Soo Pong and Li Xiu Hua; scenery, Myung Hee Cho; lighting, Jose Lopez; costumes, Anita Yavich; sound, Nathan Wang; production stage manager, Victoria Gathe.

CAST: Emily Kuroda, Page Leong, Jeanne Sakata.

SISTER MATSUMMOTO. By Philip Kan Gotanda. January 23, 2002. Director, Chay Yew.

CAST: Thomas Boyle, Elaine Kao, Emily Kuroda, Randall Mark, Nelson Mashita, Natsuko Ohama, Sab Shimono, Ryun Yu.

Evidence Room, Hollywood

Dog Mouth. By John Steppling. January 12, 2002. Director, Mr. Steppling; scenery, Jason Adams; lighting, Rand Ryan; costumes, Ames Ingham; music and sound, Karl Lundeberg. Presented in association with Padua Playwrights.

Dog Mouth .... Stephen Davies
Nyah .... Nia Gwynne

Becker .... James Storm
Weeks .... Hugh Dane

Falcon Theatre, Burbank

Kathleen Marshall producer, Rowan Joseph managing director

HOUSE. By Thomas McCormack. June 18, 2001. Director, Steve Zuckerman; scenery, Yael Pardess; costumes, Mimi Maxmen; lighting, Rand Ryan; sound, Kevin Goold; music, Donald J. Markowitz; projection design, Jenny Okum; stage manager, Jennifer Scheffer.

Griff .... Christopher Curry
Cora .... Maree Cheatham
Grover .... Neil Vipond
Kay .... Christine Estabrook
Sheila .... Abigail Revasch

Josh .... William Schallert
Sara .... Stacey Martino
Bart; Ram .... J. Kenneth Campbell
Hope; Ross .... David Starzyk
Ted .... Harry Hamlin

  One intermission.

Geffen Playhouse, Los Angeles

Randy Arney artistic director, Stephen Eich managing director

HE HUNTS. By Georges Feydeau; translated and adapted by Phillip Littell. April 17, 2002. Director, David Schweizer; scenery, Christopher Barreca; costumes, David Zinn; lighting, Anne Militello; sound, Jonathan Burke; music, Peter Golub.

Leontine .... Valarie Pettiford

Moricet .... Stephen Nichols

Duchotel .... Maxwell Caulfield
Gontreins .... Daniel Kucan
Babet .... Cathy Lind Hayes
Cassecul .... V.J. Foster

Madame Latour .... Carol Kane
Bridois .... Alan Mandell
Cops .... Paul Ellis, Robert Porch

Time: Late-19th-century. Place: Paris.

The Globe Theatres, San Diego
Jack O'Brien artistic director

THE BOSWELL SISTERS. Musical by Stuart Ross and Mark Hampton. July 28, 2001 (world premiere). Director, Mr. Ross; lighting, David F. Segal; scenery, James Youmans; costumes, Ann Hould-Ward; sound, Paul Peterson; musical director, Brad Ellis; orchestrations, Peter Matz; arrangements, Joseph Baker; stage manager, D. Adams.

Connee Boswell .... Elizabeth Ward Land
Martha Boswell .... Amy Pietz

Vet Boswell .... Michelle Duffy

STONES IN HIS POCKETS. By Marie Jones. February 3, 2002 (West Coast premiere). Director, Ian McElhinney; designer, Jack Kirwan; lighting, James C. McFetridge; production stage manager, Zoya Kachadurian.

CAST: Christopher Burns, Bronson Pinchot.

COMPLEAT FEMALE STAGE BEAUTY. By Jeffrey Hatcher. April 5, 2002 (major revision). Director, Mark Lamos; scenery, Michael Yeargan; costumes, Jess Goldstein; lighting, York Kennedy; sound, Paul Peterson; fight direction, Steve Rankin; stage managers, D. Adams and Joel Rosen.

Miss Frayne .... Christine Marie Brown
Samuel Pepys; Mistress Revels ...... Ryan Dunn
Sir Charles Sedley .... Steve Hendrickson
Thomas Betterton .... Jonathan Fried
Maria .... Laura Heisler
Charles II .... Tom Hewitt
Margaret Hughes .... Krista Hoeppner
Villiars; Duke of Buckingham ... Quentin Mare
Nell Gwynn .... Kwana Martinez

Hyde; Sir Peter Lely .... David McCann
Edward Kynaston .... Robert Petkoff
Courtier .... D'Vorah Bailey
Mrs. Elizabeth Barry; Courtier .... Deb Heinig
Ruffian .... Brian Ibsen
Ruffian; Drunk; Courtier ..... Antonie Knoppers
Ruffian; Thug; Courtier;
Sir Thomas Killigrew .... Lucas Rooney

AN INFINITE ACHE. By David Schulner. May 25, 2002 (West Coast premiere). Director, Brendon Fox; scenery, Yael Pardess; lighting, Jennifer Setlow; costumes, Holly Poe Durbin; sound, Paul Peterson; stage manager, Raúl Moncada.

Hope .... Samantha Quan

Charles .... James Waterston

La Jolla Playhouse, La Jolla
Des McAnuff artistic director; Terrence Dwyer managing director

Page to Stage Program.

I AM MY OWN WIFE. By Doug Wright. July 10, 2001. Director, Mr. Wright; scenery, Paul Eric Pape; costumes, Rebecca Lustig; lighting, Shaoann Yo; sound, Casi Pacilio; dramaturg, Shirley Fishman; stage manager, M. William Shiner.

Charlotte von Mahlsdorf et al. . Jefferson Mays

Time: The Nazi years; the Stasi years.

THE LARAMIE PROJECT. By Moisés Kaufman and the members of Tectonic Theater Project. July 31, 2001 (regional premiere). Director, Mr. Kaufman, with additional staging by Leigh Fondakowski; scenery, Robert Brill; costumes, Moe Schell; lighting, Betsy Adams; sound, Matthew Spiro; music, Peter Golub; dramaturgs, Amanda Gronich, Sara Lambert, John McAdams, Maude Mitchell, Andy Paris, Barbara Pitts, Kelli Simpkins; production stage manager, Steven Adler. Presented in association with Berkeley Repertory Theatre.

Himself; Doc O'Connor;
  Matt Galloway; Andrew Gomez;
  Russell Henderson's Mormon Home Teacher;
  Reverend Fred Phelps;
  Ensemble (7/31–8/19) .... Stephen Belber
Herself; Eileen Engen (Act I); Trish Steger;
  Marge Murray; Baptist Minister;
  Ensemble .... Amanda Gronich
Reggie Fluty; Rebecca Hilliker;
  Ensemble .... Mercedes Herrero
Moisés Kaufman; Stephen Mead Johnson;
  John Peacock; Harry Woods;
  Philip Dubois (Act I);
  Ensemble .... John McAdams
Himself; Jedediah Schultz;
  Doug Laws; Matt Mickelson; Shannon;
  Kerry Drake; Philip Dubois (Act II),
  Ensemble .... Andy Paris

Himself; Sgt. Hing;
  Rob DeBree; Father Roger;
  Rulon Stacey; Phil LaBrie;
  Ensemble .... Greg Pierotti
Herself; April Silva;
  Catherine Connolly; Zubaida Lila;
  Lucky Thompson; Eileen Engen (Act II);
  Ensemble .... Barbara Pitts
Leigh Fondakowski; Zackie Salmon;
  Romaine Patterson; Aaron Kreifels;
  Tiffany Edwards; Jen,
  Ensemble .... Kelli Simpkins
Stephen Belber; Doc O'Connor;
  Matt Galloway; Andrew Gomez;
  Russell Henderson's Mormon Home Teacher;
  Reverend Fred Phelps;
  Ensemble (8/21–9/2) .... James Asher

  Two intermissions.

BE AGGRESSIVE. By Annie Weisman. July 29, 2001 (world premiere). Director, Lisa Peterson; scenery, Rachel Hauck; costumes, Audrey Fisher; lighting, James F. Ingalls; sound, Laura Grace Brown; dramaturg, Carrie Ryan; stage manager, Elizabeth Lohr.

Laura .... Angela Goethals
Hannah .... Daisy Eagan
Phil .... Mark Harelik
Leslie ....Jennifer Elise Cox
Judy .... Linda Gehringer
Cheerleader Chorus .... Tamala Horbianski,
                                                          Carly Kleiner,
                                                          Joy Osmanski

  Place: A world of smoothie shops and affluence. One intermission.

DRACULA. Musical with book and lyrics by Don Black and Christopher Hampton; music by Frank Wildhorn. October 21, 2001 (world premiere). Based on the book by Bram Stoker. Director, Des McAnuff; choreography, Mindy Cooper; scenery, John Arnone; costumes, Catherine Zuber; lighting, Howell Binkley; sound, Acme Sound Partners; projections, Michael Clark; orchestrations, Michael Starobin, Doug Besterman; music direction, Constantine Kitsopoulos; fight direction, Steve Rankin; dramaturg, Shirley Fishman; production stage manager, Frank Hartenstein.

Jonathan Harker ....Tom Stuart
Dracula .... Tom Hewitt
Mina Murray .... Jenn Morse
First Vampire................................. Jodi Stevens
Second Vampire .... Jenny-Lynn Suckling
Third Vampire........................... Emily Kosloski
Renfield .... William Youmans
Jack Seward .... Joe Cassidy
Lucy Westenra .... Amy Rutberg
Quincey Morris .... Lee Morgan
Arthur Holmwood .... Chris Hoch
Abraham Van Hellsing .... Tom Flynn
Child (alternating) ....Michael Cullen,
                                                          Angelo Scolari

  Ensemble: Margaret-Ann Gates, Emily Kosloski, Guy LeMonnier, Lynnette Marrero, Tracy Miller, Jodi Stevens, Jenny-Lynn Suckling; Sara Tobin.

Musical numbers, Act I: Prologue, "A Quiet Life," "One More Lonely Night," "First Taste," "Fresh Blood," "The Master's Song," "How Do You Choose?" "The Mist," "There Is a Love," "One More Lonely Night" (Reprise), "The Wedding Song," "Nosferatu," "The Invitation," "Prayer for the Dead," "Van Helsing's Proposal," "Prayer for the Dead" (Reprise). Act II: "The Mist" (Reprise), "Risks Worth Taking," "The Master's Song" (Reprise), "The Heart Is Slow to Learn," "There's Always a Tomorrow," "Deep in the Darkest Night" (Reprise), "Before the Summer Ends," "I'll Be Waiting for You," "Deep in the Darkest Night" (Reprise), "The Heart Is Slow to Learn" (Reprise), Finale.

One intermission.

DIVA. By Howard M. Gould. September 16, 2001 (world premiere). Director, Neel Keller; scenery, Andrew Jackness; costumes, Candice Donnelly; lighting, David Lee Cuthbert; sound, Robbin E. Broad, dramaturg, Shirley Fishman, stage manager, M. William Shiner.

Deanna Denninger	Susan Blakely	Kurt Fast	Jonathan Hogan
Isaac Brooks	Jere Burns	Ezra Twain	Tim Maculan
Barry Joshua	Paul Provenza	Petey Ryan	Timothy Warmen

Time: The present. Place: Various locations. One intermission.

A workshop of *Diva* was produced by Williamstown Theatre Festival in July 2001.

Magic Theatre Northside, San Francisco
Larry Eilenberg artistic director

THE AMERICAN IN ME. By Rebecca Gilman. June 15, 2002 (world premiere). Director, Amy Glazer; scenery, John Wilson; costumes, Fumiko Bielefeldt; lighting, Jim Cave; sound, Scott DeTurk.

Jeannie	Bethanny Alexander	Betty; Theresa; Cheryl;	
Winnie	Anne Darragh	Margaret; Nurse	Laura Hope Owen
Louise; Elise;		Ben	Jeff Parker
Ellen; Marie	Nicole Fonarow	Russ; Owens; Stephen	Robert Parsons
Cory; Tim;		Don; Lyle; Mike;	
Russell; Paul	Richard Gallagher	Donald; Gene	Michael Ray Wisely
Leeth	Julian Lopez-Morillas		

Place: Support group for infertile couples in Birmingham, Alabama. One intermission.

Mark Taper Forum, Los Angeles
Gordon Davidson artistic director, Charles Dillingham managing director

THE BODY OF BOURNE. By John Belluso. June 6, 2001 (world premiere). Director, Lisa Peterson; scenery, Rachel Hauck; costumes, Candice Cain; lighting, Geoff Korf; sound, Darron L. West; projections, Christopher Komuro; production stage manager, James T. McDermott.

Randolph Bourne	Clark Middleton	Emmy; others	Ann Stocking
Sara Bourne; others	Jenny O'Hara	Beulah Amidon; others	Heather Ehlers
Esther Cornell; others	Jodi Thelen	Carl Zigrosser; others	Stephen Caffrey
Uncle Halsey; others	Nicolas Coster		

With: Mitchell Edmonds, Lisa Lovett-Mann, Michele Marsh, Jill Remez, Michael Eric Strickland, Christopher Thornton.

One intermission.

IN REAL LIFE. By Charlayne Woodard. July 29, 2001 (world premiere). Director, Daniel Sullivan; scenery, John Lee Beatty; costumes, James Berton Harris; lighting, Kathy A. Perkins; sound, Christopher Walker; music, Daryl Waters; production stage manager, Mary K. Klinger. Presented in association with Seattle Repertory Theatre.

Performed by Charlayne Woodard.
One intermission.

FLOWER DRUM SONG. Musical with book by David Henry Hwang; music by Richard Rodgers; lyrics by Oscar Hammerstein II; based on the original book by Mr. Hammerstein and Joseph Fields, based on the novel by C.Y. Lee. October 13, 2001. Director and choreographer, Robert Longbottom; scenery, Robin Wagner; costumes, Gregg Barnes; lighting, Brian Nason; sound, Jon Gottlieb and Philip G. Allen; production stage manager, Peter Cline.

Mei-Li .... Lea Salonga	Harvard .... Allen Liu
Wang .... Tzi Ma	Linda Low .... Sandra Allen
Chin .... Alvin Ing	Madame Liang .... Jodi Long
Ta .... Jose Llana	Chao .... Ronald M. Banks

With: Charlene Carabeo, Rich Ceraulo, Eric Chan, Marcus Choi, Michael Dow, Thomas C. Kouo, Keri Lee, Blythe Matsui, Jennifer Paz, Robert Pendilla, Chloe Stewart, Kim Varhola, Christine Yasunaga.

Musical numbers, Act I: "A Hundred Million Miracles," "I Am Going to Like It Here," "I Enjoy Being a Girl," "You Are Beautiful," "Grant Avenue," "Fan Fan Fannie," "Gliding Through My Memoree," "The Next Time It Happens." Act II: "Chop Suey," "My Best Love," "Don't Marry Me," "Love Look Away," "Like a God."

MY OLD LADY. By Israel Horovitz. December 19, 2001 (West Coast premiere). Director, David Esbjornson; scenery, John Lee Beatty; costumes, Elizabeth Hope Clancy; lighting, Scott Zielinski; sound, Jon Gottlieb; music, Peter Golub.

Mathias "Jim" Gold .... Peter Friedman	Chloe Giffard .... Jan Maxwell
Mathilde Giffard .... Sian Phillips	

One intermission.

SORROWS AND REJOICINGS. By Athol Fugard. May 22, 2002 (West Coast premiere). Director, Mr. Fugard; scenery and costumes, Susan Hilferty; lighting, Dennis Parichy; production stage managers, Alison Cote, James T. McDermott; stage manager, David S. Franklin.

Allison .... Judith Light	Rebecca .... Brienin Nequa Bryant
Marta .... Cynthia Martells	Dawid .... John Glover

Time: The present. Place: The living room of large house in a Karoo village in South Africa.

Mountain View Center for the Arts, Mountain View
Robert Kelley artistic director

SUMMER OF '42. Musical with book by Hunter Foster; music and lyrics by David Kirshenbaum; based on novel and screenplay by Herman Raucher. June 23, 2001 (world premiere). Director and choreographer, Gabriel Barre; musical direction, orchestrations, vocal arrangements, Lynne Shankel; scenery, James Youmans; costumes, Pamela Scofield; lighting, Tim Hunter; sound, Garth Hemphill. A TheatreWorks presentation.

Hermie .... Ryan Driscoll	Osey .... Brett Tabisel
Dorothy .... Kate Jennings Grant	Benjie .... Jason Marcus
Miriam .... Megan Valerie Walker	Mr. Sanders; Walter Winchell .... Bill Kux
Aggie .... Celia Keenan-Bolger	Pete .... Greg Stone
Gloria .... Erin Webley	

Musical numbers: "The Summer You'll Always Remember," "Unfinished Business," "You're Gonna Miss Me," "Little Did I Dream," "Will That Ever Happen to Me?" "Losing Track of Time," "The Walk," "Like They Used To," "I Think I Like Her," "Make You Mine," "The Movies," "Someone to Dance With Me," "The Heat," "The Drugstore," "The Campfire," "Promise of the Morning," "Oh Gee, How I Love My GI," "The Dance," "Finale."

Time: World War II. Place: Summer on New England coastal island. One intermission.

KEPT. Musical with book by Stephen Chbosky and Bill Russell; music by Henry Krieger; lyrics by Mr. Russell. Based on *Camille* by Alexandre Dumas. April 13, 2002. Director, Scott Schwartz; choreography, Andy Blankenbuehler; scenery, Robert Brill; costumes, Beaver Bauer; lighting, Pamila Gray; sound, Cliff Caruthers; musical director, Sam Davis; orchestrations, Harold Wheeler. A TheatreWorks presentation.

Caleigh	Christiane Noll	Mrs. Foster	Karen Murphy
Ian	Will Swenson	Glitterati	Emily Hsu, Brian Shepard,
Blake	Barrett Foa		Nicole Ruth Snelson, Andre Ward,
Brigitte	Brenda Braxton		Romar De Claro, Murphy Hart,
Marshall	Dennis Parlato		Val Kasvin, Nicole A. Tung

Musical numbers: "The Velvet Rope," "Let's Stay Out and Play," "I Wonder What You're Up To Now," "The Party's Just Begun," "Loving Me," "Every Breath and Thought," "This Woman Is Kept," "Why Are the Wrong People Rich?" "Something Isn't Right," "Seize the Night," "Escape," "Dancin' on the Shore," "Why Don't We Stay in Bed?" "I Like Knowing Where You Are," "A Little Loan," "Sacrifice," "When It's Time to Go," "It All Comes Down to Money," "A Cold Day in Hell," "Kept." One intermission.

Pasadena Playhouse, Pasadena

Sheldon Epps artistic director

FOREVER PLAID: A SPECIAL HOLIDAY EDITION. Musical revue by Stuart Ross. November 10, 2001 (world premiere). Director, Mr. Ross; music supervision and arrangements, James Raitt; scenery, Neil Peter Jampolis; costumes, Debra Stein; lighting, Jane Reisman; sound, Frederick W. Boot; production stage manager, Jill Gold.

Jinx	Leo Daignault	Sparky	Steve Gunderson
Smudge	John-Michael Flate	Frankie	Michael Winther

Musicians: David Snyder, piano; John Smith, bass.

THE BLUE ROOM. By David Hare; adapted from Arthur Schnitzler's *La Ronde*. March 17, 2002 (West Coast premiere). Director, David Schweizer; scenery, Christopher Acebo; costumes, Maggie Morgan; lighting, Geoff Korf; sound and music, Stafford Floyd; production stage manager, Lurie Horns Pfeffer.

The Woman	Arabella Field	The Man	Lenny Von Dohlen

A CLASS ACT. Musical with book by Linda Kline and Lonny Price; music and lyrics by Edward Kleban. May 13, 2002 (West Coast premiere). Director, Lonny Price; choreography, Marguerite Derricks; scenery, James Noone; costumes, Carrie Robbins; lighting, Yael Lubetsky (based on design by Kevin Adams); sound, Frederick W. Boot; musical direction, Steve Orich; production stage manager, Jill Gold.

Ed Kleban	Robert Picardo	Sophie	Luba Mason
Lehman Engel	Lenny Wolpe	Felicia	Nikki Crawford
Bobby; Michael Bennett	Andrew Palermo	Lucy	Donna Bullock
Charley; Marvin Hamlisch	Will Jude	Mona	Michelle Duffy

San Jose Repertory, San Jose

Timothy Near artistic director, Alexandra Urbanowski managing director

BY THE BOG OF CATS. By Marina Carr. September 14, 2001. Director, Timothy Near; scenery and costumes, Joe Vanek; lighting, Peter Maradudin; sound design, Jeff Mockus; music, Lunasa, Susan McKeown; stage manager, Jenny R. Friend.

Hester Swane .... Holly Hunter	Carthage Kilbride .... Gordon MacDonald
Ghost Fancier .... James Carpenter	Caroline Cassidy .... Gretchen Cleevely
Monica Murray .... Wanda McCaddon	Xavier Cassidy .... J.G. Hertzler
Josie Kilbride .... Jillian Lee Wheeler	Young Dunne; Waiter .... Alex Moggridge
Mrs. Kilbride .... Carol Mayo Jenkins	Father Willow .... Stuart Rudin
Catwoman .... Joan MacIntosh	Voice of Josie Swane .... Susan McKeown

One intermission.

LAS MENINAS. By Lynn Nottage. March 22, 2002. (world premiere). Director, Michael Donald Edwards; choreography, Carolyn Houser Carvajal, Marcus Cathey; scenery, Gordano Svilar; costumes, B. Modern; lighting, Robert Jared; sound, Jeff Mockus; stage manager, Nina Iventosch.

Louise Marie-Thérèse ... Rachel Zawadi Luttrell	Queen Mother;
Queen Marie-Thérèse .... Mercedes Herrero	Mother Superior .... Carol Mayo Jenkins
King Louis XIV .... Mark H. Dold	Painter; Doctor .... Ken Ruta
Nabo Sensugali .... Daniel Bryant	La Valliere .... Bren McElroy

With: Justin Buchs, Scott Nordquist, Eryka Raines, Kim Saunders, Megan Smith, Bryan Trybom.

Time: Louis XIV's reign. One intermission.

South Coast Repertory, Costa Mesa

David Emmes producing artistic director, Martin Benson artistic director

THE BEARD OF AVON. By Amy Freed. June 1, 2001 (world premiere). Director, David Emmes; choreography, Art Manke; scenery, Christopher Acebo; costumes, Walker Hicklin; lighting, Chris Parry; sound, B.C. Keller; music, Dennis McCarthy; dramaturgs, Jerry Patch, Jennifer Kiger; stage manager, Scott Harrison.

William Shakespeare .... Douglas Weston	Henry Condell; Walter Fitch;
Old Colin; Richard Burbage;	Sir Francis Bacon .... Robert Curtis Brown
Sir Francis Walsingham .... Richard Doyle	John Heminge; Lord Burghley;
Anne Hathaway .... Rene Augesen	Ben Jonson .... Don Took
Geoff Dunderbread;	Edward de Vere .... Mark Harelik
Lady Lettice .... Lynsey McLeod	Henry Wriothesley .... Todd Lowe
Michael Drayton; Ensemble .... Mark Coyan	Queen Elizabeth .... Nike Doukas
Ensemble .... Jessica Stevenson	

One intermission.

4th Annual Pacific Playwrights Festival, June 22–July 1, 2001.

CALIFORNIA SCENARIOS. By Luis Alfaro, Joann Faría, Anne Garcia-Romero, José Cruz González and Octavio Solis. Director, Juliette Carrillo.

NOSTALGIA. By Lucinda Cox. Director, Loretta Greco.

SWEATY PALMS. By Alejandro Morales. Director, Lisa Portes.

OUR TIGHT EMBRACE. By Jorge Ignacio Cortiñas. Director, Ruben Polendo.

HOLD PLEASE. By Annie Weisman. Director, Mark Rucker.

EYE TO EYE. By Kevin Heelan. Director, Seret Scott.

South Coast Repertory 2001–2002 Season

Above: Jillian Bach, Linda Gehringer, Kimberly King, Tessa Auberjonois in Hold Please. *Photo: Cristofer Gross*

Right: Laura Hinsberger, JD Cullum, Nicholas Hormann, Heath Freeman, Jennifer Griffin; (foreground) Assaf Cohen and Dileep Rao in Making It. *Photo: Henry DiRocco*

Below: Larry Drake, Susannah Schulman in Nostalgia. *Photo: Ken Howard*

GETTING FRANKIE MARRIED—AND AFTERWARDS. By Horton Foote. Director, Martin Benson.

SCAB. By Sheila Callaghan. Director, Olivia Honegger.

THE FALLS. By Hilary Bell. Director, Liz Diamond.

HOLD PLEASE. By Annie Weisman. September 21, 2001 (world premiere). Director, Mark Rucker; scenery, Christopher Acebo; costumes, Joyce Kim Lee; lighting, Geoff Korf; sound, Aram Arslanian; dramaturg, Jerry Patch; stage manager, Andy Tighe.

Erika .... Tessa Auberjonois   Jessica .... Jillian Bach
Agatha .... Kimberly King   Grace .... Linda Gehringer

NOSTALGIA. By Lucinda Coxon. November 2, 2001 (world premiere). Director, Juliette Carrillo; scenery, Myung Hee Cho; costumes, Alex Jaeger; lighting, John Martin; sound, Christopher Webb; dramaturg, Jennifer Kiger; stage manager, Vanessa Noon.

South Coast
Repertory
2001–2002
Season

Above: Kevin Corrigan and Simon Billig in Lobby Hero. *Ken Howard*

Left: Juliana Donald, Nan Martin and Joel Anderson in Getting Frankie Married—and Afterwards. *Photo: Ken Howard*

Buddug .... Susannah Schulman	Will .... Michael James Reed
Tom .... Daniel Blinkoff	Arthur .... Larry Drake

MAKING IT. By Joe Hortua. January 25, 2002 (world premiere). Director, David Emmes; scenery and costumes, Angela Balogh Calin; lighting, Geoff Korf; dramaturg, Jerry Patch; stage manager, Vanessa Noon.

Dora .... Jennifer Griffin	Mo .... Dileep Rao
Jack .... Heath Freeman	Haji .... Assaf Cohen
Paolo .... JD Cullum	Leonard .... Nicholas Hormann
Claire .... Laura Hinsberger	

LOBBY HERO. By Kenneth Lonergan. February 22, 2002 (West Coast premiere). Director, Olivia Honneger, scenery, Tony Fanning; costumes, Amy Hutto; lighting, Tammy Owens; sound and music, Aram Arslanian; stage manager, Scott Harrison.

Jeff .... Kevin Corrigan	Dawn .... Tessa Auberjonois
William ....T.E. Russell	Bill .... Simon Billig

THE DAZZLE. By Richard Greenberg. March 29, 2002 (West Coast premiere). Director, Mark Rucker; scenery, Darcy Scanlin; costumes, Nephelie Andonyadis; lighting, Geoff Korf; music and sound, Karl Fredrik Lundeberg; stage manager, Jamie A. Tucker.

Langley Collyer .... JD Cullum	Milly Ashmore .... Susannah Schulman
Homer Collyer .... Matt Roth	

    Time: Early to mid-20th century. Place: Collyer brownstone in Harlem. One intermission.

GETTING FRANKIE MARRIED—AND AFTERWARDS. By Horton Foote. April 5, 2002 (world premiere). Director, Martin Benson; scenery, Michael Devine; costumes, Maggie Morgan; lighting, Tom Ruzika; sound, Dennis McCarthy; dramaturg, Jerry Patch; stage manager, Randall K. Lum.

Constance .... Annie LaRussa	S.P. .... Hal Landon Jr.
Laverne .... Jennifer Parsons	Mrs. Willis .... Nan Martin
Mae .... Barbara Roberts	Isabel .... Kristen Lowman
Frankie ....Juliana Donald	Helen .... Sarah Rafferty
Fred .... Joel Anderson	Bill .... Jason Guess
Georgia Dale .... Linda Gehringer	Carleton .... Randy Oglesby

5th Annual Pacific Playwrights Festival, April–August 2002.
Readings, April 26–28, 2002.

    99 HISTORIES. By Julia Cho. April 26, 2002. Director, Chay Yew.

    EXPOSED. By Beth Henley. April 26, 2002. Director, Mark Rucker.

    INTIMATE APPAREL. By Lynn Nottage. April 27, 2002. Director, Kate Whoriskey.

    TRUTH AND BEAUTY. By Steven Drukman. April 27, 2002. Director, Douglas C. Wager.

    OUR BOY. By Julia Jordan. April 28, 2002. Director, Lisa Peterson.

COLORADO

Denver Center Theatre Company, Denver
Donovan Marley artistic director, Barbara E. Sellers producing director

CYRANO DE BERGERAC. By Edmond Rostand. New translation and adaptation by Nagle Jackson. October 4, 2001. Director, Mr. Jackson; scenery, Rosario Provenza;

costumes, Andrew V. Yelusich; lighting, Dawn Chiang; sound, David R. White; fight direction, J. Steven White.

Cyrano de Bergerac .... Bill Christ	Father; Bertrandou .... Louis Schaefer
Christian de Neuvillette .... Ryan Shively	Son; Apprentice; Cadet .... Justin Yorio
Count de Guiche .... Mario Cabrera	Pickpocket;
Roxanne .... Libby West	Spanish soldier .... M. Ben Newman
Ragueneau ....John Innes	Lady; Lise ....January Murelli
Le Bret .... Greg Thornton	Lady; Mother
Captain Carbon de Castel............. Scott Meikle	Marguerite .... Tracy Shaffer Witherspoon
Ligniere; Sentry .... Randy Moore	Columbina .... Sara Gwyn Lane
Montfleury; Pastry Cook;	Flower Girl; Sister
A Capuchin Monk .... Christopher Leo	Claire .... Sarah Wayne Callies
Jodelet .... Tony Church	Pierrot; Cadet; Servant .... Jason Henning
A Musketeer; Cadet .... Erik Tieze	Citizen; Cadet ....Chad Henry
Valvert; Spanish Officer .... Gareth Saxe	Citizen; Cadet ....Jonathan Clapham
The Duenna .... Gabriella Cavallero	Soldier; Cadet .... Dan O'Neill
Yellow Marquis; Pastry Cook;	Harlequin;Cadet .... Adam Gordon
Cadet .... Scott Janes	Boy .... Matt Waysdorf
Blue Marquis; Cadet .... Raymond L. Chapman	Girl ....Chelsea Cusack

Act I: An evening at the theater. Act II: The poet's pastry shop; Act III: The kiss. Act IV: The siege of Arras; Act V: Cyrano's Gazette. One intermission.

THE IMMIGRANT. Musical with book by Mark Harelik; music by Steven M. Alper; lyrics by Sara Knapp; based on the play by Mr. Harelik. January 24, 2002. Director, Randal Myler; scenery, Ralph Funicello; costumes, Andrew V. Yelusich; lighting, Don Darnutzer; sound, David R. White.

Haskell ....Adam Heller	Milton .... Walter Charles
Leah ....Jacqueline Antaramian	Ima .... Cass Morgan

Time: 1909. Place: Hamilton, Texas. One intermission.

ALMOST HEAVEN: SONGS AND STORIES OF JOHN DENVER. Musical adapted by Peter Glazer; songs by John Denver and others. March 28, 2002 (world premiere). Director, Mr. Glazer; scenery, James Dardenne; costumes, Michael Krass; lighting, Dawn Chiang; sound, Tony Meola; musical direction, Jeff Waxman; video and projection design, John Boesche. Presented in association with Harold Thau.

Ensemble: Lisa Asher, Emily Bauer, Allison Briner, Sean Jenness, Bryan Scott Johnson, David Ranson.

Musicians: Jeff Waxman, David DeMichelis, Tony Marcus, Johnny Neill, Tony Pantelis, Mark Simon, Chris Soucy.

One intermission.

PIERRE. By Jeffrey Hatcher; adapted from Herman Melville's *Pierre, or the Ambiguities*. May 16, 2002 (world premiere). Director, Bruce K. Sevy; choreography and fight direction, Colleen Kelly; scenery, Vicki Smith; costumes, Kevin Copenhaver and Andrew V. Yelusich; lighting, Don Darnutzer; sound, David R. White; music, Gary Grundei; stage manager, Lyle Raper.

Pierre Glendinning .... Christopher Kelly	Servants ....Jillian LaVinka, Khris Lewin,
Mary Glendinning .... Gordana Rashovich	Richard Liccardo, John Pieza,
Dorothea Glendinning .... Caitlin O'Connell	Christopher Webb
Glen Glendinning .... John G. Preston	Lucy Tartan .... Shannon Koob
Dates... Randy Moore	Captain Fred Tartan .... Erik Tieze
Young Pierre .... David Strouse	The Reverend Falsgrave ...... Marcus Waterman
Party Guests .... Lindsay Campbell,	The Miss Pennies .... Gloria Biegler,
Steven Cole Hughes	Kathleen M. Brady

Denver Center
Theatre
2001–2002
Season

*Above: Bill Christ and
Libby West in* Cyrano.
Photo: Terry Shapiro

Right: Adam Heller in
The Immigrant. *Photo:
Terry Shapiro*

*Below: Kathleen M. Brady,
Gloria Biegler and Morgan
Hallett in* Pierre. *Photo:
Terry Shapiro*

Wretches .... Catie Baumer,
Lindsay Campbell, Jillian LaVinka,
Richard Liccardo, David Strouse,
Roslyn Terré
Isabel .... Morgan Hallett
Delly Ulver .... Catie Baumer
Charlie Millthorpe .... Aaron Serotsky
Tavern Denizens .... Steven Cole Hughes,
Khris Lewin, John Pieza,
Christopher Webb
The Waif .... Lindsay Campbell
The Sexton .... Chad Henry
The Keeper .... Bill Christ
His Henchman .... Khris Lewin
Denizens of Five Points .... Gloria Biegler,
Kathleen M. Brady, Lindsay Campbell,
Chad Henry, Jillian LaVinka, Khris Lewin
One intermission.

Denizens of Five Points .... Richard Liccardo,
Randy Moore, Caitlin O'Connell,
John Pieza, Roslyn Terré, Christopher Webb
Glen's Maid .... Kathleen M. Brady
Glen's Party Guests .... Lindsay Campbell,
Jillian LaVinka
Van Renssalaer Vanderhost .... Bill Christ
Savoyard Boy .... David Strouse
A Policeman .... Steven Cole Hughes
The Auctioneer .... Christopher Webb
Woman in Turban .... Kathleen M. Brady
Mademoiselle Huvert .... Gloria Biegler
Jailer .... Chad Henry
Auction Clients: Lindsay Campbell, Chad
Henry, Steven Cole Hughes, Jillian LaVinka,
Khris Lewin, Richard Liccardo, Randy Moore,
Caitlin O'Connell, John Pieza, Roslyn Terré.

New Play Readings, June 12–15, 2001

CAROL MULRONEY. By Stephen Belber. Director, Anthony Powell.

Carol Mulroney .... Catie Baumer
Joan Camden .... Tracy Shaffer Witherspoon
Lesley Dane .... Erik Tieze
Ken .... Bobby Daye
Hutton .... William Whitehead

THE CATERERS. By Nagle Jackson. Director, Mr. Jackson.

The Hostess .... Kate Levy
The Host .... Randy Moore
Crystal .... Ora Jones
Elsbeth .... Sara Gwyn Lane
Ravi .... Billöah Greene
Billy .... John Pieza
Ernie .... Jennifer Schelter

SOMEPLACE SOFT TO FALL. By S.M. Shephard-Massat. Director, Israel Hicks.

Beverly Print .... Kim Staunton
Louise Trimming .... Vivian Reed
Jessie Hubble .... January Murelli
William Samuel Print .... Roger Robinson
Morris Joseph Hubble .... Keith L. Hatten

GREEK HOLIDAY. By Mayo Simon. Director, Mr. Simon.

Alex .... Marcus Waterman
Debra .... Caitlin O'Connell
Janet .... Annette Helde

8 BOB OFF. By Gary Leon Hill. Director, David Dower.

Bob Plum .... Jamie Horton
Donna .... O-Lan Jones
Bobby .... Alton Fitzgerald White

SHOVE. By Mark Eisman. Director, Bruce K. Sevy.

Genette .... Kimberly JaJuan
Cathy .... Kathleen M. Brady
Selden .... Richard Liccardo
Lowell .... Jonathan Clapham

TWO FUGUES AND AN ARIA: MAGDA, JAN AND DANIELA. by David F. Eliet. Director, Donovan Marley.

Knocking

Magda .... April Shawhan
The Investigator .... Ron Cephas Jones
The Voice of the Others ...... Dennis Robertson

Shadows

Jan .... John Innes
The Prompter .... Dennis Robertson

Daniela's Aria

Daniela .... Gordana Rashovich
The Listener .... Betty Low

THE GENIUS OF THE SYSTEM. By John W Lowell. Director, Larry Hecht.

David .... John Hutton
John .... Mark Rubald

Eric .... Jason Henning

THE DEBATING SOCIETY. By Michael R. Murphy. Director, Randal Myler.

Drew Arquette .... Christopher Webb
Gil Hernandez .... Khris Lewin
Lane Schemerinski .... Sarah Wayne Callies

Tom Fabiani .... Adam Gordon
Nathan Anderson .... Justin Yorio

CONNECTICUT

Goodspeed Opera House, East Haddam

Michael P. Price executive director, Sue Frost associate producer, Michael O'Flaherty music director

ACTOR, LAWYER, INDIAN CHIEF. Musical with book by David H. Bell; music and lyrics, Craig Carnelia. May 15, 2002 (regional premiere). Director, Mr. Bell; choreography, Kay Cole; scenery, Robert Little; costumes, Susan E. Mickey; lighting, Diane Ferry Williams; sound, Jay Hilton; production stage manager, Robert V. Thurber.

Jim .... Mark Edgar Stephens
Jimmy (at 9 years old) .... Jacob Heimer
Benjamin Gurney .... Hal Robinson
"Red Rock" Brody .... Brad Anderson
Jenny Gurney .... Lisa Brescia
Barry .... Reed Birney
Stanage .... Doug Ballard

Jon .... Hunter Bell
Grant Parker .... Blake Adams
The Three Cowboys
  Boss .... Craig Carnelia
  Shep .... Kevyn Morrow
  Billy .... Roger Seyer

Musicians: Dennis Arcano, Steve Gilewski, Sonny Landolfi, Heather Luellen, Lisa Rautenberg.

Hartford Stage, Hartford

Michael Wilson artistic director, James Ireland managing director

THE CARPETBAGGER'S CHILDREN. By Horton Foote. September 7, 2001. A co-production with the Alley Theatre in Houston and the Guthrie Theater in Minneapolis. See the Alley Theatre (Houston, Texas) for production details.

NECESSARY TARGETS. By Eve Ensler. December 5, 2001 (world premiere). Director, Michael Wilson; scenery, Jeff Cowie; costumes, Susan Hilferty; lighting, Howell Binkley; music and sound, John Gromada; production stage manager, Wendy Beaton. Presented by special arrangement with Harriet Newman Leve and Willa Shalit.

J.S. .... Shirley Knight
Melissa .... Catherine Kellner
Jelena .... Alyssa Bresnahan
Azra .... Sally Parrish
  No intermission.

Nuna .... Maria Thayer
Zlata .... Diane Venora
Zeada .... Marika Dominiczyk

TEA AT FIVE. By Matthew Lombardo. February 13, 2002 (world premiere). Director, John Tillinger; scenery, Tony Straiges; costumes, Jess Goldstein; lighting, Kevin Adams; music and sound, John Gromada; production stage manager, Christa Bean.

Katherine Hepburn .... Kate Mulgrew

Time: Act I: September 1938. Place: Katharine Hepburn's "cottage" in Fenwick, Conn., on Long Island Sound. Act II: February 1983, after Hepburn was injured in a car crash.

CONSTANT STAR. By Tazewell Thompson. April 26, 2002. (New England premiere). Director, Mr. Thompson; scenery, Donald Eastman; costumes, Merrily Murray-Walsh; lighting, Robert Wierzel; sound, Fabian Obispo; musical direction and musical arrangements, Dianne Adam McDowell.

Tina Fabrique, Cheryl Freeman, Janeece A. Freeman, Gail Grate and Shona Tucker played the role of Ida B. Wells in various ages and circumstances.

Brand: NEW Festival of New Works. May 16–May 19, 2002.

DIOSA. By Edwin Sanchez. Director, Melia Bensussen.

THE SAVAGES OF HARTFORD. By David Grimm. Director, Shelley Butler.

CONVICTIONS! By Eve Ensler. Director, Michael Wilson.

WELL. By Lisa Kron. Director, Leigh Silverman.

Long Wharf Theatre, New Haven
Greg Leaming acting artistic director, Michael Ross, managing director

AN INFINITE ACHE. By David Schulner. December 19, 2001. (world premiere). Director, Greg Leaming; scenery, Marjorie Bradley Kellogg; costumes, David Zinn; lighting, Dan Kotlowitz; music and sound, Fabian Obispo; production stage managers, Kevin E. Thompson, Stephen McCorkle.

Hope .... Angel Desai   Charles .... Peter A. Smith

Place: An empty bedroom. No intermission.

YELLOWMAN. April 10, 2002. By Dael Orlandersmith. A co-production of McCarter Theatre (Princeton, New Jersey) and Wilma Theater (Philadelphia, Pennsylvania). See production details under McCarter Theatre.

In the Works Series

GONE NATIVE. By Steven Drukman. October 29, 2001. Director, Greg Leaming.

ROSEMARY & I. By Leslie Ayvazian. January 7, 2002. Director, Rebecca Bayla Taichman.

LIGHT RAISE THE ROOF. By Kia Corthron. May 17, 2002. Director, Michael John Garcés.

Yale Repertory Theatre, New Haven
Stan Wojewodski Jr. artistic director

It Pays to Advertise. By Roi Cooper Megrue and Walter Hackett. December 4, 2001. Director, Stan Wojewodski Jr.; scenery, Robin Vest; costumes, Melissa McVay; lighting, Paul Whitaker; sound, Mimi Epstein; stage manager, Cynthia Kocher.

Mary Grayson .... Sarah Rafferty
Johnson; George McChesney .... Bob Freschi
La Contesse de Beaurien .... Henny Russell
Rodney Martin .... Adam Greer
Cyrus Martin .... Jack Davidson

Ambrose Peale .... Michael McGrath
Marie; Miss Burke .... Marnye Young
William Smith; Arthur Bronson ..... Drew Scott
Ellery Clark .... Matthew Humphreys

One intermission.

Connecticut Repertory Theatre, Storrs

Gary M. English artistic director, Robert Wildman managing director

WINGS. Musical with book and lyrics by Arthur Perlman; music by Jeffrey Lunden; based on the play by Arthur Kopit. July 20, 2001 (New England premiere). Director, Gary M. English; scenery, Tim Hunter; costumes, Melissa C. Richards; sound, Nick Borisjuk; musical director, Ken Clark; production stage manager, Melinda Lamoreux.

Emil Stilson	Florence Lacey	Amy	Wendy Saver
Doctor; Mr. Brambilla	Ken O'Brien	Billy	Richard Ruiz
Nurse; Mrs. Timmins	Mary E. Hodges		

Musical numbers: Prologue, "Catastrophe," "Globbidge," "Wait-Stop-Hold-Cut," "My Name Then," "All in All" (I), "Make Your Naming Powers," "I'll Come Back to That" (I), "I'll Come Back to That" (II), "Yum Yummy Yum," "I'll Come Back to That" (III), "Tither," "All in All" (II), "I Don't Trust Him," "Malacats," "Needle," "Out on the Wing," "I Wonder What's Inside," "Let Me Call You Sweetheart," "A Recipe for Cheesecake," "Like the Clouds," "Preparing for Flight," "Snow," "Wings."

No intermission.

BRUTALITY OF FACT. By Keith Reddin. November 1, 2001. (Connecticut premiere). Director, Kristin Wold; scenery, Vilai Bouttaphom and Tim Saternow; costumes, Pamela Ann Prior; lighting, Brendon D. Boyd; sound, Nathan Leigh; stage manager, Carola Morrone.

Jackie	Rebecca Mikan	Chris	David Polanski
Maggie	Briana Trautman-Maier	Corinne; Kate	Leah Fine
Val	Judy Baird	Harold	Stephen Graybill
Judy; Amy; Janet	Dana L. Wilson	Marlene	Meredith Bowen, Julie Stein

One intermission.

THE TROJAN WOMEN. By Euripides; adapted by Eric Hill. February 28, 2002. Director, Mr. Hill; scenery, Tim Saternow; costumes, Olivera Gájic; lighting, Brendon D. Boyd; sound, Jason A. Tratta; production stage manager, Bradley G. Spachman.

Poseidon	Eric Hill	Greek Soldier	Kevin DeChello
Hecuba	Geraldine Librandi	Greek Soldier	Willie Dixon-Peay
First Woman	Dana L. Wilson	Greek Soldier	Michael McComiskey
Second Woman	Chriselle Almeida	Greek Soldier	Andrew McLeod
Third Woman	Maire-Rose Conlon	Greek Soldier	Joe Therrien
Fourth Woman	Victoria Caciopoli	Cassandra	Tara Franklin
Fifth Woman	Jackie Burns	Priam's Ghost	Robert McDonald
Sixth Woman	Lindsay Benner	Andromache	Jill Michael
Talthybius	Chris Bolden	Menelaus	John Lysaght
Greek Soldier	Rich Clemens	Helen	Tamara Williams

No intermission.

Eugene O'Neill Theater Center, Waterbury

James Houghton artistic director, Howard Sherman executive director, Thomas Viertel chairman of the board, George C. White founder, Paulette Haupt artistic director of the Music Theater Conference.

O'Neill Playwrights Conference (Staged Readings, June 28–July 22, 2001)

SMASHING. By Brooke Berman.

BLACK SHEEP. By Lee Blessing.

LUCY AND THE CONQUEST. By Cusi Cram.

MRS. PLENTY HORSES. By Judy GeBauer.

GUINEVERE. By Gina Gionfriddo.

SODOM AND GOMORRAH. By Jean Giraudoux, translated by Michael Feingold.

YES, PLEASE AND THANK YOU. By Kirsten Greenridge.

GOING HOME. By Karen Hartman.

OLD WOMAN FLYING. By Susan Johnston.

THE BREAD OF WINTER. By Victor Lodato.

EIGHTEEN. By Allison Moore.

MOVING PICTURE. By Dan O'Brien.

FINER NOBLE GASES. By Adam Rapp.

FRAME 312. By Keith Reddin.

Directors: Daniel Aukin, Melia Bensussen, Walter Bobbie, Stephen Beckler, Susan V. Booth, Carolyn Cantor, Liz Diamond, David Esbjornson, Daniel Fish, Gerald Freedman, Michael John Garcés, Melanie Martin Long, Pam MacKinnon, Ethan McSweeney, Jerry Mitchell, Evan Yionoulis, Harris Yulin.

O'Neill Music Theater Conference (Staged Concert Readings, July 20–August 11, 2001)

TAKE FLIGHT. Musical with book by Marsha Norman, lyrics by Richard Maltby Jr., music by David Shire.

THE ROAD TO HOLLYWOOD. Musical with book by Michael Pace and Walter Bobbie; music and lyrics by Rob Preston and Mr. Pace.

Directors: Stephen Beckler, Walter Bobbie, Jerry Mitchell.

Seven Angels Theatre, Waterbury
Semina De Laurentis artistic director

BREAKING OUT OF SUNSET PLACE. By Patricia Barry Rumble. November 10, 2001 (world premiere). Director, Dante Albertie; scenery, Tom Gleeson; costumes, Irene V. Hatch; lighting, Nicole Coppinger; sound, Asa F. Wember; production stage manager, Stacy A. Blackburn.

Olivia Wilson	Georgia Creighton	The Female .... Rose McGuire
Emmy Montalbano	Jayne Heller	The Male .... William Watkins
Maudie Martinette	Sharita Hunt	

Time: Present. Many locations from Texas to Georgia. One intermission.

Westport Country Playhouse, Westport
Joanne Woodward artistic director

TEMPORARY HELP. By David Wiltse. August 31, 2001. Director, Gordon Edelstein; scenery; Derek McLane; costumes, Jennifer von Mayrhauser; lighting, Kenneth Posner; sound, Jerry M. Yager; sound design, Stephen LeGrand; music, Bill Frisell; production stage manager, Adrienne Willis. Originally workshopped at New Haven's Long Wharf Theatre in 1990–91. Presented by special arrangement with ShadowCatcher Entertainment.

Karl Streber	Jeffrey DeMunn	Ron Stucker .... Sam Freed
Faye Streber	Karen Allen	Vincent Castelnuovo-Tedesco .... Chad Allen

White Barn Theatre, Westport
Vincent Curcio producer

THE COLOSSUS OF RHODES. By Carey Perloff. August 3, 2001 (world premiere). Director, Loy Arcenas; scenery and lighting, Leo B. Meyer; costumes, James Parks Jr.; music, Catherine Reid, sound, Fabian Obispo; musical director, Stephen Hinnenkamp; production stage manager, Kimothy Cruse.

Barney Barnato	Dennis Boutsikaris	James Anderon; John Ruskin;	
Cecil Rhodes	Reg Rogers	Dr. Leander;	
Charles Rudd	Michel R. Gill	Starr Jameson	Sam Tsoutsouvas
Randall Pickering	David Adkins	Piano Man	Stephen Hinnenkamp

One intermission.

SAD HOTEL. By David Foley. August 24, 2001 (world premiere). Director, Burry Fredrik; scenery and lighting, Leo B. Meyer; costumes, Katherine Hampton; production stage manager, Patrick Ballard.

Tom	Sam Tsoutsouvas	Pedro	Jai Rodriguez
Kit	Angela Pietropinto	Mary	Gwendolyn Lewis
Frank	Omar Prince	Nurse	Marilyn Moore

Time: 1970. Place: A house on the Florida coast. One intermission.

SHEBA. Musical with book and lyrics by Lee Goldsmith; music by Cliff Ballard Jr.; based on the play *Come Back, Little Sheba* by William Inge. August 31, 2001 (regional premiere). Director, Leslie B. Cutler; choreography, Donald Saddler; scenery and lighting, Leo B. Meyer; costumes, Katherine Hampton; sound, Kevin McMahon; orchestrations, Ralph Burns; musical director, Glen Clugston; production stage manager, Kimothy Cruse.

Lola	Donna McKechnie	Ed Anderson	Alden Fulcomer
Doc	Mark Peters	Elmo	Don Rey
Marie	Rachel Hardin	Lola's Dream Suitors	Alden Fulcomer,
Turk	Braden Miles		Thomas J. Miller, Don Rey,
Milkman	Thomas J. Miller		Billy Hartung

Place: A shabbily furnished kitchen and living room. One intermission.

DISTRICT OF COLUMBIA

Arena Stage, Washington, D.C.
Molly Smith artistic director, Stephen Richard executive director

AGAMEMNON AND HIS DAUGHTERS. By Kenneth Cavander; adapted from the plays of Aeschylus, Euripides and Sophocles. September 7, 2001. Director, Molly Smith; choreography, Karma Camp; scenery and lighting, Pavel Dobrusky; costumes, Lindsay Davis; sound, Fabian Obispo; dramaturg, Michael Kinghorn.

Agamemnon	Jack Willis	Kassandra	Tsidii LeLoka
Klytaimestra	Gail Grate	Achilles; Pylades	Ezra Knight
Iphigeneia	Marta Ann Lastufka	Pythoness	Colleen Delany
Elektra	Natascia Diaz	Artemis	Naomi Jacobson
Chrysothemis	Maia DeSanti	Lookout	Rebecca Rice
Orestes	Paolo Andino	Menelaos; Thoas	Kurt Rhoads
Aigisthos; Talthybios	Andrew Long	Priest; Soldier	Stephen Patrick Martin

The Greek chorus: Saskia DeVries, Paula Gruskiewicz, Rosemary Knower, Greta Pemberton.

THE SOUTHWEST PROJECT. November 3, 2001. With Rebecca Rice. An oral history-based performance using stories, histories and ideas of the Southwest.

POLK COUNTY. By Zora Neale Hurston and Dorothy Waring; adapted by Kyle Donnelly and Cathy Madison. April 5, 2002 (world premiere). Director, Kyle Donnelly; scenery, Tom Lynch; lighting, Allen Lee Hughes; costumes, Paul Tazewell; music director, Stephen Wade; stage manager, Susan White.

Big Sweet	Harriett D. Foy	Bunch	Ida Elrod Eustis
Lonnie	David Toney	Laura B	Gabrielle Goyette
Leafy Lee	Gin Hammond	Few Clothes	Bus Howard
My Honey	Clinton Derricks-Carroll	Do-Dirty	Keith N. Johnson
Stew Beef	Andre Montgomery	Maudella	Sherri LaVie Linton
Ella Wall	E. Faye Butler	Boxcar	Yusef Miller
Nunkie	Rudy Roberson	Preacher	S. Robert Morgan
Sop-the-Bottom	Carl J. Cofield	Quarters Boss	Hugh Nees

One intermission.

Readings: First Glance

HORTENSIA AND THE MUSEUM OF DREAMS. By Nilo Cruz. October 18, 2001. Director, Molly Smith.

BLACK SHEEP. By Lee Blessing. October 19, 2001. Director, Wendy C. Goldberg.

BEAUTIFUL AGAIN. By Melanie Marnich. October 20, 2001. Director, Tim Vasen.

WHEN GRACE COMES IN. By Heather McDonald. October 26–27, 2001. Director, Eric Schaeffer.

Building Bridges. A reading series dedicated to new Latin American plays and playwrights.

I REGRET SHE IS MADE OF SUGAR. By Rogelio Martinez. March 15, 2002. Director, Jose Carrasquillo.

TIGHT EMBACE. By Jorge Ignacio Cortiñas. March 16, 2002. Director, Michael Kinghorn.

Discovering the Future. A reading series dedicated to the next generation of American playwrights and their mentors.

APPRECIATION. By Francine Volpe. March 28, 2002. (The Juilliard School)

THE MYSTERY PLAYS. By Roberto Aguirre-Sacasa. March 29, 2002. (Yale School of Drama).

LAST DANCE. By Marsha Norman. March 30, 2002.

SUMMER. By Edith Wharton; adapted by John Strand. April 6, 2002.

The Kennedy Center Sondheim Celebration
Eric Schaeffer artistic director, Max Woodward producer

SWEENEY TODD. Musical with book by Hugh Wheeler; music and lyrics by Stephen Sondheim. May 12, 2002. Director, Christopher Ashley; choreography, Daniel Pelzig; scenery, Derek McLane; costumes, David C. Woolard; lighting, Howell Binkley; sound, Tom Morse; musical direction, Larry Blank.

Anthony Hope	Hugh Panaro	Mrs. Lovett	Christine Baranski
Sweeney Todd	Brian Stokes Mitchell	Judge Turpin	Walter Charles
Beggar Woman	Mary Beth Peil	The Beadle	Ray Friedeck

Johnanna .... Celia Keenan-Bolger	Jonas Fogg .... Steven Cupo
Tobias Ragg .... Mark Price	Bird Seller .... Tim Tourbin
Pirelli .... Kevin Ligon	Gravedigger .... Eric Lee Johnson

With: Alan Araya, Ilona Dulaski, Daniel Felton, Michael L. Forrest, Janine Gulisano, Deanna Harris, Larry Hylton, Bob McDonald, Jane Pesci-Townsend, Teresa Reid, Nanette Savard, Susan Wheeler.

COMPANY. Musical with book by George Furth; music and lyrics by Stephen Sondheim. May 19, 2002. Director, Sean Mathias; choreography, Jodi Moccia; scenery, Derek McLane; costumes, Catherine Zuber; lighting, Howell Binkley; sound, Tom Morse.

Joanne .... Lynn Redgrave	Amy .... Alice Ripley
Robert .... John Barrowman	Paul .... Matt Bogart
Kathy .... Elizabeth Zins	

With: Christy Baron, Dan Cooney, Kim Director, Marcy Harriell, Jerry Lanning, Keira Naughton, David Pittu, Emily Skinner, Marc Vietor.

Florida

Caldwell Theatre Company, Boca Raton
Michael Hall artistic and managing director

CONCERTINA'S RAINBOW. By Glyn O'Malley. November 4, 2001 (world premiere). Director, Michael Hall; scenery, Tim Bennett; costumes, Penny Koleos Williams; lighting, Thomas Salzman; sound, Steve Shapiro; stage manager, Marci A. Glotzer.

Maureen ....Jacqueline Knapp	Stewardess; Elfriede;
Woolfie; Waiter; Pedja .... Jason Field	Anne; Frau Steiglitz .... Jessica K. Peterson
Maisy .... Elizabeth Perry	Little Maisy;
Mrs. Slakovanjik .... Harriet Oser	Concertina .... Tiffany Leigh Moskow

Place: En route to Vienna.

OUT OF SEASON. By Elinor Jones. February 17, 2002 (world premiere). Director, Michael Hall; scenery, Tim Bennett; costumes, Patricia Burdett; lighting, Thomas Salzman; sound, Steve Shapiro; stage manager, Lisa Lamont.

Ginnie....................................... Lisa Bansavage	Florence .... Sloane Shelton
Bess ....Elizabeth Dimon	Sally Ann .... Nancy Hess
Cora ....Angie Radosh	

SONGS OF PARADISE: A "NEWISH" MUSICAL. Book and additional lyrics by Miriam Hoffman and Rena Borow; music by Rosalie Gerut; lyrics by Itzik Manger; English translation by Avi Hoffman; based on stories from the book of Genesis. April 7, 2002 (world premiere). Director, Mr. Hoffman; choreography, Barbara Flaten; scenery, Tim Bennett; costumes, Estela Vrancovich; lighting, Thomas Salzman; sound, Steve Shapiro; stage manager, James Danford.

Cast: Elizabeth Dimon, Jason Field, Avi Hoffman, Margery Lowe, Lisa Neubauer.

Musicians: Michael Larsen musical director and pianist, Rupert Ziawinski bass, Julie Jacobs bass.

Asolo Theatre Company, Sarasota
Howard J. Millman producing artistic director

THE TALE OF THE ALLERGIST'S WIFE. By Charles Busch. March 15, 2002 (regional premiere). Director, Josephine Abady; scenery, Jeffrey W. Dean; costumes, Vicki S. Holden; lighting, James D. Sale; sound, Matthew Parker; stage manager, Juanita Munford.

Mohammed .... Jimmie Galaites
Marjorie Taub .... Carolyn Michel
Ira Taub.............................. Howard J. Millman
Frieda .... Barbara Winters Pinto
Lee Green .... Sharon Spelman

Time: Today. Place: Manhattan. One intermission.

GEORGIA

Alliance Theatre Company, Atlanta
Susan V. Booth artistic director, Gus Stuhlreyer managing director

SLEEPWALKERS. By Jorge Ignacio Cortiñas. April 17, 2002. Director, Ruben Polendo; scenery, Scott Spahr; costumes, Carol Bailey; lighting, Dawn Chiang; sound, Clay Benning; stage manager, Lark Hackshaw; dramaturg, Megan Monaghan.

Tito .... Nick Bixby
Soldier .... Mateo Gomez
Skinny Woman .... Michelle Rios
Pionera, age 12 .... Sophia Salguero
Charley .... Rafael Sardina
Orderly; Bloody Butcher;
   Tourist .... Liam Torres

Time: 1993. Place: central Havana.

ILLINOIS

Court Theatre, Chicago
Charles Newell artistic director, Diane Clausen executive director

THE CHAIRS. By Eugène Ionesco; translated by Martin Crimp. November 17, 2001. Director, Martin Platt; scenery, Geoffrey Curley; costumes, Mara Blumenfeld; lighting, Joel Moritz; sound, Lindsay Jones; dramaturg, Celise Kalke; production stage manager, Ellen Hay.

Old Woman................................... Hollis Resnik
Old Man .... Jeff Still
The Orator .... Brendan Averett

Place: A tower surrounded by water.

MY FAIR LADY. Musical with book and lyrics by Alan Jay Lerner, music by Frederick Loewe; adapted from George Bernard Shaw's play and Gabriel Pascal's film of *Pygmalion*. April 18, 2002. Director, Gary Griffin; scenery, John Culbert; costumes, Nan Cibula-Jenkins; lighting, Christine Binder; sound, Bruce Holland; musical direction, Tom Murray; dramaturg, Celise Kalke; production stage manager, Eric Eligator.

Professor Henry Higgins .... Kevin Gudahl
Costermonger; Charles .... Jason Sharp
Eliza Doolittle .... Kate Fry
Freddy Eynsford-Hill...................... Ned Noyes
Mrs. Freddy Eynsford-Hill;
   Angry Woman .... Kymberly Mellen
Colonel Hugh Pickering .... John Reeger
Alfred P. Doolittle .... Bradley Mott
Mrs. Pearce .... Ora Jones
Butler; Zoltan Karpathy .... Neil Friedman
Mrs. Higgins........................ Marilynn Bogetich
Conductor; Piano 1 .... Ritch Keitel
Piano 2 .... Jamie Schmidt

Musical Numbers, Act I: "Why Can't the English," "Wouldn't It Be Loverly?" "With a Bit of Luck," "I'm An Ordinary Man," "Just You Wait," "The Rain in Spain," "I Could Have Danced All Night, " "Ascot Gavotte," "On the Street Where You Live," "The Embassy Waltz." Act II: "You Did It," "Show Me," "The Flower Market," "Get Me to the Church On Time," "Hymn to Him," "Without You," "I've Grown Accustomed to Her Face."

Time: 1912. Place: London, England. One intermission.

Goodman Theatre, Chicago
Robert Falls artistic director, Roche Schulfer executive director

BLUE SURGE. By Rebecca Gilman. July 9, 2001 (world premiere). Director, Robert Falls; scenery, Walt Spangler; costumes, Birgit Rattenborg Wise; lighting, Michael Philippi; sound, Richard Woodbury; production stage manager, Alden Vasquez.

Curt	Joe Forbrich	Heather	Rebecca Jordan
Sandy	Rachel Miner	Beth	Amy Landecker
Doug	Steve Key		

Place: Small Midwestern City. One intermission.

THE VISIT. Musical with book by Terrence McNally; music by John Kander; lyrics by Fred Ebb. October 1, 2001 (world premiere). Based on the play by Friedrich Dürrenmatt. Director, Frank Galati; choreography, Ann Reinking; scenery, Derek McLane; costumes, Susan Hilferty; lighting, Brian MacDevitt; sound, Robert Milburn, Michael Bodeen; orchestrations, Michael Gibson; musical direction, vocal and dance arrangements, David Loud; production stage manager, Joseph Drummond.

Claire Zachanassian	Chita Rivera	Young Claire	Tina Cannon
Anton Schell	John McMartin	Mathilde Schell	Ami Silvestre
The Schoolmaster	Steven Sutcliffe	Karl	Guy Adkins
The Mayor	Mark Jacoby	Ottile	Cristen Paige
The Mayor's wife	McKinley Carter	Rudi	James Harms
The Doctor	Jim Corti	Louis Perch	Mark Crayton
The Priest	Jonathan Weir	Jacob Chicken	Raymond Zrinsky
The Police Inspector	Joseph Deliger	Lenny	Rob Hatzenbeller
Young Anton	Brian Herriott	Benny	Matt Orlando

With: Scott Calcagno, Tina Cannon, Roberta Duchak, John Eskola, Rosalyn Rahn Keirns, Leisa Mather, Adam Pelty, Greg Walter, Bernie Yvon.

Musical numbers: "Out of the Darkness," "At Last," "A Happy Ending," "You, You, You," "I Know Claire," "You Know Me," "Look at Me," "All You Need to Know," "A Masque," "Eunuchs' Testimony," "Winter," "Yellow Shoes," Chorale, "A Confession," "I Would Never Leave You," "Back and Forth," "The Only One," "A Car Ride," "Winter" (Reprise), "Love and Love Alone," "In the Forest Again," Finale.

HOLLYWOOD ARMS. By Carrie Hamilton and Carol Burnett. Based on Carol Burnett's memoir, *One More Time*. April 28, 2002 (world premiere). Director, Hal Prince; scenery, Walt Spangler; costumes, Judith Dolan; lighting, Howell Binkley; sound, Robert Milburn, Michael Bodeen; production stage manager, Joseph Drummond.

Nanny	Linda Lavin	Malcolm	Nicolas King
Louise	Michele Pawk	Alice	Emily Graham-Handley
Young Helen	Sara Niemietz	Bill	Patrick Clear
Older Helen	Donna Lynne Champlin	Jody	Frank Wood

With: Barbara Robertson, Christian Kohn, Steve Bakunas.

Place: Burnett's apartment. One intermission.

Northlight Theatre, Skokie
BJ Jones artistic director, Richard Friedman managing director

HEARTS: THE FORWARD OBSERVER. By Willy Holtzman. March 25, 2002 (regional premiere). Director, BJ Jones; scenery, Geoffrey Curley; costumes, Nan Zabriskie; lighting, Bob Christen; sound, Lindsay Jones; dramaturg, Gavin Witt; stage manager, Tom Guerra.

Donald Waldman	Mike Nussbaum	Herbie; Ensemble	William Norris

Babe; Ensemble .... William Dick
Ruby; Ensemble .... John Sterchi

Evelyn; Ensemble .... Linda Kimbrough
Ensemble .... Ryan Spector, Sean Van Vleet

Pegasus Players, Chicago
Arlene Crewdson artistic director

MUSCLE. Musical with book by James Lapine; music by William Finn; lyrics by Ellen Fitzhugh. June 13, 2001. Director, Gareth Hendee; choreography, Ann Filmer; scenery, Jack Magaw; costumes, Nan Zabriskie; lighting, David Lander; sound, Steve Mezger; production stage manager, Kay R. Shu-Cleaves.

Max .... Rob Hancock
Mother .... Anita Hoffman
Father .... Dan Loftus

Alice .... Audrey Yeck
Mousie .... Chuck Karvelas

With: Jane Blass, Cory James, Timothy Jon, Carrie McNulty, Henry Michael Odum, Brad Potts, Chavez Ravine, Michael Reyes, Eddie Schumacher, Kate Staiger, Joel Sutliffe, Megan Van De Hey.

Musical Numbers: "Nothing Like a Beginning," "Street Scene," "Almost Perfect," "This Is Not Cornell," "Arnold Schwarzenegger," "The Brain and the Body," "Never Look Back," "Muscle," "Theory," "A Day at the Office," "Athlete," "Now I Understand," "California," "Beauty," "Home," "Too Far," "A Nice Thing," "Judges," "Now I Understand," Finale.

One intermission.

Steppenwolf Theatre Company, Chicago
Martha Lavey artistic director, Michael Gennaro executive director

MOTHER COURAGE. By Bertolt Brecht; adapted by David Hare. September 23, 2001 (US premiere). Director, Eric Simonson; scenery, Allen Moyer; costumes, James Schuette; lighting, Kenneth Posner; sound, Barry G. Funderburg; music, T. Bone Burnett and Darrell Leonard; musical director, Mark Weston; stage manager, Laura D. Glenn.

Cook .... Robert Breuler
Swiss Cheese .... Joe Foust
Kattrin .... Sally Murphy
Farmer's Wife;
  Old Woman; Peasant's Wife .... Wendy Robie
Chaplain .... Nicholas Rudall
Sergeant; Peasant; Lieutenant ...... John Sierros
Mother Courage .... Lois Smith
Recruiting Officer;
  Older Soldier; Peasant .... Jeff Still
Yvette .... Amy Warren

Regimental Clerk; Soldier ... E. Milton Wheeler
Eye Patch;
  Young Soldier;Young Man ...... Jay Whittaker
Commander;
  Fur Coat; 1st Soldier .... Larry Yando
2nd Sergeant;
  Singing Soldier in Bar;
  Peasant's Son .... Eric Avilés
Eilif .... Jan Brennan
Old Colonel .... Leonard Kraft
Armourer; 2nd Soldier; Singer ...... Bruch Reed

Ensemble: Sara Antunovich, Hans Fleischmann, Jesse Geiger, David Gray, Russell Heller, Elizabeth Levy, Michael Macias, Taj McCord.

Time: During the 30 Years War between 1624-1636. Place: Sweden, Poland, Saxony and Bavaria. One intermission.

WISHES, SUSPICIONS AND SECRET AMBITIONS: THE STORIES OF CARL SANDBURG. By Ann Boyd; based on Mr. Sandburg's stories. October 2, 2001 (world premiere). Director, Ms. Boyd; scenery, Matthew York; costumes, Michelle Lynette Bush; lighting, Jaymi Lee Smith; sound, Cecil Averett; stage manager, Deborah Sullivan.

Blixie Blimber; Paula; various ...... Kati Brazda
Sandburg .... Aaron Christensen
White Horse Girl; various .... Manao DeMuth
Gimme the Ax; various . Aaron Todd Douglas

Shoulder Straps; various .... Scott Duff
Deep Red Roses, various .... Ann Joseph
Blue Wind Boy, various .... Anthony Wills Jr.
Potato Face Blind Man .... Cedric Young

Time: Now and then in the early 20th century. Place: Here and there in Illinois and the Rootabaga country.

WAVING GOODBYE. By James Pachino. December 15, 2001 (world premiere). Director, Jeremy B. Cohen; scenery, Richard and Jacqueline Penrod; costumes, Kristine Knanishu; lighting, Jaymi Lee Smith; sound and music, Lindsay Jones; dramaturg, Sarah Gubbins; stage manager, Erin Wenzel. Presented in association with Naked Eye Theatre.

Lily Blue	Liesel Matthews	Boggy	James McKay
Jonathan Blue	Brian Shaw	Perry	Alexandra Billings
Amanda Blue	Julia Neary		

Place: The New York City loft apartment of the Blue family. One intermission.

MARIA ARNDT. By Elsa Bernstein; translated by Curt Columbus with Tina Landau. February 10, 2002 (world premiere). Director, Tina Landau; scenery, John Lee Beatty; costumes, Catherine Zuber, lighting, Scott Zielinski; music and sound, Robert Milburn and Michael Bodeen, dramaturg, Rachel Shteir; stage manager, Malcolm Ewen.

Maria Arndt	Molly Regan	Council President	Bradley Armacost
Gemma	Greta Sidwell Honold	Amanda	Brett Korn
Tekla	Courtney Shaughnessy	Otto	Brad Eric Johnson
Gerhardt Claussner	Christopher Innvar	Maid	Juliana Thornton
Agatha Lovera	Marilynn Bogetich		

Time: The beginning of the 20th century. Place: An old country estate in a section of a southern German University town. One intermission.

WINESBURG, OHIO. By Eric Rose; adapted from the novel by Sherwood Anderson. February 19, 2002 (world premiere). Director, Jessica Thebus; settings, Brian Sidney Bembridge; costumes, Sarah Pace; lighting, J.R. Lederle; sound, Joshua Horvath; music, Andre Pluess and Ben Sussman; stage manager, Erin Wenzel.

Kate Swift; others	Lesley Bevan	Rev. Curtis Hartman; others	Jeff Parker
Elizabeth Willard; others	McKinley Carter	George Willard	Patrick Sarb
Tom Willard; others	Chris Farrell	Wing Biddlebaum; others	Fred A. Wellisch
Helen White; others	Kristina Martin	The Writer; The Stranger	Andrew White

Time: 1890s and after. Place: Winesburg, Ohio.

JESUS HOPPED THE 'A' TRAIN. By Stephen Adly Guirgis. March 3, 2002. (Midwest premiere). Director, Ron OJ Parson; scenery, Brian Sidney Bembridge, costumes, Sarah Pace; lighting, J.R. Lederle; sound, Joshua Horvath; stage manager, Sascha Connor.

Angel	Eric Avilés	D'Amico	Keith Kupferer
Valdez	Ricardo Gutierrez	Lucius	E. Milton Wheeler
Mary Jane	Stephanie Childers		

Time: The present. Place: New York City's Criminal Justice System. One intermission.

THE DAZZLE. By Richard Greenberg. May 18, 2002 (Midwest premiere). Director, David Cromer; choreography, Birgitta Victorson; scenery, Joseph Wade; costumes, Kristine Knanishu; lighting, Jaymi Lee Smith; musical composition and sound, Andre Pluess and Ben Sussman; stage manager, Laura D. Glenn.

Langley Collyer	Tracy Letts	Milly Ashmore	Susan Bennett
Homer Collyer	David Pasquesi		

Time: Early to mid-20th century. Place: Collyer brownstone in Harlem. One intermission.

KENTUCKY

Actors Theatre of Louisville, Louisville

Marc Masterson artistic director, Alexander Speer executive director

MACBETH. By William Shakespeare. February 1, 2002. Director, Marc Masterson; scenery, Steve O'Hearn; costumes, Connie Furr-Soloman; lighting, Tony Penna; sound, Darron L. West; videographer, Valerie Sullivan Fuchs; dramaturg, Amy Wegener; stage manager Alyssa Hoggatt.

The First Witch; others .... Kim Martin-Cotten	The Third Witch; others .... Mark Mineart
The Second Witch; others .... Will Bond	

    No intermission.

26th Annual Humana Festival of New American Plays.

THE MYSTERY OF ATTRACTION. By Marlane Meyer. March 3, 2002. Director, Richard Corley; scenery, Paul Owen; costumes, Christal Weatherly; lighting, Tony Penna; sound, Martin R. Desjardins; dramaturg, Tanya Palmer; production stage manger, Paul Mills Holmes.

Ray .... Steve Juergens	Roger .... Robert Ian Mackenzie
Warren .... David Van Pelt	Larry .... Lee Sellars
Denise .... Claudia Fielding	Vickie .... Laura Masterson

    Time: The present. Place: Carson, California. No intermission.

FINER NOBLE GASES. By Adam Rapp. March 8, 2002. Director, Michael John Garcés; scenery, Paul Owen; costumes, Christal Weatherly; lighting, Tony Penna; sound, Vincent Olivieri; dramaturg, Amy Wegener; stage manager, Charles M. Turner III.

Staples .... Robert Beitzel	Speed .... Ray Rizzo
Chase ....Dallas Roberts	Gray .... Jeffrey Bean
Lynch .... Michael Shannon	Dot .... Alaina Mills

    Time: Winter. Place: An East Village apartment near Tomkins Square Park in New York.

LIMONADE TOUS LES JOURS. By Charles L. Mee. March 12, 2002. Director, Marc Masterson; scenery, Paul Owen; costumes, Katherine Hampton; lighting, Tim Saternow; sound, Vincent Olivieri; video, Valerie Sullivan Fuchs; dramaturg, Tanya Palmer; stage manager, Heather Fields.

Jacqueline .... Christa Scott-Reed	Waiter ....Josh Walden
Andrew .... Tom Teti	

    Time: The present. Place: Paris, in the springtime. No intermission.

A.M. SUNDAY. By Jerome Hairston. March 16, 2002. Director, Timothy Douglas; scenery, Paul Owen; costumes, Christal Weatherly; lighting, Tony Penna; sound, Vincent Olivieri; dramaturg; Amy Wegener; stage manager, Cat Domiano.

Denny .... H.J. Adams	Jay .... Jason Cornwell
R.P. .... Ray Anthony Thomas	Lorie .... Tarah Flanagan
Helen .... Barbara Gulan	

    Time: Early November. Place: A home; a bus stop; the woods. No intermission.

2002 Humana
Festival of New
American Plays

Above: Steve Juergens and David Van Pelt in The Mystery of Attraction. *Photo: Fred Furrow III*

Right: Christa Scott-Reed and Tom Teti in Limonade Tous Les Jours. *Photo: Larry Hunt*

Below: Robert Beitzel in Finer Noble Gases. *Photo: Fred Furrow III*

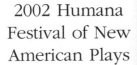

2002 Humana
Festival of New
American Plays

*Above: Barbara Gulan
and Jason Cornwell in
a.m. Sunday. Photo:
Fred Furrow III*

Left: Tom Nelis in Score.
Photo: Larry Hunt

*Below: Penny Fuller,
Josef Sommer and Fred
Major in* Rembrandt's
Gift. *Photo: Larry Hunt*

SCORE. Conceived by Anne Bogart; adapted from the writings of Leonard Bernstein by Jocelyn Clarke; created by SITI Company. March 21, 2002. Director, Ms. Bogart; scenery, Neil Patel; costumes, James Schuette; lighting, Christopher Akerlind; sound, Darron L. West; dramaturg, Stephen Moulds; stage manager, Elizabeth Moreau.

Performer .... Tom Nelis

REMBRANDT'S GIFT. By Tina Howe. March 26, 2002. Director, John Rando; scenery, Paul Owen; costumes, Jane Greenwood; lighting, Tim Saternow; sound, Kurt B. Kellenberger; fight direction, Rick Sordelet; dramaturg, Tanya Palmer; stage manager, Alyssa Hoggatt.

Polly Shaw .... Penny Fuller   Rembrandt .... Fred Major
Walter Paradise .... Josef Sommer

Time: The present. Place: Walter and Polly's top floor in downtown Manhattan.
No intermission.

Ten Minute Plays.

BAKE OFF. By Sheri Wilner. April 7, 2002. Director, Sullivan Canaday White; scenery, Paul Owen; costumes, John White; lighting, Paul Werner; sound, Colbert Davis; dramaturg, Stephen Moulds; stage manager, Heather Fields. Presented by special arrangement with Harden-Curtis Associates.

Paul .... Jeffrey Bean   The Pillsbury Doughboy ...... Michael Shannon
Rita .... Kim Martin-Cotten   Voice of the Announcer .... Tom Teti

Time: 1997. Place: The cooking floor of the Pillsbury Bake-Off.

CLASSYASS. April 7, 2002. By Caleen Sinnette Jennings. Director, Rajendra Ramoon Maharaj; scenery, Paul Owen; costumes, John White; lighting, Paul Werner; sound, Colbert Davis; dramaturg, Timothy Douglas; stage manager, Heather Fields. Presented by special arrangement with the playwright.

Ama .... Jason Cornwell   Miles .... Robert Beitzel
Big B .... Nikki Walker
Place: A room that serves as a modest radio studio at Bellmore College.

NIGHTSWIM. April 7, 2002. By Julia Jordan. Director, Rajendra Ramoon Maharaj; scenery, Paul Owen; costumes, John White; lighting, Paul Werner; sound, Colbert Davis; dramaturg, Stephen Moulds; stage manager, Heather Fields. Presented by special arrangement with Writers and Artists Agency.

Rosie .... Kate Umstatter   Christina .... Stacy L. Mayer

SNAPSHOT. March 29, 2002. A dramatic anthology by Tanya Barfield, Lee Blessing, Michael Bigelow Dixon, Julie Jensen, Honour Kane, Sunil Kuruvilla, David Lindsay-Abaire, Victor Lodato, Quincy Long, Deb Margolin, Allison Moore, Lynn Nottage, Dan O'Brien, Val Smith, Annie Weisman, Craig Wright and Chay Yew. Director, Russell Vandenbroucke; scenery, Paul Owen; costumes, John White; lighting, Tony Penna; sound, Colbert Davis; dramaturgs, Amy Wegener and Tanya Palmer; stage manager, Sarah Hodges.

With: Colette Beauvais, Joey Belmaggio, Matt Bridges, Camilla Busnovetsky, Ryan Clardy, Ellie Clark, Kristi Funk, Jake Goodman, Amy Guillory, Christopher Illing, Barbara Lanciers, Anthony Luciano, Alan Malone, Stacy L. Mayer, Elisa Morrison, Melanie Rademaker, Dave Secor, Donovan Sherman, Colin Sullivan, Kate Umstatter, Lindsey White, Tom Wooldridge.

MASSACHUSETTS

American Repertory Theatre, Cambridge

Robert Brustein artistic director, Robert J. Orchard managing director

JOHAN PADAN AND THE DISCOVERY OF THE AMERICAS. Monologue by Dario Fo; translated by Ron Jenkins. September 9, 2001 (US premiere). Director, Mr. Jenkins; costume coordinators, Jeanette Hawley and Karen Eister; lighting, John Ambrosone; sound, David Remedios. Presented in association with Provincetown Playhouse and the Underground Railway Theater.

Johan Padan .... Thomas Derrah
    One intermission.

ENRICO IV. By Luigi Pirandello; adapted by Robert Brustein, from a literal translation by Gloria Pastorino. December 12, 2001. Director, Karin Coonrod; scenery, Riccardo Hernández; costumes, Catherine Zuber; lighting, Christopher Akerlind; sound, David Remedios; stage manager, Victoria Sewell; dramaturg, Walter Valeri and Helen Shaw.

Enrico .... David Patrick Kelly	Londolfo .... Sean Haberle
Matilde .... Stephanie Roth-Haberle	Arialdo .... Craig Doescher
Frida .... Ayca Varlier	Ordulfo .... Sandro Isaack
Carlo de Nolli .... Sean Dugan	Bertoldo .... Remo Airaldi
Tito Belcredi .... Stephen Rowe	Giovanni .... Bill Salem
Dionisio Genoni .... Alvin Epstein	

    No intermission.

STONE COLD DEAD SERIOUS. By Adam Rapp. February 6, 2002 (world premiere). Director, Marcus Stern; scenery, Christine Jones; costumes, Catherine Zuber; lighting, John Ambrosone; sound, David Remedios and Mr. Stern; stage manager, Jennifer Rae Moore.

Wynne Ledbetter .... Matthew Stadelmann	Linda Ledbetter .... Deirdre O'Connell
Cliff Ledbetter .... Guy Boyd	Jack Gam .... Robert Runck
Shaylee Ledbetter;	Voice of Randall
Sharice .... Elizabeth Reaser	"Randy Man" Rockyjohn .... Philip Graeme

    Place: Illinois. One intermission.

ABSOLUTION. By Robert William Sherwood. March 31, 2002. Director, Scott Zigler; scenery, Christine Jones; costumes, Karen Eister, lighting, John Ambrosone; sound, David Remedios; fight direction, Robert Walsh; stage manager, Wendy Beaton; dramaturg, Kyle Brenton.

David .... Brennan Brown	Gordon .... Jordan Lage
Lorraine .... Peggy Trecker	Peter .... Benjamin Evett
Anne .... Sarah Howe	

    Time: Present. Place: Toronto and Vancouver.

LYSISTRATA. Musical adapted by Robert Brustein and the American Repertory Theatre Company; music by Galt MacDermot; lyrics by Matty Selman; additional material by Gilbert Seldes; based on the play by Aristophanes. May 15, 2002 (world premiere). Director, Andrei Serban; scenery, Michael Yeargan; costumes, Marina Draghici; lighting, John Ambrosone; sound, David Remedios; stage manager, Chris De Camillis; dramaturgs, Gideon Lester and Julie Felise Dubiner. A co-production with the Prince Music Theater of Philadelphia.

Lysistrata	Cherry Jones	Leander	Alvin Epstein
Kalonika	Karen MacDonald	Damon	Jeremy Geidt
Myrrhina	Chelsey Rives	Pythias; Spartan Envoy	Remo Airaldi
Penelope	Hannah Bos	President of Athenian Senate	Will LeBow
Lampito	Stephanie Roth-Haberle	Kinesias	Benjamin Evett
Dipsas	Amber Allison	Spartan Delegate	Craig Doescher
Belphragia	Paula Plum	Manes	James Dittami
Helion	Thomas Derrah		

Place: Athens and Sparta. No intermission.

Barrington Stage Company, Sheffield
Julianne Boyd artistic director, Bonnie English general manager

CIAO! By Anonymous. August 11, 2001. (world premiere). Director, Julianne Boyd; scenery, Matthew Maraffi; costumes, Louisa Thompson; lighting, Jeff Croiter; sound, Joe Jurachak; fight direction, Tony Simotes; production stage manager, Renee Lutz.

Arthur Alliman	David Rasche	Woman	Joanna Glushak
Man	Michael Countryman		

No intermission.

Berkshire Theatre Festival, Stockbridge
Kate Maguire producing director

THE SMELL OF THE KILL. By Michele Lowe. August 1, 2001. Director, Christopher Ashley; scenery, David Gallo; costumes, Linda Fisher; lighting, Kenneth Posner; sound, Dan Moses Schreier; stage manager, Mona El-Khatib. Presented in association with Elizabeth Ireland McCann, Nelle Nugent and Milton and Tamar Maltz.

Molly	Katie Finneran	Nicky	Kristen Johnston
Debra	Claudia Shear		

POUND OF FLESH. By Michael Bolus. August 9, 2001 (world premiere). Director, Peter Wallace; scenery, Jeremy Woodward; costumes, Wade Laboissonniere; lighting, Tammy Owens Slauson; sound, Jason A. Tratta; production stage manager, Peter Durgin.

Ezra Pound	Patrick Husted	Female Voice	Kate Maguire
Private Cooper	Jonathan M. Woodward		

Time: 1945. Place: US Army prison camp in Pisa, Italy. No intermission.

Market Theater, Cambridge
Greg Carr founder, Tom Cole director

FAMILY STORIES. By Biljana Srbljanovic, translated by Rebecca Ann Rugg. April 24, 2002. Director, Annie Dorsen; scenery, Jeff Cowie; costumes, Miguel Angel Huidor; lighting, Matthew Richards; sound, Jonah Rapino; fight direction, Robert Walsh; stage manager, Jenny Peek.

Milena	Danielle Skraastad	Andrija	Corey Behnke
Vojin	Brandon Miller	Nadezda	Emma Bower

Shakespeare & Company, Lenox
Tina Packer artistic director

A TANGLEWOOD TALE. By Juliane and Stephen Glantz. September 15, 2001 (world premiere). Director, Michael Hammond; scenery, Lauren Kurki; costumes, Govane Lohbauer; lighting, Steve Ball; sound, Mark Huang.

Herman Melville .... Dan McCleary
Hawthorne .... James Goodwin Rice
Sophia Hawthorne .... Elizabeth Aspenlieder

Lizzie Melville .... Celia Madeoy
Hawthorne children .... Gabriel Vaughan,
                                 Allison Collins, Tolan Aman

GOLDA'S BALCONY. By William Gibson. May 18, 2002 (world premiere). Director, Daniel Gidron; scenery, Lauren Kurki; costumes, Govane Lohbauer; lighting, Stephen D. Ball; sound, Mark Huang; stage manager, Matthew Alan Simons.

Annette Miller .... Golda Meir

Williamstown Theatre Festival
Michael Ritchie producer

BUFFALO GAL. By A.R. Gurney. June 13, 2001 (world premiere). Director, John Tillinger; scenery, James Noone; costumes, Laura Churba; lighting, Kevin Adams; sound; Jerry M. Yager; music, Barclay Stiff.

Roy .... Michael Mastro
Debbie .... Michi Barall
Jackie .... Becky Ann Baker
    One intermission.

Amanda .... Mariette Hartley
James .... Peter Francis
Dan .... Michael Gross

THE MAN WHO HAD ALL THE LUCK. By Arthur Miller. July 19, 2001. Director, Scott Ellis; scenery, Allen Moyer; costumes, Michael Krass; lighting, Kenneth Posner; sound, Eileen Tague; music, Tom Kochan; stage manager, Grayson Meritt.

David Beeves .... Chris O'Donnell
J.B. Feller .... Richard Riehle
Shory .... Dan Moran
Aunt Belle .... Barbara Sims
Patterson Beeves .... James Rebhorn
Amos Beeves .... Ryan Shively
    Time: 1938. Place: Midwest town. Two intermissions.

Hester Falk .... Jennifer Dundas
Dan Dibble .... Mason Adams
Andrew Falk .... Edward James Hyland
Gus Eberson .... Sam Robards
Augie Belfast.................................. David Wohl

MICHIGAN

BoarsHead Theater, Lansing
John Peakes founding artistic director

MOTHER'S DAY. By Jeff Baron. April 19, 2002. (North American premiere). Director, John Peakes, scenery and lighting, Rob Eastman-Mullins; costumes, Kirsten Wilcox; stage manager, K. Jayson Bryan.

Estelle .... Carmen Decker
Marilyn .... Evelyn Orbach
Jonathan .... Brooke Behmke

Leslie .... Adrianne Cury
Wendy .... Susan Felder
Carmen .... Rebecca Covey

MINNESOTA

Guthrie Theater, Minneapolis
Joe Dowling artistic director, Susan Trapnell managing director

THE CARPETBAGGER'S CHILDREN. By Horton Foote. August 8, 2001. Director, Michael Wilson; scenery, Jeff Cowie; costumes, David C. Woolard; lighting, Rui Rita; sound, John Gromada; stage manager, Amy Knotts. A co-production with the Alley Theatre (Houston, Texas) and Hartford Stage (Hartford, Connecticut); see production details under Alley Theatre.

THIEF RIVER. By Lee Blessing. February 20, 2002 (regional premiere). Director, Ethan McSweeney; scenery, Michael Sims; costumes, Rich Hamson; lighting, Jane Cox; sound, Michael Roth; fight direction, Peter Moore; stage manager, Martha Kulig; dramaturg, Michael Bigelow Dixon.

1948

Ray, 18 years old	Alex Podulke
Gil, 18 years old	Bard Goodrich
Harlow	James Shanklin
Anson; Ray's granddad	William Whitehead

1973

Ray, 43 years old	Bernie Sheredy
Gil, 43 years old old	James Shanklin

Kit	Alex Podulke
Perry; Ray's father-in-law	Richard Ooms

2001

Ray, 71 years old	William Whitehead
Gil, 71 years old	Richard Ooms
Jody	Bard Goodrich
Reese, related to Harlow	Bernie Sheredy

Place: An abandoned farmhouse outside of Thief River. One intermission.

Theatre de la Jeune Lune, Minneapolis

Barbra Berlovitz, Vincent Gracieux, Bob Rosen, Dominique Serrand, Steven Epp artistic directors, Steve Richardson producing director

THE DESCRIPTION OF THE WORLD. By Robert Rosen and Luverne Seifert in collaboration with the cast; based on book by Marco Polo. September 29, 2001. Director, Mr. Rosen; scenery, Michael Sommers; costumes, Sonya Berlovitz; lighting, Marcus Dilliard; music, Eric Jensen; stage manager, Liz Neerland.

Marseo	Jon Morris	Kajor	Julian McFaul
Fredrico	Paul Thureen	Venice	Annie Ennekind
Rusticello	Luverne Seifert	Marco Polo	Robert Rosen
Massina	Katie Kaufman		

COSI FAN TUTTE. New stage adaptation by Theatre de la Jeune Lune; based on the opera by Wolfgang Amadeus Mozart, with libretto by Lorenzo Da Ponte. December 27, 2001. Director, Dominique Serrand; scenery, Mr. Serrand with Vincent Gracieux and Dan Lori; costumes, Sonya Berlovitz; lighting, Marcus Dilliard; musical direction, Barbara Brooks; stage manager, Liz Neerland.

Fiordiligi	Jennifer Baldwin Peden	Ferrando	Sean Fallen
Dorabella	Christina Baldwin Fletcher	Guglielmo	Marshall Urban
Despina	Janet Gottschall Fried	Don Alfonso	Bradley Greenwald

Musicians: Barbara Brooks conductor and keyboard, Joanna Shelton violin I, Beth Wolfe violin II, Laurel Browne viola, Lucia Magney cello.

MEDEA. Adapted by Steven Epp and Barbra Berlovitz; from Euripides. March 2, 2002. Director, Mr. Epp; scenery and lighting, Dominique Serrand; costumes, Sonya Berlovitz.

Nurse	Sarah Agnew	Chorus	Isabell Monk
Singer	Janet Gottschall Fried	Medea	Barbra Berlovitz
Older Son	Nathan Keepers	Creon	Allen Hamilton
Younger son	Max Friedman,	Jason	Vincent Gracieux
	Miles Tagtmeyer	Aegeus	Charles Schuminksi

NUNS. By Eduardo Manet; translation by David Bell. May 17, 2002. Direction, collectively by the company; scenery, Steven Epp and Vincent Gracieux; costumes, Sonya Berlovitz; lighting, Robert Rosen; stage manager, Liz Neerland.

Mother Superior	Robert Rosen	Sister Inez	Steven Epp
Sister Angela	Vincent Gracieux	Señora	Barbra Berlovitz, Jon Morris

MISSOURI

Missouri Repertory Theatre, Kansas City
Peter Altman producing artistic director

MORNING STAR. By Sylvia Regan. October 17, 2001. Director, Risa Brainin; scenery, Nayna Ramey; costumes, Devon Painter; lighting, Michael Klaers; sound, Tom Mardikes; composer, Seongah Shin; production stage manager, D. Christian Bolender.

Becky Felderman	Geraldine Librandi	Sadie Felderman	Molly Jo McGuire
Fanny Felderman	Amy J. Carle	Irving Tashman	Dann Fink
Aaron Greenspan	Frank Anderson	Benjamin Brownstein	Barry Finkel
Esther Felderman	Stephanie Timm	Myron Engel	Gary Neal Johnson
Hymie Felderman (as a boy);		Hymie Felderman,	
Hymie Tashman	Tony Cordaro	as a young man	Michael Andrew Smith
Harry Engel	Jeffrey Cribbs	Pansy	Lisa Louise Langford

THE WINTER'S TALE. By William Shakespeare. February 6, 2002. Director, Henry Godinez; choreography, William Whitener; scenery, Christopher Acebo; costumes, Holly Poe Durbin; lighting, Rita Pietraszek; sound, Tom Mardikes; composer, John Kamys; production stage manager, D. Christian Bolender.

Leontes	Brent Harris	A Jailer	Larry Greer
Mamillius	Spencer Wilson	Time	Gary Neal Johnson
Camillo	Jeff Talbott	Hermione	Seana McKenna
Antigonus	Richard Wharton	Perdita	Sandra Delgado
Cleomenes	Mark Robbins	Paulina	Carmen Roman
Dion	Lorenzo Hughes	Emilia	Anne Dillon
Polixenes	Neil Maffin	Mopsa	Alicia Atkins
Archidamus	Phil Fiorini	Dorcas	Brianne Rose
Old Shepherd	Larry Paulson	Lady	Taylor Clearman
Young Sheperd	Joe Foust	Lord	Jeffrey Cribbs
Autolycus	Mark D. Espinoza	Lord	James Knight
Florizel	Manu Narayan	Servant	Michael Fisher
A Mariner	Joe Price	Servant	Adam Scally

WORK SONG: THREE VIEWS OF FRANK LLOYD WRIGHT. March 13, 2002. By Eric Simonson and Jeffrey Hatcher. Director, Mr. Simonson; choreography, Jennifer Martin; scenery, Kent Dorsey; costumes, Karin Kopischke; lighting, Phil Monat; sound, Barry G. Funderburg; production stage manager, Jenny Paul. A co-production with Arizona Theatre Company.

Frank Lloyd Wright	Lee E. Ernst	Julian Carlton; Draftsman;	
Edwin Cheney; draftsman; farmer;		Leelai	Leon Addison Brown
Otto Freundlich	Peter Silbert	Tommy Cheney;	
Louis Sullivan; Overton	Mark Robbins	John Brooks	Andrew Rohleder
George Brodelle; William Brooks;			David Gomez
Farris; Wes Peters	Sean Dougherty	John Wright; Draftsman;	
Anna Wright; Farmer's Wife;		Grant	John Hoogenakker
Olgivanna Wright	Wendy Robie	Dan Burnham;	
Catherine Wright; Britta;		Alexander Woollcott	Benjamin Stewart
Carolyn Brooks	Kirsten Potter	Riley; Draftsman; Reporter;	
Mamah Cheney; Ayn Rand	Kate Goehring	Sheriff; Stout	Joshua Bevans

Ensemble: Susan Glennemeier, Kate Molly Gumowitz, Stephen Moore, Patrick M. Reynolds, Roger Strong, Natalie Sullivan, Robert Winstead.

JOE TURNER'S COME AND GONE. By August Wilson. May 8, 2002. Director, Marion McClinton; scenery, Neil Patel; costumes, Jennifer Myers Ecton; lighting, Donald Holder; sound, Robert Milburn and Michael Bodeen; music, Orebert Davis; production stage manager, William Carey.

Seth	Al White	Mattie Campbell	Tracie Toms
Bertha Holly	Cheryl Lynn Bruce	Reuben Scott	Aaron Thomas,
Bynum Walker	Adolphus Ward		Joseph Samuels
Rutherford Selig	Larry Paulsen	Molly Cunningham	Heather Alicia Simmons
Jeremy Furlow	Edward Blunt	Martha Loomis	Natasha Charles
Herald Loomis	John Earl Jelks		
Zonia Loomis	Breanna Ransburg,		
	Chera Hishaw		

NEW JERSEY

Centenary Stage, Hackettstown
Carl Wallnau producing director

MARY TODD—A WOMAN APART. By Carl Wallnau. March 1, 2002. Director, Mr. Wallnau; choreography, Carolyn Coulson-Grigsby; scenery, Ani Blackburn; costumes, Brenda Lightcap; lighting, Ed Matthews; sound, Sara Bader; stage manager, Kimothy Kruse.

Mary Todd	Colleen Smith Wallnau	Attendants	Cynthia Clemansky
Attendants	Doug Spaulding		

One intermission.

George Street Playhouse, New Brunswick
David Saint artistic director, Michael Stotts managing director

WAITING FOR TADASHI. By Velina Hasu Houston. January 11, 2002 (world premiere). Director, David Saint; choreography, Yass Hakoshima; scenery, James Youmans; costumes, Theoni V. Aldredge; lighting, Joe Saint; music and sound, David Van Tieghem; production stage manager, Patti McCabe.

Shape Shifter—Dazzler	June Angela	Chikako; Kuroko	Sabrina Le Beauf
Satomi	Takayo Fischer	Shape Shifter—Confuser	Sue Jin Song
Tadashi	Clark Jackson	Matsuko; Kuroko	Mia Tagano
Vincent	Danny Johnson		

CTRL+ALT+DELETE. By Anthony Clarvoe. March 22, 2002. (East Coast premiere). Director, Ethan McSweeney; scenery, Mark Wendland; costumes, Michael Sharpe; lighting, Jeff Croiter; sound, Bruce Ellman; production stage manager, Patti McCabe. Presented in association with San Jose Repertory Theatre and the Wharton Center.

Marie	Sarah Avery	Eddie Fisker	James Ludwig
Carbury Grendall	Sam Gregory	Tom Xerox	Daniel Pearce
Gus Belmont	Jonathan Hogan	Torio Bruno	KJ Sanchez

One intermission.

PUBLIC GHOSTS–PRIVATE STORIES. By Ain Gordon. April 26, 2002 (world premiere). Co-directors, Michael Rohd and Eric Ruffin; scenery, R. Michael Miller; costumes, Brenda King, lighting, Christopher J. Bailey; sound, Rudy Veltree; music, Jason Berg. Presented in association with Cornerstone Theater Company, Los Angeles.

Josephine; Ensemble	Sue Barancik	Robert	Shawn Elliott
Hammond; Ensemble	Egan Paul Davson	Mrs. Kovash	Helen Gallagher

John Bartley .... Victor Love	Henry; Ensemble .... Lamont Stephens
Rose .... Anne O'Sullivan	Bridget .... Mara Stephens
George K. Parsell; Ensemble .... Wayne Peck	Maria; Ensemble .... Maria Tola
Dolores .... Socorro Santiago	Miguel; Ensemble .... Daniel B. Utset
Zena .... Cherene Snow	Mr. Corie; Ensemble ...... Richard Waddingham

McCarter Theatre, Princeton
Emily Mann artistic director, Jeffrey Woodward managing director

YELLOWMAN. By Dael Orlandersmith. June 13, 2002 (world premiere). Director, Blanka Zizka; scenery, Klara Zieglerova; costumes, Janus Stefanowicz; lighting, Russell H. Champa; music, Elliott Sharp; dramaturg, Janice Paran; production stage manager, Paul-Douglas Michnewicz. A co-production with the Wilma Theater and Long Wharf Theatre.

Alma .... Dael Orlandersmith	Eugene .... Howard W. Overshown

HUMPTY DUMPTY. By Eric Bogosian. March 29, 2002 (world premiere). Director, Jo Bonney; scenery, Robert Brill; costumes, Ann Hould-Ward; lighting, Kenneth Posner; sound, John Gromada; production stage manager, Cheryl Mintz.

Nicole .... Kathryn Meisle	Troy .... Patrick Fabian
Max .... Bruce Norris	Spoon .... Reiko Aylesworth
Nat .... Michael Laurence	

DON JUAN. By Molière; translated and adapted by Stephen Wadsworth. May 3, 2002 (East Coast premiere). Co-produced with Seattle Repertory Theatre; see production details listed there.

New Jersey Shakespeare Festival, Madison
Bonnie J. Monte artistic director

HAMLET. By William Shakespeare. August 11, 2001. Director, Tom Gilroy; scenery, Michael Schweikardt; costumes, Miranda Hoffman; lighting, John Lasiter; production stage manager, Elizabeth Moloney.

Bernardo; Gravedigger 2 .... Jay Leibowitz	Queen Gertrude .... Maggie Low
Marcellus; Lucianus .... Sam Wellington	Ophelia .... Lili Taylor
Horatio .... Ken Leung	Reynaldo .... Dale Ho
Ghost of Hamlet's father .... Richard Harris	Guildenstern; Osric .... Adam Stein
Claudius .... Bill Raymond	Rosencrantz; Priest .... Gregory Jackson
Voltemand; Captain .... Kevin Rolston	Player Queen .... Erin Lynlee Partin
Laertes .... Jason Weinberg	Player King; Gravedigger 1 .... Eric Hoffman
Polonius .... William Bogert	Guard .... David Foubert
Hamlet .... Jared Harris	Attendant to the King .... David Jimenez
One intermission.	

Playwrights Theatre of New Jersey, Madison
John Pietrowski artistic director

THE BOOK OF CANDY. Musical with book and lyrics by Susan Dworkin from her novel; music by Mel Marvin. November 2, 2001. Director, Ahvi Spindell; choreography, Jennifer Paulson Lee; scenery, Richard Turick; costumes, Melissa C. Richards; lighting, Charles S. Reece; sound, Jeff Knapp; musical director, Vadim Feichtner; stage manager, Fern-Marie Aames. A co-production with Passage Theatre Company.

Candy .... Lauren Mufson	Maida; Carol .... Connie Day
Alex .... Jonathan Brody	Florie; Mrs. Shapiro .... Beth Glover

George Street
Playhouse
2001–2002
Season

Above: Jonathan Hogan, Sam Gregory, Daniel Pearce and James Ludwig in Ctrl+Alt+Delete. *Photo: T. Charles Erickson*

Right: Mara Stephens in Public Ghosts–Private Stories. *Photo: T. Charles Erickson*

Below: Sue Jin Song and Clark Jackson in Waiting for Tadashi. *Photo: T. Charles Erickson*

Things in heaven: Jared Harris in Hamlet *at the New Jersey Shakespeare Festival. Photo: Gerry Goodstein*

Caterer; Shaul	Ted Grayson	Heimlich; Jack; Orpheo	Martin Vidnovic
Marty; Sam	Adam Heller	Roxie; Dalia; Odie; Ethel	Jill Abramovitz

Musical Numbers: "The Book of Candy," "When You're a Little Girl," "Kosher Style," "Pirke Maida," "A Slender Thread," "Fractures," "Mazel Tov," "Heimlich," "The Ultimate Aphrodisiac," "Rugalach," "The Tower," "The Surgeon's Lullaby," "Leviathan," "Hadassah Luncheon," "I've Seen a Door," "All This is Garbage," "The Song of Exile," "The Garden Reprise," "And How Shall I Endure," "Winning," "The Song of the Remnant."

One intermission.

NEW YORK

Arena Players Repertory Company, East Farmingdale
Frederic DeFeis producer

DOES ANYONE KNOW WHO MY FATHER IS? By Jack Donohue. February 7, 2002 (world premiere). Director, Frederic DeFeis; scenery, Fred Sprauer; costumes, Lois Lockwood; lighting, Al Davis; stage manager, Evan Donnellan.

Ellen	Carolyn Popadin	Mr. Testa	Wolfen DeKastro
Nelle	Sherry Mandery	Susan	Phyllis Kaye
Mr. Mason	Michael Lang	Ellen as a child	Darcy Donnellan

Helen Hayes Theatre Company, Nyack

THUMBS. By Rupert Holmes. March 9, 2002. Director, Marcia Milgrom Dodge; scenery, Dan Kuchar; costumes, Nan Young; lighting, Jeff Croiter; sound, Rafe Carlotto; stage manager, Eileen F. Haggerty.

Marta Dunhill	Kathie Lee Gifford	Sheriff Jane Morton	Diana Canova
Freddie Bradshaw	Brad Bellamy	Male Visitor	Hardy Rawls
Todd Monroe	Brian Lerscher	Female Visitor	Nicola Royston
Wilton Dekes	Tom Beckett		

Studio Arena Theatre, Buffalo
Gavin Cameron-Webb artistic director, Ken Neufeld executive director

CITY OF LIGHT. By Anthony Clarvoe; based on the novel by Lauren Belfer. September 13, 2001 (world premiere). Director, Gavin Cameron-Webb; scenery, William Barclay; costumes, Mariann Verheyen; lighting, Phil Monat; sound, Tom Mardikes.

Louisa Barrett	Kate Heasley	John G. Milburn;	
Tom Sinclair	Michael Chaban	Karl Speyer; Rolf	Robert Rutland
Grover Cleveland;		Franklin Fiske; Peter Fronczyk;	
William McKinley;		Richard Watson Gilder	Paul Todaro
Theodore Roosevelt	Eric Devine	John J. Albright;	
Frances Coatsworth;		James Fitzhugh;	
Maria Love	Carolyn Swift	Billy	Richard Wesp
Frederick Krakauer;		Mary Talbert	Emily Yancy
Dexter Rumsey; Daniel Henry;		Grace Sinclair;	
Bates; Prof. Barrett	Lee Moore	Young Louisa	Brianna Larson,
Susannah Rile;			Hillary Malone
Margaret Sinclair	Angela Pierce		

Time: 1901. Place: Buffalo, New York. One intermission.

LAKE EFFECT. By Tom Dudzick. November 29, 2001 (world premiere). Director, Terence Lamude; scenery, Douglas Huszti; costumes, Martha Hally; lighting, Tom Sturge; sound, Tom Gould.

Rudy Pazinski	Karl Kenzie	Aunt Marge	Darlene Pickering Hummert
Eddie Pazinski	Sean Dougherty	Dinty Shanagan	Dane Knell
Georgie Pazinski	Ryan Patrick Bachand		
Annie Pazinski	Babo Harrison		
Ellen Pazinksi	Eileen Schuyler		

BUFFALO GAL. By A.R. Gurney. March 21, 2002. Director, John Tillinger; scenery, James Noone; costumes, Laura Churba; lighting, James Vermeulen; sound, Rick Menke.

Amanda	Betty Buckley	Roy	Eddie Korbich
Jackie	Mary Beth Fisher	Debbie	Aiko Nakasone
Dan	Julian Gamble	James	Jonathan Earl Peck

Syracuse Stage, Syracuse
Robert Moss artistic director, James A. Clark producing director

A LESSON BEFORE DYING. By Romulus Linney; adapted from the novel by Ernest L. Gaines. February 14, 2002. Director, Timothy Douglas; scenery, Tony Cisek; costumes, Tracy Dorman; lighting, Dan Covey; sound, Jonathan Herter; production stage manager, Stuart Plymesser.

Paul Bonin	Charlton James	Emma Glenn	Lizan Mitchell

Grant Wiggins .... Charles Parnell   Vivian Baptiste .... Rochelle Hogue
Sam Guidry .... Larry John Meyers   Reverend Ambrose .... William Charles Mitchell
Jefferson .... Dyron Holmes
    Time: 1948. Place: Bayonne, Louisiana. One intermission.

Ohio

Cincinnati Playhouse in the Park, Cincinnati
Edward Stern producing artistic director, Buzz Ward executive director

MEN ON THE TAKE. By Carter W. Lewis. February 14, 2002 (world premiere). Director, Edward Stern; scenery, Paul Shortt; costumes, Gordon DeVinney; lighting, John Lasiter; sound, Jill B.C. DuBoff; fight direction, Drew Fracher; stage manager, Suann Pollock.

George .... Tony Campisi   Woman .... Karen Radcliffe
Jake .... Walter Hudson
    One intermission.

BARBARA'S BLUE KITCHEN. By Lori Fischer. March 28, 2002. Director, Martha Banta; scenery, Eric Renschler; costumes, Gordon DeVinney; lighting, Matthew Frey; stage manager, Emily McMullen.

Barbara Jean; Jeanette;   Disc Jockey; Guitarist .... Kurt Ziskie
  Melissa; Miss Tessie;
  Miss Morris; Tommy Lee;
  Lombardo .... Lori Fischer
    Musicians: Laura Hazelbaker, Don Aren, Steve Flora.
    Place: Barbara's Blue Kitchen on a hot day in Watertown, Tennessee. No intermission.

KING O' THE MOON. By Tom Dudzick. April 25, 2002. Director, Terence Lamude; scenery, Bill Clarke; costumes, Martha Hally; lighting, Tom Sturge; sound, Tom Gould; fight direction, Drew Fracher; production stage manager, Bruce E. Coyle; stage manager, Suann Pollock.

Georgie Pazinski .... Geoffrey Molloy   Maureen Pazinski .... Kelly Mares
Rudy Pazinski .... Christopher Drescher   Annie Pazinski .... Rachel Fowler
Eddie Pazinski .... Charlie Pollock   Walter .... Steve Brady
Ellen Pazinski .... Cheryl Giannini
    Time: July 1969. One intermission.

DIRTY BLONDE. By Claudia Shear; conceived by Ms. Shear and James Lapine. May 16, 2002. Director, Loretta Greco; choreography, Susan Tenney; scenery, Myung Hee Cho; costumes, Elizabeth Hope Clancy; lighting, James Vermeulen; sound, Robert Kaplowitz; stage manager, Jenifer Morrow.

Frank Wallace;   Jo; Mae .... Adinah Alexander
  Ed Hearn; others .... Jeffrey Kuhn   Charlie; others .... Darrin Baker
  No intermission.

Cleveland Play House, Cleveland
Peter Hackett artistic director, Dean R. Gladden managing director

THE TIN PAN ALLEY RAG. By Mark Saltzman; with music and lyrics by Irving Berlin and Scott Joplin. November 30, 2001 (major revision). Directed and choreographed by Lynne Taylor-Corbett; David Evans; scenery, Christine Jones; costumes, Judanna Lynn; lighting, Michael Korsch; sound, Jeremy Lee; stage manager, Corrie Purdum.

Teddy Snyder; Alfred Ernst .... Bob Ader
Irving Berlin .... Fred Berman
Dorothy Goetz; others .... Betsy DiLellio
Freddie Alexander;
   Treemonisha; Hattie .... Karen Gardner
Scott Joplin .... Robert Jason Jackson

Gitlo; others .... Allie Laurie
Miss Esther Lee;
   others .... Janelle Anne Robinson
John Stark; others .... Tom Souhrada
Tate; others .... Dathan B. Williams

Extras: David Lemoyne, Tina Thompkins, James C. Workman.

Time: December 1915. Place: New York office of Berlin and Snyder, music publishers. No intermission.

2002 Next Stage Festival of New Plays. February 23–March 14, 2002.

FOREST CITY. By Bridgette A. Wimberly. February 23–24, 2002. Director, Seth Gordon.

NIGHT BLOOMERS. By Sarah Morton. March 2, 2002. Director, Eric Schmiedl.

BRIGHT IDEAS. By Eric Coble. March 3, 2002. Director, David Colacci.

THE BLUE CRANBERRY HOUR. By Ted Esborn. March 4, 2002. Director, Andrew Maya.

ARTS & ANXIETY. By Seth Greenland. March 9, 2002. Director, David Colacci.

THE PLANETARIAN. By Julia Jordan. March 10, 2002. Director, Seth Gordon.

THE MAGICAL RED SHOES. Book and lyrics, Joe Miloscia; music, Ken Kacmar. Director, Kenneth Elliott. March 13, 2002.

Great Lakes Theater Festival, Cleveland
James Bundy artistic director

LONE STAR LOVE, OR THE MERRY WIVES OF WINDSOR, TEXAS. Musical with book by John L. Haber; music and lyrics by Jack Herrick with contributions from Michael Bogdanov, Bland Simpson and Tommy Thompson; based on *The Merry Wives of Windsor* by William Shakespeare. October 20, 2001. Director, Mr. Bogdanov; choreography, Randy Skinner; scenery, Derek McLane; costumes, Jane Greenwood; lighting, Mary Jo Dondlinger; sound, Tom Morse; fight direction, Malcolm Ranson; dramaturg, Margaret Lynch; production stage manager, Debra A. Acquavella.

Colonel Joseph E. Johnson .... John Jellison
Sergeant John Falstaff .... Jay O. Sanders
Robin .... Sean Dooley
Frank Ford .... Joseph Mahowald
Aggie Ford .... Sara Gettelfinger
George Page .... John Jellison
Margaret Anne Page .... Allison Briner
Missanne Page .... Christeena Michelle Riggs
Sheriff Bob Shallow .... Nick Sullivan
Abraham Slender .... Brandon Williams
Doctor Caius .... Stephen Temperley
Miss Quickly .... Brenda Braxton

Fenton .... Clarke Thorell
Lucas .... Kevin Bernard
Chester .... Peter Connelly
Consuela .... Robin Irwin
Caitlin .... Jennifer Clippinger
Grace .... Tracee Beazer
Corporal Nym .... Clay Buckner
Private Bardolp .... Chris Frank
Host of the Garter Saloon .... Gary Bristol
Sticks .... Shannon Ford
Miss Libby .... Emily Mikesell
Captain Pistol .... Jack Herrick

Musical numbers: "Carry Me Home," "The Ballad of Falstaff"/"Leavin' Dixie," "Texas Cattlemen," "Prairie Moon," "Caius's Theme," "Slender's Lesson," "Chicken Fried Barbeque Steak," "Hard Times," "The Cowboy's Dream," "World of Men," "By Way of Frank Ford," "Lone Star Love," "A Man for the Age," "Count on My Love, " Code of the West," "Quail Bagging," "Texas Wind," "The Wild Cat Moan."

372 THE BEST PLAYS OF 2001–2002

OREGON

Oregon Shakespeare Festival, Ashland

Libby Appel artistic director, Paul Nicholson executive director

HANDLER. By Robert Schenkkan. April 6, 2002 (West Coast premiere). Director, Bill Rauch; scenery, Richard L. Hay; costumes, Alex Jaeger; lighting, Robert Peterson.

Terri .... Robynn Rodriguez	Young Girl .... Maya L. Nerenberg
Geordi .... Jonathan Haugen	Burning Man; Congregant;
Bob .... Ken Albers	Reporter .... Armando Durán
Alice; Reporter .... Catherine E. Coulson	Ensemble; Congregant;
Samuel; Reporter .... Brad Whitmore	Reporter .... Kal Poole, Patrick Chew,
Larry; Congregant .... U. Jonathan Toppo	Nancy Lee-Painter

MACBETH. By William Shakespeare; adapted by Lue Morgan Douthit. February 26, 2002. Director, Libby Appel; scenery, Richard L. Hay; costumes, Deborah M. Dryden; lighting, Robert Peterson.

Macbeth .... G. Valmont Thomas	Second Witch; Macduff;
Lady Macbeth .... B.W. Gonzalez	Ensemble .... Terri McMahon
Banquo ....Jeffrey King	First Witch; Duncan
Third Witch; Malcolm;	Ensemble .... Suzanne Irving
Ensemble .... Julie Oda	
No intermission.	

New Play Reading:

LORCA IN A GREEN DRESS. By Nilo Cruz. March 14, 2002.

Lord With Blood .... Armando Durán	White Suit .... Robert Vincent Frank
Guard .... Deidrie Henry	Green Dress ....Jim L. Garcia
Bicycle Pants .... Kevin Kenerly	Flamenco Dancer .... Conja Abdessalam
Woman .... Vilma Silva	

PENNSYLVANIA

Arden Theatre Company, Philadelphia

Terrence J. Nolen producing artistic director, Amy L. Murphy managing director

BABY CASE. Musical with book, music and lyrics by Michael Ogborn. October 16, 2001 (world premiere). Director, Terrence J. Nolen; choreography, Denise Direnzo; scenery, Tony Cisek; costumes, Richard St. Clair; lighting, John Stephen Hoey; sound, Jorge Cousineau; video, Tobin Rothlein; dramaturg, Amy Lincoln; production stage manager, Patricia G. Sabato.

Walter Winchell .... Scott Greer	The Studio Sisters .... Jennie Eisenhower,
Charles Lindbergh ....Jeffrey Coon	Becky Gulsvig,
Ann Morrow Lindbergh .... Sharon Sampieri	Victoria Matlock
Bruno Hauptmann .... Ben Dibble	

With: Charles Antalosky, Tony Braithwaite, Kristine Fraelich, Gary Giles, Marybeth Gorman, Benjamin D. Hickernall, Tracie Higgins, Michael Thomas Holmes, Scott Langdon, Kristin Purcell, Aaron Ramey, Richard Ruiz, Violet Sharpe, Suzanne H. Smart, Todd Waddington, Denise Whelan, William Whitehead.

Time: 1932. One intermission.

Philadelphia Theatre Company, Philadelphia
Sara Garonzik producing artistic director

DINNER WITH FRIENDS. By Donald Margulies. October 17, 2001 (Philadelphia premiere). Director, Mary B. Robinson; scenery, David Gordon; costumes, Michael Krass; lighting, Ann G. Wrightson; music, Robert Maggio; dramaturg, Michele Volansky.

Gabe	Brian Dykstra	Beth	Jennifer Rohn
Tom	Boris McGiver	Karen	Nancy Williamson

THE INFIDEL. By Bruce Norris. January 30, 2002 (East Coast premiere). Director, Anna D. Shapiro; scenery, Todd Rosenthal; costumes, Janus Stefanowicz; lighting, Ann G. Wrightson; sound, Eileen Tague; dramaturg, Michele Volansky.

Garvey	John Seitz	Casper	Joe Guzman
Moss	Robert Breuler	Alma	Jessica Leccia
Helen	Pamela Burrell	Guard	Al Espinosa

THE PLAY ABOUT THE BABY. By Edward Albee. March 20, 2002 (Philadelphia premiere). Director, Pam McKinnon; scenery, Tony Straiges; costumes, Janus Stefanowicz; lighting, Robert Perry; dramaturg, Michele Volansky.

Man	Munson Hicks	Girl	Devon Sorvari
Woman	Lucy Martin	Boy	Matthew Stinton

Stages Festival: New Play Readings.

GUINEVERE. By Gina Gionfriddo. October 29, 2001.

CAROL MULRONEY. By Stephen Belber. November 5, 2001.

SPILL THE WINE. By Brian Dykstra. November 12, 2001.

Pittsburgh Public Theater, Pittsburgh
Ted Pappas artistic director

PAPER DOLL. By Mark Hampton and Barbara J. Zitwer. November 16, 2001. Director, Leonard Foglia; scenery, Michael Garty; costumes, Martin Pakledinaz; lighting, Brian Nason; sound, Zach Moore; production stage manager, Jim Ring.

Jacqueline Susann	Marlo Thomas	Irving Mansfield	F. Murray Abraham

With: Joanne Genelle, Armando Rodriguez.

One intermission.

Prince Music Theater, Philadelphia
Marjorie Samoff producing artistic director, Joseph M. Farina managing director

ME AND MRS. JONES. Musical with book by Charles Randolph-Wright and Kathleen McGhee-Anderson; music and lyrics by Kenny Gamble, Leon Huff and others; based on an idea by Murray Schwartz. November 16, 2001 (world premiere). Director, Mr. Randolph-Wright; choreography, Ken Robinson; scenery, Thomas Lynch; costumes, Paul Tazewell; lighting, Michael Gilliam; sound, Nick Courtides; production stage manager, Bernita Robinson.

Tammy	Orfeh	Harry; Tony	Andy Karl
Calvin	Bobby Daye	Tyrone	Andrew Wright
Miss Trina	Stacie Precia	Cookie	Anika Noni Rose

Lillian	Darlene Love	Fontaine	Cornell E. Ivey
Judge	Lou Rawls	Carolotta	Lorna Ventura
Angie	Victoria Cave	Prosecutor	Joe Langworth
Rita; Glynnis	Judine Richard	Mrs. Jones	'Nita Whitaker
J.C.	Eugene Fleming	Mr. Jones	David St. Louis
Luis	Juan Betancur	Jen Roberts	Nicole Bridgewater

One intermission.

Walnut Street Theatre, Philadelphia
Bernard Havard producing artistic director, Mark D. Sylvester managing director

CAMILA. Musical with book, music and lyrics by Lori McKelvey. September 12, 2001. Director, BT McNicholl; choreography, Richard Stafford; scenery, Riccardo Hernández; costumes, Suzy Benzinger; lighting, Brian Nason; sound, Scott Smith; stage manager, Debi Marucci.

Camila O'Gorman	Elizabeth Sastre	Señora O'Gorman	Alma Cuervo
Ladislao Gutierrez	Michael Hayden	Señor O'Gorman	David Brummel
La Perchona	Jane Summerhays		

With: Jason Adamo, Renee Bonadio, Rosa Collantes, Angela DeCicco, Enrique Cruz De Jesus, Sylvia Roldan Dohi, Kevin Duda, Maria Feeley, Laurie Ferdman, Francisco Forquera, Angel Garcia, Michael Licata, Dean Malissa, Mary Martello, Wilson Mendieta, Michael Oberlander, William Parry, Spencer Rowe, Rebecca Schall, Ellen Sowney, Bruce Winant.

Time: 19th-century. Place: Argentina. One intermission.

The Wilma Theater, Philadelphia
Blanka Zizka and Jiri Zizka producing artistic directors, Naomi Grabel managing director

PATIENCE. By Jason Sherman. September 24, 2001 (US premiere.) Director, Blanka Zizka; scenery, Jeremy Woodward; costumes, Janus Stefanowicz; lighting, Russell H. Champa; sound, Eileen Tague; dramaturg, Nakissa Etemad; stage manager, Patreshettarlini Adams.

Reuben	David Chandler	Donna; Frank	Sonja Robson
Peter; Phil	Jeffrey Hayenga	Paul; Mike; Janice; Rabbi	Jay Edwards
Sarah	Lise Bruneau	Pianist; Liz	Christina Ross

One intermission.

YELLOWMAN. By Dael Orlandersmith. February 20, 2002. Co-production with McCarter Theatre, Princeton, New Jersey; and Long Wharf Theatre, New Haven, Connecticut. See production details under McCarter Theatre.

INDIAN INK. By Tom Stoppard. May 8, 2002 (Philadelphia premiere). Director, Jiri Zizka; scenery, David Gordon; costumes, Janus Stefanowicz; lighting, Jerold R. Forsyth; sound, Adam Wernick; stage manager, Patreshettarlini Adams; dramaturg, Nakissa Etemad.

Coomaraswami; the Rajah; Politician	Wayman Ezell	Nazrul	Omar Mullick
Resident's Wife	April Feld	Nirad Das	Manu Narayan
Eleanor Swan	Barbara Haas	Resident	Buck Schirner
Eric; Englishman	Sam Henderson	Dilip; Questioner	Ashok Sinha
Anish Das	Sean T. Krishnan	Nell; Englishwoman	Elizabeth Webster
David Durrance	Richard G. Lyntton	Flora Crewe	Grace Zandarski
		Eldon Pike	William Zielinski

TEXAS

Alley Theatre, Houston
Gregory Boyd artistic director, Paul R. Tetreault managing director

THE CARPETBAGGER'S CHILDREN. By Horton Foote. June 6, 2001 (world premiere). Director, Michael Wilson; scenery, Jeff Cowie, costumes, David C. Woolard; lighting, Rui Rita; sound and music, John Gromada; stage manager, Amy Knotts. Co-production with the Guthrie Theater, Minneapolis, and Hartford Stage, Hartford, Connecticut.

Sissie	Hallie Foote	Grace Anne	Jean Stapleton
Cornelia	Roberta Maxwell		

Place: Harrison, Texas. No intermission.

UTAH

Utah Shakespearean Festival, Cedar City
Douglas N. Cook and Cameron Harvey producing artistic directors; R. Scott Phillips, managing director

AROUND THE WORLD IN 80 DAYS. By Mark Brown. Based on the novel by Jules Verne. September 14, 2001 (world premiere). Director, Russell Treyz; scenery, Christopher Pickart; costumes, Margaret E. Weedon; lighting, Brad Nelson; sound, Todd Ross; fight direction, Christopher Villa; production stage manager, Karen K. Wegner.

Foley Artist;		Phileas Fogg	Ian Stuart
Newspaperman	Bradley Dean Whyte	Sir Francis Cromarty;	
Auoda; James Forster	Enid Atkinson	Gauthier Ralph; others	Sam Stewart
Passepartout;		Detective Fix; others	Richard Kinter
John Sullivan	Alexander Ward		

Place: Various locations around the world. One intermission.

VERMONT

Dorset Playhouse, Dorset
Jill Charles artistic director, John Nassivera producing director

O THE DAYS! By Sheila Walsh. July 5, 2001 (world premiere). Director, John Morrison; scenery, Wm. John Aupperlee; costumes, Barbara A. Bell; lighting and sound, Bryan Miller; stage manager, Will Marquardt.

Nancy McGuire	Kathy Gail MacGowan	Widow Jones	Melissa Hurst
Una McQuire	Debra Whitfield	Thadden Mullen	Michael MacCauley
Moira Baines	Virginia Roncetti	Frances McQuire	Christopher Graham
Gramps	Ron Crawford		

Time: Spring 1975. Place: Small town in the west of Ireland. One intermission.

VIRGINIA

Barter Theatre, Abingdon
Richard Rose producing artistic director

MACBETH. By William Shakespeare; adapted by Richard Rose. March 13, 2002. Director, Mr. Rose; scenery, Mark DeVol; costumes, Amanda Aldridge; lighting, David Freidl;

sound, Bob Beck; fight direction, Robert Walsh; dramaturg, Peter Yonka; stage manager, John Hall.

Macbeth .... John Hedges
Lady Macbeth .... Karen Sabo
Macduff .... Will Bigham
Lady Macduff .... Catherine Gray
Banquo .... John Hardy
Duncan .... Michael Ostroski
Malcolm .... Peter Yonka

 Place: Scotland; England. One intermission.

Signature Theater, Arlington
Eric Schaeffer artistic director

THE GOSPEL ACCORDING TO FISHMAN. Musical with book and lyrics by Michael Lazar and Richard Oberacker, music by Mr. Oberacker. January 21, 2002 (world premiere). Director, Eric Schaeffer; scenery, James Kronzer; costumes, Rhonda Key; lighting, Daniel MacLean Wagner; orchestration, David Kreppel; musical staging, Karma Camp; musical direction, Paul Raiman; vocal arrangements, Keith Thompson.

Nehi Taylor .... E. Faye Butler
Alan Fishman .... Tally Sessions
Jolene Cooper .... Ta'Rea Campbell
Bunny Fishman .... Florence Lacey
Howard Fishman .... Harry A. Winter

 With: Almonica Caldwell, Chrystyna Dail, Eleasha Gamble, Gabrielle Goyette, Rodney D. Hussey, Larry D. Hylton Wendell Jordan, Susan Lynskey, Sean McLaughlin, Paul Morella, Cedric Sanders, Brian Quenton Thorne, Letitia Williams.

 Musical Numbers: "Glory," "My Son, the Writer," "One Step Closer," "Meet at the Gate," "How Many Times," "My Secret," "Start All Over Again," "Ready," "Two Weeks," "My Place at the Table," "Find Faith," "This Feels Like Home," "I Remember," "The Gospel According to Fishman," "You Love You," "Find Your Own Voice."

 Time: 1960s. Place: The segregated south. One intermission.

WASHINGTON

ACT Theatre, Seattle
Gordon Edelstein artistic director, Jim Loder managing director, Vito Zingarelli producing director

POLISH JOKE. By David Ives. July 12, 2001 (world premiere). Director, Jason McConnell Buzas; scenery, Loy Arcenas; costumes, Rose Pederson; lighting, Mary Louise Geiger; sound, Dominic CodyKramers; stage manager, Anne Kearson.

Roman; others .... Richard Ziman
Jasiu .... Ted deChatelet
Voytck; others .... Leslie Law
Helen; others .... Nancy Bell

 One intermission.

MISS GOLDEN DREAMS. By Joyce Carol Oates; based on Ms. Oates's novel *Blonde*. August 3, 2001. Director, Kurt Beattie; scenery, Scott Weldin; costumes, Carolyn Keim; lighting, Ann Ciecko; sound, Aaron Welch; fight direction, Geoffrey Alm; stage manager, Michael B. Paul.

Norma Jeane .... Carolyn Baeumler
Magi; others .... Frank Corrado
Otto; others .... Peter Crook
Young Norma Jeane .... Hilary Scheibert

WAITING TO BE INVITED. By S.M. Shephard-Massat. August 23, 2001 (West Coast premiere). Director, Israel Hicks; scenery, Bill Curley; costumes, David Kay Mickelsen; lighting, Allen Lee Hughes; sound, Dominic CodyKramers; stage manager, Jeffrey K. Hanson.

Miss Louise .... Demene E. Hall
Miss Odessa .... Ebony Jo-Ann
Miss Delores .... Cynthia Jones
Miss Ruth .... Michele Shay
Palmeroy Bateman .... Keith L. Hatten
Miss Grayson .... Jane Welch

    Time: Summer 1961. Place: Atlanta, Georgia. One intermission.

GRAND MAGIC. By Eduardo de Filippo; translated by Thomas Simpson. October 25, 2001. Director, Mladen Kiselov; scenery, Narelle Sissons; costumes, Marcia Dixcy Jory; lighting, Chris Parry; music and sound, John Gromada; dramaturg, Kurt Beattie.

Signora Locascio;
  Rosa Intrugli .... Laura Kenny
Signora Zampa;
  Mathilde Di Spelta .... Beth Andrisevic
Marta Di Spelta .... Mari Nelson
Calogero Di Spelta .... John Procaccino
Mariano D'Albino;
  Roberto Magliano .... Paul Morgan Stetler
Waiter; Oreste Intrugli .... Peter A. Jacobs

Gervasio Penna;
  Gennarino Fucecchio .... Clayton Corzatte
Arturo Recchia .... Richard Ziman
Amelia Recchia .... Winslow Corbett
Otto Marvulgia .... Ken Ruta
Mariannina Marvuglia .... Marianne Owen
Police Inspector;
  Gregorio Di Spelta .... David Pichette

    Time: Summer 1948; 1952. Place: Naples.

THE RACE OF THE ARK TATTOO. By W. David Hancock. October 26, 2001. Director, Melanie Joseph.

Featuring Matthew Maher.

FULLY COMMITTED. By Becky Mode. January 31, 2002. Director, Kurt Beattie; scenery, Scott Weldin; costumes designer, Carolyn Keim; lighting, Ann Ciecko; sound, Dominic CodyKramers; stage manager, Jeffrey K. Hanson. Presented in association with ShadowCatcher Entertainment.

Featuring R. Hamilton Wright.

THE SINGING FOREST. By Craig Lucas. February 1, 2002. Director, Gordon Edelstein; stage manager, Nat Whitten.

Loë Rieman;
  Marie Bonaparte .... Zoaunne LeRoy
Gray Korankyi;
  Walter Rieman .... Michael Black
Dr. Shar Unger;
  Dr. Max Schur .... Kevin Donovan
Dr. Oliver Pfaff;
  Martin Rieman .... Laurence Ballard
Lazslo Fickes;
  Gerhardt Zeiszler .... Daniel Eric Gold

Beth Adler;
  Young Loë Rieman .... Kristin Flanders
Bertha Ahmad;
  Anna Freud .... Marianne Owen
Jules Ahmad;
  Simon Hirsch .... Jay Goede
Bill; Sigmund Freud .... Clayton Corzatte
Stage directions .... Eric Mayer

    Time: 2000; 1930s. Place: New York; Vienna. Two intermissions.

MOURNING BECOMES ELECTRA. By Eugene O'Neill. April 25, 2002. Director, Gordon Edelstein; scenery, Andrew Jackness; costumes, Paul Tazewell; lighting, Jennifer Tipton; sound, John Gromada; dramaturg, Beatrice Basso; stage manager, Jeffrey K. Hanson.

Ezra Mannon .... Michael MacRae
Christine Mannon .... Jane Alexander
Lavinia Mannon .... Mireille Enos
Orin Mannon .... Steven Sutcliffe
Captain Adam Brant .... Thomas Schall
Captain Peter Niles .... Jason Cottle
Hazel Niles .... Liz McCarthy
Seth Beckwith .... Clayton Corzatte

    With: Chris Blanchett, Jonathan Frank, Paul Ray, Peter Sill.

    Time: Spring and summer, 1865–66. Two intermissions.

Women's Playwright Festival. May 9–11, 2002.

SLOW FAST WALKING ON THE RED EYE. By Caridad Svich. Director, Valerie Curtis-Newton.

ONE WOMAN, ONE CHILD. By Leanna Brodie. Director, Rita Giomi.

KATZMAN AND THE MAYOR. By Jessica Goldberg. Director, Leslie Swackhamer.

WAIT! By Julie Jensen. Director, Ellen Graham.

Empty Space Theatre, Seattle
Allison Narver artistic director

GREAT MEN OF SCIENCE, NOS. 21 & 22. By Glen Berger. June 6, 2001 (Northwest premiere). Director, Dan Fields; scenery, Louisa Thompson; costumes, Nanette Acosta; lighting, Timothy Wratten; sound, Nathan Anderson.

Spallanzani	Eric Ray Anderson	Housekeeper	Lori Larsen
Vaucanson	Burton Curtis	Abbé; Condorcet	Brian Thompson
Gabrielle	Mara Hesed	Le Cat	Seanjean Walsh

Time: 18th century. Place: France.

THE LARAMIE PROJECT. By Moisés Kaufman and the members of the Tectonic Theater Project. November 20, 2001 (Northwest premiere). Director, Chay Yew; scenery, Craig Wollam; costumes, Chela Scott Webber; lighting, Patti West; sound, Nathan Anderson.

With: Ian Bell, Susanna Burney, Kathy Hsieh, Duke Novak, Scott Plusquellec, Shelley Reynolds, Stephanie Shine, Ron Simons.

VALLEY OF THE DOLLS. By Jason Cannon, Burton Curtis and Allison Narver; based on the book and movie by Jacqueline Susann. January 9, 2002 (world premiere). Directors, Mr. Curtis and Ms. Narver; scenery, Richard Lorig, costumes, Dennis Milam Bensie; lighting, Timothy Wratten; sound, Nathan Anderson.

Helen Lawson	Suzanne Bouchard	Henry Bellamy	Ian Bell
Anne Wells	Nick Garrison	Lyon Burke	Kelly Boulware
Neeley O'Hara	Sarah Harlett	Ted Casablanca	Basil Harris
Jennifer North	Michelle Lewis	Tony Polar	John Kauffman

THE WAVERLY GALLERY. By Kenneth Lonergan. March 6, 2002. (West Coast premiere). Director, Kip Fagan; scenery, Peggy MacDonald; costumes, Rose Pederson; lighting, Patti West; sound, Nathan Anderson.

Gladys Green	Marjorie Nelson	Howard Fine	Mark Jenkins
Ellen Fine	Joyce Stettler	Don Bowman	David Gehrman
Daniel Reed	Michael Chick		

VERA WILDE. Musical with book, music and lyrics by Chris Jeffries. April 24, 2002 (world premiere). Director, Allison Narver; choreography, Wade Madsen; scenery, Carol Wolfe Clay; costumes, Rose Pederson; lighting, Timothy Wratten; sound, Nathan Anderson.

With: Nick Garrison, Julie Rawley, Basil Harris, Bhama Roget, Robert Shampain.

5th Avenue Theatre, Seattle
David Armstrong producing artistic director, Marilynn Sheldon managing director

THE PRINCE AND THE PAUPER. Musical with book by Ivan Menchell, music and lyrics by Marc Elliot and Judd Woldin; additional lyrics by Mr. Menchell; based on the novel by Mark Twain. November 29, 2001 (regional premiere). Director, Russell Kaplan; choreography, Casey Nicholaw; scenery, G.W. Mercier; costumes, Nanette Acosta; lighting, David Neville; sound, Lew Mead; fight direction, David Boushey; production stage manager, Cherese Campo. A co-production with the Ordway Center for the Performing Arts.

Tom Canty .... Cameron Bowen	Lord #2 .... Emil Herrera
Anne Canty .... Caroline Innerbichler	Lord #3 .... John Patrick Lowrie
Father Andrew;	Guards .... David Austin,
Archibishop .... Scott Watanabe	Cheyenne Jackson,
Edward Tudor .... Asher Monroe Book	Eric Polani Jensen,
King Henry VIII .... Perry L. Brown	Alec Stephens III
Lady Jane .... Kaitlyn M. Davidson	Witnesses .... Katie O'Shaughnessey,
Hertford .... Alan Coates	Aaron Shanks
John Canty .... Peter Lohnes	Miles Hendon .... Marc Kudisch
Mrs. Canty .... Stacia Fernandez	Mrs. Gibbons .... Claudia Wilkens
Lord #1 .... Dennis Bateman	Sheriff .... David Earl Hart

With: Kari Lee Cartwright, Daniel Cruz, Kevin Dunnigan, Lakeetra Gilbert, Billy Kimmel, Anna Lauris, Ann McCormick, Crystal Dawn Munkers. Charlie Parker, Stanley Perryman, Nikki Cardona-Rigor, Logan Denninghoff, Markell Effimoff, Meaghan Foy, Timmy McCauley, Teru McDonald, Codie Michaels, Rebecca Orts, Adriane Owens, Jordan Rosin, Thomas Wakefield.

One intermission.

Seattle Repertory Theatre, Seattle
Sharon Ott artistic director, Benjamin Moore managing director

THE BEARD OF AVON. By Amy Freed. November 12, 2001. Director, Sharon Ott; scenery, Kent Dorsey; costumes, Anna Oliver; lighting, Robert Jared; sound, Christopher Walker; stage manager, Joseph Smelser.

Colin; Player;	Code; Fitch;
Lucy; Johnson .... Eric Ray Anderson	Bacon; Peasant .... Peter Crook
De Vere; Peasant .... Laurence Ballard	William Shakespeare .... Dan Donohue
Anne; Wardrobe;	Dunderbread; Lettice;
Woman; Court Woman .... Julie Briskman	Lucy's Assistant .... Nick Garrison
Burbage;	Minstrel .... David Gehrman
Walsingham; Drayton .... Ron Campbell	Queen Elizabeth I .... Lori Larsen
Wriothesley;	Heminge;
Earl of Derby; Peasant .... Jason Cottle	Burleigh; Peasant .... Robert Sinclair

DON JUAN. By Molière; translated and adapted by Stephen Wadsworth. March 18, 2002. Director, Mr. Wadsworth; choreography, Daniel Pelzig; scenery, Kevin Rupnik; costumes, Anna Oliver; lighting, Amy Appleyard; sound, Christopher Walker; fight direction, Geoffrey Alm; dramaturg, Janice Paran; production stage manager, Joseph Smelser. A co-production with McCarter Theatre.

Gusman .... Gilbert Cruz	Pierrot .... Burton Curtis
Sganarelle .... Cameron Folmar	Mathurine .... Laura Kenny
Don Juan .... Adam Stein	Don Carlos .... Bruce Turk
Donna Elvira .... Francesca Faridany	Don Luis .... Frank Corrado
Charlotte .... Mary Bacon	

Ensemble: Cleopatra Bertelson, Ray Gonzalez, Sean Mitchell.

One intermission.

THE LAST TRUE BELIEVER. By Robert William Sherwood. February 18, 2002 (world premiere). Director: Leonard Foglia; scenery, Michael McGarty; costumes, David C.

Woolard; lighting, Brian Nason; sound, Christopher Walker; composer, Peter Golub; stage manager, Michael B. Paul.

Kevin Anderson	Coby Goss	Jessica Daniels	Liz McCarthy
Margaret Daniels	Lisa Harrow	Phillip Daniels	Terence Rigby
Jurgen Matheus	Peter A. Jacobs		

OBON: TALES OF RAIN AND MOONLIGHT. By Ping Chong; based on the stories of Lafcadio Hearn. April 15, 2002 (world premiere). Director, Mr. Chong; puppet creator, Atsushi Yamato; puppet choreography, Fred Riley III; lighting, Randy Ward; sound, David Meschter; composer, Guy Klucevsek; stage manager, Stacey Roberts. A co-production with Spoleto Festival USA, John F. Kennedy Center for the Performing Arts and Conversation & Company.

Performers: Jodi Eichelberger, Aya T. Kanai, Jennifer Kato, Fred Riley III, Sam Word.

Voices: Esther Chae, Ping Chong, Brian Hallas, Jennifer Kato, Michael Rohd, Jeffrey Rose, Louise Smith, Ching Valdes-Aran.

Hot Type: Sizzling New Plays, May 1–5, 2002.

SUGAR PLUM FAIRY. By Sandra Tsing Loh.

THE SÉANCE. By Philip and Belinda Haas; adapted from the novella *The Conjugal Angel* by A.S. Byatt.

BEOWULF. Book and lyrics by Robert O'Hara, music by Eric Schwartz.

MALEDICTION. By Bruce Hurlbut.

INVENTING VAN GOGH. By Steven Dietz.

EURYDICE. By Sarah Ruhl.

THE HOME OF POLAR BEARS. By Hilly Hicks Jr.

WISCONSIN

Milwaukee Repertory Theater, Milwaukee
Joseph Hanreddy artistic director, Timothy J. Shields managing director

8-TRACK: THE SOUNDS OF THE '70S. Musical revue by Rick Seeber. September 8, 2001 (regional premiere). Director, Mr. Seeber; choreography, Nicholas Sugar; scenery, Sarah L. Hunt-Frank; costumes, Tina Campbell; lighting, Chester Loeffler-Bell; production stage manager, Judy Berdan.

Featuring Teddey Brown, Tonya Phillips, Nik Rocklin, Liana Young.

THE MAGIC FIRE. By Lillian Groag. October 19, 2001 (regional premiere). Director, Ms. Groag; scenery, Michael Ganio; costumes, Tracy Dorman; lighting, Robert Wierzel; sound, Paul Peterson; dramaturg, Paul Kosidowski; production stage manager, Judy Berdan.

Lise	Kandis Chappell	Paula Guarneri	Mary Stark
Young Lise	Lillian Cummings	General Henri Fontannes	Lee E. Ernst
Otto Berg	Marcelo Tubert	Alberto Barcos	Torrey Hanson
Amalia Berg	Sharon Lockwood	Maddalena Guarneri	Melinda Peterson
Elena Guarneri	Laura Gordon	Rosa Arrura	Linda Stephens
Gianni "Juan" Guarneri;		Clara Stepaneck	Denise duMaurier
Giovanni	Peter Silbert	Leila	Kimberly Irion

Time: 1952. Place: Buenos Aires. Two intermissions.

MY WAY: A MUSICAL TRIBUTE TO FRANK SINATRA. Musical revue by David Grapes and Todd Olson. November 10, 2001 (regional premiere). Director and choreographer, Pam Kriger; scenery, Rick Rasmussen; costumes, Valerie Pruett; lighting, John Frautschy; production stage manager, Judy Berdan.

Featuring Ray Jivoff, Sheri Williams Pannell, Michele Smith, Branch Woodman.

ANNA CHRISTIE. By Eugene O'Neill. January 9, 2002. Director, Eric Simonson; scenery, Kent Dorsey; costumes, Kärin Kopsichke; lighting, Nancy Schertler; sound, Barry G. Funderburg; fight direction, Lee E. Ernst; dramaturg, Paul Kosidowski; production stage manager, Judy Berdan.

Johnny-the-Priest;	Larry; Sailor .... Paul Hurley
Sailor .... Jonathan Gillard Daly	The Postman .... James Pickering
Longshoreman #1;	Chris Christopherson .... Jim Baker
Johnson .... David Lee	Marthy Owen .... Rose Pickering
Longshoreman #2;	Anna Christopherson .... Deborah Staples
Sailor .... David Douglas Smith	Mat Burke .... Jeremy Holm

Time: Early 20th century. Place: New York; Provincetown; Boston. Two intermissions.

LITTLE BY LITTLE. Musical with book by Annette Jolles and Ellen Greenfield; music by Brad Ross, lyrics by Ms. Greenfield and Hal Hackady. January 12, 2002. Director and choreographer, Ed Burgess; scenery, Megan Wilkerson; costumes, Pamela J. Rehberg; lighting, Kurt Schnabel, musical direction, Richard Carsey; production stage manager, Judy Berdan.

Woman #1 .... Johnna Allen	Woman #2 .... Kay Stiefel
Man .... Michael Herold	

A SKULL IN CONNEMARA. By Martin McDonagh. January 18, 2002 (regional premiere). Director, Paul Barnes; scenery, Robin Stapley; costumes, Rosemary Ingham; lighting, Kenton Yeager; sound, Barry G. Funderburg; fight direction, Lee E. Ernst; production stage manager, Judy Berdan.

Mick Dowd .... Joseph Hanreddy	Mairtin Hanlon .... Brian Vaughn
Maryjohnny Rafferty .... Laurie Birmingham	Thomas Hanlon .... Michael Daly

Setting: Rural Galway. One intermission.

LOVERS AND EXECUTIONERS. By John Strand. February 22, 2002 (regional premiere). Director, Edward Morgan; scenery, Michael Frenkel; costumes, Helen Q. Huang; lighting, Joseph Appelt; sound, Barry G. Funderburg; fight direction, Colleen Kelly.

Bernard .... Jonathan Smoots	Octavius .... Michael Daly
Guzman .... John McGivern	Don Lope .... Mark Corkins
Julie; Frederic .... Laura Gordon	Don Lope's Squire .... David Lee
Beatrice .... Jacquelyn Ritz	The Tailor .... Ken Baldino
Constance .... Deborah Staples	The Tailor's Helper .... David Chrzanowski

With: John Walski, Paul Hurley, Ken Baldino, David Chrzanowski, David Lee.

Time: The mid-1660s. Place: A seaside town in France. One intermission.

BEACH BLANKET BASH! By Roger Bean. March 16, 2002 (world premiere). Director, Mr. Bean; choreography, Darci Brown Wutz; scenery, Sarah L. Hunt-Frank; costumes, Alex Tecoma; lighting, Chester Loeffler-Bell; production stage manager, Judy Berdan.

Frankie .... Ben Cherry	Annette .... Dorothy Elias-Fahn
Johnny .... David Coolidge	Candy .... Sarah Sokolovic

THE SHAUGHRAUN. By Dion Boucicault. April 3, 2002 (regional premiere). Director, Edward Morgan; scenery, Kent Dorsey; costumes, Martha Hally; lighting, Tom Hase; sound, Lindsay Jones; music, Maria Torres and Brett Lipshutz; production dramaturg, Paul Kosidowski; production stage manager, Judy Berdan.

Dion Boucicault;	Captain Molineux .... Ted Deasy
Conn the Shaughraun .... Brian Vaughn	The Sergeant .... David Chrzanowski
Robert Ffolliott .... Reese Maddigan	Corry Kinchela .... Jim Baker
Claire Ffolliott .... Jeannie Naughton	Harvey Duffy .... James Pickering
Artie O'Neal .... Deborah Staples	Paddy Reilly .... Mark Corkins
Mrs. O'Kelly .... Rose Pickering	Sullivan .... David Lee
Tatters .... Basel	Doyle .... John Walski
Father Dolan .... Jonathan Gillard Daly	Biddy Madigan .... Laurie Birmingham
Moya Dolan .... Laura Gordon	Nancy Malone .... Jennifer Fitzery

Musicians: Turner Collins, Brett Lipshutz, Maria Terre.

British Soldiers, Irish Constables, Keeners and Villagers: Ken Baldino, Michelle Brooks, David Chrzanowski, Jennifer Fitzery, Lorri Hamm, Paul Hurley, Kimberly Irion, David Lee, Marika Mashburn, Nickolas Rapaz, David Douglas Smith, John Walski, Leah Zhang.

Time: 1867. Place: In and around the village of Suil-a-beg, County Sligo. Two intermissions.

FACTS AND
FIGURES

LONG RUNS ON BROADWAY

○ ○ ○ ○ ○

THE FOLLOWING SHOWS HAVE RUN 500 or more continuous performances in a single production, usually the first, not including previews or extra non-profit performances, allowing for vacation layoffs and special one-booking engagements, but not including return engagements after a show has gone on tour. In all cases, the numbers were obtained directly from the show's production offices. Where there are title similarities, the production is identified as follows: (p) straight play version, (m) musical version, (r) revival, (tr) transfer.

THROUGH MAY 31, 2002

PLAYS MARKED WITH ASTERISK WERE STILL PLAYING JUNE 1, 2002

Plays	Performances	Plays	Performances
Cats	7,485	Born Yesterday	1,642
*Les Misérables	6,281	The Best Little Whorehouse in Texas	1,639
A Chorus Line	6,137	Crazy for You	1,622
*The Phantom of the Opera	5,984	Ain't Misbehavin'	1,604
Oh! Calcutta! (r)	5,959	Mary, Mary	1,572
Miss Saigon	4,097	Evita	1,567
42nd Street	3,486	The Voice of the Turtle	1,557
Grease	3,388	Jekyll & Hyde	1,543
*Beauty and the Beast	3,306	Barefoot in the Park	1,530
Fiddler on the Roof	3,242	Brighton Beach Memoirs	1,530
Life With Father	3,224	Dreamgirls	1,522
Tobacco Road	3,182	Mame (m)	1,508
Hello, Dolly!	2,844	Grease (r)	1,503
My Fair Lady	2,717	Same Time, Next Year	1,453
*Rent	2,540	Arsenic and Old Lace	1,444
Annie	2,377	The Sound of Music	1,443
Man of La Mancha	2,328	Me and My Girl	1,420
Abie's Irish Rose	2,327	How to Succeed in Business	
*Chicago (m)(r)	2,311	Without Really Trying	1,417
Oklahoma!	2,212	Hellzapoppin'	1,404
Smokey Joe's Cafe	2,036	The Music Man	1,375
Pippin	1,944	Funny Girl	1,348
*The Lion King	1,932	Mummenschanz	1,326
South Pacific	1,925	Angel Street	1,295
The Magic Show	1,920	Lightnin'	1,291
Deathtrap	1,793	Promises, Promises	1,281
Gemini	1,788	The King and I	1,246
Harvey	1,775	Cactus Flower	1,234
Dancin'	1,774	Sleuth	1,222
La Cage aux Folles	1,761	Torch Song Trilogy	1,222
Hair	1,750	1776	1,217
*Cabaret (r)	1,707	Equus	1,209
The Wiz	1,672	Sugar Babies	1,208

Plays	Performances
Guys and Dolls	1,200
Amadeus	1,181
Cabaret	1,165
Mister Roberts	1,157
Annie Get Your Gun	1,147
Guys and Dolls (r)	1,144
The Seven Year Itch	1,141
Bring in 'da Noise, Bring in 'da Funk	1,130
Butterflies Are Free	1,128
Pins and Needles	1,108
Plaza Suite	1,097
Fosse	1,092
They're Playing Our Song	1,082
Grand Hotel (m)	1,077
Kiss Me, Kate	1,070
Don't Bother Me, I Can't Cope	1,065
The Pajama Game	1,063
Shenandoah	1,050
Annie Get Your Gun (r)	1,046
The Teahouse of the August Moon	1,027
Damn Yankees	1,019
Never Too Late	1,007
Big River	1,005
The Will Rogers Follies	983
Any Wednesday	982
Sunset Boulevard	977
A Funny Thing Happened on the Way to the Forum	964
The Odd Couple	964
Anna Lucasta	957
Kiss and Tell	956
Show Boat (r)	949
Dracula (r)	925
Bells Are Ringing	924
The Moon Is Blue	924
Beatlemania	920
The Elephant Man	916
*Aida	910
Kiss of the Spider Woman	906
*Contact	903
Luv	901
The Who's Tommy	900
Chicago (m)	898
Applause	896
Can-Can	892
Carousel	890
I'm Not Rappaport	890
Hats Off to Ice	889
Fanny	888
Children of a Lesser God	887
Follow the Girls	882
Kiss Me, Kate (m)(r)	881
City of Angels	878
Camelot	873
I Love My Wife	872
The Bat	867
My Sister Eileen	864

Plays	Performances
No, No, Nanette (r)	861
Ragtime	861
Song of Norway	860
Chapter Two	857
A Streetcar Named Desire	855
Barnum	854
Comedy in Music	849
Raisin	847
Blood Brothers	839
You Can't Take It With You	837
La Plume de Ma Tante	835
Three Men on a Horse	835
The Subject Was Roses	832
Black and Blue	824
The King and I (r)	807
Inherit the Wind	806
Anything Goes (r)	804
Titanic	804
No Time for Sergeants	796
Fiorello!	795
Where's Charley?	792
The Ladder	789
Forty Carats	780
Lost in Yonkers	780
The Prisoner of SecondAvenue	780
M. Butterfly	777
Oliver!	774
The Pirates of Penzance (1980 r)	772
Woman of the Year	770
My One and Only	767
Sophisticated Ladies	767
Bubbling Brown Sugar	766
Into the Woods	765
State of the Union	765
Starlight Express	761
The First Year	760
Broadway Bound	756
You Know I Can't Hear You When the Water's Running	755
Two for the Seesaw	750
Joseph and the Amazing Technicolor Dreamcoat (r)	747
Death of a Salesman	742
For Colored Girls . . .	742
Sons o' Fun	742
Candide (m, r)	740
Gentlemen Prefer Blondes	740
The Man Who Came to Dinner	739
Nine	739
Call Me Mister	734
Victor/Victoria	734
West Side Story	732
High Button Shoes	727
Finian's Rainbow	725
Claudia	722
The Gold Diggers	720
Jesus Christ Superstar	720

Plays	Performances
Carnival	719
The Diary of Anne Frank	717
A Funny Thing Happened on the Way to the Forum (r)	715
I Remember Mama	714
Tea and Sympathy	712
Junior Miss	710
Footloose	708
Last of the Red Hot Lovers	706
The Secret Garden	706
Company	705
Seventh Heaven	704
Gypsy (m)	702
The Miracle Worker	700
That Championship Season	700
The Music Man (m)(r)	698
Da	697
Cat on a Hot Tin Roof	694
Li'l Abner	693
The Children's Hour	691
Purlie	688
Dead End	687
The Lion and the Mouse	686
White Cargo	686
Dear Ruth	683
East Is West	680
Come Blow Your Horn	677
The Most Happy Fella	676
Defending the Caveman	671
The Doughgirls	671
The Impossible Years	670
Irene	670
Boy Meets Girl	669
The Tap Dance Kid	669
Beyond the Fringe	667
*Proof	665
*The Full Monty	664
Who's Afraid of Virginia Woolf?	664
Blithe Spirit	657
A Trip to Chinatown	657
The Women	657
*The Tale of the Allergist's Wife	654
Bloomer Girl	654
The Fifth Season	654
Rain	648
Witness for the Prosecution	645
Call Me Madam	644
Janie	642
The Green Pastures	640
Auntie Mame (p)	639
A Man for All Seasons	637
Jerome Robbins' Broadway	634
The Fourposter	632
The Music Master	627
Two Gentlemen of Verona (m)	627
The Tenth Man	623
The Heidi Chronicles	621

Plays	Performances
Is Zat So?	618
Anniversary Waltz	615
The Happy Time (p)	614
Separate Rooms	613
Affairs of State	610
Oh! Calcutta! (tr)	610
Star and Garter	609
The Mystery of Edwin Drood	608
The Student Prince	608
Sweet Charity	608
Bye Bye Birdie	607
Riverdance on Broadway	605
Irene (r)	604
Sunday in the Park With George	604
Adonis	603
Broadway	603
Peg o' My Heart	603
Master Class	601
Street Scene (p)	601
Flower Drum Song	600
Kiki	600
A Little Night Music	600
Art	600
Agnes of God	599
Don't Drink the Water	598
Wish You Were Here	598
Sarafina!	597
A Society Circus	596
Absurd Person Singular	592
A Day in Hollywood/ A Night in the Ukraine	588
The Me Nobody Knows	586
The Two Mrs. Carrolls	585
Kismet (m)	583
Gypsy (m, r)	582
Brigadoon	581
Detective Story	581
No Strings	580
Brother Rat	577
Blossom Time	576
Pump Boys and Dinettes	573
Show Boat	572
The Show-Off	571
Sally	570
Jelly's Last Jam	569
Golden Boy (m)	568
One Touch of Venus	567
The Real Thing	566
Happy Birthday	564
Look Homeward, Angel	564
Morning's at Seven (r)	564
The Glass Menagerie	561
I Do! I Do!	560
Wonderful Town	559
The Last Night of Ballyhoo	557
Rose Marie	557
Strictly Dishonorable	557

Plays	Performances	Plays	Performances
Sweeney Todd,		Fences	526
the Demon Barber of Fleet Street	557	The Solid Gold Cadillac	526
The Great White Hope	556	Biloxi Blues	524
A Majority of One	556	Irma La Douce	524
The Sisters Rosensweig	556	The Boomerang	522
Sunrise at Campobello	556	Follies	521
Toys in the Attic	556	Rosalinda	521
Jamaica	555	The Best Man	520
Stop the World—I Want to Get Off	555	Chauve-Souris	520
Florodora	553	Blackbirds of 1928	518
Noises Off	553	The Gin Game	517
Ziegfeld Follies (1943)	553	Sunny	517
Dial "M" for Murder	552	Victoria Regina	517
Good News	551	Fifth of July	511
Peter Pan (r)	551	Half a Sixpence	511
How to Succeed in Business		The Vagabond King	511
Without Really Trying (r)	548	The New Moon	509
Let's Face It	547	The World of Suzie Wong	508
Milk and Honey	543	The Rothschilds	507
Within the Law	541	On Your Toes (r)	505
Pal Joey (r)	540	Sugar	505
The Sound of Music (r)	540	Shuffle Along	504
What Makes Sammy Run?	540	Up in Central Park	504
The Sunshine Boys	538	Carmen Jones	503
What a Life	538	Saturday Night Fever	502
Crimes of the Heart	535	The Member of the Wedding	501
Damn Yankees (r)	533	Panama Hattie	501
The Unsinkable Molly Brown	532	Personal Appearance	501
The Red Mill (r)	531	Bird in Hand	500
Rumors	531	Room Service	500
A Raisin in the Sun	530	Sailor, Beware!	500
Godspell (tr)	527	Tomorrow the World	500

LONG RUNS OFF BROADWAY

Plays	Performances	Plays	Performances
The Fantasticks	17,162	One Mo' Time	1,372
*Perfect Crime	6,254	Grandma Sylvia's Funeral	1,360
*Tubes	5,212	Let My People Come	1,327
*Tony 'n' Tina's Wedding	§ 4,654	*Naked Boys Singing!	1,206
Nunsense	3,672	Driving Miss Daisy	1,195
*Stomp	3,464	The Hot l Baltimore	1,166
The Threepenny Opera	2,611	I'm Getting My Act Together	
*I Love You, You're Perfect,		and Taking It on the Road	1,165
Now Change	2,448	Little Mary Sunshine	1,143
Forbidden Broadway 1982–87	2,332	Steel Magnolias	1,126
Little Shop of Horrors	2,209	*Late Nite Catechism	1,115
Godspell	2,124	El Grande de Coca-Cola	1,114
Vampire Lesbians of Sodom	2,024	The Proposition	1,109
Jacques Brel	1,847	*The Vagina Monologues	1,105
Forever Plaid	1,811	Beau Jest	1,069
Vanities	1,785	*Our Sinatra	1,037
You're a Good Man, Charlie Brown	1,597	Tamara	1,036
*De La Guarda	1,549	One Flew Over the Cuckoo's Nest (r)	1,025
The Blacks	1,408	The Boys in the Band	1,000

Plays	Performances	Plays	Performances
Fool for Love	1,000	Penn & Teller	666
Other People's Money	990	Dinner With Friends	654
Cloud 9	971	America Hurrah	634
Secrets Every Smart Traveler Should Know	953	Oil City Symphony	626
		The Countess	618
Sister Mary Ignatius Explains It All for You & The Actor's Nightmare	947	Hogan's Goat	607
		Beehive	600
Your Own Thing	933	The Trojan Women	600
Curley McDimple	931	*The Syringa Tree	583
Leave It to Jane (r)	928	The Dining Room	583
*The Donkey Show	862	Krapp's Last Tape & The Zoo Story	582
Hedwig and the Angry Inch	857	Three Tall Women	582
Forbidden Broadway Strikes Back	850	The Dumbwaiter & The Collection	578
When Pigs Fly	840	Forbidden Broadway 1990	576
The Mad Show	871	Dames at Sea	575
Scrambled Feet	831	The Crucible (r)	571
The Effect of Gamma Rays on Man-in-the-Moon Marigolds	819	The Iceman Cometh (r)	565
		Forbidden Broadway 2001: A Spoof Odyssey	552
Over the River and Through the Woods	800	The Hostage (r)	545
A View From the Bridge (r)	780	Wit	545
The Boy Friend (r)	763	What's a Nice Country Like You Doing in a State Like This?	543
True West	762	Forbidden Broadway 1988	534
Forbidden Broadway Cleans Up Its Act!	754	Gross Indecency: The Three Trials of Oscar Wilde	534
Isn't It Romantic	733	Frankie and Johnny in the Clair de Lune	533
Dime a Dozen	728		
The Pocket Watch	725	Six Characters in Search of an Author (r)	529
The Connection	722	All in the Timing	526
The Passion of Dracula	714	Oleanna	513
Adaptation & Next	707	Making Porn	511
Oh! Calcutta!	704	The Dirtiest Show in Town	509
Scuba Duba	692	Happy Ending & Day of Absence	504
The Foreigner	686	Greater Tuna	501
The Knack	685	A Shayna Maidel	501
Fully Committed	675	The Boys From Syracuse (r)	500
The Club	674		
The Balcony	672		

§ ERRATUM IN 2000–2001 EDITION: Through an editing error, the 2000–01 edition showed an incorrect number of performances for the Off Broadway production of *Tony 'n' Tina's Wedding*. The correct number through May 31, 2001 should have been 4,384 performances. The totals in this edition reflect the corrected tally.

NEW YORK DRAMA CRITICS CIRCLE
1935–1936 TO 2001–2002

○ ○ ○ ○ ○

L ISTED BELOW ARE THE NEW YORK Drama Critics Circle Awards from 1935–1936 through 2001–2002 classified as follows: (1) Best American Play, (2) Best Foreign Play, (3) Best Musical, (4) Best, Regardless of Category (this category was established by new voting rules in 1962–63 and did not exist prior to that year).

1935–36 (1) *Winterset*

1936–37 (1) *High Tor*

1937–38 (1) *Of Mice and Men*, (2) *Shadow and Substance*

1938–39 (1) No award, (2) *The White Steed*

1939–40 (1) *The Time of Your Life*

1940–41 (1) *Watch on the Rhine*, (2) *The Corn Is Green*

1941–42 (1) No award, (2) *Blithe Spirit*

1942–43 (1) *The Patriots*

1943–44 (2) *Jacobowsky and the Colonel*

1944–45 (1) *The Glass Menagerie*

1945–46 (3) *Carousel*

1946–47 (1) *All My Sons*, (2) *No Exit*, (3) *Brigadoon*

1947–48 (1) *A Streetcar Named Desire*, (2) *The Winslow Boy*

1948–49 (1) *Death of a Salesman*, (2) *The Madwoman of Chaillot*, (3) *South Pacific*

1949–50 (1) *The Member of the Wedding*, (2) *The Cocktail Party*, (3) *The Consul*

1950–51 (1) *Darkness at Noon*, (2) *The Lady's Not for Burning*, (3) *Guys and Dolls*

1951–52 (1) *I Am a Camera*, (2) *Venus Observed*, (3) *Pal Joey* (Special citation to *Don Juan in Hell*)

1952–53 (1) *Picnic*, (2) *The Love of Four Colonels*, (3) *Wonderful Town*

1953–54 (1) *The Teahouse of the August Moon*, (2) *Ondine*, (3) *The Golden Apple*

1954–55 (1) *Cat on a Hot Tin Roof*, (2) *Witness for the Prosecution*, (3) *The Saint of Bleecker Street*

1955–56 (1) *The Diary of Anne Frank*, (2) *Tiger at the Gates*, (3) *My Fair Lady*

1956–57 (1) *Long Day's Journey Into Night*, (2) *The Waltz of the Toreadors*, (3) *The Most Happy Fella*

1957–58 (1) *Look Homeward, Angel*, (2) *Look Back in Anger*, (3) *The Music Man*

1958–59 (1) *A Raisin in the Sun*, (2) *The Visit*, (3) *La Plume de Ma Tante*

1959–60 (1) *Toys in the Attic*, (2) *Five Finger Exercise*, (3) *Fiorello!*

1960–61 (1) *All the Way Home*, (2) *A Taste of Honey*, (3) *Carnival*

1961–62 (1) *The Night of the Iguana*, (2) *A Man for All Seasons*, (3) *How to Succeed in Business Without Really Trying*

1962–63 (4) *Who's Afraid of Virginia Woolf?* (Special citation to *Beyond the Fringe*)

1963–64 (4) *Luther*, (3) *Hello, Dolly!* (Special citation to *The Trojan Women*)

1964–65 (4) *The Subject Was Roses*, (3) *Fiddler on the Roof*

1965–66 (4) *The Persecution and Assassination of Marat as Performed by the Inmates of the Asylum of Charenton Under the Direction of the Marquis de Sade*, (3) *Man of La Mancha*

1966–67 (4) *The Homecoming*, (3) *Cabaret*

1967–68 (4) *Rosencrantz and Guildenstern Are Dead*, (3) *Your Own Thing*

1968–69 (4) *The Great White Hope*, (3) *1776*

1969–70 (4) *Borstal Boy*, (1) *The Effect of Gamma Rays on Man-in-the-Moon Marigolds*, (3) *Company*

1970–71 (4) *Home*, (1) *The House of Blue Leaves*, (3) *Follies*

1971–72 (4) *That Championship Season*, (2) *The Screens* (3) *Two Gentlemen of Verona* (Special citations to *Sticks and Bones* and *Old Times*)

1972–73 (4) *The Changing Room*, (1) *The Hot l Baltimore*, (3) *A Little Night Music*

1973–74 (4) *The Contractor*, (1) *Short Eyes*, (3) *Candide*

1974–75 (4) *Equus* (1) *The Taking of Miss Janie*, (3) *A Chorus Line*

1975–76 (4) *Travesties*, (1) *Streamers*, (3) *Pacific Overtures*

1976–77   (4) *Otherwise Engaged*, (1) *American Buffalo*, (3) *Annie*
1977–78   (4) *Da*, (3) *Ain't Misbehavin'*
1978–79   (4) *The Elephant Man*, (3) *Sweeney Todd, the Demon Barber of Fleet Street*
1979–80   (4) *Talley's Folly*, (2) *Betrayal*, (3) *Evita* (Special citation to Peter Brook's Le Centre International de Créations Théâtrales for its repertory)
1980–81   (4) *A Lesson From Aloes*, (1) *Crimes of the Heart* (Special citations to *Lena Horne: The Lady and Her Music* and the New York Shakespeare Festival production of *The Pirates of Penzance*)
1981–82   (4) *The Life & Adventures of Nicholas Nickleby*, (1) *A Soldier's Play*
1982–83   (4) *Brighton Beach Memoirs*, (2) *Plenty*, (3) *Little Shop of Horrors* (Special citation to Young Playwrights Festival)
1983–84   (4) *The Real Thing*, (1) *Glengarry Glen Ross*, (3) *Sunday in the Park With George* (Special citation to Samuel Beckett for the body of his work)
1984–85   (4) *Ma Rainey's Black Bottom*
1985–86   (4) *A Lie of the Mind*, (2) *Benefactors* (Special citation to *The Search for Signs of Intelligent Life in the Universe*)
1986–87   (4) *Fences*, (2) *Les Liaisons Dangereuses*, (3) *Les Misérables*
1987–88   (4) *Joe Turner's Come and Gone*, (2) *The Road to Mecca*, (3) *Into the Woods*
1988–89   (4) *The Heidi Chronicles*, (2) *Aristocrats* (Special citation to Bill Irwin for *Largely New York*)
1989–90   (4) *The Piano Lesson*, (2) *Privates on Parade*, (3) *City of Angels*

1990–91   (4) *Six Degrees of Separation*, (2) *Our Country's Good*, (3) *The Will Rogers Follies* (Special citation to Eileen Atkins for her portrayal of Virginia Woolf in *A Room of One's Own*)
1991–92   (4) *Dancing at Lughnasa*, (1) *Two Trains Running*
1992–93   (4) *Angels in America: Millennium Approaches*, (2) *Someone Who'll Watch Over Me*, (3) *Kiss of the Spider Woman*
1993–94   (4) *Three Tall Women* (Special citation to Anna Deavere Smith for her unique contribution to theatrical form)
1994–95   (4) *Arcadia*, (1) *Love! Valour! Compassion!* (Special citation to Signature Theatre Company for outstanding artistic achievement)
1995–96   (4) *Seven Guitars*, (2) *Molly Sweeney*, (3) *Rent*
1996–97   (4) *How I Learned to Drive*, (2) *Skylight*, (3) *Violet* (Special citation to *Chicago*)
1997–98   (4) *Art*, (1) *Pride's Crossing*, (3) *The Lion King* (Special citation to the revival production of *Cabaret*)
1998–99   (4) *Wit*, (3) *Parade*, (2) *Closer* (Special citation to David Hare for his contributions to the 1998–99 theater season: *Amy's View*, *Via Dolorosa* and *The Blue Room*)
1999–00   (4) *Jitney*, (3) *James Joyce's The Dead*, (2) *Copenhagen*
2000–01   (4) *The Invention of Love*, (1) *Proof*, (3) *The Producers*
2001–02   (4) *Edward Albee's The Goat, or Who is Sylvia?* (Special citation to Elaine Stritch for *Elaine Stritch at Liberty*)

NEW YORK DRAMA CRITICS CIRCLE VOTING 2001–2002
Michael Sommers (*The Star-Ledger*, Newark), President

AT ITS MAY 7, 2002 MEETING the New York Drama Critics Circle declined to honor a musical for the 2001–02 season, voting a best-play award to *The Goat, or Who Is Sylvia?* and a special citation to *Elaine Stritch at Liberty*—the latter award voted just hours after *Best Plays* announced that it would honor Stritch and collaborator John Lahr with a special citation. It was the first season since 1994–95 that no musical was honored and the first since 1993–94 that no work from abroad was honored.

Seventeen members of the Circle were present for the voting. Among the absent, Linda Winer of *Newsday* was the sole voter by proxy (Ben Brantley of

The New York Times and Elysa Gardner of *USA Today* were the two absent members who did not vote). The first ballot voting for best play was divided as follows: *The Goat, or Who Is Sylvia?* 6 (Michael Feingold, *The Village Voice*; Charles Isherwood, *Variety;* Michael Kuchwara, The Associated Press; Ken Mandelbaum, Broadway.com; Michael Sommers, *The Star-Ledger*/Newhouse Newspapers; Bruce Weber, *The New York Times*), *Fortune's Fool* 5 (Clive Barnes, *New York Post*; Howard Kissel, *Daily News*; Jacques le Sourd, Gannett *Journal News*; Donald Lyons, *New York Post*; John Simon, *New York*), *Metamorphoses* 2 (Robert Feldberg, *The Bergen Record*; Richard Zoglin, *Time*), *Homebody/Kabul* 1 (John Heilpern, *The New York Observer*), *The Guys* 1 (Frank Scheck, *The Hollywood Reporter*), *Breath, Boom* (David Sheward, *Back Stage*), *Topdog/ Underdog* (Linda Winer, *Newsday*), *The Dazzle* (Jason Zinoman, *Time Out New York*).

No play received a majority of votes on the first ballot, so the Circle went to a weighted system for the second round, which allowed voters to select first, second and third choices. No winner emerged in the second round. A third ballot matched the top vote-getters of the previous round. With 17 members present *The Goat, or Who Is Sylvia?* received 9 votes in the final round to 8 votes for *Fortune's Fool*. Edward Albee and Elaine Stritch were honored for their respective accomplishments at a May 21 cocktail party.

PULITZER PRIZE WINNERS
1916–1917 TO 2001–2002

1916–17   No award

1917–18   *Why Marry?* by Jesse Lynch Williams

1918–19   No award

1919–20   *Beyond the Horizon* by Eugene O'Neill

1920–21   *Miss Lulu Bett* by Zona Gale

1921–22   *Anna Christie* by Eugene O'Neill

1922–23   *Icebound* by Owen Davis

1923–24   *Hell-Bent fer Heaven* by Hatcher Hughes

1924–25   *They Knew What They Wanted* by Sidney Howard

1925–26   *Craig's Wife* by George Kelly

1926–27   *In Abraham's Bosom* by Paul Green

1927–28   *Strange Interlude* by Eugene O'Neill

1928–29   *Street Scene* by Elmer Rice

1929–30   *The Green Pastures* by Marc Connelly

1930–31   *Alison's House* by Susan Glaspell

1931–32   *Of Thee I Sing* by George S. Kaufman, Morrie Ryskind, Ira and George Gershwin

1932–33   *Both Your Houses* by Maxwell Anderson

1933–34   *Men in White* by Sidney Kingsley

1934–35   *The Old Maid* by Zoe Akins

1935–36   *Idiot's Delight* by Robert E. Sherwood

1936–37   *You Can't Take It With You* by Moss Hart and George S. Kaufman

1937–38   *Our Town* by Thornton Wilder

1938–39   *Abe Lincoln in Illinois* by Robert E. Sherwood

1939–40   *The Time of Your Life* by William Saroyan

1940–41   *There Shall Be No Night* by Robert E. Sherwood

1941–42   No award

1942–43   *The Skin of Our Teeth* by Thornton Wilder

1943–44   No award

1944–45   *Harvey* by Mary Chase

1945–46   *State of the Union* by Howard Lindsay and Russel Crouse

1946–47   No award

1947–48   *A Streetcar Named Desire* by Tennessee Williams

1948–49   *Death of a Salesman* by Arthur Miller

1949–50   *South Pacific* by Richard Rodgers, Oscar Hammerstein II and Joshua Logan

1950–51   No award

1951–52   *The Shrike,* by Joseph Kramm

1952–53   *Picnic* by William Inge

1953–54   *The Teahouse of the August Moon* by John Patrick

1954–55   *Cat on a Hot Tin Roof* by Tennessee Williams

1955–56   *The Diary of Anne Frank* by Frances Goodrich and Albert Hackett

1956–57   *Long Day's Journey Into Night* by Eugene O'Neill

1957–58   *Look Homeward, Angel* by Ketti Frings

1958–59   *J.B.* by Archibald MacLeish

1959–60   *Fiorello!* by Jerome Weidman, George Abbott, Sheldon Harnick and Jerry Bock

1960–61   *All the Way Home* by Tad Mosel

1961–62   *How to Succeed in Business Without Really Trying* by Abe Burrows, Willie Gilbert, Jack Weinstock and Frank Loesser

1962–63   No award

1963–64   No award

1964–65   *The Subject Was Roses* by Frank D. Gilroy

1965–66   No award

1966–67   *A Delicate Balance* by Edward Albee

1967–68   No award

1968–69   *The Great White Hope* by Howard Sackler

1969–70   *No Place To Be Somebody* by Charles Gordone

1970–71   *The Effect of Gamma Rays on Man-in-the-Moon Marigolds* by Paul Zindel

1971–72   No award

1972–73   *That Championship Season* by Jason Miller

1973–74   No award

1974–75   *Seascape* by Edward Albee

1975–76   *A Chorus Line* by Michael Bennett, James Kirkwood, Nicholas Dante, Marvin Hamlisch and Edward Kleban

1976–77   *The Shadow Box* by Michael Cristofer

1977–78   *The Gin Game* by D.L. Coburn

1978–79   *Buried Child* by Sam Shepard

1979–80   *Talley's Folly* by Lanford Wilson

1980–81   *Crimes of the Heart* by Beth Henley

1981–82   *A Soldier's Play* by Charles Fuller

1982–83   *'night, Mother* by Marsha Norman

1983–84   *Glengarry Glen Ross* by David Mamet

1984–85   *Sunday in the Park With George* by James Lapine and Stephen Sondheim

1985–86   No award

1986–87   *Fences* by August Wilson

1987–88 *Driving Miss Daisy* by Alfred Uhry
1988–89 *The Heidi Chronicles* by Wendy Wasserstein
1989–90 *The Piano Lesson* by August Wilson
1990–91 *Lost in Yonkers* by Neil Simon
1991–92 *The Kentucky Cycle* by Robert Schenkkan
1992–93 *Angels in America: Millennium Approaches* by Tony Kushner
1993–94 *Three Tall Women* by Edward Albee
1994–95 *The Young Man From Atlanta* by Horton Foote

1995–96 *Rent* by Jonathan Larson
1996–97 No award
1997–98 *How I Learned to Drive* by Paula Vogel
1998–99 *Wit* by Margaret Edson
1999–00 *Dinner With Friends* by Donald Margulies
2000–01 *Proof* by David Auburn
2001–02 *Topdog/Underdog* by Suzan-Lori Parks

TONY AWARDS 2002

○ ○ ○ ○ ○

THE AMERICAN THEATRE WING'S 56th annual Tony Awards, named for Antoinette Perry, are presented in recognition of distinguished achievement in the Broadway theater. The League of American Theatres and Producers and the American Theatre Wing present these awards, founded by the Wing in 1947. Legitimate theater productions opening in 39 eligible Broadway theaters during the present Tony season—May 3, 2001 to May 1, 2002—were considered by the Tony Awards Nominating Committee (appointed by the Tony Awards Administration Committee) for the awards in 22 competitive and 2 special categories. The 2001–2002 Nominating Committee included Maureen Anderman, actor; Price Berkley, publisher; Robert Callely, administrator; Betty Corwin, archivist; Gretchen Cryer, composer; John Cunningham, actor; Jim Dale, actor; Jerry Dominus, executive; David Marshall Grant, actor; Micki Grant, composer and lyricist; Carol Hall, composer and lyricist; Sheldon Harnick, lyricist; Betty Jacobs, script consultant; Robert Kamlot, general manager; Louise Kerz, historian; Theodore Mann, producer and director; Peter Neufeld, general manager; Gilbert Parker, agent; David Richards, journalist; Aubrey Reuben, photographer; Arthur Rubin, producer; Judith Rubin, arts executive; Meg Simon, casting director; Rosemarie Tichler, casting director; Arnold Weinstein, educator; George C. White, artistic director; Jon Wilner, producer.

The Tony Awards are voted from the list of nominees by members of the theater and journalism professions: the governing boards of the five theater artists' organizations—Actors' Equity Association, the Dramatists Guild, the Society of Stage Directors and Choreographers, the United Scenic Artists and the Casting Society of America—the members of the designated first night theater press, the board of directors of the American Theatre Wing and the membership of the League of American Theatres and Producers. Because of fluctuation in these groups, the size of the Tony electorate varies from year to year. For the 2001–2002 season there were 731 qualified Tony voters.

The 2001–2002 nominees follow, with winners in each category listed in **bold face type**.

BEST PLAY (award goes to both author and producer). *The Goat, or Who Is Sylvia?* **by Edward Albee, produced by Elizabeth Ireland McCann, Daryl Roth, Carole Shorenstein Hays, Terry Allen Kramer, Scott Rudin, Bob Boyett, Scott Nederlander, Jeffrey Sine/ZPI**. *Fortune's Fool* by Ivan Turgenev, adapted by Mike Poulton, produced by Julian Schlossberg, Roy Furman, Ben Sprecher, Ted Tulchin, Aaron Levy, Peter May, Bob Boyett, James Fantaci. *Metamorphoses* by Mary Zimmerman, produced by Roy Gabay, Robyn Goodman, Allan S. Gordon, Élan V. McAllister, Dede Harris/Morton Swinsky, Ruth Hendel, Sharon Karmazin, Randall L. Wreghitt/Jane Bergère, Second Stage Theatre, Carole Rothman, Carol Fishman. *Topdog/Underdog* by Suzan-Lori Parks, produced by Carole Shorenstein Hays, Waxman Williams Entertainment, Bob Boyett, Freddy De Mann, Susan Dietz/Ina Meibach, Scott Nederlander, Ira Pittelman, Hits Magazine, Kelpie Arts, Rick Steiner/Frederic H. Mayerson, The Joseph Papp Public Theater/New York Shakespeare Festival.

BEST MUSICAL (award goes to the producer). *Mamma Mia!* produced by Judy Craymer, Richard East and Björn Ulvaeus for LittleStar, Universal. *Sweet Smell of Success* produced by Clear Channel Entertainment, David Brown, Ernest Lehman, Marty Bell, Martin Richards, Roy Furman, Joan Cullman, Bob Boyett, East of Doheny, Bob and Harvey Weinstein. *Thoroughly Modern Millie* **produced by Michael Leavitt, Fox Theatricals, Hal Luftig, Stewart F. Lane, James L. Nederlander, Independent Presenters Network, Libby Adler Mages/ Mari Glick, Dori Berinstein/Jennifer Manocherian/Dramatic Forces, John York Noble, Whoopi Goldberg**. *Urinetown* produced by the Araca Group and Dodger Theatricals, TheaterDreams, Inc., Lauren Mitchell.

BEST BOOK OF A MUSICAL. Catherine Johnson for *Mamma Mia!*, John Guare for *Sweet Smell of Success*, Richard Morris and Dick Scanlan for *Thoroughly Modern Millie*, **Greg Kotis for *Urinetown***.

BEST ORIGINAL SCORE (music and lyrics). Marvin Hamlisch (music) and Craig Carnelia (lyrics) for *Sweet Smell of Success*; Jeanine Tesori (music) and Dick Scanlan (lyrics) for *Thoroughly Modern Millie*; Harry Connick Jr. (music & lyrics) for *Thou Shalt Not*; **Mark Hollmann (music), Mark Hollmann and Greg Kotis (lyrics) for *Urinetown***.

BEST REVIVAL OF A PLAY (award goes to the producer). *The Crucible* produced by David Richenthal, Manocherian/Leve/Boyett, Max Cooper, Allan S. Gordon, Roy Furman, Us Productions, Élan V. McAllister, Adam Epstein, Margo Lion, Dede Harris/Morton Swinsky, Clear Channel Entertainment, Old Ivy Productions, Jujamcyn Theaters, Jeffrey Ash, Dori Berinstein/Roni Selig, Margaret McFeeley Golden/Michael Skipper, Gene Korf, Robert Cole, Roundabout Theatre Company. *Morning's at Seven* produced by Lincoln Center Theater under the direction of André Bishop and Bernard Gersten. *Noises Off* produced by Ambassador Theatre Group and Act Productions, Waxman Williams Entertainment, Dede Harris/Morton Swinsky, USA Ostar Theatricals and Nederlander Presentations, Inc., The Royal National Theatre. *Private Lives* **produced by Emanuel Azenberg, Ira Pittelman, Scott Nederlander, Frederick Zollo, Nicholas Paleologos, Dana Broccoli/Jeffrey Sine, James Nederlander, Kevin McCollum, Jeffrey Seller, Duncan C. Weldon and Paul Elliott for Triumph Entertainment Partners, Ltd**.

BEST REVIVAL OF A MUSICAL (award goes to the producer). *Into the Woods* **produced by Dodger Theatricals, Stage Holding/ Joop van den Ende and TheaterDreams, Inc**. *Oklahoma!* produced by Cameron Mackintosh, The Royal National Theatre.

BEST SPECIAL THEATRICAL EVENT. *Bea Arthur on Broadway, Just Between Friends* produced by Daryl Roth, M. Beverly Bartner, USA Ostar Theatricals. *Elaine Stritch at Liberty* **produced by John Schreiber, Creative Battery, Margo Lion, Robert Cole, Dede Harris/Morton Swinsky, Cheryl Wiesenfeld, The Joseph Papp Public Theater/New York Shakespeare Festival**. *Barbara Cook in Mostly Sondheim* produced by Lincoln Center Theater under the direction of André Bishop and Bernard Gersten. *Sexaholix . . . a Love Story* produced by Tate Entertainment Group, Inc.

BEST PERFORMANCE BY A LEADING ACTOR IN A PLAY. **Alan Bates in *Fortune's Fool***, Billy Crudup in *The Elephant Man*, Liam Neeson in *The Crucible*, Alan Rickman in *Private Lives*, Jeffrey Wright in *Topdog/Underdog*.

BEST PERFORMANCE BY A LEADING ACTRESS IN A PLAY. Kate Burton in *Hedda Gabler*, **Lindsay Duncan in *Private Lives***, Laura Linney in *The Crucible*, Helen Mirren in *Dance of Death*, Mercedes Ruehl in *The Goat, or Who Is Sylvia?*

BEST PERFORMANCE BY A LEADING ACTOR IN A MUSICAL. Gavin Creel in *Thoroughly Modern Millie*, John Cullum in *Urinetown*, **John Lithgow in *Sweet Smell of Success***, John McMartin in *Into the Woods*, Patrick Wilson in *Oklahoma!*

BEST PERFORMANCE BY A LEADING ACTRESS IN A MUSICAL. **Sutton Foster in *Thoroughly Modern Millie***, Nancy Opel in *Urinetown*, Louise Pitre in *Mamma Mia!*, Jennifer Laura Thompson in *Urinetown*, Vanessa Williams in *Into the Woods*.

BEST PERFORMANCE BY A FEATURED ACTOR IN A PLAY. **Frank Langella in *Fortune's Fool***, William Biff McGuire in *Morning's at Seven*, Brian Murray in *The Crucible*, Sam Robards in *The Man Who Had All the Luck*, Stephen Tobolowsky in *Morning's at Seven*.

BEST PERFORMANCE BY A FEATURED ACTRESS IN A PLAY. Kate Burton in *The Elephant Man*, **Katie Finneran in *Noises Off***, Elizabeth Franz in *Morning's at Seven*, Estelle Parsons in *Morning's at Seven*, Frances Sternhagen in *Morning's at Seven*.

BEST PERFORMANCE BY A FEATURED ACTOR IN A MUSICAL. Norbert Leo Butz in *Thou Shalt Not*, Gregg Edelman in *Into the Woods*, **Shuler Hensley in *Oklahoma!***, Brian d'Arcy James in *Sweet Smell of Success*. Marc Kudisch in *Thoroughly Modern Millie*.

BEST PERFORMANCE BY A FEATURED ACTRESS IN A MUSICAL. Laura Benanti in *Into the Woods*. **Harriet Harris in *Thoroughly Modern Millie***. Spencer Kayden in *Urinetown*. Judy Kaye in *Mamma Mia!*, Andrea Martin in *Oklahoma!*

BEST SCENIC DESIGN. John Lee Beatty for *Morning's at Seven*, **Tim Hatley for *Private Lives***, Daniel Ostling for *Metamorphoses*, Douglas W. Schmidt for *Into the Woods*.

BEST COSTUME DESIGN. Jenny Beavan for *Private Lives*, Jane Greenwood for *Morning's at Seven*, Susan Hilferty for *Into the Woods*, **Martin Pakledinaz for *Thoroughly Modern Millie***.

BEST LIGHTING DESIGN. Paul Gallo for *The Crucible*, David Hersey for *Oklahoma!*, Natasha Katz for *Sweet Smell of Success*, **Brian MacDevitt for *Into the Woods***.

BEST CHOREOGRAPHY. **Rob Ashford for *Thoroughly Modern Millie***, John Carrafa for *Into the Woods*, John Carrafa for *Urinetown*, Susan Stroman for *Oklahoma!*

BEST DIRECTION OF A PLAY. Howard Davies for *Private Lives*, Richard Eyre for *The Crucible*, Daniel Sullivan for *Morning's at Seven*, **Mary Zimmerman for *Metamorphoses***.

BEST DIRECTION OF A MUSICAL. James Lapine for *Into the Woods*, Michael Mayer for *Thoroughly Modern Millie*, Trevor Nunn for *Oklahoma!*, **John Rando for *Urinetown***.

BEST ORCHESTRATIONS. Benny Andersson, Björn Ulvaeus and Martin Koch for *Mamma Mia!*, **Doug Besterman & Ralph Burns for *Thoroughly Modern Millie***, William David Brohn for *Sweet Smell of Success*, Bruce Coughlin for *Urinetown*.

SPECIAL TONY AWARD FOR LIFETIME ACHIEVEMENT IN THE THEATRE. **Julie Harris**; **Robert Whitehead**.

REGIONAL THEATRE TONY AWARD. **Williamstown Theatre Festival, Williamstown, Massachusetts**.

TONY AWARD WINNERS, 1947–2002

LISTED BELOW ARE THE ANTOINETTE PERRY (Tony) Award winners in the catgories of Best Play and Best Musical from the time these awards were established until the present.

1947—No play or musical award

1948—*Mister Roberts*; no musical award

1949—*Death of a Salesman*; *Kiss Me, Kate*

1950—*The Cocktail Party*; *South Pacific*

1951—*The Rose Tattoo*; *Guys and Dolls*

1952—*The Fourposter*; *The King and I*

1953—*The Crucible*; *Wonderful Town*

1954—*The Teahouse of the August Moon*; *Kismet*

1955—*The Desperate Hours*; *The Pajama Game*

1956—*The Diary of Anne Frank*; *Damn Yankees*

1957—*Long Day's Journey Into Night*; *My Fair Lady*

1958—*Sunrise at Campobello*; *The Music Man*

1959—*J.B.*; *Redhead*

1960—*The Miracle Worker*; *Fiorello!* and *The Sound of Music* (tie)

1961—*Becket*; *Bye Bye Birdie*

1962—*A Man for All Seasons*; *How to Succeed in Business Without Really Trying*

1963—*Who's Afraid of Virginia Woolf?*; *A Funny Thing Happened on the Way to the Forum*

1964—*Luther*; *Hello, Dolly!*

1965—*The Subject Was Roses*; *Fiddler on the Roof*

1966—*The Persecution and Assassination of Marat as Performed by the Inmates of the Asylum of Charenton Under the Direction of the Marquis de Sade*; *Man of La Mancha*

1967—*The Homecoming*; *Cabaret*

1968—*Rosencrantz and Guildenstern Are Dead*; *Hallelujah, Baby!*

1969—*The Great White Hope*; *1776*

1970—*Borstal Boy*; *Applause*

1971—*Sleuth*; *Company*

1972—*Sticks and Bones*; *Two Gentlemen of Verona*

1973—*That Championship Season*; *A Little Night Music*

1974—*The River Niger*; *Raisin*

1975—*Equus*; *The Wiz*

1976—*Travesties*; *A Chorus Line*

1977—*The Shadow Box*; *Annie*

1978—*Da*; *Ain't Misbehavin'*

1979—*The Elephant Man*; *Sweeney Todd, the Demon Barber of Fleet Street*

1980—*Children of a Lesser God*; *Evita*

1981—*Amadeus*; *42nd Street*

1982—*The Life & Adventures of Nicholas Nickleby*; *Nine*

1983—*Torch Song Trilogy*; *Cats*

1984—*The Real Thing*; *La Cage aux Folles*

1985—*Biloxi Blues*; *Big River*

1986—*I'm Not Rappaport*; *The Mystery of Edwin Drood*

1987—*Fences*; *Les Misérables*

1988—*M. Butterfly*; *The Phantom of the Opera*

1989—*The Heidi Chronicles*; *Jerome Robbins' Broadway*

1990—*The Grapes of Wrath*; *City of Angels*

1991—*Lost in Yonkers*; *The Will Rogers Follies*

1992—*Dancing at Lughnasa*; *Crazy for You*

1993—*Angels in America, Part I: Millennium Approaches*; *Kiss of the Spider Woman*

1994—*Angels in America, Part II: Perestroika*; *Passion*

1995—*Love! Valour! Compassion!*; *Sunset Boulevard*

1996—*Master Class*; *Rent*

1997—*The Last Night of Ballyhoo*; *Titanic*

1998—*Art*; *The Lion King*

1999—*Side Man*; *Fosse*

2000—*Copenhagen*; *Contact*

2001—*Proof*; *The Producers*

2002—*The Goat, or Who is Sylvia*; *Thoroughly Modern Millie*

LUCILLE LORTEL AWARDS 2002

THE LUCILLE LORTEL AWARDS for outstanding Off Broadway achievement were established in 1985 by a resolution of the League of Off Broadway Theatres and Producers, which administers them and has presented them annually since 1986. Eligible for the 17th annual awards in 2002 were all Off Broadway productions that opened between April 1, 2001 and March 31, 2002. Winners were selected by a committee comprising David Cote, Mark Dickerman, Maria DiDia, Susan Einhorn, Beverly Emmons, George Forbes, Barbara Hauptman, Walt Kiskadden, Michael Kuchwara, Sheila Mathews, Gerald Rabkin, Marc Routh, Donald Saddler, David Stone, Anna Strasberg.

PLAY. *Metamorphoses* by Mary Zimmerman.

MUSICAL. *Urinetown* music and lyrics by Mark Hollmann, book and lyrics by Greg Kotis.

REVIVAL. *Cymbeline* by William Shakespeare, produced by Theatre for a New Audience.

ACTOR. **Reg Rogers** in *The Dazzle*.

ACTRESS. **Linda Emond** in *Homebody/Kabul*.

FEATURED ACTOR. **Keith Nobbs** in *Four*.

FEATURED ACTRESS. **Kathleen Widdoes** in *Franny's Way*.

DIRECTION. **Mary Zimmerman** for *Metamorphoses*.

CHOREOGRAPHY. **John Carrafa** for *Urinetown*.

SCENERY. **Douglas Stein** for *36 Views*.

COSTUMES. **Elizabeth Caitlin Ward** for *Cymbeline*.

LIGHTING. **T.J. Gerckens** for *Metamorphoses*.

SOUND. **Scott Lehrer** for *Franny's Way*.

BODY OF WORK. **Second Stage Theatre**.

LIFETIME ACHIEVEMENT. **Edward Albee**.

EDITH OLIVER AWARD. **Ruby Dee**.

UNIQUE THEATRICAL EXPERIENCE. ***Elaine Stritch at Liberty***.

2002 INDUCTEE: PLAYWRIGHTS' SIDEWALK. **Romulus Linney**.

LORTEL AWARD WINNERS 1986–2002

LISTED BELOW ARE THE LUCILLE LORTEL Award winners in the categories of Outstanding Play and Outstanding Musical from the time these awards were established until the present.

1986—*Woza Africa!*; no musical award
1987—*The Common Pursuit*; no musical award
1988—No play or musical award
1989—*The Cocktail Hour*; no musical award
1990—No play or musical award
1991—*Aristocrats*; *Falsettoland*
1992—*Lips Together, Teeth Apart*; *And the World Goes 'Round*
1993—*The Destiny of Me*; *Forbidden Broadway*
1994—*Three Tall Women*; *Wings*

1995—*Camping With Henry & Tom*; *Jelly Roll!*
1996—*Molly Sweeney*; *Floyd Collins*
1997—*How I Learned to Drive*; *Violet*
1998—*Gross Indecency*, and *The Beauty Queen of Leenane* (tie); no musical award
1999—*Wit*; no musical award
2000—*Dinner With Friends*; *James Joyce's The Dead*
2001—*Proof*; *Bat Boy: The Musical*
2002—*Metamorphoses*; *Urinetown*

AMERICAN THEATRE CRITICS/STEINBERG NEW PLAY AWARDS AND CITATIONS

○ ○ ○ ○ ○

INCLUDING PRINCIPAL CITATIONS AND NEW PLAY AWARD WINNERS, 1977–2002

BEGINNING WITH THE SEASON of 1976–77, the American Theatre Critics Association (ATCA) has cited one or more outstanding new plays in United States theater. The principal honorees have been included in *Best Plays* since the first year. In 1986 the ATCA New Play Award was given for the first time, along with a $1,000 prize. The award and citations were renamed the **American Theatre Critics/Steinberg New Play Award and Citations** in 2000 (see essays on the 2002 ATCA/Steinberg honorees in the Season Around the United States section of this volume). The award dates have been renumbered beginning with this volume to correctly reflect the year in which ATCA conferred the honor.

New Play Citations (1977–1985)

1977—*And the Soul Shall Dance* by Wakako Yamauchi

1978—*Getting Out* by Marsha Norman

1979—*Loose Ends* by Michael Weller

1980—*Custer* by Robert E. Ingham

1981—*Chekhov in Yalta* by John Driver and Jeffrey Haddow

1982—*Talking With* by Jane Martin

1983—*Closely Related* by Bruce MacDonald

1984—*Wasted* by Fred Gamel

1985—*Scheherazade* by Marisha Chamberlain

New Play Award (1986–1999)

1986—*Fences* by August Wilson

1987—*A Walk in the Woods* by Lee Blessing

1988—*Heathen Valley* by Romulus Linney

1989—*The Piano Lesson* by August Wilson

1990—*2* by Romulus Linney

1991—*Two Trains Running* by August Wilson

1992—*Could I Have This Dance?* by Doug Haverty

1993—*Children of Paradise: Shooting a Dream* by Steven Epp, Felicity Jones, Dominique Serrand and Paul Walsh

1994—*Keely and Du* by Jane Martin

1995—*The Nanjing Race* by Reggie Cheong-Leen

1996—*Amazing Grace* by Michael Cristofer

1997—*Jack and Jill* by Jane Martin

1998—*The Cider House Rules, Part II* by Peter Parnell

1999—*Book of Days* by Lanford Wilson.

ATCA/Steinberg New Play Award and Citations

2000—*Oo-Bla-Dee* by Regina Taylor
Citations: *Compleat Female Stage Beauty* by Jeffrey Hatcher; *Syncopation* by Allan Knee

2001—*Anton in Show Business* by Jane Martin
Citations: *Big Love* by Charles L. Mee; *King Hedley II* by August Wilson

2001—*The Carpetbagger's Children* by Horton Foote
Citations: *The Action Against Sol Schumann* by Jeffrey Sweet; *Joe and Betty* by Murray Mednick

ADDITIONAL PRIZES AND AWARDS 2001–2002

THE FOLLOWING IS A LIST of major awards for achievement in the theater this season. The names of honorees appear in **bold type**.

2000–2001 GEORGE JEAN NATHAN AWARD. For dramatic criticism. **Laurence Senelick**.

21st ANNUAL WILLIAM INGE THEATRE FESTIVAL AWARD. For distinguished achievement in American theater. **John Kander and Fred Ebb**. New voice: **Dana Yeaton**.

2002 M. ELIZABETH OSBORN AWARD. Presented by the American Theatre Critics Association to an emerging playwright. **Mia McCullough** for *Chagrin Falls*.

24th ANNUAL KENNEDY CENTER HONORS. For distinguished achievement by individuals who have made significant contributions to American culture through the arts. **Julie Andrews**, **Van Cliburn**, **Quincy Jones**, **Jack Nicholson**, **Luciano Pavarotti**.

5th ANNUAL KENNEDY CENTER–MARK TWAIN PRIZE. For American humor. **Bob Newhart**.

2001 NATIONAL MEDALS OF THE ARTS. For individuals and organizations who have made outstanding contributions to the excellence, growth, support and availability of the arts in the United States, selected by the President from nominees presented by the National Endowment. **Alvin Ailey Dance Foundation**, **Rudolfo Anaya**, **Johnny Cash**, **Kirk Douglas**, **Helen Frankenthaler**, **Judith Jamison**, **Yo-Yo Ma**, **Mike Nichols**.

2002 DRAMATIST GUILD AWARDS. 2001 Elizabeth Hull–Kate Warriner Award to the playwright whose work deals with social, political or religious mores of the time, selected by the Dramatists Guild Council. **Tony Kushner** for *Homebody/Kabul*. Frederick Loewe Award for Dramatic Composition: **Cy Coleman**. Flora Roberts Award: **Neal Bell**. Lifetime Achievement: **Betty Comden and Adolph Green**.

2002 HEWES DESIGN AWARDS (formerly American Theatre Wing Design Awards). For design originating in the US, selected by a committee comprising Tish Dace (chair), Glenda Frank, Mario Fratti, Randy Gener, Mel Gussow, Henry Hewes, Jeffrey Eric Jenkins and Joan Ungaro. Scenic design: **Louisa Thompson**, *[sic]*. Lighting design: **T.J. Gerckens**, *Metamorphoses*. Costume design: **Susan Hilferty**, *Into the Woods*. Unusual Effects: **David Gallo**, *Wonder of the World* (repeating clouds against blue sky).

24th ANNUAL SUSAN SMITH BLACKBURN PRIZE. For women who have written works of outstanding quality for the English-speaking theater. **Gina Gionfriddo** for *U.S. Drag*; **Susan Miller** for *A Map of Doubt and Rescue*. Honorable mention: **Julia Jordan** for *Our Boy*.

2002 FRANCESCA PRIMUS PRIZE. Presented by the Francesca Primus Foundation and the Denver Center Theatre Company. **Alexandra Cunningham** for *Pavane*.

2001 GEORGE FREEDLEY MEMORIAL AWARD. For the best book about live theater published in the United States the previous year. ***Harlequin Unmasked: The Commedia Dell'Arte and Porcelain Sculpture*** by **Meredith Chilton**.

21st ANNUAL ASTAIRE AWARDS. For excellence in dance and choreography, administered by the Theatre Development Fund and selected by a committee comprising Douglas Watt, Clive Barnes, Howard Kissel, Michael Kuchwara, Donald McDonagh, Richard Philp, Charles L. Reinhart and Linda Winer. Choreography: **Susan Stroman** for *Oklahoma!* Female dancer: **Sutton Foster** in *Thoroughly Modern Millie*. Male dancer: **Justin Bohon** in *Oklahoma!* Dance teachers: **Frank Hatchett**, **Luigi**, **Phil Black**, **Gabriela Taub-Darvash**.

57th ANNUAL CLARENCE DERWENT AWARDS. Given to a female and a male performer by Actors Equity Association based on New York work that demonstrates promise. **Anne Hathaway** and **Sam Robards**.

2002 RICHARD RODGERS AWARDS. For staged readings of musicals in nonprofit theaters, administered by the American Academy of Arts and Letters and selected by a jury including Stephen Sondheim (chairman), Lynn Ahrens, Jack Beeson, Sheldon Harnick, R.W.B. Lewis and Richard Maltby Jr. Richard Rodgers Development Awards: *The Fabulist* by David Spencer and Stephen Witkin; *The Tutor* by Maryrose Wood and Andrew Gerle.

68TH ANNUAL DRAMA LEAGUE AWARDS. For distinguished achievement in the American theater. Play: *Metamorphoses*. Musical: *Urinetown*. Revival of a play or musical: *The Crucible*. Distinguished performance: **Liam Neeson** in *The Crucible*. Julia Hansen Award for excellence in directing: **Richard Eyre**. Achievement in Musical Theatre: **Elaine Stritch**. Unique contribution to theater: **Julia Hansen**.

2002 GEORGE OPPENHEIMER AWARD. To the best new American playwright, presented by *Newsday*. **Cornelius Eady** for *Brutal Imagination*.

2002 NEW DRAMATISTS LIFETIME ACHIEVEMENT AWARD. To an individual who has made an outstanding artistic contribution to the American theater. **Barbara Cook**.

13TH ANNUAL OSCAR HAMMERSTEIN AWARD. For lifetime achievement in musical theater. **Cameron Mackintosh**.

2002 *THEATRE WORLD* AWARDS. For outstanding debut performers in Broadway or Off Broadway theater during the 2001–2002 season, selected by a committee including Clive Barnes, Peter Filichia, Harry Haun, Frank Scheck, Michael Sommers, Douglas Watt and Linda Winer. **Emma Fielding** in *Private Lives*, **Spencer Kayden** in *Urinetown*, **Gretchen Mol** in *The Shape of Things*, **Anna Paquin** in *The Glory of Living*, **Louise Pitre** in *Mamma Mia!*, **Rachel Weisz** in *The Shape of Things*, **Justin Bohon** in *Oklahoma!*, **Simon Callow** in *The Mystery of Charles Dickens*, **Mos Def** in *Topdog/Underdog*, **Adam Godley** in *Private Lives*, **Martin Jarvis** in *By Jeeves* and **David Warner** in *Major Barbara*.

47TH ANNUAL DRAMA DESK AWARDS. For outstanding achievement in the 2001–2002 season, voted by an association of New York drama reporters, editors and critics from nominations made by a committee. New play (tie): *Metamorphoses* and *The Goat, or Who Is Sylvia?* New musical: *Thoroughly Modern Millie*. Revival of a play: *Private Lives*. Revival of a musical: *Into the Woods*. Book of a musical: **Elaine Stritch** and **John Lahr** for *Elaine Stritch at Liberty*. Music: **Jason Robert Brown** for *The Last Five Years*. Lyrics: **Jason Robert Brown** for *The Last Five Years*. Music in a play: **Willy Schwarz** for *Metamorphoses*. Actor in a play: **Alan Bates** in *Fortune's Fool*. Actress in a play: **Lindsay Duncan** in *Private Lives*. Featured actor in a play: **Frank Langella** in *Fortune's Fool*. Featured actress in a play: **Katie Finneran** in *Noises Off*. Actor in a musical: **John Lithgow** in *Sweet Smell of Success*. Actress in a musical: **Sutton Foster** in *Thoroughly Modern Millie*. Featured actor in a musical: **Shuler Hensley** in *Oklahoma!* Featured actress in a musical: **Harriet Harris** in *Thoroughly Modern Millie*. Solo performance: **Elaine Stritch** in *Elaine Stritch at Liberty*. Director of a play: **Mary Zimmerman** for *Metamorphoses*. Director of a musical: **Michael Mayer** for *Thoroughly Modern Millie*. Choreography: **Susan Stroman** for *Oklahoma!* Orchestrations: **Doug Besterman** and **Ralph Burns** for *Thoroughly Modern Millie*. Set design of a play: **Tim Hatley** for *Private Lives*. Set design of a musical: **Douglas W. Schmidt** for *Into the Woods*. Costume design: **Isaac Mizrahi** for *The Women*. Lighting design: **T.J. Gerckens** for *Metamorphoses*. Sound design: **Dan Moses Schreier** for *Into the Woods*. Special awards: **Paul Huntley**, lifetime achievement in hair and wig design; **Billy Rosenfield**, contributions to the preservation of musical theatre recordings; **Mint Theater Company**, presenting and preserving little-known classics; **Worth Street Theater Company** for its Stage Door Canteen shows for workers at Ground Zero.

52ND ANNUAL OUT3ER CRITICS CIRCLE AWARDS. For outstanding achievement in the 2001–2002 season, voted by critics on out-of-town periodicals and media. Broadway play: **The Goat, or Who Is Sylvia?** Off-Broadway play: **The Dazzle.** Revival of a play: **Morning's at Seven.** Actor in a play: **Alan Bates** in *Fortune's Fool.* Actress in a play: **Mercedes Ruehl** in *The Goat, or Who Is Sylvia?* Featured actor in a play: **Frank Langella** in *Fortune's Fool.* Featured actress in a play: **Katie Finneran** in *Noises Off.* Director of a play: **Mary Zimmerman** for *Metamorphoses.* Broadway musical: **Urinetown.** Off-Broadway musical: **Tick, Tick . . . Boom!** Revival of a musical: **Oklahoma!** Actor in a musical: **John Lithgow** in *Sweet Smell of Success.* Actress in a musical: **Sutton Foster** in *Thoroughly Modern Millie.* Featured actor in a musical: **Shuler Hensley** in *Oklahoma!* Featured actress in a musical: **Spencer Kayden** in *Urinetown.* Director of a musical: **John Rando** for *Urinetown.* Choreography: **Susan Stroman** for *Oklahoma!* Scenic design: **Anthony Ward** for *Oklahoma!* Costume design: **Isaac Mizrahi** for *The Women.* Lighting design: **David Hersey** for *Oklahoma!* Solo performance: **Elaine Stritch** in *Elaine Stritch at Liberty.* John Gassner Playwriting Award: **Suzan-Lori Parks** for *Topdog/Underdog.* Special Achievement Award: **Mos Def** and **Jeffrey Wright** in *Topdog/Underdog.*

47TH ANNUAL *VILLAGE VOICE* OBIE AWARDS. For outstanding achievement in Off and Off-Off Broadway theater. Performance: **Bill Camp** in *Homebody/Kabul;* **Reg E. Cathey, James Himelsbach, Karen Kandel, Anthony Mackie, John Seitz, Maria Tucci** in *Talk;* **Christopher Donahue** in *Monster;* **Linda Emond** in *Homebody/Kabul;* **Raúl Esparza** in *Tick, Tick . . . BOOM!;* **Juliana Francis** in *Maria del Bosco;* **Peter Frechette** and **Reg Rogers** in *The Dazzle;* **Yvette Ganier** in *Breath, Boom;* **Martha Plimpton** in *Hobson's Choice;* **Jeffrey Wright** in *Topdog/Underdog.* Direction: **George C. Wolfe** for *Topdog/Underdog;* **Mary Zimmerman** for *Metamorphoses.* Sustained excellence in lighting design: **Kevin Adams.** Set and lighting design: **Angela Moore** and **Michael Schmelling** for *Drummer Wanted.* Video:

Marilys Ernst for *Talk.* Sound design: **Whit MacLaughlin** for The Fab 4 Reach the Pearly Gates. Playwriting: **Melissa James Gibson** for *[sic];* **Tony Kushner** for *Homebody/Kabul.* Sustained achievement: **Caryl Churchill.**

Special Citations: **ART/NY** for support of Off Broadway theater; **Daniel Aukin** and **Louisa Thompson** for direction and set design of *[sic];* **Ingmar Bergman** and the **Royal Dramatic Theatre of Sweden** for The Ghost Sonata; **Daniel MacIvor** for *In on It;* **Charles L. Mee** and **Les Waters** for playwriting and direction of *Big Love;* **Elaine Stritch** for *Elaine Stritch at Liberty;* **The Wooster Group** for *To You, the Birdie!* Grants: **Ma-Yi Theater Company, Salt Theater Company.** Ross Wetzsteon Award: **PS 122.**

12TH ANNUAL CONNECTICUT CRITICS CIRCLE AWARDS. For outstanding achievement in Connecticut theater during the 2001–2002 season. Production of a play (tie): **Hartford Stage** for *Seascape* and **Long Wharf Theatre** for *Yellowman.* Production of a musical: **Downtown Cabaret Theatre** for *Smokey Joe's Cafe.* Actress in a play: **Dael Orlandersmith** in *Yellowman.* Actor in a play: **Howard W. Overshown** in *Yellowman.* Actress in a musical (tie): **Lovena Fox** in *Jekyll and Hyde* and **Florence Lacey** in *Wings.* Actor in a musical: **Michael McGrath** in *They All Laughed.* Direction of a play: **Rob Ruggiero** for *The Laramie Project.* Direction of a musical: **Semina De Laurentis** for *My Way: A Musical Tribute to Frank Sinatra.* Choreography: **Jamie Rocco** for *Smokey Joe's Cafe.* Set design: **John Coyne** for *You Never Can Tell.* Lighting design: **Mimi Jordan Sherin** for *Seascape.* Costume design: **Mirena Rada** for *Pera Palas.* Sound design: **David Budries** for *Seascape.* Ensemble performance: Michael Anderson, Mary Bacon, Natalie Brown, Matthew J. Cody, Antoinette LaVecchia, Duane Noch, Susan Patrick and Jeremy Webb in *The Laramie Project.*

Debut award: **Patrick O'Sullivan** and **Philip Piarrot** in *Lost in Yonkers.* Special award: **International Festival of Arts and**

Ideas, presenter of the Abbey Theatre's *Translations*. Tom Killen Memorial Award: **Steve Campo**, artistic director of TheaterWorks.

20TH ANNUAL ELLIOT NORTON AWARDS. For outstanding contribution to the theater in Boston, voted by a Boston Theater Critics Association Selection Committee comprising Terry Byrne, Carolyn Clay, Iris Fanger, Joyce Kulhawik, Jon L. Lehman, Bill Marx, Ed Siegel and Caldwell Titcomb. New play: **Adam Rapp** for *Nocturne*. Norton Prize: **Barbara Meek**. Productions—Visiting company: *The Glass Menagerie* from Hartford Stage; Large resident company: *Homebody/Kabul* produced by Trinity Repertory Theatre Company; Small resident company: *Twelfth Night* produced by Commonwealth Shakespeare Company; Local fringe company: *The Laramie Project* produced by Boston Theatre Works. Solo performance: **Catherine Samie** in *The Last Letter*. Musical production—Large company: *Contact* produced by Broadway in Boston; Small company: **Sunday in the Park with George** produced by Lyric Stage Company. Actor—Large company: **Simon Russell Beale** in *Hamlet*; Small company: **Robert Pemberton** in *Much Ado About Nothing*, *Lobby Hero* and *Shel's Shorts*. Actress—Large company: **Andrea Martin** in *Betty's Summer Vacation*; Small company: **Nancy E. Carroll** in *Bailegangaire*. Director—Large company: **Nicholas Martin** for *Betty's Summer Vacation*; Small company: **Carmel O'Reilly** in *The Lonesome West* and *Bailegangaire*. Scene design: **Alexander Dodge** for *Twelfth Night* and *Heartbreak House*. Costume design: **Gail Astrid Buckley** for *Curse of the Bambino*, *Much Ado About Nothing*, *Twelfth Night*, *Shel's Shorts*.

Guest of Honor: **Julie Harris**. 20th Anniversary Award: **Robert Brustein**. Special citation: **Eliza Rose Fichter** for her remarkable portrayal of children in *A Russian Tea Party, One Flea Spare, The Miracle Worker* and *Reason*.

18TH ANNUAL HELEN HAYES AWARDS. In recognition of excellence in Washington, D.C., theater, presented by the Washington Theatre Awards Society.

Resident productions—Play: *Home* produced by Round House Theatre. Musical: *Blues in the Night* produced by Arena Stage. Lead actress, musical: **Bernardine Mitchell** in *Blues in the Night*. Lead actor, musical: **Brian Childers** in *Danny & Sylvia: A Musical Love Story*. Lead actress, play: **Jenifer Deal** in *The Muckle Man*. Lead actor, play: **Nigel Reed** in *The Judas Kiss*. Supporting actress, musical: **Kadejah Oni Higdon** in *Spunk*. Supporting actor, musical: **Michael Sharp** in *Grand Hotel*. Supporting actress, play: **Mia Whang** in *Far East*. Supporting actor, play: **Helmar Augustus Cooper** in *Jitney*. Director, play: **Thomas W. Jones II** for *Home*. Director, musical: **Mary Hall Surface** for *Perseus Bayou*. Set design, play or musical (tie): **Tony Cisek** for *The Judas Kiss* and **Ming Cho Lee** for *Don Carlos*. Costume design, play or musical: **Robert Perdziola** for *Don Carlos*. Lighting design, play or musical: **Chris Parry** for *Don Carlos*. Sound design, play or musical: **Daniel Portaix** for *Les Cloisons (Partitions)*. Musical direction, play or musical: **Jon Kalbfleisch** for *Grand Hotel*. Choreography: **Ilona Kessell** for *Damn Yankees*.

Non-resident productions—Production: *Mill on the Floss* produced by the Kennedy Center. Lead actress: **Jodi Capeless** in *Late Nite Catechism*. Lead actor: **Jason Watkins** in *A Servant to Two Masters*. Supporting performer: **Tom Riis Farrell** in *Dirty Blonde*.

Charles MacArthur Award for outstanding new play: *In the Garden* by Norman Allen.

33ND ANNUAL JOSEPH JEFFERSON AWARDS. For achievement in Chicago theater during the 2000–2001 season, given by the Jefferson Awards Committee in 28 competitive categories. Twenty-six producing organizations were nominated for various awards. The Lookingglass Theatre Company, in association with the Actors Gymnasium, topped all other companies by winning five awards. Marriott Theatre in Lincolnshire followed closely with four.

Resident productions—New work: *The Pagans* by **Ann Noble**; *The Ballad of Little Jo* by **Mike Reid** and **Sarah Schlesinger**. New Adaptation: *Hard Times* by **Heidi Stillman**. Production of a play:

Lookingglass Theatre Company in association with **Actors Gymnasium** for *Hard Times*. Production of a musical: **Marriott Theatre in Lincolnshire** for *The King and I*. Director of a play: **Heidi Stillman** for *Hard Times*. Director of a musical: **Gary Griffin** for *Big*. Director of a revue: **Marc Robin** for *And the World Goes 'Round*. Actor in a principal role, play: **Greg Vinkler** in *King Lear*. Actress in a principal role, play: **Carmen Roman** in *Wit*. Actor in a supporting role, play: **David Darlow** in *Endgame*. Actress in a supporting role, play: **Laura T. Fisher** in *Early and Often*. Actor in a principal role, musical: **Rod Thomas** in *Big*. Actress in a principal role, musical: **Mary Ernster** in *The King and I*. Actor in a supporting role, musical: **Gordon McClure** in *Being Beautiful*. Actress in a supporting role, musical: **Alene Robertson** in *Mame*. Actor in a revue: **Mark Townsend** in *The Nat King Cole Story*. Actress in a revue: **E. Faye Butler** in *Could It Be Magic?* Ensemble: *The Incident* produced by Next Theatre. Scenic design: **Linda Buchanan** for *House*. Costume design: **Nancy Missimi** for *The King and I*. Lighting design: **Brian Sidney Bembridge** for *Hard Times*. Sound design: **Mike Frank** and **Andre Pluess** for *Macbeth*. Choreography: **Sylvia Hernandez-DiStasi** for *Hard Times*. Original music: **Alaric Jans** for *The Two Gentlemen of Verona*. Musical direction: **Patrick Vaccariello** for *The Ballad of Little Jo*.

Non-resident productions—Production: **Marshall Cordell**, **Q Brothers** and **Mary Lu Roffe** for *The Bomb-Itty of Errors*. Actor in a principal role: **Nick Garrison** in *Hedwig and the Angry Inch*. Actress in a principal role: **Marilu Henner** in *Annie Get Your Gun*.

Special Awards—**Irv Kupcinet** and the late **Essee Kupcinet** for "six decades of working together to make Chicago a fertile ground for careers in the arts and for nurturing the talents of Chicago actors and artists." ***Artbeat Chicago***, a program of WTTW television, for "its intelligent, witty and compassionate celebration of the depth, diversity and talent in Chicago theatre."

29TH ANNUAL JOSEPH JEFFERSON CITATIONS WING AWARDS. For outstanding achievement in professional productions during the 2001–2002 season of Chicago area theaters not operating under union contracts. Productions: *The Crucible* produced by **TimeLine Theatre Company**; *Who's Afraid of Virginia Woolf?* produced by **Shattered Globe Theatre**. Ensembles: *Corpus Christi*; *The Crucible*; *The Life and Times of Tulsa Lovechild*; *Who's Afraid of Virginia Woolf?* Directors: **Nick Bowling** for *The Crucible*; **Louis Contey** for *Who's Afraid of Virginia Woolf?*; Nathaniel Swift for *2*. New work: **Mia McCullough** for *Chagrin Falls*; **Jim O'Connor** for *Rosemary*. New adaptation: **Page Hearn** for *Jeeves and the Mating Season*; **Michael Thomas** for *With or Without Wings*. Actress in a principal role: **Kati Brazda** in *The Life and Times of Tulsa Lovechild*; **Michelle Courvais** in *Rosemary*; **Linda Reiter** in *Who's Afraid of Virginia Woolf?* Actor in a principal role: **Darrell W. Cox** in *Some Voices*; **Steven Fedoruk** in *2*. Actress in a supporting role: **Jennifer Kern** in *Who's Afraid of Virginia Woolf?*; **Beth Lacke** in *The Life and Times of Tulsa Lovechild*. Actor in a supporting role: **Marc Jablon** in *Sexual Perversity in Chicago*; **Jim Slonina** in *Fortinbras*; **Joseph Wycoff** in *Jeeves and the Mating Season*. Scenic design: **Heather Graff** and **Richard Peterson** for *The Crucible*; **Stephanie Nelson** for *Unbinding Isaac*. Costume design: **Michelle Lynette Bush** for *Les Liaisons Dangereuses*; **Jeffrey Kelly** for *Nine*. Lighting design: **Heather Graff** and **Richard Peterson** for *The Crucible*. Sound design: **Joseph Fosco** for *The Return of the King*. Original music: **Poh'ro and the Ministers of the New Super Heavy Funk** for *Kosi Dasa*. Musical direction: **Chris Staton** for *Pippin*.

THE THEATER HALL OF FAME
○ ○ ○ ○ ○

THE THEATER HALL OF FAME was created in 1971 to honor those who have made outstanding contributions to the American theater in a career spanning at least 25 years, with at least five major credits. Honorees are elected annually by members of the American Theatre Critics Association, members of the Theater Hall of Fame and theater historians. Names of those elected in 2001 and inducted January 28, 2002 appear in ***bold italics***.

GEORGE ABBOTT	JOHN BARRYMORE	RICHARD BURTON
MAUDE ADAMS	LIONEL BARRYMORE	MRS. PATRICK CAMPBELL
VIOLA ADAMS	HOWARD BAY	ZOE CALDWELL
STELLA ADLER	NORA BAYES	EDDIE CANTOR
EDWARD ALBEE	SAMUEL BECKETT	MORRIS CARNOVSKY
THEONI V. ALDREDGE	BRIAN BEDFORD	MRS. LESLIE CARTER
IRA ALDRIDGE	S.N. BEHRMAN	GOWER CHAMPION
JANE ALEXANDER	NORMAN BEL GEDDES	FRANK CHANFRAU
MARY ALICE	DAVID BELASCO	CAROL CHANNING
WINTHROP AMES	MICHAEL BENNETT	RUTH CHATTERTON
JUDITH ANDERSON	RICHARD BENNETT	PADDY CHAYEFSKY
MAXWELL ANDERSON	ROBERT RUSSELL BENNETT	ANTON CHEKHOV
ROBERT ANDERSON	ERIC BENTLEY	INA CLAIRE
JULIE ANDREWS	IRVING BERLIN	BOBBY CLARK
MARGARET ANGLIN	SARAH BERNHARDT	HAROLD CLURMAN
JEAN ANOUILH	LEONARD BERNSTEIN	LEE J. COBB
HAROLD ARLEN	EARL BLACKWELL	RICHARD L. COE
GEORGE ARLISS	KERMIT BLOOMGARDEN	GEORGE M. COHAN
BORIS ARONSON	JERRY BOCK	ALEXANDER H. COHEN
ADELE ASTAIRE	RAY BOLGER	JACK COLE
FRED ASTAIRE	EDWIN BOOTH	CY COLEMAN
EILEEN ATKINS	JUNIUS BRUTUS BOOTH	CONSTANCE COLLIER
BROOKS ATKINSON	SHIRLEY BOOTH	***ALVIN COLT***
LAUREN BACALL	PHILIP BOSCO	BETTY COMDEN
PEARL BAILEY	ALICE BRADY	MARC CONNELLY
GEORGE BALANCHINE	BERTOLT BRECHT	BARBARA COOK
WILLIAM BALL	FANNIE BRICE	KATHARINE CORNELL
ANNE BANCROFT	PETER BROOK	NOEL COWARD
TALLULAH BANKHEAD	JOHN MASON BROWN	JANE COWL
RICHARD BARR	***ROBERT BRUSTEIN***	LOTTA CRABTREE
PHILIP BARRY	BILLIE BURKE	CHERYL CRAWFORD
ETHEL BARRYMORE	ABE BURROWS	HUME CRONYN

RUSSEL CROUSE

CHARLOTTE CUSHMAN

JEAN DALRYMPLE

AUGUSTIN DALY

E.L. DAVENPORT

GORDON DAVIDSON

OSSIE DAVIS

RUBY DEE

ALFRED DE LIAGRE JR.

AGNES DEMILLE

COLLEEN DEWHURST

HOWARD DIETZ

DUDLEY DIGGES

MELVYN DOUGLAS

EDDIE DOWLING

ALFRED DRAKE

MARIE DRESSLER

JOHN DREW

MRS. JOHN DREW

WILLIAM DUNLAP

MILDRED DUNNOCK

CHARLES DURNING

ELEANORA DUSE

JEANNE EAGELS

FRED EBB

FLORENCE ELDRIDGE

LEHMAN ENGEL

MAURICE EVANS

ABE FEDER

JOSE FERRER

CY FEUER

ZELDA FICHANDLER

DOROTHY FIELDS

HERBERT FIELDS

LEWIS FIELDS

W.C. FIELDS

JULES FISHER

MINNIE MADDERN FISKE

CLYDE FITCH

GERALDINE FITZGERALD

HENRY FONDA

LYNN FONTANNE

HORTON FOOTE

EDWIN FORREST

BOB FOSSE

RUDOLF FRIML

CHARLES FROHMAN

ROBERT FRYER

ATHOL FUGARD

JOHN GASSNER

PETER GENNARO

GRACE GEORGE

GEORGE GERSHWIN

IRA GERSHWIN

JOHN GIELGUD

W.S. GILBERT

JACK GILFORD

WILLIAM GILLETTE

CHARLES GILPIN

LILLIAN GISH

JOHN GOLDEN

MAX GORDON

RUTH GORDON

ADOLPH GREEN

PAUL GREEN

CHARLOTTE GREENWOOD

JOEL GREY

GEORGE GRIZZARD

JOHN GUARE

OTIS L. GUERNSEY JR.

TYRONE GUTHRIE

UTA HAGEN

LEWIS HALLAM

T. EDWARD HAMBLETON

OSCAR HAMMERSTEIN II

WALTER HAMPDEN

OTTO HARBACH

E.Y. HARBURG

SHELDON HARNICK

EDWARD HARRIGAN

JED HARRIS

JULIE HARRIS

ROSEMARY HARRIS

SAM H. HARRIS

REX HARRISON

KITTY CARLISLE HART

LORENZ HART

MOSS HART

TONY HART

JUNE HAVOC

HELEN HAYES

LELAND HAYWARD

BEN HECHT

EILEEN HECKART

THERESA HELBURN

LILLIAN HELLMAN

KATHARINE HEPBURN

VICTOR HERBERT

JERRY HERMAN

JAMES A. HERNE

HENRY HEWES

AL HIRSCHFELD

RAYMOND HITCHCOCK

HAL HOLBROOK

CELESTE HOLM

HANYA HOLM

ARTHUR HOPKINS

DE WOLF HOPPER

JOHN HOUSEMAN

EUGENE HOWARD

LESLIE HOWARD

SIDNEY HOWARD

WILLIE HOWARD

BARNARD HUGHES

HENRY HULL

JOSEPHINE HULL

WALTER HUSTON

EARLE HYMAN

HENRIK IBSEN

WILLIAM INGE

BERNARD B. JACOBS

ELSIE JANIS

JOSEPH JEFFERSON

GERALD SCHOENFELD	*ISABELLE STEVENSON*	DAVID WARFIELD
ARTHUR SCHWARTZ	ELLEN STEWART	ETHEL WATERS
MAURICE SCHWARTZ	DOROTHY STICKNEY	CLIFTON WEBB
GEORGE C. SCOTT	FRED STONE	JOSEPH WEBER
MARIAN SELDES	TOM STOPPARD	MARGARET WEBSTER
IRENE SHARAFF	LEE STRASBERG	KURT WEILL
GEORGE BERNARD SHAW	AUGUST STRINDBERG	ORSON WELLES
SAM SHEPARD	ELAINE STRITCH	MAE WEST
ROBERT E. SHERWOOD	*CHARLES STROUSE*	ROBERT WHITEHEAD
J.J. SHUBERT	JULE STYNE	OSCAR WILDE
LEE SHUBERT	MARGARET SULLAVAN	THORNTON WILDER
HERMAN SHUMLIN	ARTHUR SULLIVAN	BERT WILLIAMS
NEIL SIMON	JESSICA TANDY	TENNESSEE WILLIAMS
LEE SIMONSON	LAURETTE TAYLOR	LANFORD WILSON
EDMUND SIMPSON	ELLEN TERRY	P.G. WODEHOUSE
OTIS SKINNER	TOMMY TUNE	PEGGY WOOD
MAGGIE SMITH	GWEN VERDON	ALEXANDER WOOLLCOTT
OLIVER SMITH	ROBIN WAGNER	IRENE WORTH
STEPHEN SONDHEIM	NANCY WALKER	TERESA WRIGHT
E.H. SOTHERN	ELI WALLACH	ED WYNN
KIM STANLEY	JAMES WALLACK	VINCENT YOUMANS
MAUREEN STAPLETON	LESTER WALLACK	STARK YOUNG
FRANCES STERNHAGEN	TONY WALTON	FLORENZ ZIEGFELD
ROGER L. STEVENS	DOUGLAS TURNER WARD	PATRICIA ZIPPRODT

THE THEATER HALL OF FAME
FOUNDERS AWARD

ESTABLISHED IN 1993 in honor of Earl Blackwell, James M. Nederlander, Gerard Oestreicher and Arnold Weissberger, The Theater Hall of Fame Founders Award is voted by the Hall's board of directors to an individual for his or her outstanding contribution to the theater.

1993 JAMES M. NEDERLANDER	1997 OTIS L. GUERNSEY JR.	2000 GERARD OESTREICHER
1994 KITTY CARLISLE HART	1998 EDWARD COLTON	ARNOLD WEISSBERGER
1995 HARVEY SABINSON	1999 NO AWARD	2001 TOM DILLON
1996 HENRY HEWES		

MARGO JONES
CITIZEN OF THE THEATER MEDAL

PRESENTED ANNUALLY TO A CITIZEN of the theater who has made a lifetime commitment to theater in the United States and has demonstrated an understanding and affirmation of the craft of playwriting.

1961 LUCILLE LORTEL
1962 MICHAEL ELLIS
1963 JUDITH RUTHERFORD MARECHAL
GEORGE SAVAGE
(University Award)
1964 RICHARD BARR, EDWARD ALBEE & CLINTON WILDER
RICHARD A. DUPREY
(University Award)
1965 WYNN HANDMAN MARSTON BALCH
(University Award)
1966 JON JORY ARTHUR BALLET
(University Award)
1967 PAUL BAKER GEORGE C. WHITE
(Workshop Award)

1968 DAVEY MARLIN-JONES ELLEN STEWART
(Workshop Award)
1969 ADRIAN HALL EDWARD PARONE & GORDON DAVIDSON
(Workshop Award)
1970 JOSEPH PAPP
1971 ZELDA FICHANDLER
1972 JULES IRVING
1973 DOUGLAS TURNER WARD
1974 PAUL WEIDNER
1975 ROBERT KALFIN
1976 GORDON DAVIDSON
1977 MARSHALL W. MASON
1978 JON JORY
1979 ELLEN STEWART
1980 JOHN CLARK DONAHUE
1981 LYNNE MEADOW

1982 ANDRE BISHOP
1983 BILL BUSHNELL
1984 GREGORY MOSHER
1985 JOHN LION
1986 LLOYD RICHARDS
1987 GERALD CHAPMAN
1988 NO AWARD
1989 MARGARET GOHEEN
1990 RICHARD COE
1991 OTIS L. GUERNSEY JR.
1992 ABBOT VAN NOSTRAND
1993 HENRY HEWES
1994 JANE ALEXANDER
1995 ROBERT WHITEHEAD
1996 AL HIRSCHFELD
1997 GEORGE C. WHITE
1998 JAMES HOUGHTON
1999 GEORGE KEATHLEY
2000 EILEEN HECKART
2001 MEL GUSSOW

MUSICAL THEATRE HALL OF FAME

THIS ORGANIZATION WAS ESTABLISHED at New York University on November 10, 1993.

HAROLD ARLEN
IRVING BERLIN
LEONARD BERNSTEIN
EUBIE BLAKE
ABE BURROWS
GEORGE M. COHAN
DOROTHY FIELDS
GEORGE GERSHWIN

IRA GERSHWIN
OSCAR HAMMERSTEIN II
E.Y. HARBURG
LARRY HART
JEROME KERN
BURTON LANE
ALAN JAY LERNER
FRANK LOESSER

FREDERICK LOEWE
COLE PORTER
ETHEL MERMAN
JEROME ROBBINS
RICHARD RODGERS
HAROLD ROME

2001–2002 NEW PUBLICATION OF PLAYS, ADAPTATIONS, TRANSLATIONS, COLLECTIONS AND ANTHOLOGIES

○ ○ ○ ○ ○

Compiled by Rue E. Canvin

PLAYS

Accused, The. Jeffrey Archer. Methuen. (paper) $10.95

Altruists, The. Nicky Silver. Dramatists Play Service. (acting ed.) $5.95

Amadeus. Peter Shaffer. HarperCollins. (paper) $15

Blood Brothers. Willy Russell. Methuen. (paper) $11.95

Blue Surge. Rebecca Gilman. Faber and Faber. (paper) $13

Book of Liz, The. Amy and David Sedaris. Dramatists Play Service. (acting ed.) $5.95

Book of Ruth, The. Deborah Lynn Frockt. Dramatic Publishing Company. (acting ed.) $5.60

Boston Marriage. David Mamet. Methuen. (paper) $14

Cellini. John Patrick Shanley. Dramatists Play Service. (acting ed.) $5.95

Contrast, The. Royall Tyler. Feedback Theatrebooks. (spiral bound) $5.95

Credeaux Canvas, The. Keith Bunin. Dramatists Play Service. (acting ed.) $5.95

Crucible, The. Arthur Miller. Penguin. (cloth) $17

Dead Eye Boy, The. Angus MacLachlan. Dramatists Play Service. (acting ed.) $5.95

Director, The. Nancy Hasty. Broadway Play Publishing. (paper) $6.95

Educating Rita. Willy Russell. Methuen. (paper) $11.95

Edwin Booth. Lance Tait. Enfield Publishing Company. (paper) $14

Far Away. Caryl Churchill. Theatre Communications Group. (paper) $11.95

Five Nickels. Jack Neary. Dramatic Publishing Company. (acting ed.) $5.60

Follies. Stephen Sondheim and James Goldman. Theatre Communications Group. (paper) $12.95

Force Continuum. Kia Corthron. Dramatists Play Services. (acting ed.) $5.95

Girl of the Golden West, The. David Belasco. Feedback Theatrebooks. (spiral bound) $5.95

Glory of Living, The. Rebecca Gilman. Faber and Faber. (paper) $12

God's Man in Texas. David Rambo. Dramatists Play Service. (acting ed.) $5.95

Haitian Trilogy, The. Derek Walcott. Farrar, Straus and Giroux. (paper) $20

Hearts. Willy Holtzman. Dramatic Publishing Company. (acting ed.) $5.60 (OK)

Hedwig and the Angry Inch. John Cameron Mitchell and Stephen Trask. Penguin. (paper) $16.95

High Dive. Leslie Ayvazian. Dramatists Play Service. (acting ed.) $5.95

Homebody/Kabul. Tony Kushner. Theatre Communications Group. (paper) $12.95

Howie the Rookie. Mark O'Rowe. Dramatists Play Service. (acting ed.) $5.95

Human Events. A.R. Gurney. Broadway Play Publishing. (paper) $6.95

In Arabia We'd All Be Kings. Stephen Adly Guirgis. Dramatists Play Service. (acting ed.) $5.95

Incorruptible: A Dark Comedy About the Dark Ages. Michael Hollinger. Dramatists Play Service. (acting ed.) $5.95

Irish Play, An. Dan O'Brien. Dramatic Publishing Company. (acting ed.) $5.60 (OK)

Japes. Simon Gray. Nick Hern. (paper) $16.95

Jesus Hopped the 'A' Train. Stephen Adly Guirgis. Dramatists Play Service. (acting ed.) $5.95

Jitney. August Wilson. Overlook Press. (cloth) $22.95

Kit Marlowe. David Grimm. Dramatists Play Service. (acting ed.) $5.95

Laramie Project, The. Moisés Kaufman and the Tectonic Theater Project. Random House/Vintage. (paper) $11

Last Christmas Carol, The. Dramatic Publishing Company. (acting ed.) $5.95

Lieutenant of Inishmore, The. Martin McDonagh. Methuen. (paper) $13.95

Like Bees to Honey. Andrea M. Green. Dramatic Publishing Company. (acting ed.) $5.60

Long Day's Journey Into Night: Revised Edition. Eugene O'Neill. Foreword by Harold Bloom. Yale. (cloth/paper) $22.95/$12.95

Looking for Normal. Jane Anderson. Dramatists Play Service. (acting ed.)

Lost Colony, The. Paul Green. University of North Carolina. (paper), $12.95

Lydie Breeze. John Guare. Overlook Press. (paper) $16.95

Metamorphoses: A Play. Mary Zimmerman. Northwestern University Press. (paper) $14

Mothering. Rebecca Christian and Tracey Rush. Dramatic Publishing Company. (acting ed.) $5.95

Music from a Sparkling Planet. Douglas Carter Beane. Dramatists Play Service. (acting ed.) $5.95

Nebraska. Keith Reddin. Dramatists Play Service. (acting ed.) $5.95

Nocturne. Adam Rapp. Faber and Faber. (paper) $13

Nowadays. George Middleton. Feedback Theatrebooks. (spiral bound) $5.95

Now Then Again. Penny Penniston. Broadway Play Publishing. (paper) $6.95

Old Money. Wendy Wasserstein. Harcourt Brace. (cloth) $23

Orpheus and Eurydice. Jeremy Dobrish. Broadway Play Publishing. (paper) $6.95

Passion Play. Peter Nichols. Nick Hern. Originally titled *Passion.* (paper) $16.95

Play About the Baby, The. Edward Albee. Dramatists Play Service. (acting ed.) $5.95

Poor of New York, The. Dion Boucicault. Feedback Theatrebooks. (spiral bound) $5.95

Praying for Rain. Robert Lewis Vaughan. Dramatists Play Service. (acting ed.) $5.95

Preface to the Alien Garden, A. Robert Alexander. Broadway Play Publishing. (paper) $6.95

Race. Ferdinand Bruckner. Adapt. Barry Edelstein. Dramatists Play Service. (acting ed.) $5.95

References to Salvador Dali Make Me Hot. José Rivera. Broadway Play Publishing. (paper) $6.95

Saved or Destroyed. Harry Kondoleon. Dramatists Play Service. (acting ed.) $5.95

Secret Service. William Gillette. Feedback Theatrebooks. (spiral bound) $5.95

Seeking the Genesis. Kia Corthron. Dramatists Play Service. (acting ed.) $5.95

Serious Money. Caryl Churchill. Methuen. (paper) $12.95

Shape of Things, The. Neil Labute. Faber and Faber. (paper) $13

Sheridan. David Grimm. Dramatists Play Service. (acting ed.) $5.95

Sleep Deprivation Chamber. Adam P. and Adrienne Kennedy. Dramatists Play Service. (acting ed.) $5.95

Sorrows and Rejoicings. Athol Fugard. Theatre Communications Group. (paper) $11.95

Stags and Hens. Willy Russell. Methuen (paper) $11.95

Summer Cyclone. Amy Fox. Dramatists Play Service. (acting ed.) $5.95

Tabletop. Rob Ackerman. Dramatists Play Service. (acting ed) $5.95

Thief River. Lee Blessing. Dramatists Play Service. (acting ed.) $5.95

Tiny Island. Michael Hollinger. Dramatists Play Service. (acting ed.) $5.95

Topdog/Underdog. Suzan-Lori Parks. Theatre Communications Group. (paper) $12.95

Trial of One Short-Sighted Black Woman vs Mammy Louise and Safreeta Mae, The. Karani Marcia Leslie. Broadway Play Publishing. (paper) $6.95

Vampire Dreams. Suzy McKee Charnas. Broadway Play Publishing. (paper) $6.95

Wake Up and Smell the Coffee. Eric Bogosian. Theatre Communcations Group. (paper) $11.95

Whiteout. Alan Newton. Dramatic Publishing Company. (acting ed.) $5.60

Yalta Game, The. Brian Friel. Dufour. (paper) $10.95

Yard Gal. Rebecca Prichard. Dramatists Play Service. (acting ed.) $5.95

ADAPTATIONS

Christmas Carol, A. Charles Dickens. Adapt. Paul Sills. Applause. (paper) $6.95

Duchess of Malfi, The. John Webster. Ed. Brian Gibbons. Norton. (paper) $15

Enrico IV. Luigi Pirandello. Adapt. Richard Nelson. Broadway Play Publishing. (paper) $6.95

Ethan Frome. Adapt by Gary L. Blackwood from the novel by Edith Wharton. Baker's Plays. (acting ed.) $5.25

Government Inspector, The. Nikolai Gogol. Adapt. Adrian Mitchell. Methuen. (paper) $11.95

Hedda Gabler. Henrik Ibsen. Adapt. Doug Hughes. Dramatists Play Service. (acting ed) $5.95

Light. Adapt. Simon McBurney and Matthew Broughton. Based on the book by Torgny Lindgren. Oberon Books. (paper) $16.95

Lulu. Frank Wedekind. Adapt. Nicholas Wright. Nick Hern. (paper) $16.95

Miss Julie and *The Stronger.* August Strindberg. Adapt. Frank McGuinness. Faber and Faber. (paper) $13

New Inn, The. Ben Jonson. Ed. Michael Hattaway. Manchester University Press. (paper) $19.95

Star Quality. Noël Coward. Adapt. Christopher Luscombe. Methuen. (paper) $13.95

Wild Duck, The. Henrik Ibsen. Adapt. Anthony Clarvoe. Broadway Play Publishing. (paper) $6.95

TRANSLATIONS

Bacchae, The. Euripides. Trans. Herbert Golder. Applause. (paper) $7.95

Blood Wedding. Federico Garcia Lorca. Trans. Lillian Groag. Dramatists Play Service. (acting ed.) $5.95

Drama Contemporary: India. Edited by Erin B. Mee. Johns Hopkins University Press. (paper) $22.50

Faust: Part One. Goethe. Trans. Randall Jarrell. Farrar, Straus and Giroux. (cloth) $22.50

Feydeau: Plays. Vol. I. Georges Feydeau. Trans. Kenneth McLeish. Methuen. (paper) $17.95

Feydeau: Plays Vol. II. Georges Feydeau. Trans. Kenneth McLeish. Methuen. (paper) $17.95

Four Major Plays Vol. II. Henrik Ibsen. Trans. Rolf Fjelde. New American Library/ Signet. (paper) $5.95

Hedda Gabler. Henrik Ibsen. Trans. Michael Meyer. Methuen. (paper) $11.95

Heiner Muller Reader, A. Heiner Muller. Trans. Carl Weber. Johns Hopkins University Press. (paper) $19.95

Life x 3. Yasmina Reza. Trans. Christopher Hampton. Faber and Faber. (paper) $13

Lysistrata. Aristophanes. Trans. Douglass Parker. New American Library. (paper) $5.95

Misanthrope, Tartuffe & Other Plays, The. Molière. Trans. Maya Slater. Oxford. (paper) $7.95

Oedipus at Colonus. Sophocles. Trans. Nicholas Rudall. Ivan R. Dee. (paper) $7.95

Oedipus. Trans. Kenneth McLeish and Michael Sargent. Nick Hern. (paper) $8.95

Phedra. Jean Racine. Trans. Wallace Fowlie. Dover. (paper) $1.50

Philoctetes. Sophocles. Trans. Judith Affleck. Cambridge. (paper) $9.95

Plays One: Lope de Vega. Lope de Vega. Trans. Michael Jacobs. Oberon Books. (paper) $20

Rabindranath Tagore: Three Plays. Rabindranath Tagore. Trans. Ananda Lal. Oxford. (paper) $16.95

R.U.R. Karel Capek. Trans. Paul Selver and Nigel Playfair. Dover. (paper) $1.50

Six Characters Looking for an Author. Luigi Pirandello. Trans. David Harrower. Methuen. (paper) $11.95

Suitors, The. Jean Racine. Trans. Richard Wilbur. Dramatists Play Service. (acting ed.) $5.95

Toller: Play One. Ernst Toller. Ed. and trans. Alan Raphael Pearlman. Oberon Books. (paper) $20.95

Trojan Women and Other Plays, The. Euripides. Trans. James Norwood. Oxford. (paper) $8.95

We Won't Pay! We Won't Pay! and Other Plays, Vol. I. Dario Fo. Ed. Franca Rame. Trans. Ron Jenkins. Theatre Communications Group. (paper) $17.95

COLLECTIONS

Adrienne Kennedy Reader, The. Adrienne Kennedy. University of Minnesota. (paper) $18.95

Cellophane: Plays by Mac Wellman. Mac Wellman. Johns Hopkins University Press. (paper) $22.50

Collected Plays of Bernard Pomerance, The. Bernard Pomerance. Grove Press. (paper) $16

Collected Works of Langston Hughes, Vol. 5: The Plays to 1942. Langston Hughes. Ed. Leslie Catherine Sanders with Nancy Johnston. University of Missouri. (cloth) $49.95

Collected Works of W. B. Yeats, Volume 2: The Plays. W. B. Yeats. Ed. by David and Rosalind Clark. Simon & Schuster. (cloth) $70

Eugene O'Neill: Early Plays. Eugene O'Neill. Penguin USA. (paper) $12

Four Plays: Abbensetts. Michael Abbensetts. Oberon Books. (paper) $5.95

George Bernard Shaw's Plays. George Bernard Shaw. Norton. (paper) $16.50

Jane Martin Collected Plays: Vol. II. 1996–2001. Ed. Michael Bigelow Dixon. Smith and Kraus. (paper) $19.95

La Bête and *Wrong Mountain.* David Hirson. Grove Press. (paper) $14

Luna Park: Short Plays and Monologues. Donald Margulies. Theatre Communications Group. (paper) $16.95

Madame Melville and *The General From America.* Richard Nelson. Grove Press. (paper) $14

Plays by Adam Rapp. Adam Rapp. Broadway Play Publishing. (paper) $11.95

Plays One: Robert Bolt. Robert Bolt. Oberon. (paper) $.20.95

Rachel's Brain and Other Stories. Rachel Rosenthal. Continuum. (paper) $24.95

Synge: The Complete Plays. J.M. Synge. Methuen. (paper) $16.95

Three Plays About Ibsen and Strindberg. Michael Meyer. Oberon Books. (paper) $20.95

W.B. Yeats: The Major Works. W.B. Yeats. Oxford World's Classics. (paper) $15.95

ANTHOLOGIES

American Political Plays: An Anthology. Ed. Allan Havis. University of Illinois. (paper) $18.95

Contemporary Australian Plays. Ed. Russell Vandenbroucke. Methuen USA. (paper) $16.95

Eighteenth-Century Women Dramatists. Ed. Melinda Finberg. Oxford. (paper) $15.95

Humana Festival 2001: The Complete Plays. Ed. Tanya Palmer and Amy Wegener. Smith and Kraus. (paper) $19.95

London Assurance and Other Victorian Comedies. Ed. Klaus Stierstorfer. Oxford. (paper) $13.95

Mysterious Actions: New American Drama. Ed. Jody McAuliffe. Duke University. (paper) $18

New Dramatists 2000: Best Plays by the Graduating Class of 2000. Ed. Todd London. Smith and Kraus (paper) $19.95

New Playwrights: The Best Plays of 1999. Ed. Marisa Smith. Smith and Kraus. (paper) $19.95

Plays and Playwrights 2002. Martin Denton. New York Theatre Experience. (paper) $15

Political Stages. Eds. Emily Mann and David Roessel. Applause. (paper) $19.95

Renaissance Drama: An Anthology of Plays and Entertainments. Ed. Arthur F. Kinney. Blackwell Publishers. (paper) $42.95

Victorian Theatricals From Menageries to Melodrama. Ed. Sara Hudston. Methuen. (paper) $24.95

Women Playwrights: Best Plays of 1999. Ed. Marisa Smith. Smith and Kraus. (paper) $19.95

Women's Project & Productions: Rowing to America and 16 Other Short Plays. Ed. Julia Miles. Smith and Kraus. (paper) $19.95

IN MEMORIAM
MAY 2001–MAY 2002
○ ○ ○ ○ ○

PERFORMERS

Aaliyah (22) – August 25, 2001

Agar, John (81) – April 7, 2002

Albright, John R. (88) – October 24, 2001

Ast, Pat (59) – October 2, 2001

Atkins, Norman (82) – January 13, 2002

Atkinson, Beverly Hope (66) – December 11, 2001

Baker, B. J. (74) – April 2, 2002

Barry, Dave (82) – August 16, 2001

Barton, Donald (76) – April 24, 2002

Barton, Steve (47) – July 21, 2001

Bass, Bobby (65) – November 7, 2001

Becaud, Gilbert (74) – December 8, 2001

Bellamy, Diana (57) – June 17, 2001

Bene, Carmelo (64) – March 10, 2002

Berenson, Berry (53) – September 11, 2001

Berle, Milton (93) – March 27, 2002

Bishop, Julie (87) – August 30, 2001

Blocksmith, Roger (56) – December 16, 2001

Bower, Beverly (76) – March 24, 2002

Brodsky, Vlastimil (81) – April 20, 2002

Brooks, Foster (89) – December 21, 2002

Broun, Heywood Hale (83) – September 5, 2001

Brown, James "Buster" (88) – May 7, 2002

Bryant, Michael (74) – April 25, 2002

Burkhart, Melvin (94) – November 8, 2001

Calvert, Corinne (75) – June 23, 2001

Cambridge, Edmund J. (80) – August 18, 2001

Caran, Lillian Green (85) – January 2, 2002

Cigna, Gina (101) – June 26, 2001

Cobb, Joe (85) – May 21, 2002

Coca, Imogene (92) – June 2, 2001

Coleman, Charlotte (33) – November 14, 2001

Conway, Bert (87) – February 7, 2002

Coombs, Ernie (73) – September 18, 2001

Cracknell, Ruth (76) – May 13, 2002

Dagmar (79) – October 9, 2001

Dale, Alan (73) – April 20, 2002

Donahue, Troy (65) – September 2, 2001

Dudley, Jane (89) – September 19, 2001

Dyer, Ruth McCullough (80) – June 15, 2001

Everett, Betty (61) – August 19, 2001

Fant, Lou (69) – June 11, 2001

Farina, Mimi Baez (56) – July 18, 2001

Farrell, Eileen (82) – March 23, 2002

Félix, María (87) – April 8, 2002

Foster, Gloria (64) – October 6, 2001

Fraser, Ruth (71) – February 5, 2002

Freeman, Kathleen (78) – August 23, 2001

Gaye, Frankie (60) – December 28, 2001

Gebel-Williams, Gunther (66) – July 19, 2001

Gordon, Gerald (67) – August 17, 2001

Gracie, Sally (80) – August 13, 2001

Greer, Jane (76) – August 24, 2001

Gurney, Rachel (81) – November 24, 2001

Gwillim, Jack (91) – July 2, 2001

Halstead, Bianca (36) – December 15, 2001

Hamilton, Carrie (38) – January 20, 2001

Hawthorne, Nigel (72) – December 26, 2001

Heckart, Eileen (82) – December 31, 2001

Hellstrom, Gunnar (73) – November 28, 2001

Hewett, Christopher (80) – August 3, 2001

Hewett, Peggy (56) – March 1, 2002

Hollis, Tommy (47) – September 9, 2001

Hubschmid, Paul (84) – December 31, 2001

Huston, Martin (60) – August 9, 2001

Ivey, Monteria (41) – December 13, 2001

Jackson, Eugene (84) – October 26, 2001

Jennings, Waylon (64) – February 13, 2002

Johnson, Raymond Edward (90) – August 15, 2001

Jones, Etta (72) – October 16, 2001

Jordan, Judith (61) – September 13, 2001

Kazantzidis, Stelios (70) – September 14, 2001

K-Doe, Ernie (65) – July 5, 2001

Knef, Hildegard (76) – February 1, 2002

Konya, Sandor (78) – May 20, 2002

Kramer, Bert (66) – June 20, 2001

Kruschen, Jack (80) – April 2, 2002
Kumar, Ashok (90) – December 10, 2001
Lamm, B. Karen (49) – June 29, 2001
Lee, Peggy (81) – January 21, 2002
Lemmon, Jack (76) – June 27, 2001
Leonard, Queenie (86) – January 17, 2002
Leotard, Philippe (60) – August 25, 2001
Loud, Lance (50) – December 21, 2001
Lund, Lucille (89) – February 16, 2002
Manson, Alan (83) – March 5, 2002
Martinez, José Vargas (70) – October 20, 2001
McBride, Vaughn (66) – November 24, 2001
McCalla, Irish (72) – February 1, 2002
McCarthy, Nobu (67) – April 6, 2002
McCutcheon, Bill (77) – January 9, 2002
McGuire, Dorothy (85) – September 13, 2001
McKay, Gardner (69) – November 21, 2001
Merrill, Scott (82) – June 28, 2001
Milligan, Spike (83) – February 27, 2002
Mitchum, John (82) – November 27, 2001
Mödl, Martha (89) – December 16, 2001
Montgomery, Reggie (54) – January 13, 2002
Moore, Dudley (66) – March 27, 2002
Moore, Pauline (87) – December 7, 2001
Mount, Peggy (85) – November 13, 2001
Music, Lorenzo (64) – August 4, 2001
Nader, George (80) – February 4, 2002
Nicol, Alex (85) – July 29, 2001
O'Connor, Carroll (76) – June 21, 2001
O'Connor, Harry (45) – April 4, 2002
O'Grady, Lani (46) – September 25, 2001
Okunyevskaya, Tatiana (88) – May 15, 2002
Pagent, Robert (87) – September 4, 2001
Piven, Byrne (72) – February 18, 2002
Puopolo, Sonia Morales (58) – September 11, 2001
Quinn, Anthony (86) – June 3, 2001
Rasnick, Marlene (57) – November 18, 2001
Reed, Walter (85) – August 20, 2001
Renan, Emile (88) – December 8, 2001
Robert, Yves (81) – May 10, 2002
Robinson, Edna Mae (86) – May 2, 2002
Rowles, Polly (87) – October 7, 2001
Russell, Harold (88) – January 29, 2002
Russell, Johnny (61) – July 3, 2001
St. Clair, Michael (79) – November 22, 2001

Salinas, "Chucho" (73) – November 8, 2001
Salter, June (69) – September 15, 2001
Sanders, Byron (76) – November 12, 2001
Saunders, Russell M. (82) – May 29, 2001
Schreiber, Avery (66) – January 7, 2002
Scott, Evelyn (86) – January 31, 2002
Seurat, Pilar (62) – June 2, 2001
Shaw, Janet (82) – October 15, 2001
Shuster, Frank (85) – January 13, 2002
Sims, Joan (71) – June 28, 2001
Smith, Darwood (72) – May 15, 2002
Smith, Howard K. (87) – February 15, 2002
Smith, Kevin (38) – February 9, 2002
Smith, O.C. (65) – November 23, 2001
Sokolova, Lyubov (79) – June 6, 2001
Staley, Layne (34) – April 21, 2002
Stanley, Kim (76) – August 20, 2001
Stearns, Johnny (85) – December 1, 2001
Stewart, Mel (72) – February 24, 2002
Stockwell, Guy (68) – February 7, 2002
Stojkovic, Danilo Bata (67) – March 16, 2002
Stricklyn, Ray (73) – May 14, 2002
Stuart, Mary (75) – February 28, 2002
Taylor, Ron (49) – January 15, 2002
Thaw, John (60) – February 21, 2002
Thomas, Henry (70) – June 29, 2001
Thomas, Rufus (84) – December 15, 2001
Thornton, Melanie (34) – November 24, 2001
Tierney, Lawrence (82) – February 26, 2002
Toll, Judy (44) – May 3, 2002
Tomaszewski, Henryk (81) – September 23, 2001
Took, Barry (73) – March 31, 2002
Townson, Ron (68) – August 2, 2001
Tutin, Dorothy (71) – August 6, 2001
Unwin Stanley (90) – January 12, 2002
Urich, Robert (55) – April 16, 2002
Uzaemon, Ichimura (84) – July 8, 2001
van der Vlis, Diana (66) – October 22, 2001
Van Ronk, Dave (65) – February 10, 2002
Vanzo, Alain (73) – January 27, 2002
Vitsin, Georgy (83) – October 22, 2001
Vohs, Joan (73) – June 4, 2001
Winbergh, Goesta (58) – March 18, 2002
Wong, Victor Keung (74) – September 12, 2001
Worth, Irene (85) – March 10, 2002

Wyllie, Meg (84) – January 1, 2002
Young, Otis (69) – October 12, 2001
Young, Tony (64) – February 26, 2002

PRODUCERS, DIRECTORS, CHOREOGRAPHERS

Abady, Josephine (52) – May 25, 2002
Angell, David (54) – September 11, 2001
Arkoff, Samuel Z. (83) – September 16, 2001
Babbin, Jacqueline (80) – October 6, 2001
Berman, Ted (81) – July 15, 2001
Beug, Carolyn (48) – September 11, 2001
Boetticher, Budd (85) – November 29, 2001
Boulting, Roy (87) – November 5, 2001
Buck, Jules (83) – July 19, 2001
Christensen, William Farr (99) – October 14, 2001
Chukhrai, Grigory (80) – October 28, 2001
Coleman, William "Herbert" – October 3, 2001
Cogan, David (78) – February 7, 2002
Davis, Dale (61) – September 13, 2001
De Cordova, Fred (90) – September 15, 2001
Demme, Ted (38) – January 13, 2002
de Rochemont III, Louis (70) – July 11, 2001
Elkin, Harvey (70) – February 5, 2002
Engel, Frederick (71) – November 28, 2001
Fay, Maura (43) – October 29, 2001
Granz, Norman (83) – November 22, 2001
Grossberg, Jack (74) – December 28, 2001
Hager, James (61) – February 8, 2002
Hemmings, Peter (67) – January 4, 2002
Houghton, Norris (92) – October 9, 2001
Jires, Jaromil (65) – October 24, 2001
Kesten, Steve (66) – December 20, 2001
Koner, Pauline (88) – February 8, 2001
LeNoire, Rosetta (90) – March 17, 2002
Levy, Ralph (81) – October 15, 2001
Long, Dwight Stanley (89) – July 3, 2001
Magner, Martin (101) – January 25, 2002
Mayer, Gerald (82) – September 21, 2001
McKenzie, James B. (75) – February 20, 2002
Padula, Edward (85) – November 1, 2001
Patterson, Ray (90) – December 30, 2001
Persky, Lester (76) – December 16, 2001

Phillips, Julia (57) – January 1, 2002
Pultz, Alan L. (64) – October 25, 2001
Radin, Paul B. (88) – October 18, 2001
Rafkin, Alan (73) – August 6, 2001
Roberts, John (56) – October 27, 2001
Rodgers, Rod (64) – March 24, 2002
Rogers, Richard P. (57) – July 14, 2001
Ross, Herbert (76) – October 9, 2001
Rostotsky, Stanislav (79) – August 10, 2001
Rothstein, Freyda (72) – October 27, 2001
Seid, Art (87) – August 9, 2001
Sidney, George (85) – May 5, 2002
Swift, David (82) – December 31, 2001
Todd, Michael Jr. (72) – May 5, 2002
Weiss, Adrian (83) – October 28, 2001
Wherrett, Richard (60) – December 7, 2001
White, John Simon (91) – November 6, 2001
Whitehead, Robert (86) – June 15, 2002
Wilder, Billy (95) – March 27, 2002
Ziv, Frederick (96) – October 13, 2001

PLAYWRIGHTS, SCRIPTWRITERS

Goetz, Ruth (93) – October 12, 2001
Goldman, Harold "Hal" (81) – June 27, 2001
Herbert, John (75) – June 22, 2001
Kempley, Walter Jr. (74) – August 11, 2001
Kesey, Ken (66) – November 10, 2001
Lessing, Norman (90) – October 22, 2001
Marcus, Lawrence (84) – August 28, 2001
Melfi, Leonard (66) – October 28, 2001
Miller, J.P. (81) – November 1, 2001
Naum, Gellu (86) – September 29, 2001
Peyser, Arnold (80) – July 1, 2001
Pine, Lester (84) – August 11, 2001
Rose, Reginald (81) – April 19, 2002
Schiffman, Suzanne (71) – June 6, 2001
Shaffer, Anthony (75) – November 6, 2001
Sherman, Stuart (55) – September 14, 2001
Silverton, Doris (73) – November 27, 2001
Sterner, Jerry (62) – June 11, 2001
Welty, Eudora (92) – July 23, 2001
Wright, Norman Hall (91) – July 21, 2001

COMPOSERS, LYRICISTS, ARRANGERS

Albam, Manny (79) – October 2, 2001
Bebey, Francis (72) – May 28, 2001
Berlinski, Herman (91) – September 27, 2001

Burns, Ralph (79) – November 21, 2001
Darion, Joe (90) – June 16, 2001
Elliott, Jack (74) – August 18, 2001
Esquivel, Juan Garcia (83) – January 3, 2002
Hague, Albert (81) – November 12, 2001
Hammond, Michael P. (69) – January 29, 2002
Hartford, John (63) – June 4, 2001
Howard, Harlan (74) – March 3, 2002
Johns, Erik (74) – December 11, 2001
Johnston, Donald (57) – January 7, 2002
Livingston, Jay (86) – October 17, 2001
Lockwood, William (69) – August 11, 2001
Lubin, Joe (84) – October 9, 2001
Mann, David (85) – March 1, 2002
Mann, Kal (84) – November 28, 2001
McGlohon, Loonis (80) – January 26, 2002
Neil, Fred (64) – July 7, 2001
O'Farrill, Chico (79) – June 27, 2001
Ornstein, Leo (108) – February 24, 2002

DESIGNERS

Abel, Robert (64) – September 23, 2001
Flowers, A.D. (84) – July 5, 2001
Maatera, Barbara (72) – September 13, 2001
Montresor, Beni (75) – October 11, 2001
Porcher, Nananne (78) – June 17, 2001
Shorr, Richard Jay (58) – August 13, 2001
Svoboda, Josef (81) – April 8, 2002

ARTS WRITERS AND CRITICS

Buckle, Richard (85) – October 12, 2001
Dance, Helen Oakley (88) – May 27, 2001
Esslin, Martin (83) – February 24, 2002
Goodman, Walter (74) – March 6, 2002
Hume, Paul (85) – November 26, 2001
Kael, Pauline (82) – September 3, 2001
Kaufman, Dave (87) – November 9, 2001
Kott, Jan (87) – December 22, 2001
Sayre, Nora (68) – August 8, 2001
Schaap, Dick (67) – December 21, 2001
Sylvester, David (76) – June 19, 2001
Tillim, Sidney (76) – August 16, 2001

CONDUCTORS

Asahina, Takashi (93) – December 29, 2001
Buketoff, Igor (87) – September 7, 2001
Garcia Navarro, Luis Antonio (61) – October 10, 2001
Nygaard, Jens (69) – September 24, 2001

MUSICIANS

Adler, Larry (87) – August 7, 2001
Atkins, Chet (77) – June 30, 2001
Austin, Sil (71) – September 1, 2001
Byrd, Billy (81) – August 7, 2001
Candoli, Conte (74) – December 14, 2001
Charles, Vince (55) – June 3, 2001
Coffman, Bill (75) – December 7, 2001
Collins, Cal (68) – August 26, 2001
Collins, John (83) – October 4, 2001
Czerny-Stefanska, Halina (78) – July 1, 2001
Dvonch, Mara Sebrionsky (87) – August 30, 2001
Ettleson, Steve (56) – June 1, 2001
Fajardo, Jose (82) – December 11, 2001
Feyer, George (92) – October 21, 2001
Flanagan, Tommy (71) – November 16, 2001
Flynn, Frank Emilio (80) – August 23, 2001
Francis, David "Panama" (82) – November 13, 2001
Fromer, Marcelo (39) – June 13, 2001
Gigliotti, Anthony (79) – December 3, 2001
Graham, Art (78) – October 24, 2001
Harrison, George (58) – November 29, 2001
Helps, Robert (73) – November 24, 2001
Henderson, Charles N. (84) – July 24, 2001
Henderson, Joe (64) – June 30, 2001
Hinton, Milt "The Judge" (90) – December 19, 2001
Hooker, John Lee (83) – June 21, 2001
Hsu, Fei-Ping (51) – November 27, 2001
Hunter, Robert (72) – September 10, 2001
Jerome, Jerry (89) – November 17, 2001
Karoli, Michael (53) – November 17, 2001
Kershaw, Russell "Rusty" (63) – October 23, 2001
Kestenbaum, Myra (69) – November 6, 2001
Kikuhara, Hatsuko (102) – September 12, 2001
Land, Harold (73) – July 27, 2001
Martin, Grady (72) – December 3, 2001
McIntyre, Makanda K. (69) – June 13, 2001
Menuhin, Yaltah (79) – June 10, 2001
Migliori, Jay (70) – September 2, 2001
Montgomery, Smokey (88) – June 6, 2001
Nelson, John (85) – August 25, 2001
Nichols, Roy (68) – July 3, 2001

Phillips, Flip (86) – August 17, 2001
Robinson, Spike (71) – October 29, 2001
Schnabel, Karl Ulrich (92) – August 27, 2001
Scott, Isaac (56) – November 16, 2001
Stern, Isaac (81) – September 22, 2001
Sutton, Ralph (79) – December 30, 2001
Szekely, Zoltan (97) – October 5, 2001
Thomas, Milton (81) – June 16, 2001
Wilkeson, Leon (49) – July 27, 2001
Williams, Chris (31) – August 5, 2001
Woodman, Coney (83) – June 20, 2001
Zelka, Charlotte (71) – October 6, 2001

OTHERS OF NOTE

Aschenberg, Bridget (73) – March 6, 2002
Agent for Arthur Miller, William Inge, Tennessee Williams, and others
Balaban, Elmer (92) – November 2, 2001
Founder of theater chain
Davies, Harry (94) – July 1, 2001
Publicist for Florenz Ziegfeld, worked with Walter Winchell
Kananack, Arthur (68) – March 9, 2002
Entertainment attorney

Kupcinet, Essee (84) – June 16, 2001
Arts advocate
Melnick, Wilt (85) – July 28, 2001
Agent for actors
Petrafesa, John (54) – July 18, 2001
Labor relations head for Walt Disney Theatrical Productions
Springer, John (85) – October 30, 2001
Renowned theatrical and film press agent
Stevenson, John Alun (87) – February 16, 2002
Film publicist, journalist and New York theater patron
Strauss, John (88) – September 21, 2001
Independent Hollywood publicist
Tyre, Norman R. (91) – January 3, 2002
Entertainment lawyer
Williamson, Alix (85) – August 26, 2001
Press agent for singers and musicians
Wooler, Bob (76) – February 8, 2002
Liverpool disc jockey, helped launch the Beatles

THE BEST PLAYS AND MAJOR PRIZEWINNERS
1894–2002

○ ○ ○ ○ ○

LISTED IN ALPHABETICAL ORDER below are all works selected as Best Plays in previous volumes of the *Best Plays* series, except for the seasons of 1996–97 through 1999–2000. During those excluded seasons, *Best Plays* honored only major prizewinners and those who received special *Best Plays* citations. Opposite each title is given the volume in which the play is honored, its opening date and its total number of performances. Two separate opening-date and performance-number entries signify two separate engagements when the original production transferred. Plays marked with an asterisk (*) were still playing on June 1, 2002 and their number of performances was figured through May 31, 2002. Adaptors and translators are indicated by (ad) and (tr), the symbols (b), (m) and (l) stand for the author of the book, music and lyrics in the case of musicals and (c) signifies the credit for the show's conception, (i) for its inspiration. Entries identified as 94–99 and 99–09 are late 19th and early 20th century plays from one of the retrospective volumes. 94–95, 95–96, 96–97, 97–98, 98–99 and 99–00 are late-20th century plays.

PLAY	VOLUME	OPENED	PERFS
ABE LINCOLN IN ILLINOIS—Robert E. Sherwood	38–39	Oct. 15, 1938	472
ABRAHAM LINCOLN—John Drinkwater	19–20	Dec. 15, 1919	193
ACCENT ON YOUTH—Samson Raphaelson	34–35	Dec. 25, 1934	229
ADAM AND EVA—Guy Bolton, George Middleton	19–20	Sept. 13, 1919	312
ADAPTATION—Elaine May; and NEXT—Terrence McNally	68–69	Feb. 10, 1969	707
AFFAIRS OF STATE—Louis Verneuil	50–51	Sept. 25, 1950	610
AFTER THE FALL—Arthur Miller	63–64	Jan. 23, 1964	208
AFTER THE RAIN—John Bowen	67–68	Oct. 9, 1967	64
AFTER-PLAY—Anne Meara	94–95	Jan. 31, 1995	400
AGNES OF GOD—John Pielmeier	81–82	Mar. 30, 1982	599
AH, WILDERNESS!—Eugene O'Neill	33–34	Oct. 2, 1933	289
AIN'T SUPPOSED TO DIE A NATURAL DEATH—(b, m, l) Melvin Van Peebles	71–72	Oct. 20, 1971	325
ALIEN CORN—Sidney Howard	32–33	Feb. 20, 1933	98
ALISON'S HOUSE—Susan Glaspell	30–31	Dec. 1, 1930	41
ALL MY SONS—Arthur Miller	46–47	Jan. 29, 1947	328
ALL IN THE TIMING—David Ives	93–94	Feb. 17, 1994	526
ALL OVER TOWN—Murray Schisgal	74–75	Dec. 29, 1974	233
ALL THE WAY HOME—Tad Mosel, based on James Agee's novel *A Death in the Family*	60–61	Nov. 30, 1960	333
ALLEGRO—(b, l) Oscar Hammerstein II, (m) Richard Rodgers	47–48	Oct. 10, 1947	315
AMADEUS—Peter Shaffer	80–81	Dec. 17, 1980	1,181

423

CONTRIBUTORS TO *BEST PLAYS*

○ ○ ○ ○ ○

Rue E. Canvin worked at the *New York Herald Tribune*, first as a secretary in the advertising department and then as an editorial assistant in the drama department for 15 years where she worked with the editors and the arts critics until the demise of the newspaper in 1966. She also worked at the *World Journal Tribune* until its demise the following year. Canvin has served as an assistant editor of the *Best Plays* series since 1963. She has also transcribed taped interviews for the Dramatists Guild and Authors League.

Richard Christiansen is a Chicago-based journalist who has reviewd and reported on theater there and elsewhere for more than 40 years. He retired from his post as chief critic of the *Chicago Tribune* in 2002 and is writing a historical memoir of theater in Chicago, due for publication in 2004. He has served on the Pulitzer Prize nominating jury for drama seven times, twice as its chairman.

Jennifer de Poyen is a theater critic for the *San Diego Union-Tribune*. She also serves as vice president of the San Diego Theatre Critics Circle, which in 2002 established the Craig Noel Awards for Excellence in the Theatre in honor of the founding father of San Diego theater and to honor the work of San Diego's diverse theatrical community. A former fellow in the National Arts Journalism Program at Columbia University, she is a regular contributor to *Full Focus*, a public television program on the arts. She lives on a sailboat in San Diego Bay with the photographer Jeffrey Lamont Brown.

Michael Feingold is chief theater critic for the *Village Voice*, to which he first contributed reviews in 1971. He is a recipient of the George Jean Nathan Award and was named a Senior Fellow of the National Arts Journalism Program at Columbia University for 2001–2002. A graduate of Columbia University and the Yale School of Drama, he is one of the few critics to work steadily in the theater while reviewing. He has translated more than 50 plays and served as Literary Manager for Yale Repertory Theatre, the Guthrie Theater, and Boston's American Repertory Theatre. His translation of Carlo Goldoni's *Venetian Twins* was recently published by Samuel French.

Jeffrey Finn Productions is an entertainment and production management company. JFP credits include *Game Show* (US and International productions) for which Jeffrey Finn is also a co-author, and Broadway National Tours including *The Who's Tommy, Leader of the Pack, Promises, Promises, Company, Chess*, Diahann Carroll in *Almost Like Being in Love*, Marilyn McCoo & Billy Davis Jr. in *Hit Me With a Hot Note!*, *A Swell Party, Puttin' on the Ritz* and *A Slice of Saturday Night*. JFP also features a Special Events Division customizing Broadway corporate entertainment.

Michael Grossberg has worked since 1985 as chief theater critic for *The Dispatch* in Columbus, Ohio. He served as vice chairman of the American Theatre Critics Association, chairman of ATCA's New Plays Committee and chairman of ATCA's Regional Theatre Committee. He is a monthly columnist for *Back Stage*, the national performing arts weekly, and has written for *Reason, Liberty, Libertarian Review, Critics Quarterly* and the *New York Times* Special Syndicate.

Mel Gussow, a cultural writer for the *New York Times*, is the author of the biography, *Edward Albee: A Singular Journey*, and of Conversations with Miller, as well as books about Harold Pinter, Tom Stoppard and Samuel Beckett. He has also written

449

Theater on the Edge: New Visions, New Voices, a collection of theater reviews and essays, and was co-editor of the Library of America's two volume edition of the plays of Tennessee Williams. In 2002, he was awarded the Margo Jones Medal and, in previous years, the George Jean Nathan Award for Dramatic Criticism and a Guggenheim Fellowship.

Hirschfeld has virtually been synonymous with Broadway since his first theatrical drawing was published in December 1926. A stay in Bali in 1932 convinced Hirschfeld of the graphic possibilities of line. He says, "It was in Bali that my attraction to drawing blossomed into an enduring love affair with line." He returned to America to record the American theater in distinct line drawings for New York newspapers. His work has appeared in virtually every publication of the last 80 years, including a 74-year relationship with the *New York Times.* In 1951, he has wrote and illustrated *Show Business is No Business,* a satirical primer on the mechanics of Broadway production. He is the subject of the Academy Award-nominated documentary, *The Line King.* Among his many awards, he has won two Tonys for lifetime achievement and been designated a "Living Landmark" in New York. Hirschfeld has appeared in *Best Plays* since the 1952–53 edition—this volume marks his 50th contribution. He died in his sleep Jan. 20, 2003, just six months before his 100th birthday when the Martin Beck Theatre was to be renamed the Al Hirschfeld Theatre.

Charles Isherwood is the chief theater critic of *Variety.* He has been with the publication for 10 years, working as an editor and critic in both the Los Angeles and New York offices. He also writes regularly about theater for the *Times* of London.

John Istel has been an arts journalist for the last 15 years, contributing to such publications as *The Atlantic, Elle, American Theatre,* and the *Village Voice.* He has worked as an editor for *Stagebill,* Billboard/Back Stage Books, and *American Theatre.* He has taught at City University of New York and New York University, and has contributed to many reference works, including *Contemporary Playwrights,* the *Reference Guide to American Literature,* and the *Best Plays of 2000–2001.* In 2002, he founded ICAP (Istel Creative Arts Publishing), which provides consulting, editorial and writing services to such arts institutions as Carnegie Hall, Lincoln Center, and Roundabout Theatre Company.

Jeffrey Eric Jenkins is the sixth editor of the *Best Plays* series founded by drama critic Burns Mantle in 1920. He has written more than 300 articles about theater and culture for a variety of publications in the past decade. He is a faculty member in the Drama Department at New York University's Tisch School of the Arts, where he has taught theater studies—with an emphasis in United States drama and theater—since 1998. Jenkins has also taught at Carnegie Mellon University, the University of Washington, and SUNY–Stony Brook. Jenkins received degrees in drama and theater arts from Carnegie Mellon University and San Francisco State University, and he has directed thirty productions in professional and educational theaters across the United States. Jenkins is a former board member of the American Theatre Critics Association (1995–2001) and served as the association's chairman from 1999 to 2001. He is a board member of the American Theatre and Drama Society and the Theater Hall of Fame, and serves on the advisory committees of the American Theatre Wing and the William Inge Theatre Festival.

Vivian Cary Jenkins spent more than 20 years working as a healthcare administrator in both the public and private sectors. She now teaches aspiring administrators in the graduate and undergraduate programs at Iona College. Prior to her work in healthcare, she was a student at the School of the American Ballet, a dancer and a Peace Corps volunteer in Honduras. Over the past decade, she has also begun to develop her skills as a theater producer, with productions of Sam Shepard's *True West* and Slawomir Mrozek's *The Emigrants.*

Chris Jones reports on and reviews theater for the *Chicago Tribune*. He has contributed reviews and articles to *Variety* for the past 15 years, specializing in out-of-town tryouts and the Broadway road. His reviews, interviews and commentary also have appeared in *American Theatre* and the *New York Times*, along with numerous other arts publications. Born in Manchester, England, Jones holds a PhD in theater criticism from Ohio State University.

Robert Kamp and his wife Kim Wu co-own I Can Do That Productions, Inc., a graphic design company. Prior to starting his own business, Bob worked for several arts and entertainment publications including *Stagebill* and *City Guide*. Bob and Kim live in Manhattan in a pre-war one-bedroom with four feline children. They spend their free time trying to develop the precise "launch sequence" of electric appliances that will allow them to print, scan and make toast at the same time.

Donald Lyons has been drama critic for the *New Criterion*, the *Wall Street Journal* and the *New York Post* (where he is now employed). He has taught Classics and English at Harvard, NYU and Rutgers. He is the author of the book *Independent Film*, and numerous articles on literature, film and drama.

Michael Phillips is the theater critic of the *Chicago Tribune*. Prior to joining the *Tribune* in 2002 he served as theater critic for the *Los Angeles Times*, the *St. Paul Pioneer Press*, the *San Diego Union-Tribune* and the *Dallas Times-Herald*. Phillips has twice served as juror on the committee that selects the Pulitzer Prize in drama, is presently on the New Plays Committee of the American Theatre Critics Association. He has taught criticism at the O'Neill Theater Center's National Critics Institute in Waterford, Connecticut. He lives in Chicago with his wife and son.

Christopher Rawson has been since 1983 drama critic and (more recently) drama editor of the *Pittsburgh Post-Gazette*. Along with local reviews, features, news and columns, he also reviews regularly in New York and London. His love of theater is partly inherited from his father, actor Richard Hart, but he started professional life in 1968 in the English Department at the University of Pittsburgh, where he still teaches Shakespeare, critical writing and satire. His BA is from Harvard and his MA and PhD from the University of Washington. A former chairman of the American Theatre Critics Association, he is a member of the executive committee of the Theater Hall of Fame, managing the selection process with Henry Hewes.

Michael Sommers is the New York theater reviewer for the *Star-Ledger* of New Jersey, the *Staten Island Advance* and other Newhouse News publications. He is a former editor of *Entertainment Design* and *Back Stage* and has written features and reviews for many other magazines since 1981. Sommers is serving his second year as president of the New York Drama Critics Circle.

Bruce Weber, a theater critic for the *New York Times*, has been on staff at the newspaper, as an editor, reporter and writer, since 1986. A former fiction editor for *Esquire* magazine, he was the editor of the collection *Look Who's Talking: An Anthology of Voices in the Modern American Short Story*, and he is the author, with the dancer Savion Glover, of *Savion! My Life in Tap*.

Margaret B. Wilkerson is Director of the Media, Arts and Culture unit of the Knowledge, Creativity and Freedom Program of the Ford Foundation. She has programmatic responsibilities for the Foundation's work in the US and overseas. Wilkerson is also Professor Emerita at the University of California at Berkeley where, during her academic career, she served as professor and chair of the Department of African American Studies and of the Dramatic Art Department, and was director of the women's research center. Wilkerson earned her PhD in Dramatic Art at Berkeley and was editor of *9 Plays by Black Women*. She is completing a biography of playwright Lorraine Hansberry.

Charles Wright reviews books and writes about theater for a variety of publications. A native of East Tennessee, he holds degrees from Vanderbilt, Oxford, and the University of Pennsylvania. During the past eight years, as a business affairs executive at A&E Television Networks, he has been involved in production and commissioning of hundreds of hours of documentary programming, including *The Farm: Angola, USA*, which received the 1998 Grand Jury Prize at Sundance and was nominated for an Academy Award as Best Documentary Feature the following year.

Index

Titles in bold are play titles.
Page numbers in italic indicate essay citations.
Page numbers in bold italic indicate Broadway and Off Broadway listings.

453